Reader Series
in Library and Information Science

Published *Readers* in the series are:

Reader in Library Administration. 1969.
Paul Wasserman and Mary Lee Bundy.

Reader in Research Methods for Librarianship. 1970.
Mary Lee Bundy and Paul Wasserman.

Reader in the Academic Library. 1970.
Michael M. Reynolds.

Reader in Library Services and the Computer. 1971.
Louis Kaplan.

Reader in American Library History. 1971.
Michael H. Harris.

Reader in Classification and Descriptive Cataloging. 1972.
Ann F. Painter.

Reader in Technical Services. 1973.
Edward L. Applebaum.

Reader in Medical Librarianship. 1973.
Winifred Sewell.

Reader in Government Documents. 1973.
Frederic J. O'Hara.

Reader in Science Information. 1973.
John Sherrod and Alfred Hodina.

Reader in Library Cooperation. 1973.
Michael M. Reynolds.

Reader in Music Librarianship. 1973.
Carol June Bradley.

Reader in Documents of International Organizations. 1974.
Robert D. Stevens and Helen C. Stevens

Reader in Library and Information Services. 1974.
Michael M. Reynolds and Evelyn H. Daniel.

Reader in Operations Research for Libraries. 1975.
Peter Brophy, Michael Buckland and Anthony Hindle.

Reader in Library Systems Analysis. 1975.
John Lubans, Jr. and Edward A. Chapman.

Reader in Social Science Documentation. 1975.
Christopher D. Needham

Reader in Media, Technology and Libraries. 1975.
Margaret Chisholm.

Reader in Library Technology. 1975.
Shirley Gray Adamovich.

Reader on the Library Building. 1975.
Hal B. Schell.

Reader on
the Library Building

edited by

Hal B. Schell

1975

 **Microcard Editions Books**
An Indian Head Company
A Division of Information Handling Services

Published by Microcard Editions Books
5500 South Valentia Way
Englewood, Colorado 80110

Printed in the United States of America

Foreword

Unlike many other academic disciplines, librarianship has not yet begun to exploit the contributions of the several disciplines toward the study of its own issues. Yet the literature abounds with material germane to its concerns. Too frequently the task of identifying, correlating, and bringing together material from innumerable sources is burdensome, time consuming or simply impossible. For a field whose stock in trade is organizing knowledge, it is clear that the job of synthesizing the most essential contributions from the elusive sources in which they are contained is overdue. This then is the rationale for the series, *Readers in Library and Information Science*.

The *Readers in Library and Information Science* includes books concerned with various broad aspects of the field's interests. Each volume has been prepared by a recognized student of the topic covered, and the content embraces material from the many different sources from the traditional literature of librarianship as well as from outside the field in which the most salient contributions have appeared. The objectives of the series are to bring together in convenient form the key elements required for a current and comprehensive view of the subject matter. In this way it is hoped that the core of knowledge, essential as the intellectual basis for study and understanding, has been drawn into focus and may thereby contribute to the furtherance of professional education and professional practice in the field.

Paul Wasserman
Series Editor

Contents

VI

STAFF SPACES

VII

MECHANICAL SPACES

VIII

SOME CONSIDERATIONS FOR NEWER MEDIA
AND AUTOMATION SERVICES IN LIBRARY BUILDING

IX

FURNISHINGS AND EQUIPMENT

Introduction

The planning of library buildings today is complicated by a set of inter-acting circumstances, each of which may be recognized but little understood. Major among these are the publications explosion and our population explosion. These, when coupled with new technologies and systems, demand a greater knowledge of the total library function on the part of the librarian, the planning agency and the architect. As library needs, services, technologies and systems are changing at an increasing pace we must strive toward an understanding that will provide the greatest possible flexibility of design, construction and utilization of library space.

The literature of general works on library physical facilities is limited. Major works have been published on academic libraries and public libraries. A few general works have been published by architects but these are mainly pictorial. This present work aims at bringing together articles of known authority on all aspects of library planning: from first planning stages through the purchase of furnishings and equipment. *Reader on the Library Building* is designed to be used by the building planner (architects and engineers as well as librarians and administrators) seeking basic information on the scope and procedure of library building planning. As an instructional tool its utility increases in the classroom when coupled with an instructor's building experiences and expertise.

Several volumes of this series have already been published and I have followed the organizational format of previous volumes. The introductions to the various sections or articles are intended to provide some continuity to the work.

Due to production costs for this volume, illustrations have been kept to a minimum; yet, to be fully appreciated the subject demands graphic representation. The reader is reminded that supplemental illustrative materials are available from the Buildings and Equipment Section, Library Administration Division, American Library Association, through the Association's Headquarters Library and from the Association's Library Technology Program. These organizations have on file for lending actual blueprints of fine library buildings, color slides of buildings (both exterior and interior) and sketches of individual pieces of furnishings and equipment.

As editor of this volume, I express my sincere gratitude to the authors and publishers represented for their generous cooperation and consent to reprint. I am deeply grateful to the staff members of Southern Methodist University and the Universities of Pittsburgh and Cincinnati for their assistance in the preparation of this work.

H.B.S.

Cincinnati, Ohio
August, 1973

Reader on
The Library Building

I

THE PAST AND FUTURE
OF LIBRARY BUILDINGS

As a point of departure on our subject, this first unit presents an overview of library facilities. Libraries, considered either as institutions or as buildings, have a future as well as a past, and it is important that this be understood before continuing with specific elements in the planning process. From the columned edifice of the ancients, through the bricks and mortar of today, toward the electronic circuitry of tomorrow, we look at the library building as a reflection of the functions it must perform.

The Library Building: an Overview

by Hal B. Schell

Libraries from ancient times to those of future times are considered in an historical perspective. An overview of present day library facilities is related. Included are public, school, academic, research and special libraries.

When man first collected knowledge in recorded form it became necessary to have a storage facility such that the recorded knowledge would be preserved but could be recalled with minimum effort. Thus, the library building form has always been determined by the nature of the stored materials, whether clay tablets, scrolls, books, films, or tapes. The form, or plan, of the building most generally follows from this storage and retrieval function.

The British librarian, Anthony Thompson, has identified a variety of historic plan types in his *Library Buildings of Britain and Europe* (London, 1963). The "classical" plan was used throughout antiquity and the Renaissance and is illustrated in the plan of the library at Ephesus (A.D. 107). At first, these libraries were generally connected with temples (see Figure 1); later they were attached to or were integral parts of cathedrals and princely dwellings. The classical plan has continued into modern times in such library buildings as those of the Boston Atheneum (1855), the Peabody Library in Baltimore (1861), and the Patent Office (1902) and Science Museum (1905) Libraries in London. The "medieval" plan calls for a simple, one-room library. It developed through several stages into a series of alcoves created by bookshelves with tables and chairs in each alcove. Very functional for small libraries or even for special collections or rooms within larger libraries, in recent years it has been most dramatically and successfully used in the greatly admired Lamont Library for undergraduate students at Harvard University (see Figure 2).

The real impetus to planning modern library buildings stemmed, according to Thompson, from designs to solve "the problem of supplying many books to many readers." Three principal types of modern libraries are identified: closed-bookstack, open-access, and various-shaped; each of these has several subtypes. The first "modern" library building was the Bibliothèque Sainte-Geneviève at the Université de Paris (1843). It is the prototype of all closed-stack libraries with reading room above and bookstacks below (see Figure 3). It solved the problem of having books and readers in close proximity, yet separated, and of providing natural light for the readers. As a building type it has been widely copied, most recently in the National Library of Medicine at Bethesda, Maryland (1962) (see Figure 4). A similar arrangement is that of the readers' spaces in front with the bookstacks behind (see Figure 5). Again, Thompson cites, as the prototype of this plan, a

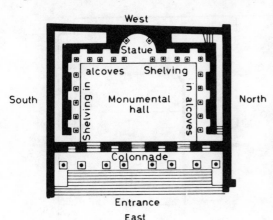

FIGURE 1 Roman library at Ephesus (A.D. 107). A typical Roman library, built mostly in towns and attached to a temple. (Reproduced from Anthony Thompson, *Library Buildings of Britain and Europe,* Butterworth, London, 1963.)

SOURCE: Originally published as "Buildings, Library" by H. B. Schell in *Encyclopedia of Library and Information Sciences,* vol. 3 (New York, Marcel Dekker, Inc., 1970). Reprinted by permission of the publisher.

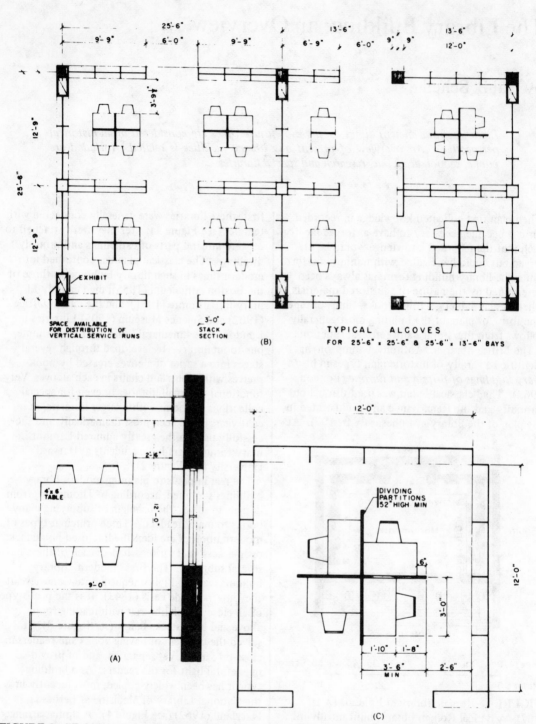

FIGURE 2   "Tables in book alcove. (A) Standard table with no partitions. (B) Tables for two to four persons, with partitions fitted in different column spacing and with exhibit space replacing a short section. (C) Nest of tables in pinwheel form to give additional privacy." Similar arrangements are used in the Lamont Library at Harvard University. (Reproduced by permission of McGraw-Hill Book Company from Keyes D. Metcalf, *Planning Academic and Research Library Buildings.* Copyright © 1965 by the American Library Association.)

building in Paris, the Bibliothèque Nationale (1854). Several later examples of this type are the libraries of the University of California (1908), the Public Library of Detroit (1921), The Free Library of Philadelphia (1927) (see Figure 6), Liverpool

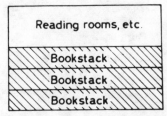

FIGURE 3 Typical section of building with closed bookstacks below reading rooms. (Reproduced from Anthony Thompson, *Library Buildings of Britain and Europe,* Butterworth, London, 1963.)

University (1938) (see Figure 7), and Cantonal Library, Lucerne (1951) (see Figure 8). The bookstack in the form of a tower (see Figure 9) has been used by major university libraries. Some fine examples are the libraries of the University of Rochester (1930) and Yale University (1931), the addition to the Ohio State University Library (1951), and the library of Moscow State University (1953). Other closed-stack plans are typified by the British Museum (1854–1857) and the Library of Congress (1886–1897) with their central reading room system (see Figure 10), and by Butler Library of Columbia University (1935) with its central bookstack and surrounding reading rooms (see Figure 11).

Open-access library building plans are a result of efforts in modern times to bring books and readers together. They developed first in public libraries, mainly from the stimulus of the many millions of

FIGURE 4 Exterior view of the National Library of Medicine, located on the campus of the National Institutes of Health, Bethesda, Maryland. A mezzanine of offices and a main floor for major library services are above grade, and three large stack levels are below grade. (Courtesy the National Library of Medicine, Bethesda, Maryland.)

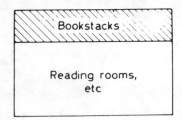

FIGURE 5 Typical plan for buildings with reader and service spaces in front and bookstacks at the rear of the building. (Reproduced from Anthony Thompson, *Library Buildings of Britain and Europe,* Butterworth, London, 1963.)

dollars contributed to public library buildings by Andrew Carnegie. Later, college and university libraries opened their collections to students (they had previously been limited to the faculty), which resulted in the further need for better open-access plans. Thompson cites the single-room plan and "Carnegie rectangle" as developing into the right/left plan, and later into the H-, U-, L-, and V-shaped building plans. The right/left plan, simply stated, is the single-room rectangular plan divided into two rooms by a loan or control desk in the middle which supervises the two halves as well as the entrance to the building. The right/left plan is

FIGURE 6 The Free Library of Philadelphia built in 1927 is typical of buildings with bookstacks at the rear and public rooms in front. (Courtesy the Free Library of Philadelphia; photo by Lawrence S. Williams, Inc., Upper Darby, Pa.)

FIGURE 7 Exterior view of the Harold Cohen Library, Liverpool, England. (Photo by Stewart Bale Ltd., Liverpool.)

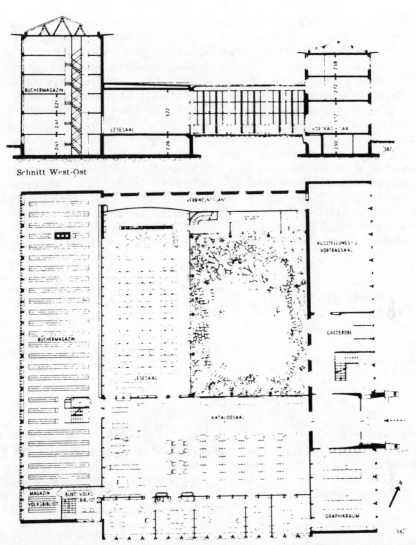

FIGURE 8 Zentralbibliothek, Luzern, Switzerland. Top, section through the building from west to east; bottom, plan of the main floor showing the entrance, card catalog room, reading room, one level of the bookstacks, the lecture hall, and the garden court.

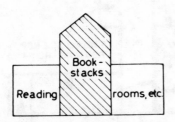

FIGURE 9 Typical section of the bookstacks in the form of a tower. (Reproduced from Anthony Thompson, *Library Buildings of Britain and Europe,* Butterworth, London, 1963).

common today in small branch libraries of all types, especially elementary and secondary school libraries, academic branch or departmental libraries, and the special libraries serving business and industry. Larger library buildings were divided vertically with lending on the ground or entrance level and reference on a second floor where the quieter surroundings were more conducive to study in depth. Subject departmentalization as a plan for buildings was developed in public library buildings in the 1920s and 1930s (although the prototype was the Public Library of Leningrad as early as 1833), and in university library buildings in the late 1930s. An example of the latter is the University of Colorado Library (1940) (see Figure 12).

Finally, there are plans of various other shapes. Among these are the square (see Figure 13), the circle (see Figure 14), the triangle (see Figure 15), the T-shape, and the hollow or ring plan with a central courtyard. Interesting examples of the last-mentioned type are the Charles Hayden Memorial Library of the Massachusetts Institute of Technology with its central courtyard open to the exterior (see Figure 16), and the Francis A. Countway Library of Medicine at Harvard with its closed interior central court and skylight above (see Figure 17). Both buildings have achieved beautiful

architectural integrity, but at the cost of complicated interior traffic patterns and a considerable waste of space. Although many library building planners prefer to work with the rectangle for interior layout, the square-type plan is less costly since it has the least amount of exterior wall construction. These types of plans listed by Thompson are helpful in identifying basic and single forms but, in practice, many library buildings incorporate several of the types. The courtyard or light-well can be fitted to most types and is used very often today. Subject departmentalization has been used in several of the types of plans. An interesting plan is that proposed for the new library of the University of Massachusetts at Amherst (see Figure 18), which utilizes the tower plan for bring-

FIGURE 10 Typical plan of building with central reading room and bookstacks on the periphery. (Reproduced from Anthony Thompson, *Library Buildings of Britain and Europe,* Butterworth, London, 1963.)

FIGURE 11 Typical plan of building with central bookstacks and reading rooms and services on the periphery. (Reproduced from Anthony Thompson, *Library Buildings of Britain and Europe,* Butterworth, London, 1963.)

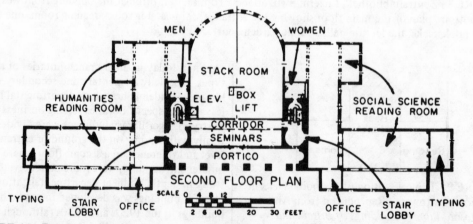

FIGURE 12 Example of subject departmentalization: original plan for the second floor of the University of Colorado Library, Boulder, Colorado.

ing together books and readers, rather than separating them as in the tower at the University of Rochester.

The rapidly expanding book collections of the twentieth century, the introduction of new media (e.g., microforms and phonograph records), changes in library service patterns, and increased library staffs have caused greater attention to the functional aspects of library buildings. Construction techniques of this century were applied to advantage and, through the efforts of many minds (particularly through Angus Snead MacDonald, praised by Ellsworth as the "originator of most of the new ideas in library planning"), resulted in

modular, or loft-type, buildings with flexibility, allowing for adaptation of the building to constantly changing needs of collections, services, and staff. Earlier, flexibility was assumed with the removal of load-bearing walls from the interior of buildings, but today architects and librarians work together to achieve complete building flexibility through careful planning of the building module and attention (through the use of expert consultants) to the details of lighting, sound, ventilation, and other electromechanical aspects of building planning. A valuable body of literature on these subjects exists in the writings of MacDonald, Githens, Thompson, Reece, Ellsworth, Wheeler,

FIGURE 13 An example of the square building: the Hillman Library, University of Pittsburgh, Pittsburgh, Pennsylvania (1967).

FIGURE 14 An example of the circular building: Chabot College, Hayward, California.

FIGURE 15   An example of a triangular-shaped building: University of Toronto, Humananities and Social Sciences Research Library and School of Library Science, scheduled for completion in 1972 (Mathers & Haldenby, Architects). (Photo by Panda Associates, Toronto.)

Metcalf, and others. Considerable attention to planning has been given by organizations such as the American Library Association (particularly its Buildings and Equipment Section of the Library Administration Division and the Library Technology Program supported by the Council on Library Resources), the Special Libraries Association, the Educational Facilities Laboratories (supported by the Ford Foundation), the Office of Education of the U. S. Department of Health, Education and Welfare, and various state and local agencies. *Library Journal* addresses itself to improved library facilities once a year with its special December architectural issue.

Flexibility continues to make greater demands on library planners today as the library function is defined to include recorded information in all its variant forms and media. Planning in several recent instances has resulted in libraries as "learning centers," utilizing much technologically advanced equipment. Examples of these centers can be found at Stephens College and Oral Roberts University. Indeed, through the introduction of more advanced systems of communication (improved

microforms; audio, video, and computer tapes; facsimile and data transmission capabilities; dial-access information systems; and the possible electro-mechanical combination of these), some writers have described the library of the future not as a building or "place" at all but rather, as suggested by C. Walter Stone (*Library Trends*, October 1967), "as a far-flung network composed of units of various sizes and types, each of which may perform similar as well as different functions, but all of which will be linked together electro-mechanically."

Thus, library building planners have always concerned themselves with function. In many notable instances they have erred when adapting the functional plan of an earlier era to the needs of a library whose function is radically different. The monument-type library was originally connected with a temple or cathedral and functioned well as such; but when this type of architecture was used in modern times to serve busy urban library needs or open-access campus libraries, they were ill-thought, ill-planned, and ill-served. All library building planning should start with carefully de-

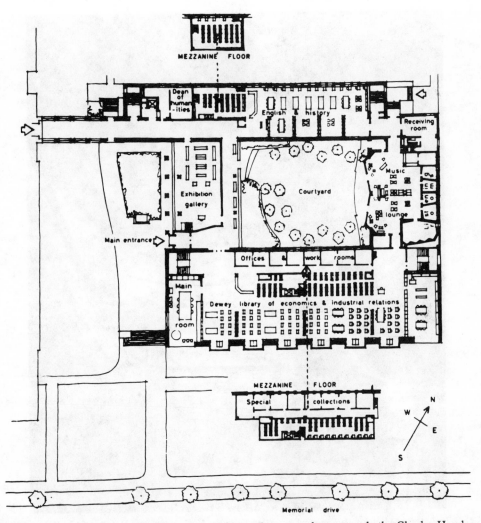

FIGURE 16 An example of the hollow or ring plan with a central courtyard: the Charles Hayden Memorial Library at the Massachusetts Institute of Technology, Cambridge, Massachusetts (1950). (Reproduced by permission from *Technology Review*, published at the Massachusetts Institute of Technology.)

tailed programming, in which the functional needs of the library are described; the proper type plan, or form, will follow. If the library building of the future is started from this base, it will be as great an accomplishment as the library at Ephesus (A.D. 107), the Bibliothèque Sainte-Geneviève (1843), or the successful John M. Olin Library at Cornell University (1961) (see Figures 19 and 20).

The public library building, i.e., the municipal library as distinct from state and federal (or national) libraries, received its greatest impetus in the early twentieth century from the Carnegie Corporation. Not only did the Carnegie Corporation give money for the construction of public library build-

ings, but it also instructed that these buildings should be community centers and issued in 1911 its *Notes on the Erection of Library Buildings.* Although the tremendous sociocultural impact and benefits of the Carnegie Corporation's work cannot be denied, it should be asserted that its *Notes* were nearly lethal to continued imaginative planning in the design of library buildings, for they tended to standardize library planning. Theirs was not only the single great force of the time; their design was emulated, or copied, by others. Thus, the Carnegie Library of Syracuse University, though much larger, is not unlike the earlier Carnegie Public Library of small communities

FIGURE 17 Interior view of the central court at Francis A. Countway Library of Medicine, Harvard University. (By permission from the Francis A. Countway Library of Medicine, Harvard University; photo by Louis Reens, New York, N.Y.)

throughout the nation, and all bear a close resemblance to the library at Ephesus, their classical prototype. The *Notes* of 1911 sought to overcome this classical plan by substituting the "Carnegie rectangle," which remained the standard of library planning until the mid-1940s.

It was the post-World War II period with its Sputnik, scientific and cultural advances, publication and population explosions, computerization, and advances in communications technology which demanded—with force—a freedom from the "Carnegie rectangle." A few notable breaks had been effected before the war through the works of Angus Snead MacDonald and Alfred Morton Githens. MacDonald, originator of the modular

concept, had been successful in creating a module equally able to accommodate books or readers for the Library of Congress Annex in the 1930s. Several of the larger public libraries in Europe and America had successfully functioning buildings at this same time, e.g., the Cleveland Public Library (1925) and the Enoch Pratt Free Library at Baltimore (1933). It was the success of the Cleveland Public Library which set the trend for subject departmentalization in the major public library buildings. Since the war, the modular concept has been used almost universally in public library buildings. Some fine postwar examples are the Grosse Point, Michigan, Public Library (1953); the Midland, Michigan, Public Library (1955) (see Fig-

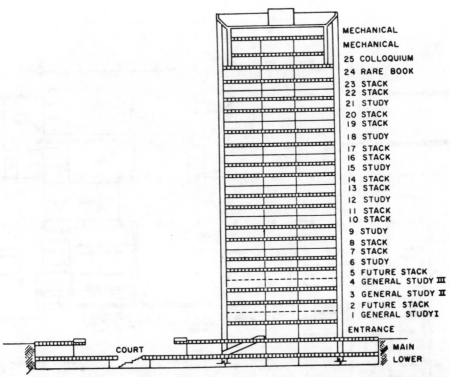

FIGURE 18 Proposed new library building, east elevation, at the University of Massachusetts, Amherst. Each reading room of the tower connects vertically to a stack level immediately above or below.

FIGURE 19 Exterior view, John M. Olin Library, Cornell University, 1961. (Photo by Photo Science Studios, Cornell University, Ithaca, N.Y.)

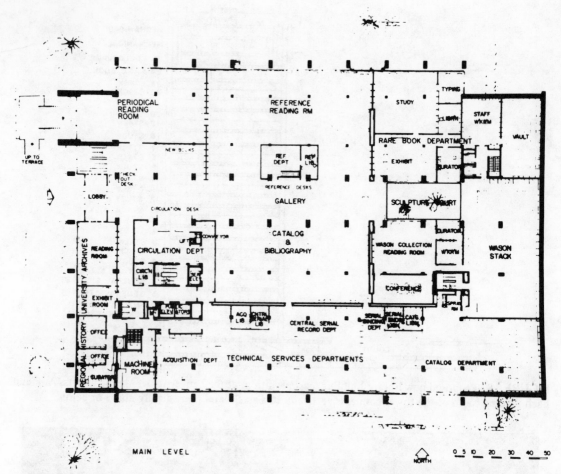

FIGURE 20 Plan of main level, John M. Olin Library, Cornell University, Ithaca, N.Y. 1961.

FIGURE 21 Exterior view of the Grace A. Dow Memorial Library, Midland, Michigan, 1955. (Photo by Bradford-LaRiviere, Inc., Saginaw, Michigan.)

ure 21); the Charlotte, North Carolina, Public Library (1956); the Seattle Public Library (1960) (see Figure 22); the Norfolk Public Library (1962); the addition to the Detroit Public Library (1963) (see Figures 23 and 24); the Buffalo and Erie County Public Library (1964) (see Figure 25); the Knoxville Branch, Carnegie Library of Pittsburgh (1965) (see Figures 26 and 27); the Edmon-

FIGURE 22   Seattle Public Library, 1960.

FIGURE 23   Exterior view illustrating the 1963 addition to the Detroit Public Library.

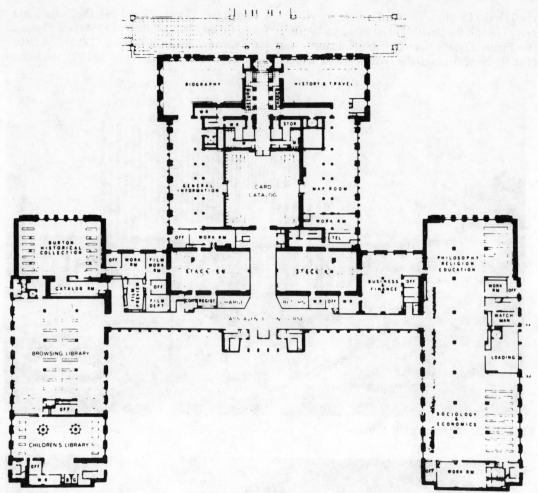

FIGURE 24 Plan of the first floor of the original building and the 1963 addition, Detroit Public Library.

ton, Alberta, Public Library (1967) (see Figure 28).

In the history of libraries, elementary and secondary school libraries are relatively recent, having their development almost completely in the present century. Imaginative planning for school library facilities is even more recent—completely post-World War II. Early established school libraries consisted of one room, often poorly located with relation to other instructional and functional facilities of the school. The school library has followed the same evolution noted for public libraries. The one-room library took the form of the right/left plan. Later, as newer instructional and communications technologies were developed, other rooms of the school building were given over to house their related facilities and services. They were sometimes adjacent to the library rooms, but more often not; in many instances, they were even administratively separated from the library function.

Recently, following an emphasis on the instructional function of the library, plans have been effected in which first-class library facilities are provided for the newer schools. These libraries provide a full range of recorded materials and instructional media. They have been carefully planned with consultants' advice on electromechanical requirements and attention to lighting, acoustics, air conditioning, and all aspects of study

FIGURE 25 Exterior view of the Buffalo and Erie County Library, Buffalo, N.Y., 1964.

FIGURE 26 Rendering of exterior, Knoxville Branch of Carnegie Library of Pittsburgh, 1965.

comfort. In a one-building school, the library has been located centrally in the main traffic areas of the building, easily accessible to students, teachers, and administrators. Work space for library staff has been provided adjacent to the materials which they service, yet removed from the student study areas (see Figure 29). In the "campus" plan for the newer secondary schools, the library is usually a separate, centrally located building (see Figures 30 and 31). Both elementary and secondary

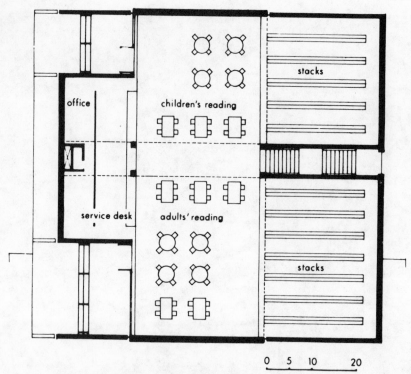

FIGURE 27 Plan of main level, Knoxville Branch of the Carnegie Library of Pittsburgh, 1965.

FIGURE 28 Edmonton, Alberta, Canada, Public Library (1968). Wall opening at right is ramp to underground parking for motor vehicles. (Photo by Richard G. Proctor, Edmonton.)

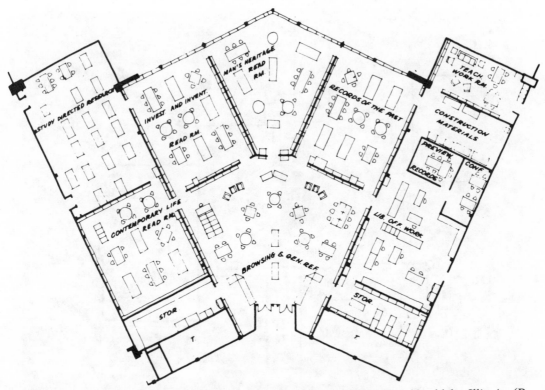

FIGURE 29 Plan of the centralized library at the West Leyden High School, Northlake, Illinois. (Reproduced by permission from Ruth Weinstock, ed., *The School Library*, Educational Facilities Laboratories, New York, 1963.)

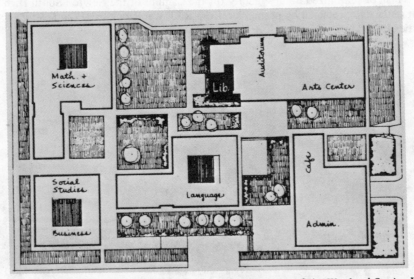

FIGURE 30 Plan for decentralized library facilities on the Campus of the Wayland Senior High School, Massachusetts. The central library is in the building marked Auditorium and Art Center. Branches of the main library form the center of the subject area buildings in this school. (Reproduced by permission from Ruth Weinstock, ed., *The School Library*, Educational Facilities Laboratories, New York, 1963.)

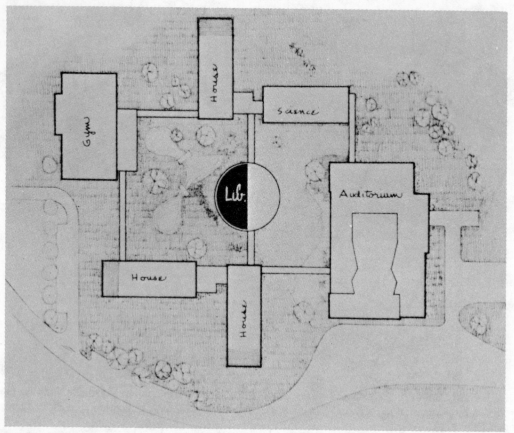

FIGURE 31   Plan of centralized library facility for the Campus of the Newton South High School, Newton, Massachusetts. (Reproduced by permission from Ruth Weinstock, ed., *The School Library,* Educational Facilities Laboratories, New York, 1963.)

FIGURE 32   Exterior view of the Lovejoy Library, Southern Illinois University, Edwardsville Campus, Edwardsville, Illinois.

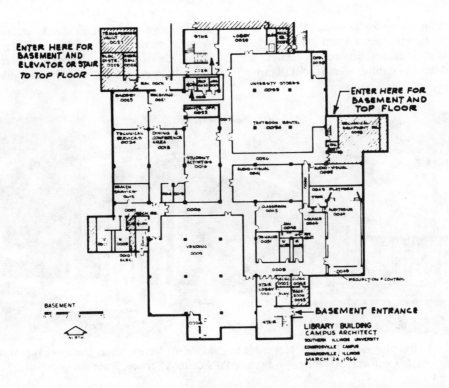

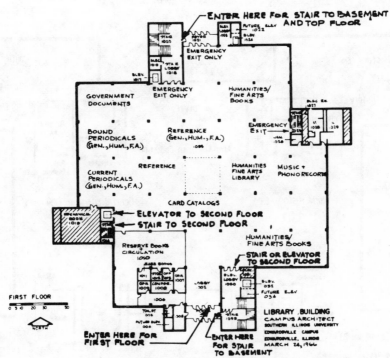

FIGURE 33 Floor plan of the Lovejoy Library, Southern Illinois University, Edwardsville Campus, Edwardsville, Illinois.

schools today recognize the need for a variety of library seating with special attention being given to individual study spaces, particularly carrels.

In an effort to establish more school libraries and improve existing ones, the American Library Association has declared, "Every child needs a school library," and has issued its *Standards for School Library Programs* (1960) as a guide to

FIGURE 34 Exterior view, J. Henry Meyer Memorial Library serving undergraduates at Stanford University, Stanford, California. (Courtesy News and Publications Service, Stanford University, Stanford, California.)

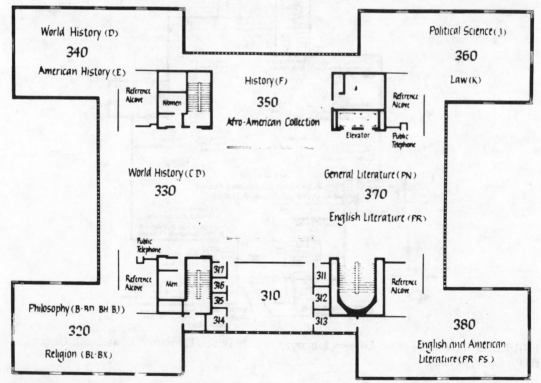

FIGURE 35 Plan of the third floor, J. Henry Meyer Memorial Library, Stanford University, Stanford, California.

school planners. This publication covers all aspects of school library services and includes as an appendix, "Policies and specifications for library quarters and equipment. . . ." The 1960 *Standards* has been replaced by *Standards for School Media Programs* (1969) which includes a chapter entitled,

FIGURE 36 The Andrew D. White Library in the Uris Undergraduate Library at Cornell University, Ithaca, N.Y. Although the building was remodeled in 1961, this room preserves the 1890 charm of the original library. (Photo by C. Hadley Smith, Ithaca, N.Y.)

FIGURE 37 The Learning Resources Center at Oral Roberts University, Tulsa, Oklahoma.

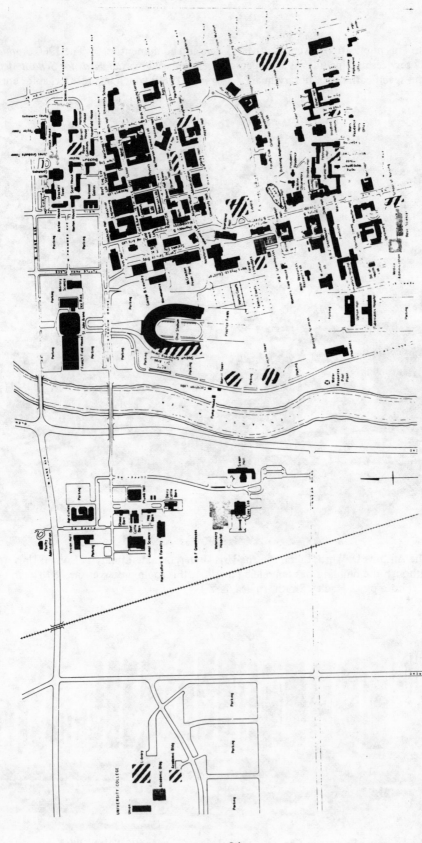

FIGURE 38 Map of The Ohio State University campus showing distribution of dial-access system from the tape banks in Denny Hall (see Figure 39) to 14 remote areas of the campus. The areas of heavy hatching indicates the locations of the dial-access system stations.

24

"Media Center Facilities." These publications were prepared by the American Association of School Librarians, a division of the American Library Association, and the Department of Audiovisual Instruction of the National Education Association in cooperation with representatives of several other library and educational associations. School library programs and quarters have improved nationally as a result of acceptance of these standards.

The work of Angus Snead MacDonald with college and university librarians was largely responsible for the concept and practice of modular planning. The Cooperative Committee on Library Building Plans, formed in 1944 at the invitation of Harold W. Dodds, President of Princeton University, was active for several years and published its *Planning the University Library Building* in 1949.

The book records the most advanced thinking of architects, engineers, librarians, and higher education administrators at that time. Its influence on library building planning has been significant and widespread.

Improvements in modular planning have concentrated on attention to interior traffic patterns and the better location of fixed service cores, not only by grouping such spaces and keeping them to a minimum, but also by actually placing them outside the building. As reported in *Bricks and Mortarboards,* an Educational Facilities Laboratories publication, plans for a building at Southern Illinois University called for ". . . pushing the service cores part way outside the walls. Thus, around the squarish three-story building rise six four-story towers. Each juts out from the wall of the building, rather than consuming space inside the wall.

FIGURE 39 Bank of tape decks for the dial-access system at The Ohio State University. From this central source information is distributed to remote locations throughout the campus (see Figure 38). (Courtesy Department of Photography, The Ohio State University.)

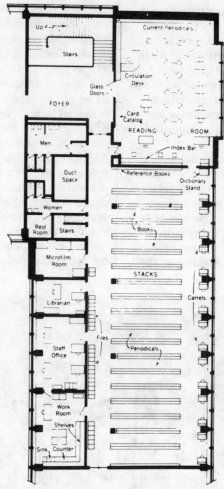

FIGURE 40 Plan of the Ford Motor Company Engineering Staff Library. [Reproduced by permission from J. L. Strauss, *Scientific and Technical Libraries,* Wiley (Interscience), New York, 1964.]

These house the elevator shafts, stairways, toilets, mechanical equipment, etc." The functional benefits to the library operations created by the uninterrupted interior spaces of such a building are at once obvious (see Figures 32 and 33).

A significant post-World-War-II development has been the establishment of separate undergraduate facilities on the large university campus. Two widely publicized examples are the Lamont Library at Harvard and the Undergraduate Library at the University of Michigan. A more recent example is the J. Henry Meyer Memorial Library at Stanford University (see Figures 34 and 35). At Cornell and the University of California at Los Angeles new research libraries have been built and the former main library is now being used as an undergraduate library. At Cornell, extensive remodeling

and renovation have resulted in a virtually new interior facility that combines the charm of the 1890 structure with all the comforts and conveniences of present-day construction. The original architecture of the building has actually been enhanced, yet its many elevations and various-sized rooms present the student with a variety of study conditions. The 1890 President Andrew D. White Library quarters have been restored, using the original tables and Thonet Vienna bentwood chairs (see Figure 36); interior stone carvings, mantles, and fireplaces have been restored; other rooms have been carpeted and have had wood paneling installed and lighting improved; the entire building has been air conditioned.

In recent years, college and university library buildings have followed the success of the "learning center" concept of the secondary schools. Notably at the newly established campuses, but also at some older campuses (e.g., Stephens College), the learning center combines in one facility the traditional library lending and reference services with the newer communications technology through electromechanical devices. Thus, at Oral Roberts University, the Learning Resources Center (see Figure 37) includes television studios, graphics studios, dial-access information systems (both audio and video), lecture halls with rear-view projection and TV monitors, classrooms with all modern teaching aids, and the full range of recorded media capabilities in the library portions of the building. Probably the heaviest used of the dial-audio systems is that located at The Ohio State University, where 40,000 calls per week are serviced through its dial-access information system. Here the system is separated from the libraries physically and administratively. The system is headquartered in Denny Hall, the liberal arts building, and information is carried by coaxial cable to points scattered about the campus: dormitories in several locations, the student union, the central library, commons (cafeterias), the music building,

and the School of Nursing. Public utility lines carry the information to several fraternity houses situated near the campus (see Figures 38 and 39). The information is stored on audio tapes which are activated through a special purpose computer by the dials at any of these remote locations. The system was planned for audio use only, but has since been adapted to include some video stations. Another interesting approach is that installed at the Oklahoma Christian College, where each of the 800 students enrolled at the college has a private carrel in the Learning Center which is capable of utilizing several types of teaching aids and an audio dial-access system. The cost of these elaborate installations is questioned by those who believe that high speed individual tape to tape duplication is more economical.

In the future, more libraries will take on the role of "instructional" or "learning" centers as dial-access systems and computer-assisted instruction systems are added to the more traditional functions of printed media. The building problems of such centers are simply those of ever-greater flexibility. To the need for providing flexibility in air conditioning, lighting, and partitioning, must be added

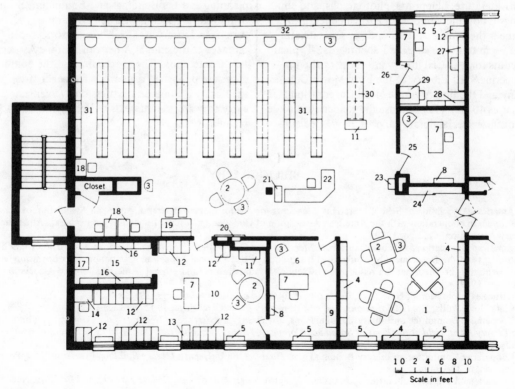

FIGURE 41 Plan of the Mead Corporation Library. [Reproduced by permission from J. L. Strauss, *Scientific and Technical Libraries,* Wiley (Interscience), New York, 1964.]

the capability of carrying audio-video signals throughout the building and, indeed, outside the building to other parts of the college and university campus. Such a building is but the first step toward an electromechanical communications network of service on a local, regional, national, and international basis. Thus, the library of the future may truly be not a "place" but a far-flung system of interconnected facilities and stations.

For a further discussion of academic library buildings, including modular planning, the reader is referred to the article by Dr. Ralph E. Ellsworth, "Architecture, Library Building" (Vol. 1, p. 491 of this encyclopedia).

Libraries organized to serve particular clientele are referred to as special libraries. Typically, they are found in the central or major plants of industrial and commercial firms, banks, hospitals, research organizations, and government agencies, but the branch or departmental libraries of the university are not unlike them in their organization, services, and physical arrangement. The nature of collections often presents special housing problems. Special shelving or storage equipment installed to house substantial collections of maps, report literature, blueprints, photographs, and clippings is not uncommon. Of special concern to some is the provision for a vault or separate storage room to house classified documents. Typical layouts for a special library are those of the Engineering Staff Library of the Ford Motor Company and the library of the Mead Corporation (see Figures 40 and 41). Because the tendency is to decentralize special library services, large special libraries are seldom found. Generally, twenty to fifty reader seats are sufficient and the total space alloted to the library is 2,000 to 10,000 square feet. Special libraries have set the pace for documentation and advanced methods for information handling, and it is not unusual to find data-processing centers near, adjacent to, or integrated with the special library. The Special Library Association has published its "Objectives and Standards for Special Libraries" (*Special Libraries*, December 1964), which includes an "Appendix: Standard Specifications," giving the physical space and equipment standards for a special library. *Special Libraries*, the association's journal, carries feature articles on library plans, layout, equipment, and organization.

The American Library Association headquarters' library and the Library Technology Program maintain collections of prints, slides, architectural drawings of buildings and equipment, and building program statements, all of which are available to librarians throughout the world through interlibrary loan. In recent years, library schools have sponsored seminars and workshops on building planning and the Buildings and Equipment Section of the Library Administration Division of the American Library Association sponsors preconferences at the annual American Library Association Conference. The proceedings of the conferences are published regularly. These activities of the library schools and professional organizations carry forward the interests of library building planners today.

BIBLIOGRAPHY

American Association of School Librarians, *Standards for School Library Programs,* American Association of School Librarians in cooperation with the American Association of Colleges for Teacher Education [and others], American Library Association, Chicago, 1960.

American Association for School Librarians, *Standards for School Media Programs,* American Association for School Librarians and the Department of Audiovisual Instruction of the National Education Association, in cooperation with representatives of The American Association of School Administrators [and others], American Library Association, Chicago, 1969.

Carnegie Corporation of New York, *Notes on the Erection of Library Buildings,* 1911.

Clark, John Willis, *The Care of Books,* 2nd ed., University Press, Cambridge, 1902 (reissued 1909).

Cooperative Committee on Library Building Plans, *The Orange Conference, a Meeting of the Cooperative Committee on Library Plans, Held at the Plant of Snead and Company, Orange, Virginia, Oct. 26-28, 1945,* Stephenson Brothers, Philadelphia, 1946.

Cooperative Committee on Library Building Plans, *Planning the University Library Building,* Princeton Univ. Press, Princeton, N. J., 1949.

Educational Facilities Laboratories, *Bricks and Mortarboards: A Report on College Planning and Building,* New York, 1964.

Ellsworth, Ralph E., *Planning the College and University Library Building: A Book for Campus Planners and Architects,* 2nd ed., Pruett Press, Boulder, Colo., 1968.

Ellsworth, Ralph E., and Hobart D. Wagener, in *The School Library: Facilities for Independent Study in the Secondary School* (Ruth Weinstock, ed.), Educational Facilities Laboratories, New York, 1963.

Lewis, Chester M., ed., *Special Libraries, How to Plan and Equip Them,* Special Libraries Association Monograph No. 2, Special Libraries Association, New York, 1963.

Library Journal, Architectural Issues (Dec. 1, annually).

MacDonald, Angus Snead, "Library of the Future." *Lib. J.,* 58, 971–975 (Dec. 1, 1933); 58, 1023–1025 (Dec. 15, 1933).

Mason, Ellsworth Goodwin, "Writing a Building Program," *Lib. J.,* 91, 5838–5844 (Dec. 1, 1966).

Metcalf, Keyes D., *Planning Academic and Research Library Buildings,* McGraw-Hill, New York, 1965.

Mevissen, Werner, *Buchereibau/Public Library Building,* Verlag Ernst Heyer, Essen, 1958.

Montgomery, Helen Grace, "Blueprints and Books: American Library Architecture, 1860–1960," *Lib. J.,* 86,4077–4080 (Dec. 1, 1961).

Reece, Ernest James, "Library Building Programs: How to Draft Them," *Coll. and Res. Lib.,* 13, 198–211 (July 1952).

Special Library Association, "Objectives and Standards for Special Libraries," *Spec. Lib.,* 55,672–680 (Dec. 1964).

Stone, C. Walter, "The Library Function Redefined," *Lib. Trends,* 16(2), 181–196 (Oct. 1967).

Streeter, Burnett Hillman, *The Chained Library,* Macmillan and Co., London, 1931.

Thompson, Anthony, *Library Buildings of Britain and Europe,* Butterworth, London, 1963.

Wheeler, Joseph L., and Alfred Morton Githens, *The American Public Library Building,* Scribner, New York, 1941 (reprinted by American Library Association, Chicago, 1951).

ABOUT THE AUTHOR–Hal B. Schell, the editor of this volume, recieved the A. B. degree from Wittenberg University in 1955 and the M.S.L.S. degree from Syracuse University in 1957. He has held administrative positions at the libraries of Cornell University, the University of Maryland, the University of Pittsburgh, Southern Methodist University and is presently Dean of Library Administration at the University of Cincinnati. Mr. Schell has consulted, lectured and written on aspects of library management and building planning.

Libraries

by Alvin Toffler

While addressing himself to "bricks and mortar" Toffler considers the broader aspects of libraries and librarianship, such as collections, services and staffing as related to planning for the library building.

Fifteen years ago a revolution swept the planning of college and university libraries. A new type of library sprang up on the grounds of many campuses —a clean-lined contemporary library that emphasized efficiency and economy, occasionally at the cost of beauty or comfort. Today the initial force of that revolution has spent itself. Campus planners, architects, and librarians are modifying its principles, softening the lines of the revolutionary model, adding grace to its form, and shaping the library to accommodate man in all his individual variety. The result is a more human library than any we have ever known. But already a new revolution is brewing, one that promises to be more profound and far-reaching than any to date. For while the changes of the recent past adapted the library to man, the coming revolution must adapt the library to the machine. And there are those who insist that this is impossible, that, in fact, the library will be completely swallowed up by the machine.

Some argue forcefully that the library and the book itself are mere relics of an inefficient past, that the job of storing, retrieving, and transmitting information will, in the future, be accomplished without either. They point out that there is nothing inviolable about the book or its storehouse, that cuneiform tablets gave way to papyrus rolls, that medieval manuscripts gave way to books, and that books are already sharing the job of communicating information with other carriers. Already most libraries store records, tapes, films, slides, and other non-book materials. The rise of the computer and the development of a whole new technology of information, these prophets charge, will inevitably transform the role of the book in modern society.

It is ironic that the death or down-grading of the book should be debated seriously today. The American higher education community is in the midst of a library-building boom of unprecedented scope and thrust. According to the U.S. Office of Education, between 1958 and 1959, 52 new campus library structures rose at a cost estimated at $29,500,000. Between 1960 and 1961 another 69 new campus libraries sprang up at a cost of $38,650,000. And in the five-year period 1961–1965, fully 504 more libraries will come into being on college or university campuses at a cost of approximately $466,600,000. This means we are spending an annual average of over $93,000,000 on these new buildings designed to bring book and scholar together. These impressive figures do not include the cost of the books themselves, of salaries, or other operating expenses.

Why, at a time when the book is for the first time in history being challenged, are we pouring so much time, energy, and money into new libraries for our institutions of higher education? Campus libraries are overcrowded. Educators believe that college and university libraries should be able to seat anywhere from 25 to 50 per cent of the total enrollment of the institution at any given time. Yet the latest figures of the U.S. Department of Health, Education and Welfare paint a stark picture of shortages in capacity: "For the aggregate United States, as of December 31, 1957, the number of students who could be seated at one time in higher education library reading rooms represented 16.2 per cent of the fall 1957 enrollment." Construction since then has done little to narrow the gap. In fact, it may have widened since this report.

Behind the shortage of teaching capacity lies the powerful surge in student enrollment. And of the swelling wave of students descending on the colleges and universities, an increasing proportion go on to graduate study. According to Francis H. Horn, president of the University of Rhode Island,

SOURCE: Reprinted from Alvin Toffler, "Libraries" in *Bricks and Mortarboard*, Educational Facilities Laboratories, 1964, by permission of the publisher.

"They require much more service than do undergraduates. More space is needed. . . .This means
that libraries cannot be expected to provide for
twice as many students in the future just by doubling present facilities, staffs, and appropriations."
Furthermore, students at all levels are using libraries more than in the past. According to an an-
nouncement from Cornell University, "Students
have been reading more books, too; during 1959–
1960 a total of 873,903 books are recorded as
having been used by Cornell students," not counting reference books. "This means that students at
Cornell on the average are consulting annually—in
addition to their regular texts—more than 80 library books each—a stack of books from 12 to 15
feet high." By 1960–1961 the average had
climbed further to 89 books per student.

An increase in library usage is reported almost
everywhere. Says Stephen A. McCarthy, director
of Cornell University Libraries: "This phenomenal
rise in library use—steady over the last few years—
apparently results from changes in teaching
methods and from a greater sense of urgency and
purpose on the part of the students." Henry
James, assistant librarian at the Lamont Undergraduate Library at Harvard adds: "Today education is more sophisticated. Assignments are made
not from a single book, but from many books,
from government documents, pamphlets, journals,
and magazine articles."

Meanwhile, another explosive force is at work.
This is the accelerating growth in the number of
books, journals, and other materials that libraries
must house. The world has never known such a
rapid proliferation of knowledge. In the words of
the *Wall Street Journal*: "Every 24 hours enough
technical papers are turned out around the globe
to fill seven sets of the 24-volume *Encyclopedia
Brittanica*. The output is rising every year. This
year's crop: some 60,000,000 pages or the equivalent of about 465 man-years of steady round-the-
clock reading." A more recent estimate by Charles
P. Bourne of the Stanford Research Institute put
the number of significant journals being published
around the world at 15,000, with perhaps
1,000,000 significant papers in them each year.
These figures do not include books and other
forms of publication. Information specialists say
that the sheer quantity of information is doubling
every 10 years.

The library that expects to serve its readers, and
especially faculty researchers, must somehow attempt to keep up with this tidal wave of data. No
library can store everything. But as intellectual

disciplines subdivide into specialties and the relationships between disciplines multiply, collections must grow. The fantastic information explosion not only means that storage space must be
expanded rapidly or some other means of storage
developed, but that the costs of cataloging, clerical
processing, and retrieving material are skyrocket-
ing. Scholars, faculty researchers, and graduate
students are drowning in a sea of data, and locating and obtaining any specific item of information
is becoming harder and more time consuming.

Under such pressures the campus library is being
transformed. The library of the University of
Illinois Chicago Undergraduate Division, for example, will have to grow 1,000 per cent in less
than 10 years, and is making preparations to do so.
Cornell's new seven-story library, completed in
1960 at a cost of $5,700,000, houses 2,000,000
volumes, is cataloging new titles at the rate of
80,000 a year, and will be hard pressed for space
again within 15 years.

At the same time, colleges and universities
themselves are undergoing changes that must affect
libraries. Colleges are becoming universities, meaning that their libraries must increase their collections to permit graduate research and more faculty
use. Universities are broadening their scope to encompass new specialties. Moreover, educational
philosophy itself is changing. As a result, according to Ralph Ellsworth, director of libraries for the
University of Colorado, and a leading consultant
on library construction: "Most libraries built before 1950 are either totally unusable or need to be
remodeled or enlarged." The challenge confront-
ing planners has never been so massive or so
complex.

How may this challenge be met? How may
the urgent demands of the present be confronted
without compromising the future? How real is
the threat to both book and library as we know
them? To answer these and similar questions, it
is necessary to cast a glance backward at the
traditional library, at the upheaval that so recently replaced it, at the mood of library planners as they consolidate the gains of the past, and
only then at the multiple possibilities of the
future.

MONSIEUR LABROUSTE'S SKYSCRAPER

Libraries have been in existence at least since
Assurbanipal, the Assyrian emperor of 2,500 years
ago, kept a crew of copyists busy collecting and

copying samples of the literature of his time. And builders have been worried about library design since the Roman Vitruvius urged that library rooms face east so that scholars might have the benefit of the morning sun as they bent over their scrolls. But the classic design of the library in modern times was established by a French architect, Henri Labrouste. M. Labrouste built a great library in Paris, the Bibliothèque Nationale, begun in 1858 and finished 10 years later. In doing so, he created a tradition that endured almost a century. The Bibliothèque Nationale was a monumental structure with vast, high-ceilinged reading rooms, elaborately decorated and covered with a huge dome. Inside it, M. Labrouste constructed what was, in effect, a small skyscraper within a building—a five-story framework of cast iron columns and wrought iron beams—a gigantic rack to house the shelving for 900,000 volumes. Since this part, the stack, was closed to the public and not visible to outsiders, M. Labrouste felt free to do away with the ornamentation that covered the public spaces, and therefore to create a truly functional building within one that was not.

This same basic concept embracing two sharply differentiated parts, one grandly elaborate, the other Spartan in its simplicity, became the model for hundreds of libraries subsequently built elsewhere, and today monumental libraries, descendants of M. Labrouste's Bibliothèque, still dominate scores of American college and university campuses.

In these, as a rule, the section open to the public is an aggregate of reading or working rooms clustered around a central reading hall whose ceiling towers as much as 30 or 40 feet above the long tables and straight-backed chairs ranged below. Natural light filters in from windows set high above the floor. Huge marble stairways wind leisurely from floor to floor, and upstairs, somewhere near the top level, there may be small, book-lined seminar rooms in which groups of students can meet with their professors. Each room is set off from the others by thick, immovable, load-bearing walls. The stack area, either housed within the main building or in a separate annex connected with the main building, consists of tier after tier of shelves, narrow staircases, and cramped aisles. Often floors are constructed of translucent glass tile so that light from a skylight in the roof may seep downward into the warehouse-like gloom.

While some of the monumental libraries that dot American campuses are, in their way, beautiful buildings, most were neither beautiful nor efficient from the beginning, and most are cripplingly inefficient today. Yet monumentalism reigned over the American campus right down through the 1930's. One after another, major new library buildings cropped up on university grounds, each a variation of the same basic theme. At Harvard, at Stanford, at Minnesota, Michigan, Illinois, and elsewhere the same lofty ceilings, impressive stairways, and ornamented walls turned up. Architects vied to make the buildings look imposing. To quote Ralph Ellsworth again, "The monumentality of a library was accepted as a symbolic measure of respect for knowledge in the minds of the university community."

The monumental library turned out to be hard to wire and light artificially, and almost impossible to heat and air condition efficiently. It was wasteful of space, too. As much as 25 per cent of its gross space was assigned to wide stairways, impressive lobbies, thick walls, and service facilities, leaving only 75 per cent for actual library functions. But its chief drawback was its rigidity. Each room or working space was designed to serve a single function and, set off by load-bearing walls, could be altered only with extreme difficulty. As functions changed with the passage of years, the rooms became increasingly inefficient.

This is illustrated by the change in the function of the stack. Throughout history, until fairly recently, the book (or the tablet or manuscript) was expensive and frequently rare. The library was primarily a repository, and the librarian's first impulse was to protect the collection from the reader. In the Middle Ages, books were chained to iron bars on library desks. In church libraries, monks wrote "book curses" into them to deter thieves. In our own country in 1667 the overseers of Harvard University ruled that "No schollar in the Colledge, under a Senior Sophister shall borrow a book out of the library." This air of possessiveness was reflected during M. Labrouste's time in the exclusion of readers from the stack.

By the 1920's, however, the whole philosophy of librarianship had begun to shift. Service to the reader became far more important than it had been. Books were cheaper, more easily available. On campuses, libraries came to be regarded less as passive repositories and more as an active part of the teaching machinery. This new emphasis was reflected in a movement to throw the stack open to the student. Educators came to believe that there is positive intellectual value in encouraging the student to browse among thousands of books.

By the 1920's the open, or at least partially open, stack had become commonplace among small-and medium-size libraries. The stack had thus become something more than just a place for storage.

This shift in the function of the stack dramatized the rigidity of the old monumental library. The tightly packed stack, created for maximum storage, lacked adequate aisle space for browsing. There was no handy place to set a table for readers to use near the shelves. Lighting and ventilation were inadequate for the increased traffic in the stack. Nor could the old–fashioned stack, designed to exclude rather than welcome people, be easily converted. The change in the philosophy of service created a conflict between function and form.

Similarly, as other concepts of librarianship changed with changing times, the frozen forms of the old monumental buildings stood more and more in the way of simple, efficient, and modern operation. Constricted by the walls around them, librarians took up the cry for more functional surroundings. During the 1930's the Depression slowed down the construction of new facilities. But by the early forties the attack on the monumental library had gained great force.

ENTER MR. MODULE

Ever since the mid-thirties Angus Snead Macdonald, a manufacturer of library shelving, had urged a radical change in library design. By 1943 he had built a mock-up of a completely new kind of library building. The contemporary library, Mr. Macdonald argued, should throw out the clichés of monumentalism. It should be built of light steel columns, beams, and panels. The columns should be hollow, providing vertical ducts for air conditioning. The cool air should flow into hollow chambers in the floors and be distributed into the rooms through registers in the ceilings. The ceilings, themselves, should be built to permit installation of flush lighting fixtures. And most important, each room should be set off, not by load-bearing walls, but by easily movable steel partitions.

Mr. Macdonald campaigned vigorously in articles and speeches for his idea of simple, wide-open spaces in libraries, broken only by impermanent walls that could be moved as functions in the library changed. Instead of thick walls to bear the weight of the upper stories,

carefully distributed columns would do the job. The spaces bounded by these columns, i.e., the structural bays, were termed "modules," and Mr. Macdonald soon became known in the library profession as "Mr. Module," a tribute to his persistence and vigor.

Mr. Macdonald's ideas struck a responsive chord in Ralph Ellsworth, then librarian at the State University of Iowa. Dr. Ellsworth, a tall, husky, outspoken man, energetically proselytized for experimentation with Mr. Macdonald's ideas, and promptly began, with the backing of his institution, to build a so-called modular library at Iowa. The dominance of monumentalism came to an abrupt end.

The swiftness of the modular revolution was amazing. From the time Dr. Ellsworth built his new library at Iowa down to the present, hardly a single major campus library has been built in this country that has not, in one way or another, followed his lead. Few accepted every jot and tittle of Mr. Macdonald's mock-up. Even Dr. Ellsworth was unable to make use of the hollow columns. But free-flowing space became an article of faith in what can now be called the modular era. The modular library made possible an easy intermixture of reading spaces and stack spaces. The stack, instead of being structurally independent, was part of the building. Readers could move freely and comfortably through those stack areas open to them. The elimination of space-wasting stairways, thick walls, and elaborate decoration proved economical. Up to 85 per cent of gross space could actually be turned to true library use. Electrical outlets and ventilating ducts were easier to install and to alter. But most important of all, the modular plan made possible libraries that, in the words of one librarian, "you don't have to blow apart with dynamite to change."

The modular revolution affected almost every physical element of the building. The stack, the most rigid element of the traditional campus library, was transformed. In the traditional multi-tier stack, a series of vertical columns thrust up from the base to the top of the stack building. Floors were built around them, usually at intervals of about $7\frac{1}{2}$ feet. The vertical columns were set in rows 3 feet apart, and the shelving actually hung on them so that all the weight was borne by these columns rather than the floors. The floors, in consequence, were relatively thin.

In the modular library the stacks are not structural elements at all. Instead, they consist of free-standing bookcases easily shifted from place to place. For standardization purposes they are still usually made in sections 3 feet long, but while the traditional stacks were made in rows set apart $4\frac{1}{2}$ feet center to center, the aisle can now be made any desired width. Ordinarily, the $4\frac{1}{2}$-foot width is still used, except where tables and other furniture are interspersed with bookcases. These dimensions, 3 by $4\frac{1}{2}$, are often used to help determine the horizontal dimensions of the module or bay. Today architects strive to make the bay as large as possible in an effort to minimize the number of columns necessary and thereby enhance the easy convertibility of the space. Architect Gyo Obata, whose firm, Hellmuth, Obata and Kassabaum, is helping to create a new $25,000,000 campus for Southern Illinois University at Edwardsville, Illinois, has designed a library that uses a 30 by 30 foot module, and at the University of Illinois at Chicago, architect Walter A. Netsch, Jr., of Skidmore, Owings and Merrill, has planned what is probably the largest module of any in the academic library field—30 by 45 feet.

One factor that limits the size of the module is floor strength. The further apart the columns are spaced, the stronger the floors have to be. This adds to cost. According to Mr. Obata, after a certain point, as the span widens, "You have to begin to do extra things like tensioning the reinforcing steel or using higher strength concrete to get the bigger span. The depth of your structural floor system gets much deeper, and you take on more height in the building." Just where the convenience of a larger bay warrants extra expenditure and where it does not is a point in hot dispute among architects and librarians, with most building planners leaning toward dimensions of $22\frac{1}{2}$ feet or 27 feet.

As the bay or module expands, the floors tend to grow fatter. In modular buildings the books may be stored anywhere, and the floors must be able to carry a load of about 200 pounds per square foot. In addition, false ceilings are often hung beneath the structural floor leaving space above to accommodate ducts, wiring, and lighting fixtures. This, too, adds thickness. Some modern libraries have floors as thick as five feet. At Washington University, whose new $3,000,000 library opened this fall, the architects, Murphy and Mackey, used flat slab concrete floors 9 inches thick, with drop ceilings hung from them only in certain parts of the building and not over the stacks.

The modular library concept also radically altered classical notions about the vertical space between floors—that is, room height. An adult can comfortably use a bookshelf that is about 7 feet tall. In traditional buildings, with the stack structure divided into stories roughly $7\frac{1}{2}$ feet high, the surrounding reading rooms were frequently built so that their floors tied into certain stack floors. This meant that room heights were almost always multiples of the basic $7\frac{1}{2}$-foot height of a single story in the stack. The lowest ceiling in a reading room was likely to be two stack levels high, or about 15 feet. The great reading hall, of course, was likely to be much taller. The consensus was that human beings are uncomfortable in rooms with low ceilings.

The modular library directly challenged this notion. According to Keyes D. Metcalf, Librarian Emeritus of Harvard and the dean of library construction consultants, the death knell of the high ceiling came when Princeton performed an unusual experiment. In preparing to build its own modular library, he says, "Princeton built a two-bay mock-up with a fake ceiling and cranked it up and down. They brought in librarians, students, architects, college presidents, faculty members, and others and asked them to holler when it got uncomfortable. They found the users could take it as low as 8'4" in a room as large as 25 by 36 feet." At Iowa, the library Dr. Ellsworth built has 8-foot ceilings. Today most modular libraries incorporate heights of about 8'6" for their reading areas.

The modular library brought with it air conditioning. The musty odor of the old-fashioned stack and the suffocating closeness of the cavernous reading room have been replaced by scientific comfort control. Libraries now being built are using air-conditioning equipment to accomplish a whole number of ends. First, temperature and humidity control make readers and staff comfortable all year round. Second, in many libraries, the air is electronically filtered to remove odors, smoke particles, and dust, thus reducing the time and money that must be spent cleaning the rooms and the collection. Many new libraries are "pressurized"—i.e., the air-conditioning level is such that when a door or window is opened air is forced out, thus keeping dirty or dusty air from rushing in. Third, the noise level of the system is so adjusted that it masks distracting sounds like the click of heels on tile, the clatter of a typewriter, or the opening and closing of doors. The air-conditioning system, in effect, maintains a comfortable backdrop noise. (Where the air-conditioning system has been set to operate too quietly, library users complain the building is noisy.)

The most important distinguishing characteristic of the modular library is the so-called loft space that is created by this type of design. Librarians are given great, wide-open spaces, whole floors broken only by a minimal number of fixed vertical elements. Architects, aware that any immovable vertical element constricts the librarian's freedom, have attempted to cluster the service areas in places where they get in the way of library functions as little as possible. In many libraries they are pushed outward toward the walls to leave the internal space clear. At Southern Illinois University this idea is to be carried one step further. Mr Obata's plans call for pushing the service cores part way outside the walls. Thus, around the squarish three-story building rise six four-story towers. Each juts out from the walls of the building, rather than consuming space inside the walls. These house the elevator shafts, stairways, toilets, mechanical equipment, etc.

The modular revolution gave the librarian economy, efficiency, and a new sense of openness never before experienced. It also gave him the freedom to adapt his buildings to change.

THE HUMANIZATION OF THE MODULAR

Today the modular revolution, having triumphed, is in a new phase. The period of revolutionary zeal is over. A period of revision has begun—a period in which architects, librarians, consultants, and planners are rethinking their principles and applying them in new ways. Modularism is undergoing humanization.

When the modular revolution began, shortly after World War II, its critics charged that it would create large numbers of standardized, factory-like libraries across the country. Similar design principles had been used in the hasty construction of air-craft plants and similar structures during the war. Characteristically, they were long, low, unrelievedly bleak, and unimaginative. The loft spaces in them were too big, emphasizing the closeness of the ceilings and giving the interiors a claustrophobic appearance. The ruthless elimination of ornament heightened their look of grim, uninviting efficiency.

It is true that the modular revolution, like most revolutions, brought with it some excesses. A number of early modular libraries shared these unpleasant characteristics. But since the mid-fifties increasing attention has been paid to making college and university libraries livable.

What might be called the new humanism of the library can be seen in the way space is cut up and put together, as well as in the way it is subsequently furnished.

Inside the library, space must be set aside for a number of basic functions. Apart from the stack and the reading rooms, there must be space for a lobby, a centrally located card catalog, a reserve book room where students can come for assigned reading of books which are stocked in multiple copies by the library, a periodicals room, a reference room, a circulation counter and work space for the staff, receiving and shipping rooms, and work space for cataloging, mending, binding, ordering, or otherwise processing books.

Most new libraries now add to the basic areas listed above, special rooms for typing, for record listening, for seminars, small offices for faculty members engaged in research, conference rooms, lounges for student and staff, rare book rooms, exhibition spaces, and special lounges and study rooms for smokers. (Some libraries now permit smoking throughout and provide a few no-smoking rooms.) The Temple University library now being built in Philadelphia will even provide special study areas for blind students. Increasing attention to the needs of the individual rather than the mass is leading to increasing variety in space assignments.

This accent on the individual is reflected also in the growing importance now placed on providing private and semi-private study space for students. The large reading room of the past, with its long wooden tables and its institutional climate, is now being replaced by smaller rooms and alcoves, some formed by imaginative stack arrangements. According to Ralph Ellsworth: "It has been proved over and over again in college libraries that students don't like to read in large open reading rooms. They like the privacy and the intimacy of small groups. They do not want to sit at flat tables in the middle of a large reading room."

This finding is strongly supported by the results of a survey conducted by four institutions, Amherst, Smith, Mt. Holyoke, and the University of Massachusetts. Nearly 400 students were polled on their preferences for certain types of study space. The results, in the words of the sub-sequent report, are a "challenge to the typical large library reading room. It may be economical in terms of the cost per student user, but it is expensive in terms of the quality of work done."

Just as the size of the reading room is growing smaller, more space is being devoted to individual seating, and especially to the use of carrels. (The study carrel is a small table with a raised partition on one, two, or three sides to screen off from the seated student visual distractions that interfere with concentration.) Says Keyes Metcalf, who planned the Lamont Undergraduate Library at Harvard and who has served as consultant to hundreds of other libraries around the world, "Since 1915 many libraries have provided large numbers of carrels for graduate students. Since 1949 we've had a great many individual seats in all parts of libraries, and I dared to put in up to 50 per cent individual seating when we were designing Lamont just after World War II. That was as far as I could go then. Today if it were done, I'd go to 75 or 80 per cent individual seating—and this for undergraduates." In university libraries, where many graduate students make use of the library, the proportion might even be higher. Carrels are often interspersed in or near the stack areas. At the just-opened Van Pelt Library of the University of Pennsylvania, individual work desks are built directly into the stack bookcases.

In many large libraries where long tables are still used, fewer students are placed at them. Thus at Washington University in St. Louis the large reading rooms are furnished with tables intended to seat eight, but only six chairs are ranged around them. At the beautiful new library of Colorado College, in Colorado Springs, the main reading room is furnished with small round tables for four.

The scaling down of space in the campus library for use by individuals or small groups rather than masses—this humanization of the modular library—has been accompanied by attempts to make the spaces themselves more inherently interesting and varied. Walter Netsch bluntly calls it "demodularization," and thinks it is a good thing. As he sees it, architects are now seeking to combine the beauties of the classical library with the efficiencies of the modular. "The classical idea of the dome is gone. But the new idea of the box is gone also," he says.

Behind this impulse toward modification of the box, Mr. Netsch says, is the need of mankind for a variety of space, rather than a uniformity of space. "You can have a world that's nine feet tall. It's technically feasible. . . . But there is no universal space. Mankind needs different kinds of spaces for different kinds of activities."

Architect Obata expresses the need for variety and beauty in other terms: "Within the essentially horizontal spaces of the pure modular library we have very little chance to create any spaces that would add a new dimension for a person going through the building."

Ralph Ellsworth sees what is happening as less of a retreat from the modular than an advance in our ability to handle it. "We went through a period," he says, "when the architects took the modular idea and wrapped it up and put a cover around it. It's ugly. But now they are viewing the structure. They're learning how to use the medium, and some of the new modular libraries are extraordinarily beautiful."

One way in which architects are striving to regain the human element, the variety they find lacking in the unrelieved horizontality of the modular libraries, is through the creation of contrasting high-ceilinged spaces. At Washington University, designed by Murphy and Mackey, this takes the form of a small court that cuts through the building like an off-center hole in a donut and reaches up to open to the sky. This small square patio is moved off toward one corner of the large building so that it interferes little with the free space within. At Colorado College, a much smaller library achieves relief from the horizontal quality by creating a reading area that is two stories high with a mezzanine running around all four sides above it and a skylight roofing it over. This atrium is, indeed, a throwback to the high-ceilinged reading room of the past. But because it is in a small building, and is carefully furnished with small tables and groupings of lounge furniture, it avoids the institutional look. Its scale is human and intimate, its appearance warm and inviting.

This same concern for warmth and individuality is evident in the way in which new libraries are being outfitted. The old library, says Ellsworth Mason, librarian of Colorado College, speaking of his campus, "kept a lot of students out simply because it was totally unaesthetic and in a style that was dead as far as these kids were concerned. So we've paid very careful attention to appearance. The looks of a building influence very greatly whether or not the student wants to come in."

Today libraries are taking on some of the

comfort of the home or of a well-furnished dormitory. The accent is on the provision of a variety of furniture forms so that each individual temperament can find some comfortable working space. As the four-college report on study habits declared: "Most institutional furniture is bought in standard sizes, but students don't come that way."

In consequence, libraries are getting away from the so-called standard items and sizes. Here is what one architect, Theodore Wofford, of Murphy and Mackey, had to say about his firm's findings after building the new Washington University library and working on several others: "In a modular building the furniture becomes very important. We found that the traditional library suppliers had standard sizes, mostly geared to high-volume high school libraries, and much of it badly designed. So we gambled and went to high-quality furniture houses. Working with the library staff, we programed each piece of furniture for them, giving them the size, its purposes, etc., and asked them if they would be interested in a no-strings-attached arrangement to develop designs to meet our requirements. Many did. And so did some of the regular library suppliers.

"This took two years. We worked with Knoll, Herman Miller, Jens Risom, Dunbar, Steelcase, General Fireproofing, and others, including Art Metal and Remington Rand. Some of the houses came up with a full line of designs. The fine furniture houses are increasingly aware of the volume of library building and are eyeing this market. This whole process paid off. We took the best furniture we could afford, and we feel we have a more attractive and comfortable library than we might have gotten by doing things the standard way."

Fabric or leather-covered armchairs, coffee tables, couches, and table lamps turn up with increasing frequency in alcoves, lounges, or lobbies of the humanized library. In the study rooms a variety of carrels are being tried out, offering different kinds of partitions, some with shelves for storing books, others with extra large surfaces, some made of wood panels, others of various kinds of peg board or composition. Says Walter Netsch: "We need to do more research on the efficiency of different kinds of study room furniture. Aside from the standard carrel, consideration should also be given to the old-fashioned stand-up carrel. Maybe some people like to work that way. Remember Thomas Wolfe wrote

standing up. And how about the big over-sized tablet arm that Ben Franklin had on his chair. We need maximum variety."

The concern for comfort is also more and more evident to anyone who looks downward in a library. Carpets, once unknown in the library, and bitterly opposed by maintenance people, are now turning as a pleasant, efficient, and economical addition to modern campus libraries. "A reference librarian walks eight miles a day," says Colorado's Mr. Mason, "and our beautiful carpeting is wonderful for the staff. But the kids love it, too. They will sit down in front of a stack right on the floor to browse through a low shelf. I find myself doing it!"

Says architect Eugene Mackey, "There's been a terrific breakthrough in carpeting, on price as well as in the kinds there are—acrilan, nylon, dacron—and others. And you can use them to provide color."

A cost analysis drawn up for the John Crerar Library at Illinois Institute of Technology shows the comparative costs of carpeting, cork tile, vinyl asbestos tile, homogeneous vinyl tile, and asphalt tile. Initial costs for carpeting are still higher than for any of the other kinds of floor covering included. But maintenance costs are significantly lower, and the most expensive grade of carpeting analyzed in the study turned out to be cheaper to own and maintain than all other types of covering in less than 8 years. The carpeting was given a life expectancy of 15 years.

Carpeted, coloful, and quiet, tastefully designed and decorated, offering a variety of spaces and furnishings for its users, the humanized modular library of today is a far cry from the rather formal, artificially hushed, poorly ventilated, and dimly lighted library of the not-too-distant past.

THE STUPIDEST MONK PROBLEM

Hundreds of years ago Leibnitz predicted that, "If the world goes on this way for a thousand years and as many books are written as today, I am afraid that whole cities will be made up of libraries." Today more books are being written than ever and although no city has yet been drowned under a sea of paper, thoughtful librarians have long been pondering whether libraries must—or can—continue to increase the size of their collections *ad infinitum*. The increase is swelling both the size and the cost of campus libraries.

A growing body of opinion holds that librarians must get over the traditional idea that the bigger the collection, the better the library. Perhaps the most vociferous critic of the size of libraries today is Mortimer Taube, a former librarian, now chairman of the board of a company called Documentation, Inc. "Libraries are too big today," Mr. Taube charges. "The question is how much of the total past are you going to embalm? The stupidest book written by the stupidest monk in the Middle Ages is a rarity today. We want to own it, not because it contains useful information but because it's a historical artifact. This attempt to embalm the living past is silly. Why, we're worse than the ancient Egyptians. We're trying to mummify the past. An enormous number of the books collected today are not collected as books at all. Nobody wants to read them. They are collected because their very existence is presumed to tell us something about the society that produced them. Is this the job of the library? And how many copies of each one do we need?"

To date no way has been found to stem the ever swelling tide of material that is finding its way into campus collections. But a number of positive steps have been taken. Libraries have begun serious programs aimed at weeding out insignificant items from their collections, and determining use patterns for the books and other materials they own.

Libraries are also banding together to carry out two other programs to help alleviate the problem of mushrooming collections. First, groups of libraries are linking up to create regional storage warehouses for their least-used materials. Thus there are today three interlibrary storage centers. The Mid-West Interlibrary Center in Chicago serves about 20 libraries from Kansas to Minnesota and Ohio; the Hampshire Interlibrary Center services Amherst, Smith, the University of Massachusetts, and Mt. Holyoke; and the New England center handles overflow from a dozen libraries in the Boston area, including Harvard, Tufts, and the Massachusetts Institute of Technology.

But putting books into storage is clearly not a final solution to the problem. While it is cheaper to store materials in warehouse space than in library space, there is a limit, too, to how much storage is practical. Says Mortimer Taube with a snort: "Dead storage is like making four copies of everything before you throw it away."

The second and more imaginative interlibrary program is designed to restrict the size of collections by birth control rather than *ex post facto* means. Called the Farmington Plan, this program brings together some 60 libraries into a systematic division of labor. Each participant is given responsibility for building its collection in a special field of knowledge. Thus Cornell has the nation's best collection of Icelandic literature; Harvard has the best collections in philosophy and law; Princeton's chief specialty is mathematics; and the University of Minnesota boasts the best Scandinavian collection. Each institution buys the periodicals in its own field, and goes lightly in other fields. In this way the nation's campuses can support first-rate collections without heavily duplicating one another's activity. All collections are recorded in the National Union Catalog so that scholars can locate their materials through a central clearinghouse.

Another step being taken by campus librarians to keep their expanding collections under control is called compact storage. Here, certain materials are stored in big drawers jammed full. They take up less space than they would if ranged on shelves in the normal manner. Though they are cumbersome to handle, some libraries find this eminently practical for books and other materials that are called for infrequently.

But the most important and most promising steps to control the physical size of collections have to do with microreproduction, that is, the reduction of the materials to diminutive size. The best-known technique for doing this is, of course, microfilm. Here, the pages of periodicals or books may be reduced to fingernail size on strips of film. These, when needed, are fed through reading machines which enlarge the image and convert it to black on white. Microfilm techniques are hardly new, but they are being used more widely than ever before. One reason for this is the availability of more and more material in this form. At St. Louis University, for example, scholars have access to 600,000 manuscripts, including histories, biographies, chronicles, annals, notes, and other documents from the famed Vatican Manuscript Library. Between 1953 and 1955 crews of technicians shot 873,000 feet of film in the Vatican to compress 11,000,000 manuscript pages into manageable proportions, and thereby, with the permission of the Vatican, brought to the United States one of the world's great collections of the history of theology, philosophy, the church, and Renaissance humanism.

Today the librarian can also use similar techniques to compress collections. Microreproductions are available on index cards—microcards—and in other shapes and sizes. These techniques are regarded as especially important today when all libraries face the problem of book embrittlement. Recent studies have shown that much of the book paper produced since the turn of the century is subject to rapid deterioration. A recent test revealed that, of 400 books manufactured between 1900 and 1939, the paper in 89 per cent of them had a fold strength less than that of newsprint. What this means is that the sheer passage of time will, before too many decades, literally destroy vast sections of present book collections. Microreproduction is looked to as a way of saving some of these doomed materials.

However, microreproduction techniques are not a panacea for the problem of sprawling collections. First, the need for a machine of some kind to enlarge the images means that users do not have the physical freedom that book users enjoy. The Council on Library Resources is supporting studies aimed at developing a simple, light-weight, and effective pocket reader—an enlarging lens and bracket of some kind that readers can carry with them anywhere. But there are a number of prickly optical problems to be solved before this can be accomplished. Secondly, many readers, especially researchers, need the convenience of a book. Study through a reading enlarger makes it difficult to flip through pages, to scan, or to browse for material. The machines often must be used in subdued light.

It is, of course, now possible to have photographic enlargements made of each frame of the microreproduction, but this is still a fairly costly and time-consuming method. However, University Microfilms, Inc., in Ann Arbor, Michigan, has started a service through which Xerox copies, in paperbound form, of microfilmed books can be obtained at $3\frac{1}{2}$ cents a page. Copies of doctoral dissertations run slightly higher—$4\frac{1}{2}$ cents a page. But the service is limited to the firm's existing microfilm collection: 15,000 books printed in English prior to 1640, 6,000 out-of-print books, and 50,000 doctoral dissertations.

From the point of view of the library planner, too, microreproduction is less advantageous than might seem at first blush. While the compression of collection material into diminutive form is, of course, a great space saver, the reading machines require space. As a result, until a library has a fairly large collection in microform, it is not likely to save much in square footage.

According to Verner W. Clapp, president of the Council on Library Resources: "Microfilm will enrich collections, not replace them. It is possible to make microfilm almost as convenient as books. But we haven't done it yet. At present it's downright abominable." Nevertheless, it is predictable that more and more use will be made of microreproduction in years to come. It is a sign of the times that the Mormon Geneological Society in Salt Lake City is building a reading room that will house 750 reading machines. The switchover to microfilm was partially responsible for a decision to abandon plans for a 15-story archives building to house the Society's records.

THE WIRED-IN STUDENT

The day is thus long past when libraries stored books alone. In addition to microform material, all new libraries now must make provision for new forms of material like phonograph records, tapes, films, slides, even, in some cases, kinescopes, and, of course, the machines needed to make use of these information carriers. Apart from special racks and storage facilities, and in some cases, special catalogs, the introduction of audio-visual equipment often brings with it the need for special areas in which it may be used. With instructors assigning spoken word LP records to their classes, so that the student may hear T. S. Eliot reading his own poetry or John Gielgud doing Hamlet, the listening booth or earphones have become commonplace in the campus library. Rooms are also set aside for the projection of movies, filmstrips, and slides.

The tape recorder is cropping up with ever greater frequency in college libraries, and the library stocks taped lectures, foreign language lessons, and similar material. In some libraries tape recorders are installed in booths or carrels. In others the student may pick up a portable unit at the reserve desk and carry it to a place set aside for listening. At Washington University a room has been set aside for mobile tape recorder units into which a number of students simultaneously may plug their earsets. With ever greater emphasis being placed on educational television, libraries are also equipping themselves for closed-circuit reception.

Another form of material that may be expected to become important in campus libraries is the teaching machine program. Librarians are talking about the day when teaching machines will be signed out as books are now.

Perhaps the most ambitious project presently in the development stage is the so-called environmental carrel. Unlike the traditional carrel which is nothing much more than a small table partially enclosed by partitions, the environmental carrel would be equipped to receive information electronically in a number of forms, and to dial out for the data needed.

Sol Cornberg, former director of studio and plant planning for the National Broadcasting Company and now head of his own firm of "designers in the communication arts," has been engaged by Grand Valley State College, a new institution near Grand Rapids, Michigan, to install the most up-to-date audio-visual equipment possible. The library now being built there will contain 256 carrels, each outfitted with a microphone, two loudspeakers, an eight-inch TV picture tube, and a telephone dial. As Mr. Cornberg describes it: "Any information stored in a 'use attitude' will be available to the student. There will be up to 310 audiotapes—that is, 310 talking books. These will be programed for self-learning. On a typical day the student would go to his class or laboratory. That is, he would participate in a group learning activity. After his lesson he goes to his carrel for individual learning. There, by simply dialing a code number, he will be able to get a repeat of the lecture, excerpts as they apply to his assigned lesson, a list of problems. He will use the microphone to record his answers on tape, erase and correct them, if necessary, then dial his instructor. He then plays the tape for the instructor."

The advantage of this system, Mr. Cornberg says, "is that it presents a controlled environment. The student works at his own pace. There is no problem of being too shy to raise one's hand or too exhibitionistic and, therefore, a disruptive influence in the class. It's a more objective learning situation."

Such carrels could, in theory, be placed anywhere on the campus, not only in the library. But even if they were not housed in the library, the library would have the responsibility for storing the tapes, videotapes, films, and other materials. A similar system is envisioned as being part of the new library now planned at Stephens College in Columbia, Missouri. So far, it must be cautioned, no such fully equipped carrel has been placed in actual operation anywhere, but the technical problems of producing them are not overwhelming. Their usefulness, of course, will depend largely on how much information will be stored "in a use attitude"—that is, how much will be available in the appropriate forms and how much of that will be properly coded for remote dialing.

With the development of such mechanical teaching aids still in its infancy, it is impossible to predict just how deeply they will affect campus libraries. But already the audio-visual invasion has created design problems for academic libraries. The biggest and most important of these is whether, in fact, the entire audio-visual function should be a part of the library. At the Southern Illinois University, where this question was thoroughly explored, the decision reached was that a separate "communications building" right next door to the library should house TV production studios and all audio-visual materials. "We felt it was developing so fast that it was important to put it in a separate building," says Mr. Obata. At Stephens College, a pioneer in the use of closed-circuit TV for teaching, the decision of the architects and planners again was that a special building was needed. "We started out to put all the audio-visual into the library," says Joseph Murphy of Murphy and Mackey, the architects. "We ended up finding that this was not as practical as it seemed. While the user in the library still has access to a full range of audio-visual resources, it was more sensible and economical to put the TV production and the master control facilities in a separate building. What we had was not a group of flexible spaces, but a group of specialized spaces and equipment that required studios and office space, and eventually needed a whole building."

In contrast, there are strong arguments for including audio-visual centers in library buildings. One is that libraries are equipped to acquire, process, and catalog the materials needed. Another argument is put forward by Keyes Metcalf, who points out that "We tend to build libraries about twice as large as they are needed at the time of construction because libraries double their collections in 16 years. This means that for the first few years you have extra space in the library. We have no idea how far audio-visual can go in the next few years, and it is therefore foolish to put up audio-visual buildings as such. The new library can give it space for the next 5 years, until we know more about how far it will go in higher education."

This fundamental policy question has not been decided by campus planners yet. It is likely to arouse heated controversy in the next few years.

FROM CLAY TABLET TO PUSH BUTTON

Reading machines, teaching machines, electronic carrels, closed-circuit television, tape recorders, motion-picture screens—the age of technology is moving into the hitherto machineless quiet of the library. At one end of the historical spectrum, a slave carving a message in a clay tablet; at the other, a whirring, computerized push-button library. Today, after nearly 3,000 years of development, the library is just now entering the machine age, and the possibilities are so cloudy and complex that no one can say with assurance how fast or how far the mechanization or automation of the library will travel in the foreseeable future. Nevertheless, for those faced with the need to finance or plan new campus libraries no issue is more significant, and even an educated guess about the future is better than none. Today librarians and architects are trying to piece together just such an educated guess. It seems inevitable that the campus library will make far greater use of machines than ever before. But for what purposes? To what end? How soon? And in what ways?

One relatively simple way in which the age of technology will make itself felt in libraries will be through the mechanization of certain clerical processes that now occupy increasing staff time in any medium or large campus library. According to Donald V. Black, director, Library Operations Survey, University of California at Los Angeles, "A lot of libraries have come to the point in their history at which they're being asked embarrassing questions. Administrations are beginning to cast a rather jaundiced eye at the vast sums of money going into operating costs."

How high these costs can run is indicated by the fact that cataloging, preparing, and shelving a new book routinely costs more than twice the price of the book itself in many libraries. One recent study put the price of book processing at between $10 and $15 per volume. It is now believed that automation can not only speed the paperwork of the library, but cut processing costs as well. In Don Black's words: "Here we have a situation very much resembling ordinary business. Take circulation records. In circulation we have something very much like inventory control. In acquisition work we get invoices from a dealer, we approve them for payment, we process them in some way, and send them on to the comptroller's office to write checks. Straightforward business. Has noth-

ing to do with libraries except the fact that the materials we are buying are library materials. Many businesses automated this kind of activity years ago."

In acquisitions work, libraries first must review the catalogs and other advertising materials submitted to them by publishers and dealers. Selections are made. Then the existing collection must be searched to determine whether or not the items to be purchased are already owned. This is sometimes tricky because the same work may appear several years later under a new title, or as part of some other volume. Large libraries today spend thousands of dollars continually searching dealers' offers and then matching them against their collections. Campus libraries often get faculty members to help make selections. But even with this help, large staffs are required just to execute the acquisitions function.

At the University of Missouri, whose librarian, Ralph Parker, has for years urged the mechanization of routine library functions, a sophisticated IBM punch card system helps cut acquisition costs. Once an item is definitely selected for purchase, an IBM card is punched for it. This card indicates the author, title, publisher, date of publication, edition, number of copies wanted, the account from which the funds are to be drawn, the dealer from whom it is to be purchased, and several other facts. The cards are machine sorted by dealer, then fed into a Cardatype machine which actually types out the order form. The cards are then re-sorted according to the account from which funds are to be drawn, and they are used to update the ledger automatically. The University of Florida library operates in similar fashion and, according to Mr. Parker, his system has brought a stream of visitors to the campus.

At the University of Colorado, IBM punch cards are used for ordering and bookkeeping, and the university is taking the lead in setting up an integrated purchasing system for all seven state-supported college and university libraries in Colorado.

A related library activity that also lends itself to automation is "serials control." This is the process of keeping tabs on which issues of periodicals arrive at the library. This sounds easy enough but, as Verner Clapp of the Council on Library Resources explains: "This is one of the messy operations in a library. The Library of Congress, for example, acquires 100,000 separate serials (i.e., periodicals) and employs 40 people just in recording them. Harvard has 28. And even so, records are unsatisfactory. This ought to be automated. It's just checking and matching. It's dumb-cluck stuff."

Yet developing a system for serials control that covers thousands of different publications issued at different rates of frequency, arriving from different sources, and printed in dozens of languages, is not simple. At the University of California, San Diego, librarian Melvin Voigt is working to crack this problem with a computer. Mr. Voigt is now able to keep tabs on 800 English and foreign titles by computer, and hopes, by the end of 1963, to boost the number to 3,000 titles. No total cost figures are available yet, but Mr. Voigt is confident that serials control by computer will prove to be economical. "Should Mr. Voigt demonstrate that he can beat the costs of doing it by hand, this application of the machine might be embraced by 100 universities tomorrow," Mr. Clapp believes.

Acquisitions and serials control involve incoming material. Circulation control involves outgoing books and materials. Just how massive a job this is can be gauged from the following statistics from the University of Illinois, Chicago Undergraduate Division Library—not one of the largest by any means. This library handles 400,000 circulations a year, sends out 30,000 to 35,000 overdue notices, plus an additional 3,000 to 9,000 faculty notices. It has been estimated that this entire record keeping job could be done by a computer operating just six minutes a day. Mr. Parker at the University of Missouri has been using punch cards to keep circulation records, and he is now at work developing an integrated system that will knit together into a single process both acquisitions and circulation control. In the process of recording the purchase order a card will be punched for each title. This card will be inserted in the pocket of the book when it arrives at the library and is shelved. In addition, each borrower will carry an identification card. At the check-out desk the borrower's card and the book card will be inserted in a machine to produce a so-called transaction card. From transaction cards it will be possible to create for each book a complete case history from the time it is ordered to the time it is finally withdrawn from inventory.

Such a system will provide not only the records needed to control circulation and acquisition, but a stream of operational statistics that will help Mr. Parker run a more efficient library. The system will kick out answers to questions like: How much duplication of materials is there in the library? What type of material is being duplicated? What proportion of the collection is in languages other than English? How much are these used? Mr. Parker estimates that his present punch card equipment is saving him between $8,000 and $10,000 a year in direct, calculable dollars. But the "operations analysis" the system makes possible creates additional savings elsewhere and, he notes, he is able to eliminate significant waste by freeing his professional staff from routine drudge work and applying their talents to more productive activities.

The time has now come, Mr. Parker believes, for his library to convert from punch card operation to computer, and he is exploring the applicability of the IBM Ramac. Computerization would eliminate much of the slow and clumsy manual manipulation of the cards, he says, and would speed up the entire process. It would also make it possible to avoid peak work loads. "For instance," he explains, "at the end of the fiscal year, when we run out of money, we traditionally hold back orders until after July 1, and after that we're swamped with work. With the speed of the computer we can go ahead and prepare much of the work in advance."

The circulation activity would be improved, too. The borrower would present his identification card and the book to be borrowed at the desk. The two cards would be inserted in a machine at the counter. In less than three seconds the transaction would be completed and the borrower on his way. At the end of the day all the transactions, both lending and return, would be fed into the computer which will maintain in its "memory" a record, not only of every book outstanding, but of every borrower. The Ramac, renting for $2,600 a month, would considerably reduce the need for people at the loan desk, and would be capable of handling all the work now being done by punch cards. Mr. Parker estimates he will be ready for his computer within two or three years.

The computer is only economical after a certain scale of operation is reached. According to Don Black, who has researched the potentials of computer operation for U.C.L.A., "if we could link these three functions—acquisitions, serials control, and circulation—into a single system for computer, which I believe is perfectly possible, then we could easily justify the cost of the computer. We would replace enough personnel and handle enough increased volume to pay for it, and probably save money to boot. Just within the circulation operation alone we believe we're going to save $8,000 a year right now, net. When an institution gets above 10,000 students, and has a book purchase budget of around $150,000 a year, and a collection of 300,000 or 400,000 titles, it has reached the point at which it warrants a small-scale computer exclusively for clerical processing."

Just what impact the coming mechanization of clerical processing will have on the design of new library buildings is still problematical. It is apparent that different interior arrangements of work space will be required for conducting the paper work of the library. The circulation desk, the acquisitions area, and the serials control space, will all probably be smaller in the future than they are now. But space will have to be provided for some of the machines themselves. More than this it is, at present, impossible to predict.

THE CASE OF THE $5,000 FILE DRAWERS

At the same time that clerical processing in the library is being automated or mechanized, steps are being taken to harness the machine for far more complex library functions. The second point of attack, one already receiving considerable attention from researchers, is the library catalog, a central determinant of the interior layout of libraries today.

The catalog, consisting of hundreds of drawers of index cards listing the books of the library by author, title, and subject matter, and located in a central place in the library, represents the key to the collection. The user, after finding the appropriate card in the catalog, reads from it the number assigned to the book he seeks. This number is, in effect, the address of the book, a code indicating its location in the stack. The catalog is an essential part of any library; it is also, librarians believe, a barrier between the user and his material. As one librarian puts it: "Particularly in large libraries the catalog becomes a mammoth thing, a monster almost."

The larger the collection grows, the more unwieldy the catalog. In big libraries whole crews of catalogers are kept busy assigning numbers to new titles and filing cards for them in the catalog drawers. As the drawers fill up, new sections must be added and the cards redistributed, a job that requires months of advance planning and weeks of work to accomplish. Moreover, as the catalog expands, the time and cost of filing each new card increases. "We believe on the basis of some studies that catalogers spend 90 per cent of their time moving back and forth between their desks and the catalog and thumbing through cards," says Donald Black. "The intellectual part of their work occupies only 10 per cent of their time. Yet catalogers are in short supply, and they are among the highest paid library workers."

The card catalog, representing a fantastic concentration of labor, time, and money, is a one-of-a-kind proposition. It is the central control of the library, and no duplicate of it exists. There is no reference point to check back against when something goes wrong with it. Thus at U.C.L.A., when four catalog drawers were stolen some time back (presumably by a prankster) the job of reconstituting those drawers took on prodigious proportions. Deducing what cards had been in them, searching the miles of stack shelving for clues, and making up and filing a new set of cards ran to an estimated $20,000 in expense—$5,000 a drawer.

The catalog is also highly expensive to house. The cases in which it is filed are usually the single largest item of cost in the furniture and equipment budget, apart from the stacks. It is estimated that these cases cost one cent per card. This means that for a library with 1,000,000 volumes, each requiring about four cards in the catalog, the cases alone run to roughly $40,000. A catalog of this size would occupy, perhaps, 1,500 square feet of choice, central space in the building, which, if it cost $25.00 a swuare foot would represent a capital expenditure of $37,500. In short, the catalog is to the library what the memory is to the mind. And its costs are commensurate with its importance.

From the point of view of cost, then, as well as from the point of view of making life easier for the library user, who is often intimidated by the sheer bulk and complexity of the catalog, anything that can be done to streamline the catalog is worth doing. Several things can be done—either now or in the foreseeable future.

One approach is described by Don Black: "You could put the catalog in a computer memory. This would be difficult and costly, but not impossible. You could then hook into this storage unit a number of what are called input-output stations. These are devices with a small television screen and a keyboard. The user looking, say, for a copy of 'Information and Communication in Biological Science' by Lowell Hattery, punches in the author and title on his keyboard. The computer is activated. It searches its memory, prints out the call number of the book, and transmits it to the station via television. You could put these stations—which, incidentally, only cost about $800 apiece—not only in the library but in each of the department offices, even in dorms."

Such a system, Mr. Black estimates, could go into operation for an expenditure of about $30,000 for equipment plus a monthly rental of about $2,400. In addition to this it would take about $20,000 to translate his catalog's 3,000,000 cards into readable language for the machine and feed it into the memory unit. These figures do not include, however, the unascertainable cost of developing the programs necessary to instruct the computer how to respond to queries. This would quite likely cost far more than the $20,000, for simply preparing the catalog and programing is by no means easy.

Nevertheless, an ambitious year-long project recently completed by librarians of the University of Illinois at Chicago, working with experts provided by manufacturers of data processing equipment, now shows the way not merely to automate the catalog, but to go beyond this and link cataloging with clerical processing functions in a single, overarching computer system that could revolutionize the field.

This system would begin with the punching of IBM cards for each new title to be purchased. These cards would be fed into a computer and the information from them stored in a magnetic tape storage unit. The computer would be programed to print out the actual order form to be sent to the publisher or book dealer, then to deduct automatically the necessary funds from the appropriate source. At this point the machine would create a weekly list of titles "in process." Once a month the machine would print out a cumulative list of new titles that have already arrived.

At the same time the entire catalog of the library's holdings would be fed into the machine, which in turn would print out a holdings catalog in book form. Duplicate copies of this book could, like the input-output stations mentioned above, be distributed around the campus at convenient places so that a student or researcher could actually do a good deal of his bibliographic research without setting foot in the library building itself. (Users could determine the catalog number of the books they want and phone the library. A messenger service would be provided to deliver the books to them.) At intervals the cumulative new titles catalog and the main catalog would both be run through the machine to create a single up-to-date book catalog, with as many duplicate copies

as are needed. The loss of a drawerful of cards would no longer be a disaster.

The computer would also create a daily list of books out on loan, and automatically print out overdue notices when necessary. Developers of this system also plan to produce magnetic tape units that store lists of faculty reading interests. These tapes would be automatically matched with titles of incoming books, and notices would be printed alerting faculty members of the arrival of new volumes in which they may have an interest. The system, its developers believe, can also be extended to carry out serials processing.

The effect of such a system on the physical layout of the library building has yet to be determined. But at present the positioning of the card catalog dictates many other interior design decisions. This is true because it must be conveniently available to users, to catalogers, to reference librarians, and others. The reduction of the catalog to tapes or discs inside a computer storage unit, and the distribution of books or input-output stations around the campus would open up many possibilities for new and varied uses of space in the library building and for possible reductions in the space needed.

THE LIBRARY OF THE FUTURE

Such developments and others, like the preparation of *Index Medicus*, an index of medical literature prepared through sophisticated machine techniques by the National Library of Medicine, all represent milestones on the path to the push-button library. By most of those who use the term, this is taken to mean a library based on a fully automatic information retrieval system. In such a library the user would rely on machines not only to tell him where to locate the book or journal article he wants, but literally to deliver to him its contents. If card catalogs can be fed into a computer memory, why can't the data now stored in books? Indeed, say many critics of the *status quo*, unless some way is found to crack this problem, data recovery will become so time consuming and costly as collections swell in size in the future, that research will grind slowly to a halt.

As a result, an intensive effort to solve the technical and intellectual problems associated with automatic information retrieval is now under way around the world. Researchers, technicians, scholars, librarians, and others are at work, not merely in the United States, but in Japan, India, Belgium, Holland, France, England, and other nations, on the host of mechanical and related problems that still bar the way to the library of the future. Information retrieval, mechanical translation, automatic indexing and classifying, optical scanning or pattern recognition, high speed photography, and printing, are a few of the subjects being probed. Much of this research is financed by military and intelligence agencies, but its potential impact on libraries is profound.

Out of this melange of research two main lines of attack emerge. In one, the actual documents—pages of books, for example—would be reduced by microreproduction techniques to pinhead size, then stored on film in what is, in effect, an information warehouse—a miniature library. Each item is coded, and a memory unit in a computer "remembers" where it is located in the warehouse. One version of this system (there are several) has been produced by IBM for the Central Intelligence Agency, and is known as WALNUT. The WALNUT system makes it possible to recover any of millions of documents or book pages within five seconds. The user starts his search by writing a few key words on a form. These might be "library," "technology," and "computer." From this form a punched tape is made, and this directs the computer to search its memory for headings related to these key words. The machine then presents the user with a list of documents relevant to his study. He indicates which he wants.

When he does, the computer locates the item and activates a mechanical device that extracts the appropriate film. The images on this film may then be enlarged and read on a viewer, or may be photographically enlarged and converted into so-called hard copy—i.e., a duplicate of the printed original.

The second line of attack condenses the information itself, not merely its physical embodiment. The ideal system based on this principle would begin with a scanning device which automatically "reads" printed matter and translates it into machine language. Next the material is abstracted, classified, and indexed automatically and stored in a computer. The user can call up relevant abstracts automatically, but he goes about getting the original documents he may want in the conventional manner. He is spared reading in full a lot of material that he doesn't really need, and the machine sharply reduces the amount of time he needs to spend searching.

Primitive systems employing both methods now exist, although most have only a relatively small capacity for data storage. Which line of research will prove the most practical and economical in the years ahead is impossible to predict with assurance. In either case, the concentrated study of the entire problem, and the growth of what might be called information science, will necessarily reshape the library.

One form that the library of the future may take has been sketched dramatically by John D. Kemeny, chairman of the Department of Mathematics at Dartmouth, in a paper read as part of the Massachusetts Institute of Technology Centennial Lecture Series. Speaking of the continuing growth of Brobdingnagian collections, Dr. Kemeny talks of the day when libraries could reach the 100,000,000 volume mark. "It is clear," he states, "that the cost of building, of purchasing volumes, of cataloging, and of servicing these monstrous libraries will ruin even our richest universities."

The only solution to the problem of mushrooming magnitude, Dr. Kemeny believes, is the creation of a national research library big enough to hold the equivalent of 300,000,000 volumes in miniaturized form. He proposes storing all this data on film tapes retrievable by computer. The user could have access to this central storage center without leaving his campus, through the help of a multi-channel cable on which data can be transmitted. "The university," says Dr. Kemeny, "will have a large number of reading units scattered around the campus, some at the university library, some in departmental reading rooms, and some in individual professors' offices"—the number to depend on the institution's size and "library" budget.

These reading machines would have within them "reading tapes" similar to Videotape, a three-inch section of which, he calculates, could hold the equivalent of 10 miniaturized volumes. The reader would dial a number to be connected with the central storage bank. From it the relevant tape would be extracted, and an image of its contents transmitted through the cable to the user's reading machine. These images would be reproduced on the strip of reading tape inside the reading machines. The reading tape could then be projected on the reading machine's screen, much as microfilm is today, or it could be photographically enlarged to make a full-scale duplicate of the original book or document.

It has been suggested that instead of a single central information storage bank, regional centers might be established at different universities, each perhaps specializing in certain fields of knowledge as the participants in the Farmington Plan already do.

Dr. Kemeny, who speaks of this centralized information bank as "the library of 2000 A.D.," does not believe that such massive information centers would necessarily do away with campus libraries, but they would, of necessity, radically transform their functions. He says, "I take it for granted that our university libraries will not be abolished, even if their role becomes secondary. Partly this will be due to the fact they will serve a limited but useful purpose, but mainly to the fact that faculty members will be reluctant to give up personal contact with books." In this connection, Dr. Kemeny urged retention on the campus of any book that might be consulted as often as once a week. This would include, he said, "present reference rooms, as well as core research libraries in all subjects. The periodicals room would still serve as useful a purpose as in the past... Students would have books on reserve...." But all of these functions, Dr. Kemeny declared, "could be fulfilled comfortably with a collection of no more than a few hundred thousand volumes," and this, he added, was a generous estimate. These small libraries might be permitted to grow slowly, but a ruthless control over their size would be exercised, and the spaces now used as libraries, but freed by automation, could be converted to faculty studies and reading rooms, in the sense indicated above—that is, rooms with receiving machines.

There are, however, those who go even further than Dr. Kemeny in predicting the contraction of the campus library. According to Sol Cornberg, perhaps the most radical prophet of the new library technology, the campus library is doomed. Books, says Mr. Cornberg, "are inefficient. It's not that we don't like them—my wife is a novelist, as a matter of fact—but they just aren't the best way to transmit information anymore. We don't like the laborious problems of finding information in them. Furthermore, to serve a thousand students you need multiple copies. You need storage space for them. The weight of the books is reflected in the architectural costs. Floors get heavier, steel supports, foundations get heavier. Yet in a cabinet the size of my desk or a bit higher we can store 20,000 volumes on microfilm. Nobody can tear a page out of them. They don't smell of old vellum or glue, but you can browse through them and sit there and read them."

Mr. Cornberg goes further. The day when reading will be a primary form of information intake is also passing, he believes. Students will learn better and faster through audio-visual techniques, with films, lectures, and other materials piped directly to them in their homes. "Reading and writing will become obsolete skills," he predicts.

At Grand Valley State College, where Mr. Cornberg is installing the latest audio-visual equipment, he conducted a successful battle to restrict the size of the library to no more than 23,000 volumes. Even this many books he considers a concession to the sentimentality of the faculty. "Today's student learns more easily from a television screen than from a book," he insists. Mr. Cornberg's advice to campus planners is explicit. "My advice is: plan no more buildings for library use. The library space is a concession to the past. Don't invest in bricks and mortar!"

WHEN IS TOMORROW?

What stands between the library of today and this smoothly efficient, precision-machined tomorrow?

Plenty.

Before the library of the future can become a reality—if, indeed, we want it to—a number of towering intellectual, technological, and economic barriers must be hurdled. This is not the place to rehearse these all in detail. But a look at only a few of them impresses one with their complexity.

As human knowledge expands, becomes ever more splintered into sub-specialty and sub-sub-specialty, and the relationships between specialties become more important, it becomes necessary to improve profoundly our system for the classification of knowledge. The utility of any system of information retrieval, whether manual or automatic, depends most heavily on how finely the data in the memory bank is classified and cross referenced. Before large masses of vital knowledge are committed to a machine mind, it is absolutely essential that systems of classification be so highly developed that nothing of significance will be lost. Yet today we do not know enough about logic, semantics, psychology, and the structure of knowledge to code all existing information so that we can safely pull it out of a storage unit.

The problem of classification is essentially an intellectual problem. It has nothing to do with nuts and bolts. But it is growing ever more difficult as the volume of information expands. As one researcher has pointed out, "The difficulty of assigning something to the *right* pigeonhole is greater, the greater the number of pigeonholes. It is thinkable that for a sufficiently large and detailed subject list, a point of considerable doubt may be reached as to whether two people (for example, cataloger and user or reference librarian) would agree on a classification assignment often enough to permit the system to work at all. This problem may be one of the most important consequences of information growth."

Today scholars at Harvard, University of Minnesota, University of Iowa, Western Reserve University, and elsewhere are digging into the terminological or classification problems of information retrieval. But until human knowledge, seen as an organic system, is better understood, and a reliable and sufficiently sophisticated system of classification is agreed upon, we are not going to be ready to use machinery, simply because, as one expert puts it, "we don't dare run the risk of losing information."

Machines have been developed that can index and classify material automatically, by recognizing certain key words in the material and matching them against a list of categories. Studies indicate, in fact, that these machines can index and catalog faster and more accurately than human catalogers. But how well they can do this depends entirely upon the refinement of the category lists fed into them and the sophistication of their programs—both dependent upon the human brain, and both not yet developed to anywhere near the point necessary for feeding whole libraries into little black boxes.

Moreover, there are certain kinds of retrieval that a human reference librarian can perform that no known machine can. This is retrieval based not on objective factors, but on associative recall, a wholly subjective process. As one information retrieval specialist has explained it: "The machine may be able to get me a copy of Shannon and Weaver on 'The Mathematical Theory of Communication' if I ask for it and describe it correctly. But it cannot, if I misidentify it. Yet I can ask a librarian for a copy of that red book by Shannon on information theory, and somehow, through a process of association she will remember that it is, in fact, an orange book, and that it is the one that has been circulated a lot recently to faculty members in the math department, and that its title is not what I said. She can find it for me despite my misinforming her." A good deal more work must be done on human psychology and perception before the machine can match this capability. "For a long time," says this expert, "the first step in information retrieval will be a conversation between a user and a librarian."

Another and related problem is the difficulty of reducing data to machine language. This is not a problem in those systems which, like WALNUT, simply reduce the physical size of the document. But for those methods that depend on reducing the *content* of books through abstraction, this problem is critical. These systems may begin with a scanning device that "reads" the data submitted for inclusion in the system and converts it into machine readable form. Automatic reading is done through "pattern recognition"—that is, the machine is constructed so that different patterns of sight or sound, say, a letter of the alphabet printed on a white background or spoken against a backdrop of silence, trigger certain responses in the machine. Optical and magnetic scanners that do this have received much publicity in the popular press. Yet the fact is that no machine yet exists that can "read" or "recognize" more than a single typeface.

Today every library of consequence contains materials printed in as many as 1,000 different typefaces, plus a great volume of data in foreign languages and in alien scripts. Donald Black of U. C. L. A. cautions: "The large academic library will have mountains of retrospective material that cannot be put into machine readable form in the foreseeable future. You can't even get catalogers nowadays who can read Sanskrit. Where are you going to get a keypunch operator who can? Or a machine?"

In addition to such intellectual and technological obstacles to the achievement of true automatic information retrieval, there are many social and economic difficulties. It is important to remember that information retrieval must do better what is done by nonautomatic means—not merely equal it—before it stands a chance of being adopted. Small systems are already being used by certain corporations and by government agencies. But for most purposes, campus libraries have no need for the speed of retrieval that automatic systems would make possible. And they do not have the money to pay the freight. Don R. Swanson, a trim, imaginative, but hardheaded researcher, manager of the Synthetic Intelligence Department, Thompson Ramo Woolridge Inc., is busy developing ways to accomplish automated information retrieval, and he serves on a committee exploring its possible application to the Library of Congress.

But Mr. Swanson cautions against the idea that automatic data recovery is around the corner.

"A complete set of Reader's Guide in conventional form," he points out, "provides 30-second access to 1-$1\frac{1}{2}$ billion bits of information stored in less than half a cubic yard of space, and a Boeing 707 filled with books and mail is so fantastically more efficient than the same amount of information transmitted electronically that it would seem a long time before electronic transmission can compete."

The idea that the book is already obsolete fills Mr. Swanson with contempt. "Right now the economics of automation are such that no present equipment economically threatens the book. This might change 10 years from now, but it'll be a long time before the book goes. What's more, any system of carrels hooked up to the Library of Congress or to regional depositories for remote TV reading of books or textual materials is visionary and impractical on a national scale in anything like the next decade or so. People who talk this way are glossing over 20 years of engineering and several billion dollars of expense. Can it be done? Sure. Technically. But you've got a lot of things other than technical problems to consider!"

One of these, of course, is economics. First there is the cost of designing the system—the so-called "software" cost. There is no way now to estimate the cost of designing the kind of vast and comprehensive systems envisaged by those who advocate fully automatic retrieval systems encompassing the data in whole libraries. One rule of thumb suggested by Dr. Robert M. Hayes, president of Advanced Information Systems Co., is that this part of the job often winds up costing roughly the same amount as the hardware—the machines themselves. These, obviously, represent the second major element of cost and may range into the multimillions of dollars when computers, printers, transmission facilities, and all related apparatus are taken into consideration. Next, there is what Dr. Hayes calls "the really significant cost—that of getting the material into a form that the machine can handle." This means the translation of text into machine language and its subsequent preparation in the form of punch cards or tapes. Finally, there are the operating costs. Too little is known about any of these factors to make any real judgments. But all commentators agree the magnitudes involved are fantastically large for the complete data recovery systems under discussion.

The application of computers and punch card systems to clerical processing functions may be accomplished for far less expenditure and far more easily than the automation of information retrieval in the popular sense. For this reason, say experts like Dr. Hayes, the machine will find its place in the library. But not for information retrieval purposes for a long time to come. How long that time may be, he suggests, is a function of how badly automation is needed. For an institution like the National Library of Medicine, whose data must be available on demand and as quickly as humanly possible, the investment in I. R. can more easily be justified than an equivalent investment for a library that serves no essential research purpose or faces no intense urgency of demand.

Frank B. Rogers, director of the National Library of Medicine, and one of the most knowledgeable experts in the country on the application of machine techniques to the library, refuses to speculate on how long it will be before automatic information retrieval becomes a fact for most libraries. "If so little exists now, how can we extrapolate from it to make a prediction?" he asks. "All I know is that it is now possible to put the entire contents of the Library of Congress into a little black box. But it would take another black box 10 times the size of the Library of Congress just to provide the juice to run it!"

BUILDINGS OF THE FUTURE

Before it committed itself to plans for a library at Edwardsville, Illinois, Southern Illinois University dispatched consultant Donald G. Moore to survey the technological advances that might affect its decision. Mr. Moore interviewed 43 experts employed by companies like IBM, Lockheed, the Martin Company, Information Handling Services, System Development Corporation, Thompson Ramo Woolridge, Teleprompter Corporation, and R.C.A., as well as at the Stanford Research Institute, and the University of California Radiation Laboratory. His preliminary report presents a striking and imaginative picture of the possibilities of the future. But his findings clashed directly with the views of Mr. Cornberg. The report declared: "There was nothing found that would conflict with the conclusion that the Edwardsville campus should have a book-containing library."

This conclusion is shared by hundreds of other librarians, architects, scientists, and technical experts. The present large-scale assault on the problems of information retrieval and storage, Mr. Moore reported, "is certain to have an impact on modern library facilities," within 10 years. But not so deep an impact as to make the library of books obsolete.

Today the library profession is watching the technological revolution with hawk-like concentration. "We know," says Ralph Ellsworth, "that the era of the 'handcraft' library is at an end." But this does not wash away the pressing need for new libraries *now*, the miracles of technology notwithstanding.

Today hundreds of colleges and universities go ahead with plans for new and better libraries than ever before. At the same time, they are keeping an eye cocked on the future, preparing for it as best they can. Hollow floors and ceilings going into new buildings are concealing miles of electrical conduit and ventilation ducting so that computers, punch card machines, TV screens, or other devices can be plugged in at any point. At U.C.L.A., alert to the possibilities, a pneumatic tube planned for a new building was increased in diameter so that it might carry IBM cards without the need for them to be folded.

At the National Library of Medicine, which has had more experience with the machine age than any other library in the country, preparations are being made for bringing in a computer so that it may improve and speed up the work now done by punch card equipment in the compilation of *Index Medicus*. The changeover has meant the installation of a false floor in the computer area to contain the wiring required and to serve as a plenum to dissipate the heat generated by the machine. Such floors now come in standard modular sections so that any section can be pulled out at will. A special 50-ton air conditioner is being readied, and another set aside for emergency service. Space is being allotted for the computer, for related machines, for parts and test equipment. A special fireproof vault is being built to store the precious magnetic tapes—the computer memory—when they are not in use.

The lack of extensive experience to date makes it impossible to predict accurately all the adjustments that must be made in the design of modern library buildings if they are to take full advantage of the coming age of automation. But the uncertainty that accompanies an age of rapid social and technological change proves the essential rightness of the modular revolution. For today, more than ever before, library buildings must avoid becoming frozen forms. They must be easily and swiftly convertible from one use to another. In the words of Ralph Ellsworth: "All we really know is that we should provide a good deal of uncommitted floor space that can accommodate rooms of varying size, each well-lighted, properly ventilated, with access to wiring ducts from which electrically powered machines can draw their power, with good soundproofing qualities. Such a building can be set up to meet the needs of the college at the present time and for the known future. This is about as far as our existing knowledge will permit us to go. . . . Our buildings should be capable of major expansion or of conversion to other uses."

The avalanche of technological discoveries, the accelerating pace of change may, as has been suggested, transform the library, eliminate the book, and provide still-unthought-of methods for collecting, storing, recovering, and communicating information. But for the foreseeable future the campus library, with all its primitive faults, will remain a vital part of our intellectual landscape. We need the know-how, money, and courage to make it just as good as is humanly possible.

ABOUT THE AUTHOR—Alvin Toffler has been a free-lance writer since 1961, contributing to such magazines as *Fortune, Life, Nation, Saturday Review*. He received a B.A. degree from New York University in 1949, was a Washington correspondent for two years, and Associate Editor of *Fortune*. Mr. Toffler has written three books: *The Culture Consumers,* 1964, *Future Shock,* 1970, and *Schoolhouse in the City,* 1968.

A Library of the Future

by Angus Snead MacDonald

Like Toffler, but 30 years earlier, MacDonald looks at the broader aspects of libraries and librarianship. Mr. MacDonald, a concerned layman, possessed a thorough understanding of the library function and even today he excites the imagination of the library planner.

A most unfortunate "pause in culture," dangerously affecting the current work and orderly growth of nearly all libraries, is being experienced during the present world wide depression. The protests of the comparatively few citizens to whom libraries are of vital interest are largely disregarded, although in America particularly, "made work" and salvaging expenditures are being lavished on the same non-cultural objectives as have already caused a top-heavy debt-structure. We are witnessing the fallacy of applying more materialism as a cure for too much materialism. We see the millions appropriated for unemployment relief expended on additional preparations for war, endless roads for aimless automobiling, financial props for over-capitalized or moribund institutions, and demoralizing doles to keep millions alive in semi-starvation. Meanwhile the fundamental tools of civilization with which a real recovery could be built—education, the arts, administration, national hygiene, research, and libraries—are criminally neglected.

What will finally come out of the economic crisis due to our bungling management no one can say. But it can safely be assumed that industrialization has come to stay and will ultimately result in the universal distribution of an unprecedented amount of leisure. The wholesome utilization of this leisure becomes a problem of vast importance, not only to the individual, but to the state and the world at large.

For the masses, the advent of this unprepared for leisure may be either a menace or the greatest boon which mankind has ever received. No small part of the responsibility for its wholesome utilization will rest on the shoulders of those directing the planning and management of our library systems. But some radical changes in Library Science are definitely indicated. Public libraries must so demonstrate their social value that they will be given equal consideration with public schools instead of being looked upon merely as luxuries for the book-loving few.

This presents a problem relating in part to library architecture and here a definite challenge must be faced. Now as never before library buildings are needed which will strongly attract and adequately serve a large and representative cross section of national population. This goal will not be easily attained as commercial interests will strive to exploit the newly found hours of leisure and will prevail over library management unless the situation is met with ingenuity and bold progressiveness.

We must admit at the outset that the use of traditional library architecture will not solve the problem. It has three fundamental faults: lack of intimate charm, inadequate accommodation, and narrow class interest. Fortunately, we have available a vast amount of talent in the fields of both library science and architecture. The principal handicap is the tyranny of long established habit. Our library buildings still follow the traditions of regal display at the expense of utility and good reading conditions; of chained books in their arrangements for close supervision; and of student-class exclusiveness in their failure to appeal to the man on the street.

To get out of this rut of tradition, architects and librarians should cooperate in developing specifications of requirements based on revised methods of library administration in order to foster the use

SOURCE: Reprinted from Angus Snead MacDonald in "A Library of the Future," appearing in *Library Journal* in two parts, December 1, 1933, pp. 971-975 and December 15, 1933, pp. 1023-1025.

of libraries by *all* classes. Many onerous restrictions should be removed, discarding the old idea that libraries were intended only for professional men, scholars and born readers.

But there must also be a definite discarding of tradition in regard to past limitation of funds available for library purposes. Specifications once developed, they must be made feasible by ample appropriations. Fortunately, public sentiment, influenced by the Depression, is beginning to see the futility of over-investing free capital in the production of consumables alone and the economic distress that results when culture is allowed to become static or decline. We are beginning to realize that through the stimulating influence of a constantly developing culture we can have a "becoming" civilization with augmented markets for all and general prosperity.

The advent of a policy recognizing the practical value of culture forces libraries to become leaders in the movement to conserve and divert to constructive ends our new leisure.

But can this be done?

For the sake of making clear the major requirements for success, let us visit in imagination a central public library of the future: one that is serving directly and through its branches a city of two hundred thousand people together with the contiguous suburban and rural territory.

We are interested to learn that the library is not located near the congested center of the city, but in a spacious park on a main avenue in the residential section, as, like the trees in the park, it is a living, growing organism requiring continually more and more room for expansion.

We find the library set well back in the park—an impressive, towering building that nevertheless avoids overwhelming us with a monumental or institutional aspect. Because of the unconventional planting of trees and shrubs bordering the paths of approach and of the informal simplicity of the architecture, we have no feeling of awe but rather one of personal interest. The walls, with the contiguous suburban and rural territory, work with random jointing, and a warm, light color effect. Glimpses of gay colored awnings and green planting on "setback" terraces and the roof stir our curiosity. The main entrance is not the imposing feature one usually expects for a large public building. There is no long flight of steps to be climbed to a series of enormous doors. Instead, we see a vine-clad, arcaded porch level with the ground, into which we are attracted as though into the home of a well known friend.

But a shower causes us to choose an underground passage from our street shelter. This, we find to our delight, is much more than a utility subway; it is a brilliantly lighted exhibit gallery along which we get a foretaste of the treats in store for us in the library itself. While passing through we catch a glimpse of an enormous automobile parking space built deep down under the roots of the trees.

From the gallery we walk up an easy ramp into an ample entrance lobby. At either side are retiring rooms and in the center an inconspicuous but capacious wrap checking machine. Directly from the lobby we enter a spacious hall which proves to be the dominant feature of the library interior. It is instantly and agreeably impressive—not on account of any rich decoration or architectural elaboration but simply through its harmonious proportions, and the color and texture of the plainly visible wall and ceiling structure. The general effect is that of the reading lounge of a luxurious club.

At one end is a great fireplace surrounded by comfortably upholstered furniture and tables with a few new books, magazines, and vases of flowers. In a nearby corner, tea is being served by an attractive hostess to a group of young people, while an animated discussion goes on about a callenging new book. We note that smoking is permitted.

In the center of the hall convenient to the entrance, there is a circular receiving and delivery desk equipped with intercommunication apparatus and a mechanical system for conveying books to and from storage in other parts of the building. At either side of the delivery deck is waiting space with restful chairs and lounges. Beyond the desk are banks of card catalog cases—the only kind of formalized furniture we will see anywhere in the building.

At the other end of the great hall, we find alcoves formed by book ranges containing fresh copies of some of the newer books. The furniture is of a kind that invites one to sit down and browze. Here again, an attractive member of the library staff is stationed ready to give informal guidance whenever requested.

Above the alcoves, approached by easy and gracefully curving stairways, we enter the space for periodical reading located on a wide mezzanine which sweeps across the whole end of the hall and continues as an ample gallery along one side. This gallery contains the general reference collection arranged in alcoves. Everywhere we are impressed with the comfortable appearance of the furniture which does not in the least suggest the public institutions to which we have been accustomed.

From this gallery we enter the suite of rooms occupied by the Director of the library and his immediate staff. The Director is well known as a far sighted, socially minded executive who, started his career as librarian for a great industry. Later he became its president and secured national recognition through his successful administration. That position he left to become director of this library—at a salary which did not involve sacrifice on the part of his family.

We sit down in his reception room while he explains to us the fundamental principles of the library plan and its administration. The conversation is opened by our remarking on the delightful quality of the air in the library—which, despite smoking and the presence of a large number of persons, possesses the freshness of a fine autumn day. The Director remarks that absolute control of air conditions, temperature, humidity, and dust-content should be accepted as a matter of course in such a building—not only for health and comfort, but also as a measure of economy in heating and book-preservation. Thirty per cent more fuel would have to be burned during the heating season were it not that the relative humidity of the air is kept close to 60 per cent. This causes such slow evaporation from the skin that the room temperature can be maintained about 10° F. lower than would be comfortable with heated but unhumidified air. At the same time rebinding costs are kept low since the books do not become over-dry and go to pieces in handling. Furthermore, with an air washing and cooling system it is unnecessary to keep any windows open during the summer season, and, as a consequence, a vast amount of cleaning labor and wear and tear on books is saved.

The Director now expounds his general theory of administration. First of all there is no regimentation of readers. Reading, he feels, is individualistic and not fostered by offering a prospective reader one of a row of chairs at a row of tables in a large, closely supervised room which is as full of movement and noise as a public street. Some people can read under such conditions but most cannot or will not even make an attempt.

"We have arranged therefore, that every regular reader may have privacy; also that nearly all of the readers shall go to the books instead of having the books brought to them—thereby lessening personnel expense and book repair costs. To that end we have provided over fifty special departments in which books on particular subjects are collected in close proximity to those on related subjects. Each department is in direct connection with a central receiving and dispatching station, which takes care of calls from remote departments, the delivery desk and branch delivery room. Underlying everything we have done is the fundamental principle that the library must serve the needs and desires of all people—not only those who want books simply as books, but also the much larger class of those who use books only as adjuncts to other interests.

"Before our architect put a line on paper he was given a few basic instructions. In both exterior and interior architecture we wanted a feeling of homelike intimacy rather than monumental impressiveness. We desired charm, not grandeur, and for aesthetic effect we preferred to depend on good proportions and the frank use of logical materials, particularly local ones, rather than on architectural splendor and decoration.

"Furthermore, aside from the great public room at the entrance, some smaller rooms for casual readers, executive offices, receiving, shipping, mechanical equipment, etcetera, all other facilities for readers' use, book storage, and staff work were to be elastic, interchangeable, and adaptable for alteration as to location and area.

"Finally, although we believe in mass production in its proper place, we especially banned furniture of a standardized institutional character and suggested that all furniture be varied in design and as comfortable and attractive as one would expect in a well equipped home or club. The allowance for furniture and equipment was fixed at about 20 per cent of the cost of the building instead of the usual 10 per cent maximum. This increased allotment we felt was necessary in order to carry out our basic policy. Besides we expected, rightly as it turned out, that the simplification of our plan and the economy of our construction and finish would allow us to spend this extra amount for furniture and still keep our total cost per cubic foot down well below that of other library buildings.

"By the simplification of our plan was meant the virtual elimination of interior dividing walls and the total absence of any light courts, skylights and other difficult expedients to obtain natural light. The economy of construction was to be derived from the fact that three quarters of our building cubage was designed for elastic, interchangeable use, requiring merely an absolute minimum of building structure."

Even with this explanation we express surprise

that such luxury as we have seen could be linked with economy. But he goes on to state:

"In actual experience we found that still greater savings, based on square feet of usable area, were derived from our non-dependence on window ventilation and light. You have already noted the agreeable atmospheric conditions and probably also the ample and pleasant illumination even in remote corners. We have windows, it is true, but we depend on them only as a means of looking out of doors. They are never opened. Consequently we do not have to make our rooms unnecessarily high so as to allow the daylight to penetrate to the opposite wall.

"Most of our work and reading is done in our 'interchangeable' stack space which is only eight feet high from deck to deck. Throughout the reading and working areas of this space we average fifty square feet or four hundred cubic feet per person. But in one of the old style monumental reading rooms with its great windows and high ceilings, perhaps sixteen hundred cubic feet or four times as much is required. And at that only about thirty square feet of floor space could be alloted to each reader. Consequently, by increasing the total volume of our building about three times as compared to one of the old type serving a community of this size, we have been able to accommodate ten times as many persons. That was our aim.

"And there were many further savings in administrative expense which helped make this project possible. For instance with our system, as compared with that of an old-fashioned library, only about one-third as much air must be conditioned as to temperature, relative humidity, and freedom from dust because the ventilation in our compact space is far more efficient.

"Also, our lighting costs are less even though we supply illumination of daylight quality and the wholesomeness of mild sunshine in amount sufficient for easily reading the finest of print. In the monumental type of reading room most of the light is absorbed by the decorative treatment of walls and ceiling or lost out the windows. The readers get all too little—and yet the cost is heavy. We feel that daylight as well as window ventilation is much too fickle and costly to receive consideration in working up a library plan.

"The tyranny of tradition in library architecture has been so great that these wastes and handicaps have continued many years after they could have been eliminated. This is particularly surprising in connection with libraries which have long had on their shelves the very books to point the way to freedom."

All this seems logical from an architectural viewpoint but we ask for an explanation as to his administration policy in such building. He continues:

"We have already mentioned the Great Hall with its Periodical Reading Room and there are two adjacent general reading rooms. One of these latter is for general literature and the other for reference books. In these rooms we accommodate under supervision, all our casual readers and newcomers. But regular readers are given the run of the library without organized supervision, after investigation has proved their worthiness. These can go where they please and take from the shelves whatever books they may wish to use. Before leaving the building they are expected to take all their books to the nearest attendant's desk where they may get a release slip for any they desire to carry out of the building.

"Our wide open shelf system greatly fosters reading and a wholesome attitude towards the library. It also enables us to lessen the cost of handling books and almost to eliminate supervision expense. The value of the books lost or wilfully mutilated is small in comparison to the expense in money and good will of trying to keep close track of the readers. Of course our more valuable books and those not easily replaced are kept under lock and key—not so much to protect them from our regular readers as to frustrate professional book thieves.

"In every department where our readers may go they will find a specialist ready to advise them authoritatively on whatever phase of a subject may be of interest. For this purpose we have the equivalent of a staff of university professors, scientists and technical experts. All the departmental routine is taken care of by assistants and clerks so the specialists are entirely free for advisory service and their own work. As a consequence we have no difficulty filling these special chairs with highly competent and oftentimes outstanding men to whom our superb facilities, adequate salaries and freedom of action appeal."

This sounds most interesting but we ask quite naturally how such a faculty can be paid for in a free public library:

"Our library is free and tax supported as to the commonly expected facilities and services but we secure a special income to take care of the important extras. This comes from our Library Association to which regular readers contribute voluntarily in accordance with their interest and ability.

The contributions total far more than we receive from taxes and enable us to conform to the cities' policy of 'pay for service.' No one, however, is denied the fullest privileges because of lack of means.

"The collection of voluntary contributions was forced on us by the organized commercial amusement interests in order to stop what they called our tax supported, unfair competition for patrons. However, it had the reverse effect from what they intended. Our patronage increased and our association members take a proprietary interest in the library and all its property. They are willing to defend it against wastage from within and political discrimination from without, and are so numerous, influential, and keen in their support that we can now get from the city anything we may ask for within reason.

"This is a pleasant contrast to the old days when the library had difficulty in maintaining its book fund and the best salaries it could pay were all too meager. We have now reached the position where we can keep our accessions right up to the minute, and our salary scale compares favorably with that of any other line of work—public, professional, or commercial. For instance, our trustees, in fixing the Director's salary, made comparisons with the responsibilities of other executive positions as to number of employees, value of the plant, size of annual budget, educational qualifications and experience. The figure arrived at made the city politicians envious but it greatly increased the prestige of the library and its range of selection.

"Another great gain derived from our Association is in gifts. Formerly most people thought that a gift should be nothing less than the endowment for a special room or even a whole building. But now we have not only an increase in donations of great value but a constant stream of smaller gifts—old books, historical and genealogical papers, letters, works of art, items of decoration, furnishings, technical tools and equipment for our special departments. Some of these latter are purchases and some the handiwork of the skilled technicians we number among our strong adherents. Anyone who visits a certain department constantly soon comes to consider it as a sort of second home for which nothing he can give is too good. This division of the library into small, intimate departments is really the secret of our greatest success.

"But now suppose you take a look at some of the things of which we have been talking. So far you have seen only the static part of the building on the entrance side which accounts for about 25 per cent of our total volume. This part is not very different from what you have seen in other cities. But the rest of the building is dynamic and unique. Aside from the floor levels and such things as elevators, conveyors, and stairs, there are no fixed locations in this major portion not even as to the walls. The walls are made of unit panels insulated against heat transmission and interlocking with window sections and with deck floors in such a way that they may be taken down and reassembled in a new location. In this way we have made an expansible building that may be enlarged peripherally (and also vertically) by adding new layers of our 'interchangeable' general utility space whenever required. These layers are analogous to the annual rings of a tree trunk except that our rings will be spaced at intervals of about a decade.

"As all this 'interchangeable' space is divided up into small units, now patrons must be helped in finding their way around; so you will see right here near the main entrance, and also in all elevator lobbies, an automatic electric guide board. As you are particularly interested in architecture, suppose you look up that heading in the list of divisions in the column at the left and press the adjacent button. The lighted line on the block plan shows us the way through the passage directly opposite the main entrance to an elevator and the 17th deck. There we turn right, through the elevator lobby, to aisle L 12 and then left to our destination.

"The elevator lobby is a low well lighted room with upholstered furniture, a book conveyor station, attendant's desk, doors to rest rooms, and openings to the right and left hand main passages. These passages are about nine feet wide, simply paneled, and lined with paintings, etchings, and prints. At intervals there are signs at doors leading into various departments."

L 12 proves to be a short passage about seven feet wide. The walls are units of steel and glass covering recessed bulletin boards, exhibit panels, and shelving for rare books. The bulletin boards announce such lecture courses, exhibitions, and tours as might be interesting to architectural readers. The panels show sketches and photographs as examples of a coming exhibit, and behind glazed doors are rows of book treasures.

The passageway widens out into an open space about twenty-seven feet wide and fifty-four feet long with windows at the far end. Softly glowing tubes on the ceiling give out light of such quality that we cannot tell where the natural daylight ends and the made daylight begins. The floor is attractively tiled with a resilient, noise deadening material and rugs here and there give a homelike touch. The smooth, beamless, pearl grey ceiling, nearly eight feet high is acoustically treated to absorb sound. Consequently our footsteps and conversation are so muted that the readers hardly notice our entrance.

The equipment of the room seems graciously to invite one to stop and study. On a long table, that might have been taken with all its belongings from the home of a well to do bibliophile, there are local and foreign magazines, a few of the latest books between sculptured book ends, writing equipment, ash trays, and a flowering plant which adds just the right friendly touch. The chairs around the room are of various kinds and sizes and all are comfortable-looking. Some are plain, some deeply upholstered, while most have adjustable book rests or convenient side tables. Along the window wall there are several attractive nooks formed by book cases and equipped with lounges or groups of chairs and tables.

The lowness of the ceiling in proportion to the size of the room is hardly noticed because the overhead expanse is broken up by slender stack columns spaced about nine feet apart in both directions. Our host explains that a height of eight feet,—or eight foot multiples—from floor to floor has been adopted as the standard throughout the building instead of the formerly orthodox seven feet six inches. The extra six inches is just enough to prevent such study spaces as we are now in from seeming oppressively low. It also permits the installation of usable mezzanine stories anywhere between main structural floors.

The space we see is not defined by walls but merges gradually with the bookstack ranges which run off at right angles from all sides. Every second range is shortened by two compartments so as to form an individual study alcove. In these are collected the most used books on special subjects, while others are housed in ranges beyond.

The Director takes us to one of the window alcoves where we are introduced to an elderly gentleman, a former architect with a strong literary bent and now the specialist in charge of this department. He takes us around his division and shows us the outdoor reading terrace with shrubs and flowers, several studies for research, rooms for society meetings and a series of rooms cut right out of the stack space, and devoted to special purposes. One has files of trade catalogs, another architectural samples, and a third contains drawing tables with drafting machines and a pantograph. In still another we find young men and women who are working on building and landscape models. There is a space devoted to a large photograph collection, compactly stored in rolling cases. Alongside we find a photographer's room completely equipped with apparatus for reproducing, developing, printing, and color work.

We are informed that the architectural department, occupying some sixty-five thousand cubic feet, can accommodate over one hundred readers and workers, fifty-four thousand books and ninety thousand photographs. The equivalent space in a great reading room of the old type would accommodate only forty or fifty readers, with a few books in wall cases, and none of the other facilities. The savings in carrying charges on invested capital, in building maintenance and administration, and in library operatives, through letting the readers go to the books, makes possible all the fine technical equipment, luxurious furniture, perfect lighting, air conditioning, and expert advisory service—all that without any increase in cost over the budget of a library having accommodations for an equivalent number of readers but built on the principle of large supervised reading rooms and segregated book storage. Furthermore, the response from the citizens in increased patronage and good will is gratifying.

While we continue on our tour of inspection, the Director explains that the Architectural Department which we have just seen is typical of some fifty other departments each catering to a particular field of interest. These are all in a constant state of growth and adjustment made possible by the fact that there are no permanent vertical divisions throughout the general utility area. As a consequence, perfect elasticity in secured and related departments may always be kept close to each other horizontally or vertically without hindering their expansion. What is stack space one day may the next day be converted to reading space or open area for the work of the library staff. The lines of division between departments are formed by movable panels and doors which interlock with the stack columns and deck floors and can be quickly transferred to a different location without noise or muss. The same is also true of the stack ranges and the various items of equipment. These units, accurately and economically fabricated by methods of mass production, are interchangeable and may be installed wherever needed. Only the furniture is variable as it must suit a host of different individuals each with his own peculiarities.

"Adjustments for department growth," explained the Director, "and the accommodation of new departments are made at least once a year, when we go right through the library, cutting down, expanding, and shifting, so that each division is adequately housed and can take in a year's accessions without any crowding. Then whenever we find that our general utility space averages three quarters full, reading, working and storage all considered, we expand the building."

At this moment we see a job of departmental readjustment going on. A new division just established for Atomic Power is being split off from, but kept adjacent to, Physics, Electricity and Chemistry. The Applied Mechanics department is being moved to another tier close to Civil Engineering, and the space vacated divided among the four closely related departments which will now have an entire tier to themselves.

We are told that the physical work of establishing this new division will all be finished by an expert moving gang in one night and they will then proceed through the tier making the necessary adjustments in the neighboring departments. Everything, including the rearrangement and shelf listing of the books, is to be completed within a week with but slight inconvenience.

We now proceed cursorily through a number of other departments—Germanics with its suggestion of a mediaeval atmosphere in the furnishings; the Music division, which contains not only bound and sheet music but also records on rolls, discs, and films, apparatus for recording and playing and a dozen or more, small studios; Elizabethan literature with a splendid collection of first editions and prints; and a well set up book bindery; Forest Products having furniture made of woods from all over the world and samples of every known commercial variety; Comparative Religions with an interesting exhibit of ritual material, primitive and civilized, ancient and modern; and the Izaak Walton room with a work shop well filled with fishermen readers tying flies and making equipment. Right here the Director calls out attention to two men working side by side on a dry-fly rod and engaged in animated conversation. One he knows to be a pattern maker and the other a leading banker. It seems that attention to a common interest or hobby is a great destroyer of class distinction. These two men can associate in an intimate special library on common ground and without inhibitions. But such association in a great general reading room where there was no recognized common interest could scarcely be expected.

Each department is built with the same space units and with identical structural members, but there is a most pleasing variety and contrast between them. The space units are combined in different ways so as to secure for each department a layout which exactly fits its special requirements. Also, each has its own individuality and charm in the design and arrangement of the furnishings. And with each we get a visual impression suggesting the literary character of the department.

Every one of several dozen special libraries seems to be complete in itself and each interlocks and cooperates with all the others to form one great smoothly functioning general library.

We next visit the children's section, which occupies three entire tiers and generally duplicates but on a minor scale, the departments for adults. It has similar, although fewer, subject divisions, with experts in charge particularly selected for their understanding of children. Also the same kind of exhibits, work shops and laboratories are available for both boys and girls. We can readily see by the appearance of the children that the appeal is strong enough to attract many who would ordinarily avoid voluntary attendance at any cultural institution. It is in this children's section that interests are awakened which will later develop steadfast library supporters and good citizens.

We are informed that there is also a day nursery occupying most of the ground floor tier and having access to an adjacent enclosed playground in the park. Here, for a small fee, mothers may leave their children under safe and wholesome conditions while they attend to their business in the library. The Director feels that the library would fall far short of its mark if it did not reach the mothers of the community.

But now for the top decks and roof! Our guide remarks that the roof of a library was formerly left quite unused but he has found it, and the space immediately below, to be the most valuable areas in the building and all too small for the need. We get out of the elevator on the second deck from the top and find just beyond the usual small but attractive lobby a large reception hall. In the center is a wide space two tiers high with ample galleries around all four sides and club-like furnishings suitable for a reception, dance or musicale.

Opening off the reception hall are several lecture rooms of different sizes with complete equipment for sound and silent pictures, and also a "band box" theatre for little shows. All of these extend up through the height of two tiers and are equipped with rows of seats on removable, sloping platforms. These are to permit this special use area being turned into the typical "general utility" space whenever the building may be extended higher.

These facilities, we are told, are for the joint use of all the various library departments for such purposes as lecture courses, society meetings, receptions for notables, or travel pictures. When the advance schedule shows any free periods, organizations outside the library are allowed to come in. This has resulted in an ever increasing acquaintance with the library throughout the city and in a longer list of staunch friends each year.

We next proceed to the roof—or, actually, the top of the main building structure. The real roof is of steel and glass and surmounts an auxiliary super-structure. The elevator lobby on the roof is much larger than those below and serves as a reception room. One door from the lobby leads out into an open air reading room having a fine view over the city. It is equipped as a terrace garden with awnings, tables, comfortable wicker furniture, a pool and tinkling fountain and delightful planting.

From the Reading Terrace we pass through a gate in a hedge into a much larger area used as an outdoor café. Here, where a skillful landscape artist has had control, one has the feeling of entering the tea garden of a fine country club. The center of attraction is a wide fish pond full of aquatic plants and partly shaded by an overhanging dogwood tree and some flowering shrubs. Beyond the stone slabbed area around the pool there are lawns and flower gardens with high planting to form a background. In one spot this planting is kept down to parapet height disclosing a charming view of the park, suburb, farmland, and forest covered hills beyond a winding river.

The café tables continue from the outdoor terrace on under a veranda and into a glass enclosed dining room. It is explained that by means of a sliding glass roof the outdoor garden can also be enclosed to make a fully protected but sunny winter garden. The quality of the glass is such as to transmit wholesome light rays and its thin hollow slab form provides excellent insulation as the interior of each slab is a vacuum.

The Director explains that the planting we see serves other purposes than mere decoration: it is really the demonstrating laboratory for the Home Gardens department:

"Here is shown in a practical way the effect of special fertilizers, inoculations, electrical currents in the soil, light and gas treatments, and insecticides. Probably no single feature in connection with the library has made more library adherents than this roof garden. Just after it was opened a series of demonstration lectures was given on the decorative home garden, kitchen garden, private greenhouse, window box planting, and aquatic plant culture. The fame of the lectures spread by word of mouth and they became so popular that they had to be repeated immediately and then continued year after year. It seemed as though every housewife and 'five-o'clock' gardener in the territory wished to attend despite the fact that a fee was charged. We do not believe that such fees are a deterrent, but rather the contrary, where the subject is handled in a way to arouse personal interest. As a result of these lectures, many gardening and horticultural books have become more in demand than fiction 'best sellers.' "

Before taking our departure we sit down at one of the tables near the pool for an appetizer and luncheon while the Director summarizes their guiding philosophy:

"It is our belief that if a library can connect books in a vital and practical way with the commercial, professional, and recreational interests of the community it serves, its patronage will be limited only by its physical capacity, up to possibly fifty per cent of the population.

"We have aimed to develop our library as a working laboratory for all kinds of people rather than as a monumental reading place for the comparatively few congenial 'book worms.' By following that policy we have actually attained the ideal of making the library the 'People's University.' We find that there are far more people who will not read except as an adjunct to other interests than there are readers to whom books in themselves are sufficiently satisfying.

"In trying to adequately take care of both we had some serious difficulties to overcome such as the avoidance of impossible bulkiness in our building and overwhelming administration costs. Our architects found the answer merely by a logical simplification.

"We feel that in nearly every person there is a certain individuality which if properly developed will allow him to stand out in some activity instead of being completely submerged. I could cite you instance after instance of 'dead ended' clerks, mechanics, and even common laborers who have been sent here to see some practical demonstration in connection with their work or hobby, and as a consequence have become steady visitors and men of some achievement in life.

"This development of human individuality we consider to be one of the best balance wheels possible for the successful operation of a democracy.

Such people are not so easily led into mob madness by mere emotional appeal as are those who derive their ideas from the mass propaganda that can be so widely and attractively offered.

"A reader of books tends to become individualistic in his ideas. Those ideas may be extravagant in any individual but collectively the average is wholesome for the community and the state. The kind of intelligence which is cultivated by the personally selective reading of books makes for a steadiness that is not reactionary and for a progressiveness that likes to feel safe footing step by step as it proceeds.

"Such has been the experience in this community. As a result our public library system has won a position in popular esteem which need yield to no political whim or take second place to any other enterprise.

"What we are doing here today might have been done long ago and may be done tomorrow almost anywhere in the civilized world. We feel that such a library as we have serves an essential purpose in helping to develop the kind of mature men and women who can be safely entrusted with responsibility for governments operated under universal suffrage."

ABOUT THE AUTHOR—Angus Snead MacDonald graduated from the Columbia School of Architecture, and joined the staff of Snead and Company in 1905. He spent 47 years with the company, advancing to the position of president. When Snead and Company was sold, Mr. MacDonald continued his work as a library building consultant from his home in Virginia. He is famous as the originator of the Snead book stack (the module concept).

The Impact of Technology on the Library Building

A position paper prepared for Educational Facilities Laboratories

"Communications and information technologists, librarians, and architects . . . met at EFL's offices in New York City on June 7th and 8th, 1967. . . . Their task was to separate rhetoric from reality, fact from fancy. Specifically, they explored the wisdom of continuing to build libraries along traditional lines, and plumbed available knowledge for cues on how to prepare buildings to adapt to the new era. . . . [They] explored four principal areas of relevance: computer technology, microform technology, communications technology and the relationship of human beings to the possible changes ahead."

The image of the library has been as immutable as the shape of the steeple in a village landscape. Time has given these forms the stamp of authenticity. Within the past decade, however, cracks have been appearing in the library's facade—and they are growing wider.

Computer technology, microform technology, and developments in communications, have created a potential for the storage, retrieval, and exchange of information beyond any means ever before attainable. Indeed, Sunday supplement writers, fired by the far-reaching visions of pioneers in these fields, declare that the book will become obsolete. It will be an artifact exhibited in museums, they tell us, its functions assumed by electronic circuitry. And libraries, as the institutions we have known them to be, will be things of the past.

This hypothesis, as Mark Twain reported on the news of his death, is greatly exaggerated. The book, which appears to have extraordinary survival power, has stood up thus far against the real and imagined threats of radio, film, and television. Witness its career since 1945, for example, when general television broadcasting began. The circulation of public library books in the United States has increased by more than 200 percent; and from 1960 through 1965, the numbers and titles of new books, and new editions of books produced in the United States, increased by more than 90 percent.[1] *Publisher's Weekly* reports that the past two years were banner years for book sales, continuing an upward trend in annual overall book figures for more than a dozen years. In 1965, dollar volume ran to over 2 billion.[2] In 1966, how to meet the bottlenecks in production and delivery caused by the demand became a major industry issue.

The survival powers of the book notwithstanding, technological changes in the making *could,* one day, profoundly alter the traditional operations of libraries—and their buildings. And those within the profession, as well as college and university presidents, trustees, governing boards of public libraries—all those responsible for planning library buildings and committing large funds to their construction, are concerned.

This concern is by no means a matter of resistance to change. On the contrary, library professionals are actuely aware of the dire need for new solutions to mounting library problems. Major among these is the flood of new information. Most of the nation's libraries are hard pressed for money to buy, and space to house, the torrent of books and journals pouring off presses around the world. There are 400,000 books published annually worldwide, roughly twice that of a decade ago.[3] In the sciences alone, where old-fashioned physics, biology, and chemistry have bred new fields like biomagnetics, macromolecular physical chemistry, and cryogenics, to name only a few, there are 35,000 separate journals published annually with over 1.5 million articles in them. The journals themselves are estimated to be growing in number at the rate of 5 to 10 percent a year; the literature in them

SOURCE: Reprinted from "The Impact of Technology on the Library Building," a position paper prepared for Educational Facilities Laboratories, 1967, by permission of the publisher.

doubling every 10 to 15 years.[4] The Library of Congress owns 54 million items. Cornell University catalogs over 85,000 titles a year. And if one considers that academic and research libraries tend to double the size of their collections every 16 to 20 years—then, in the words of mathematician J. G. Kemeny, "the cost of building, of purchasing volumes, of cataloging, and of servicing these gigantic libraries could eventually ruin our richest universities." This says nothing of the difficulties that lie in wait for the user as he approaches the card catalogs of awesome dimensions, or the reference librarian who is estimated at the present time to walk an average of eight miles a day on the job.

How to cope with it all is by itself a subject of prolific literature in the library world. Librarians themselves are the first to recognize that the solution is not simply more books, more buildings, and more librarians. What they look forward to, and *need*, is a change in the very concept of what a library is: that is, beyond its function as a depository of books, the library must become a source of active information transfer. The new technologies offer the long-range hope of realizing this concept, and librarians, above all, welcome it. Through computer storage and retrieval, microforms, long-distance transmission, and the like, it may yet be possible to multiply the usability of every information unit, to transcend the physical and geographic limitations of the library building, and ultimately, perhaps, to make one's home or office in Kimberly, Idaho as fruitful a place for learning as the best public, academic, or research libraries in major centers.

But to what extent this will ever be a reality is the big question. Almost as important is the question of when.

The answers are urgent because well-planned, flexible buildings erected today can serve for 100 years; because current construction costs per square foot for library building space range from $25 to $40 per square foot depending on the region of the country and other variables, with total project costs running roughly a third more, including fees, furnishings, and the like; and finally, because we are in a period of intensified activity in library construction.

Increased population, greater numbers of young people going farther in higher education, federal assistance, the opening of new fields of employment, greater leisure time—and present library deficiencies which are acute—are behind the building surge.

The Office of Education reports that, among public libraries, though capital outlay soared from $12.3 million in 1956 to $103 million in 1965, prospective capital expenditures to construct 68 million gross square feet of public library space by 1975 come to $1.9 billion.[5] Still, this will not satisfy the full needs, estimated to be more than 90 million square feet by 1970.

For libraries in public and nonpublic schools, estimates are that more than 3.4 billion square feet of space will be necessary by 1972.

And in institutions of higher education, the indications are that more than 135 million new square feet of space will be required by the same date.[6] Scheduled for construction in two- and four-year colleges are 1,200 buildings to go up between 1966 and 1970. Their anticipated cost, including furniture, comes to $2.17 billion.[7]

Given the magnitude of monies already committed, and the additional sums likely to be so allocated, it is little wonder that librarians are deeply concerned. If it is a fact that in the future the bulk of knowledge will be stored on magnetic tapes or greatly reduced microforms and fed into computers; that information transactions will be negotiated through terminals located at home, in the dormitory, the classroom, the office, or in service stations remote from where information is stored; and that information will be transmitted to users over long distances, then indeed it is imprudent if not illogical to plan costly structures to house nonexistent books and their readers.

The questions that hang over the heads of library planners are (a) the probability of these propositions, and (b) whether they will be true for all types of information, in all types of libraries, in small ones as well as large, (c) whether they will be economically practical or prohibitively expensive, and (d) the speed of change.

Between the myths and the realities, between the over-simplifications of the space-age writers and the arcana of the new sciences, planners are caught in a web of dilemmas.

It is not uncommon to encounter representatives of small liberal arts colleges, influenced by the space-age prose, who are afraid they have fallen behind the times because their libraries lack automated information systems. In fact, such highly sophisticated operations are at present confined to a very few specialized national libraries such as the National Library of Medicine or the American Chemical Society. These deal mainly with bibliographic material, not text, and almost all of them are in some important aspects still experimental or developmental. Similar misconceptions exist in relation to automated "housekeeping" processes such as circulation, acquisitions, serials control, and the like. While these chores are in fact automated in many libraries, it is at present more economical in small ones to manage them in the traditional mode. There are still other stiuations where new library facilities are desperately needed, but planners are sitting tight, chary of committing sizable funds to structures that may turn out to be anachronisms.

Clearly, there is a need for shared expertise and for common sense in its application. Those with responsibility for decision-making must be informed of the implications of the new technology and provided with guidelines so they can proceed with confidence that the buildings they plan today will be usable in the future. The present state of the art of library architecture, based on modular principles which allow for interior flexibility, has until now provided that confidence. We knew that such buildings, appropriately located, capable of expansion, and with provisions for the addition of electric and air-conditioning loads, could serve as well in the year 2067 as they do today.

But in the light of the unfolding possibilities for the management of information, do these principles remain sound and adequate?

To probe for viable answers, EFL arranged a symposium of experts from the relevant disciplines. Communications and information technologists, librarians, and architects (see appended list of participants) met at EFL's offices in New York City on June 7th and 8th, 1967. Broadly, they addressed themselves to the impact of technology on library buildings. Their task was to separate rhetoric from reality, fact from fancy. Specifically, they explored the wisdom of continuing to build libraries along traditional lines, and plumbed available knowledge for cues on how to prepare buildings to adapt to the new era.

Two days of discussion explored four principal areas of relevance: computer technology, microform technology, communications technology, and the relationship of human beings to the possible changes ahead.

Other points dealt with, in addition to those noted earlier, were the cost of envisioned programs; patterns of library use; how the library may absorb particular innovations or be absorbed by them; centralization, decentralization, and networks; the implications for space requirements, mechanical provisions, and the physical environments of buildings.

Every question could not be fully answered either for lack of time or because there are no answers at this point in time. The critical questions, however, were covered. What follows represents the consensus of views expressed concerning the impact of technology on library buildings over the next 20 years or so, beyond which period forecasts would take on aspects of pure speculation. It is EFL's hope that they will resolve for the present some of the uncertainties that beset the profession, and provide a guide to assist planners in the approach to their task.

COMPUTERS

The first substantial application of the computer to library processes began in 1959, propelled by the scarcity of librarians, the rapidly soaring costs of processing books, and the increasing flood of publications. Since that time there has been a great deal of pioneering work in most areas of library operations, usually in large libraries, and with varying degrees of success. These early attempts have been to a great extent random and unrelated to each other, even competitive, with programming developed for local operations only and with scant or immature reports of results.

Four areas of library activities have been repeatedly attempted—bookkeeping operations connected with the ordering and receiving departments (in many libraries); the handling of catalog data for books, sometimes accompanied by book catalogs printed by computer (such as that at the University of Toronto); circulation control (such as that at the University of California at Los Angeles); and information retrieval of technical data, law citations, bibliographical citations, and most ambitiously, the MEDLARS program at the National Library of Medicine. The latter results in computer production of the *Index Medicus* and the searching of information contained in it on demand. The Library of Congress now has under way in Project MARC a series of ambitious experiments in computerized library processes, concentrated at present on the handling of catalog data. Since the Library of Congress is pivotal, to the degree that these experiments are successful they will affect the entire library world.

Many of the results obtained to date are impressive, but conflicting claims have created confusion about the entire field of computerization in libraries. The questions facing any library interested in computerization today are—Should we computerize, when, and why? What should we computerize? What are the costs involved, and should we accept them? What relation will local computerization have to regional or national computer projects, such as those of the Library of Congress? What information about library computerization can we depend on?

The course of computer development and use within the library over the next 20 years is likely to proceed as follows.

Its first general impact will be in the area of housekeeping chores—order records and reports, fiscal control, circulation systems, etc. Application of the computer to bookkeeping operations, such as buying and receiving, is the easiest to accomplish. Moreover, it is the area in which considerable experience in many libraries to date indicates clear cost advantages in large operations.

The second field of general application—and impact—will be the computerization of the library card catalog. Some aspects of this are now technologically feasible. The promise is that this will extend greatly the usefulness of information contained in the present card catalog. Its advantages lie in its accessibility to users beyond the library, in permitting the interchange of catalog information between libraries, and in mobility within the library itself for checking holdings, changing location records, and the like. While the conversion of any library operation to automation must be undertaken with the greatest care and planning because of the very large costs involved, this is especially so with regard to computerization of the card catalog.

Totally aside from costs, there are technological and intellectual problems of the greatest magnitude to be overcome before computerized catalogs will be generally usable. Direct access files of larger storage capacity than presently available in computer systems will be required to store the catalogs of great research libraries. The capability of simultaneous consultation of the catalog by very large numbers of users must be expanded (the present limit is about 30). · Problems of what terms and how many to use in describing catalog information must be resolved. Programs to retrieve only the materials specifically required by a user must be developed. But, despite these problems it is expected that within 10 to 20 years, the use of computerized catalogs will be widespread.

When dealing with the storage and retrieval of text, equally formidable problems exist. Data or factual evidence of small unit size is easily manipulable by the computer, but much more complex bodies of thought or of knowledge are not. As of the present, it would appear that most of the literature in the humanities and social sciences will remain primarily useful in book form. There is no signal advantage in converting Plato's dialogues to machine readable form and retrieving them or juxtaposing them by the computer. It is therefore economically senseless to attempt a massive conversion of existing library books to machine readable form, since the advantages of doing so are minimal in many subject fields, and the costs enormous. The change to computer storage of full texts, when it comes, will be evolutionary, not revolutionary, and it is unlikely that the library as a repository of books will be replaced in the near future by a computer in the basement consulted by remote consoles.

The first phase of development in information retrieval will use the computer to store and retrieve highly used specialized data, probably in nonalphabetical languages, in the physical and life sciences—as is now being done on a limited scale. Sometime later, perhaps within 10 years, the texts of some highly used materials selected from current science and non-science publications will be originally published in computerized form. But for the next 20 years or more, the great bulk of publication will be in conventional print form, with a gradual increase in the production of microform texts. Retrospective conversion of texts to machine readable form is not expected to any great degree for a very long time in the future. Therefore, the bulk of a scholar's negotiations in a library will be with books even 30 years from now.

MICROFORMS

The vision of carrying the Library of Congress around, in miniaturized form, in a shoebox, has long been held—and in a smaller way, projected and abandoned at Wake Forest College.

The use of microfilm to preserve deteriorating material, to reduce the size of bulky materials such as newspapers, and to facilitate transfer of texts from one library to another, dates back to about 1935. The microfilm was soon joined by the microcard, heralded as a great space saver for research collections. For about 20 years, the principal use of microforms in libraries was to store the texts of newspapers and periodicals to save space (and to preserve the text). With the proliferation of printed material, especially of technical reports, in the fifties, pressures for space generated many new types of microforms and experiments to reduce their size. One of the latest of these is that recently announced by the National Cash Register Company, which has succeeded in writing a two-micronline width (a size equal to about half the width of a red blood cell) with a laser beam. In terms of storage, this means that 10,000 pages could be recorded on an area the size of one page. The distribution by the government of NASA and Atomic Energy Commission reports in microfiche added further impetus to the microform world. And recently, there have been repeated attempts to adapt microforms to computer systems for automatic retrieval of documents.

At present, the usefulness of microform technology is minimized by the fragmented nature of the industry. This has resulted in a lack of standardization in the production of microforms. The past few years have seen a rapid multiplication in the kinds and shapes of microforms which are not compatible, have little or no relationship to each other, and are in fact mutually exclusive. Advances in use will depend on standardization of a reasonably restricted number of kinds of microforms, and on the production of a system of machines interrelated so that their output can be automatically converted, quickly and cheaply, from one form to another. It must be possible to convert from micro to micro, micro to large, and large to large, producing retention copies of such quality that copies of the copies can be made with no deterioration of the image. In addition, and most important, there must be equipment for consulting microforms that is inexpensive, easy to use, and that has excellent legibility.

These developments do not seem likely to occur in the near future. Progress in the field is slow since there is no single firm in the industry that plays a dominant role in setting the pace for all of the others, as was the case with IBM in the computer field.

In the view of the participants, the long-range effect of microfilm technology on the book and library building will be greater than that of the computer. In the short run, i.e. the next 20 years or so, while the use of microforms will gradually increase, they will not replace the book in a significant way.

COMMUNICATIONS

Facsimile transmission of text over long distances holds enormous implications for the library world. Contained within it is the potential solution to the problems of duplication, unmanageable growth, and rapid access.

While it has been possible since the advent of television to transmit images of text over long distances, the impermanence of the image makes this unsatisfactory for library use. The recent development of machines for facsimile transmission which print out text at the receiving end has added a new dimension to communications technology. And there are now experimental projects under way which substitute the transmission of text for interlibrary loan: one between the campus of the University of California at Berkeley and the University's Davis campus; the other among libraries in New York State.

Facsimiles of text printed at the receiving end are transmitted by conventional telephone cables or microwave stations. Since this requires a broad band transmission channel, the line costs are very high. The costs of microwave transmission are still higher. Even more restrictive is the lack, at present, of a national switching system that would allow rental of a broad band channel for a few minutes of time to any geographic location, which interlibrary transmission requires. And even if educational communication satellites were available today to facilitate transmission, the lack of an adequate switching system on a national scale would prevent facsimile transmission of text from becoming a common means of information exchange for libraries.

Eventually, a common carrier network, equipped with adequate switching, is likely to be set up to accommodate such developments as the PICTURE-PHONE and the transmission of data between computers. If this develops, the system would serve well for library needs.

Such a common carrier network is within the present technology, but the economic basis of the service has yet to be established. Initially, the service may be too expensive for libraries. Also, such a network cannot be suddenly created but must grow over a period of years.

Regional, national, and special purpose libraries

will become increasingly important. To be effective, adequate communications must make these centralized facilities available over a wide geographic area. An initial arrangement practical with present communications, consists of published or microform catalogs plus distribution of the documents by mail. (Witness MEDLARS, for example, the most sophisticated computerized retrieval system, which now sends the results of its bibliographic retrieval by mail.) The catalogs could be widely distributed and enable remote users to locate documents which they would then receive in a day or two. As a broad band network develops, fast electrical transmission of both bibliographic and textual material will gradually evolve to replace mail service. The time scale will depend very much on the particular region. Big cities like New York, Boston, Washington, Chicago, Denver, San Francisco, and Los Angeles may be firmly interconnected within 5 years, but it may take 30 to 40 years to reach Peru, Nebraska.

When it materializes, the use of facsimile text transmission between libraries may be economically practical. It would be unwise, however, for the next generation of libraries to depend on its general availability. It would appear at present that, while bibliographic citations will be exchanged electronically, in the face of competition from more conventional and vastly cheaper forms of haulage like trucking and mailing, facsimile transmission of books and documents will be restricted for a long time.

Pertinent too, is the matter of copyright ownership of text and other intellectual products, as applied to electronically stored and transmitted materials as well as to all forms of photoduplication. Legislation pending in Congress acknowledges the need to extend copyright protection from the traditional to the new formats. The problem is not one that lends itself to easy solution, however, and until viable arrangements are evolved, this will pose a barrier to realizing the potential of the new technologies.

With regard to the implications for buildings, since facsimile text transmission is simply a newer and better form of interlibrary loan, it would have no significant effect on the interiors of library buildings. It would, however, slow down the rate of expansion since research materials easily obtainable from regional and national resource centers would not need to be bought for local storage.

IMPLICATIONS FOR BUILDINGS

Computers: Even if a library were completely computerized, there would be no necessity to locate the central computer equipment within the library building. If local considerations should make it desirable, however, a total of some 2,000 square feet apportioned as follows, along with the environmental conditions described, would provide the needs for a library of a million volumes.

1. The central processing room: This does not need to be large since the processing needs of even a large research library are well within the capacity of quite small computers (in terms both of physical size and of processing speed). A thousand square feet is adequate, but the space should be planned to accommodate a progression of facilities. (That is to say, a library might opt initially for a punch card installation or a small-scale computer, and would use this facility for certain clerical functions for two or three years. At that time it might decide to employ a machine of larger capacity. Some years after that, it might decide to incorporate on-line processing in the facility, and then, at a later date, establish on-line connection to a much larger utility computer located elsewhere—such as in the computer center of the university or a commercial computer utility which may possibly be in existence by 1980.)

The central processing room should be located away from all reading areas and acoustically controlled to contain the noises produced by the machines. It should have a double floor, with a one-foot space below the standing floor to carry computer cables. Also, a separate air-conditioning system to hold the temperature at 75°F. and relative humidity at 50 percent. (This has particular significance for the magnetic tapes which tend to change their operating characteristics under excessively low or high temperatures.) There should be a continuous recorder for both temperature and humidity, with an alarm set to indicate dangerous variations of either, and a cut-off for the air-conditioning system located within the room. It should have the best possible filtration system to remove dust from the air, such as a pad filter backed by high efficiency bag strainers rated at 95 percent. Dust control is necessary, again, primarily because of its effect upon the reliability of magnetic reading and recording systems. Power requirements will depend on the machines used, but a typical load is 20 KVA at 175 amps. Because a stable power source is essential, surges must be controlled to within 5 to 10 percent. A continuous voltage recorder should be provided, again with an alarm set to indicate dangerous variations and a cut-off for the power located within the room.

For connection to peripheral terminal units throughout the building, there must be a flexible system of electrical conduits both vertically between floors and horizontally on each floor. Likely locations for terminals are the catalog, acquisitions, circulation, and serials departments, and the card catalog itself. Any terminals that involve cardhandling or typewriter equipment will make noise, and provisions must be made to control it. There must also be provisions for running cables out of the building from both the computer processing room and the peripheral terminals, to reach a larger computer facility for special or rapid processing—or, in the remote future, to tie into computer networks.

2. Ancillary spaces required, are these: Two offices convenient to the central processing room. One, for the computer director, operators, and programmers, should allow 150 square feet per person; the other, for key-punch operators, 75 square feet per person. Immediately adjacent to the processing room should be two additional rooms of 100 square feet each; one for mechanized storage forms such as punched cards, tapes, etc., the other for spare parts and testing equipment. Finally, storage of cards, forms, and other supplies should be provided in still another room of about 200 square feet near the processing center. The entire complex of rooms should be provided with the same atmospheric conditions as the central processing room itself.[8]

Seating: The impact of technology on seating in academic libraries is likely to be slight. With an increase in the use of electronic carrels, dial retrieval, computerized retrieval of texts, and teaching machines, the formula for square footage allowed per reader will have to increase. Even with a great increase in the ability to receive information from remote sources, the dormitory room is not likely to replace the library. The present surge of students to the library for concentrated, disciplined study, especially at times of academic pressure, is not likely to be rendered less by technology, and will probably increase. Demand for seating in the science sections may diminish, however, since that class of information will be most heavily computer-stored and re-

trievable in laboratories, offices, and points on the campus remote from the library. The more that technology facilitates access to information, the more will information and libraries be used, which will tend to increase, not reduce, library workloads and the size of library facilities.

The Card Catalog: Changes in the card catalog will generate physical objects to take its place— multiple copies of book catalogs or many consoles. Great change in the form of the catalog would not involve much change in planning a library building at this time.

Shelving: Modification or redesign of shelving now provided for books will be necessary to hold forms of information of smaller unit size than books, i.e., microforms, magnetic tapes, etc. The smaller unit size will not reduce total space requirements, however. As microforms become easier to use—as they must if they are to replace books to any significant degree—the very ease of their use will then accelerate their purchase. Together with the installation of machines for their retrieval, the result will be a shift in space or even an expansion of space requirements. Since shelving will have to be moved, the preferred practice of using free standing stacks will be even more important in the future.

While a library built today is not condemned to early obsolescence by the new technology, the changes in store do place a greater premium than ever on planning buildings to be adaptable. The column system should be coordinated with the lighting layout, and with stack and furniture modules, so that shifts between seating and shelving are easy to make, and rearrangements of partitioning inexpensive. Perimeter and underfloor ducts should be provided large enough and in sufficient numbers to allow access to cables and electrical wiring at unpredictable locations on the floor, and to run easily from one floor to another. Air-conditioning shafts throughout the building should be oversized to provide room for additions to the airconditioning system.

It is also important to avoid illumination levels above 70-80 footcandles, maintained, which tend to bleach out the image on computer display terminals, television screens, microfiche projectors, and other rear-screen projection equipment. Indeed, it will be necessary to lower the light intensities in areas of the library as they become occupied by these machines.

In sum, it is the consensus of those who participated in the conference that for at least the next 20 years the book will remain an irreplaceable medium of information. The bulk of library negotiations will continue to be with books—although the science and technology sections will gradually shrink. Remote retrieval of full texts in large amounts over long distances will not be generally feasible, and the continued use of a central library building will still be necessary.

It follows, therefore, that library planners can proceed at this time with confidence that technological developments in the foreseeable future will not alter radically the way libraries are used. In planning library buildings today, we should start with the library as the institution we now know it to be. Any departures in the future should be made from this firm base.

To be sure, technology will modify library buildings. But the changes will involve trade-offs in space and demands for additional space, rather than less. Thus, buildings planned now must be planned for expansion. And at the same time, it is imperative that an added cost factor of three to five percent should be allowed in order to assure adaptability, especially in the electrical and air-conditioning systems.

This should not invite complacency, however. Predictions in a swiftly changing society are a risky business and must be hedged with caveats. All the fields of technology are swirling with action, and it is certain that, in every individual library, planners and administrators must be constantly alert to innovations, to local potential for assimilating developments, to the possibilities for interaction between libraries. On a broader scale, continued research, experimentation, and study must be carried on to help solve today's planning problems. Technological progress perforce will continue. But it is not break-throughs that are going to make a new world so much as the constant accumulation of new experiences over a considerable period of time.

Finally, we need much more consideration than has yet been given to the library user. Any applications of technology to library activities will have to be engineered to be humanly acceptable, since there will be resistance to them all—to the use of microforms in place of books, to console typed texts instead of print, to engaging in complicated interaction with a machine, to reading in a fixed place without moving around. The machines will breed their own resistance to the extent that they place restrictions on people.

Now, more than ever, it is important to design library buildings so they will be inviting and comfortable for people to use. The library building itself will gradually change, but people, who use libraries, are a constant factor.

CONFERENCE PARTICIPANTS

Baker, William O.	Vice President for Research, Bell Telephone Laboratories
Blackburn, Robert	Chief Librarian University of Toronto
DeGennaro, Richard	Associate Librarian for Systems Development, Harvard University
Ellsworth, Ralph	Director of Libraries, University of Colorado
Fussler, Herman	Director, the University of Chicago Library
Gores, Harold B.	President, Educational Facilities Laboratories
Hayes, Robert M.	Director, Institute for Library Research, University of California at Los Angeles
King, Jonathan	Vice President and Treasurer Educational Facilities Laboratories
Licklider, J. C. R.	Consultant to Director of Research, Thomas J. Watson Research Center of IBM at Yorktown Heights, New York
Lowry, W. K.	Manager of Technical Information Libraries, Bell Telephone Laboratories

Mason, Ellsworth	Director, Hofstra University Library
Mathews, M. V.	Director, Behavioral Research Laboratory, Bell Telephone Laboratories
Netsch, Walter A., Jr.	Skidmore, Owings & Merrill, architects, Chicago
Rooney, Walter J., Jr.	Curtis and Davis, architects, New York
Singer, Ira	Assistant Superintendent, West Hartford Public Schools
Swinburne, Herbert H.	Nolen, Swinburne and Associates, architects, Philadelphia
Toan, Danforth	Warner, Burns, Toan and Lunde, architects, New York
Ulveling, Ralph A.	Director, Detroit Public Library
Weinstock, Ruth	Research Associate, Educational Facilities Laboratories

NOTES

1. *Illinois Libraries,* Vol. 48, No. 7 (September, 1966), pp. 562-63, as quoted in R. J. Blakely, "The Wit to Win," *ALA Bulletin,* Vol. 61, No. 2 (February, 1967), p. 168.

2. "Statistics, News, and Trends in the Industry," *Publisher's Weekly,* Vol. 191, No. 5 (January 30, 1967), p. 46.

3. Figures for 1964, from *Statistical Yearbook, 1965* (Paris: UNESCO, 1965).

4. "The Literature of Science and Technology," *Encyclopedia of Science and Technology,* Vol. 7 (1960 ed. updated in 1966; New York: McGraw-Hill, 1966), p. 542.

5. Nathan M. Cohen, "Public Libraries," *Public Facility Needs* ("State and Local Public Facility Needs and Financing," Vol. 1. Study prepared for the Subcommittee on Economic Progress of the Joint Economic Committee, Congress of the United States [Washington, D.C.: Government Printing Office, 1966]), pp. 616-624.

6. Estimates of need in public, school, and college and university libraries, prepared by Henry Drennan, Acting Chief, Library Planning and Development Branch, U.S. Office Education, 1967.

7. Data from unpublished report, "Projected Construction and Financing of College and University Libraries, Fall 1966 to Fall 1970," prepared for EFL by Consultants to Industry, Inc., Stanford Professional Center, Palo Alto, California, in 1967.

8. Architects recommend that computer manufacturers be consulted in the programming and planning of these spaces, as well as in the mechanical and electrical requirements necessary in each situation.

II

THE USE OF CONSULTANTS

There are many "experts" around today each of whom because of his experience while seeing "his" building to completion will now consider himself a qualified consultant. Nothing could be further from the truth. A consultant in any field must be one of broad and diversified experience rather than one of single or limited experience. A library building consultant must have had several building experiences, preferably with buildings of various sizes and quality of materials; must be knowledgeable of the furnishings and equipment available—both the good and the bad; must be widely traveled, having visited (and studied) many library buildings and investigated fabrication plants of library equipment; and he must be experienced in dealing with administrative agencies, architects, specialty consultants, contractors, and, of course, other librarians.

We look now at the writings of several expert building consultants who address themselves to the philosophy, practice and ethics of their professional endeavor. The section closes with a discordant note from one not so convinced of their philosophy, practice and ethics.

A word of caution: If one must go it alone without the use of consultants then that one should travel, observe, study other library buildings. If travel is not possible, then a similar procedure should be followed in looking at recent local construction: banks, office buildings, hospitals, schools. Consultants should be employed if at all possible; but if not, then a little knowledge must surely be stretched as far as it can.

Consultants for College and University Library Building Planning

by Ralph E. Ellsworth

Whether in the conference room or at the evening cocktail party, the library building consultant must be ready to make his pitch straightforward, where, and when, it is most likely to be received. His advice may be accepted, or it may be rejected, but he must state the needs of the institution as he sees them, based on his wide experience.

During the years just before World War II, there was no college and university librarian alive who could, today, qualify as a building consultant in the college and university field. There were a few who had been through one building experience, but none who had been through a sufficient number to build up cumulative experience. Indeed, from the time the Bibliothèque Saint Genevieve Library was built in the middle of the nineteenth century until after World War II, it was rather generally accepted, in colleges and universities at least, that architects planned libraries without much help from librarians. There were exceptions: Theodore Koch at Northwestern, Louis R. Wilson at North Carolina, and Edna Hanley at Agnes Scott, for example. Joseph Wheeler and Alfred Githens had, of course, done outstanding work in the public library field, but there was no one in the college and university field of their stature and experience.

It was not until after 1940 in ALA that anyone realized the need for specialized planning for college and university libraries. Prior to that time the ALA Building Committee included representatives from all types of libraries—on the assumption (which ALA seems to be drifting back into) that a library is a library. Indeed it was only after strenuous objections were raised by A. F. Kuhlman, William H. Jesse, and myself that ACRL established its own separate committee. To be sure, there are certain heating, ventilation, and lighting problems that are common to all libraries, but that is about as far as the "Togetherness" theory applies.

It was the Cooperative Committee on Library Building Plans that firmly established the idea of using building consultants. Today, practically all projects have used consultants.

Who is a building consultant? Unfortunately, it is anyone who thinks he knows how to plan buildings and can persuade an institution to hire him! There are no qualifying examinations to pass, no boards to be interviewed by, no criteria to meet. If one may judge them by the results, one must admit that consultants can get away with bad, sloppy work with no one the wiser. There is no organized follow-up work by any individual or organization. Here perhaps, is a service ACRL could perform.

Officials at ALA nominate, upon request, consultants on the best information they have, but frequently this means nothing more than that they know the individuals and have a general idea of their competence. Yet, I have seen lists that nominate men I would not trust to design a dog house.

Seldom is a building failure labeled as such. For example, in one of the newest college buildings in the Midwest I found more planning mistakes than I have seen in recent years. Yet the man who served as consultant for that building has a good reputation as a consultant. How come? Could it be that librarians can't distinguish between a good and bad building? Or could it be that consultants are sometimes ignored?

In this article I shall attempt to state what a consultant is supposed to do, how he works, how he should be selected and paid, and how his work should be evaluated.

First, it should be understood that a consultant

SOURCE: Reprinted from Ralph E. Ellsworth in "Consultants for College and University Library Building Planning," *College and Research Libraries*, vol. 21, July, 1960, pp. 263–268, by permission of the publisher.

never finds the needs of any two problems to be alike. Sometimes the consultant is needed to sell the need for a new building to the trustees; sometimes it is to get faculty thinking channeled along certain lines; sometimes his primary task is to reason with a dean who for one reason or another has picked up an unworkable but fascinating conception of a library; and sometimes his job is to fill in for the librarian who may be incompetent, ornery, uninterested, or otherwise a problem.

I know of one instance in which the consultant made his big contribution at a cocktail party by persuading one of the college officials that the building should be turned ninety degrees. He earned his fee on that act alone because this change opened up the solution to many other problems that had blocked the planning.

Each new library consultation is a new challenge. After having worked on more than twenty assignments I have yet to find any two that come close to being alike. From this one may conclude, correctly, that the first thing a consultant does on a new assignment is to find out why his services have been requested. This may or may not coincide with what was told him in his correspondence with the officials. He will, after a time, develop special skill at getting at the heart of the problem and at finding out what's going on and who's in control. The normal situation, however, is that the institution has decided it needs a library building, has hired an architect, and wants to know what to do next.

How shall an institution pick the right consultant? Perhaps the safest way is to inquire of some six or eight librarians in charge of the kind and size of library involved. After obtaining, in this manner, a consensus on two or three consultants, one should ask each of them for (1) a list of the buildings for which he has served as consultant; (2) copies of these building programs for which the individual was responsible (under no circumstances should one choose a consultant who has done fewer than three buildings, either alone or with a colleague); and (3), a statement on what projects the consultant is already working.

Representatives should then be sent to inspect these buildings and to discuss with the librarian—if he or she was in charge at the time the building was planned (the problem of how to evaluate the comments of a second generation librarian is a baffling one, partly because this librarian won't know what the consultant did and partly because one of the generally present but less admirable traits of present-day head librarians is their habit

of blaming the past for mistakes that usually stem from their own weaknesses)—the contribution made by the librarian.

At this point one must consider the question of how much blame can be placed on the consultant for mistakes that were made in planning. Or, to put the question another way, should a consultant stay with a project all the way, keeping mistakes to a minimum, when things are not going right, or is there a point at which it would be better for the institution concerned if he would resign and publicly disassociate himself from the project? How far should a consultant go in refusing to let a client have things in a building he knows to be wrong?

If the problem appears to be one of choice between several workable plans or ideas, the client's choice should always be respected. But if the consultant knows (and if he doesn't know enough to judge he shouldn't be a consultant) the client's or architect's decision will result in a building that is unworkable or full of major defects, or that will in a few years be a handicap to the institution, he should so inform the client in writing and, if necessary, withdraw from the project and state publicly why he has done so, unless by so doing he would be harming the institution unnecessarily or unwisely.

It can be argued that it's the consultant's job to give the client what he wants even if what he wants is wrong. A better case can be made for the position that the consultant should stay with the project to the bitter end, saving as much as possible out of the situation. One should remember that a building lasts a long time and that basic faults, if present, will last an equal length of time.

As to fees, the first question is why pay a consultant? Why not bring your plans to ALA and have some expert tell you what to do, free and no questions asked? This is done, and for minor problems it is not a bad idea.

But this has nothing to do with planning. Each college or university is different from all others. It has its unique geography, traditions, character, pocketbook, and desires. These must be carefully isolated, analyzed, and synthesized before one can develop a library plan. This cannot be done around the ALA convention halls. Furthermore, people will respect and use the things they pay for and disregard the things that are free. And if the payment is large enough to cause a little self-sacrifice, the advice given will be taken just that much more seriously. We have all seen some of our colleagues who came to the ALA with their building plans and go from one "expert" to another, like bees sucking honey from flowers, asking advice from all and then going home and taking advice from none, or possibly assembling a hodge-podge of unharmonious elements.

A library building is a complicated machine that will work only when all its elements are designed to fit the whole. It is not likely that more than one or two people can maintain a sense of the whole while the plans are being developed. There is a place, of course, for group criticism, but this does not come in the creative stage of planning.

Fees vary from consultant to consultant according to the needs of the job and the amount of experience the consultant has had. One learns, with experience, how to work fast and to avoid typical errors. One hundred and fifty dollars a day, plus expenses, is a standard fee for an experienced consultant for ordinary, uncomplicated program writing and blueprint reading. A wise consultant will put in his contract a statement saying that if extraordinary situations arise (such as trouble with the architect) that call for more than ordinary service, he will so notify the client in advance and will ask for extra compensation of a specific amount. The fee will vary, too, depending on how much supervision is wanted.

The amount of time a consultant spends on a typical (if there is such a thing) college problem would be somewhat as follows: a preliminary visit of three days to study the local problem and to work out the first draft of a program; a second visit of one day with the architect on the site problem in relation to the program; and another two days on the final draft of the program. After the architect has developed plans there will usually be a series of one-day meetings to discuss the plans. (I am talking about a college library problem—a university problem usually requires three times as much time.) From this point on the consultant should check all blueprints against departmental requests for the local needs; he may or may not be asked to choose furniture and equipment; and he may or may not do floor layout. A college planning a $1,500,000 building should budget $1,500 for the consultant. He may use much less.

The question arises about the use of a single consultant or an organization of consultants such as Library Building Consultants, Inc. If the choice is between a relatively inexperienced consultant and an organization group, the latter should be chosen. The virtue of the group consulting service is that it makes fewer errors because more than one person works on the problem. The limitation of the group is that it is no better than the individuals who make up the group. The problem is comparable to that of choosing an architect. You may get better results from an individual architect who has the particular kind of ability and time your job requires. On the other hand, a larger firm that can run your problem through its highly specialized departments—programming, design, layout, construction, landscaping, equipment, etc.—may be better for your job. Some architects work better as individuals and some work better as members of a team. So it is with consultants. If an individual is chosen, it is most important that the owner satisfy himself on the quality of work the individual has done.

A good consultant—individual or group—will save the client a great deal of money, and, of even more importance, he will see to it that the building will do the work the client expects it to do.

The first task of the consultant is to help the institution prepare a written program—a document that will include answers to all the questions the owner, the donor (or the taxpayer), the architect, and the future users of the library could possibly ask.

The program should begin by asking the question of why a new building is necessary. Here the consultant should help the college or university think through a campus-wide system of reading resources or facilities, taking into consideration all the possible developments in micropublishing, mechanization of bibliographic searching, audio-visual devices, paperback books. Such questions as these should be raised: Are there to be departmental libraries, study hall facilities in academic buildings? In dormitories? What is the geography of the campus? What are the lines and flows of student movements?

Next comes the question of site. It has been my experience that there is usually one best site that can be spotted quickly, but that, for one reason or another (and these reasons frequently seem quite inconsequential to an outsider) the library can not be put there. And so one must hunt for the second best site.

Fortunately, on most college campuses distances are so short that the site is not a matter of great importance. But in a large university the problem is almost always critical. Unfortunately, none of us knows enough about the elements that should determine a library's location to be very certain of our advice. I am, for example, coming more and more to the conclusion that the single most important element is whether or not the faculty members who should use the library find the site easy and convenient. If they don't, they will, in one way or another, find ways of avoiding the library and they will not see to it that their students use the library as much as they would if the faculty were happy about the situation—even though all other elements are optimum.

The consultant will need to know how to find out which departments or colleges will use the library and where the center of gravity of this use will be; he will need to find the confluence of student traffic; he will need to study the campus master plan—where growth is to take place and to what extent; and he will need to be certain that the site plan is large enough to permit expansion and that it can be committed to library use.

Next comes the question of what kind of a building the institution wants. What is to be its mood, its style, and its symbolic place on the campus? What is the intellectual climate of the campus? The prestige of reading? The degree of reading sophistication of the students? The balance between teaching and research in the faculty? The relation between the library and the student union on the facilities for browsing should be determined if possible.

Having determined these background facts, the main part of the program should be written. This will be a description, considering proper relationships, of the various parts of the building with an estimation of the quantities required for each part. This will begin with an analysis, based on data supplied by the institutions, of the seating capacity derived, as well as the number of books that are to be housed, now and in the future.

In doing this the consultant should not forget that he is not an architect and that he should not try to design a building. Rather, he should try to tell the architect everything he should know so that he will know "what the function is the form must follow," if I may twist Louis Sullivan's dictum around. The consultant should stay out of the architect's way as long as the architect is expressing the program faithfully. Too often in the past, we librarians have blamed architects for mistakes that really are the result of faulty programming, not of architectural ineptitude.

Consultants should realize that today architects are striving mightily to create new styles that will be richer than the so-called "International" boxes we have had since World War II. Let us hope they will be able to do better than merely cover up a barren structure with a stone-like lattice of cement or iron. (And by this I am not referring to the New Orleans Public Library, where the use of iron lattice work had a local *raison d'etre*.) Surely we need not lose all we have gained the last twenty years in our concept of organic architecture.

Each part of the building should be described clearly in terms of its purpose, operations, special needs, and its spatial relations to other parts.

The consultant, in writing this part of the program, will try to follow the institution's wishes and ideas if it has any, but more frequently he will be expected to tell the institutions about the best of the new ideas to be found in the newer libraries. He must be careful not to ride his own hobbies, or to impose concepts that would limit the freedom of choice in the future for the institution. If there is someone in the institution who wants to, and is capable of writing the program, by all means let him do it. The consultant's sole responsibility is to see to it that the program is written completely and accurately.

At this point a word on copying or borrowing ideas from other libraries is in order. It is my opinion that so many mistakes have been made in so many buildings that when we can find something done properly we should repeat the success—if it is relevant—and not worry about the repetition. We need not worry about the monotony for the simple reason that there are too few good examples to follow.

● ● ● ●

The style and arrangements of a good program need not be standardized. I offer as a model the program for Colorado College, written by Dr. Ellsworth Mason, librarian:

   I. The Nature of the College
  II. General Description of the Library
 III. Specifications of the Library Area

Introduction to the Library:

  1. Vestibule
  2. Lobby and control
  3. Circulation:
      Desk
      Office
  4. Reference
  5. Periodical indexes
  6. Periodicals
  7. Card catalog
  8. Reference office
  9. New book browsing

Technical Processes and Administration:

10. Receiving and shipping
11. Technical processes:
    Order department
    Cataloging and mending
    Serials
    Documents
12. Librarian
13. Librarian's secretary

Books and Readers:

14. Bookstacks and reading areas:
    Stacks
    Readers
15. Special collections
16. Bibliography
17. Microcard room
18. Listening area
19. Locked faculty studies
20. Student conference rooms

Miscellaneous:

21. Seminar rooms
22. Lock section

23. Staff room
24. Staff toilet and washroom
25. Smoking rooms:
    Studies
    Lounges
26. Typing rooms
27. Supply room
28. Toilets and washrooms
29. Elevator
30. Book return slot
31. Photo dark room
32. Reshelving stations
33. Student telephone
34. Fire exit

Summary of space requirements

• • • •

If a consultant can be successful in developing a good program, the major part of his work is accomplished. Architectural competence is so high these days that one can be fairly safe in assuming that a good program will be well expressed. The consultant will, of course, follow each stage of the project through to completion and, if all goes well, he may occupy a seat in the back row at the library dedication and he will share in the pleasure of seeing a job well done.

ABOUT THE AUTHOR–Ralph E. Ellsworth received his A.B. degree from Oberlin College in 1929; his B.S. in L.S. degree from Western Reserve in 1931, and his PhD from the University of Chicago in 1937. Before 1937, he held positions at Adams State Teachers College and Colorado State College of Education. Since that time, he has been Director of Libraries and Professor of Library Science at the University of Iowa and the University of Colorado, from which position he retired in 1972. He has written a number of books on library planning and building for both schools and colleges, among them *Planning the College and University Library Building* (1960. 2nd ed. 1968). Mr. Ellsworth is also the author of numerous articles in library and educational journals.

The Library Building Consultant; Five Questions

by Keyes D. Metcalf

The five questions are stated in the first paragraph. "The Dean of Library Building Consultants" then proceeds to answer his own questions for us.

This discussion on library building consultants will center upon five questions: (1) Why have a consultant? (2) How do you select him? (3) At what stage in the planning should he be selected? (4) What do you pay him? (5) What should he do?

WHY HAVE A CONSULTANT?

In spite of the large number of libraries that have been planned and constructed since the war, the average librarian rarely has an opportunity to participate in the planning of more than one building during his career. Until very recent years, comparatively few architects had specialized in library planning. An institution may well appoint a consultant in order to place at the disposal of its planning team knowledge and experience that would not otherwise be available.

The institution may have special planning problems which make a consultant particularly desirable. There may be a trustee who wants what his grandfather wanted, and only a monumental or a Gothic building will satisfy him. There may be a professor with a German background who believes in seminar rooms for his advanced classes, in which the basic collections in his special field are shelved. There may be a science professor who is convinced that no library is going to be needed in the future because of technological developments. The institution that has the over-all responsibility for the building, or its representative, will find that an outsider can provide the needed ballast.

In most cases, however, a consultant is wanted because of the realization that special knowledge is not locally available. Since the cost of a library building is very great—sometimes double the investment in the library—mistakes would be ex-

tremely serious. Before the use of a library consultant, which is a development of the last twenty years, libraries were generally planned with the librarian having little to say about the details. Since the architect was primarily interested in the aesthetic side and knew little of library problems, results were not satisfactory functionally.

The chief reasons for a library building consultant, then, are to make available special knowledge of the functional needs and requirements in a library building, and to have an effective voice on its planning problems.

HOW DO YOU SELECT A CONSULTANT?

Experience is a most important consideration. Ralph Ellsworth says never to take a man who has not already had at least three assignments of this kind.[1] This sounds a little like trade unions that do not want to admit young workers. It is easier to demand higher wage rates when there is no competition. Experience is desirable, but how does a new man get his apprenticeship and training? It is important for those of us who are now doing consultation work to bring in younger men to help us so that a new crop will be available in the years ahead. The same rule applies to administrative work of any kind. One of the most important things that a head librarian can do is to train others to take his own or another administrative position.

Yet, it is desirable to select a consultant with experience. Investigate the results of work that he has done elsewhere. Keep in mind his knowledge of building planning, and his ability to influence the people with whom he deals and to make them understand the basic problems involved.

SOURCE: Reprinted from Keyes D. Metcalf, "The Library Building Consultant; Five Questions" in *Problems in Planning Library Facilities,* Chicago, American Library Association, 1964, pp. 9–11, by permission of the publisher.

He should have the ability to explain the reasons for his point of view, and to persuade those with whom he works of the importance of carrying out his suggestions. He must be a good salesman who is fearless in expressing his views. He must avoid undue aggressiveness and not be overly dogmatic.

While you cannot expect the consultant to be an architect and an engineer, he must understand their problems well enough to avoid unsuitable and impractical suggestions. He must also keep in mind the present situation and prospective future library developments as well.

The right consultant should be picked for the particular job at hand. A man under consideration for the position may be very suitable for one institution and not for another. The proper qualifications for a good librarian do not necessarily make a good library building consultant. You should not pick a building consultant because he is the successful administrator of a large library. Neither should you do so just because he is in the same city or state. The fact that he may have worked successfully on a public library building does not necessarily mean that he can do the same on a college library, or vice versa. Pick a man who you think has the knowledge, experience, and broad-gauge mind that will enable him to understand your particular problem and to help in the places where you need help. If you need someone to influence the governing board, the library committee, or your administrative officers, rather than a person to help with the details of the building planning, pick someone who you believe can do this job.

AT WHAT STAGE SHOULD THE CONSULTANT BE SELECTED?

If you are going to have a consultant, select him just as soon as possible. He can be of use in deciding whether you should erect a new building or add to an old one. He can help select the site. He can properly give advice in connection with the selection of an architect. While he will not be in a position specifically to recommend the firm to be selected, he can offer suggestions for the qualifications of the man to be chosen. He may be able to prevent various mistakes if he is appointed before important decisions have been made which it will be impossible, embarrassing, or expensive to change. This does not mean that it is unwise to have a consultant unless he is chosen at the be-

ginning. A situation may often develop which makes the appointment imperative and better late than never.

WHAT DO YOU PAY THE CONSULTANT?

There is no accepted schedule of payments for library consultants as there is for architects. The latter are almost always employed on a percentage basis, the percentage varying with the type of building and its location. Library building consultants are not in an organized and accepted profession as yet and may never be. Yet, they may properly consider themselves to be like physicians, who adapt their charges to the patient with whom they deal.

There are three fairly definite methods used in charging. One is a percentage basis, the percentage varying according to what is expected of the consultant. Is he to follow the procedures through from beginning to end, as the architect does, supervising the construction as well as making the preliminary plans, the working drawings, and the specifications? Or will his assignment be completed when working drawings are authorized? The answer makes a difference in the percentage.

The second method is an agreement by which the work will be done for a definite sum. Ralph Ellsworth very modestly suggests that for a $1,500,000 college library one tenth of 1 percent, or $1,500, might be budgeted for the consultant.

The third method is for the consultant simply to say that his charges will be so much a day plus expenses. The per diem rate may vary from $50 up, according to the experience of the consultant and the job at hand. As an illustration, a small college library or a branch library costing $200,000 might need a consultant. A tenth of 1 percent of the total, or $200, would not be adequate, but $150–$200 a day would be too much if too many days were involved. On the other hand, a man with a great deal of experience might feel that in a situation where there could be complications, $200 or more a day would not be unreasonable. Also, a team of consultants, working together and contributing between them expert knowledge in various fields, might require altogether a larger percentage of the total cost but perhaps less per day per person.

Consultant work is not sufficiently well organized or established at present for us to say that a definite scale for any of these methods can or should be proposed. Some consultants do a great deal without any charge except for expenses, particularly with institutions in which they are interested.

There are two definite suggestions in connection with charges. The institution should not base its selection primarily on the cost, but on the person that it wants. The consultant should not try to bargain and charge as much as traffic will bear, but should set his rate for the particular job and let the institution accept or decline.

WHAT SHOULD THE CONSULTANT DO?

The consultant should do everything that he can to bring about a better building. He should make available his knowledge and experience to those concerned, moving ahead when necessary and holding back temporarily or permanently, if he believes that someone else's voice on a particular point at a particular time can be more valuable. He should defer to the specialist in the field for which he is not qualified, although if he has a definite opinion based on good authority, he should state his case as quietly and persuasively as he can.

To be more specific, if the consultant is hired at the very beginning, as his first task he should go over the whole situation in general terms. This means that he must learn enough about the institution, its history and background, and its objectives so that the framework of the library's requirements becomes reasonably clear. Then these requirements should be translated into approximate square footage.

A consultant may have basic formulas for use in this way. Different formulas are required for different types of institutions. In a small academic library ten to twelve volumes can be shelved in 1 square foot of gross floor space. In a larger library up to fifteen may be a safe figure. Fifty square feet or a little more will accommodate a reader. This 50 square feet will provide not only space for the reading room but also space for the staff to serve the readers, the processing work space, and the architectural space as well. The two added together—the space for books and readers, and that for services to readers—will give the gross square feet if no unusual special facilities are required. Features such as an auditorium, audio-visual areas, an exhibition room beyond normal lobby space, classrooms, more than a limited number of seminars or faculty studies, and special lounges are extras and must be added to the previous figure.

Other important factors to be kept in mind are the special features that the institution wants to incorporate, such as all-night study areas, open or closed stack access, seminars and studies, smoking rooms, lounges, exit controls, auditoriums, exhibition areas, and the like.

With an approximate total of space requirements available, the present building should be carefully investigated, the consultant asking himself whether, with rearrangements, the space required could be provided for a few years more within that building, or a wing could be added without leaving the building in an undesirable position aesthetically or functionally. The possibility and advisability of an addition should always be considered so that no interested person can say that such a plan has been left out of consideration. It is necessary at this stage to decide for how many years in the future the plans are to be made, since it is not only the present but the future requirements which are of interest.

After the decision has been reached as to the total space requirements, the site problem should be settled. Do not permit this decision to become definite until you know what is needed, and can be assured that a building of the size required can be placed on the plot selected. Also, if the long view is to be taken, thought must be given to the next stage when the new building will outgrow its space.

The next step is to return to the program and complete it for the architect. It should provide, if not the exact size of each area, an indication of the required size in terms of readers, staff, and collections to be housed and the desired spatial relationships between the different areas.

The program should be written locally by the librarian or his building committee. It is almost impossible for an outsider to obtain the required information in a short time. The consultant can, however—and generally should—take a leading part in the program writing, primarily by asking questions that should be answered and by seeing that important points are not omitted. In other words, he should be the guide and critic rather than the author. If the program is written by those who have to live with the results, it should be more satisfactory. The building committee and the librarian will understand the program better if they have written it, and will then be able to explain it more successfully to the faculty, students, the governing boards, and the public in general.

Help in selecting the architect after or before the program has been completed can, in many cases, be provided by the consultant. The consultant generally confines himself to suggestions on the type and the characteristics of the architect to be selected, rather than to the recommendation of a particular architect.

The consultant or the institution should ordinarily not prepare schematic drawings or preliminary sketches for the architect beyond those which indicate desired spatial relationships. It is important, however, for the consultant to see and discuss with those concerned the drawings that the architect makes, particularly those that have to do with spatial relationships and function. Comment should be made by the consultant on the adequacy of the space assignments proposed and whether they fulfill the program requirements. He certainly should be involved with equipment layouts and traffic patterns, floor loads, floor coverings,

lighting, acoustic problems, ventilation, and related problems. All of the architect's proposals should be studied. Furniture design, particularly sizes, are within his province, and, to a limited extent, color and finish.

During the planning stage, if the architects and other members of the planning team visit various libraries to learn how and how not to solve planning problems, this can often be done under the sponsorship and direction of the consultant, who can suggest libraries to be visited and points to be kept in mind during the visits. Finally, the consultant should be available by telephone and by letter as questions and problems arise throughout the working drawing stage and during construction as well, even if he does not appear on the scene himself.

NOTES

[1] Ralph Ellsworth, *Planning the College and University Library Building: A Book for Campus Planners and Architects* Boulder, Colo.: Pruett Pr., 1960), p. 24.

ABOUT THE AUTHOR—Keyes D. Metcalf received the B. A. degree from Oberlin College in 1911; a certificate and diploma from Library School, New York Public Library, in 1914. He was assistant and later Chief Librarian of the Reference Department of the New York Public Library, 1919-1937; Librarian of Harvard College and Director of Harvard University Library, 1937-1955, and Librarian Emeritus since 1955. Mr. Metcalf has been consultant for library administration and building planning in a number of foreign countries as well as in the United States. He was ALA President, 1942-43. Mr. Metcalf has written much on library buildings, notably *Planning Academic and Research Library Buildings* (1965).

The Role of the Building Consultant

by Warren J. Haas

A building consultant delineates the value, advantages, and significance of the outside consultant with library competence.

The story is told of the woodpecker who became bored with the routines of his life and embarked on a cross-country trip to a distant point and a change of scene. After flying many miles, the bird was forced by an approaching storm to land in a tall oak. True to the instincts of his kind, he took a tentative tap at the tree just as a bolt of lightning split the trunk full-length. After recovering his composure, the bird surveyed the damage and was awed by what he saw. "Isn't it amazing," he said to himself, "what an ordinary woodpecker can accomplish once he gets away from home."

This story has a message for both building consultants and the colleges and universities that employ them. For the institutions involved, it demonstrates that proper timing in the matter of involving a consultant is essential if ordinary efforts are to produce exceptional results. For the consultant, the story warns that artificially induced delusions of grandeur tend to push the limits of confidence beyond the realities of competence.

But these two observations are by no means the only ones that might be made concerning consultants in the programming and design of academic buildings. The comments that follow explore the relationship between the consultant and the employing institution and suggest a few guidelines for making that relationship fully effective. While library planning experience provides the basis for this decision, the points made are likely to be generally pertinent to other areas as well.

At the outset, it should be noted that the role of the consultant changes with each assignment. The degree of involvement is governed by institutional needs and policy, and since these are bound to vary, it follows that there is no fixed pattern governing the relationship between a college or university and its consultant. In an effort to identify most of the areas in which a consultant might participate, five distinct stages in the planning process are considered and the nature of the contributions a consultant might be expected to make in each phase is suggested.

1. THE INITIAL PROGRAM

The importance of timing has already been noted. In general, the earlier a consultant is involved, the better will be the results. The fundamental thinking that serves as a basis for the initial program document on a new library building should reflect conclusions of those responsible for long-range campus planning, senior institutional administrators, and the library. The product of this planning phase might be a simple statement of need (for example, we need a new one million volume library with two thousand seats) arrived at on the evidence of a few obvious facts. At the other extreme, the initial program might be a complex document outlining the institution's projected educational activities and pedagogical techniques to be employed, along with a detailed description of the library operations projected to support those activities.

In established colleges and universities, a consultant is often not involved in the conversation and studies that lead to the recommendations incorporated in the initial program, simply because this work is a part of continuing institutional planning activity. For this very reason, it is important that the consultant review the conclusions to

SOURCE: Reprinted from Warren J. Haas, "The Role of the Building Consultant," vol. 30, no. 4, July, 1969, p. 365–368. The original paper was copyrighted in 1968 by the Society for College and University Planning and was reprinted from their *Quarterly*; it is reprinted here with permission from the Society.

verify that they are in fact as valid when viewed from the outside as they seem to those within. Because the prescription for action and the supporting philosophy of this initial program are in a real sense the foundation from which the detailed program and ultimately the building itself rises, their importance should not be underestimated. The consultant needs to satisfy himself that the conclusions incorporate the best of all possible options, or at least that all possible options were considered. This requires an intensive effort on the part of the consultant to gain historical perspective as well as to understand the future objectives of the institution. In large universities especially, the consultant has an obligation to verify that any projected building reflects the existence of and is consistent with a long-range program for the development of library service. More and more, it is important to assess regional needs, as distinct from strictly internal needs, in programming and planning library facilities, simply because many aspects of library and information services are by their very nature best viewed regionally rather than parochially.

While the role of the consultant relative to the initial program is most often that of a reviewer, there are many instances in which he is in fact a participant in, and at times even primarily responsible for, program development. In the case of new colleges, and colleges undergoing dramatic change, a library consultant often finds himself the most experienced person in the planning group and heavily involved in policy formulation. It is critically important in such cases that the consultant avoid being drawn into the decision-making process; this is not properly his role. He must concentrate instead on providing facts and establishing options for those who are responsible. In these circumstances especially, the consultant needs to serve in a kind of educational capacity to provide the institutional participants with pertinent facts and examples of alternatives, as well as an understanding of the implications of different courses of action.

Whether reviewing initial program recommendations made prior to his involvement or participating in the basic planning process, the objective is the same—to assure that the basis for action is sound when viewed in the light of both educational objectives and library management. In effect, an acceptable initial program for a library building is evidence of a proper and realistic institutional commitment to library support.

2. PROGRAM DEVELOPMENT

If the initial program is the place for formulation of broad elements of basic policy, the process of program development and refinement is one requiring meticulous attention to an infinite number of details. If the breadth and depth of the consultant's wisdom is tested in the first case, his technical knowledge gained from practical building experience is of paramount importance here. In many instances, the detailed program is developed in the institution, with the consultant providing substantial assistance at all stages of the work. Often, the architect for a building is engaged before the program is completed, opening the way for participation by three parties (institutional representatives, architects, and the consultant) in final program formulation. Inclusion of the architects as a new voice in the final stages of program development can stimulate the planners to refine carefully and evaluate the elements of the program and often can promote inclusion of information of importance to the architect that would otherwise be omitted. The architects, by their early participation, come to comprehend more quickly the nature of their assignment. The consultant can often play an important role in the early stages of the dialogue between architects and the institutional planning team by retaining his "third party" isolation with the purpose of seeing to it that "architectural considerations" do not begin to dominate educational objectives before the program itself is finally developed.

The consultant needs to verify that terms used in the program are defined with precision; that standards used in relating specified capacities (for studies, book storage, staff space, etc.) to actual areas are valid; that all buildings and operating functions are enumerated and their relationships described; that anticipated traffic volumes and patterns are established; that qualitative requirements for building components as well as for environmental elements are clearly established; that such considerations as ease of maintenance and housekeeping are precisely treated; and, where appropriate, that provisions are made for building expansion. In the case of specialized buildings like libraries, a wide range of distinctive equipment must often be included as part of the program, and the consultant's knowledge of many installations is often a valuable resource in this aspect of program formulation.

From the above, it is evident that the role of a consultant in the program development stage has several aspects. He is a source of up-to-date facts; he can help both his institutional employers and the architects, if they are involved, to learn about alternate solutions by directing them to existing buildings or written material that bear on the problem at hand; and he can often help maintain effective communication among the parties involved, both within the institution and between the institution and the architectural firm.

3. EARLY DESIGN

Program refinement and preliminary design work often overlap in time. In a sense, the early design phase is not unlike the initial period of program preparation, in that one ends in the formulation of the governing educational and operating philosophy and the other culminates in the form of the architectural solution. With this phase, principal responsibility shifts from the institutional planners to the architect. The consultant's role also changes. Given reasonable success by the architect in arriving quite quickly at a solution acceptable to the client, the consultant might be involved only to the extent of verifying for the college or university concerned that the proposed design is compatible with program specifications, and at the same time provides the flexibility and the versatility required to meet the unknown needs of the future.

Generally, it is unwise for the consultant to assume any more than a proportionate share of the responsibility for judging design suggestions from the point of view of aesthetics. It is equally unwise in most cases for the consultant to prepare anything more than schematic layouts of major spaces because he runs the risk of dampening architectural imagination and thus producing less than optimal solutions to the problems involved. Architects are not normally interested in plans from consultants' desks.

There are times, however, when an architect has difficulty in finding a building form that provides a space configuration consistent with program requirements and institutional criteria. In such situations, the institution can, and often does, turn to its consultant for advice on how to resolve the problem. It is here especially that a consultant's experience and demonstrated ability are of prime importance, for finding and promoting acceptance

for the right course of action often hinges on his statesmanship as well as his architectural instincts.

4. FINAL DESIGN

Assuming the consultant has done his work well in previous stages of the project, his role towards the end of the period of final design is to verify for his employer that the design reflects the general objectives as well as the details of the program.

The review process, whether done at one time or in phases over an extended period, is best carried out in close consultation with the responsible people. It is meticulous work, and often difficult. Give and take on all sides is required, since graphic interpretation of prose specifications is as much an art as it is a science. Further, the "art" in architecture and the requirements of the structural approach chosen both carry their own catalog of restraints that must be comfortable with program requirements, but not obviously subservient to them. In brief, the consultant must help the institution verify that the design in fact reflects the program, even though at times the form of the recommended architectural solution might be something unpredicted and perhaps even unpredictable.

5. WORKING DRAWINGS
AND SPECIFICATIONS

In most cases, the consultant is no longer involved once this phase of a project is reached. On occasion, however, he is asked to review specific details to verify that certain program elements have been properly incorporated. Examples include specifications and installation details for technical equipment, as well as those items that indicate proper attention has been paid program admonitions for ease of maintenance and the quality of staff and user environment (for example, the characteristics of window glass specified, security provisions, signs and directional aids, etc.).

These notes suggest the possible range of the consultant's role. Ideally, he adds to the talent devoted to a project. He is a balance wheel working to resolve divergent views represented within the institution employing him, not by seeking compromise solutions, but by helping establish which is the best solution and developing support for it. He is a source of facts in his own special area of expertise, but not an oracle either in or outside of that field. Most important, perhaps, he is a kind of mirror helping college and university planners see their institution in a somewhat different light, amplified and focused specifically on the problem at hand. The consultant does not make decisions, but he can help, and at times force, the decision-making process.

ABOUT THE AUTHOR—Warren J. Haas received degrees from Wabash College (AB, 1948) and the University of Wisconsin (BLS, 1950). Following some early university and public library experience, he held administrative positions at the Johns Hopkins University and Columbia University before becoming Director of Libraries at the University of Pennsylvania. He has recently returned to Columbia where he is Vice President and University Librarian.

Survey of Library Buildings and Facilities

by Donald E. Bean

If the previous three authors "tell it like it is" then Mr. Bean tells it as it should be. Of particular significance is the closing section of this article, "Some Suggestions for Improving Consulting Standards."

SOME HANDICAPS TO CONSULTATION WORK

Despite the well-known fact that there is rapidly increasing demand for consultants in library building projects, there are many projects which are erected with little, if any, consultation service. For this there may be several possible causes. One is the unwillingness of the librarian to make a forthright declaration in favor of the engagement of consultants. This unwillingness may stem from the naïve and incorrect belief that the librarian is quite capable of writing an adequate statement of program and checking the architect's plans without outside assistance except from published information and perhaps a few conferences; or it may be the result of the librarian's equally unfounded belief that a request for consulting assistance may be construed by his employers as an admission of weakness; or it may be caused by pure ego.

All of these reasons for the librarian's hesitancy to recommend consultants are sometimes supplemented by an architect who may not like the idea of engaging consultants unless he can control them. Again, the need for paid building consultants is sometimes minimized in the minds of the clients by well-meaning but overzealous representatives of some state library extension departments who do not realize the harm they do a library when they say "Why pay for consultants? We'll give you the service free of charge."

These attitudes may have been reinforced by the fact that until comparatively recently much library literature has treated in a rather casual manner the question of engaging building consultants. Fortunately, these attitudes are changing rapidly. There is more than ample evidence that no one librarian's, indeed no one consultant's, opinions can safely be accepted as solutions to library building problems. At least one large state now requires the engaging of a library building consultant before an application for financial assistance for a library building is considered.

THE ANALYSIS OF BUILDING NEEDS

There is a wide difference of opinion among consultants as well as among clients as to the nature and the amount of consultation service which a library building project requires; all are agreed that there should be a written library building program of some sort. However, some believe that the statement of program can be limited to very general statements covering, for instance, the number of total volumes and a few general categories, the number of periodicals, the total quantity of seating and a few general areas, and a few other suggestions about various aspects of the building. The librarian of a very large library once told me that a written library program need require no more than four and a half pages.

Some believe that consultation service regarding a statement of program is sufficient if it consists of advice, verbal or written, given to the librarian, who then proceeds to write his own program, no matter whether he has had sufficient experience in this or not. Others, and I believe their number is increasing, believe that the analysis of building needs is a problem so important and so complex that a solution requires a thorough, comprehensive, written, detailed statement of program which may occupy 75 to 150 doublespaced typewritten pages.

SOURCE: Reprinted from Donald E. Bean, "Survey of Library Buildings and Facilities" in *Library Surveys,* New York, Columbia University Press, 1967, pp. 90–108, by permission of the publisher.

Let us recount some of the things which a good statement of program for a library building should attempt to describe:

1. The service which the library may be required to render in future years—say twenty years hence—both in extent and in nature.
2. The quantities of library materials that may be needed in order to render that service. This point includes not only books and periodicals but also all other library materials including such items as audiovisual materials, documents, maps, ephemeral materials, etc.
3. The future departmental organization of those library materials.
4. The future library staff required to render the needed service, in detail, department by department.
5. A detailed list of furniture and equipment that will be needed to carry out the future service.
6. The estimated square footage, department by department, complete and in detail, that will be required to house the materials and equipment.
7. The relationship of each area in respect to other areas, both horizontally and vertically.
8. Other aspects of the building design and structure which are likely to affect the cost of operation of the library or the effectiveness of its service or both.

What are some of the characteristics of a good statement of program, one or more of which are likely to be missing from many of these reports? There are several.

The statement of program should be a statement of *future need,* not merely of current need. It should be entirely unrelated to the amount of money available for the building. Any standard formulas which are used should be adjusted to the future. Furthermore, the statement of program should recommend that the site to be selected and the earliest architectural sketches to be prepared should be based upon this described future need, again without any reference to funds for current building. The statement of program should be based upon the library needs of the particular community or the particular college being studied, not based on average formulas. The statement of program should avoid the indiscriminate application of favorite preference in building design. The reports should be written in complete detail. The statement of program should contain no attempt to draw outline

sketches for the architect. Finally, the statement of program should include a complete equipment list geared to the future insofar as possible. Some of these remarks require further development.

Future Needs

It has been said that the statement of program should be a statement of future need. In its basic recommendations it should ignore entirely the amount of money which may be currently available for building. Yet much of the effort of some consultants has been concerned with the problem of specifying a building which is limited to the size and design for which funds are available. Indeed some library literature of twenty years ago gave this as a laudable objective.

Yet the first objective of the statement of program should be to estimate the nature and extent of the service that will be required of that library in future years; only when that need is assessed can planning go forward logically. It is difficult to over-emphasize this practical point.

Another common error in statements of program prepared by some consultants, or nonconsultants, is the use, without adjustment, of average standards. The published standards for both public and college libraries—splendid guides though they are—are current guides. Yet a public library building is supposedly planned for at least twenty years in the future and a college or university building for at least ten to fifteen years in the future and in almost all cases the buildings will have to serve for fifty years or more.

Furthermore, as we all know, we are only at the beginning of an educational revolution in which the library is at the very center, and which presages greatly increased per capita use of the public library and of the college library. In ten years, with a much better educated generation growing up, the current standards will be as far out of date as the standards of 1930 are now. It is the job of the consultant to assess future trends, yet in case after case future trends are given no more than casual reference and the statement of program is based upon current standards.

It may be worth emphasizing that we are not talking about the erecting of a library building; we are not even talking about the final planning of the library. In respect to this point we refer only to the written statement of program and the earliest preliminary sketches of the architect.

Furthermore, as has been said before, the statement of program should insist that the site to be selected and also the earliest architectural sketches to be prepared should be based upon this described future need. Only after those earliest sketches for the ultimate building have been reviewed and approved should the attempt be made to cut down the size of the building to fit the present funds or present needs.

The reason, of course, is that there are certain features of most library buildings which may be very difficult and expensive to change once the structure has been erected. These are fixed features such as stairways, booklifts, elevators, entrance details, and circulation areas.

The ultimate size and shape of the building may affect the original size and location that should be given these features. In college libraries, for instance, the location of the technical processes area may be affected. Frequently it is difficult to enlarge these areas or change their locations at a later date. The original planning should be done with the ultimate building in mind so that these adjustments can be made in the future.

Seldom is this point stressed sufficiently in statements of program. In many it is not even mentioned. A further handicap is that the architect may not relish the extra cost of designing, even in preliminary sketches, a larger building than he may be paid for designing.

Individual Studies

The statement of program should be based on the library needs of the particular community or the particular college being studied. For example, it is well known that the educational status of the community is perhaps the most important factor in the amount of use that is made of a public library. Yet program after program is based on average standards, without adjustments for variation in the educational status of the community.

The work and the insight which went into the establishment of these various published standards are truly magnificent. However they *are* averages and should be considered as such. A library building designed on those standards in a community in which the educational average is one third or more above the national average is likely to prove inadequate very shortly after it is erected. We have seen that unfortunate situation occur many times.

Favorite Designs

It is a habit of some who prepare statements of program to attempt to apply, in almost all cases, one's own favorite preference in building design. Some are wedded to extreme versions of the modular design in the mistaken belief that this is the answer to all problems of flexibility.

Some planners are tied to the core arrangement in which a main stairway, an elevator, and a book-stack arrangement of two levels or more are grouped in one area of the building. However, in some cases these very features are obstructions to flexibility and future expansion.

Some who emphasize, as we all do, the necessity of a grade level entrance, are fond of mezzanines in reading rooms in spite of several facts: that mezzanines are usually a handicap to flexibility, that older public library users will find it difficult to climb the stairs, that the percentage of these older public library users (who are also taxpayers) is rapidly increasing, and finally, that the high area not covered by the mezzanine constitutes a cubic footage which will have to be heated in winter and cooled in summer yet is not used.

Written Reports

To some it may seem axiomatic and therefore superfluous to say that all consultants' reports should be in writing. Yet there are librarians, active as consultants, who avoid written reports as much as possible. One told me quite frankly that he did not wish to undertake any consulting work which involved written reports. He would contract for a day's service, visit the community and the library in the morning, discuss the problem with the librarian and/or the board in the afternoon and perhaps evening, and then go home and send a bill. This practice is wrong; this practice is very wrong, but this practice is not at all unusual in college libraries as well as in public libraries. It is not uncommon for a college administration, faced with an urgent library expansion problem, to call in half a dozen individual consultants on different days. Each goes over the same problem with the library staff and the architect in the morning, meets with various committees in the early afternoon, and about 4:00 P.M. gives his views verbally to a full meeting of the building committee, the architect's representative, and university officials.

Now I suppose that this procedure might be dignified by the term "consultation service" for lack of any other label. However, it cannot be called library building consultation service in the sense in which I am attempting to discuss the term. This is not to say that in such a case the consultant's advice is not good; it is probably excellent. It is simply that there is not enough of it. When a library is spending hundreds of thousands and often millions of dollars on a library building the project needs and deserves more than the casual haphazard consultation service furnished by a few verbal discussions.

Furthermore, sometimes it is difficult for us to remember that reports should be written, not for librarians, but for library laymen, who may be board members or other local leaders or architects, or college officials, and who often have a high intelligence sharpened by skepticism, and are not likely to accept as "manna from Heaven" a bald statement unsupported by reason.

Sketches for Architects

Some consultants like to draw outline plans for architects. This practice is of such questionable advantage that it may not be too extreme an admonition to say: *Never* attempt to draw a sketch for a client in order to illustrate an idea. It can be expressed clearly enough in writing, if sufficient care is taken.

Designing a plan is an architect's responsibility and prerogative. Often an architect, trained as he is, can come up with a solution to a problem that is quite different from the sketch a consultant or a client might draw, and yet is a better solution, provided the requirements and possible alternatives have been accurately and fully set forth in writing.

Within these limits the architect's imagination should be allowed free rein, unconstricted by those unacquainted with problems of architectural design and structure. On the other hand, it is important that the client and the librarian should retain their dominant positions and their freedom of choice as critics and judges.

One of the most practical aids to an architect is a full discussion of the projected arrangement of facilities. Too many statements of program do not go into sufficient detail in this respect. For instance, in a public library project for an average-sized library, the survey may stop with a few general remarks such as;

> It is advantageous if all public service departments can be kept on one floor. If this is impossible, the Children's Room of X number of square feet may be moved to another level.
> Beyond this, if adult public services must be split, the first and, hopefully, the only department to be moved to another floor should be Arts and Music.

It would be of much more assistance to the architect if, for instance, Arts and Music, in the case cited, were specifically expressed in square feet, shelving needs, and seating. In most public libraries it is helpful if the entire departmental organization is discussed in its relationship, department to department.

In the college field, the situation is a little more difficult. The typical academic library will frequently have more stories or floors devoted to public services than the average public library. The architect needs information as to the future needs of major book classifications and related seating, expressed in square feet. If land is limited, or if the new building must be an addition, the architect may be very much in need of this information.

Consultants are often loathe to make such detailed guesses. This is understandable, for nobody can foretell the future with accuracy. As Stephen McCarthy says: "It is almost impossible to keep books and readers in phase as the years pass." Yet somebody should try to make these future estimates for the guidance of the architect. For example, in the case of one undergraduate college library, the report divided the books into three main classes by related subject, and an estimate was made that Group A subjects might constitute approximately 42 percent of the future book stock, Group B subjects, 41 percent, Group C subjects, 17 percent. After explaining the advantages of the intermixing of books and readers, it was estimated on the basis of comparative amount of use, that Group A might require 50 percent of the seats, Group B, 35 percent, and Group C, 15 percent.

Translating these percentages into books and reader seats, and then into square feet, the report recommended 31,000 square feet for Group A, 26,000 square feet for Group B, and 11,000 square feet for Group C.

Following this were a few paragraphs explaining how, in a small floor area, subject classes of books become divided more frequently and, because of lack of space, related material must be shelved on different floor levels, constituting an obstruction to the effective use of the resources, and explaining further that librarians have found that these obstructions inhibit the use of the materials.

Equipment Lists

Very few statements of program contain equipment lists based on future needs. Yet an equipment list, provided it is complete, is a very effective check against the calculations for square footage of the various rooms and areas, and also of the entire building.

It is interesting to note that in a great percentage of cases the total building measurements for a public library need to be 10 to 25 percent more than one would expect from the formulas expressed in library literature in various sizes of communities. This points up the remark made earlier that these formulas, splendid helps that they are, nevertheless suffer because they are averages, and because they are based on the past.

These formulas would prove to be even more inadequate were it not for the fact that many of the buildings on which the statistics are based were constructed during the time when library architecture was characterized by rotundas, grand staircases, and other waste space, part of which modern architecture has been able to eliminate.

As has been stated, the equipment list is not effective unless it is complete. *Every* piece of equipment which requires floor space should be included. It is sometimes surprising how much extra space is found to be needed beyond the usual requirements for shelving and seats. It may be well to follow the principle, that if there is any question regarding the need for an item, the question should be answered in the affirmative. This stage of the planning is not the time for compromises.

It may be objected that it is impossible to estimate accurately the amount of equipment that will be needed in the building twenty years hence. This may be the case. Nevertheless, the attempt should be made; otherwise, why try to plan at all?

Admittedly, preparing an equipment list is a very slow and painstaking process. It means more costly consulting work. It also means the consulting work will be that much more valuable to the client.

REVIEWS OF PLANS

It is frequently assumed, by those inexperienced in dealing with architects (and by "inexperienced" I mean those who have worked on fewer than five or six library buildings) that, given a reasonably adequate statement of program, the architect can proceed to devise a good library plan, and the client will need very little further assistance from the consultant. On the contrary, experience indicates that at least one third of the total consultant time on the project, and sometimes as much as one half, should be devoted to reviews of plans. The reviews, like the statement of program, should be in writing and in detail.

One such review can best take place immediately after the architect prepares his earliest sketches. This is the time in which the architect can make changes in his sketches with comparative ease. Sometimes the review may cause him to change his entire concept of his design. It is not fair to the architect to allow the designing to proceed too far without making a thorough review of the plan. The architect's drafting room is his factory, and in most cases he receives no more compensation for having to do a job over again.

Here is where the first compromises may need to be made, where the consultant needs a true sense of perspective, to know when and on what items to agree to a compromise, and where many mistakes can be made by failing to be sufficiently stubborn and insistent about important points.

Perhaps it will be worthwhile at this point to consider the approach which most architects take toward their assignments and the attitude which the consultant should have. The architect must be an artist but also a businessman. After he obtains the client's initials in the lower righthand corner of his drawings it becomes increasingly difficult and sometimes expensive for the client to have changes made. This is as it should be. However, consider that fact in the perspective of the architect's training; that training is largely in aesthetics. It is true that the architectural schools and colleges spend a great deal of time and effort in teaching the budding architect the theory of the functional approach. Perhaps they do every bit as well with it as can be expected. The fact remains that in any conflict between the aesthetic and the functional, most architects are by inclination and training likely to lean toward the aesthetic.

There is nothing wrong with this. On the contrary, I would not have it any other way, for we all want beauty in our architecture and who is to supply it if not the architect.

What is needed in any conflict between the aesthetic and the functional, and there are always several such conflicts, is a person who is trained and knowledgeable in the functional aspects of library buildings and who knows how to interpret plans, to uphold the functional interest just as capably as the architect will look out for the aesthetic. That person must be the consultant. It is naïve to think that the college administration or the public library board can do it; it is also usually futile to hope that the client librarian can do it.

This job requires much training and it requires experience on many library projects. It requires an ability to read and understand the drawings with facility. More important, it requires an ability to put into proper perspective the problem at issue, to know when to compromise, when to give up the functional in favor of aesthetic considerations, and, on the other hand, when to stand firmly for the functional and insist that the architect should find some other aesthetic solution than the one he is advocating. This is one reason why the consultant should be engaged by and work for the owner, not the architect. Otherwise, the architect will be free to accept or ignore the consultant's recommendations, as he sees fit; whereas it is the owner who should reserve the right to make these decisions. This is why those consultants who are content to spend a day here and a day there examining sketches with clients are doing a most unfortunately superficial job and may do their clients more harm than good.

Before passing on to the next phase of this discussion it may be pertinent to consider also the reviews of plans offered by the various Building Institutes held in connection with ALA Conventions. No doubt everybody will agree that those reviews of plans have done a tremendous amount of good, not only for the institution whose plans are discussed, but also for the several hundred librarians, faculty, and trustees who listen to and sometimes participate in the discussions.

It would be advantageous, however, if some way could be found to emphasize sufficiently, and officially, to all concerned that no more than a very superficial analysis can be offered in this manner; that bad advice as well as good advice may be given, because any one is privileged to speak; and that those who offer plans for analysis should not assume, therefore, that they are getting authoritative consulting service gratis. It is surprising how many librarians think this casual advice is all they need. Consultants who had furnished the Statement of Program for a large library received a letter which said in part: "I had not planned on a review of our plans prior to presenting them at [ALA] since the content of that program is in the nature of a review and criticism. . . . I will discuss with [the Board] whether we feel further general consultation is desirable in view of the costs involved."

CONSULTANTS' QUALIFICATIONS AND CHARACTERISTICS

Keyes Metcalf, in a paper delivered at a Building Institute a few years ago, gave an excellent outline of the qualifications a consultant should have, and no repetition is needed here. It may be worth mentioning, however, that a person can be an excellent library administrator and yet be a poor library building planner—and that a person can be a good library planner and yet be a poor consultant. Sometimes this is because, as Metcalf says, the consultant is not articulate; often it is because of other personal characteristics.

A good consultant must be able to see the other side of the question, willing to have his views questioned critically without being offended, and willing to admit error and yet stand firmly for his opinions if the issue is important enough. In short, he must be objective.

The dominant need of many consultants today, though some obviously do not realize it, is training and experience. There are some who are ambitious for consulting work, including some on the so-called ALA list of consultants, who are definitely lacking in the necessary experience.

It is unfortunate that with many millions of dollars being spent on library buildings throughout the country, this important matter should be treated in such haphazard fashion. Admittedly, ALA should not set itself up as a judge of the qualifications of building consultants. However, the inference, if not an actual statement, is that all those on the ALA list of building consultants are qualified. It is unfortunate if this list is sent to inquirers without an accompanying statement that no attempt has been made to judge the experience or the capability of those on the list. A few examples may serve to illustrate this.

There is, for instance, a statement of program, prepared by a consultant who is on the ALA's list. The statement attempts to describe the public library needed by a certain city with an estimated future population of 55,000 people. For this population, the statement recommends a library with a total area of only 20,000 square feet. Even the twenty-five-year-old Wheeler and Githens formula recommends about 50 percent more space than that.

Furthermore, there is, in this particular statement of program, no attempted substantiation of the recommended size. Then again, no detail whatsoever is given to break down this recommended square footage into its component parts.

As another example, there is a statement of program for a certain college library, which specifies · a number of doublefaced book stack units, for each of which is allocated an area of 13 1/2 square feet. Now this is adequate for the average book stack unit and its lengthwise aisle. However, the total square footage needed for book stacks as recommended in this statement of program was obtained merely by multiplying the recommended number of book stack units by this average of 13 1/2 square feet. No consideration was given to any cross-aisles. The omission was, in fact, recognized, but it was avoided by stating that the end aisles would probably be shared by table aisles. No consideration was given to the possibility that, in some areas, the length of book stack ranges might have to be quite short, depending upon the arrangement of the area, thus requiring considerable space for cross-aisles. No consideration was given to the possibility that it might be desirable or even necessary to utilize wider aisles in some arrangements; no consideration was given to the possibility that it might be desirable or even necessary to utilize, in some arrangements, book shelving less than seven shelves high.

In the same statement, there was a recommendation of 25 square feet per reader for all reading areas and this was supposed to be sufficient to cover, in addition to tables and chairs, all other reference equipment such as atlas cases, dictionary stands, map cases, microfilm readers, attendants' desks, and a host of similar items.

As a third example, there is a statement of program, also written by a consultant on the ALA suggested list—and, I may add, one who has had many assignments—which specifies approximately 30,000 total square feet for a new public library building. There is neither an indication of the future population estimate upon which this recommendation was based, nor an indication of the educational or financial level of the community. In fact, there is no background information whatsoever.

A recommendation is offered regarding the location of the future building, but no evidence is offered to support the recommendation. For architectural requirements, items such as stairways, elevators, corridors, heating and ventilation, wall thicknesses, custodial requirements, and rest rooms, the statement allows less than 10 percent of the total building area.

In general, it may be said that among the many statements of program examined in the preparation of this paper, it was quite common to find recommendations for a quantity of book housing or seating without square footage recommendations; or to find square footage recommendations without any substantiating detail. Then there are recommendations like these: "Shelf space for six sets of encyclopedias should be available," with no information given the architect about the space required. Again, "Three or four tables are needed in this immediate area," but there is no indication of how large the tables should be, how many seats there should be, or how many square feet are required.

There are naïve assumptions that it is sufficient to indicate the floor size of a piece of equipment without considering the space needed around it. One obtains the impression from some of these statements that the architect is expected to be a magician and thus be able to fill in the gaps between the general guidelines offered.

THE COST OF CONSULTING WORK

Some qualified consultants charge very little; in fact, some consultants have been known to give consulting service on library buildings to neighboring libraries free of charge. This laudable generosity may be unwittingly misleading, if the client thinks he is getting complete and adequate consulting service. On the other hand, at least two consulting organizations exist whose total fees average three-fourths of 1 percent of the total project cost.

Some qualified consultants may make trips away from their home bases, spending a day or so with the client and then another very few days writing a report, and this practice too, may result in a very superficial piece of work and one that can cause positive harm. I am sure most, if not all, of these men are genuinely interested in doing a thorough job, but have different ideas than do some others as to what constitutes thorough consulting work.

This situation is well illustrated by statements which appear in Ellsworth's book, *Planning the College and University Library Building:*

> One hundred and fifty dollars a day plus expenses is a normal nominal fee for an experienced consultant. . . .
> The amount of time a consultant spends . . . would be somewhat as follows: A preliminary meeting of three to five days—studying the local problem and getting a first draft of the program written . . . a second meeting of one or two days on the site problem and another two days on the final draft of the program. After the architect has developed preliminary plans there will usually be a series of short meetings to discuss the plans. From this point on, careful studies of the plans should be made with the librarian and other local officials not just for layout but for all aspects of lighting, heating and ventilation, location of control, etc. A college planning a million and one half dollar building should budget $1,500.00 for this kind of consultation service [pp. 24–25].

In other words, ignoring consideration of travel expenses for the moment, we are to assume that consultant service for a total of ten days would be sufficient to write the program, analyze the preliminary plans, and study the later plans in detail. How are we to reconcile this thinking with that of others, which would indicate that something like ten times the Ellsworth estimate is needed for a thorough job?

Ralph Ellsworth does not mind having his view questioned, and so I wrote him, and after a couple of exchanges of correspondence I received this letter: "I think the answer to the question about the time required for a consultation is that we are talking about different kinds of problems. I am talking about the kind of situation when there is a competent and experienced architect and a librarian who has ideas and knows how to get the job done."

Ah, but Ellsworth made no such qualification in his book, and who is to judge whether the librarian "knows how to get the job done" when he has had little or no building experience? Furthermore, the reference was quoted without any qualification whatsoever in a paper delivered by Metcalf at a Building Institute and printed in the *ALA Bulletin* of December 1963. Perhaps a great many librarians, both college and public, may have included in their budgets an allowance for building consultation service which is grossly inadequate.

It is certain that the depth of consulting service which has been discussed in this paper simply cannot be rendered for any such paltry sum as one tenth of 1 percent of the building budget. As Charles Mohrhardt has said, ten times that percentage is more accurate for a mediumsized building.

There may be valid objections to the theory that the statement of program should be written by the local librarian with some help from the consultant. The program, to be truly and certainly objective, should be written by an outside consultant. For best results, the consultant should serve the owner, the institution, not the librarian. The librarian, as a representative of the owner, should remain in a position to recommend acceptance or rejection of any recommendation in the statement, and he should be a part of the consulting team; but he should desire, for best results, that the original recommendations come from the outside.

SOME SUGGESTIONS FOR IMPROVING CONSULTING STANDARDS

Two suggestions come to mind for the improvement of consulting service for library buildings.

One is to have the consulting service performed by groups of three or four consultants who can check each others' work. Without exception, there is no one person in the country who is knowledgeable enough and experienced enough to be entrusted with the preparation of a complete statement of program for a library, and to review its architectural sketches, without considerable experienced assistance. One may be splendid at setting up a future departmental organization; another may be expert at technical processes; a third may excel at estimating detailed space requirements; and a fourth may be better at interpreting plans and suggesting improvements. One of the four may be adept at writing. A group operation takes advantage of the strong points of each consultant and will avoid errors of judgment which almost inevitably occur in a one-person consultantship.

The other suggestion is prompted by this question: How can the conflicts of opinion of which we have previously spoken, and which are confusing to a librarian who is seeking assistance, be clarified and brought into reasonable control for the benefit of both clients and consultants? I realize that I may be treading on thin ice when I suggest adding yet another set of initials to the many which now cover various aspects of librarians' activities. However, might it not be feasible to have an Association of Library Consultants which could do the sort of thing that the AIA (American Institute of Architects) does so well for the architectural profession?

What could such an association do? A few objectives may be listed for library consultation work alone; there may be others for other types of library consultation. Such an association might:

1. Define the extent of good consultation work.
2. Set standards for qualification of individuals as members of the Association of Library Consultants.

3. Provide means whereby those who are interested in consultation work can achieve much needed training and experience, to replace the hit-or-miss methods of today.
4. Clarify the percentage of the building budget which should be allocated to consultation work if a qualified consultant is to participate.
5. Provide a clearing house of building information for the benefit of its members.

It seems to me that library consulting work, and in particular that part of it which has to do with library buildings, needs some sort of organized effort to establish and maintain high standards.

ABOUT THE AUTHOR—Donald E. Bean is President of Library Management and Building Consultants, Inc., of Evanston, Illinois. After receiving the B.A. degree from the University of Illinois in 1921, he was library planning specialist on the staff of the Library Bureau, a division of Remington Rand, until 1958 when he accepted his present position. Mr. Bean has served on many library committees, been library building consultant, and written several books, notably *Modular Planning for College and Small University Libraries* (with Ralph E. Ellsworth).

Super-Librarian and Sub-Architect: The Anomaly of the Role of the Building Consultant

by Nancy R. McAdams

Mrs. McAdams has provided us with one of the most provocative articles in the litera-ture of library buildings. Even while accepting its provocation one wonders if at the time of its writing, Mrs. McAdams was perhaps too long an architect and too short a librarian.

Who are library building consultants? What do they do, for whom, and how? How are they paid, and how do they promote their services? How have they prepared for this kind of work?

These and related questions led to a detailed study, in the Spring of 1965, of the library build-ing consultant, for presentation as a master's re-port at the University of Texas Graduate School of Library Science. The study consisted of an analy-sis of the small body of available literature on the topic, and a parallel analysis of a questionnaire sur-vey of 99 practicing consultants. The survey in-cluded only librarians (and library school faculty members) who had acted as library building con-sultants either to architects or to libraries. It did not include architects, interior designers, library equipment manufacturers' representatives, or other nonlibrarians, nor did it include staff con-sultants of state or regional libraries.

Of the 99 respondents to the questionnaire, there were 88 men and 11 women. Most were em-ployed full-time as the directing officers of public or university libraries, or were retired from such positions. The consultants averaged over 24 years of experience in librarianship, and on the average had been concerned with about 18 building proj-ects, a third of these for their own libraries and two-thirds for other libraries. Almost all the re-spondents conducted their consulting practices alone, from their own offices in their employing libraries. They averaged 21.4 work days per year for an average fee of $107 per day plus expenses.

Many of the questionnaire respondents replied at some length, adding remarks and opinions, and

sometimes sending material about themselves or their work, even complete building programs. This additional information helped to define rather ac-curately the nature of their consulting practices. Because of several discrepancies between the litera-ture view of what the consultant should do, and what the consultants themselves reported actually doing, the following comments and recommenda-tions were developed.

There is general agreement in the literature that the library building consultant should, whenever possible, be brought into planning for a new proj-ect at the very beginning, during the initial con-sideration of whether or not to build. He should assist in the selection of the site, and of the archi-tect; should perhaps make a survey of the library as a basis for programing, and should assist or guide the preparation of the building program without actually writing it. He should then see that a satisfactory form is devised for the building by critical reviews of the architect's preliminary plans, working drawings, and specifications; should assist in the layout of specialized library equip-ment and furnishings, perhaps in collaboration with an interior design specialist; should inspect the building occasionally during construction; and finally should assist the librarian in adapting to the new quarters after completion of the building.

However, the respondents to the survey indi-cated very little participation in projects prior to the program-writing stage, and the majority sug-gested that, more often than not, programs were written by the consultant himself rather than co-operatively. In addition, only a few of the con-

SOURCE: Reprinted from Nancy R. McAdams, "Super-Librarian and Sub-Architect: The Anomaly of the Role of the Building Consultant," *Library Journal*, vol. 91, December 1, 1966, pp. 5827–5831, by permission of the publisher and the author.

sultants continued to participate in projects after commencement of construction. Thus it would seem that, in current practice, the actual function of the library building consultant is the production of a building program and the interpretation of that program to the architect during plan development.

This present role of the library building consultant has come about because of the supposed inadequacies of others: the inability of the librarian to formulate program requirements, whether through lack of experience, time, knowledge, or confidence; and a collateral inability of the architect to comprehend the program statement, either because of lack of experience with library buildings or lack of vision. The consultant's services have been sought to compensate for these supposed inadequacies by the application of his specialized knowledge and experience with library buildings.

Despite what may be, in some cases, a real need for these services, the increasing volume of library construction, due in part to the Library Services and Construction Act, will force many projects to proceed without the benefit of consulting advice. Since a rapidly growing library cannot afford to wait for a consultant to tell it what to do, more knowledgeable participation in planning will be required of the librarian, along with a strengthening of his confidence in his own ability and that of his architect.

If it is true that the consultant is needed because the librarian lacks the time, staff, or funds for adequate study for preparation of the building program, or is really incapable of performing the work, the librarian's need for assistance should be recognized. Help should be provided, not by engaging a consultant to do the librarian's thinking for him, but by employing an additional staff member specifically for research in planning, or for administrative assistance to free the librarian for planning. Since an increase in size of staff almost always takes place on completion of a new building, it should simply be moved forward to the beginning of planning.

In addition, if planning were viewed as a continuing process of administration, planning for physical change would be less traumatic. Large libraries and systems with rapid expansion would do well to employ a regular staff planner especially qualified for this work. A high-level example of this practice is furnished by the Library of Congress, which this year added to its staff a former library building consultant to work exclusively on physical planning for the library.

In the literature and in the questionnaire comments, consultants have made much of the difficulty for the librarian in determining the future physical requirements of the library, but in practice the librarian need not solve this problem alone. Planning projection can be made more easily and accurately by a statistician (who is often part of the academic or municipal administration), using the statistical methods routine to planning for business development, schools, utilities, and other community facilities, than by a librarian consultant. A sound statistical projection should certainly carry as much influence with the library's administrative body as the opinion of a library consultant, no matter how authoritative.

Consultants have also emphasized their usefulness in guiding the librarian through the unfamiliar procedures of building. Since the procedures for implementing construction of a library building (site acquisition, funds procurement, construction permits, contracts, etc.) are essentially the same as for other public buildings, the architect to whom these are routine matters can be of more help than a consultant because he knows the local conditions and requirements while a visiting consultant may be unaware of them.

Librarians seem to believe that the library building possesses a special quality, not perceptible to others, which demands superior performance or inspiration from its architect. This is an unrealistic notion, for the usual library building cannot begin to compare in difficulty with some other building types. It is simpler functionally and mechanically than the modern hospital or industrial plant, and is less rapidly obsolescent or outgrown; its architectural character is less exacting than that of a church; it presents fewer structural problems than any high-rise building; and it makes no unusual demands of its materials, beyond those of other public or institutional buildings. Viewed without sentimentality, the library building is a fairly ordinary structure, requiring no special magic of its designer, and it is fully within the capabilities of most architectural firms, with or without prior library planning experience.

Two strong trends in the practice of architecture should help to dispel the librarian's reluctance to trust the architect. One is the increasing specialization of architectural firms in a single building type, such as schools or hospitals; it is hoped that more firms will develop specializations in library buildings. The other trend is the concept of expanded professional practice called "comprehensive architectural services." A firm offering comprehensive services should be prepared to perform, in addition to the usual architectural services, complete project analysis, using staff and consultant specialists for location analysis and site selection, economic feasibility studies, budget estimating, human factors analysis, operations planning, and building programing. Under these circumstances, the major functions of the library building consultant, as they are now performed, would be assumed by the architect.

Consultants are believed to be required to explain library functions to the architect who has never designed a library building, and to assist him in the allocation of space for these functions and the placement of equipment. Such repeated explanation would be unnecessary if there existed a body of concise, up-to-date literature on functional planning and equipment, in a form *readily available to architects.*

Hopefully, books by library consultants, recently published or in preparation, may help to fill this need. (Keyes D. Metcalf's *Planning Academic and Research Library Buildings* [McGraw Hill, 1965] contains a wealth of information applicable to other types of libraries as well, but its size and verbosity discourage its use in the drafting room, where data is needed for detailed planning.) However, a long-range program of technical research in library operations, and the space requirements of patrons and staff, should be implemented. Perhaps this could be accomplished by the establishment of an interprofessional agency to sponsor such research, publish the findings for distribution to both professions, and sponsor interprofessional seminars or conferences. A comparable agency has recently been organized as the Center for Research on Religious Architecture, a nonprofit corporation for interfaith research governed by representatives of the American Institute of Architects and the three major religious bodies.

Another approach might be the encouragement by the library profession of the establishment of a committee within the American Institute of Architects, parallel to its existing Committee on Hospital Architecture, Committee on Religious Architecture, Committee on School and College Architecture, and its Committee on Auditorium and Theatre Architecture. These groups maintain close contact with their related professional organizations (American Hospital Association, American Association of School Administrators, etc.) and have been responsible for the publication of several regular report series, such as a monthly newsletter for hospital planners, "School Plant Studies," and planning guides for churches of various denominations.

It is no longer a once-in-a-lifetime event for a librarian to be faced with the problems of planning a new building. Indeed, many librarians must handle these problems repeatedly in the same library position, and some encounter them again and again as they advance through administrative positions in different libraries. The library building boom will undoubtedly offer the present library building consultants many more opportunities for employment of their services. At the same time, it will of necessity produce a number of librarians and architects capable of developing a satisfactory library building without the use of consultant services, especially if the suggestions above, for local assistance for the librarian and published assistance for the architect, are followed. The need for the library building consultant's services as they now exist would then be obviated. However, it is not intended that he quietly disappear; rather, he should consider a transition in his role in order to meet other needs of libraries and architects which are liable to continue.

The consultant's present role is something of an anomaly—he attempts to be a combination of super-librarian and sub-architect. It is not reasonable to expect such versatility, nor is it necessary. The consultant has been concerning himself to a great extent with details of the physical form of the library, matters which are after all the special province and the ultimate responsibility of the architect. Therefore, it would seem advisable for the consultant to turn his attention to the broader problems of library growth, policies, and practices, and to concentrate on administrative consulting. Reorganization of campus-wide or community-wide services, advice on staff utilization, suggestions for changes in service systems or recommendations for financial campaigns to support building projects are some of the functions which could be included under this concept of consulting.

There are, and probably always will be, certain planning situations which contain problems only a consultant can help to overcome. In these situations the consultant's contribution is not so much his knowledge as it is his professional reputation, the force of his personality, his public relations know-how, or his persuasiveness.

The members of the planning team work in a complexity of personal and professional relationships. When comparable ability and mutual respect are present, planning can proceed smoothly, but this is frequently not the case. It is not too unusual for the librarian's recommendations to be ignored by an administration which doubts his capability, or to be suppressed by a domineering architect. Nor is it unheard of for an aggressive librarian to promote ideas which are outmoded or unworkable in the new building situation. Occasionally the librarian and his administrative officers may disagree on far-reaching decisions about the course of their library's development. When the consultant's services are requested to resolve conflicts of this kind, it should be recognized that he has been engaged to lend strength to a combatant, to mediate an agreement, to dictate a solution, or to size up a situation with the objectivity possible only to an outsider.

The consultant could also fill a role in "comprehensive architectural services." The architect engaged in complete project analysis for a library could benefit from the direct employment of a library consultant, particularly in the performance of location analysis, human factors analysis, and building programing.

The advent of advanced library techniques for information handling will probably bring a need for yet another kind of consultant, a technical consultant. Working with systems engineers, the technical consultant could assist the librarian in adapting present library systems to automation, and could advise the architect in the space requirements and mechanical needs of automated systems. It is unlikely that more than a few of the present library building consultants are prepared to assume this kind of work.

Among library building consultants, part-time practice is the prevailing mode, but this is not true for other types of consultants for building planning. School consultants, hospital consultants, industrial consultants, and the like are almost invariably representatives of independent consulting firms or architectural firms; consulting work constitutes their sole employment and receives their full attention. A school board would not engage a neighboring school administrator, nor would a hospital board expect to employ the administrator of another hospital as its consultant. It cannot be understood, then, why a library board should ask another librarian for assistance, and expect him to accomplish satisfactory work for it in time borrowed from his regular employment.

How is the consultant's regular work conducted in his absence? Is his library board indulgent of his absences? If they consider consulting work an extension of his library duties, is it ethical for him to accept payment for the work? These questions have not been satisfactorily answered by the study, and could not have been asked of the respondents without seeming impertinent. Nevertheless, the conclusion must be drawn that an active consulting practice and the conscientious administration of an important library (and most of the questionnaire respondents hold such posts) are beyond the capacities of most people.

It is recommended, therefore, that serious consideration be given to reducing the workload of practicing consultants who are fulltime library administrators, and to developing a corps of consultants, experienced in administration, who are free of regular library responsibility. The several practicing consultants who are retired from library service already constitute the nucleus of such a corps. Perhaps administrative consulting could most reasonably be combined with library school teaching. (The questionnaire survey showed that approximately a third of the respondents were already engaged in regular or occasional library school teaching, indicating a definite parallel of interests. Perhaps both consultants and teachers are simply people who like to tell others what to do.) If such a combination were effected, it might help to narrow the gap between school and work which exists in every professional field. Consulting might also be conducted as an extension of the work of a research agency, such as that proposed above, where it would strengthen the contact between research and practice.

The acknowledged "deans" of library building consulting have already generously shared their knowledge with the profession through publication. Their works probably form the basis for much of the advice given by other consultants, conditioned as librarians are to relying on the printed word for authority. However, library building planning is not, or should not be, static. New developments in the storage and handling of printed materials, and in other systems of communicating knowledge, will inevitably make obsolete much of what is now standard library building practice. The availability of information to librarians and to their architects must keep pace with these developments if libraries are to enjoy the benefits of contemporary technology in buildings which permit its fullest use.

ABOUT THE AUTHOR—Nancy R. McAdams received her Bachelor of Architecture degree in 1951 and her Master of Library Science in 1965, both from the University of Texas. She has worked with several architectural firms (1961–62), and is a registered architect in Texas. Mrs. McAdams has been architectural librarian at the University of Texas since 1965.

III

THE BUILDING PROGRAM

At the conclusion of his article, included here, Mr. Mason states that "... properly done, the production of a good library building program can be the librarian's greatest intellectual achievement." Nothing could be more true. Good library buildings stand or fall upon the programs on which they are based.

Ideally the librarian will prepare his building program with the aid of a qualified consultant before an architect is appointed. A well conceived program should include information on the following elements:

1. The parent institution or agency (its history, philosophy and goals)
2. How the library will aid in carrying out this philosophy and in achieving these goals
3. A description, in layman terms, of the various areas, departments, or functions of the library with attention to spatial relationships
4. Summary of space needs (the net square foot requirements)
5. A listing of special mechanical or library equipment of significance

Obviously if careful consideration is given to these five elements of planning before the project is handed to an architect, the resultant building scheme should be relevant to the library's needs.

In describing the building's functions, the librarian and library staff are given an opportunity to depart from the old, the existing, to the new and the ideal. At least in the programming stage, physical barriers are non-existent. The best of all possible worlds may be considered here—until budget considerations are brought into play.

Although only two articles are reprinted on the subject of programming, the deed of programming itself is of paramount significance to the whole of library buildings.

Library Building Programs: How to Draft Them

by Ernest J. Reece

The following is a classic in the literature of library building planning. Thorough and scholarly, though nearly twenty-five years old, it remains the best there is to both instruct in the method and at the same time evaluate the method itself.

Two forward steps have marked the recent practice of librarians in their work on building projects. One is the formal conferring on mutual problems, exemplified by the activities of groups in the university and public library fields respectively. The other is the preparing of programs, or statements of requirements, setting forth the features desired in contemplated structures.

Both of these steps have seemed overdue. A person need only scan the proceedings of the Cooperative Committee on Library Building Plans to realize how much reason there was for joint attack on the issues facing its members. Essential knowledge could be passed along, experiments reported, and proposals sifted out, with prospect that fewer unfortunate decisions would be built into stone and steel and fewer libraries forced to endure unsuitable quarters. While the task of such groups never can be finished, the reports and the book they already have produced are useful fruit and suggest a pattern for future undertakings.

In the drafting of programs the benefits have been less recognized and the developments so far less conclusive. It is true that their use apparently is becoming established, perhaps because the heads of libraries are accepting a new degree of responsibility for buildings. However, librarians seem not wholly agreed and clear about procedure. Uncertainty and debate have arisen as to how to render statements of requirements most fitting and effective. What should go into them, and how should it be organized and presented? And just what is the part of the librarian in the matter? The present paper deals with these queries, in the hope of clarifying the program-drafter's course. Its sources are the writings, programs and architects listed at its close.

In dealing with statements of requirements it is to be remembered that those for library buildings are only one branch of a large family, that the purposes and the relations of parties in projects of various kinds run parallel, and that what holds for one type is good in principle for all. Little seems to have been said about building programs in general, however, which has not come into the discussions concerning libraries. Librarians apparently have been justified, therefore, in centering attention on their particular sector, and the ensuing treatment follows them in this. At the same time all interested may gain by watching for examples and suggestions in other fields and gleaning what is possible from them.

SOME FUNDAMENTALS

Whatever the differences regarding library building programs a few aspects seem generally accepted, beginning with the intention of furnishing the architect the data useful as a guide in his work, and thus making more likely the results sought. Almost everyone recognizes too that programs should be prepared by or with persons knowing intimately the libraries concerned; that they should reflect careful preliminary study of needs and conditions; that they ought to embody more or less information about the institutions; and that if they are to be sufficiently definite they must indicate the facilities necessary, with some quantitative clues. Finally, all doubtless would see the advisability of insisting upon practicality, easy and economical operation, adaptability, and allowance for expansion.

SOURCE: Reprinted from Ernest J. Reece, "Library Building Programs: How to Draft Them," *College and Research Libraries,* July, 1952, pp. 198–211, by permission of the publisher.

So far so good; but the composer of a program is likely to find soon that these points need to be particularized or amplified, and perhaps supplemented by others similarly self-evident. Also, he may meet questions on which they shed no light. In trying to fill the gaps it is simplest to start with the points at agreement.

BENEFITS TO BE REAPED

First as to the values of a program. Supplying the architect with information means several things, viz., setting forth at the outset the requirements for service, with the conditions and reasons behind them; defining the enterprise in such ways that oversights and misunderstandings can be prevented and the work expedited; exposing the ideas of the owner to the architect, for criticism and mutual understanding; and, if necessary and discreet, fixing the relative importance of the various specifications so that it will be clear what to give up in case there must be sacrifices. Incidental benefits may be that if it is careful and systematic the statement affords the architect a better chance to save time, to do a reasoned job, and to make a profit, and shows possible donors that the project is well thought through. As for effects upon the framers, its development hardly can fail to crystallize their ideas and add to their comprehension of the situation and of the problems entailed.

PUTTING NEEDS FIRST

To realize these values fully librarians are warranted in assuming a free hand in the early stages of their planning. Much may be lost if a program is not shaped originally according to needs and without such limitations as those of funds and site. It may be difficult to hypothecate an ideal situation; and as far as can be judged there are few existing programs which deliberately disregard the restraints mentioned, unless it be where sites are not fixed or restricting and where no figure for expenditures has been set. Obviously one way to forestall the difficulty is to frame and publicize a program before hampering decisions have been made by higher authorities. Subsequently it may be softened by a scale of precedences, as already suggested, so that the total requisitions can be set

forth even though their parts must be diversely weighted. Whatever the situation it is only sensible to define the requirements on their merits, rather than according to extraneous factors. Thereafter, if they must compete against other claims they can do so with everything on the table and with a chance to justify themselves. If the aim is adequate planning, any other course seems like too easy yielding.

THOSE WHO DO THE WORK

As for authorship, a word will be in order later as to possible joint production by owner and architect. Whether the architect enters thus early or not, a large part of the labor and matter naturally must be supplied by representatives of the institution. The record shows that the work is done variously by the librarian; by a committee or members from corporation or staff, or from faculty in case of a college or university; or by the librarian and such a committee in team. Leadership and the bulk of the responsibility commonly lodge with the librarian whatever the machinery, and may be formalized where there is a committee by his membership ex-officio and/or as chairman. Apparently neither librarians nor architects are greatly concerned about the method so long as it accomplishes the job and does so without friction. Doubtless librarians are glad to have it remembered that normally they know the conditions and needs more intimately than do others, and that their insight deserves full credence and utilization.

PRELIMINARY STEPS

Whoever has the task of compiling a building program, the preparatory study necessary is the same. It embraces review of relevant data; scrutiny of the prospective operations and uses; consultation with staff and clientele, and with the librarians and building committees of kindred libraries; and examination of comparable buildings, as the best means of strengthening or correcting ideas already held, and of securing candid reports as to what has succeeded and what has not. Actual programs cite less use of such procedures than might be anticipated, their emphasis being mainly on conferences with committee members, staff and patrons. However, it may be suspected that in gathering material for decisions available resources were drawn upon generally, and that sometimes fairly systematic investigations were made. This would seem especially likely in colleges and universities, where conditions and demands can be gauged with some precision and where it is hardly thinkable that a head librarian or building committee would omit to canvass them thoroughly and to consider the views of the faculty regarding them, whether as part of the functioning of a committee or otherwise. Again, advising with librarians in similar institutions and inspection of other library buildings are known to have been prominent in some cases where such programs fail to mention them.

LIGHT ON THE PROJECT

One of the likely products of the study alluded to above is a store of background information. This consists of whatever facts about the library would affect its operations and accordingly call for specific features—notably its aims and policy; its plan of service and functioning, present and future; and, assuming prerequisite decisions have been made, an outline of the organization intended, perhaps in the shape of charts. A resumé of its history also sometimes is thought relevant. Presumably the more complete such matter can be in a program, without extending to undue length, the better. Architects again and again say it is useful and can not be too full; and librarians as a rule give it space, even though this is not always large. Aside from the orientation and explanations it provides, it makes possible an understanding of a situation not gainable from a sheer recital of needed particulars, since similar facilities may serve in different ways in different libraries, and therefore may not in themselves indicate too definitely what is sought by them. There of course is no claim that presentation of underlying facts can obviate that independent enquiry and thought through which some architects like to round out their knowledge and thus raise the chances of achieving over-all harmony and usefulness in their buildings. Still less can it take the place of such discussions as may best transmit the "librarian's enthusiasm for his institution and its background and its . . . methods."[1]

FUNCTIONS AND PARTS

From the general background material just referred to may come definitions of particular responsibilities and activities, and then of the units of organization and work they indicate. Incidentally, the processes preceding formulation of the program should follow this order, otherwise conventional departments and rooms may be assumed without considering whether they accord with the library's objectives and duties and should have a place in the new quarters. The definitions afford the breakdown desirable for initial thinking about the plan, and explain such estimates of capacities as usually accompany them. Instances occur in which departmental capacity specifications are offered without allusion to the business to be performed, but such requests are apt to lack conviction.

SERVICEABILITY

The urgency of making buildings simple, practical and economical often permeates building programs, especially in application to spaces, the relation and placing of parts, and lines of communication and transportation where these are considered. More pointed insistence on such necessities, however, might help to drive home their importance. They merit the same emphasis commonly given to the kindred principles of flexibility and expandability. In most cases the authors of programs wish the way left open and easy for rearrangements, sometimes through unit construction but not necessarily so, and make that desire clear in their statements. The possibility of adding capacities likewise is paramount, although if it is not so generally pressed this may be because so often locations already provide for the space which is its major requisite.

COST AND SITE

Besides the more or less axiomatic points thus far treated there are several less commonly mentioned which doubtless would command equally wide agreement. If feasible without prejudice to the thinking about requirements it should be useful to tell what funds are in prospect. Often there is no reference to these, whether because the facts are unknown or indefinite, or through anxiety not to be fettered by them. Such figures seem to be desired by architects, however, who naturally wish to know the proposed limits of expenditure, and likewise whether construction alone or other items as well are to be covered within them. Then too they might make a program look more complete and intelligent, providing any discrepancies between demands and costs were explained.

Similarly, if an architect is to understand a project he may have to know something about its location. Recommendations on site accordingly are important where it is not settled, and a description may be helpful if a choice has been made. Such matter frequently is missing from programs, however. While this may be because so often locations are predetermined and familiar it can be a loss, especially as concerns exposures. The placing of an edifice in relation to external traffic lines and to points of the compass is likely to affect vitally the access to it, its interior arrangement, and its supply of daylight. Proposals covering this hence may be important, whether in selecting a location or deciding how to use it. So far as they reflect urgent requirements, librarians hardly can afford to neglect them in their statements.

Lines of movement, communication and transportation, or what architects call circulation, also seem worthy of more express treatment than generally they have received. It likely is true that ideas respecting them are interwoven widely with prescriptions as to the relations and situations of parts. They influence compactness and efficiency so closely, however, and account for so large a fraction of the tare, that a librarian may slight part of his problem unless he recognizes and stresses their needs.

FURNISHINGS FOR THE STRUCTURE

The directions in a program regarding equipment and furniture apparently do not have to be extensive. There doubtless should be indication of the pieces suited to carry out the purposes of the building and of the departments and rooms planned, to guide the architect in any decisions he has to make on dimensions. Detailed inventories and layouts seem not essential, however, assuming that the assignments of space desired can be secured without them. Such compilations are requisite later, of course, for reference in drawing up specifications for equipment by whoever bears

that responsibility. On these matters a librarian is entitled to remember that he is more nearly an authority than he can be on some aspects and components of a building, especially since much of the furniture is peculiar to libraries in its qualities and application.

BEAUTY VS. USE

Esthetic quality receives mention in a few library programs, although usually in a somewhat negative way. The treatments suggest that the authors feared to be thought unduly utilitarian, yet realized that artistic effects belong in the domain of the architect. At any rate they mainly urge such beauty as inheres in simplicity, harmony and dignity, and contributes to effective functioning and an inviting atmosphere, and stop there. Perhaps such guarded advocacy veils a fear of reverting to monumentality, but while such an attitude is comprehensible, librarians might gain by giving it a more positive turn.

As addendum to what without much question should be in a building program, a note is in order as to what definitely ought to be out, viz., features and proposals not adequately authorized. Covering these an architect very pertinently has stressed the need for clearing programs in detail with governing bodies, to make sure that implied requirements involving "costs, site and other controlling considerations" are wholly approved, in order to forestall later "disappointment and waste of time."[2]

APPROACH TO CONTROVERSY

So much for matters which raise no sharp issues. There are others on which librarians' opinions or practices vary and about which there appear enough uncertainties otherwise to suggest going into their pros and cons. A few of these bear closely upon the designer's province and task, hence prompted the effort in preparation for the present article to secure viewpoints from a group of architects. Most of the professional men approached had had to do with library buildings, and so were presumed able to furnish significant responses. Naturally they do not agree completely; but most of their advice is pertinent, especially since rules suited to all situations are neither to be expected nor desirable.

AREAS AND DIMENSIONS

The first of the mooted questions stems from the specifying of capacities for departments and rooms, which has been alluded to above as a normal feature of a program and which proves in most cases to be welcomed by architects. Shall there be added calculations of the square and/or cubic footage necessary, with stipulations as to dimensions? In some cases librarians seem satisfied with statements of capacities, perhaps supplemented by such quantitative norms as the number of square feet required per reader, to help in translating the estimates into usable space figures. Commonly, however, they favor showing areas and volume and act accordingly, although sometimes only where the reckonings relate definitely to operation, and for functional divisions rather than for particular rooms and comparable parts. Some would go further and propose dimensions, at least where effective performance is at stake.

Architects differ on the point; and it could be inferred that some do not attribute much importance to it, perhaps anticipating that the information they need will soon develop or be amended in conference, whatever clues as to sizes get into the program. In a few instances they seem to consider mere capacities sufficient, and in contrast one holds that areas and dimensions both are needful; but the majority wish requisite capacities and appropriate areas—a "space budget," as one put it—or these plus suggested measurements and shapes. Their preference is made subject often to the condition that specific figures, when offered, should seek to convey approximate ideas and be open to adaptation, "in the spirit of willing compromise—of 'give and take.' "[3] They would avoid such rigid prescription as might interfere with the process of composition. Considerable latitude thus is open to the program-drafter, so long as he provides data that will suffice and yet will neither confuse nor bind the designer.

PLACING OF PARTS

Again, in treating the sections of a building should the framer of a program go beyond indicating the desired relations of parts—a process which generally seems taken for granted—and detail their positioning? Librarians lean to more or less designating of locations, although in practice they are likely to do it department by department, and

with a view to getting these put on appropriate floors, rather than through a complete building layout. Architects on the other hand appear pretty much agreed that clear exposition of functional relations, perhaps with charts showing the connections and the flow of work and traffic among the elements, is the greatest aid toward devising a suitable physical arrangement. Anything more implies attempting what the designer is best fitted to do; besides which it may discourage discussion and the attendant clarifying and evolving of a solution, and perhaps cause a plan to jell prematurely. One respondent goes so far as to say that "if you find an architect who is willing to take the librarian's direction as to the location of the various parts and not their relation, then you have a draftsman, and you are not getting the best out of the architect."[4] Direction, it may be noted, is too much—not relevant facts and opinions. Some point out that beneficial processes and results need not be endangered and that definite ideas on the positioning of components may be helpful, if they are shown to rest on operational plans and if they are made in general terms and as suggestions to be considered for and against in later conference.

SKETCHES, OR TEXT ONLY?

When positions are to be shown one way to do it is to introduce sketches, and regarding these there is marked difference of view both among librarians and architects. Of the two groups architects have been the more assertive, which is not strange considering that drawings are for them a chief means of expression and the making of plans one of the techniques included in their training. At the same time librarians have been prone to put their ideas into sketch form as well as into words, perhaps even before the day when John Shaw Billings outlined on the back of a discarded envelope a floor arrangement for the central building of the New York Public Library.

In favor of sketches in programs librarians claim that they may carry what words could not transmit, especially to an architect who is unacquainted with library practice; further, that they may be more stimulating to a designer's imagination than verbal presentation, and that they may save him time and money. Some aver that they need not involve such detail as to be beyond the powers of a librarian to produce, suggesting that if incongruities show up these can be corrected by the architect. According to that belief, too, work on drawings helps to give a librarian an appreciation of the designer's problems. Architects strengthen the argument by saying not only that sketches conform to their manner of thinking and are effective in conveying general concepts and as incentive, but that they sometimes tell more about the librarian's view than many words, aiding for one thing his understanding of "the way in which the librarian would like to operate." One adds: "Sketches as suggestions . . . are extremely valuable not only in passing on the experience of the librarian, but even in stimulating the architect to see if he can make a better one. Interchange of ideas often results in something better than previously was thought of by either."[5]

There are plenty who do not concur. The disclaimers from architects are that sketches may stifle their freedom of thought and criticism and deaden their inventive faculties, whereas a verbal statement challenges their mental resources; and that if they are impeded in the tasks for which they are especially equipped, the client fails to get the grade of service he should enjoy. Hence it is doubtful, states a member of their group, that "sketches are a proper part of a formal program except where they are the only means of showing a relationship."[6]

Psychological factors may play a part here, including the possible reluctance of an architect to pick flaws in a scheme which has become fixed in its proposer's mind, even though he feels that it oversteps bounds and has been built up to undue importance. Again, one of that calling puts much in few words by urging that the architect have opportunity to reach his solution "without the prejudicial influence of a sketch."[7]

Librarians who are on this side of the fence recognize the imprudence of invading the architect's field. Further, they insist not only that laymen are unfitted to draft plans, but that such efforts tend to reflect traditional rather than original ideas. Whether or not because of such reasoning, sketches seldom appear in available programs.

Since both of the above viewpoints are positive and credible, the program-drafter supposedly will be wise to choose between them in the light of his own conditions. Much could depend on his own skill, with the pencil and with the written and spoken word; and on his willingness to have an architect treat any drawing he might prepare merely as a tentative semblance of the way spaces might be arranged, and "push it around."[8] He might feel freer too if he was disposed to offer variants, as one designer suggested, all to be taken as experimental and subject to comparison and rejection in the interest of the best solution. If an architect already has been designated still more might hinge on his particular feeling about sketches, if that could be ascertained without adverse consequences. In any event what the librarian needs to remember is to keep to his part of the job and to discharge that in the most effectual and considerate manner he can.

TECHNICAL ASPECTS OF BUILDINGS

The debatable matters touched so far lie close to the librarian's field of expertness and intimate knowledge. What of those in which he is not a specialist, but on which he nevertheless may hold legitimate preferences and even supply apposite advice? That is, how far should his program refer to architectural style, design, building materials, decoration, general equipment, furnishings, floor coverings, air treatment, lighting and noise control?

This question is one largely for architects to answer; and among them are men who feel strongly that to treat the subjects concerned even tentatively in an owner's program may set the minds of the parties too early and thus hinder the reconciliations called for by the problem as a whole. One says in this relation, "It is very hard to make . . . development [of the project] a success if specific recommendations are made before the client has had the opportunity of seeing his plan grow with the architect."[9] There is alleged to be danger too that secondary considerations will be exalted above utility. All of this perhaps is especially true in reference to style.

In contrast, some endorse expressions on the matters listed, particularly where they bear upon administrative requirements or "have a definite relation to library operation and use."[10] "It is essential," the argument runs, "if for no other reason than that an issue is presented, a discussion follows, and a conclusion is reached through understanding of costs, maintenance, criteria of comfort, and the other factors."[11] And insofar as the subjects concerned are disputable, it aids by bringing them to attention and prompting their consideration in good time, and before decisions have been made which it would be costly to alter.

Specifically, the voicing of opinions on technical

topics may enable the architect to show why certain proposals are meritorious and others are not, and clear the way for the owner's wishes where they are appropriate, in pursuance of his "duty . . . to plan a building incorporating as many ideas of the client as are practical and possible."[12] It also may help the architect to "visualize the sort of building desired," restrain him from going to extremes, and facilitate consideration of preferences throughout the planning process and in the interest of harmony in the "over-all picture." One respondent furnishes a reminder too that occasionally a stipulation on the matters concerned needs to be presented clearly and in mandatory form because an endowment or some comparable arrangement depends upon it.[13]

Those architects who welcome preferences on technical matters of course feel nevertheless that their own opinions should "have considerable weight." Further, they join others in stressing that the librarian's desires may well be presented later and in a different way. In this connection one suggests that what goes into a statement of requirements be of a general nature, with more specific advices to come subsequently. Others urge full conference, where a plan may be worked out and the style and related topics developed in collaboration between themselves and the library authorities; and where "the sympathetic architect will be able either to adopt the suggestions where they fit in or to explain to the client why some of the preferences perhaps contradict other parts of the program or violate vital economy or lead to illogical results."[14]

In general librarians seem restrained in treating style, materials and the cognate topics, being content usually to tell what the requirements are and what qualities and effects are desired. Indeed, in view of what architects have said they might be more explicit, at the suitable time and with realization that the main thing is the result, and that this can be achieved best by leaving the means to the specialist.

MULTIPLE PROPOSALS?

In his specifying the composer of a program may ask himself how catagorical it is wise to be. Shall he stick to single-barreled directives, or shall he advance alternatives? While anxious to get at what is in the minds of clients, architects in general naturally are eager for whatever options may enhance their leeway and give rein to their own thinking, and doubtless would wish to introduce them whether or not any came from the owner. One says, "a single recommendation does not lend much to the imagination," and advocates getting numerous suggestions and then using the opportunity "to evaluate them and pick out the ones that you think answer your problem."[15] Another comments that in an atmosphere of discussion "it is possible to make all kinds of suggestions and eliminate those which seem to be developing illogically."[16]

The case for variant proposals is that "the architect lives in a world of alternatives,"[17] and that if they are offered—perhaps ranked for relative desirability—they may add to his comprehension of conditions, broaden the discussion of the issues posed, render it easier to avoid premature decisions, and lead to a solution which would not have found favor at first but may turn out to be preferred. Also, where quantities are involved optional figures may help to reveal the minimum which will suffice—information possibly obscure otherwise. Such benefits do not prove that any alternatives forthcoming need have place in a program. If they can be offered that early, however, readjustments may less likely be necessary later and when changes have become expensive. Everything is put into the picture, for consideration at the suitable time, and decisions still can be postponed so far as that is advantageous. Whenever broached, the choices of course should not be inconsistent with each other in purpose, lest they be confusing rather than helpful to one who is not a librarian.

Despite the above, the programs examined concentrate as a rule on single and unqualified specifications. One librarian advocates this on the ground that a flat-footed directive spurs healthy debate. However general that aim, the process of thinking through their enterprises must often have led composers to firm opinions, and to focusing on such conclusions as a means of impressing readers and fortifying their case. They even may have thought of the requirements they arrived at as scarcely subject to discussion; or if they felt uncertainty, feared nothing would be gained by betraying it.

Probably with all their earnestness, however, the compilers of programs have not meant to be exigent, realizing that they are not infallible, that an architect can be a helpful partner, and that adaptation is inevitable. They may have hoped to invoke in their negotiations the qualities once attributed to a New York state governor, of being "firm, moderate, . . . conciliatory in non-essentials, unwavering in matters of principle." With that attitude, and assuming they included some proposals of which they would not make an issue, they normally might count on respecting the architects' interest and at the same time attaining their chief objectives.

COOPERATIVE PROGRAMS

Some readers of this paper may be wondering whether building programs need be framed by owners alone, and whether in the case of libraries some of the questions so far discussed would not vanish if they were prepared jointly with architects. Such collaboration should be possible, and might save time and eliminate or reduce points of disagreement. That it would find considerable favor with architects can be gathered from the emphasis some of them place on close and continued consultation supplementing a program. One endorses it in the following words: "the making of a program is a definite creative act and should be a part of the process of design. Ideally, the program should be the joint and cooperative effort of the architect and the client working together in the fullest mutual confidence. For this reason it is most advantageous to all parties concerned to have the architect chosen work along with the authorities who prepare the final formal program of a building in advance of its actual issuance. This does not mean that the good architect wishes in any way to impose upon the client's ideas in opposition to the client's interests or desires; it is only by having the advice of an architect during the process of program-making that the individual or committee concerned will be able to save itself from many points of confusion and from a program which may unconsciously contain mutually exclusive elements."[18]

This is a strong plea, and librarians hardly can deny it credence. However, a librarian or committee certainly needs to have threshed out its problem before going into conference, and this effort naturally would produce some kind of a program, even if not a final and written one. Also, one librarian has suggested that the statement of requirements should be shaped up before an architect is designated, since situations may arise in which it ought to influence that selection. There furthermore is a warning against too early association in the comment that "the architect is by training persuasive and as a collaborator is likely to talk the librarian out of ideas which are important and which should be preserved for discussion at a more concrete stage."[19]

These lines of reasoning may beg the question in part, yet can carry a good deal of force. In some instances librarians might have ground to fear premature and unnecessary compromise. In others there might be simple anxiety that full weight be accorded their views, as those of the parties who know the needs and what is requisite to meet them, and who are responsible for ultimate success or failure. Frustration certainly is in the offing where an ill-adapted scheme for a building, and with it perhaps an unsuitable plan of work for the library itself, is forced upon institutional officers, as might happen if the joint effort was dominated by persons having no concern in eventual operation. Representatives of libraries seem to realize this, for they show by expression and action that they prefer to keep the drafting of programs in their own hands.

With all their desire to work alone at the start, librarians still may be ready and glad to have an architect shape up a program based on his own study of conditions, hoping that he thus can contribute to a better consummation than cooperative work throughout could produce. Neither they nor architects suggest, however, that the latter should prepare programs except by way of defining the approach as they see it. One architect has stated that a member of his calling, unless in unusual circumstances, "could not possibly write a program for a library . . . the librarian is the only one that knows what is required,"[20] and another that an architect does not have his problem until the program has been "completely developed by an expert,"[21] meaning the librarian.

IS A PROGRAM A "MUST"?

Again with thought of the issues they raise, how indispensable are programs? Confirming the values cited earlier, architects generally say or imply that such statements have an unquestionable place, at least as a basis for dealings between themselves and owners. For example, one declares that if "clear and intelligent" they can be most helpful guides, and another says they are essential if the architect is not to go wrong at the start. Then too their use is spreading, which must mean something, even though it seems confined largely to college and university libraries.

On the other hand the programs that can be gathered so far are few as compared with the buildings constructed, hence they hardly can be the sole means of accomplishing their task. Presumably adequate conferring can remove much or all of the occasion for written statements, especially in case of small and simple structures. Architects again and again stress the importance of close and constant consultation with clients, from early stages on. This they regard as imperative even with the best of formal memoranda—something in fact which no amount of "programming" can replace, and which probably they would give first rank if there had to be a choice. The summation may be that while it is desirable for librarians to count on compiling statements of requirements as a normal step, they should recognize that the business of getting their ideas across does not depend wholly on that, nor end with it.

OPEN SECRETS

There remain for notice a few tricks of the program-drafter's trade, of a sort which are elementary but might be overlooked. For instance, the citing of examples from other buildings may gain readier consideration for a librarian's suggestions, whether because the features concerned have proved successful or because of respect for precedent. It is not known why so few available statements of requirements employ such illustrations; but if they were pertinent and their authors possessed the information for them, it seems a loss that they were not used to strengthen the programs.

Composers of statements also may need to think often of the way readers are going to be impressed. A compiler labors over his draft in the mood of playing for keeps. What can he do to invest it with such character and tone and form that it will convince the architect? How build it so that the library's interests will be advanced if it is used to win the approval of the committees, officers and others who hold purse strings or have power to make controlling decisions, as sometimes happens?

The answers to these questions look didactic, yet they are pertinent enough to bear reciting. To a large extent they center in correct, forthright, logical writing. This of course necessitates selectivity and conciseness, so far as they do not hamper adequate presentation; with recognition that the readers who count may expect to get their information in brief time and with little study, and that a statement which has been boiled down is likely to be more comprehensible than a discursive or over-detailed one. It also implies phrasing which, while definite in purport, is free from jargon, understandable to laymen, and suggestive of sophistication and perspective. Finally, it means a tone which is clear and assured, yet tactful and forbearing. On the whole existing programs measure up fairly well on these points, the composition and organization being generally creditable and evidences of myopia and provincialism not pronounced.

DIVISION OF LABOR

Finally, some of a program-drafter's success in carrying his points may lie in realizing just what his job is and where it ends. Summarizing much that already has been said, he is or he represents one party, and but one, in an undertaking; and his responsibility, while real and inescapable, is only a segment of the whole. On the one hand it is to provide a platform for the work of all the participants in the project, with thought of the architect's views if occasion arises as early as the period for shaping the program, but without being overborne by them. On the other hand it is to avoid imposing even his desiderata upon his associates as unarguable law, to leave the way open for the architect's suggestions, and to keep from trenching upon the province or prerogative of that partner. To adopt phrasing which is becoming encouragingly conventional, the librarian's role is to give the architect the problem and leave to him the solution; to tell him what to build—not how to build it, which is his business. Common sense and modesty and consciousness of their own limitations of course should be enough to keep librarians on their own side of the line in all of this, and happily it seems as a rule to work so. If anything, the framers of library programs appear overly solicitous not to poach upon the preserves of architects.

Even though programs reveal a punctilious attitude toward designers' rights, however, architects apparently have had experience with librarians or other patrons which lead them to emphasize the conditions and demands they face, as explaining the need for accommodation. They wish it clear that often they must be definite in the positions they take. They show concern lest the librarian's zeal to do the best he can for his institution make him forget that the architect is expected to reconcile a variety of requirements, of which the librarian's are only one section, and to produce an integrated building satisfactory to all. As one put it, "The best results will be obtained if the architect is given a free hand to develop a scheme which will be functionally suitable to the needs . . . and to the conditions of the site."[22]

Moreover, architects repeatedly point out that the terms and necessities of the problem as a whole take precedence over specific items. Hence the owner's readiness to yield where possible on his stipulations, already shown to be consonant with positiveness at other points, now appears essential to an acceptable over-all solution. Without it an architect may be handicapped in exercising his peculiar skills, i.e., those in "the arrangement of rooms, the study of daylighting and orientation, the economic use of space, the use of materials, the proper application of color, the routine of service," and the like, and thus be hindered in his "duty to weld all these functional factors into a pleasing and attractive building."[23] All of which is doubly relevant because every undertaking is individual, and has to be approached without preconceptions traceable to previous cases or experience.

This earnestness of architects does not lessen their appreciation of the part librarians can play. Adequate presentation by the latter of administrative needs is desired and "invaluable," not only in a program and otherwise at the outset, but in criticism and suggestions on sketches as the project develops, so that the results will be "workable" and in accordance with the way the members of a staff plan their activities. By way of standing invitation to such expression one respondent in the enquiry for this paper said, "a state of flux and willingness to change or harbor new ideas is extremely valuable . . . this applies to the architect even more than librarian or board members."[24]

THE GUIDING RULE

The keys to effective relations therefore are consultation and team-work, with respect by each party for the competence of the other, beginning at whatever stage may be agreed upon—"the librarian advising and informing the architect as to his particular needs, and the architect evaluating these data and placing them on paper for study and review"[25]; the librarian allowing the architect the necessary leeway in his task, and the architect not attempting "to dictate function and specify allotments."[26] With such understanding a kind of comradeship can develop, based on united effort in meeting difficulties, seeking lessons in the failures and successes of others, and exploring possible solutions. Narrowed down in application to a building program this viewpoint suggests that it be "the simplest possible statement of the problem, as definite as it can be in all matters dealing with the purpose, function and conditioning of the building, and as free as possible in all matters dealing with plan arrangements and design."[27]

BIBLIOGRAPHY

1.–Chief Books and Articles

American Institute of Architects. *Library Buildings,* 1947, p. 1–20. (Building Type Reference Guide No. 3. A I A File No. D-5). Partially also in *Bulletin of the American Institute of Architects* 1:3:25–43, July 1947.

Bean, D. E. and Ellsworth, R. E. *Modular Planning for College and Small University Libraries.* 1948, p. 1–4.

Burchard, J. E. "Post-war Library Buildings." *College and Research Libraries* 7:118–26, April 1946.

Burchard, J. E. et al., eds. *Planning the University Library Building.* Princeton, Princeton University Press, 1940, p. 121–26.

Fussler, H. H., ed. *Library Buildings for Library Service.* Chicago, University of Chicago Press, 1947, p. 22–24, 97–100, 188–89, 194–96.

Gerould, J. T. *The College Library Building.* New York, Scribner, c1932, p. 18, 26–27.

Green, B. R. "Planning and Construction of Library Buildings." *Library Journal* 25:677–83, Nov. 1900.

Lyle, G. R. *The Administration of the College Library.* New York, Wilson, 1949, p. 540, 544–54.

Randall, W. M. "Some Principles for Library Planning." *College and Research Libraries* 7:319–25, Oct. 1946.

Randall, W. M. and Goodrich, F. L. D. *Principles of College Library Administration.* Chicago, ALA and University of Chicago Press, c1941, p. 172–74.

Schunk, R. J. *Pointers for Public Library Building Planners.* Chicago, ALA, 1945, p. 9–13.
Smith, H. D. "What the Architect Expects of the Client." *American School and University,* 1949–50, p. 39–42.
Wheeler, J. L. and Githens, A. M. *The American Public Library Building.* New York, Scribner, 1941, p. 15–23, 75–81.
Wilson, L. R. and Tauber, M. F. *The University Library.* Chicago, University of Chicago Press, c1945, p. 460–61.

2.–Available Programs

Blanchard, J. R. "Preliminary Statement Prepared for the Architect of the College of Agriculture Library Building, University of Nebraska." 1950.
"Building Program for Greenville College Library." 1948?
Burchard, J. E. "Program for a New Library Building at the Massachusetts Institute of Technology." 1945.
Brown, C. M. "Requirements for a Library for the University of Southern California." 1930.
California University. Santa Barbara College. "Program for the First Units of a New Library Building." 1950.
Cornell University. New York State College of Agriculture and Home Economics. "Considerations in Planning the Library Building." [1945?]
Goucher College, "Requirements for the Proposed Library at Goucher College, Prepared for Use in a Competition to Select an Architect." *ALA Bulletin* 34:145–51, Aug. 1940.
——— . "A Library for Goucher College." [1946]
North Carolina. University. Women's College. "Statement of the Requirements for a New Library Building. . . ." 1947.
Pennsylvania. University. Library. "Program for the Architects, University of Pennsylvania Library Building." 1949.
Queens College. Library Building Committee. "Proposed Library Building for Queens College, Flushing, N.Y." 1944.
[Sanderson, C. R.] "New Northern Branch . . . " [of the Toronto, Canada, Public Libraries].
Virginia. State Library. "Proposed Requirements for a New State Library Building." 1938.

3.–Contributing Architects

Mr. C. C. Briggs, of Emerson, Gregg and Briggs, Peoria, Illinois.
Mr. Arthur H. Eadie, Toronto, Canada.
Mr. H. Sage Goodwin, of Schutz and Goodwin, Hartford, Connecticut.
Prof. Talbot F. Hamlin, School of Architecture, Columbia University, New York, New York.
Mr. Karl B. Hoke, Toledo, Ohio.
Mr. George L. Horner, Superintendent, Physical Plant Department, State University of Iowa, Iowa City, Iowa.
Mr. Louis E. Jallade, New York, New York.
Mr. Walter H. Kilham, Jr., of R. B. O'Connor and W. H. Kilham, Jr., New York, New York.
Mr. Carl Koch, of Carl Koch Associates, Cambridge, Massachusetts.
Mr. H. Abbott Lawrence, of Lawrence, Tucker and Wallman, Portland, Oregon.
Mr. John C. B. Moore, of Moore and Hutchins, New York, New York.
Mr. Truman E. Phillips, of Wolff and Phillips, Portland, Oregon.
Mr. James Gamble Rogers II, Winter Park, Florida and New York, New York.
Mr. Henry R. Shepley, of Coolidge, Shepley, Bullfinch and Abbott, Boston, Massachusetts.
Mr. H. D. Smith, University Architect, The Ohio State University, Columbus, Ohio.
Mr. Ernest L. Stouffer, Architect, Physical Plant Department, University of Illinois, Urbana, Illinois.
Mr. Ralph Walker, of Voorhees, Walker, Foley and Smith, New York, New York.
Prof. William Ward Watkin, Dept. of Architecture, The Rice Institute, Houston, Texas.

NOTES

[1] Letter of September 26, 1951 from Mr. H. Abbott Lawrence, of Lawrence, Tucker and Wallman, Portland, Ore.
[2] Letter of October 11, 1951 from Mr. John C. B. Moore, of Moore and Hutchins, New York, N.Y.
[3] Letter of September 25, 1951 from Mr. H. Sage Goodwin, of Schutz and Goodwin, Hartford, Conn.
[4] Letter of October 31, 1951 from Mr. Louis E. Jallade, New York, N.Y.
[5] Letter of September 26, 1951 from Mr. W. H. Kilham, Jr. of R. B. O'Connor and W. H. Kilham, Jr., New York, N.Y.
[6] Letter of September 27, 1951 from Professor Talbot F. Hamlin, School of Architecture, Columbia University, New York, N.Y.

[7]Smith, H. D. "What the Architect Expects of the Client." *American School and University,* 1949-50, p. 39-42 (41).

[8]Letter of September 26, 1951 from Mr. Lawrence.

[9]Letter of September 26, 1951 from Mr. Kilham.

[10]Letter of October 25, 1951 from Mr. Henry R. Shepley, of Coolidge, Shepley, Bullfinch and Abbott, Boston, Mass.

[11]Letter of September 26, 1951 from Mr. Lawrence.

[12]Letter of September 17, 1951 from Mr. Karl B. Hoke, of Toledo, Ohio.

[13]Letter of October 8, 1951 from Mr. H. D. Smith, University Architect, The Ohio State University, Columbus, Ohio.

[14]Letter of September 27, 1951 from Professor Hamlin.

[15]Letter of October 31, 1951 from Mr. Jallade.

[16]Letter of October 30, 1951 from Mr. Ralph Walker, of Voorhees, Walker, Foley and Smith, New York, N.Y.

[17]Letter of September 26, 1951 from Mr. Lawrence.

[18]Letter of September 27, 1951 from Professor Hamlin.

[19]Burchard, J. E. et al. *Planning the University Library Building.* Princeton, Princeton University Press, 1949, p. 122.

[20]Githens, A. M. "The Architect and the Library Building," in Fussler, H. H. *Library Buildings for Library Service.* Chicago, University of Chicago Press, 1947, p. 94-106 (p. 100).

[21]Jallade, L. E. "Are You Prepared to Plan a New Building?" *Library Journal* 69:1077-79 (p. 1078), Dec. 15, 1944.

[22]Letter of October 5, 1951 from Mr. Arthur H. Eadie, Toronto, Can.

[23]*Ibid.*

[24]Letter of September 25, 1951 from Mr. Goodwin.

[25]Letter of September 18, 1951 from Mr. James Gamble Rogers II, Winter Park, Fla. and New York, N.Y.

[26]Letter of October 2, 1951 from Mr. Truman E. Phillips of Wolff and Phillips, Portland, Ore.

[27]Letter of September 27, 1951 from Professor Hamlin.

ABOUT THE AUTHOR—Ernest James Reece received the PhB degree from Western Reserve in 1903. He attended graduate schools at Western Reserve, Oberlin and the University of Illinois. Mr. Reece authored several books, including *Task and Training of Librarians* (1949), contributed to various journals and was an editor of *College and Research Libraries* and *Library Trends.* He taught at the University of Illinois, New York City Training School and Columbia, where he served from 1926-48 (Melvil Dewey professor, 1938-48), and returned to Illinois as visiting professor from 1949-54. He now resides in Boulder, Colorado.

Writing a Building Program

by Ellsworth Mason

It was almost fifteen years before the work of Reece was updated in an equally fine addition to the literature. Mr. Mason understands well the importance of the programming function. "Ideally, the program should be written by the librarian, because only if he has struggled with the thought involved in projecting imaginatively the dynamics of the operation for the period the building is intended to serve, can he respond with full understanding and sensitivity to the plans as they are developed."

Let me set up a straw man, or rather a straw situation, to show what really passes for building planning in the academic world, at least a great percentage of the time, and to bring into focus some of the elements centrally important in planning a library building.

Our hypothetical situation begins with a meeting at which are present representatives of the architect, the administration, the faculty, and (we sincerely hope) the librarian. Everyone is charged with a buoyant optimism, based on the fact that 40 percent of the funds reasonably required are at hand, and the fact that Old Caesar, the present library, laden to the point of groaning floors, has become so forbidding that one could become a hero, conceivably, by putting it to the torch. Everyone is in favor of building a Great Library, something short of Harvard's of course, but one to include everything that has ever been done and praised in any library of all times.

Everyone is Intelligent. Everyone has a Good Heart. And no one knows anything about buildings or their planning, with the exception of the architect. The buildings erected by the administration have left them completely unhampered with knowledge of them. The faculty member's experience is anchored to that wonderful seminar room in grad school at Old State U., where everything he ever needed was, like loaves and fishes, immediately available at his fingertips on wall shelving. The librarian has never planned a building; few survive to plan more than one. In this great updraft of emotion surrounding a vacuum of knowledge, the architect is the key person, and that is why he has been hired. It is made clear to the architect that he is to plan a great library; in fact, he is commanded to build a library that everyone ought to want. Meeting adjourned! The architect, like Flaubert's God, is to creep into his handiwork and create a world. That's what he was hired for!

Let us examine the architect. He is a good craftsman, if he has been chosen well, but left to feed on himself, he is likely to spin out of his innards a sticky web that will entrap, rather than help, the library user. The architect has his own problems, and the dynamics of his office constitute the central reason for writing a program that tells him meticulously what is wanted in a building, and why it is wanted.

First of all, the architect is a businessman; he has to make money to live. He runs an expensive operation, and cannot work exclusively on one project until it is finished, before he takes up the next one. At any one time he has about five times the load that he can handle. Every client pushes to have his job done fast, so the architect lives by rotating his neglect among the clients, working on one job periodically, in turn with the seven others he has on the line.

This pressure makes for two dislocations. The best men in the firm work only occasionally on *your* plans. Although these are the men you will see in your negotiations, most of the work is done much lower on the ladder. At peaks of great pressure students from schools of architecture are hired to work part-time on plans; this is a practice in highly reputable architects' offices. (One version of the plans for the Colorado College Library, I conjectured, had been drawn by the doorman's wife, at home.) Secondly, the gaps in time

SOURCE: Reprinted from Ellsworth Mason, "Writing a Building Program," *Library Journal,* vol. 91, December, 1966, pp. 5838-5844, by permission of the publisher and the author.

between the spurts of working on a set of plans make for discontinuity in the architect's mind. This is why flaws carefully discussed and agreed upon in one set of plans are not corrected in the succeeding set. Within the broad limits of professional conscience, the architect will do your job as rapidly and as easily as possible. One more factor complicates the planning in the architect's office. Despite the evidence of their neat, meticulous drawings, architects are not orderly thinkers, like good librarians. Their temperament is essentially artistic, and such grubby things as counting, to make sure that there are still seats for the programed 200 students, do not come naturally to them.

Since the process of planning in the architect's office is more random than controlled, the process of negotiating with architects involves detecting when they are falling short of reasonable performance and jacking them up to a higher level by insisting on better solutions. In order to be able to negotiate, the architect must be told precisely what is expected of him, and the librarian must understand, himself, what he wants. For these reasons the program is written.

A library building program is a multiheaded document. It tells the architect what you are trying to achieve. You are not likely to get everything you want, but the program is your basic position in negotiating with the architect. Although its demands should be reasonable, it should not compromise; the time for compromise is later.

The program provides meticulous notes from the librarian to himself. When the 10,000 details have faded from his mind during the two-year period of planning and building, the program will remind him of what he originally intended, and how he conceived of various segments of the building. He should save his backing papers—the calculation sheets and the preliminary drafts of the program— because he will sometimes have to pursue his thoughts back that far to clarify a decision a year and a half later.

The program is a reference handbook for the architects to use throughout their planning. The easier it is to use, the more likely they are to use it. It should, therefore, contain such reference elements as a table of contents, an index, summary lists of space requirements, and other useful summaries. It is easier to use if no more than one library unit is detailed on a page. This will waste some paper, but save the librarian and the architects a great deal of time. A program is also a checklist, like one used to assemble equipment for a camping trip, to make sure that nothing is left behind at the last moment, when all looks complete. Finally, if it is at all good, the program will be a public relations document, because it will be borrowed by other schools that are planning libraries. It should be typed in meticulous graphic form, and mimeographed in a generous number of copies.

I have referred to the process of working out building plans as a negotiation, which implies that there should be valid teams on both sides of the table, and I take it as axiomatic that it is not possible to develop satisfactory plans for a library building unless 1) there is a good librarian on the spot, thoroughly familiar with the dynamics of the present operation; 2) there are clear-cut administrative decisions on such matters as maximum student body for the period the new building is to serve, etc.; and 3) the librarian is placed clearly in control of the university's representation in the negotiations. If the librarian is weak and does not understand the library's needs, or if the architect is allowed access to someone behind the librarian's back to circumvent him (such as the president or business manager, who cannot possibly know what is going on in the negotiations), the planning negotiations will break down.

The first requirement for the program, therefore, is a good librarian who has been given free reign, within reason and subject to responsible elements in his community. What do we do if there is no good librarian on the spot? Who, then, will write the program? Some architects will do it, buy my view of the negotiations in building planning insists on an interaction of counterbalancing skills, and in this case, the program should be written by a library building consultant, called in and briefed fully on the dynamics of the institution, and allowed to get from the library staff and the librarian something of the feel of the operation.

Ideally, the program should be written by the librarian, because only if he has struggled with the thought involved in projecting imaginatively the dynamics of the operation for the period the building is intended to serve, can he respond with full understanding and sensitivity to the plans as they are developed. Most poor buildings fail because whoever is the dominant voice in the planning has not been able to see what movements, what materials, what equipment and furnishings, what kinds of feeling are required in each unit of the library building.

The purpose of the program is to define the

library building for the architect as interacting separate units of the library operation. Each unit must be specified in terms of square footage, and in terms of relationships to each other. This information enables the architect to mass the building by knowing which units must be grouped together on a common floor and which units allow leeway in their placement. Without this information (and buildings are sometimes planned without it), he cannot intelligently estimate either how many floors the building should have, or what the overall size should be. The program must further make the architect understand what will go on in each unit, and why, since the internal arrangement of each depends centrally on human movements, which govern the arrangement of the equipment. If the program states clearly and intelligently 1) what units must be included in the library, 2) how large each one should be, and which must be grouped together, and 3) what will go on in each, and why, the basic planning of the building has been substantially completed. The subsequent problems involve getting the architect to respond to the program, which now provides the librarian with a basis of carefully developed thought that allows him to understand what he must require of the architect, and for what reasons.

CONFUSION AND DESTRUCTION

Let me emphasize what the program should *not* do. It should not usurp the proper function of the architect. It should not, for instance, tell him how many floors the building should have. If there is a height limitation above ground, for zoning or other reasons, tell the architect. If you want a low building, or a high building, tell him why, but let him propose how many floors the building should have. Then the proposal can be discussed. Confusing oneself with the architect is like confusing oneself with God, and that is the essence of *hubris* in the Greek tragedies, which leads only to destruction.

The architect will do his job as easily as possible, within the limits of professional conscience, and if you give him an excuse to slack off on his own thinking (and a building requires an incredible amount of thought), he may do so. On the other hand, you will probably find that the architect has a low opinion of academicians as planners, which is justified by his past experience, and if he finds you telling him what only he has the knowledge to tell you, he will consider you, and treat you, as an inferior in the negotiation process. If the program indicates clearly that you know what you want, and why you want it; if it shows that you have thought out your problems intelligently, but that you know your own limitations, he is likely to respond well to your requirements. Therefore, do not play architect at any time in the planning process, and especially in the program. It should not be necessary to give this warning, but there is something about the entire building process that leads people to mad and pretentious actions far beyond their field of competence. Recently, I saw a building, all laid out by the client in an uninformed and unimaginative way, being pushed on the architect before he had been told what the client wanted and before he had a chance to think about it at all. In this direction madness lies.

Assuming, therefore, that the librarian knows what he is doing, and that he understands what he does not know, the program should do three central things: it should describe the dynamics of the institution that are shaping the library operation; it should pinpoint respectfully for the architect some elements of the building that need special attention; and it should specify each unit of the building.

The dynamics should be defined by a brief history of the institution, and a statement of its projections for the visible future. This statement should be short, and rigidly selected for the purpose of making the architect understand what will be going on in the library in the future, and why it will be going on. Long-windedness is the enemy here; a five-page history of Old State U., replete with details of athletic triumphs, is more likely to confuse the explanation than clarify it, but there is nothing like a hired captive audience to bring out the divine afflatus in people, as some recently written programs show. Think pithily, write succinctly, and focus your statements sharply on the library and its needs.

The more library buildings one studies, the more one will see the same mistakes repeated by many architects, and these will vary from period to period. At one time it was the Greek columns, the monumental stairway, and the 80-foot ceilings. These days it is likely to be lighting, ventilation, and over-use of glass that are the failures. It is appropriate and necessary, after the inspection of a number of library buildings that should precede the writing of a program, to call the architect's attention to problems commonly left unsolved in building and ask him to pay particular attention to them in your building.

INTERRELATED AREAS

The specification of the library areas is the most important part of the library program. It should list the units to be provided in the library building, grouped to encourage the architect to think of those within each group as related to each other. There is no absolute rule for these groups. I like to use the four categories: Introduction to the Library, Technical Processes and Administration, Books and Readers, and Miscellaneous. Included in the Introduction to the Library are those units that should be located just inside the main entrance, plus the keys to the library materials—the common reference sources and services that the student will use in his preliminary exploration of the library's resources. There is a good deal of movement and noise connected with these preliminary explorations, and the student is likely to move from one unit to another before he proceeds to the stacks or a seating area. Consequently, they should be thought about in relationship to each other. This section of the program includes the vestibule, the lobby and control area, the circulation desk and office, the card catalog, the reference and bibliography area and reference office, and the periodical index and abstracts area.

The Technical Processes and Administration grouping includes the order department, catalog department, documents department, shipping room, mending and labeling room, card-reproduction room, and any other satellites of the technical processes. I also include, somewhat arbitrarily, the administration office complex, partly because the head librarian is a technician of sorts; partly because, given the possibility, he is likely to be near his technical operations; and partly because if we don't group him here, the only other place for him is in "Miscellaneous," and that would never do.

In the Books and Readers group, those library units that provide reader spaces specifically related to library materials are included. These units do not necessarily belong near each other, but they are similar in that each contains library materials and readers. They include the periodicals area (however this is organized in a library), the reserve book room, the special collections area (and any other special materials-reader collections, such as curriculum collection, record collection, etc.), the micro-reading room, and the bookstacks and reading areas not already included in the specialized units.

The service units—smoking areas, typing rooms, toilets, and the library staff areas—are listed under the miscellaneous category.

So much for the principal of grouping the library units. How does the librarian projecting plans ambitiously beyond his present building, decide which units he will program in his library plans? The easiest way is to borrow a good existing program designed for a good building somewhere in the range of the size and nature of the one he is planning. A careful study of such a program, added to the experience of studying several library buildings, which should precede the writing of the program, plus much conversation with the librarian's faculty and staff, plus some imaginative projection of his own conception of the new library, should supply the list of units to be included in it.

LOCAL CONSULTATION

Let me emphasize here the necessity for local consultation and exploration before the program is finally written. It should go through a number of versions—three or four—before it is final, and each should be mimeographed and distributed widely among the staff and faculty for comments. One never knows where the good ideas will come from. Some of the best I received in developing the program for the Colorado College library came from a young girl, barely twenty-two years old, who had just begun to work for me as a circulation subprofessional assistant. She had almost no experience with libraries, but had imagination and the ability to visualize, and some of her vision is embodied three-dimensionally and functionally in that building.

Invite comments from the faculty and listen carefully to what they say. Along with the book-lined seminar-room with its never-failing stock of materials, you are likely to find something new about ways in which your present operation fails to meet the needs of the institution, and you are almost certainly going to hear some interesting new ideas from points of view quite different from your own. Of these you can use what makes sense and forget what does not, and the faculty are likely to feel much better just for having been consulted. Their ultimate reaction to the new building will depend not on whether you have accepted their suggestions, but on how well-stocked it is, how pleasant it is, and how easy it is to use.

Three statistics underlie the writing of Specifications of the Library Areas—the total number of student seats to be provided, the total staff to be accommodated, and the total number of books to be shelved in the new building, at peak capacity for the period of time it is intended to serve. The number of students seated will be a portion of the largest student body that the institution plans to enroll during this period. A firm statement on this basic fact must come from the top administration. Colleges try to seat no less than one-third of the total peak enrollment and press to get nearer to 50 per cent. If hammered by the black forces of obstruction or the evils of budget, they fall back to 25 per cent and stand there until the death.

The tendency in universities is much less uniform because their library system is much more complex, involving a division between undergraduate libraries, graduate libraries, and divisional libraries. The problem involves analyzing the numbers projected for those segments of the student population that will use the building most heavily. Such a prediction is difficult in the present state of education, when the borderline between undergraduate and graduate level needs for books is rapidly disappearing, and when subject disciplines themselves are becoming far less definable than they have been in the past. Nevertheless, from experience, and in hope, predictions have to be made, on the basis of enrollment projections, of the maximum number of students that the new library building will accommodate. Whatever figure is produced is likely to fall short of the ultimate demand.

The total shelving requirement can be arrived at by assuming an ambitious aim, computing how many volumes must be added on the average per year for the projected period of the building's use to attain this figure, and extrapolating from this yearly average the peak number to be added in any one year. The reverse method is to extrapolate from current acquisitions the annual acquisitions, year by year, through the period the building is intended to serve. The total of these figures, added to the present collection, will indicate the ultimate size of the collection for which you must build. The peak annual acquisitions figure is crucial in determining peak staff. Guidelines for the ultimate size of collections are available in the statistics reported by other similar institutions of about the same student enrollment that yours intends to achieve, but they must not be accepted literally.

These three basic figures—total seating, shelving, and staff—are applied to each of the units in the program, to estimate square footage, and to define the function of the units. At this point in the planning, it is extremely important to understand the human movements of each unit—the likely traffic patterns, and how much noise will result from them. The necessary and the desirable arrangements between units must be described. Tell the architect what other areas each must be near, and what areas it would be helpful to be near. Beyond that, say nothing about arrangements. Do not tell him that the documents area must be in the basement if there is no cogent reason, beyond personal preference, why it must be there. The architect's job in arranging good floor layouts is difficult enough without depriving him of what flexibility is possible because of personal whim.

The building you are planning is not built for now, but for the ultimate future, and not for one head librarian, but for any head librarian. If you insist on an arrangement that fits your personal preference, make sure that it is a reasonable preference in light of standard library practices, or that it can be easily changed. One library now under construction is very idiosyncratic in its layout because of the peculiar way its librarian likes to arrange his collection. This librarian will probably go on to four other jobs before retirement, leaving in his wake a building that no one else will be able to live with. I think of the shift in administration at the University of Illinois, Chicago Circle campus library, that changed the decision to have a computerized print-out catalog and found inadequate space for a conventional catalog. I think of a bothersome fixed wall in the technical processes area of the University of California, Los Angeles graduate library, built solely to accommodate a drinking fountain that a department head insisted be placed near the door of his office. This department head soon departed for another job, leaving the wall firmly behind.

The next to last step in thinking out each unit involves determining precisely what furnishings and equipment are required for its function, staff, seating, and shelving. These must be included in the program, because as soon as the architect gets beyond schematic drawings into floor plans, he must be required to lay out the furniture and equipment. Until this is done, it is impossible to know whether the space assigned to each unit is adequate. Without a definition of the furnishings and equipment, the librarian is completely lost in appraising spaces in a floor layout.

The final step in specifying library areas is to

analyze whether each unit has special requirements in terms of mechanical elements—special ventilating, special lighting, special noise problems, special fire hazards, special protection of any kind. A statement of what is required must be included in the specification of each unit.

At this point, the librarian has been extended to his limit. I have assumed along the way that a good deal of guidance in working out the steps detailed above will have been given by an experienced library building consultant, and now the estimation of square footage requirements should be turned over to him. It is possible to use gross formulas for estimating shelving, seating, and furnishings, and Keyes Metcalf's book supplies a number of them. However, any such formula must be used with a great deal of discretion, and altered to fit the different requirements of different units. For instance, whether it is possible to shelve in book ranges ten books per square foot or 15 depends on the length and width of the block of ranges, the book capacity per square foot increasing as the dimensions increase. This means that it is necessary to predict how long book ranges are likely to be in any area, or what their most effective length should be, at a time when there are no floor layouts as guidance at all. In making square footage estimates for library units, I block them out with formulas, then refine them by making imaginary layouts of all the furnishings and equipment, and adding together the space required by each. After that, it is advisable to compare the actual square footage for a similar area in a comparable library that is already known.

The librarian-programmer's final step is to tidy up the program, compile summaries of seating, shelving, and area requirements, make an index and table of contents, and send it for mimeographing. It is a happy day that sees it finished.

DIGESTION AND REGURGITATION

Writing the program is a long, arduous, time-consuming, soul-searching process, which will take about three months to complete, assuming that the existing library operation is in reasonably good condition and that the new buildings will house no more than a million volumes. Larger, and more expansive and more complex university libraries can take a year or more to program. During this entire time, the mills of the mind will be grinding problems of library buildings consciously or unconsciously most of the time. Seventh and eighth thoughts about these problems are infinitely better than first thoughts, and the mind should be given time to digest and regurgitate them. Half the librarian's usual work load should be turned over to someone else; if it isn't, either the program or the librarian will suffer greatly. But properly done, the production of a good library building program can be the librarian's greatest intellectual achievement.

ABOUT THE AUTHOR—Ellsworth G. Mason has been Director of Libraries at the University of Colorado since 1972. With B.A., M.A., and PhD degrees from Yale, he has been active in the fields of English and library science, and has chaired committees in various aspects of library work. Mr. Mason was serials librarian at the University of Wyoming, 1952–54; reference librarian and later librarian at Colorado College, 1954–63; and Director of Library Services at Hofstra University, 1963–72. He also is a specialist on the writings of James Joyce, having written a number of books on that author, and he is a consultant on library buildings for educational institutions.

IV

SITE CONSIDERATIONS

Equal to programming in successful building endeavors is site selection. Hopefully the librarian and his consultant will be involved in the consideration of the building's site; however, the actual choice of the particular site remains the responsible decision of a higher authority or authorities. The mayor, city manager, the city council or county commissioners and a planning commission or board—all are responsible for the broader aspects of planning rather than the local public librarian. Correspondingly in the choice of site on the college or university campus the president, the board of trustees or regents, a firm of "campus master planning" architects, and many others are involved and have responsibilities broader than those of the campus librarian. In both cases, a major donor may also carry substantial influence. In either situation other units of the city or campus are competing for the best site for buildings with other functions. It is perhaps folly for the librarian to insist on one particular site (even though that site is the best). The librarian can be most effective in the decision for site when he can articulately state the *criteria* for site selection and then successfully defend against opposing arguments or competitors.

Following are two articles, one each on public and academic libraries, by such highly respected authorities on site selection that no further comment is needed.

A Reconsideration of the Strategic Location for Public Library Buildings

by Joseph L. Wheeler

1. THE 1958 REPORT

Libraries today are living, changing things. Particularly so are public libraries, the 10,000 dynamic service centers which try to provide the nation's population with the stimulating ideas and the information which help America move steadily forward.

Librarians today have to be alive to today's changes. Services have broadened and deepened even in the last five years. We are more concerned and responsive to social and cutural problems and challenges. We are rushed along by the pressures of state and federal aid. We assume that current developments like regional systems and automation will help solve major problems, but attention should always be given to more efficient administration and better service to readers and their needs in each local library, whether it be a branch of a system or not.

And it seems well to know what libraries are doing. Though no adequate statistics were available as to how many public library books were being borrowed annually, we published a 1961 estimate of "more than 550 million."[1] Evidently this was too conservative, for USOE recently estimated that in 1965 public libraries lent 836 million books to 65 million registered borrowers at a cost of $650 million annually.[2] Incidentally, if the USOE estimate is fairly accurate, this would mean a cost of about $10 per registered borrower and 78 cents per circulation. Some librarians can remember a national average of 12 cents per circulation.[3]

One wonders how large a part the good or bad location of the library building and its good or bad interior arrangement play in what seems a high present service cost. Or does it make any particular difference to the taxpayer, or to society, that the usual elementary cost unit, i.e., dividing expenditures by number of books lent, is so high? One needs no reminder that circulation is only one library function. The time-consuming, highly important reference function is growing rapidly in volume and in intensiveness, but is not as yet being realistically measured as widely as it should be. An acceptable 1967 standard is $\frac{3}{4}$ to 1 reference question per capita.[4]

In 1958, the University of Illinois Graduate School of Library Science published the pamphlet, *The Effective Location of Public Library Buildings.*[5] It has been reprinted four times, and several thousand copies have been distributed. The author, without grant or royalty, and at considerable personal expense, gathered considerable data and examples, waited for hard facts in the form of detailed check-ups in two cities, and presented a large array of opinions of an almost unanimous belief, on the part of heads of over one hundred large and smaller libraries, that the most effective location for a public library, in the mid-1950's, was in the heart of the downtown pedestrian crowd. There was considerable evidence, and numerous cases were cited, to attest to the validity of this conviction.

In this 1958 report several librarians were quoted as favoring some concession, usually a site at a less costly and not so congested location, in order to make the parking problem less difficult. Parking was a major problem in library use in the 1950's.

The present report should be used in connection

SOURCE: Reprinted from Joseph L. Wheeler, "A Reconsideration of the Stategic Location for Public Library Buildings," *Occasional Papers,* no. 85, July 1967, University of Illinois, Graduate Library School, by permission of the publisher.

with the 1958 report because many special topics are there covered in more detail than can be given space here. In Section 8 of the present report we do present additional discussion on several special topics, supplementing material in the 1958 report.

Editor's note: Contrary to this statement the present report is sufficient for the needs of the Reader in Library Buildings. *The 1958 report does contain specifics and details not covered here and the interested reader is referred to the author's earlier report, entitled "The Effective Location of Public Library Buildings" (University of Illinois. Graduate School of Library Science.* Occasional Papers, *Number 52, July 1958).*

2. A FRESH REVIEW OF CHANGING FACTORS

Nine years have passed since that report was published, and twelve or fourteen years since some of the materials for the 1958 report were actually gathered. In the intervening period great changes, already visible then, have become even more evident in American cities and towns. In particular, automobiles in use have increased more than 50 percent since 1955 (see figures below). A general belief twelve years old has to be looked in the face again to see how much validity it has in 1967. A complete change in ideas and decisions on this important matter may be necessary.

This review seems to fall under three main heads:

(a) What are the present objectives of the American public library, and what changes are in sight which would seem to affect its desirable location?
(b) What is happening to the downtown business center of our cities which would seem to affect public library location therein?
(c) Recognizing the great increase in automobile registration and use, and the ever greater difficulty in parking, how is this affecting the library visiting habits of the public?

Unquestionably there are attitudes and beliefs on the part of librarians which cannot be overlooked in weighing either opinions or facts.

Also, it is not easy to come up with specific facts and statistics except those so obvious or well known that they may be interpreted in quite opposite ways.

For example, the Public Library Inquiry of 1947–1950 found that the segments of the population with the best educational background and per family income produced the highest percentage of actual and potential readers and library users.[6] This is entirely compatible with the widely held conviction that a good library and a good librarian are indefatigable in attempting to bring library service into the life of every citizen, regardless of social, economic, or educational status. Now a great national campaign is on, to bring education to the underprivileged, to reduce the number of drop-outs, and to encourage everyone to read. Who can foresee just how effective these efforts will be? On the one hand, though failure in ability to read is characteristic of drop-outs, one psychologist reminds librarians that flaunting the very idea of books and reading in the face of the underprivileged person is a further wound to his personality and a cause of even deeper feelings of inferiority.[7] On the other hand, we have a few cities where perceptive, outgoing members of library staffs are finding great response and appreciation for their efforts, and are increasing reading and the ability to read among previously neglected children.

These variations in social philosophy assuredly influence library objectives. The missionary element of library promotion which was widespread in the 1920's and 1930's is not so evident today. It may well be that there is too much current preoccupation with the forms and mechanics of organization and operation, e.g. regional library systems (with whose objectives all agree) and data processing, which are diverting attention from the individual customer. Some librarians are convinced that by taking heed thereto they can and should greatly increase the proportion of library users to total population. Other librarians do not seem to care, and say in effect, "Everyone who's going to read will find the opportunity," which seems a bit like, "No one can convince me that people won't walk a few blocks to use the library," as a Denver trustee argued, who favored a bad site about half a mile from the downtown center. On the other hand, by concentrating on its public services, the Baltimore Public Library doubled its circulation in two years, at the same time greatly increasing the proportion of non-fiction in its adult circulation.[8]

Clearly, the library building, in its location, planning, design, attractivenss, atmosphere and sense of welcome, will make a vast difference in how many citizens will use it. We venture to stress this because so many public officials, trustees, architects, and real estate men (many of them with an axe to grind, or with uncomprehending preconceptions), completely overlook the library's objectives and welfare in considering the project only in terms of "an impressive building in a beautiful setting."

Another changing factor which needs to be considered is expressed in a point of view opposed to that expressed in the 1958 report, *The Effective Location of Public Library Buildings*: "*Do not follow outdated principles in choosing a library site.* A quarter-century or more ago, the principle was laid down and broadly accepted that a library should be at the main intersection of the downtown area. . . . but . . .our social patterns . . . have changed [and] no one . . . has challenged the appropriateness of that dictum for today's conditions, as I do now." The tremendous growth in automobile use is cited as influencing "the growth of great outlying shopping centers, suburban living, the threatened collapse of good public transportation, and the downgrading in importance of the downtown areas of cities generally. In . . . hundreds of communities, the busiest corner is no longer a downtown intersection but a place miles . . . out from the city center where automobiles by the thousands pass every hour . . . . I am merely decrying acceptance of the slick, easily-mouthed formula of earlier years."[9] This does sound logical indeed, except as to whether being on a suburban automobile stream really generates library use.

In most cities, the facts are nearly as quoted, except that it may be an exaggeration that "hundreds" of the busiest spots are "miles" from the downtown centers, if we mean busy pedestrian crowds and not merely cars whizzing by. It sounds as though reluctance to change the "dictum" is a matter of stubborn refusal to change, whereas, as everyone should know, change is an inexorable principle of life, and of living habits, of good administrative methods, even of scientific theories.

On the other hand, in the recent views of many librarians there is plentiful evidence that the heart of downtown is still the major concentra-

tion spot. They are quoted below and their opinions are in direct refutation of the foregoing statement, as are the statements of many city planners, real estate men and observers of urban America.

Numerous librarians strongly believe that their colleagues who advocate placing a new library anywhere else than in the heart of downtown are merely rationalizing their disinclination to struggle for a good site, because of frequent local opposition, much greater cost for a good than for a poor site, or lack of concern with the library's major objective.

As one of the "downtown" advocates puts it, they are "rationalizing without realizing it . . . making the best of a bad situation where the main library moved from the heart of the city . . . to put the beautiful new building in a park setting."[10] Or, as another librarian puts it, "Many librarians, influential or not, tend to rationalize their own situations and find ways of defending a condition which they cannot change."[11]

3. WHAT IS THE PUBLIC LIBRARY'S MAIN OBJECTIVE?

Useful recurring attempts to rephrase the function of the American public library give varying emphasis to its educational, informational, and recreational services, but they all imply the powerful constructive value of books, reading and information use. They do not overlook the value of other media, some of which, like films and phonorecords, many libraries service effectively. They currently recognize the library's obligation to the underprivileged. But they are almost certainly neglecting the promotion of individual library use among the 60 percent of the population over twenty-one, in favor of a national campaign to get all public libraries into regional systems, as a means to greater efficiency and economy. We are impressed by the significant phrase used by an Argentine educator, Ernesto Nelson, who studied American public libraries and wrote a book in Spanish about them; he calls one of his chapters "The Social Penetration of the Book."[12] Most librarians would agree, and the present author assumes, that promoting "the social penetration of the book" is the library's main purpose, with all the implications and obligations of the most specialized, most enlightening types of library service.

The selection, preparation and servicing of printed matter is and promises to continue to be the chief element of public library service, with major emphasis on widening the circle of library users while improving and deepening the service to each patron. The library's fundamental objective in 1967 is "The best materials and the best service to be used by the largest number of citizens, old and young, at the least service cost." This is a fair rephrasing for today of the ALA's 1876 motto: "The best books for the greatest number at the least cost."

In seeking to give better service to more citizens, trustees and librarians must inevitably strive to get adequate budgets, adequate staffing, and adequate book and materials collections. All this investment of dollars deservedly needs to be measured in the returns for the overhead. In the case of a bookstore, the owner would buy, build or rent space where he expected to do the largest business, in crowded retail pedestrian centers.[13] We have seen or heard no valid argument or case which indicates that this same criterion does not apply equally to the public library.

In the 1958 *Effective Location of Public Library Buildings,* it was pointed out that the larger the number of users in a library, the lower the cost per transaction, including overhead, such as the capital investment in the building. It is difficult to see how anything can change this basic principle: that an increased number of customers means increased turnover and service including reference service, at less cost per unit. Nevertheless many libraries are being badly located each year because little attention is being paid to this administrative and cost aspect of the library's operations.

The best example we have found of a potential service cost estimate as influenced by several possible sites, was the 1959 study made by Queens Borough Public Library (cited in Section 8, below) which resulted in the interesting tabulation reproduced here as Table 1. As noted in Tucker's comments below, it is based primarily on pedestrian counts and on the assumption (with which the present writer completely agrees) that placing the library where the pedestrians are, and not where they are not, is the major test of an excellent location. The difficulty is that a few librarians, many city planners and most public officials, are not accustomed to thinking in terms of reaching the

TABLE 1

QUEENS BOROUGH PUBLIC LIBRARY CENTRAL BUILDING SITE STUDY:
ANALYSIS OF SITES IN RELATION TO USE AND COST OF PUBLIC
SERVICES TO DETERMINE BREAKING POINT[14]

Site (1)	Estimated circulation per year (2)	Cost per item circulated (3)	Yearly circ. loss relative to Site X (4)	Increase in cost per circ. over Site X (5)	Overhead loss for one year in comparison with Site X (Col. 4 × Col. 5) (6)	Overhead loss for life of building (Col. 6 × 30 years) (7)
X*	1,660,000	0.275	0	0	0	0
F	1,500,000	.304	160,000	.029	$4,640 per year	$ 139,000
A	1,250,000	.365	410,000	.090	36,900	1,107,000
B	860,000	.53	800,000	.255	204,000	6,103,000
D	860,000	.53	800,000	.255	204,000	6,103,000
E	860,000	.53	800,000	.255	204,000	6,103,000
Present	860,000	.53	800,000	.255	204,000	6,103,000
13	730,000	.625	930,000	.350	326,000	9,770,000
C	730,000	.625	930,000	.350	326,000	9,770,000

*Site X is the ideal location at Jamaica Avenue and 193rd Street, the point of 100 percent pedestrian saturation in the Jamaica shopping area.

Notes: Circulation per year is estimated on the basis of a new building of approximately 200,000 sq. ft. Unit costs are computed on the basis of public service staffing only, at $456,500 per year and by the arbitrary device of dividing total estimated circulation into estimated total annual staffing expenditures.

Source: A release from the Queens Borough Public Library.

most readers with the best books at the least cost, but only in terms of how difficult it is to park a car where others besides specifically library users park.

4. INFLUENCE OF GROWTH OF AUTOMOBILE USE

The Ulveling quotation above ties increased car use to other urban changes. This is well justified; in a general way the suburbs are a product of the automobile, though the influx of underprivileged is another factor in the move to suburbia. The figures for auto registration are for 1955, 62,688,792; for 1960, 73,868,682; and for 1966, 94,179,000.[15] The resulting congestion and parking difficulties mount even while many cities are building downtown public parking space at an increasing rate.

Obvious also is the influence of the automobile in the nationwide development of the large and small outer city and suburban shopping center. The rapid growth and increasing number of these convenient outlying centers is phenomenal. Librarians are well aware that such shopping centers are often the strategic location for branch libraries, though here again it does not suffice to be merely in the vicinity of one; the library needs to be where the people are and not five or six blocks from the center of the shopping center. In the 1958 report on *Effective Location* . . . (p. 13) the case of San Diego's El Cerrito branch was cited as an example of moving four blocks to get better parking, and then having to fold up the branch. Another problem encountered in several cases is that of choosing for branch location a shopping center which is not large enough or not successful enough to generate sufficient crowds and business to continue operations.

The front foot value of ground for a library building where it will generate the most business is so high, either downtown or for a branch in a neighborhood shopping district, that in most cases it is necessary to arrange for parking space nearby, e.g. on a side or rear street, rather than on the building plot.

There are recent cases where parking space has been built in under the library building. At Nashville the library plot in the business district slopes to the rear; the front half of the basement in this 1965 building houses a solid bookstack while the down-hill half provides a large parking space. At Tulsa's recent city-county library there is underground parking for 183 cars. The new District of Columbia library will occupy most of a large city block in the heart of the business district; the main floor will be at sidewalk level but there will be two underground levels. The upper will include the schools division and a large auditorium, while most of the lower level will be a large parking area for a hundred cars; this could later be used when needed for book storage depending on the availability of parking space close by. Upper basement-level space is highly valuable for storing library materials frequently used but crowded off the main floor.

Many problems are involved in providing outdoor parking on the library's grounds. These include:

Whether to provide space at front, sides or rear?

How to estimate the number of spaces to provide?

How to collect parking fees without paying the salary of an attendant?

How to supervise two exits, one for a rear or side parking lot, if such a second entrance cannot be avoided, without detriment to the plan?

How to prevent secondary activities (such as group programs and meetings of outside organizations), and the resultant need for extensive parking, from dictating a bad location?

In many cases libraries have been badly placed, outside of congested areas, primarily because local enthusiasts wished to be sure that crowds attending meetings and group programs at the library would have easy parking. Usually these persons were simply not acquainted nor concerned with a public library's chief services.

Just how important is the parking problem? The evidence is overwhelming that it is not nearly such an important factor as some persons imagine. In saying this we would recognize the library's obligation to help find or create adequate parking, but not at the expense of good location. Automobile traffic has drastically increased, and so have parking difficulties. But one cannot discount nor evade the examples recited in the 1958 report nor the quotations as to 1966 situations, included below. The 1958 report cited San Diego and Dallas, both of which had such spacious temporary quarters (San Diego in an exposition building, Dallas in a disused but attractive railroad station) while their new downtown buildings were being constructed. In both cases these temporary locations not only doubled their previous space and were much better arranged and more efficient quarters

TABLE 2

REFERENCE USE AND CIRCULATION OF THE DALLAS CENTRAL LIBRARY, 1955–1964[16]

Years	Reference	Circulation	Years	Reference	Circulation
1955/56	220,522	319,819	1960/61	515,317	627,662
1956/57	317,563	422,097	1961/62	553,682	602,985
1957/58	346,576	509,679	1962/63	585,285	614,355
1958/59	412,852	585,448	1963/64	614,355	582,626
1959/60	474,072	603,566	1964/65	660,836	544,397

than their former library buildings, but both had 100 percent easy generous parking. Both carried on a heavy program of publicity to promote library use during the construction period, but both had a great drop in circulation and reference service. On the other hand, both had a tremendous increase (Dallas 140 percent in its reference use) for the first year in their new buildings over their temporary quarters, even though their customers had to brave downtown traffic, had not an inch of parking on library property, and parking within a block was hard to come by.

The sad stories about parking problems and the impressive statistics on ever more automobiles in use imply that reference service should be slowing down by now, but they are belied by the figures in Table 2 on reference usage of Dallas' central building, opened September 1955.

Some advocates of providing generous parking for readers have in the past claimed that putting a library where the crowds of people are is only a device to roll up circulation figures, or as one city planner put it, "nothing but light fiction for office clerks." Nothing could be further from the truth; strategic location affects the most consequential informational services of the library.

In contrast to Dallas, with an estimated city population of 802,600 in 1966, Houston with a 1966 city population estimated at 1,142,000 lent only 451,230 books from its central library in 1965, and looked up only 144,311 reference questions at central. The major obvious reason is that Dallas' central building has an excellent downtown location, whereas Houston's library is in a "civic center" ten blocks or so from the major downtown pedestrian intersection. A 1964 poll of 2,021 patrons of Akron's central library, which was downtown a few short blocks from Main Street, showed that 67 percent drove to the library in their own cars, 16 percent in someone else's car, and 39 percent did other errands on their downtown trip; though 83 percent came by car, only 2 percent said that library parking was a necessity.[17] People who go downtown undoubtedly need parking space, but it is not necessary for the library or any other single agency to provide such space on its own. We believe that more can be done than most cities have done to provide better parking at strategic downtown sites.

We have not been able to find any figures to show that in libraries located in these outlying, easy-to-park neighborhoods the proportion of women users is much greater than downtown, but we surmise so, and raise the question whether it is desirable for a public library to attract more women than men. Figures from the well-located San Diego central library in February 1965 showed 70 percent male and 30 percent female users.[18] We do not imply anything more estimable in serving men than women with library materials, but the assumption may be valid that a larger proportion of consequential materials are used by men, as predominantly salary earners, than by women.

It is argued that in some large cities "downtown is dead" after business hours. If so, it would logically seem to mean easy parking; perhaps this is one reason why many central city libraries have such busy evenings.

We shall shortly quote considerable testimony on the optimum location of public library buildings, but much of it combines the subject of parking with the great question as to what is happening to the heart of downtown, the central business district.

5. WHAT'S HAPPENING TO DOWNTOWN?

Impressive figures from various sources indicate that retail sales in the central business district are declining: "Money and brains keep draining out of every core city into the suburbs in every metro-

politan area of America."[19] At the same time
many articles in the general magazines and newspapers, in books on urban problems, and in the
real estate, retail trade, city planning, architectural
and other periodicals, make it equally clear that a
tremendous program of downtown renewal is now
going on in hundreds of large and small cities, that
the downtown city core is coming back and has a
bright future, and that every city with intelligent
leadership can find ways to renew downtown and
protect the enormous investment in downtown
real estate and business.

To anticipate the conclusions on this point,
there are two incontrovertible facts which bear directly on library location:

1. Downtown is still and by far the area where
the greatest number of people are; we shall
support this partly by quotations, source
documents and cases below.
2. The front foot value of downtown property
is far higher than that in any outlying shopping center or in any other location. The reason it continues to be most valuable is that it
attracts the greatest number of persons.

The figures for 116 Standard Metropolitan Statistical Areas show decreases in 1963 dollar retail
sales totals in their central business districts in 90
of these cities, as compared with 1958.[20] The fact
might be expected that in almost every SMSA
there has been a continuing decline in the proportion of central business district sales to total area
sales because of the increasing number and size of
suburban shopping centers and the populations
around them. However, store sales in the central
business district have increased in numerous cases.
No one can overlook another fact: many city
downtown stores have made additions, remodelled
and otherwise prepared for larger downtown business. And new buildings and stores are also being
added; Woolworth for example is placing most of
its new stores in downtown areas instead of suburbs, because President Kirkwood senses "a trend
of rejuvenation in the center city."[21] In Dallas a
major new downtown department store was recently opened.

The significant factor in all library planning,
both of services as well as locations, is the widespread rebuilding of the heart of our cities, large
and small. It is true that many cities have not got
into stride on downtown renewal, but any city
which has civic leadership and backbone is either
busily at it or getting plans ready to embark on
such a program. Nor does this always require ex-

tensive rebuilding; in at least a few cities there is a
tremendous downtown redevelopment that involves demolition on only a minor scale. One of
the best examples of the latter is Atlanta, one of
America's fastest growing cities, with five successive building boom years.[22] In 1965, in downtown Atlanta, fourteen large building projects
were underway including eight multi-story office
and organizational buildings. The two big downtown department stores are ringing up heavy sales;
one had just opened a multi-level parking garage.
The central library is next door. And the continued and accelerated growth farther and farther
into the suburbs has not been at the expense of
downtown Atlanta. In contrast was Boston in
1960, where "the central business district looked
to be on its last legs."[23] But it is coming back.

In the first paragraph of this report we reminded
ourselves to try and be aware of what is going on
in our society. Any librarian, trustee, city planner
or other responsible official who thinks it sensible
to leave behind all this activity, this crowd of intelligent people, these office and business employees, these shoppers and errand doers, this day-by-
day gathering of the major constructive segments
of the population, just to place the library where
parking is easy, is guilty of violating this principle.

Space is lacking to summarize adequately this
nationwide movement to renew and strengthen
the inner city core. This includes bringing back
great numbers of middle class residents and not
abandoning downtown to the underprivileged.[24]
The International Downtown Executives' Association is a stimulant to this renewal. The literature
is overwhelming, including Jane Jacobs' *The Death
and Life of Great American Cities*,[25] whose iconoclastic ideas about paying more attention to the
daily living habits of the average family, before up-
rooting it and forcing it into unrealistic surroundings, gave many city planners a jolt. One should
see also Victor Gruen's classic interpretation, *The
Heart of Our Cities; the Urban Crisis, Diagnosis
and Cure*,[26] and the 672-page, 1966 collection of
twenty-six selected articles edited by James Q.
Wilson, cited above.[20]

After false starts, wasted funds, unfortunate experiments with many failures, including wholesale demolition of both residence and downtown
areas where much could have been salvaged, the
present Federal Housing and Renewal Acts and
their administrators are encouraging and producing more selective and resultful downtown rebuilding. "[T]he downtown section must be vital, exciting, and economically sound for the sake of the

whole city. To date, downtown urban redevelopment has been a factor in sparking the renaissance of more than a score of . . . cities."[27] A score is not very many, but the Weaver article was written in 1965 and the Wilson book notes that, in early 1966, 1,600 renewal projects were underway in 770 communities, many of them without federal aid.[28] Increasingly they include smaller cities like Rutland, Vermont (20,000 population), where without federal aid an extensive shopping center on the main downtown street has replaced old buildings and railroad tracks, while the library, six long uphill blocks away in a residential area, still suffers from underuse despite a recent addition.

The present rejuvenation of city centers is involving billions of dollars a year and Congress is considering a greatly accelerated program: "The downtowns . . . hold the key to reshaping urban America."[29] In several cities, like Norfolk and Yonkers, high-rise apartments are bringing back downtown the kind of residents who use books and libraries. A recent account summarizes the main features in nineteen large cities, including Pittsburgh's Golden Triangle, the early 1950's forerunner of all the others.[29] An increasing part is being played by private capital not only in financing but perhaps more importantly in the realistic planning of these huge undertakings.[30] Responsible financiers who decide on major investment funds, for example the most trusted insurance companies, are now pouring millions into the central business districts of many cities.[31] This is strangely inconsistent with the notion that all these "downtowns" are going to perish and die because of parking difficulties. Numerous other changes will characterize the renewed downtown, such as decreased loft and industrial space and increased office and apartment space, both of which mean increased per capita library use, but they need not be detailed here, except to note that large scale downtown parking is being increasingly provided as basic to all downtown renewal.[32] In 1967 Congress is considering diversion of highway construction funds to speed up downtown parking facilities, and Governor Rockefeller is working to create state-sponsored cultural and recreational centers in core areas of New York cities. Unfortunately the substantial part which a new central library building can play in downtown renewal is overlooked by most officials and real estate men because they have never thought of the library in those terms.

A more recent development consists of the considerable and increasing number of new "general" centers in outlying areas, not only for shopping but for office buildings, apartments and civic and cultural activities. While Atlanta's central business district is growing at a great rate, as noted above, a new development, Executive Park, is already in use ten miles out on an expressway, based on a master plan and occupied largely by southeastern branch offices of national concerns, at lower per foot rentals than downtown.

This example, however, is not typical of what some other cities are planning as well as doing, such as Northland Center just northwest of Detroit, where "a common meeting place" has developed, planned by Victor Gruen in 1954,[33] and including stores, offices, a post office, a community auditorium, etc. Such a general community center is also being used as a device to develop or to redevelop a large area, preferably having some original coherence, part of which is now a large city (such as Georgetown, D.C.) on a planned basis and carefully incorporating the more worthy existing elements.[34] There is also the likelihood of completely new cities being undertaken, on a large scale.

This is assuredly an important, promising and already successful trend. May one conclude or deduce from it that: (a) This is one more pull away from downtown, but (b) parking will again be at a premium because success means crowds and tough parking, (c) nevertheless one of these large-scale overall outlying centers may well become itself an ideal outlying branch library location, if large enough and far enough away from the larger city center, and (d) no large city central library can be placed successfully in such a suburban center, but a major branch of the city or regional system may very well be?

6. SUMMARY OF CONCLUSIONS FOR THE LATE 1960'S

1. The library's objective continues to be to reach the largest proportion of citizens with the best library materials and services, at the lowest unit cost.

2. The informational services of the library are becoming more and more important in proportion to its total services.

3. As 60 percent of the population is over 21, public libraries need more attention and promotion for their adult services; strategic library loca-

tion, efficient plan arrangement and attractive design are major factors in reaching this objective.

4. Automobile use has increased markedly, 50 percent, from 1955 to 1966. So has the parking problem. The library has to pay attention to and help solve this problem. Some new libraries provide underground parking.

5. The movement of population is from the downtown city center to the suburbs. And the number and size of outlying shopping centers increase daily, so that the relative importance of downtown has diminished in the last decade.

6. On the other hand, several hundred cities, large and small, are in the midst of central business district renewal on a large scale, and this return to downtown promises to accelerate.

7. In any case, downtown continues to be the chief area for transacting most business, banking and office work. It still attracts the greatest number of people, and indications are that it will continue to do so in the foreseeable future.

8. Increasing provision is being made for downtown parking. Planners, real estate men and business leaders recognize that downtown parking problems can and must be solved.

9. The public library, to serve most people, should be where most people congregate. That continues to be downtown. "While the suburban shopping center development has continued unabated, the Central Business District still attracts multitudes of people, and there are more people *there than in any other single part of the city.*" says a city planning sociologist who has continuously studied and reported developments in this field for some years[35] (emphasis added). This seems to be indicated by the front foot valuations; they are higher there than those anywhere else in the city.

10. The basic factors as stated in the foregoing paragraph lead to the inevitable conclusion that the main public library building in a city should be placed in, or kept in, or rebuilt in, the heart of the downtown business and office district.

11. Similarly, branches should be not where parking is easiest, but where the busiest crowds of people are, generally in the heart of outlying shopping centers or retail districts which bid fair to continue in popularity, and not at some distance away from them. Later, in Section 7, we shall try to deal with the question, "How do all these crowds of people get to these business centers, despite parking problems and when nearly all suburban residents have automobiles?"

7. SOME ILLUSTRATIVE CASES

The writer has seen numerous bitter battles over sites. The pressures, the personal selfish interests, subordinating the library to some other cause such as an effort to create a civic center or "cultural center," the animosities, the compromises, the final decisions sometimes completely satisfying, sometimes completely wrong and destructive to the library's welfare, give this controversial subject its great significance.

One librarian, explaining a civic center site which is nothing short of dismaying, writes, "The location, according to the city manager, was selected because it was available, because it was in the civic center site, because it was closest to the geographical center of the city that could be purchased with enough acreage . . . chosen by selecting all available sites and starting to eliminate the most desirable because of different problems—until this site was left. . . . The heaviest patronage would require building in the most densely populated area and upon a transportation line." One might wonder, why eliminate the most desirable? What's wrong with a densely populated area and a transportation line? One might wonder why there seemed some opposition to generating "the heaviest patronage" for the library; that is exactly what any library should seek. One might wonder why "enough acreage" is needed for the library site in a city which will hardly have 50,000 people in 1985; one acre would more than suffice. This letter expresses some extremely bad reasons for selecting a library site. Every one of the reasons given appears to be exactly wrong, and the site should never have been approved. One may venture the opinion that no state library agency should permit such a project to be approved. Rather, it definitely should be rejected.

There is substantial agreement on the part of librarians as to what constitutes the most desirable site for a building. Thus the 1966–67 New York State requirements for federal aid for public library buildings include the following: "*Site.* The annual return from the capital investment and from annual library budgets is controlled to a large degree by good or poor location of the library building. A project for a new building for direct reader service will be favored if the site chosen is within two or three blocks of the busiest pedestrian intersection of the downtown area or in the case of branches . . . on the major street near the major intersection of the neighborhood. The library site should, therefore, cost or be worth a fourth to a third as much as the building. . . . A project will be disapproved if the site is not central. Parking is important and the library has to meet local parking requirements. Parking for the staff can be provided a block or two away on less valuable ground. In choosing a suburban library site, give careful consideration to shopping patterns and accessibility to the population to be served."[36]

It is the present author's belief that every librarian and especially every consultant, who cares about his library's welfare and the welfare of libraries everywhere, needs to have some convictions on this matter and to stand up to the difficulties which almost always threaten the choice of a good site and too often result in a bad location. One bad location is too many; for the next sixty or seventy years that library will suffer the frustrations, the underuse, the heartbreaking disappointments of each successive conscientious librarian who attempts to get a full return from the taxpayers' library dollar.

In 1964 the International City Managers' Association published a volume on *Local Public Library Administration*; in the chapter on "Public Library Buildings," Keith Doms cites various cases to support his contention that the library should be where the crowd is thickest (pp. 296–300).

This conclusion seems to be supported also by the following cases as discussed by their library directors. With permission from each public library head, we include excerpts from letters to the author, dated August and September, 1966, and based on 1966 experience (not that of 1958). They are unanimous in indicating without compromise that a public library should be placed in the busiest downtown pedestrian center, despite the problems of parking. The growth of automobile use, parking difficulties, business district changes, and suburban growth seem to be clearly understood by these library heads. Each considers that the library should be definitely active in helping to find a solution to the problem of parking. We have inserted pertinent comments in brackets.

Editor's note: Here follows in the original edition of the article twelve pages of excerpts from eighteen letters to the author. These letters are from librarians throughout the U.S. (and one from Vancouver, B.C.) which are documentary support for the conclusions of the author. These excerpts are somewhat repetitive and though they support the author's conclusions, they offer little clarifica-

tion. These twelve pages are therefore omitted here. The interested reader will find them on pages 14 to 25 of the original publication.

8. SPECIAL PROBLEMS

Ratio of Site Cost to Project Cost

Perusal of the questionnaires returned to ALA Headquarters as to the details of more than fifty recent buildings, and of 1965 Michigan data[37] and of *Library Journal's* annual building issues for 1960–66, gives no definite or average relationship between cost of site and the total cost of public library building projects.

One notices immediately the numerous cases where the land cost was zero, because the city owned the land on which both central libraries and branches were built. Surely, there should be other site criteria than a piece of free ground in a bad location. The second thing noticed was the low site cost for so many new libraries. It is evident that in many communities the importance of good location is overlooked in the attempt to save money on the site. The writer has been taken to see sites in various cities and towns, many of them in residential sections where neither a main library nor branch could possibly flourish; in several cases they had been purchased as "bargains" or under pressure from real estate interests or by friends of the owners, or had even been given to the library, and no one protested using them.

In a few cases the site has cost a third or half as much as the building. In our 1958 report we cited the case of Denver where city officials paid $1,100,000 for a very large site on which to place a $1,900,000 building, at a location which three consultants each independently had protested as being too far from the downtown heart of the city. In other words, the large sum was spent for a large tract to "show off" the new library as part of a special civic group, but not to make it more convenient and useful to its community. In contrast the District of Columbia case, cited above, is an example of paying over $3 million for a central business district site, partly or largely due to the insistence of the director, who on taking charge in 1947, inherited a comparatively recent library building which had been built on Pennsylvania Avenue in the impressive style of the other government buildings located there. It had been designed without regard to economical and convenient library operation, with a large interior court as an architectural *tour de force*. A library consultant, protesting but foreseeing approval of this plan, had declined to be associated with the project. The first unit of the building, the only one ever constructed, was being used for federal wartime purposes. The newly arrived director persuaded the library board to refuse to accept or occupy the building because of its bad location and its bad plan. The long wait has well repaid the community, for plans are now ready for a good building in a strategic location, 9th and G Streets, as discussed above.

Keith Doms has suggested inquiring into the value of air rights over valuable downtown sites as a help to overcome cost and land scarcity problems.[38]

Branch Library Location

In a recent article, Garrison feels that the 1958 *Effective Location* . . . report touches on branch location problems only summarily, and is not concerned with overall systems.[39] A study of branch library operations and services and their costs is badly needed. Some of the problems are suggested in Sealock's chapter in the city managers' library administration book,[40] particularly his statement that "the average branch library is serving too few people"; he also cites Lowell Martin's recommendation of 70,000 population per branch. The present author has studied the proposed and actual locations and buildings of over two hundred branches in many cities, and feels fully as concerned with branches as with central libraries. Unquestionably more, but more profitable, branches are needed in numerous cities, some of them to replace currently unprofitable ones. Some studies on branch location by inexperienced persons have disregarded basic administration factors, such as whether a given branch should be created at all, whether or not it is financially feasible on the basis of the number of persons who will actually use it, and the types of service users will desire and obtain.[41] If the branch is to be a social-service center for example, and only in part a library, then the librarians of the country should discuss and come to some conclusions as to the policies involved; they will need also to consider their functions as drastically altered, and an increased obligation to see that the library services as such are better rather than less well financed. These questions greatly influence library location. Many librarians keenly sympathetic to social services will nevertheless continue to believe that each library branch must justify its creation, its size and cost, its location, and its annual operating and maintenance costs by the number of persons it will serve with consequential library materials and services.

In numerous cities, e.g., Chicago, San Francisco, Philadelphia, Los Angeles, Syracuse and many smaller ones, the central library building is so inefficient as well as overcrowded, that a firm policy is plainly needed, that there will be no more branches until an adequate and strategically located new central library has been provided, no matter how great the pressure or the branch needs. Laymen cannot be expected to realize, as most librarians do, that every branch customer is affected by the staff abilities and activities and the depth of service at the central library, and by the adequacy and convenience of the central building. It may be held also, as has been pointed out by Sealock and others, that no city of less than 50,000 population and few cities of less than 75,000 can justify a separate branch—or any branch which will lend less than 80,000 or 100,000 volumes a year.

It is unfortunate that, especially in older eastern states, so many smaller cities deplete their annual budget by continuing or even adding to their weak and unprofitable branches which have been permitted over the years, especially in the New England states. This "spreading too thin" inevitably results in: (a) inadequate local staffing, especially by trained personnel, (b) inexcusably low local salaries which retard library service in the whole state, with rare exceptions, and discourage recruiting, (c) the embryonic status of reference and informational service, (d) a high proportion of children's and adult fiction circulation, (e) almost universal failure to aim at or attain excellence in informational and other substantial library objectives, and (f) neglect of the central library on which every branch depends. As to library location, one result of too many branches is the prevalent feeling of penury, as a result of which library and public officials shrink from paying enough to insure a good site.

The case for drastic restrictions on new branches becomes more valid each month with the increased costs of salaries, books and maintenance. It is also supported better as time passes, by the argument that "everyone has a car and doesn't mind driving a long way to use the library."

More specifically as to branch location, the basic principle which applies to locating central libraries seems to apply equally to any branch, namely: its location should be at the major pedestrian center of its section of its city, where the public chiefly congregates, and not where there is no one except those who make a special auto trip just to use the library. This holds true whether the branch belongs to a city system, a county system or a regional system; we find no evidence or cases to justify an alternative policy. It does not seem necessary to analyze a large number of individual branch locations to prove this basic principle. The quotations from the Dallas and Atlanta cases (Sections 4 and 7 above) include their branch locations. Atlanta cites their four busiest branches, where location has unquestionably been a major factor in their success. The necessity for getting good branch sites is also emphasized in such branch surveys as Martin's for Dallas.[42] At this writing Pittsburgh "expects to participate in a multiple-use program in the Squirrel Hill section where property is exceedingly dear. A branch library, a bank, a high rise apartment, and parking facilities, will be built on a small but choice piece of ground.[39] That sounds like a busy neighborhood with the library in its center and the site costs reduced by pooling interests.

"Coordinating" the City Plan and Civic Centers

In our 1958 report we discussed (pp. 35–38) relationships with city planners and the city plan, as affecting library location. There is considerable evidence that many city planners, as well as architects, studied the 1958 report; numerous planners have played an active part in assuring that the library would be placed where it actually would be most useful to its community, and not in some theoretically "coordinated" location, or on a piece of ground which could be had for nothing.

Under the pressure of federal aid, however, city planners, especially in the midwest, have recently been consulted or have been permitted to influence the discussions on library location, without taking the time to study the problems and objectives of libraries and the travel and visit habits of library users. This has been worsened by a revival of the idea that a civic center or cultural center, just because it involves "coordinating," is necessarily a sound project. Some librarians and library boards are impressed with such a statement as "The site of the public library should be coordinated with general area planning."[43] Yet, as noted in our 1958 report, "coordination" of the library generally means placing the library in some group of civic buildings, where it does not belong. It is noticeable that few local post offices are placed in civic centers because usually it would be an inconvenience to their customers.

A growing number of clear-thinking city planners do not agree with the civic center idea, especially in competition with other aspects of current urban renewal. Some of them disagree also with the "cultural center" idea, a more recent and more popular variation of the civic center. To a considerable segment of Americans, culture means art, musical and dramatic programs for group enjoyment, though there is little real culture without books and reading, which involve totally different attitudes and procedures.

Librarians want to cooperate with other leaders and groups, and are reluctant to oppose attempts to force the library into a location which is illogical for library purposes. There is also the parallel idea that the public library might well be placed on what usually are newly bought and spacious public school grounds, regardless of the fact that schools are almost always away from the downtown center of things, even in small cities and towns.

Generally it is inconvenient for adults and high school students to travel to such a "community grade school house"—plus library, just as it is often for adults and grade school pupils to walk or travel to a high school "community center" area when the public library has been unwisely placed on this piece of usually free ground. If the school and the library's allotment of ground are in the heart of town, on the main pedestrian street, where adults are constantly passing on their day's errands, a school grounds site may be successful. This seldom happens, for school grounds have to be spacious and are costly downtown, and most states' requirements make sites in the center of town impracticable.[44]

It needs to be realized that people and crowds going to a public meeting or entertainment, or to art or musical programs, in a cultural or community center, are not likely to find the time, be in the mood, or have any great interest in trying to use the library at the same time. Almost always they are intent on getting home as promptly as possible after the group program is concluded, which is usually after the library has closed. We have recently studied numerous library situations where the library has been victimized by being forced to accept civic center sites; in every case the results have been as unfortunate as those recited in our 1958 report. As one example, the discussion and comparative figures from Dallas and Houston central libraries in Section 4 above, will indicate the penalty paid by Houston as a result of being coordinated in a civic center.

At San Diego recently, a report on effective location opposed any connection with civic centers and received the support of the city manager and the major newspaper which refused to compromise even when the library board seemed to waver for fear of defeat at the bond issue election. It was better to lose the bond issue, for in the following year the proposition for the new building at the old downtown location was approved by the voters and the project went ahead merrily. The rapid growth of San Diego was foreseen, but its good central location has brought even greater use than was anticipated and in 1966 the voters approved a loan for branches and for adding an extra floor to the central building, as provided in the architect's original plans.

In a 1965 nationwide mail survey by Fort Worth Public Library, with responses from 338 branches, the sixty-two branches located more than two blocks from a shopping center or business district averaged an annual circulation of 103,000. The 276 branches located within two blocks of a shopping center or business district averaged an annual circulation of 125,000. The 136 branches located in or at the edge of a shopping or business district averaged an annual circulation of 132,000. The thirty-nine branches located in or at the edge of a contemporary shopping center averaged 186,000. The nine branches located in a contemporary shopping center, in a building owned by the library, averaged an annual circulation of 311,000. These returns indicate three points: (a) that most librarians have recognized and acted on the strategic value of locating branches where the pedestrian crowd is, (b) that these in-pedestrian centers have generated the greatest patronage, (c) that where an adequate library building has been erected by the library for a branch in this strategic location, the resulting library and book use has far exceeded that in the average of other branches (eleven branches in contemporary shopping centers, but in rented quarters had only 102,000 average circulation).[45] The penalties of renting branch quarters were noted in the 1958 report; it is usually resorted to as an escape from difficult decisions and almost always the library is the loser both of money and of a strategic site.

The word "coordinating," as generally applied in city planning, is a dangerous and misleading one when it fails to recognize the objectives and distinctive needs of the library. In several of the cities discussed in Section 7, such as Dallas, South Bend, and Vancouver, there were long and bitter attempts to use the proposed new central library building to start a civic center project. The statements from their directors quoted above in Section 7, suggest the penalty which they would have paid if they had acceded to the pressure to place the library anywhere else than in the heart of downtown.

Split-Personality Libraries

In the 1958 report (p. 24), Memphis was cited as a library where the old central building had been left as a busy reference library very close to the heart of downtown, while a new central library had been built in a major shopping center four miles from downtown. In the intervening years the penalties have been great even though the older building has been renovated. The chief penalty comes from attempting to separate the circulating and reference services to readers; those downtown are deprived of the use of the major non-fiction circulating books which are essential for answering many informational questions on all subjects. And the users of the new central library have been deprived of good reference service; at the time the 1958 report was written, the new central library had only about 1,000 reference books and no trained reference librarian.

One fundamental principle of public library service is the essential unity of reference and adult non-fiction materials, and their joint servicing by trained and experienced librarians. Further, this service is drawn on by adults, college students and high school students, and they are served by reference librarians whose objective is to know as much as possible about the subject literature, including periodicals. To duplicate the reference staff for these three reader groups or for the two categories of materials is costly and inefficient.

Since our 1958 report a new director has taken charge at Memphis who is deeply concerned about the situation and is attempting to rectify it. The Memphis library recently retained an experienced library administrator, Harold Hamill of the Los Angeles Public Library, as consultant, to recommend a solution. In a news interview in September 1966, he is quoted as "finding the division of

Memphis main library and the city's reference library shocking. . . . It is shocking that the general reference collection—about 50,000 volumes, is outside of the main and central library. . . . I will recommend that the reference and circulating books be put together."[46] But where? To take the major reference materials and services from downtown would create a grievous vacuum of informational help where it is chiefly sought and be a major disservice to that community. To save space downtown, suggestions are sometimes made to separate the administrative offices and the preparation of books from the rest of the central library and place them on less expensive land elsewhere. But the costly time loss in daily operations which would result is inexcusable, as demonstrated in the separation of these functions in the District of Columbia Public Library. A central library organization can only be split apart at great expense and inconvenience; it is one complete and interrelated organization, with a logic in the interrelation of its parts. It is better and less costly to have a building with an additional upper floor if it is in a good location and no additional ground can be had.

Another variety of split-personality libraries has resulted in new library buildings in several cities being poorly located, for various reasons. At Flint, Michigan, pressure resulted in relating the public library to the local college "eight blocks from the main street at its busiest section," to create a "cultural center," leaving the old library in its more central location, as a branch, for a few months, then in rented and very inadequate floor space thus increasing the operating costs for the library system. Steps are now being taken to rectify the general situation at Flint, probably by establishing a new "branch" where central should have been. But it will not be easy or inexpensive; almost certainly the taxpayers will be penalized by operating two libraries within a few blocks of each other, and the major collections and services will not be where the major adult public would use them most conveniently.

Orientation and Placement on Site

There is a basic conflict between two ideas: (a) that the library building should be a beautiful building, located, designed and placed on its site to attract the entire intelligent community to use it, and therefore easily approached and entered and not set back from the sidewalk, nor raised up on an elevated base requiring any steps to enter it, but on the contrary giving a view to passers-by of the interesting and busy interior of the library in action, and (b) that the library should be "set off" in landscaped grounds, set up on a base or pedestal to make it more impressive, and given an aura of "dignity," often false and inappropriate because a good library has an inherent dignity derived from effective performance of its essential function of serving its community. It seems obvious that the latter concept must inevitably reduce the library's visual attraction to that considerable segment of a community's population, especially adults, which should but does not use it. It may well be that the entire impression of their library as a public institution has been that of the traditional Morgue of Culture, the Great Stone Face, or the Stuffed Shirt, which characterized so many public library buildings of the past.

It is most regrettable, but true, that in the 1960's the pressures from architects and public officials who are making decisions without comprehending the consequences, are now resulting in a reversion to some of the former attempts at "show off" buildings, some of which are even receiving architectural awards.

One prefers a site where the building will not face south or west, on account of the sun's glare and heat. But ideal orientation is by no means as important as an otherwise strategic site, and it often happens that one side of the same street is much busier than the other. There are numerous ways to overcome difficulties from too much sunlight, but one way—using a blank masonry wall along the front—should not be used. In other words, good orientation means placing the modern library and designing its front so that everyone may look into its interior and see what goes on, as a matter of public relations. The quotation above in Section 7 from South Bend, illustrates the value of using the space along the sidewalk as a display medium.

Recently, some strange things have been done as a result of increasing concern for the numerous citizens with physical handicaps serious enough to make stair climbing difficult or impossible. Though 12 percent of the population has permanent physical disabilities, by no means is this proportion unable to use the library easily, and a considerable segment are housebound and are not part of those who visit the library.[47] The easiest and most sensible way to meet this need is by the simple device of designing the library with its main floor at sidewalk level, rather than raising it up on a base, requiring several steps to reach it, and then having to make up for this penalty by a ramp or other device which in several buildings has complicated and detracted from their design.

Circular Library Buildings

One of the architectural excesses recently being committed is the circular building. A careful study of the plans for six circular libraries does not encourage the belief that a circular library can be either efficient or economical. Considerable space is wasted because the rectangles of bookcases, tables and other equipment do not fit into curved spaces and because curved structure and equipment are more costly. Most circular buildings support a heavy domed roof structure, and in three of the six cases this necessitates a circle of closely-spaced columns which cut off the supervisory view, reduce interior flexibility, and increase the per foot cost of usable space. In three cases, in order to justify radial stacks (whose vogue ended a half-century ago) on the ground that one person posted centrally can see what goes on between all the bookcases, the procession of users is routed all the way from the entrance at the perimeter to the service desk in the center of the building, a noisy, spacewasting, and inefficient solution. We omit discussion of numerous other weaknesses of circular buildings, and note only the waste of valuable ground lost by setting a round building on a square or rectangular plot.

NOTES

[1] Wheeler, Joseph L., and Goldhor, Herbert. *Practical Administration of Public Libraries*, New York, Harper and Row, 1962, p. 3.

[2] Drennan, Henry T., *et al*. "Statistics of Public Libraries Midway Through the 1960's." In *Bowker Library Annual*, 1966, p. 13.

[3] "Municipal Library Expenditures and Circulations Per Capita," *Library Journal*, 45:73, Jan. 15, 1920.

[4] The basis for raising the ALA Postwar Standard of "$\frac{1}{2}$ to 1 reference question per capita" (In *Post-War Standards for Public Libraries*. Chicago, ALA, 1943, p. 27) are discussed in Wheeler and Goldhor. *Practical Administration . . . op. cit.*, p. 332; also in Wheeler, Joseph L. "Bettering Reference Service," *RQ*, 6:99–114, Spring 1967.

[5] Wheeler, Joseph L. *The Effective Location of Public Library Buildings.* (University of Illinois Library School Occasional Papers, No. 52). Urbana, University of Illinois Graduate School of Library Science, 1958.

[6] Leigh, Robert D. *The Public Library in the United States.* New York, Columbia University Press, 1950. (*See* Chapter 3, especially pp. 46–50.)

[7] "Editorial. Precious Irrelevance," (comment on Kenneth B. Clark address), *Library Journal*, 90:2772, June 15, 1965.

[8] *The Reorganization of a Large Public Library: Ten Year Report . . . 1926-1935.* Baltimore, Enoch Pratt Free Library, 1937, p. 8.

[9] Ulveling, Ralph A. "Problems of Library Construction," *Library Quarterly*, 33:95–96, Jan. 1963.

[10] Archer, Leonard. Letter dated Sept. 1, 1966.

[11] Munn, Russell. Letter dated Sept. 3, 1966.

[12] Nelson, Ernesto. *Las Bibliotecas en los Estados Unidos.* 2d ed. New York, Carnegie Endowment, 1927.

[13] "K[roch's] & B[rentano's] Completes Major Expansion Program in Chicago Area," *Publisher's Weekly*, 191:49–52, Jan. 2, 1967.

[14] Release from the Queens Borough Public Library dated April 17, 1959. (Processed.)

[15] *World Almanac*, 1967. Edited by Luman H. Long. New York, Newspaper Enterprise Association, Inc., p. 805.

[16] Dallas Public Library. *Annual Reports.* (For fiscal year ending April 30.)

[17] "Poll Reassures Library Board It Needn't Build Parking Lot," *Akron Beacon Journal*, April 5, 1964, p. 2E.

[18] Wheeler, Joseph L. *Report on a Proposed Regional Library System for the San Diego Area.* The S.D.P.L., Feb. 1965, p. 4.

[19] "Editorial," *Cleveland Plain Dealer*, Dec. 27, 1966, p. 12, col. 1.

[20] "Retail Sales in the Central Business District Still Declining," *Real Estate Analyst*, 34:437–452, Dec. 22, 1965. (Based on surveys in these SMSA's made every five years by the Census Bureau.) *See also* Vernon, Raymond. *The Changing Economic Function of the Central City.* 1959. Reprinted in James Q. Wilson, ed. *Urban Renewal: The Record and the Controversy.* Cambridge, Mass., M.I.T. Press, 1966, pp. 3–23. This book also cites the decreasing *proportion* of central cities' retail, wholesale and manufacturing production employees.

[21] "Merchandising. Strength in Variety," *Time*, 84:63, Nov. 20, 1964.

[22] "Atlanta, the Hopeful City," *Fortune*, 74:155–56+, August 1966.

[23] McQuade, Walter. "Boston: What Can a Sick City Do?" *Fortune*, 69:132, June 1964.

[24] Faltermayer, Edmund K. "What it Takes to Make Great Cities," *Fortune*, 75:118–123+, Jan. 1967.

[25] Jacobs, Jane. *The Death and Life of Great American Cities.* New York, Random House, 1961.

[26]Gruen, Victor. *The Heart of Our Cities; the Urban Crises, Diagnosis and Cure.* New York, Simon and Schuster, 1964.

[27]Weaver, Robert C. "New Directions in Urban Renewal." Reprinted *in* James Q. Wilson, ed., *Urban Renewal . . . , op. cit.*, p. 671.

[28]Wilson, James Q., ed. *Urban Renewal . . . , op. cit.*, p. xiii.

[29]"Comeback of 'Downtown': Big Plans in Big Cities," *U.S. News & World Report*, 59:64, July 26, 1965.

[30]"Money and Politics in Downtown Development," *Stores, the NRMA Magazine*, March 1966, pp. 17–18; *see also* Link, David E. "Milwaukee: Investor Confidence Helps Downtown . . . ," *National Real Estate Investor*, Nov. 1965, pp. 91–96.

[31]Murray, Thomas F. "The Resurgence of Downtown," *Urban Land*, 23:1–6, July–Aug. 1964.

[32]Edwards, Arthur W. "Central Business Districts Undergoing Changes; Renewal Can Bring Changes for the Better," *Journal of Housing*, 21:86–189, May 1964; *see also* Shenkel, William M. "Downtown Redevelopment: a Critical Review," *Journal of Property Management*, 30:140–52, May–June 1965.

[33]Gruen, Victor. "From the Shopping Center to the Planned City," *Stores, the NRMA Magazine*, March 1966, pp. 14–17.

[34]Perloff, Harvey S. "New Towns Intown," *American Institute of Planners Journal*, 32:155–61, May 1966. Followed by a report on "The Harper Court Experience," an example of such a development in the Hyde Park section of Chicago, pp. 161–62.

[35]Jonassen, C. T. Letter dated June 22, 1966.

[36]New York. State Library–Library Extension Division. *Criteria for Selection of Public Library Building Projects to Receive Federal Grants-in-Aid.* (New York Library Services and Construction Act Plan, Title II, Construction.) Albany, 1966, p. 7.

[37]Wheeler and Goldhor, *op. cit.*, p. 554.

[38]*Michigan Library Building Statistics.* Lansing, Michigan State Library, 1965.

[39]Doms, Keith. Letter dated Nov. 3, 1966.

[40]Garrison, Guy. "Some Recent Public Library Branch Location Studies by City Planners," *Library Quarterly*, 36:151–55, April 1966.

[41]Bowler, Roberta, ed. *Local Public Library Administration.* Chicago, The International City Managers' Association, 1964. (*See* Ch. 12: "Extending Services," especially p. 267.)

[42]Grundt, Leonard. *An Investigation to Determine the Most Efficient Patterns for Providing Adequate Public Library Service to All Residents of a Typical Large City.* Ph.D. Thesis, Rutgers Library School, 1965. This was summarized in his article, "Branch Library Inadequacies in a Typical Large City," *Library Journal*, 90:3997–4001, Oct. 1, 1965. In contrast to Grundt *see* Wetzel, Frank J. *Considerations of Retailers of Interest to Public Library Systems in Locating New Units in Medium to Large Metropolitan Areas.* M.A. Thesis, Catholic University Library School, 1965. Wetzel assumes, with seeming justification, that the objective of a public library branch is to attract the largest number of potential users of high quality library materials and services, in order to serve best its entire community with the funds available. Also *see* Nelson, Richard L. *Selection of Retail Locations.* New York, Dodge Corporation, 1958. Nelson analyzes in detail the principles, criteria and procedures for successful store location (relevant here since the library is a distributing agency for a highly valuable commodity).

[43]Martin, Lowell. *Branch Library Service for Dallas.* Dallas Public Library, 1958.

[44]"Public Library Service Standards for California," *News Notes of California Libraries*, 58:299, Spring 1963.

[45]Sealock, Richard B. "Extending Services." *In* Roberta Bowler, ed. *Local Public Library Administration, op. cit.*

[46]Jones, Wyman. Preliminary summary letter dated Aug. 10, 1965, from Director Jones of the Fort Worth Public Library to the participants in the survey. (Up until April 1967 no additional report had been issued from Fort Worth.)

[47]Memphis *Commercial Appeal*, Sept. 20, 1966, p. 19, col. 6.

[48]Noakes, Edward H. "Making Libraries Usable," *Wilson Library Bulletin*, 40:851–53, May 1966.

ABOUT THE AUTHOR—Joseph L. Wheeler received the A.B. degree (1906) and the M.A. degree (1907) from Brown University; and the B.L.S. degree (1909); an honorary M.L.S. degree in 1924 from New York State Library School. He has held administrative positions at five large public libraries, has been surveyor or consultant for over 175 administrative or building projects. In 1961 Mr. Wheeler received the Joseph W. Lippincott award. He has been President of the Ohio Library Association and is author of numerous outstanding books on library buildings and administration, including (with A. M. Githens) *American Public Library Buildings* (1941) and with (Herbert Goldhor) *Practical Administration of Public Libraries* (1963). Mr. Wheeler died December 3, 1970.

Selection of Library Sites

by Keyes D. Metcalf

In providing a new library building for a college or university it might be supposed that the logical order of procedure would be to decide that it is needed, then to decide what sort of building it ought to be, and finally to decide where it should be placed. Unfortunately, however, the situation is practically never as simple as this. The availability or nonavailability of a satisfactory site is one of the factors that affect the decision on whether or not to build; this was the case at Harvard when replacement of the central library building was given up more than twenty years ago.[1]

One can hardly determine how much space is necessary for an adequate site unless one has studied the objectives of the library and projected its future growth. One can hardly judge whether or not a particular location will be reasonably convenient for those who use the library unless one can predict the extent and direction of future physical growth of the institution served by the library. If the institution is in its infancy and there is ample room, it may be wise to select the library site first and to plan the future building program for the whole college or university around it. More often, however, the problem is one of fitting a large building into an existing pattern that may have made no provision for it.

It should be emphasized also that one cannot design a satisfactory building and then look about for a parking space, if one is required, that is large enough and sufficiently convenient. Instead, many features of a good building are determined by its site. In order to compare the advantages of two sites, one must compare the two somewhat different buildings that could be erected on them.

The problems that have been outlined in the preceding paragraphs indicate that the selection of a library site is so important for an institution as a whole that it should be preceded in many instances, if not most, by the preparation of a master plan for physical development of the campus. This master plan should consider among other things the following:

1. The objectives of the institution.
2. The estimated prospective size of the student body and faculty, including separate figures for graduate and undergraduate students and professional schools, if there are any.
3. The size of the physical plant that will be required in the next generation and, if possible, for a longer period.
4. The parking facilities required for faculty, staff, and students.
5. The general landscaping plan for the campus.
6. Policy decisions in regard to the type and architectural style of the buildings to be erected.

Without a master plan for development of the institution's physical plant, the difficulties of selecting a satisfactory site for a new library will be greatly increased. It should be noted that there are architects and landscape architects who make a specialty of preparing master plans for the development of colleges and universities.

There are five major factors that should be taken into account in evaluating a site. First, is its size adequate? Second, what is its relation to neighboring buildings and to the whole population distribution and traffic flow of the institution? Third, what orientation is possible for a library building erected on it? Fourth, are there advantages or disadvantages in the slope of the land? Finally, what complications will arise from the nature of the ground beneath the building?

It may be, of course, that only one site will be available that is large enough and in an acceptable

---

SOURCE: Reprinted from Keyes D. Metcalf, "Selection of Library Sites," *College and Research Libraries,* May, 1961, pp. 183–192 and 222, by permission of the publisher.

location. Even so, the other factors should be examined to determine how they will affect the proposed building. How, in other words, can it be designed to make the most of favorable circumstances and to overcome the difficulties presented by this site?

SIZE OF THE BUILDING

A new building ought to provide for present collections, staff, and readers, plus anticipated growth for at least twenty-five years to come, and preferably for twice that period. There may be cases where for one reason or another it is impossible to build a new library large enough to be adequate for even twenty-five years. California planning authorities, because of the tremendous demands for additional space in the tax-supported institutions of higher learning in that state, have in certain instances ruled that new buildings constructed at this time should be large enough for five years only, after which a second stage of their construction should be proposed. In many rapidly growing state universities throughout the country the size of an addition to an old building or of the first stage of a new building is determined by the size of the appropriations that the university administration is able to obtain from the states' fiscal authorities, rather than by prospective needs during a specified number of years ahead. In private institutions also the sums that can be made available, rather than the needs, are too often the determining factor. Two points concerning future needs for space should be emphasized here.

1. If a new library or an addition to an old one is inadequate for space requirements for the next twenty-five years, disadvantages will result, and their cost should not be overlooked.
2. Serious as the disadvantages in question may be, an even more important consideration is selection of a site where a suitable and functional addition can be added at a later time. The site selected, wherever it is, should be large enough for additions that will extend the useful life of the building as long as it is adequate functionally.

Even when a minimum square footage has been determined for a building and its prospective additions, there is, alas, no formula that will translate this into the minimum dimensions for the site. A building does not look good if it fills a plot too full. Spacing of buildings is an aesthetic problem and is affected by what has been done already on a campus or is planned for the future. Proper landscaping can often help to make space go farther than has been expected, and its possible usefulness in this connection should not be neglected.

It may not be out of place here to remind librarians, administrative officers of educational institutions, and even, in a few cases, architects, that a college or a university that prides itself in providing its students with a good liberal education should appreciate the fact that a handsome, comfortable, and functional library building may have an important contribution to make in bringing about the desired results of the whole educational process. A library should not be a monument. It should not be wasteful of space. It should be economical in construction, always taking the long view and considering the cost of maintenance, as well as the original building costs; but it should provide also an atmosphere that encourages and helps to make possible good hard work on the part of students and faculty.

The size of the plot that is needed also depends on the height of the building, which involves functional as well as aesthetic considerations. The number of floors that will be satisfactory from the functional standpoint cannot be determined without taking account of the total square footage, the type of library, its collections, and use.

A library requiring ten thousand square feet or less, and often considerably more, will usually be more satisfactory if it is all on one floor. In larger libraries, it is often desirable that the entrance level and the one above, plus the one below, particularly if it has windows, be large enough to house the central services[2] and provide seating for at least 75 per cent of the readers—particularly those who come and go at short intervals. If this is practicable, there will usually be no serious problems with public elevators. The most heavily used books ought to be shelved comparatively close to the entrance. Other things being equal, the majority of readers should not have to travel any longer distances than necessary, either horizontally or vertically, within the building.

Sometimes a site will prove to be large enough for a building and its additions only if expansion takes the form of additional floors. This is expensive and inconvenient, but, even so, may be preferable to any alternative. At the Louisiana State University, for example, the library has a central location in the heart of the campus and fills the available plot almost completely. This was realized and accepted when the building was planned; the architect provided for construction that will make it possible to add two more floors when they are needed.

The total height of a building above ground is determined by four factors: the percentage of the building that is below ground level, the number of stories above ground level, the height of these stories, and the thickness of the floors between finished ceilings and finished floors above. If a large part of a building can go below the entrance level, as at the Princeton University Library, which in some ways resembles an iceberg with the major fraction of its square footage in its three basement floors, the total height will be correspondingly reduced. It should be noted that the percentage of space required for stairs and elevators increases with each story that is added. Also, three stories with eight-foot ceiling heights require no more height than two stories with twelve-foot ceilings, except for the thickness of one additional floor. In buildings with as many as five stories above ground the thickness of floors is an important factor in its total height; if each one, for instance, is five feet thick instead of two, the five would take 5×5, or 25 feet, instead of 5×2, or 10 feet, making a difference of 15 feet, or enough space to provide two additional stack levels. Thick floors make it easy to plan ducts and services that can be run almost anywhere, but it is more economical of space and gross cubature to run services vertically in so far as possible, rather than horizontally.

CENTRAL OR ECCENTRIC?

The library has often been called the heart of the university; it is visited frequently by nearly everyone in the institution and, if a good library, will be used at least as much as any other building on the campus. Obviously, its location ought to be convenient. Does this mean near the dormitories, the classroom buildings, the laboratories, the student union, or the athletic field?

No one answer is correct for all institutions. If most students commute to the campus, it may be best to place the library near the transportation center, enabling the student to return books on

his way to classes and borrow others as he is leaving. The location of lockers for commuting students may also be an important consideration.

A location near the classroom center is usually preferable to one near the dormitory center; to lengthen the walk to the library between classes by two minutes is more disadvantageous than to lengthen by five minutes the time required to reach the library in the evenings from dormitories.[3] If there are dormitories on opposite sides of the campus, as in many coeducational institutions, a location near classroom buildings may be approximately equidistant from the dormitories. If a choice must be made, it is preferable to place the library near classrooms for the humanities and social sciences, rather than near those for the sciences. If it is much easier, either in the daytime or evening, to reach the student center than the library, a temptation to defer study has been left in the student's path.

Convenience evidently implies a central location, but it is possible for a site to be too central. Some campuses still have a large unoccupied space in their central squares, and this might at first glance seem to be an ideal site for a new library. In fact, however, there are usually serious drawbacks.

First, because the space is so centrally located and conspicuous, the donor, and less frequently, the officers of the college and even the architect may be tempted to decide that it is the place for the single monumental building on the campus. To be sure, it is possible for a good library to be a monument, but it is less likely to be a good functional library if it is planned primarily as a monument. The successful combination is rare. Moreover, a monumental building usually costs much more than one that is simply functional. If funds available for library construction are limited, it may be impossible to pay for the space that is needed if this space has to be housed in a building that is to be the showpiece of the campus.

Second, if a library is in the center of the campus, with students approaching it from all directions, there will inevitably be demands for public entrances on all sides. One objection is that each entrance, with the lobby attached to it and the corridors leading from it to the circulation desk and other central services, takes valuable space. If, for example, an extra entrance requires an outside lobby of only 100 square feet, plus a small inside lobby of 500 square feet, plus a corridor (otherwise unnecessary) 100 feet long and 10 feet wide, there is a total of 1,600 square feet that adds nothing to the building's seating or

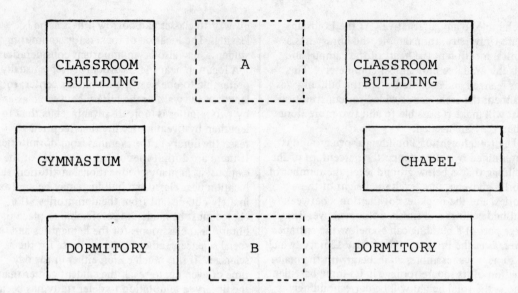

FIGURE 1   A—Suitable site for library, near classroom buildings. B—Possible site for library, but one closer to classrooms is to be preferred.

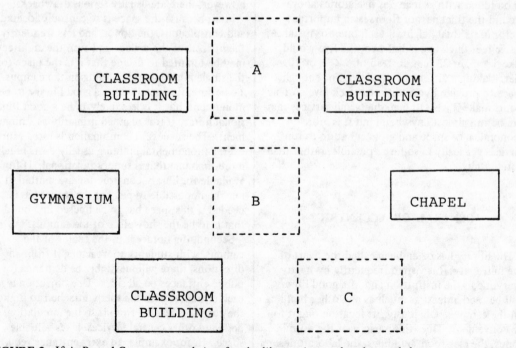

FIGURE 2   If A, B, and C are proposed sites for the library, it may be observed that—

A   is too small a space, and an addition would be difficult, if not impossible.
B   would also be hard to expand, and would call for entrances on all sides; its central location would increase the temptation to erect a monumental structure.
C   appears to be the most desirable location for the library.

shelf capacity, which may also interfere, sometimes seriously, with its functional properties, and
costs perhaps $20,000. This is only 4 per cent of
the total in a $500,000 building, but it would
provide space for shelving 25,000 volumes or,
used as endowment, would bring in an income of
$1,000 per year for books or services.

The extra entrance will prove to be still more
expensive if the library decides, as more and more
libraries have done, that the cheapest and most
effective way to supervise the building is not to
have an attendant in each reading area, but to
check all readers at the exits as a means of dis-
couraging unauthorized borrowing. If this is done
in a building open eighty hours per week, a very
modest number of hours today when student and
faculty pressure is for a midnight or later closing
time, each exit may increase the payroll by $4,000
or $6,000 annually. It will be hard to resist the
demand for additional entrances and exits if the
building is too centrally located; students and
professors do not like to walk around a building
and then have to return part of the way as soon as
they enter.

The third, and, in many ways, the most serious
objection of all to a location at the exact center
of things is that it increases the difficulties of
making an addition to the building that will be
aesthetically and functionally satisfactory. Often,
indeed, it makes an appropriate addition difficult
if not impossible. A central building tends to be
symmetrical, and an addition usually threatens to
destroy this symmetry. If it is also monumental,
the cost of an addition will be greatly increased.
Perhaps it should be emphasized once more that
most library buildings, if they continue to serve
the purpose for which they were designed, have
to be enlarged sooner or later, and ought to be
planned with this in mind.

What is wanted, then, is a convenient location,
but not one so central that it calls for an un-
reasonably expensive, monumental, and unfunc-
tional structure. The accompanying drawings
illustrate some of the points that have been made.

ORIENTATION

No single orientation is ideal for all seasons,
climates, and other conditions; but orientation is a
factor to be considered, particularly in areas where
extremes of heat or cold, hard winds, or intense
sunlight may be expected. Near the tropics the
sun shines in east and west more than in south
windows. As one goes farther north, the southern
sun becomes more and more of a problem; the
situation is reversed, of course, south of the
equator.

The extent to which sunlight penetrates into
rooms at the hottest time of day is a matter of
some importance in most areas. The problem is
minimized if it is usually cloudy, and, in a country
where central heating is not customary, the winter
sun may be a useful source of heat. More commonly, however, when direct sunlight streams into
a building it creates glare and overheating; if there
is air conditioning, it adds to costs. An architect
should be able to provide drawings showing the
penetration of sunlight into a room at any latitude
during any month of the year for any proposed
orientation of a building.

The amount of direct sunlight, as well as heat
and cold, that enters a room depends also, of
course, on the height of windows, the percentage
of wall space that they occupy, and the depth of
the room from windows to inner walls. Prevailing
winds and extremes of heat and cold should also
be taken into account; double windows and
certain special kinds of glass may do much to
counteract unfavorable conditions, but they are
expensive and sometimes difficult to replace. Outside screens have been developed in recent years to
reduce the problems resulting from excess sunlight.

In most parts of the United States the western
sunlight is the most difficult to control. The
eastern sunlight generally presents much less of a
problem because it is rarely as hot and the sun is
ordinarily higher above the horizon and so penetrates a room a shorter distance by the time the
library is open or is heavily used. The southern
sunlight becomes more of a problem as distance
north from the equator increases. Sunlight rarely
causes trouble in northern windows of this hemi-
sphere, as it occurs only in early mornings and
late afternoons when the sun is not at its brightest,
and can usually be kept out during the summer
months by relatively inexpensive landscaping.

The use of special glass and screens of one kind
or another some distance beyond the outside walls
has already been mentioned as a means of protection from glare and heat. In addition, there are
awnings, louvres projecting horizontally from the
building above windows, and metal, vertical
venetian blinds outside the building. The screens
may be of metal, hollow tile, or wood. They may
be placed a few feet beyond the outside wall and

can protect windows from direct sunlight except, possibly, for a few minutes at the end of the day on a western exposure. Examples of such screens can be found in the undergraduate library of the University of South Carolina, the new University of South Florida in Tampa, and the New Orleans Public Library, to mention only a few. Inside the windows, venetian blinds (vertical or horizontal), curtains, or drapes will help, but these sometimes tend to interfere with the circulation of air in an unexpected fashion, and may add to the air conditioning load in summer and heating in winter. All cost something and often a good deal. An engineer should be asked to supply estimates for the specific locality.

It should not be forgotten that a reduction in the percentage of glass in the walls will reduce considerably the heat and cold that is transmitted to the inside. Some architects prefer all-glass buildings, which can be very effective aesthetically. Others prefer to have no windows at all, or very few, with a wall pattern to provide the architectural effects desired. Though small window areas produce savings on heating and air conditioning, they may necessitate lighting over a longer period, but the additional resulting cost is rarely great. A library open for fourteen hours a day in a climate with an average amount of sunlight will require artificial lighting for reading approximately half the time it is open, even if it has large windows, and, while many readers feel the need of windows or tend to have claustrophobia without them, it should be remembered that the light that comes from windows is not for reading but for readers.

It has been said that the western sunlight is the most objectionable throughout most of the United States. It follows that a rectangular building with long north and south sides and short east and west walls is to be preferred if practicable in other respects. If the long axis runs directly east and west, objectionable effects of sunlight will be minimized. If a building faces to the southwest or southeast, it will usually suffer from both the southern and western sunlight even more than if it faces straight south. In addition, the eastern sunlight will be more troublesome, and, in late afternoons, it will come in on the northwest side. In other words, a building that is placed at a forty-five degree angle from north to south tends to have much greater difficulty from excess sunlight than one that has its main axis either straight north and south or east and west.

If the north side of a building is the best area for reading, it will be preferable, other things being equal, to have the main entrance on the south, leaving the entire north side free for reading space. Furthermore, if the stronger winds and storms usually come from the north and west, an entrance on the south or east is preferable and may require a smaller entrance lobby than would otherwise be needed.

It should be kept in mind that direct sunlight, with its ultra-violet rays, is harmful to book bindings and paper. Book ranges should not extend to a wall where the sunlight can come through windows between them; if ranges extend to any wall, they should do so only on the north. The ranges should be at right angles to walls that have windows; if they parallel such walls the full force of the sunlight will strike the volumes in the first range with full force.

It is obvious that the ideal for most of the United States—a library with its entrance on the south and its long axis running directly east and west—is impractical in many cases because of other considerations. A convenient location is more important than an ideal orientation; but orientation is a factor to be considered, and its effect on building costs should not be overlooked. If other factors dictate a particularly undesirable orientation, special attention should be given to avoiding the complications that would arise from large areas of unprotected glass.

THE SLOPE OF THE LAND

If a campus is flat, as many are, one site is like another as far as slope is concerned. In other cases, however, the extent to which the ground slopes and the direction of the incline may be important considerations.

A flat site is not ideal; it has distinct disadvantages. If the main entrance is to be at ground level or only one step up, it will probably be difficult, if not impossible, to have windows in the basement. This may not be of too great importance, but it is true that, even with the best of air conditioning and lighting, some persons are inclined to think that reading and staff accommodations without any outside light are substandard. This is particularly likely to be true if the rooms also have low ceilings, as they often do in basements. A basement is not essential, and may be impractical because of ground and soil conditions; but a basement can provide a large amount of space comparatively inexpensively. Indeed, with central heating and air-conditioning plants for whole campuses, basement space is often not needed for machinery, and there may be as many square feet to be assigned to readers or books in the basement as on any other floor—more, usually, than on the main floor, where a large entrance lobby is almost always needed. If the basement has windows, this space may be highly attractive, and it has the great advantage of being only a short flight of steps from the entrance level. It may also make possible a separate entrance and, if so, can house facilities that are open at times when the rest of the building is closed.

It should be noted that a short flight of steps leading to the entrance on the main floor may make it possible to have a basement with windows all around, but it should be remembered that a building without such steps, entered directly from the grade level, is likely to be more inviting. Areaway windows can sometimes provide nearly as much light as those above ground, but they entail problems of landscaping and drainage. If the first floor is approximately thirty inches above ground level on a flat site, a loading platform at the rear is automatically available; this is not essential, but it is a convenience, even now when most shipments reach a library in small parcels rather than in the tremendous packing cases that used to prevail. Shipments leave the library also, it should be remembered.

One further observation on flat sites may be made. If soil conditions permit, modern earthmoving machinery can change ground levels a few feet at small expense, and, with adequate landscaping, the results may be excellent. It may thus be possible to have a front entrance at ground level, but with a loading platform at the rear.

A considerable slope may be a distinct advantage or disadvantage, depending on its location. In a given site, there is usually one side where it is obvious that the main entrance ought to be—a point at which traffic to the library naturally converges. If there is a fairly steep downward slope from this entrance to the back of the building, it should be possible to have windows in the basement—possibly on as many as three sides and even part of the fourth. Indeed, if the slope is sharp enough, there may also be windows in a subbasement or, as it is sometimes called, the "minus-2" level. At Princeton, even the "minus-3" level has windows at the rear. A slope of this kind offers the further advantage of reducing the height of the building above the entrance level. One may enter a five-story building at the middle of its five levels; this may make it possible to dispense with a public elevator if there is a service elevator for the transfer of books and for persons who cannot climb stairs.

In order to avail themselves of a basement or "minus-1" level, some libraries have an entrance set back from the top of a hill and reached by a bridge, as at the Carleton College library in Northfield, Minn. Construction of a short ramp up to the front entrance can serve the same purpose. At the Grinnell College library there is a ramp and then a bridge to the entrance; the result is that, though the campus is relatively flat, windows could be provided wherever wanted in the basement.

On the other hand, if there is a sharp upward slope toward the rear of a building, the back of the first floor may have to be sunk into the ground; windows may not be possible on one or more sides of the first floor and there will be none at all in the basement. This may be a disadvantage if natural lighting is desired, and may also involve difficult drainage problems.

If the ground falls off to one side of an entrance and rises on the other side, it may facilitate basement fenestration on one side but make it impossible to provide windows on the other side of the main floor. It will probably complicate the landscaping and make architectural planning of the building more difficult. It may also seriously complicate plans for a subsequent addition.

In general, then, a site is to be avoided if the ground slopes upward from the entrance or if it slopes from one side of the entrance to the other. A flat site is to be preferred to one that slopes objectionably; but it is better yet if the ground slopes from the entrance downward toward the back of the building. No one of these factors is of first importance. But, other things being equal, they may prove to be the deciding considerations on site selection.

SOIL AND GROUND CONDITIONS

A site for a library should never be selected without some knowledge of ground conditions. When general information on this subject is not available, at least one or two and in many cases a larger number of preliminary borings should be made. This may seem expensive, but it will cost hundreds rather than thousands of dollars at most, and will be well worth the cost if it prevents great unanticipated expenses for excavation and foundations—misfortunes that have been much too common in library building. One university library had spent more than $60,000 on its plans before it realized that foundations alone for its library would cost approximately $500,000 extra because of ground conditions.

This is not an engineering treatise, and it should suffice to give a brief summary of the points that ought to be considered.

If the foundation runs into ledge or boulders over one-half cubic yard in size, there may be substantial additional costs for removing this material. The extra costs which would result from placing a building in this type of soil should be carefully estimated by a qualified professional estimator or a contractor familiar with this kind of work. On the other hand, it should be kept in mind that solid rock makes a fine foundation for a library; books are heavy, and stack areas in particular need a firm foundation. In excavating for the Lamont Library at Harvard shale was reached before the foundation was excavated to the proper depth, but practically all of it was friable enough to be handled by a power shovel, and, as it was removed, an excellent foundation of harder rock was exposed for the footings.

If loose, fine sand, soft clay, silt, or peaty materials are encountered, piles or caissons may have to be driven down great distances in order to provide an adequate foundation. Along the Charles River in Cambridge and in the Back Bay section of Boston (areas that once were tidal swamps) it may be necessary to go two hundred feet or more below the surface to reach a solid bottom, and the cost of driving piles or sinking caissons to this depth is great. Under certain conditions it is possible to pour a concrete mat on which the building will "float." The library of the Massachusetts Institute of Technology is floated in this way, but adoption of this method dictated the construction of the building around a large court in order to spread the weight, and this resulted in a disadvantageous circulation pattern. The Yale University library is built over quicksand on which a concrete slab was poured, but conditions were such that it was possible to build a tower stack, despite the great weight of such a structure.

In many sections of the country there are numerous springs, sub-surface ground water flow, or other water conditions to complicate the construction of foundations. It is possible to excavate for a foundation, keep the water pumped out,

and waterproof the building either outside or in; but this is expensive and, unless the construction is of highest quality, difficulties will arise sooner or later. During flash floods, the water table around the Widener Library at Harvard occasionally rises above the sub-basement floor; on two occasions during nearly fifty years water has come up through the concrete slab in small sections of the floor.

Another problem sometimes occurs on hillsides, which have been particularly recommended, if they slope the right way, as building sites. In certain ground formations, however, the whole side of the hill may begin to slide in wet weather, as has happened occasionally in canyons of the Los Angeles region.

The Louisiana State University library at Baton Rouge is built on Mississippi River delta land that can carry only a limited weight per square foot of surface. It was necessary to reduce the pressure on the bearing strata by removing the over-burden. This made it necessary to include a basement in the building, and this involved a drainage problem. The basement and the drainage difficulties could have been avoided if the site had not been so small that it was necessary to plan for a five-story building.

SUMMARY

A specific example illustrating some of the considerations involved in the selection of a site may be provided by the Lamont Library at Harvard. This site was selected from four possibilities after some weeks of discussion and preparation of rough sketches of a suitable building in each location. Its actual position was chosen because:

1. It was the only remaining available site in the Yard large enough for a building of the desired size. A location in the Yard close to the two other central library buildings, Widener and Houghton, to which it could be connected by tunnel, was an important factor.

2. It was so placed that the freshmen had to pass its front entrance six times a day going to and from their meals in the Freshmen Union. It was on a main walk between the houses where the upper classmen lived and the classrooms, and closer to the latter.

3. It had a long east-west axis, giving the most desirable long north and south exposures for the reading areas.

4. The ground slope was such that two levels

with windows below the main entrance, which was only one short step up, were possible, with two more without windows below them. It was possible to have the entrance level, plus its mezzanine, a full second floor, and a penthouse with a good deal of useful space in it; even the latter is closer to the ground than the main reading room in Widener. Moreover, the building, which would have been a little large for its site if it had been taller, does not give that impression.

5. Policy decisions on the part of the university permanently limiting the size of the undergraduate college and on the part of the library limiting the size of the undergraduate book collection meant that provision did not have to be made for a future extension.

To recapitulate, the site must be large enough to provide for the building and for projected additions, and it must be in as convenient a location as possible. This does not mean that it ought to be in the exact center of the campus; but it ought to be readily accessible from classroom buildings, particularly those for the humanities and social sciences. The orientation, ideally, should be on a long axis running directly east and west, with the entrance on the south. A site that slopes downward from the entrance to the rear may be advantageous, and costs of construction may be greatly increased if ground conditions are unsatisfactory. Parking and delivery problems should not be forgotten. Since a site will rarely be found that is ideal in every respect, careful assessment of the advantages and disadvantages of each possible site is called for before a decision is made.

NOTES

[1] The only available site for a new central library at Harvard was more than a quarter of a mile off center. This was not the only reason for the decision that was reached; tremendous costs were involved, and a building large enough to provide for another generation would have had to be so large that professors and graduate students, to say nothing of undergraduates, would have found it difficult to use.

[2] The central services referred to here are generally considered to include the circulation and reference desks, with the offices and service areas that go with them, the bibliography and reference collections, with such reading space as they require, the public catalog and in many cases the current periodical collections, with an attached reading area, and also accommodations for the use and storage of microreproductions if it is desired to service them from one of the service desks mentioned above. To this should be added at least the work areas housing those members of the processing staff (particularly acquisition and catalog) who have frequent need for using the catalog and the reference and bibliography collections.

[3] Some librarians disagree with this argument, on the basis that evening study is on the whole more important and that the library should be as close to the dormitories as possible.

ABOUT THE AUTHOR–(See biographical note on page 79.)

V

SOME GENERAL
PLANNING CONSIDERATIONS

The literature of library buildings contains many articles of a general nature. While these may cover information better handled in more specific matters, still the very generality of these works is important to the understanding of the total library building. On the other hand a few subjects covered are so specific they do not fit under any heading other than "miscellanea." "Miscellanea" however are often confused with "trivia." But by no means are traffic patterns, interior design, and consideration of the handicapped to be confused with trivia in library planning.

What follows then in this section is a series of articles either too general or too specific to be included elsewhere. They are too significant however to be delayed further in the *Reader*.

Problems of Library Construction

by Ralph A. Ulveling

"It is a relatively small matter to remove a wall on a drawing by means of an eraser. But once the wall is built. . ." We need not complete the sentence—the point has been made. Busy as the librarian and his staff may be, they cannot give too much time to the planning process. Dual purposes of space, flexibility, horizontal versus vertical traffic, changed, improved or new services—all must be considered before the building is constructed. In this article attention is focused on these matters for the public library building.

The planning of a new library building or a major enlargement of an existing library is a project of such dimensions that the institutional investment involved will likely not be repeated for half a century or more. Most librarians who are confronted with such a problem have had no experience to prepare them for it. They may have attended one or more ALA building institutes, and they probably have heard a few lectures on building planning as part of an administration course in library school years before. These are a helpful introduction to planning, but sometimes they give a false sense of security to both the librarians and their governing boards. These same boards and librarians would recognize at once the folly of allowing someone with such a very meager background to assume the responsibility for cataloging the library's books. I point to this incongruity even though it must be obvious to all that cataloging errors would lend themselves to easy correction in a way that a building error would not.

Today, a library board confronted with a new building project would probably engage the services of a library building consultant, just as school administrators turn to school consultants, hospital administrators to hospital consultants, and industrialists to factory layout consultants. Wheeler and Githens have written:

The planning of a library is an intricate matter. It is too much to expect anyone, in the few months while a library plan takes shape, to master the intricacies of a complex and rapidly developing subject in which only a few architects and librarians are fairly competent after a lifetime of study and practice. Most businessmen agree that technical advisors are well worth the cost. It is an evidence of good judgment and no reflection on the intelligence of trustees to call in an experienced advisor before starting sketch plans, thus preventing unnecessary expense, inefficient service, and lasting regret.[1]

That statement was made more than two decades ago. However, in a recent issue of the *Library Journal*, we find new evidence of the failure of a librarian and architect to comprehend fully the ideas of one another. In that issue a prominent architect of White Plains, New York, said:

Where the library director and the architect present as differing a report on one aspect of the library planning as we find here, there has obviously been a failure in communication somewhere along the line. . . . The language of an architect in communicating his designs to others must remain basically the language of his drawings. To most who are laymen in respect to architecture and building, this is a foreign language to greater or less degree.[2]

It is true, unfortunately, that many laymen who profess the ability to read architectural plans see them in two dimensions only. They often fail to see differences in elevation. Yet, it is the height of objects, such as freestanding shelving or other visual obstructions, as well as variations in floor levels, etc., that can create real operating difficulties and deep-seated disappointments for the librarian and the board.

In general, a good library consultant can be expected to do many things: (*a*) aid in clarifying

---

SOURCE: Reprinted from Ralph A. Ulveling, "Problems of Library Construction," *Library Quarterly*, vol. 23, January, 1963, pp. 91–101, by permission of the publisher and the author.

the library's service requirements, being sure to bring up for consideration services, or methods, or programs that may have been overlooked but that should be considered; (*b*) translate the library's needs into terms that can be readily grasped by the architect; (*c*) clarify for the librarian and board the architectural limitations that must be recognized in developing a plan; (*d*) confer with the librarian and architect—first in developing and then in refining the building plans; and (*e*) give guidance and counsel to the librarian and board on all problems that may be related to the building project. I emphasize the words "guidance and counsel" simply because there are some things no building consultant can be expected to do, such as convincing city officials or the townspeople of the need to provide funds for a new library building. Nor can a building consultant work out the interior decoration and furnishing of the building, though this is often expected. However, in both of these matters and in many similar ones, his broad experience will make it possible for him to give knowledgeable advice.

With this background let us consider the three phases of a building project: the preliminary planning of the services and methods; the principles to follow in building layout; and the creation of the plan.

PRELIMINARY PLANNING OF THE SERVICES AND METHODS

The time to begin modernizing operating methods and planning new services is *before* rather than *after* the building plans are drawn. It is not unusual to hear librarians say: "After we get into the new building, the next thing we are going to do is investigate various charging and registration systems with a view to modernizing ours. Right now we are so busy we can't think about such things." That is the wrong time to do it. Why provide the space for a mass of slip trays and registration files if a year after going into a new building all the processes are to be streamlined? It has happened that the useless space thus provided at considerable extra expense actually militates against whatever compact plan may be instituted.

Similarly *new* services to be added should be anticipated before even schematic plans are prepared. Will the library have a collection of circulating sound recordings? If so, ample space

for examining each recording at the charge-out and return desks must be provided and a place for listening equipment and special shelving must be included in one of the rooms. If a film service is to be maintained, a place for checking, repairing, and cleaning the films will be essential. Some provision for previewing the films, either by the staff, the public, or both, must be made. Will the book collection be continued as one central collection or will one or more special departments be created? Regardless of the number of administrative offices required currently, in a growing community it is likely that more will be needed before long. Provide space now which can later be divided by movable partitions.

Likewise, prepare the best estimates you can make of the size of the book collection to be housed eventually, with separate figures for the adult and juvenile collections; the number of periodicals that will be received currently; the number of seats to be provided in each department; the number of persons you feel is the maximum to be seated in the meeting room at one time; and the number of staff members for whom provision should be made. The latter figure should be divided into male and female, so that lavatory and locker spaces may be anticipated. Through the years the proportion of one sex to another will change; the quarters for each should provide leeway.

These are the facts and figures that any librarian should have before a consultant is brought in. The figures may be revised in the course of discussion with the consultant. But since no two libraries are exactly alike, and since no two library programs are identical, it is basic that the ideas and the plans of the local administration be the starting point for all that follows.

PRINCIPLES TO FOLLOW IN BUILDING LAYOUTS

John Burchard, architect-librarian-educator, once said: "Librarians, like cooks, know what they do but not *why* they do it nor *how* they could do it better."[3] This is not a very flattering statement and one which surely does not apply to services, though it may to building considerations. In any case, I shall try to state some principles to consider in planning a building.

1. *Patrons can be moved horizontally more easily than vertically and with greater safety and*

economy. Ideally then, public services should, if possible, be kept on one floor—the ground floor. This, of course, is not even possible, or desirable, for libraries that have become quite large. Availability of land for sites also affects the extent to which a library can apply this principle.

From a cost standpoint, I point out that if only one public department is moved off the ground floor, that fact may entail a building expense out of all proportion to the size of the service area required. Local building safety regulations almost uniformly would require two stair exits from an upstairs or a basement public room. If a stairwell occupies a minimum of 125 square feet on one floor, it will require a total of 250 square feet on two floors. Double that for two stairwells and you find that at $20 per square foot (I am using this figure for explanatory purposes only) you are spending $10,000 just to get to the other level. For that much money you could have had a very significant enlargement for one of the main floor departments.

2. To provide the maximum future flexibility for the library, *keep all unmovable building features in one area instead of being scattered through the building.* I am referring to such items as stairways, elevators, toilets, etc. Avoid built-in seats, desks, decorative borders in floors around book stacks or other designated areas. Fixed elements such as these tend to freeze the plan and make the building less flexible to meet future needs.

Librarians, too, must control what seems to be a group characteristic—that of wanting to separate each different kind of activity by a wall. For example, instead of a built-in closet for supplies, use a free-standing supply cabinet. This has many advantages: it saves the cost of the closet walls and door; it permits the supply space to be enlarged later; and it permits the supply space to be moved to another location. You may be surprised to learn that the amount of space occupied by walls is often as much as 10 per cent of the total floor area. Further, walls not only reduce the aggregate available space within a building, but they lessen the usability of the areas that remain. Open spaces can be used far more efficiently than space divided into smaller parcels.

3. *As far as possible, strive to make things serve two purposes instead of one.* Toilet rooms can often be so located as to be readily accessible to readers using the library and also available to the audience using the meeting room after the library proper has closed. In locating toilets, however, place them where the entrances can be supervised during the time the library is open for general service. A storyhour room used only for a weekly story hour is a luxury few libraries can afford. Such a room, however, should be so placed as to have direct easy access from both the children's and the adult areas; it may serve as a meeting room for people of various ages. The corollary to this is that the room should not be decorated in a fairy tale or similarly childish motif. It is quite possible to develop an interesting decor that will be equally appropriate for adults and for children.

A single workroom placed between two departments where it can be shared will be less costly to build than two separate workrooms. A jointly used workroom will also permit operating economies. For example, one typewriter and one typist may be all that are necessary, whereas two separate workrooms would almost surely necessitate the purchase of two typewriters and possibly would necessitate duplication of typists.

4. One subject that might have been included under shared facilities is so important that it demands separate mention. I refer to the question of *whether or not children's books should be charged at the library's general control desk or in the children's room.* In the light of a long and extensive experience in library consulting, I believe I can say that nothing is more hotly championed one way or the other, and that nothing is farther from reaching a commonly accepted solution. Some children's librarians resent the idea that children should come through a separate door and be treated any differently than any other person. They imply, without putting it into words, that anyone who supports another position just "hasn't seen the light." Those who champion separate charging arrangements for children seem to think that someone who knows children's books must pass on the book being taken by each little patron lest he get something unsuitable for him or her. I feel that this position is untenable, simply because it seems to me that any supervision or help in selecting reading matter should be given *before* the child makes his choice rather than after. I have not attempted to assemble comparative figures, but I have a feeling that the number who favor having all children's books charged by clerks at the general control desk is now numerically larger and that that group will eventually become dominant.

5. A principle that requires repeated enunciation is to *avoid emulating special building features of other types of institutions* unless they can logically be defended as sound for libraries. I believe the somewhat popular conception that public libraries

should have driveup windows like the progressive new banks is fallacious. Book drops for the return of books is an unquestioned service to the borrower. But these require no more than a slit in the wall or door, certainly not a window with an attendant. The patron's relationship to a bank is altogether different from that of his relationship to a library. I know of no place where the patron is so completely independent of the need for consultation as in his normal banking activities. Either he will deposit money, cash checks, or withdraw money. He alone can make these decisions. The patron in these cases needs no counsel from the banker. But if he does need counsel, either on investments or the taking out of a mortgage or on anything more than the deposit or withdrawal of money, he would never attempt to get it at a drive-up window. He would park his car and go in. Likewise, he would go into a store to select the merchanise he wants. And the store with its big array of products on display surely would not feel it was sensible, as a business practice, to make it possible for customers to remain in their automobiles while on a buying expedition. Similarly, libraries that are concerned with guiding readers in a meaningful way would not be content to restrict their contact with patrons to a short telephone message followed later by passing a package of books through a window. Much could be said, too, of the unsound economics of this kind of service procedure, but I do not wish to attach undue importance to it here. Suffice it to say that libraries do not enhance their service or their standing in the community by adopting the ill-fitting ways of other organizations. People believe, and rightfully so, that librarians are quite capable of devising sound, progressive practices for their institutions, and that they will provide normal new conveniences as was done when drop boxes and book-return slots were taken up widely. Artificial copying of others is neither necessary nor desirable.

6. Another principle I wish to recommend is to *leave some space "unassigned"* in any new building. Developments are coming so fast that the little leeway thus provided is frequently used up before the building is three years old. It is not wasteful; it is good sense to recognize openly that the building under construction must provide for more than today's requirements.

7. Finally, I turn to a very controversial matter —the location of the library site. If the decision has been made to rebuild on the old library site, then what follows will have no bearing on your problem. However, if the existing library lot is too small, or too poorly located to serve successfully for a new building, choices will have to be considered. *Do not follow outdated principles in choosing a library site.*

A quarter-century or more ago, the principle was laid down and broadly accepted that a library should be at the main intersection of the downtown area. We have learned much since that time, but even more significant is the fact that our social patterns nationally have changed. However, no one to my knowledge has challenged the appropriateness of that dictum for today's conditions, as I do now. During the Hoover administration, we were much aware of a popular slogan that referred to a chicken in every pot and a car in every garage. That was used to suggest the optimum in abundance. Today, even in the homes of quite modest salaried workers, it is becoming common to find a car for every worker. A man and wife each holding jobs may well have two cars. Grown sons and daughters in a household increase the need for, and the number of, cars. This had resulted in a kind of population mobility that has brought on the growth of great outlying shopping centers, suburban living, the threatened collapse of good public transportation, and the downgrading in importance of the downtown areas of cities generally. In Detroit and in hundreds of communities, the busiest corner is no longer a downtown intersection but a place miles and miles out from the city center where automobiles by the thousands pass every hour. I am not saying that the library must be located remote from the downtown area. I am merely decrying acceptance of the slick, easily mouthed formula of earlier years that the main intersection downtown is the ideal site for a main library. Each city must be analyzed as a separate problem. The close proximity of large municipal parking lots may be far more important in choosing a library site than other factors.

I am sure that all of you are well aware of the frustration of trying to find a place to leave an automobile while you go into a bank, a post office, or any other similar building. I am sure, too, that you have found it far easier to pass your usual drug store and drive a mile beyond to another if you are assured of a parking space when you get there. There is nothing compulsive about using a library. If you have difficulty finding a place to park your car every time you go, or if parking fees are unreasonable in commercial parking grounds near the library, you will gradually forego frequent trips to it, and so will others. Parking is not the only factor to be considered in site selection, but be sure to consider it when you locate your building, and do not be guided by principles that may have been good in the 1930's but are now no longer valid.

CREATION OF THE PLAN

As you approach the actual work of getting your hopes on paper in definite realizable form, of necessity you create a planning team. The care and judgment applied in developing that team will largely determine the results you obtain. The librarian, the architect, and the building consultant will each have a principal part in the undertaking. A fourth member—the interior designer—will be discussed later. The building consultant is to see that a sound functional plan is devised, one which will adequately meet the service needs the library is to provide for. The architect is to develop a suitable and pleasing form for housing the activity. Neither of these should trespass on the field of the other and usually they do not. The librarian represents the owner and, as such, is in position to veto the proposals of either of the other two members if those proposals seem unsuitable for the community. He must, however, remain open-minded and receptive to suggestions.

"The best consultant," says a prominent North Carolina architect, "is an experienced administrator in the particular field for which a building is being planned. If neither the architect nor the client is familiar with the problems inherent to a building of highly specialized use, such as a library, then in lieu of research by the architect and owner a consultant would be desirable. . . . I treasure the recollection of Charles Mohrhardt's performance when the planning of the Winston-Salem Public Library was bogging down in a confusion of professional and amateur advice. After studying overnight the proposed plans, which were in advanced working drawing stage, Mr. Mohrhardt [who had just been called into consultation at that point in the library's planning] recommended a completely new approach. His reasons were sound and convincing. His advice was followed."[4]

HOW TO CHOOSE A CONSULTANT

Since the term "consultant" has many applications, a few words on the selection of a consultant may be in order. Two points of possible confusion need clarification: (1) Eminence in the library profession is not synonymous with experience in planning buildings. Not infrequently, however, one will hear a board speak of engaging some librarian of a nearby city to guide its building project. The choice is sometimes made for no better reason than that the librarian is close at hand and is well known in the state. (2) Similarly, the consultants from the state library who periodically tour the state are for the most part service and operational advisors, not building experts. They fill a very important function but that function must be recognized for what it is.

Before discussing the kind of services various consultants provide, it is necessary to define some commonly used terms that may be misunderstood unless the trade use of the terms is known.

The *building program* is usually a written statement of the philosophy, principles, requirements, and limitations that are prepared to guide the architect. (Some library building consultants limit their services largely to preparation of the building program.)

Schematic plans are proposed floor layouts that have been developed in the light of all the requirements that have been given. They represent a possible solution for the problem that is set up in the building program. Sometimes several schematic plans must be prepared. When one plan is acceptable, it will be used as the basis for the preliminary plans.

Preliminary plans, though based on the approved schematic plan, are developed by the architect in much greater detail. These plans show the location and space requirements for everything to be contained in the building, including the structural building requirements. The preliminary plans together with an *outline of specifications* prepared by the architect provide the basis for preparing a preliminary cost estimate for the entire structure.

Working drawings together with *specifications* are the detailed contract documents used by builders for the preparation of bids and for erection of the building. Working drawings include elevations, sections, and details. Further, these drawings show architectural, structural, and mechanical work.

Specifications include a written description of the scope of the work, general conditions, the materials to be used, and the workmanship involved in the project.

Shop drawings are drawings of details prepared by the fabricator of special features of the building. These are done for the contractor at no added expense to the library. They must be submitted to the architect for his approval before the work can go forward.

Thus, in selecting the consultant, find out in what form his reports will be presented—as a written building program that in effect defines the problem, or as a schematic drawing with accompanying explanatory reports, which are proposed solutions to the building problem. The latter, which are more difficult to prepare, are usually more readily understood by the librarian and the board and they convey to the architect a more definite conception of what will be needed. (A word of warning, however, should be included here. Architects usually welcome a well-prepared schematic plan, but they become annoyed when confronted with a proposed scheme that is an amateurish hodgepodge of rooms stuck together without the discipline of a controlled plan.)

Also, you should get a record of the consulting work he has done in the past. Examine this as to extent and variety. Visit some of the libraries referred to, if possible. Find out from the librarian of one of these buildings how well the consultant works with the board and with the architect. One librarian made a somewhat more thorough analysis of the work of various consultants and found out that the actual building costs per square foot for one consultant were usually less than for others, regardless of which architectural firm he worked with.

Further, make sure that your consultant will not consider his responsibility ended when he presents a typed report for handing to an architect. A fully satisfying consultant will not disassociate himself from the project until the building is occupied. Weigh all these factors and then make your selection.

WHEN SHOULD A CONSULTANT BE BROUGHT IN?

The first person to be added to your building team should be the building consultant. This should be done long before an architect is engaged. The time for this is when the librarian and board begin serious consideration of a building project. Very often this is before the financing of a new building has been provided—when the board is often uncertain about what moves to make. Should the present building be enlarged? Would a small branch relieve the main library sufficiently? Or should someone do an over-all library survey and in that way find out just what should be done about the building? Let me speak briefly of each of these points, beginning with the last:

1. A general library survey may be needed to get some appraisal of its services, its operating methods, the quality and extent of its book collection. But if it is recognized that a more adequate building is needed, a survey is usually only an instrument for deferring the coming to grips with a decision that sooner or later must be made.

2. A branch library or many branch libraries will duplicate in part some of the service of the main library and thus make these services available to more people more conveniently. But it will very seldom diminish the pressures at the main library sufficiently to affect that library's building requirements. The raised educational level of people throughout this country, the growth of reading interests both in breadth and especially in depth or specialization, require far bigger, broader, and better main libraries everywhere. A branch can to an extent relieve the student load but, except in the case of large branch libraries (larger than I have envisioned for the cities under consideration), it cannot provide the range of reading matter demanded by an educated adult clientele.

3. Should the present building be enlarged? Though each building presents a unique problem, some generalizations can be made. An amazing number of libraries in medium-sized cities are in Carnegie buildings that were erected fifty or more years ago, when the communities they serve were far smaller. Most of these buildings are literally unsuitable for major expansion. The basements usually have a veritable forest of supporting columns, thus making it completely impossible to assemble enough open area at that level to locate a service. Many of these early buildings have already had additions so badly planned and placed that all possibility of further expansion is precluded. Nearly all have the main service area far above the ground level, thus making it difficult or even impossible for many elderly people and people with heart ailments to use the library. And frequently the service areas of these buildings are so difficult to integrate into a unified, open plan that operating costs will inevitably be higher than would be necessary in a better organized structure. An over-all admonition then would be: Do not be misled by the fact that the present building is in

excellent physical condition. Uniformly, such buildings have been so well maintained and are nearly always so monumental in design that a serious resistance can develop to any proposals concerning replacement. Usually, however, when sentiment has forced the retention of the existing building, the over-all construction costs have been nearly as large as if an entirely new building had been erected. And often the operating cost for staffing is larger.

The last member of the planning team—the interior designer—may be unfamiliar to many. I begin my comment by warning that interior designers resent being confused with interior decorators. The basic difference, I believe, is in the scope of the work which each is prepared to handle. I have heard, too, that there is a fundamental difference in the amount and kind of training of each; I cite this only as hearsay, for I have no intention of making myself the target of a controversy on this point. The interior decorator is concerned with adding equipment and color to a completed building. The interior designer is concerned not only with all equipment and color but, further, with the choice of materials for floors and walls, with lighting equipment, and with all those building features that become a part of the total symphony of parts in a finished room.

One of his great strengths is that he is competent and often very ingenious in suggesting or even designing new kinds of special equipment to meet special needs. Many architects like to control all the finish detail for their buildings, and some of the very large architectural firms, therefore, maintain interior-design departments within their own organizations. Many other architects are very happy to work with any recognized interior designer. Be certain, however, that the interior designer you engage is not representing one single manufacturer and that he is free and ready to draw from the products of all and is in the employ of none.

My advice regarding the final phase of your building project would be to avail yourself of the services of a competent interior designer. If you wish your building to have a smart appearance as opposed to the look of an amateur decorator, I strongly urge you not to rely on any staff member, even though one may have a reputation for being very clever in handling colors. A good librarian has neither the time nor the opportunity to keep up with all the new thinking and new developments in a field so unrelated to our own.

HOW MUCH MONEY SHOULD BE REQUESTED FROM THE CITY?

I begin this section by saying that the standard indexes of construction costs—the engineering News-Record Building Cost Index and the Building Commodity Index—show that these costs have been rising steadily and sharply since 1950 or before. This, plus the fact that people have a natural inclination to allow their desires to influence their judgment when estimating prices, results in some early surprises on probable costs for a building. Some board member, at this point in the planning, is quite likely to say: "This is a very conservative community." In other words, cut the price. But a board must be realistic. If the schools and other local interests pay standard rates for construction, the library will have to do so, too. The building rates cannot be cut. And if the estimates of the library's needs were correct, they can be cut only a very little.

Because the consultant has a degree of detachment not enjoyed by the members of the board who have the responsibility for providing the needed funds, he can sometimes be helpful in giving general counsel. I remember one board that was quite perturbed to learn that the building they wanted would cost about $500,000. Gradually, conversation led around to a proposal that "we ask for $350,000 which is the figure we discussed a year ago." Their attitude changed, however, when it was pointed out that as a board they have a responsibility to tell the community the facts as they know them. Otherwise, if it should become known that the new building is inadequate and the board knew it would be at the time it was planned, the people will feel that the library board was incompetent and irresponsible. On the other hand, if the board stated the true needs and then the city fathers or the townspeople allowed only a lesser amount, the good faith and the confidence of all would have been preserved. There is real danger in altering any facts merely to make them palatable. Amazingly, too, most communities, once they pass the point of early surprise, are willing to provide for all reasonable needs for the library just as they do for the schools.

CONCLUDING STATEMENT

A well-planned building not only provides for all needs of readers and staff but it has a simplicity of layout that permits patrons, even on their first visit, to grasp easily the service plan. It is difficult to devise a plan in which services are so located that each may function with the least interference possible from the users of other services in the building. It is difficult, too, to arrange a layout that gives the maximum access by all departments to the library resources they will need and to do this while making it possible to supervise the building with a minimum of staff. In short, it is difficult and time-consuming to devise a satisfactory, functional, appealing plan that is also a simple plan. For this reason allow plenty of time in the early stages both for creating a plan and then for studying it. It is a relatively small matter to remove a wall on a drawing by means of an eraser. But once the wall is built, its removal is not so simple. Changes in a plan that are made after a construction contract has been awarded also create complications and will necessitate "change orders." Such late changes are expensive, and often they affect more separate trades working on the building than most laymen realize. Avoid them by disciplining your early eagerness to get the work going. Control that very strong urge to get the digging started before the project has been fully matured in the planning stage. The dividends for early patience are large.

NOTES

[1] J.L. Wheeler and A.M. Githens, *The American Public Library Building* (New York: Charles Scribner's Sons, 1941), p. 59.

[2] W.H. Heidtmann, "Haste and Misunderstanding," *Library Journal*, LXXXVII, No. 9 (May 1, 1962), 1718.

[3] Quoted in C.M. Mohrhardt and R.A. Ulveling, "Public Libraries," *Architectural Record* ("Building Types," Study No. 193) CXII (December, 1952), 150.

[4] L. Lashmit, "The Architect's Function in Preliminary Planning," *Proceedings of the Institute sponsored by the American Library Association Buildings Committee* (Chicago: American Library Association, 1954), p. 16.

ABOUT THE AUTHOR—Ralph A. Ulveling is a graduate of DePaul University with a PhB degree earned in 1922, and Columbia, with a B.S. degree in 1928. After graduation, he went to the Detroit Public Library, becoming Director in 1941 and Director Emeritus in 1967. Mr. Ulveling has been Professor of Library Science at Wayne State since 1968. He has made surveys of U.S. libraries both at home and abroad, and acted as a consultant in the planning of many library buildings. A member of many commissions and boards, he was also President of the Michigan Library Association, 1937–38 and of ALA, 1945–46. He has written numerous articles and received both the Lippincott award and the Palmer citation.

New Library Buildings: Some Strengths and Weaknesses

by William H. Jesse

Fortunes and misfortunes, attention and neglect, understanding and misunderstanding, enlightenment and blindness, planning and lack of planning, use and abuse—yes, both strengths and weaknesses are found in the newer library building. The significance is in what we learn from both the good and the bad. "Anything should go in a new library which improves it, is justifiable budgetarily and will do the job faster and easier than the thing it replaces." Here attention is focused primarily on the academic library building.

The most widely experienced disappointments in new library buildings today come from engineering failures. However carefully and cooperatively a building is planned, if it does not work well because of physical plant failures—especially in the heating, ventilating, air conditioning, and humidity control equipment—everything else seems to fade into relative unimportance. Patrons know something is wrong and the staff feels either apologetic or disgusted, sometimes both, with the new facility. After frustrating weeks, months, and often years, the mechanical parts are adjusted, repaired, or replaced, and the building may begin to operate in a satisfactory manner. But by this time most of the sheen is worn off, and the disappointment which has been experienced cannot be forgotten.

Modular planned buildings, unless they are very small, must have deep interiors and should have relatively low ceilings, both of which call for actual, not theoretical, performance from the machinery. The fault is not always with the building client, nor the owner, nor the architect, nor even the engineers. It varies. In many instances, everything would be all right if the owner had put *qualified* maintenance personnel on the payroll.

Flexibility is much greater than it has ever been before, particularly when it has been kept in mind as one of the prime, rather than secondary, motives for modular planning. A great many new buildings, however, are limiting or crippling their flexibility by the overuse and misuse of mezza-

nines. The number of mezzanines going into new buildings is almost frightening. In many cases, the only reason for having a mezzanine is a presumed aesthetic gain. Whether architects and librarians realize it or not, they are reverting to the cause of the problems of many years ago: creating fixed-function areas, making portions of their buildings relatively inflexible. Some librarians (and even some library building consultants) recommend mezzanines because of the economy they feel is involved. If this trend continues, then the big battle for modular slab-floor construction either has been forgotten or is being lost. A mezzanine involves the simple principle of crowding extra books on an intermediate partial floor. Actually, if the floor will take readers or books or other functions for the width of the mezzanine, it will take them for the width of the building. The mezzanine is simply a throwback to multitier stacks with off-height rooms adjacent to them. The arguments for and against them have apparently been forgotten. As a result, history is repeating itself and we have in such widely read "model" library building literature as *Bricks and Mortarboards* (Educational Facilities Laboratories, 1964) one of the great anomalies of the day, as far as library architecture is concerned. One illustration in this most excellent book points to the old Bibliotheque Nationale as the horrible pattern which started all our woes. Another illustration of a new college library shows the same architectural features, except that the stacks are free-standing

SOURCE: Reprinted from William H. Jesse, "New Library Buildings: Some Strengths and Weaknesses," *Library Journal*, vol. 89, December 1, 1964, pp. 4700–4704.

instead of self-supporting. The result is the same: we still have two ceiling heights. Modular planning has demonstrated time and again that this is not only unnecessary but undesirable. The modification of complete modular planning, or "humanizing" as it is sometimes called, actually is a step back to relative inflexibility, which in a small library, or even in a medium-sized one, is a functional disruption of some magnitude.

Frequently, people say they feel that a building should "open up" when they enter it, especially if it is a large building. A library does not need to "open up" at all. The interior should keep the patron's eyes and even his mind on the level of the books, which is the height to which attention should be called. There are exceptions, as in multipurpose buildings, but to say a building needs to open up because it is a large one is ridiculous. Most of our skyscrapers don't open up at all. You merely walk in and your perspective becomes adjusted to a floor level. I am no aesthete and certainly no architect, but when I walk into a very large building that makes a feeble stab of "opening up" with only the entranceway so treated, the thing that seems out of proportion is the impression I get of a two or more story height from a relatively small elevator and stair lobby. This kind of thing in a library can badly damage it functionally, especially if the stair halls become monumental in design and size. It is usually necessary to enclose these, at least with glass, for the noise factor keeps such a function as reference from being conducted satisfactorily on even the upper level. The monumental stairway is a compromise with the two-story height entrance lobby. Neither of these, however, is as bad as carrying the wastefully high ceiling throughout most, or in some cases all, of the entrance level to the library.

A tremendous factor for improvement in library buildings is the wide participation in its planning. Almost all librarians now have a major share in the planning, and so do others who are appropriate to a planning team. There is no question but that this cooperative approach to planning is resulting in much more functional buildings. In the 38 buildings I have worked on, I have found only two uncooperative architects. This average is probably higher than for librarians themselves. Administrative officers rarely take the reins and run off with the architect and the building too early in the planning period. There are, of course, exceptions and always will be.

The factor of expansion in new libraries varies tremendously. No "trend" can be detected, but as far as weakness and strength is concerned, there seem to be two extremes. Most college and university libraries are apparently completely conscious of the need for expansion. Growth space is provided and the building is constructed to take an actual rather than a merely theoretical addition. On the other hand, particularly in the field of school libraries, but also in many public and higher education libraries, the treatment of the library as a separate, completely finished building is widely prevalent.

Theoretically, the school library does not need to be expanded because the collection can be kept to a minimum by proper weeding; and the student body, it is assumed, will grow only to a certain size and then another school will be built. According to school librarians, however, this is not always the case. They find that their neatly conceived, well balanced little structure has to accommodate more students and books than the planners said it would. Colleges and universities have encountered this problem for so long that seldom does anyone go ahead and "complete" a building. It is the complete building, or what used to be called the "jewel of a building," which causes a lack of expansibility. Either the building itself cannot be added to functionally or the site has been treated in such fashion that expansion is undesirable from the total campus point of view. It is much better to locate a building on slightly less than an ideal site, if such a move is necessary to insure that the expanded building, rather than the first unit, is properly situated in its relationship to the campus.

Odd-shaped buildings can be quite attractive, especially from the outside, but for the most part they make expansion difficult, if not impossible. If the odd shape is in the form of several joint, roughly circular buildings forming a complex, all sorts of problems can arise. Some of these have already been stated in connection with the school library. In addition, and perhaps even worse, is the problem of each of the several preconceived units having to accommodate not the anticipated amount of materials and number of readers, but entirely different ones. This results in some of the individual units being much overused, some much underused. Such a structure makes successful planning more difficult because there are more variables.

There are undoubtedly places where oddshaped buildings are in order: the branch library in an already fully populated section of the town; many limited-enrollment, small private schools; and a college "house" library. Such libraries will probably serve an already complete community with a given number of patrons.

The architect must have the freedom to suit his building to the site, and although their methods vary, most architects today seem to keep in mind not only the total effect of the total mass but also what this will do to the interior of the building. One of the most encouraging things about today's university libraries is that the architects seem to be able to place a very large building in what once would have been considered too crowded a site. If this site is well suited to the library (and often it is the *only* one which is suited), then the educational gain for the institution is tremendous. An architect should also be encouraged (not that they usually need it) to decide what part the library building is going to play in the overall "statement" of the campus. If this results in a building that is odd-shaped, or too high, or too low to be functional, then the campus statement ought to take second place to the educational needs. On many campuses the library does much more than merely fit it, it has a lot to "say." This is also true of the public library. As a matter of fact, I have one AIA/ALA/NBC award winner (the Sequoyah Hills branch library in Knoxville—*see* Lj, Dec. 1, '61, pp. 4108–09) which not only improved, but actually *made* the area around it take on a highly attractive character.

For many libraries, a cantilevered type of construction is solving several vital problems. In a university library, the main floor is apt to be above the entrance level. Usually this main floor, which must house so many functions, materials, and people needs to be a very large one, which this type of construction permits. Sometimes the reasons for cantilevering are a crowded site or the desire to "suspend" a building to make it appear smaller and lighter in an area where architectural differences or closeness of other buildings will not permit a "typical" building to go. In very hot or cold climates and wherever it rains, a covered walkway is provided, perhaps all the way around the building. However few entrances might be employed, the user gets the impression that he is approaching an inviting and open building. This type of building has resulted in some of the better libraries which have been constructed recently.

MISUSE OF GLASS

Overuse and misuse of glass in library construction was, especially a few years ago, an alarming thing. It seems to have slowed down a bit, but since some of the architectural award buildings use so much glass, some people feared this might be taken as a recommendation. Generally, glass is not for libraries, just as too many windows are not for libraries, and largely for the same reasons. In many cases buildings were designed with an overhang which presumably would take care of any overuse, at least for the ground level. This turned out to be mostly theory. Solar screens are used with various degrees of success. They are expensive because in essence the building has two walls instead of one. Unless careful fenestration studies are made—and they should be required in such cases—large portions of the building may be almost unusable a great amount of the time.

Another disadvantage of using glass and large windows is that shelving the book collection becomes difficult. It should be possible to put either readers or books along the wall, but it is not possible when there are too many windows of the wrong kind and size and on the wrong side of the building. It would be dangerous to generalize, but my own impression from seeing many new buildings is that more careful attention is now being given to windows with better results than was formerly the case, but that the overuse and misuse of glass is almost counteracting this gain.

In general, library lighting is still unsatisfactory. There are a few exceptions, but good lighting is often accomplished at the cost of proper acoustical treatment of the building, so here again the loss is almost as great as the gain.

After a long period of being completely unsatisfactory, floor coverings are swinging back to a plus factor. Cork had been a fine floor covering for public areas, but ladies began wearing needle heels and suddenly floor installations which had been satisfactory for years were ruined. Many of the relatively soft vinyl asbestos tiles, if properly maintained, are working out very well, and carpeting is making a contribution of a most unexpected nature. In addition to having most of the good features of a library floor covering, carpeting also permits much greater freedom in providing proper light, for the simple reason that its sound-killing qualities preclude all or most of the acoustical treatment being done in the ceiling.

The present academic library permits furnishings in a fashion which give the reader a sense of privacy yet leaves him in a generally social situation. He is not out in a big reading room at a table with a half-dozen other students, nor is he locked off in a separate room. Increasingly, new buildings are so constructed as to multiply the opportunities to place the reader in an individual carrel or carrel cluster. This trend, in my opinion, is one of the better features of our new buildings.

CHECKING POINTS

More new buildings provide exit checks for the reader. This allows the book charging function to be deeper in the interior where it is more accessible to the public catalog and other necessary library functions. The exit check also relieves a great deal of the congestion formerly experienced when a patron leaving the library was held up by people charging books. I think that this is a great improvement because one of the worst features of our older buildings, especially the small and intermediate-sized ones, was this congestion of an exit which combined the functions of bookcharging and reader-checking points.

There are fewer large divisional-plan university libraries, and generally speaking I think this is a gain. There should still be some divisional-plan libraries, but the big "trend" has been stopped and few people are following it blindly as they were for many years.

The university undergraduate library facility is a new and good thing. Whether it is housed in the main building or in a separate building, it permits the undergraduates to be introduced to the large university research collection gradually. Many of these facilities are much more than an undergraduate "library." They are all sorts of things: study centers, total learning media centers, etc. But whatever they are called they seem to provide a good solution for many campuses. Like divisional planning and some other things, each university should question severely whether or not it should build one.

Vertical transportation in most of the new buildings is much improved. More thought goes into the number and placement of stairways; and where traffic justifies it, escalator installations are an excellent innovation. Elevators are no longer merely for the staff and disabled, but for everybody. There is no reason on earth why a library staff member or user should not have the advantage that is enjoyed in almost every other type of building he enters. The substitution of elevators for other types of book carriers is a good trend, though there are certainly some libraries which could use vertical book carriers.

One by one the "austerity" approaches to library planning are being eliminated, or at least reduced, according to the owner's budget. Anything should go in a new library which improves it, is justifiable budgetarily, and will do the job faster or easier than the thing it replaces. Whereas this once seemed to be a rather exceptional point of view, it is fairly widely encountered now. Luxury items, if the patron wants and can afford them, are being included without apology. In many cases where criticism has been heard, funds for luxury items were given by a donor who was not interested in anything other than adding something which would make the building more beautiful, more pleasing to see, to be in, and to work in. The monumental entrances or great, beautiful lobbies are not the best ways to spend the luxury dollar if it should become available. It has become increasingly easy to persuade donors to allow their gift money to be spent for more attractive and more comfortable furniture, more and better decoration, and art objects which enhance rather than damage the atmosphere being sought.

Another improvement along this same line is the use of color. Not that all libraries want or even should use it. In some buildings color has provided the brightness that was lacking. In very few instances have I seen buildings where the use of color in stacks, furniture, etc., damaged the whole appearance.

Most new libraries going up today are inviting, both outside and in. In addition to an attractive appearance, there is a further invitation to the reader to use particular materials and facilities through open shelving and the wise selection and arrangement of furnishings. In an effort to invite students to use books, some large university libraries arranged their books in such a manner as to make finding one's way about extremely difficult. This is being corrected by using a greater number of tables and especially carrels, which are not intermingled with stacks to the extent that was done—or overdone—a few years ago. Traffic patterns are much more generally studied than formerly, making the building much easier to use and causing less interruption to the other users. With the exception of the overuse of mezzanines (where there is a cubic-foot waste as well as a linear functional disruption), the space available is exploited much more fully.

ARCHITECTURAL ADVENTURE

If we librarians and library building consultants want architects and others to listen carefully to our ideas of what goes on in a building, we must in turn respect the other members of the planning team. Where the overall building is concerned, the architect must and does decide whether or not he should merely build a building in a given place to do a certain thing—or is there something else involved? Sometimes it is necessary for him to make a statement with the building itself. This statement is something strong enough to be called a declaration. A whole building which is a declaration is quite a gamble, but one which should be taken on occasion. Some of these strong statements are not going to come out well, but when one does, then you really have quite a library building. Some library building consultants feel that we are going back to a period of too much monumentality. I think I know what they mean but I would use a different word where a declaration is in order. Monumentality, to me, means a declaration merely for the declaration's sake. To such I am strongly opposed, but despite some rather startling experiences, I personally feel that more strong statements should be made and that there should be more adventuresomeness in library architecture than we have thus far had. The adventuresomeness may result in the solution to some very practical as well as aesthetic, problems.

ABOUT THE AUTHOR—William H. Jesse was a graduate of the University of Kentucky (A.B., 1933); Columbia (B.S., 1938); and Brown (M.A., 1945). He was Chief of the Reader's Division at Brown, Assistant Director of the University of Nebraska Libraries, Head of the Reader's and Reference Division of the U.S. Department of Agriculture Library, and from 1943 until his death in 1970, Director of Libraries and Professor of Bibliography at the University of Tennessee. A consultant on the construction of library buildings, Mr. Jesse contributed to various journals.

A Well-Wrought Interior Design

by Ellsworth Mason

Metcalf has written in Planning Academic and Research Library Buildings: *"Comfort, to oversimplify, might be said to require conditions that enable the occupant to forget about such matters as temperature, humidity, drafts, lighting, visual and auditory distraction and to go about his work oblivious to his physical surroundings." Mason tells us in the following article, "If a library feels good to be in, it will be used . . ." Both quotations point to the fact that the planners must do more than to define functions and put them in a box. Truly successful library buildings have fine interiors as well as fine exterior architecture. Unfortunately, as Mason notes further, ". . . if anything has to go by the board through pressure of the budget, it is the interior." The planners must bear the responsibility to insist on a building of total integrity: interior as well as exterior, comfort as well as beauty, functional as well as being within the budget.*

Furniture—which I construe in the Mediterranean sense of the word: French, *meubles;* Spanish, *mobilario;* Italian, *mobilia*—refers to those things in a building which can be moved. The *movables* or furniture in a library include all those objects which are not fastened to the floor and which cannot walk by themselves. These objects are of the greatest importance in establishing the feeling produced by the interior design—the carefully planned visual interrelationship between the objects in the building.

The interior design is the most important single element in any library dedicated to serving undergraduates. (Graduate and professional students are more highly motivated, and less addicted to the luxuries of feeling, for they take the vow of poverty, chastity, and obedience with their entrance exams.) If a library feels good to be in, it will be used even though the air conditioning freezes, the lighting dims, the bookstock dwindles, and the staff offends. Though the architect lead him through awkward labyrinths, yet will he follow if it feels good to be there.

If I am right in this contention, it is a national tragedy that most library interiors, as a witty friend of mine notes, "feel like yogurt." They have no interior design in the sense of objects brought together in a visual relationship. Most libraries are bland in color and flat or aggressively ugly in furniture design, the ill-feeling heirs to a

long tradition of interior ugliness in libraries. In one of his finest poems, "Under Ben Bulben," William Butler Yeats, analyzing his contemporary world, dismisses a whole generation with magnificent contempt as "baseborn products of base beds." He was referring to my generation, but I like to think that he would describe modern library interiors in similar words.

What has gone wrong, aside from the fact that good taste is one of the rarest gifts in human affairs? First of all, we are still locked, in a way, to the concept of the scholar of the middle ages, gathering blear-eyed wisdom under a dwindling candle, on a bare bench, stooped over a slanting board, in a monk's cell. We have come a little way since then, but embedded in many a school board's mind is the certainty that the harder the seat the less the temptation to relax, and sybaritic things like carpeting still produce shudders throughout the land. Consequently, if anything has to go by the board through pressure of budget, it is the interior.

I have reviewed the plans of a remarkably ambitious high school library in Illinois which promises to be exciting *if* its interior is successful, but the librarian indicated that they had thrown the interior to their purchasing agent, not wishing to spend money on the "fancy frills" an interior decorator would insist on. The purchasing agent is to good interior design as the real estate agent is

SOURCE: Reprinted from Ellsworth Mason, "A Well-Wrought Interior Design, *Library Journal*, vol. 92, February 15, 1967, pp. 743-747, by permission of the publisher and the author.

to orderly zoning. Ask him to buy furniture that is indestructible at the lowest possible price, and he does it well. Ask him to buy a good looking chair costing four dollars more than the monstrosity he has been foisting off on his school, and he quivers. And yet, most interiors are left to the mercies of the purchasing agent. In this direction, madness lies.

Having decided to save money on the interior, some schools still have sense enough not to trust the sensibilities of the purchasing agent; instead, they choose the second way guaranteed not to achieve a good interior—placing the advising of furniture combinations in the hands of a library supply house furniture expert. He will do a lot of work for you, be solicitous of your wishes, will give you his best advice, within the range of furniture made by his company; and it will cost you nothing, except the purchase of his furniture. Across the board, this is well-made furniture, and almost without exception, it is quite poorly designed. The best of the lot is still not good, and without well-designed furniture you cannot have a well-designed interior. That most libraries are dominated by library supply house furniture is the second reason why our interiors are so bad.

If we are, then, in Dante's dark wood, having missed the right path, how do we find our way out? We hire an interior designer, and make clear to the architect from the start that we intend to do so. If the architect's staff does not have an interior designer, and only the very large ones do, the task is to find an independent one, and there are very good ones available. Do not hire one accustomed to do houses; your designer must be a specialist in larger buildings. The architect will try to control the interior design if he can, on the assumption that a designer becomes automatically superior by virtue of being part of an architectural firm. This theory is false; some of them are not very good. Whether you hire a designer from within the architect's firm or from the outside, test him by carefully looking over at least two jobs he has designed before you sign a contract.

At least five important elements enter into the interior design of each unit in the library:

1. The character of the building—the feeling it achieves visually outside and inside, which should enclose an interior in harmony with it. No Louis XIV interiors in a building of modern design, to give a crass example. But more positively, the feeling of the interior design should reflect the building itself.

2. The function of the library unit. If it is a reference room, the feeling must be different, for a number of reasons, from that of a smoking lounge.

3. The dynamics of the unit's use, especially the typical movements of readers in the room. The predominant traffic patterns will dictate to a certain degree the feeling of the furniture to be placed in a given spot.

4. The needs of the readers in the unit—for smoking or nonsmoking, for standing, sitting, reading, talking, etc.—will dictate what objects must be included.

5. Finally, the most important of all, the relationship of every object to every other object in the room, and to the surrounding walls, ceilings, and floors, in terms of position, shape, color, and texture, in such a way that the whole produces a feeling of pleasantness appropriate to the circumstances of the room.

We are, you will note, if not actually in the realm of art, certainly approaching it, and requiring of the designer a wide range of artistic talents, plus a great deal of understanding of libraries, and a wide knowledge of the furniture market. In a well-wrought interior design, every single detail is heavily laden with thought, and it is impossible, for example, to change a chair used in large numbers without considering carefully the effect of the substitution on everything else it is related to in the building. It may take an entire afternoon to discuss the complexities of locating specially designed dictionary stands in a building and the effect of their location on the design.

To plan an interior with a designer will take about four or five months. The procedure involves gradually narrowing down, by the process of weeding out, the range of choices to those that, used together, will produce the kind of feeling that reflects the five governing considerations already noted. All of this process, of course, is worked out within the framework of utility—that is, we select the furniture that has been detailed, unit by unit, in the program. We select a desirably shaped and sized filing case not because we want an object that size in the room but because we need a filing case there. As the interior design develops, the quantities stated in the program will undoubtedly change. As the units begin to shape into living spaces, some furniture will probably be added for different reasons. But the library must be completely functional, as well as pleasant, so let's switch our consideration from the esthetics of interior design, not forgetting its paramount importance, to items of furniture.

FURNITURE FOR READERS

Numerically, there will be more chairs in a library than any other single item. They will, therefore, influence to a considerable degree the feeling of the entire building, and must be chosen with the greatest care. For side chairs, the choices involve wood frames or metal frames; wood backs and seats or plastic backs and seats; plastic upholstery or fabric upholstery, and just on the seat or on the back as well; with arms or without arms.

To a considerable extent, the choice will be restricted by the budget. Plastic chairs with metal legs are the cheapest, and are now sturdy and quite colorful. Wood chairs, especially in teak or walnut, and if fabric upholstered, are the most expensive. There is a place for more expensive side chairs—special collections rooms, for example—but in general, chairs should be selected to meet the requirements, visually and functionally, at the most reasonable price.

A variety of chairs is needed, partly because one chair will not feel comfortable to all readers, and partly to vary the feeling of the building in different areas. There should not be too much variety, however, or the feeling of the building itself will fragment into scattered units. Three different side chairs, of which two can be different versions of each other, will provide enough variety. It is often possible to get the same style chair with arms and without arms. Chairs with arms cost a little more, but they are popular with readers. If arm chairs are used at tables, be sure that the arms slide easily under the type of table used, even after the table has sunk a little into the carpeting.

I plead for some arm chairs at tables, and also for upholstery at least on the seats to ease those long hours that so compact even well-padded flesh. Naugahyde, or similar plastic materials, make colorful seat covers. They tend to sweat, i.e., condense evaporation from the body, in hot weather, as do plastic seats of the shell kind, but both wear like iron. Fabric materials provide a much wider range of color and texture in seats, but wear out faster. If plastic fabrics such as nylon weave are used, make sure that the weave is tight, for loose weaves are picked at by readers with pencils, and by their nature they wear out faster than tight weaves. Nylon threads have a tendency to absorb dirt through their open ends, and it cannot be

removed. Therefore, when using some of the more brilliant colors, such as bright yellow, make sure that a constant maintenance program is provided for them. If they are allowed to get dirty at all, they will become impossible to clean. Bright fabrics of a solid color can be kept looking immaculate if they are gone over lightly about once a week, with a little cleaning fluid tinted with a dye the identical color of the fabric. All fabrics should be Scotch-guarded, a word describing a process of spraying the fabric to make it easier to keep clean.

This brings up the maintenance problem for furnishings as a whole. Obviously, if you have a poor or ill-informed maintenance program, the interior of your library will rapidly deteriorate, and within a year look seedy. The plant department should be alerted to the need for learning how, and on what regular schedule, they should maintain the different furniture items in the new library. The librarian should collect data about maintenance needs of the furniture and present it to the plant department. Of course, furniture that is extremely difficult to maintain should not be bought, but on the other hand, maintenance should not be the governing factor in selecting furnishings. If it is well-designed, it is very much worth extra maintenance, and the college should be sold this idea.

All chairs should be equipped with glides that suit the surface on which they rest; they will be different for carpeting and tile. All chairs must be sturdily built to absorb the violent energy that young students discharge so casually. In lesser used areas, such as staff lounges or library offices, sturdiness is of much less importance in choosing the furniture.

A hard-nosed purchasing agent can be most helpful in testing the construction of a chair, and of course he will demand a sample of every item of furniture before signing a contract for their purchase, and preferably before the selection for the interior design is final. It is quite impossible to tell what a chair really looks or feels like from even a good photograph; it must be seen in the flesh, and it is startling how different it will look from the photograph which may have led the buyer to it.

Lounge chairs should be used in general library areas only near materials that invite their use, such as periodicals, newspapers, fiction, poetry, etc. They will also be used, but not exclusively, in smoking lounges, and other relaxation areas. They present no problems different from those involved in choosing side chairs, except in smoking areas, where the question is whether they are to be used at all, and if so, what kind of upholstery will resist cigarette burns. No upholstery will resist cigarette burns, except perhaps lead sheathing. Wool and plastics burn and melt, and whatever is used will have holes burned in it soon, including the carpeting. Shall you, therefore, use it? Is not stark wood good enough for such slovenly habits? Morally, I suppose it is, but I nevertheless recommend the use of both carpeting and colorful fabric upholstery in smoking lounges, without worrying about the fact that they will surely be burned. Students must be lured away from sneaking cigarettes in the stacks, which they tend to do, and the tradition must be established as soon as the building opens that smoking lounges are the places to let down hair and let off tensions. A pleasant room will set such a tone. Don't worry about maintaining the burn spots until they become numerous. A well-designed room can absorb many holes and still look good.

Other seating will include sofas, stools, and stacking chairs. Sofas present the problem of choosing between seating for two and seating for three or more. Two-seaters may be usurped by one reader, while three-seaters may accommodate two, one at each end. The longer sofas invite sleeping, belly-sprawling, or more heterosexual activities, depending on the occupancy of the room. Rarely will sofas be seated to capacity, so they should be used sparingly. Backless stools are useful in areas where readers are not invited to linger—low ones at periodical index tables and high ones at card catalog tables. Hard seats are recommended. A few low stools in front of a mirror in the women's rest rooms will be much appreciated. Low stools scattered throughout open stacks will be much used. Stacking chairs should be used only where they must be removed periodically; there is no point in using them as permanent chairs anywhere.

TABLES

I grew up in a reserve room that had long tables for about 30 students, with a center rail running down the entire length. How I remember those tortured hours during which one student in that 30 tapped the center rail steadily with his foot, but which one I knew not. For such reasons, we have abandoned multiple seaters, and there is a steady move in the direction of single-seaters in libraries, as well as in plumbing. Single carrels threaten to

take over the world. On these I will comment later, but I plead here for some multiple seating, and in fact, for as much variety in the grouping of seating as possible.

Tables for four and even a few tables for six have their place in a library. The larger tables should be used in reference rooms, map rooms, and other spread areas that are not likely to be crowded with readers. Tables for four should be mixed throughout all reading areas and especially where many books are shelved. It can never be predicted when the reader will find on the shelves not the one book he is seeking, but eight more that he wants to gather and spread over a large area. Sometimes the reader wants to sit for a while at an area that feels more luxurious than the $2' \times 3'$ space provided by single seating.

On the other hand, seating for more than six should not be used. Since I do not envision six people sitting together at these tables often (though they may sometime), I am willing to accept $3' \times 8'$ tables with three chairs on each side for such seating. This is less than the $2' \times 3'$ space for each reader at multiple-seating tables that is clung to like Mother by some librarians, and they should choose larger tables; but after carefully observing, for the past three years, the acceptance of $3' \times 8'$ tables for six in my current periodicals reading room, I am convinced that they have their use in libraries, in limited quantities, located for variety in areas where the spreading of library materials is likely to occur. In group study rooms, where students want to be close rather than separated from each other, $3' \times 6'$ tables with two chairs on each side and one at each end are more than adequate for six. Needless to say, if two tables for four are placed touching each other, they form in effect a table for eight, and this should be avoided by allowing at least two feet between tables juxtaposed laterally. In its new central library, Yeshiva University is considering using tables that are $3'$ wide, to accomodate four and six with readers seated on one side only. I have not seen tables like this in use, but the idea seems attractive.

Tables as long as $8'$ pose problems of construction, if they are made of wood. It is possible to carry this length in a heavy bar metal frame without difficulty, but to support it with wood requires either a fifth central leg, which makes the table more difficult to move, or central bracing. Reading tables should never have a deep apron to knock knees or chairs against; and table legs should be at the corners, to avoid reader straddle. All tables should be equipped with adjustable glides to suit the surface on which they will rest, *and* the glides should be adjusted after the tables are properly placed.

Since table surfaces are the largest horizontal reflecting surfaces in the building other than the floor, it is extremely important for good lighting that they be light-colored. Of course, this goes directly against the wishes of many architects to make them of wood, fine grains being available only in dark tone wood. It is possible to have an elegant table made with wooden legs and frame, and a Formica or similar plastic-covered top edged with a thin strip of wood. (It should be noted here that the idea is quite false that custom-built furniture of good construction and design is expensive in comparison to the cost of good quality stock furniture. In units of two, it is somewhat more expensive; in units of 50, it is about the same price; in larger units, it is likely to be cheaper. The prices on each item of the custom built furniture—about half of the total—in the new Hofstra library were the most reasonable in the entire furniture bid.)

If Formica is used on the table top, the bottom side as well as the top should be covered to prevent warping; some furniture designers do not seem to know this. The Formica should be light-colored to help produce the kind of good quality lighting discussed in the second article of this series (*LJ*, January 15, p. 201-6). If it is of satin finish, it will have a high gloss which produces bad glare; therefore, it should be of suede or matte finish, which does not glare and helps diffuse the light. In smoking areas, Formica has the added advantage of resisting cigarette burns.

The question arises as to whether light Formica tops invite penmanship and other forms of deface-ment. At the Colorado College library, all tables and carrels have a putty-grey suede Formica top, which under fluorescent light looked white. The students at that college live in a highly permissive atmosphere and are self-indulgent in many ways. They abuse furniture in other buildings. I recently checked with the plant director about his experi-ence with these tops after the library had been in service four years. He reported that, although there was occasional writing on the surfaces with ball-point pens, it was easily removable by light treatment with Bon Ami. The custodian who takes care of the building stated that if the choice were left to him, he would choose this kind of sur-facing. From such a source, there can be no higher recommendation.

Coffee-type tables should be used in lounge areas. In small conference rooms, such as we have in the new Hofstra University library, for reference librarians to use in working with students, a 2' × 3' table is suitable. At the card catalog, stand-up tables should be used for consulting drawers of catalog cards; the tables should be 3' wide to be graceful. A similar standup table can be used in reference areas to hold multiple large dictionaries. In the staff lounge, if stacking tables for four are used, this area can be easily cleared to provide re-ception space. None of these tables pose special problems other than selecting a suitable design.

CARRELS

A carrel is a single table with a baffle at the far end at least 19 inches high. Its writing surface should not be smaller than 2' × 3' clear dimen-sions if it is rectangular. A bookshelf on the baffle is useful, and side baffles extending at least eight inches beyond the front table edge will provide the ultimate in privacy short of an enclosed booth. Carrels can be larger and much more complex. In some schools, they include coat lockers, book lockers, television receivers, jacks for ear-phones, tape players, and typing-height wings; in short, a kind of work-area for every conceivable educa-tional activity that the student can engage in alone. This more complex kind of carrel, to date, has turned out to be pretty bad looking, and it is still in the process of jelling, as the field of multi-media instruction comes gradually into focus at the uni-versity level. Just what it will turn out to be I can-not predict; but I can state that the carrel as a seating unit will come to dominate college and university libraries.

I am not entirely happy about this. I am fond of carrels; I grew up on the old graduate stack carrel in the Yale library. For the Colorado Col-lege library, we developed one of the best looking carrels I have seen, and for the new Hofstra library, we have developed a handsome quarter-octagonal carrel that has a wonderfully inviting feeling, and nests in twos and fours in a most pleasing way. Nevertheless, I am convinced that the needs of different students, or of the same student at differ-ent times and for different purposes, are so varied that the reading furniture should be quite varied in a library. It does not make sense to talk about individual study, which implies that student needs are different, and then force everyone into identi-cal seating units, as is done in some libraries. At the Colorado College, we alternated baffled carrels with similar $2' \times 3'$ open tables, and found that the students used each kind about equally. About one-half of the seating should be provided in single carrels, the rest in twos, fours, and a few sixes, and some lounge seating.

OFFICE FURNITURE

I will not use space to cover office furniture, since manufacturers who respond to the needs of the office world have produced a number of well-designed lines of reasonably priced furniture, in contrast to the manufacturers who respond to the needs of librarians. Working with a good interior designer, it is comparatively easy to select attractive desks, swivel chairs, filing cases, and similar office furniture with the single exception of typing stands. It is preferable to provide typing wings on desks for fixed typing stations, but in libraries, it is often necessary to have a stand that can be wheeled around for typing. It may be necessary to have one specially designed. There are good examples at Colorado College and at Hofstra University.

SPECIALIZED FURNISHINGS

Charging Desks. Besides being the most utilitarian pieces of furniture in the building, charging desks will also, if of any size, greatly influence the feeling of the area in which they are located. Therefore, as much care should be taken with their looks as with their function. There are two or three library supply houses that can provide reasonably good-looking charging desks, unitized if desired. It is not greatly important that they be in units unless more than one desk height is required. If it is at all possible, this massive piece of furniture should be custom designed by the interior designer.

Card Catalog Cases. All of the locally designed cases I have seen in recent years have had difficulty with sticking drawers. The level of cabinet-making necessary to produce good card catalog drawers you can be sure of finding only in the reputable library supply houses. I make a distinction between the drawer units and the completed catalog cases, which include the surrounding cabinet. Only a few library supply houses can provide complete cases that are reasonably good looking, and it may be advisable to have the cabinet enclosure designed.

Periodical Index Tables. These tables should be double-sided and double-headed. None of the standard periodical index tables I have seen are completely satisfactory in appearance, and to get a really good looking one, it will probably be necessary to have one designed. The best one I know of is, again, at Colorado College.

Microfilm Reading Tables. The only satisfactory ones I have seen are at Washington University Library in St. Louis. We are developing a similar one for the new Hofstra library. It is $2' \times 4'$, with the table top divided into three panels. The center panel is fixed, and either the left or right panel pulls out a foot and a half to form a writing surface located in the right place. The other two panels form the surface to support the reading machine. Light is provided by individual Tensor lamps.

Booktrucks. Don't think that booktrucks are unimportant in establishing the feeling of the building as they will be located all around the library. Therefore, make sure that a good looking one is selected. The larger and the smaller size trucks tend to be unesthetic; but there are some good looking ones in the medium size range. Choose yours carefully.

I will say nothing about stacks, although they have a great effect on the feeling of a library, because they are a world to themselves, and it would take another article to do them justice. I am also leaving out such peripheral but important items as mirrors, ashtrays, pencil-sharpeners, bulletin boards, signs, and the like, but they *must* be taken into consideration in planning the interior design. Nothing short of the most painstaking, thoughtful, time-consuming, repeatedly revised, empirically tested planning of every single item to be included in the library can produce the kind of interior design that is necessary for and worthy of a library. Although a crucially important part of the total planning, the interior is usually shunted aside or jerry-built on a spatch-cocked basis. To achieve a truly outstanding interior is one of the most worthy goals of the library planner, and it will lend distinction to his building more easily than any other single factor.

ABOUT THE AUTHOR–(See biographical note on page 116.)

Two Aspects of Readers' Services Areas: Recommendations to Library Planners

by Robert M. Pierson

This article is not by a building specialist but rather by one who has experienced building handicaps in serving the library user effectively and efficiently. Though greatly to be desired, it is difficult to attain much of what is requested of planning in Mr. Pierson's article. While perfection in any endeavor is elusive, still we all strive toward it. This article does indeed contain substantive recommendations to library planners.

In many library buildings, utility—the achievement of some practical goal—is the primary consideration rather than the stimulation of amusement, awe, or some other complex of feeling and attitude; and it is lucidity rather than mystery which is thus chiefly to be valued, even if it can be achieved only at the expense of charm. Unless a library building is to be used only by the fully initiated, pains should be taken, in planning it, to achieve utmost clarity so that the least experienced patron may be informed at every step in his progress, not only in respect to where he is, but also to where he is going. Signs, exhibits, and guidebooks help; a large reference staff is even better; best of all (but too seldom achieved) is the kind of library planning which enables the building itself—through barriers, vistas, contrasts, repetitions, and the like—to help keep the patron informed.

In getting down to cases—in imagining precisely how built-in information service, so to speak, might function—I have found myself constantly touching upon a second problem in planning readers' services areas: supervision (by which I mean whatever the librarian does to control and facilitate the activities of patrons while on duty, while "at the desk," as opposed to what he does while absent from the public areas). Architectural features which make for clarity *may* make for ease of supervision; but the latter success is by no means an automatic by-product of the former. It is possible to design entrances, service centers, reading rooms, stacks, and other areas which are clearly laid out but which are unmanageable.

The extent to which the following suggestions regarding these two problems can be applied will vary from library to library. Exceptional situations are to be found. A building recently visited seemed altogether too mysterious: the patron wishing to renew a book had to cross a large lobby, enter a second lobby, climb a flight of stairs invisible from the first lobby, cross a hall, enter a large catalog and bibliography area, cross it, and enter a "circulation room," the door to which is not visible from the head of the stairs. A second building which I visited seemed to be laid out just as impractically. On the first floor were service desks facing a lobby. This was good but otherwise the building—several floors of cozily integrated stack and study areas—was utterly unsupervised. Yet at both libraries, staff members assured me that their arrangements cause no difficulties.

EASE IN FINDING AND ACCESS

The library should be easy to find. Public libraries should stand where patrons will pass; college libraries should dominate campuses; libraries within multi-function buildings need not spill into main lobbies, but neither should they be hidden away. But easy to find is not enough; easy to identify is also important: the library should suggest a library—or at least nothing else: not a church, not a prison, nor a court house, not even a country club. One common way to label a li-

SOURCE: Reprinted from Robert M. Pierson, "Two Aspects of Reader's Services Areas: Recommendations to Library Planners," *College and Research Libraries,* September, 1962, pp. 398-401 and 404, by permission of the publisher.

brary is to plan it so that books and readers are visible from without. Another way is to be frank about its structure. I am impressed by the number of university libraries whose facades suggest nothing in particular. But go around to their backs—ah, the stacks, like nothing else in academic architecture: multi-windowed blocks obviously featuring seven- or eight-foot ceilings, with glimpses of books within: structures as true to themselves as are greenhouses.

The library should be easy to reach. A driveway that takes one past the front door so that one may pick up and deliver passengers and books and even, at least momentarily, park, is not a pointless luxury—certainly not in a shopping area and not even on a college campus. Hilly campuses should reserve their summits for observatories, presidential mansions, war memorials, and other incidentals; getting to the library should not necessitate a long climb, however impressive the edifice eventually reached.

Glass doors dispel mystery, as does a place in which to pause to get one's bearings, and as do clear indications that one is in the right place. In even a large building it should be possible for the incoming patron to see (1) a person, obviously a staff member, who is ready to help him, (2) a counter (not a charming desk more suited to a parlor) or other piece of equipment at or through which books may be returned, (3) a catalog or evidence as to where one is, (4) a place to sit and read, and (5) books. If the library is so arranged that the main service floor is not the floor at which the patron enters, care must be taken that the lobby (1) is so designed as to direct, even impel him to the service area (lest he wander down blind alleys into classrooms, staff lounges, etc.) and (2) is staffed with a person competent to direct him or is furnished with a readable directory and has space for exhibits that proclaim the character of the institution in unmistakable terms, i.e., exhibits that tell about the library and its collections and services—not about the Boy Scouts, the Red Cross, the garden club, the school band, and the like.

For various reasons, it may not be possible for the incoming patron to behold the collection, i.e., the main collection, as opposed to reference books, rentals, new books, and other items more or less on exhibit. Such is generally the case in sizable buildings with separate stack areas. Two things will help: (1) a librarian stationed conspicuously and (2) a conspicuous stack entrance. Reading areas should be visible or at least clearly

indicated and should be adjacent to or within the stack area but not, I should think, between the incoming patron and the stack area. Ideally, too, the stack area should be clearly accessible from whatever point in the building from which the patron may need to approach it. Once within the stack area, no matter where he came in, the patron should be able to determine easily: (1) how the sequence of shelving runs, (2) where tables and chairs are, and (3) where to go when he is ready to leave. What is needed is a simple rectangle (no aisles to cross) with aisles on all four sides, with ranges open at both ends, with study tables along one or more of the surrounding aisles, and with conspicuous stairs and exits. If there is a stack assistant, it should be obvious where he is normally to be found. Some sort of fenestration should be provided, if only because there are few rooms more mysterious than a cave-like stack room when the power fails.

If the library contains several reading rooms, these should, if possible, be placed according to some simple and repeated pattern, so that the patron may learn, for example, that reading rooms are at the east and west ends of each floor. Within rooms, a similar uniformity will aid the reader, e.g., files always to the right, service desk always opposite the door. Incidentally, the fact that every part of a room is visible from the entrance will not only simplify supervision, but will also enable a patron to spot a librarian who has momentarily left his post to go to a remote part of the room. The location of the service desk in relation to the door is also important: it should intercept but not block the patron's progress, if such a distinction may be made; i.e., it should either be at the end of a brief vista or just a third of the way across the patron's view, so that although he may easily pass it by, he cannot very well ignore it.

And so on throughout. Color variations will provide a clue to which of several virtually identical areas one is in. Counters that look like counters will tell the patron where public areas leave off and staff areas begin. The route to take to get to the librarian's office, the catalog room, and other areas occasionally visited by the public should be easy to follow. Continuous shelving in reading rooms does not cause the confusion inherent in a series of detached ranges set on various planes. Furniture which avoids the hotel lounge look will, to younger patrons in particular, communicate the fact that a library is not a recreation center. Smoking rooms, typing rooms, and rest rooms need not display themselves to passersby; but from "serious readers" who have penetrated the outer barriers such conveniences should certainly not be concealed.

EASE OF SUPERVISION

We have noted some ways in which clarity may be achieved. In considering our second problem, ease of supervision, it will be helpful to think of it under four headings: visibility; accessibility; maintenance of silence in areas where silence is needed; and economy of personnel. Visibility is an obvious aid to supervision. Although we blanch at the thought of installing a system of mirrors such as chills the air of many a ten-cent store, we can imagine a situation, in at least one respect ideal, in which the deskbound librarian can see every inch of the public area (this suggests a large fan, with shelves on the periphery and, conceivably, along the spokes—the librarian sufficiently raised that he can see over nearby patrons and penetrate, like Big Brother, the heights and depths). For various reasons, this too Orwellian effect some may not wish to adopt; but the principle need not be altogether discarded. Four practical suggestions for increasing visibility are:

1. Long narrow items, like catalogs, banks of vertical files, and ranges of shelving, should be placed either flat against walls opposite service desks or endwise; if they stand crosswise there will be hidden areas behind them.
2. Exits from building—or from areas where control must be maintained—should require patrons to pass service desks.
3. Subsidiary service desks, e.g., those in special reading rooms, should be so placed that librarians can see into adjacent halls.
4. Reading areas should include a minimum of remote alcoves, secluded mezzanines, and the like (my impression being that library planners sometimes adopt a too idealized view of human nature or have an undue admiration for informal effects).

When I speak of accessibility I have in mind not how far the librarian must walk but rather how far and how fast he must run if he is to watch the door, stay near the phone, greet the public, help at the index table, prepare bibliographies, inspect stacks, encourage research, discourage romance, etc., etc.,—in other words, function as the one

person on duty in a library (or in a reading room therein) must ordinarily function.

In planning details of readers' services areas, various points should be kept in mind—if the librarian is to have access to what he needs to have access to. Stack entrances, even if uncontrolled, should be adjacent to service counters. Counters should be so constructed that one may emerge from behind them readily, without having to cut back through work areas, around pillars, etc. If books and briefcases are to be inspected, some means must be found of forcing patrons to come all the way up to counters rather than stroll by out of reach. Most important, main entrances, charging desks, catalogs, index and bibliography areas, vertical files, reading areas, and shelf areas should all be as accessible as possible to reference librarians—whose role, when fully realized, is to give service at all these points, not just at two or three.

CONTROLLING NOISE

How can library planning help control noise? Obviously, through well-designed floors, walls, and ceilings. Some other ways are as follows:

1. By so placing auditoriums, classrooms, and the like that traffic in and out of them does not enter library service areas.
2. By arranging the various areas so that the least frequented will be the most remote.
3. By avoiding traffic lanes that cross reading areas.
4. By erecting banks of rooms—offices, restrooms, stairs, elevators, seminar rooms, and the like—between quiet and noisy areas.
5. By separating reference (i.e., inquiry) areas from study areas.

This last suggestion is, I gather, somewhat iconoclastic. I agree that reference and study areas should be adjacent, so that the transition from "look it up" to "read about it" and its converse may be easily achieved; but it should not be necessary always to answer *sotto voce*, nor always to try to answer Patron A's question while considering how best to discourage the conversation of Patrons B and C.

Economy of personnel is a consideration of particular importance in library planning. My study of library plans suggests to me that buildings are sometimes designed with expectations of considerable increases in staff. Years may pass before such expectations are fulfilled. In many libraries, especially those with considerable subdivision, the minimal staff for minimal service is enormously large in proportion to the number of people employed by the library or the number of patrons likely to be in the building at certain times. "Here I sit, chaperoning five couples, when I could be helping out at the catalog downstairs" is a typical comment; one difficulty is that one never knows at what point the couples may need bibliographical assistance. A sign saying, in effect, "No one on duty here; go to the Circulation Desk for help" is not an ideal solution; nor is closing the area; nor is placing an incompetent person at the desk. Some better solutions are these:

1. Placing the reference desk and the circulation desk next to each other so that one person can man both.
2. Placing the reference desk so that the same person can assist with indexes, supervise the catalog, and direct incoming patrons.
3. Placing two reading rooms with their service desks contiguous or continuous, so that one person can supervise both rooms.
4. Relating service desks and offices so that a person working in an office is readily visible to the patron at the desk and so that patrons, whether incoming or seated, are visible from the office.
5. Avoiding unnecessary duplications of such control points as building exits.

Careful planning can thus smooth the patron's path and can assist the librarian in guiding the patron and in maintaining an appropriate atmosphere. In other words, careful planning can facilitate reference service. In the foregoing recommendations (recommendations which, if not particularly novel, bear repetition) a point of view regarding reference service is implicit which has been expressed before but acceptance of which is not always implicit in library plans. Reference service should be pervasive. Library activities can scarcely survive inadequate acquisition, catalog, and circulation service; but they can—and do—survive inadequate reference service. Why is reference service so often inadequate? Because for one thing, it is, unlike Mount Everest, so often simply not *there.* In too many libraries, reference service is available in the sense that it is on call (if you know how to call it) but is not present at various points, e.g., front doors, catalogs, stack entrances, where it is needed. One solution is to station nonprofessional help at such points and to train it to call on professional help when uncertain how to answer inquiries: surely a rather roundabout approach—and hardly foolproof, as so often it is just the thing one is least correct about that he is most certain about. A second solution is to hire more professional librarians, but this may result in a waste of professional skill (as one sits and waits for people to wait on); and, in any case, who has that much money? Still another solution is the one offered in this paper: to plan buildings so as to make arrangements of rooms, services, and collections easy to apprehend and so as to enable reference service, however small the reference staffs, to be as nearly as possible ubiquitous.

ABOUT THE AUTHOR—Robert M. Pierson received his B.A. degree in 1946 from DePauw University, his M.A. degree in 1949 and his PhD in 1951 from Duke University, and his M.S. in L.S. from Catholic University in 1955. After teaching at Ohio State University and later at the University of Maryland where he has also held several library positions, Mr. Pierson is currently Assistant Director for Administration at the University of Maryland Libraries.

Traffic Patterns

by Keyes D. Metcalf

Supervision and control are both major matters of concern in library planning. Communication, both directly and by remote means must be considered. In multi-story buildings the relative costs and effectiveness of vertical transportation means must be weighed. The noise and distractions of traffic must be limited as much as possible. All must be carefully developed in the planning stages of the building. In his major publication, Planning Academic and Research Library Buildings, *Mr. Metcalf, in quoting Stephen A. McCarthy concerning the new research library at Cornell University, notes that "the disposition of many of the facilities in the building flows naturally from the traffic patterns." It might be added that this was not an accident.*

Library buildings are designed to be used, and use obviously implies traffic. One of the essential characteristics of a functional building is accessibility with a minimum of effort and minimum of disturbance. If planning is to produce satisfactory traffic patterns, it must take into account problems of supervision and control of the building and its exits, facilities for communication and vertical transportation, and means of minimizing noise and other distractions. Spatial relationships are also involved, but these cannot be considered in this article.

SUPERVISION AND CONTROL

Most librarians would rather help than supervise those who use their buildings; they have no desire to act as police officers, and are eager to make controls as inconspicuous as possible if they cannot be eliminated. It is good to be able to add that less supervision is required now than was thought to be necessary a generation ago. Today's students, both graduates and undergraduates, seem to be more serious than their predecessors and come to the library to study rather than for social purposes. Better acoustic materials have reduced the disturbance that results from whispering and talking. Many libraries now admit students to the stacks, where close supervision is almost impossible; consequently it is hard to justify intensive supervision of reading rooms. At least three out of four students prefer individual seating, and seating of this kind, which is being provided more and more generously, discourages conversation in reading areas and hence reduces the need for supervision. Better traffic patterns and seating layouts which reduce noise and confusion help to create an atmosphere conducive to orderly behavior. Finally, there is a growing realization that the most economical and, in many ways, the most satisfactory location for supervision and control is at a building's exit or exits.

It should be emphasized that no one advocates control, even at exits, if it can be eliminated without serious consequences. Unfortunately, as students grow increasingly serious and need less supervision within the building, they seem to be tempted more and more to appropriate library materials extralegally; the problem is particularly serious in the case of reserved books. Attendants at the exits can not search everyone who leaves the building; books can be concealed in clothing, particularly during the winter. Experience indicates, however, that, if it is known that unauthorized borrowing is a serious offense punishable by dismissal or suspension, inspection at the exits can be more effective than the traditional method of reading-room supervision. Most new buildings provide either for control at the exits or for no control at all.

Control at the exits is no safeguard against theft

SOURCE: Reprinted from Keyes D. Metcalf, "Traffic Patterns," *College and Research Libraries*, vol. 24, January, 1963, pp. 19–30, by permission of the publisher.

of rare books by professional thieves; the only satisfactory procedure is to keep very valuable materials in closed stacks, supervise their use by persons who have signed for them, and check them in immediately on their return, before the reader leaves, in order to make sure that they have not been mutilated. Exit controls can be expected, however, to prevent unauthorized borrowing by absent-minded students and professors and to deter deliberate theft because, if an individual must conceal a book to get it past the controls, he can hardly pretend to himself or, if apprehended, to others that he has taken it thoughtlessly, rather than deliberately.

It may be suggested also that though controls may not seem necessary at the time a building is planned, conditions may change. It is desirable, therefore, to plan the building so that exit controls can be provided at some later date without expensive alterations and without ruining the appearance of lobbies.

Various methods of exit control are possible. Turnstiles were used for some years in the Widener library at Harvard and have been used at the New York Public Library for a long period. It should be noted that persons entering a building may also be required to pass through turnstiles, as at Princeton's Firestone library. Either electric eyes or turnstiles can be used to count those who enter, though neither can be relied upon for a completely accurate count.

Chains or railings of some kind can be used to channel readers through a narrow lane past a desk. At the Lamont library as many as four exit lanes can be opened at one time in the main entrance, and two in the secondary entrance, but only half of these have proved to be necessary in order to handle the traffic without forcing students to line up.

A third method, which has been used in the Widener library since the unattractive turnstiles were removed, is to leave a passage more than six feet wide with a counter on the right-hand side behind which an attendant sits on a high stool. This has proved to be reasonably satisfactory at Widener, where much of the use is by professors and graduate students. In an undergraduate library, where there is very heavy traffic just before each class period begins, narrow passages seem to be preferable.

Control counters may also serve as information desks where the stranger can obtain directions, which are often needed in any large library. Counters rather than desks are suggested, because

it is not convenient for readers to show books on a low surface; a height of forty-two or even forty-three inches is preferable to thirty-nine, and the increased height makes possible a reduction in width. For use when he is not standing, the attendant should be provided with a high stool having a back and a footrest or a platform in the kneehole of the counter. It should be possible for the attendant to reach the outside door quickly if necessary, but it is preferable that this feature be inconspicuous.

In some cases it is possible to install a long control desk at the exit that serves also as the main circulation desk and even as the desk for service of books on closed reserve. If this is possible there are significant advantages. The noise and confusion that circulation services always entail is confined to the entrance lobby; the number of staff members who must be on duty during quiet periods is reduced, which may be an important financial consideration; and the reader may avoid having his books checked twice, once when he signs for them and again when he leaves the building.

Nothing has been said thus far of how many entrances and exits may be needed. Most libraries, of course, must have a separate shipping and receiving entrance, which may be available for use by members of the staff. Each public entrance and exit is expensive; attendants must be paid and floor space must be provided in the building plans. Moreover, the whole traffic problem within the building can be simplified if there is a single entrance and exit. In a large library, however, traffic is often so heavy and distances so great that a second entrance and exit is essential. Fire laws may require it; if they do not, emergency exits with crash locks should be available.

Control of each additional exit may require payment of two or three additional salaries in a library that is open for seventy-five to one hundred or more hours per week. Moreover, a secondary exit will normally be used considerably less than the main one, and may not be a suitable place for circulation or reserved-book services. There may be a problem in keeping the attendant profitably occupied. In the Lamont library at Harvard a portion of the reserved-book collection is kept behind the desk at the secondary entrance, which is on a different floor level from the main entrance. Those using the bottom level of the building need not climb an additional seventeen feet if they come in at the side entrance, and division of the traffic load is desirable. It can be noted also that traffic is so heavy that two checking-out posts would be needed most of the time at the main entrance if it were the only one.

In the Widener library also the second entrance is on a different level from the front door, and controls a secondary entrance to the book stack, which is a great convenience in a ten-level stack. Fire regulations require that two exits be provided in each building at all times when it is open; elsewhere, however, there are equally large buildings operating under regulations that call for emergency exits only. These can be controlled by glass that must be broken to open the door. An exit of this sort at Princeton has been the victim of unauthorized use only once in fifteen years.

Glass can be broken, of course, and a thief or errant student can escape unless there is an effective alarm system. If the exit door is at the end of a fairly long corridor, an alarm may sound at the other end of this corridor, at the nearest service desk, and perhaps in the janitor's quarters. If the library is near a main gate to the campus where an attendant is on duty at all times, an alarm may ring in his station.

A discussion of problems of control and supervision would be incomplete if it did not mention the difficulties that sometimes occur when there are outdoor reading terraces. These can be attractive and some architects delight in them, but their disadvantages ought not to be overlooked. Books can be dropped from them to a waiting confederate or to the ground if a secluded spot is available. Dust and air pollution may make them unsatisfactory places to read and, in most sections of the country, the number of dry and warm days when they can be used is discouragingly small.

Entrances and exits are where traffic patterns begin and end. The decisions that are made regarding them also affect the security of the library's collections and its operating costs. It is important, therefore, that entrance lobbies be designed with a view to installation of control desks in the future if not at once, with space for rush-hour traffic and provision for channeling those who are leaving past a desk.

COMMUNICATION AND VERTICAL TRANSPORTATION

Unless a library is very small, mechanical devices for communication will probably be needed. Unless the whole library is on a single level books and people will have to move from one floor to another. To consider communication and vertical transportation is to consider stairs, ramps, booklifts, conveyor belts, escalators, elevators, telephones, public-address systems, telautographs, and teletypes. The uses of these varied devices will be discussed as a means of helping the librarian to decide what is needed and of indicating something of library requirements to architects and engineers.

The number of stairways that is desirable will depend, of course, on the amount of traffic, the size of floor levels, and, to some extent, the total square-footage of the building; local building regulations and fire codes may also impose specific requirements. They often state that no place in a building shall be more than a certain number of feet—sometimes the figure is one hundred—from a stairway providing direct access to an exit from the building. The codes often permit only one open stairway—i.e., only one outside a fireproof enclosure with closed doors at each level. They may also permit the open stairway to connect only two levels; in this case it may be open from the first to the second floor, but if the same stairway continues down to a basement or up to a third floor, it must be enclosed at these levels.

Some buildings do not come under code restrictions, either because there is no applicable state law or local regulation or because the institution is exempted; sometimes a limited exemption can be obtained if sprinkler systems are installed. Fire risks will not be discussed here, but it should be emphasized that no building should be planned without checking the codes and regulations to which it must conform.

Architects may recommend that open stairways, often monumental ones, rise from the main floor as an architectural and aesthetic feature. A monumental stairway in a small library may be out of proportion, but it can be attractive as well as functional in a large building. Contemporary fashion favors stairways as light and seemingly insubstantial as possible, apparently hanging in air and completely open except for hand railings to prevent accidents. The University of Miami library at Coral Gables has a stairway of this kind.

The location of both main and subsidiary stairways is important; indeed, it is usually a primary factor in determining floor layouts. They should be convenient for use, and reasonably conspicuous if students are to find them readily and use them instead of looking for mechanical transportation; on the other hand, they should not be allowed to obstruct the major traffic arteries on each floor.

Stairways are often placed in a central building core, together with elevator shafts, toilets, and other fixed services, leaving the remainder of the building as flexible and adaptable as possible. This plan also reduces the extent of the interior walls that will be required. Another possibility is to place the main stairway immediately adjacent to the main entrance and next to an outside wall, leaving the rest of the building unobstructed by a permanent installation. As has been noted, however, fire laws usually necessitate at least one secondary stairway, and large buildings require more than this; in some cases a stairway in each corner may be desirable in addition to the central stairway.

Decisions on the steepness of stairs involve questions of design, comfort, and the use of space. If the ascent is too gradual, space will be wasted and many persons will find it awkward to climb. If stairs are too steep, many persons will find them difficult to climb. In general, the most acceptable height for risers is no more than seven and one-half inches, and risers of less than six or more than eight inches should be avoided. The following simple formula is often used:

1. The product of the riser and the tread should be between seventy and seventy-five.
2. The risers plus the tread should be from seventeen to seventeen and one-half inches.
3. The sum of the tread plus twice the riser should be between twenty and twenty-five inches.[1]

Decisions on stair widths depend primarily on the traffic expected at times of peak load. Indeed, many decisions in library planning must be based on anticipated peak loads, and, particularly in academic institutions, these normally come when classes change. Emergencies such as fire should also be kept in mind; in times of emergency, traffic can be expected to move in a single direction, making the full width available. Building codes often stipulate the minimum width as well as the maximum width permissible without a railing down the center. Eight feet is often set as the maximum between railings. The minimum for floor-to-floor stairs is usually three and one-half feet clear between rails, though narrower stack stairs are often considered adequate. The legal width may depend upon the number of occupants on the other floors served.

If a stairway is to be a fire exit, it must lead as directly as possible to an outside door, and this door must always be made to open without a key from the inside during periods when the building is open to the public. All library stairways should have hand railings, ordinarily thirty to thirty-two inches above the intersection of the tread and riser at the front end of the steps. This will bring the railing to from two feet ten inches to three feet above the floor at landings. Some architects recommend heights as much as six inches greater than these. A railing that goes a short distance beyond the bottom step will help those who are handicapped, but must be so installed that it is not a hazard for normal persons rounding the corner to go up the stairs.

Architects sometimes propose circular stairs because of their aesthetic advantages, but they are to be avoided in most cases. If the narrow edge of the circular stair tread is to be wide enough to be reasonably safe, considerable space must be left in the center; legal requirements often set a minimum. The total square-footage of floor space required by an adequate circular stair well is considerably greater than would be needed for a direct stairway or for one going around one, two, three, or even four corners, particularly if it is considered that the space immediately outside the circle is usually useless for library purposes. If a circular stairway is to be installed in spite of these disadvantages, it should be so designed, in countries where pedestrians normally keep to the right, that the person going upstairs on the right uses the narrow end of the tread; this will reduce to some extent the dangers presented by any nonrectangular stair tread. Likewise, of course, where pedestrians keep to the left, a stairway rising counterclockwise is indicated. Few architects, it appears, have taken this principle into account.

Apropos of stairways and safety, one further warning may be offered: Avoid like the plague a flight of only two steps; a single step is worse yet. In some places it is illegal to offend in this way, but it is hard to excuse the infraction whether it is an offense against the law or only against common sense. If a library is afflicted with such stairs, they should be properly marked and lighted; in some cases it may be possible to replace them by ramps as was done in the Widener building at Harvard, where accidents had occurred, on the average, once a week for forty years. Obviously it should be possible to move books by truck throughout a library building with a minimum of trouble, yet architects of earlier days sometimes placed short flights of steps at a variety of points in a building. The old library at Cornell, now completely rehabilitated as the Uris undergraduate library, was an example.

It has been noted that the substitution of ramps for stairs helped to improve the Widener building. Steep ramps are to be avoided if book trucks must traverse them, and any slope greater than 5 per cent will be difficult for a person on crutches. A 5 per cent incline entails eighty feet of ramp for only four feet in altitude; a 10 per cent gradient would take only half this space for the same rise, and 10 per cent should be the limit even for very short ramps. A nonskid surface is essential on all ramps, and hand rails should usually be provided. If a change in level is required at the approach to a staff elevator, a ramp is to be preferred to stairs, but the change in level should be avoided altogether if possible. A ramp may be the lesser evil when an addition is made to an old library and it is impossible to make floor levels match.

Escalators, which can handle a large volume of traffic and use relatively little power, can be useful in some cases. They function continually without requiring an operator. It is doubtful, however, that any library can afford to install them between as many as four levels, and it seems out of the question to go beyond that. For heavy traffic between only two levels they may be both useful and economical, as in the new Columbia Law School library, where every reader must go up one floor to reach the library. In the University of Miami library at Coral Gables escalators go from the first to the third floor, with three separate lifts, as two were used between the first and second floors. These escalators go up only, so they cost only half as much and require only half as much space as if they went both up and down. It is estimated at Coral Gables that, though only of medium width, these escalators have a greater capacity than four elevators, and cost less for space, installation, and operation; it is doubtful, however, that four elevators would have been necessary.

The location of escalators calls for careful consideration, and each end should be located where it will not obstruct traffic. Particular care is indicated if more than two levels are involved. It is also essential that escalators be very carefully installed; they must be tailor-made for the building if they are not to be unduly noisy. Special fire protection devices may also be required.

Book lifts, sometimes called dumbwaiters, vary widely in size; some are only large enough to hold a folio volume; others will take a loaded book truck. A few book lifts survive that must be operated manually by pulling a rope, but electric power and push-button controls now prevail. One disadvantage of any book lift is that, if there is no staff member at the level to which the lift is sent, the person who loads the lift must climb up or down stairs to unload it. Even in a large library, where an attendant is stationed at each level, confusion may result if the attendant is temporarily absent from his post. If the lift is too small to handle a truck, its use almost inevitably involves at least one or two extra handlings of each book transported. Many libraries rarely use the book lifts they have.

Wear and tear in handling is an important consideration. Pages, particularly when working under pressure, are inclined to throw books into a lift. For many years thousands of books, sometimes five thousand a day, at the New York Public library were transported between the stacks and the main reading room by book lift, and the resultant damage to bindings was serious. Yet, if an elevator is beyond the library's means, a book lift, particularly if large enough to carry a truck, may be better than nothing. Building codes may require fire-resistant shafts, and insurance rates may be affected. If the lift is to carry a book truck, it must, of course, open at floor level on each floor.

Elevators are clearly preferable to book lifts in every respect but one—they are more expensive. Their cost, in a small library, may represent a substantial fraction of the total expenditure for construction. The cost will be affected by several factors. Is the elevator propelled by cables or by water- or oil-driven pistons? What is the size of the cab? What is the maximum weight to be carried? What is the total length of the rise? What speed is required? How complex are the controls required in order to provide service without an operator? Is there to be an accurate leveling device?

Electrically operated cables are always used in high buildings and often in others. Elevators propelled by a water- or oil-driven piston are less expensive to install and operate when a lift of fifty feet or less is required. They are relatively slow, but may well be considered for freight, and, occasionally, for public use.

The machinery for electrically operated cable elevators is usually located in a penthouse rather than in the basement; this saves in costs of installation and operation, reduces wear and tear on the machinery, and helps to minimize noise enough to obviate special acoustic treatment. When heavy loads are to be handled and speed is not important, what is known as two-to-one roping is used instead of one-to-one.

The number of passenger-elevator cabs that will be needed depends on the volume of traffic and the waiting period that will be tolerated, the capacity of the cabs, and their speed. Traffic customarily is measured by the number of persons to be transported in a five-minute peak-load period, and there are standard formulas that can be used. These take into account the time required for a full-speed round trip without stops, plus time for accelerating and slowing down at each stop, time for leveling at each stop, time for opening and closing gates and doors, time for passengers to move in and out, lost time resulting from false stops, standing time at top and bottom floors, and reaction time of the operator if there is one. The wider the doors, the more rapidly passengers can move in and out. Doors that open at the center speed up operation to some extent.

If wages are to be saved by eliminating operators, automatic elevators must be installed. These are of three principal types. The simplest responds to the first button pushed and does not "remember" any other calls. The selective-collective type answers only calls in the direction in which the car is moving. Finally, a fully automatic system can be adjusted to operate in a variety of ways designed to suit traffic demands of different levels and types depending upon the time of day. The more complicated the controls, the more they cost. Small libraries are rarely justified in installing anything but the simplest type. Safety devices, however, should always be used to prevent the car from moving when doors are open. Car speed should be increased in high buildings.

Two elevators in one bank will carry more traffic without undue delay than three widely separated ones, and three together in a large building will probably be as satisfactory as five or six widely separated elevators. In the Widener library, where there are five automatic elevators, each something like 125 feet from the others, it is often necessary to wait five minutes or more for a car. Three elevators in a single bank would give better service, though passengers on the average would have to walk greater distances to reach them.

A major question in locating elevators is whether or not to place them in a part of the building not open to the general public. Traffic will be heavy if they are used by undergraduates going up or down only one or two floors. Use can be restricted by having elevator doors and call buttons operate only by key, and distributing keys only to members of the staff and physically handicapped readers. Another possibility is to locate elevators behind a desk where an attendant is always on duty. Control has been facilitated in several new buildings where the bank of elevators is at the rear of the circulation desk lobby or in the central core of the building. If stairways leading to restricted levels are also located in this space, there are considerable advantages. Control, it should be emphasized, may be needed for two purposes—to restrict stack access to professors, librarians, and graduate students, and to relieve the load on elevators, which are very expensive to duplicate.

The gravity of the problem will be recognized by anyone who has waited fifteen minutes for an elevator in the University of Pittsburgh's cathedral of learning, as well as by anyone who has helped to plan an eighteen-story library building in which it will cost $500,000 to provide six elevators for passengers and one for freight. It should be added that, when an automatic elevator is pushed too hard by heavy traffic, its nervous system is likely to break down, and remedial treatment is costly.

One means of reducing the load on elevators is to confine the library's most heavily used facilities to the entrance level and the levels immediately above and below, which readers can be expected to reach by stairways. If this can be done, it will be much easier to provide satisfactory elevator service for the professors and graduate students who use the library even more intensively than undergraduates but do not rush in and out in such large numbers between classes.

A leveling device is of great importance, particularly if elevators are used for transportation of heavily laden book trucks. Without such a device, it is difficult for even a skilled operator to stop a car in exactly the right place, and a loaded truck going up or down even an inch as it enters or leaves an elevator is subjected to more wear and tear in a few seconds than during days of operation on the level. The books it contains are also likely to fall off.

If the reader is inclined to think that questions of cab size and elevator speed, or the number of cars and their location are minor matters, he is urged to reflect that an elevator in a five-level building will cost $35,000 in addition to the space occupied by its shaft and by the lobby in front of it. This is an investment large enough to warrant careful consideration.

Conveyors should be considered if there is a fairly continuous flow of books or other library materials through a multi-tier building. They may provide a more satisfactory solution than either book lifts or passenger elevators. An endless-belt conveyor is similar mechanically to an escalator, but it goes straight up and down. Like elevators, conveyors should be enclosed in fire-resistant shafts. Attached, usually at approximately nine-foot intervals, to the chains that go up and down are carrier prongs on which books can be placed as the prongs go past. It is desirable to provide light trays in which the books can be placed; otherwise, there is danger of books falling down the shaft. The books or trays laden with books can be placed on the conveyor at any level. They then go to the level that has been indicated by pushing a button when they were loaded. If this level is below their starting point, they first go to the top, swing around, and then come down.

It should be noted that the simplest conveyor installations have proved to be the most satisfactory; those that pick up material at any level but deposit it at only one—e.g., the reading-room level—are least likely to get out of order. Two conveyors of this sort have been in operation at the New York Public library for nearly forty years with very few difficulties. More complicated types are to be found at Yale and in the old Library of Congress building, where, because the stack is not directly above, below, or adjacent to the charging desk or reading room, the conveyors have to travel horizontally for a considerable distance. A central location for conveyors is highly desirable, of course. Installation by a stair well is advantageous because it may facilitate access for servicing and repair. Precautions should be taken to make conveyors as quiet as possible; many have caused trouble by creaking and groaning.

Pneumatic tubes have been used for many years to transfer call slips from circulation desks to attendants in the stacks. Propulsion is by air pressure, and slips can be delivered much more rapidly than by elevator or conveyor. Many new charging systems, however, use punched cards of one kind or another for call slips, and these cards, which should not be bent, cannot readily be inserted in the pneumatic tube containers that have been used heretofore.

Much larger pneumatic tubes have been used for transporting books over considerable distances when vertical or horizontal endless-belt conveyors do not seem to be practicable. The connection between the Library of Congress Annex and the main building is an example; containers used there are approximately a foot in diameter and eighteen inches in length. The difficulty is that they stop at their destination with an abrupt jar, and books are likely to be damaged unless they have been tightly strapped in place; moreover, of course, to

strap the books tightly does them no good. Hence, there is a real question as to whether or not pneumatic tubes for transportation of books can ever be entirely satisfactory, in spite of the great advantages in speed that they offer over long horizontal distances. When the final section of the Australian National Library has been constructed, books may have to travel as much as five hundred feet horizontally before they reach vertical conveyors to bring them up to readers. If they move at a rate of eighty feet per minute, which is approximately the maximum safe speed for an endless-belt conveyor, it will take them seven minutes to reach the transfer point, and the total time from stack attendant to reading-room desk will be about nine minutes—this, of course, after the time that has been taken for the call slip to reach the stacks and for the attendant to find the book and place it in the conveyor.

Telephones are essential in any college or university library. The large library may have its own central switchboard, or house the switchboard for its college or university. It is important to facilitate communication within the library, and money may be saved if any instrument in the building can be connected with any other there without going through an outside switchboard.

Decisions must be reached on how many telephones are needed, and how many of these can be extensions without a separate main line to the outside. Location of telephones is an important matter. Unauthorized calls can be expensive—directly, in the case of toll calls, and indirectly when they waste the time of employees. Faculty members have also been known to take advantage of unsupervised instruments in order to make long distance calls free of charge. Except for telephones in private offices, therefore, each instrument in the library ought to be placed where a responsible member of the staff can see and hear how it is being used. If one is located at a desk that is in use only part of the day, it should be safeguarded against misuse at other times, either by locking the dial or arranging for it to be cut off by the switchboard.

In planning the conduits for wiring that are to be installed at the time the building is constructed, it should be remembered that installation at any later date will be much more expensive. Both extensions and regular stations are costly and should not be provided before they are needed, but it is uneconomical in the long run not to install at the outset all the outlets that will eventually be wanted.

Pay telephones are usually desirable in a library,

and the telephone company will gladly install as many of them as promise to be profitable. In some cases the library receives a commission on receipts, but it may be worth while to provide pay telephones even if the institution must make up a small deficit in order to have them. They should be located where they will not disturb readers, which usually suggests a hallway or lobby, though preferably not too secluded a place.

Other means of communication are to be found in a few large libraries. The telautograph, which may be observed in some railway terminals, enables a person to write by hand a message that is reproduced elsewhere in the same form, but it is awkward enough to interfere with legibility, and few libraries have found it useful. Teletype, by which a typewritten message is made available in the same form at the other end of the line, has been used at the Midwest Inter-Library Center, the Library of Congress, and elsewhere. It is expensive, particularly for intercity communication, and should not be considered unless heavy and important traffic is anticipated; for less frequent communication, long distance telephone, or commercial telegraph is cheaper.

Loudspeaker and public-address systems, as well as two-way radio installations (as in taxi-dispatching systems) have been used in some libraries, particularly for direct communication between the circulation desk and stack attendants. Care should be taken to avoid creating a disturbance either at the desk or in the stack, especially if the stack is one to which readers are admitted. In a research library, complications may arise from communications relating to materials in foreign languages with which members of the staff are unfamiliar.

Large libraries, particularly those with open stacks, may also find it difficult to notify readers of closing time in order to clear the building. Warning gongs or public address systems may be useful. In planning stack layouts it should not be forgotten that it will be necessary to make sure that all readers have left before the building is closed.

NOISE AND OTHER DISTRACTIONS

Noise has been mentioned at various points in the preceding discussions of supervision and control and of communications and vertical transportation, but noise and other distractions are not incidental matters; they fully deserve to be considered as fundamental problems in any survey of traffic patterns. Sound-absorbing materials can do much to minimize noise, but it is better to prevent noise rather than try to absorb it. Visual distractions are a closely related subject.

It should be conceded that there are fortunate individuals for whom noise and motion are no problem; those who have grown up amidst large families or have worked from an early age in large open offices may be nearly immune to distractions. Many undergraduates, however, are not immune, and undergraduates may deserve particular consideration in this respect. The professor can usually find a secluded corner in his own home even if he does not have a private study in the library. The graduate student in many institutions is now provided with a reasonably quiet and secluded cubicle or carrel. But for the younger student, the only alternative to a library reading room may be his own dormitory, where his roommate may operate on a different timetable and gregarious friends may be plentiful. The reading room is likely to be crowded with his contemporaries, and table space available to him there may be no more than thirty inches wide by eighteen inches deep, which is not enough for spreading out books or, indeed, for opening more than one if space for taking notes is also needed. The chair may be unsatisfactory; its arms may be designed for comfort, but a needlessly deep apron beneath the table may prevent the chair from being drawn close. In one large college library two out of three readers must straddle chair legs within a few inches of the edges of the tables. Lighting may leave something to be desired.

Fully as serious as any of the handicaps that have been suggested is the fact that the reading room may be in almost constant turmoil. It may settle down twenty minutes after a class period begins, only to be disrupted again fifteen minutes before the period ends as students begin to leave. Afternoons and evenings may be disturbed by more continual, though less concentrated, coming and going. In many ways the contemporary undergraduate may be worse off than his predecessors; the great monumental reading rooms of earlier days absorbed noise and tended to engulf the reader just as a large stadium filled with cheering crowd may leave the athlete oblivious of everything but his immediate surroundings. The new, more intimate reading rooms, continue to be surrounded by shelves holding heavily-used reference books that attract steady traffic. Entrance to the room is often through a single doorway in the center of the long side or, worse still, at one end; few readers can enter or leave without going past many tables at which others are attempting to study.

The foregoing account of the undergraduate's woes may be enough to indicate why the following principles need to be emphasized:

1. *Noise and confusion should be kept out of reading areas in so far as possible.* Circulation and reference desks should be elsewhere, with books, walls, distance, or acoustic materials—perhaps more than one of these barriers—to separate them from readers. The public catalog and, to a lesser extent, shelves holding reference collections are also areas of relatively heavy traffic. Use of current periodicals involves a good deal of motion. If periodicals or reference books must be in the reading room, they should at least be placed at one side or one end, with adequate acoustic insulation.

2. *Access to reading areas should be provided through as many well distributed entrances as possible.* If the student can usually find a seat near the point at which he enters the room, he can be expected to leave the same way, and both visual and auditory disturbance can be kept to a minimum.

3. *Individual seating accommodations are highly desirable.* They will be most satisfactory if a barrier at the back of each individual table can be built up to a height of fifty-two to fifty-four inches, which is enough to prevent the reader from seeing the head of the person in front of him. In a seat of this kind he should be able to turn slightly away from the rest of the room and obtain visual privacy if he wishes.

4. *Table surfaces should be large enough to permit the student to spread out the materials on which he is working.* Space on an individual table goes farther than space on a large table; a surface measuring twenty-two by thirty-three inches is as useful in an individual table as a segment measuring twenty-four by thirty-six on a table that must be shared.

5. *Noise and other distractions should be kept in mind when planning traffic lanes throughout the building.* Stairs in the vicinity of reading areas should be well sealed off. Elevators, which are also noisy, are a similar problem, and elevator lobbies must be separated from reading areas.

6. *A plan designed to avoid disturbing readers should not make a maze of the library.* Devious and complicated traffic lanes will discourage use of the building and cause frustration and wasted time.

7. *Traffic patterns in book stacks also vitally affect the welfare of readers.* The tendency is to locate a larger and larger percentage of total reading accommodations in the stacks. It is important to avoid main traffic arteries that go past open carrels along a wall.

These are obvious principles, but few libraries have not disregarded one or more of them. Good traffic patterns, plus adequate lighting and ventilation, are essential if the library is to be a satisfactory place for study.

NOTES

[1]Frederick S. Merritt, ed., *Building Construction Handbook* (New York: McGraw Hill, 1958).

ABOUT THE AUTHOR—(See biographical note on page 79.)

Architectural Barriers and the Handicapped, the Infirm, the Elderly, and the Physically Limited

by Donald E. Fearn

Although a very small percentage of library users are physically handicapped, not to plan the building for their use is like erecting the building and then locking the door. Mr. Fearn suggests a few ways in which we can open up the library to these very special citizens.

Picture, if you will, an island which is extremely small and which contains only one house—yours! Let us now assume that for some reason you have no access to the mainland, which can easily be seen across the water. The island itself constitutes your total life space or environment. Let us also assume that you wish for a chance to go to the mainland. However, as it is, everything you do in terms of learning, working, socializing, and playing is confined to this island—this very limited life space.

Suppose some group on the mainland learns about you and decides to build a footbridge over to your island. You now have the opportunity to expand your life space to include the mainland and all the cultural, social, vocational, educational, and recreational opportunities that are available there but are not present on your island. Whether you do or not is your choice. But now you have a choice!

In effect, we have placed many of the handicapped and older persons in our communities on just such an island. We do not see them on the mainland—or in the community—because we have unconsciously failed to provide them with an opportunity, a footbridge, to function as first-class citizens in the community. The few that do venture out are often forced, not so much by their disability as by concrete, steel, and wood, to be dependent on others. Seeing very few such persons among us, therefore, we falsely assume that this minority is so small that it really is no community-wide problem.

To give some concept of how large this group is, it has been estimated that there are over 250,000 persons confined to wheel chairs; 200,000 with heavy leg braces; 139,000 with artificial limbs, 5,000,000 with heart impairments; and 17,500,000 men and women over sixty-five years of age who would benefit by easier access and function within buildings *used by the public,* not just public buildings.

Not too long ago the severely disabled and aged were given very little assistance and were often relegated to a rear room or an institution. Yet, in the last few decades, America has come a long way in the care and treatment of disabilities through a variety of programs aimed at total rehabilitation. However, professional people in the rehabilitation fields are becoming increasingly frustrated on finding that rehabilitated clients are returning to community life only to find that they are blocked from putting training into practice. The purpose of our Architectural Barriers Project is simply the correction and prevention of this problem. It is intended to give these people an opportunity to participate as full-fledged members of the community.

Combating the Problem

How are we proceeding to combat this problem? First, a major step was taken in October of 1961, when the American Standards Association adopted

SOURCE: Reprinted from Donald E. Fearn, "Architectural Barriers and the Handicapped, the Infirm, the Elderly and the Physically Limited," in *Problems in Planning Library Facilities,* edited by William A. Katz, Chicago, American Library Association, 1964, pp. 207–208, by permission of the publisher.

specifications for making buildings and facilities accessible to and usable by the physically handicapped. This was an excellent example of inter-agency cooperation, since over fifty groups and organizations joined with the President's Committee on employment of the Handicapped and the National Society for Crippled Children and Adults in the research and development of these standards. However, as pointed out by President Kennedy in a letter of commendation to the Honorable Joseph Foss, then president of the National Society, this effort is valuable only if the specifications are transformed into the modification of present buildings and incorporated into new construction.

Briefly, the recommended specifications include:

1. *Site development.* Grading of the ground for one or more ground-level entrances should be planned. Walks should be at least 48 inches wide with a grade no greater than 5 percent.
2. *Parking lots.* Some parking spaces 12 feet wide should be reserved and identified for use by the handicapped. Care should be exercised in planning so that individuals are not compelled to wheel or walk behind parked cars.
3. *Ramps.* A ramp, interior or exterior, should not have a slope greater than 8.33 percent. Ramps should have nonslip surfaces, at least one handrail, a level space at the top, and at least 6 feet of clearance at the bottom.
4. *Entrances.* One primary entrance should be usable by persons in wheel chairs, and, if there is an elevator, it should be accessible from this entrance.
5. *Doors.* A clear opening width of no less than 32 inches for all interior and exterior door-ways is needed. All doors should be operable by a single effort. Revolving doors cannot be used by those in wheel chairs or on crutches. Thresholds should be as nearly level with the floor as possible.

6. *Stairs.* These are, of course, the number one enemy of the wheel-chair user, the crutch-walker, and the cardiac. Where they must be used, it is recommended that the height of the riser be not more than 7 inches and that the commonly used nosing be discarded for a type of riser and tread without any abrupt change of surface. At least one handrail should be extended 18 inches beyond both the top and the bottom steps.
7. *Rest rooms.* There should be adequate space for individuals in wheel chairs to enter. At least one toilet stall, with the door opening out, should be wide and deep enough to accommodate a wheel chair. This stall should be equipped with handrails on each side.
8. *Other features.* Water fountains should have spouts and controls usable by persons handicapped or in wheel chairs. The new designs of wall-mounted drinking fountains, when placed at the proper height, meet the requirements for use by the handicapped. A telephone equipped with volume controls for the hard-of-hearing and within reach of those in wheel chairs should be available.

In their entirety, the American Standards Association specifications are much more inclusive and specific with respect to dimensions, use of materials, and methods of construction for the physically handicapped and the aged.

Many of the newer libraries of all kinds have been designed and built with many of these features included. In some buildings, a few minor adaptations would make the difference between barring the handicapped and the aged and welcoming them with *open doors*. Other older buildings may require ramps or other changes to make them accessible. The planning or modification of any library to make it accessible and usable by the handicapped and aged will accrue benefits to all who visit and use it.

ABOUT THE AUTHOR—At the time this article was written (1964) Mr. Fearn was Survey Director, Architectural Barriers Project, National Society for Crippled Children and Adults.

VI

STAFF SPACES

The shift from monumental structures in library buildings has been accompanied by concern for staff work spaces. It is not uncommon today to see carpet on the floor and draperies at the windows of the technical services rooms. Comfort, including proper control of air, acoustics and lighting is recognized as not just desired but actually required for the cataloger or bibliographer as well as for the reference or information staff serving the public.

In the planning stages attention must be given not only to the comfort and aesthetics of staff spaces but also to flexibility to prepare for new and different processing services and to accommodate the ever increasing number of staff required as collections, services and programs are increased. In one major research library the large processing room was programmed to house eighty staff members even though only sixty-three were employed. By the time the building was occupied the processing staff to be housed in this room numbered eighty-four. The room was forced to hold one hundred six staff before other space within the building (a remodeled basement area) was made available. In the example cited less than ten years had elapsed from the period of planning. One cannot emphasize too much the need for careful planning for the enlargement of staff work spaces.

In the articles which follow in this section we look primarily at the planning for the technical, or processing, areas of the library building.

The Technical and Administrative Functions of the Library

by Robert A. Miller

Mr. Miller provides here much detailed information for the planning of spaces for administrative and processing services. Scattered throughout will be found a number of basic principles for all planners, for example: ". . . the quality of public service depends directly upon the internal organization and efficiency of the library." Or, "the only valid basis upon which to rest a plan for an interior is that of function." Or, ". . . the pressures of personality, whim, or precedent (should not) prevail against a proper layout." And, "it is the responsibility of the architect to provide a physical solution for an imperative need; it is not required of the librarian that he must revise procedure or scramble a layout to serve an architectural appetite." These are powerful statements of basic planning philosophy.

A careful analysis of building and space requirements for technical and administrative functions is most important because the quality of public service depends directly upon the internal organization and efficiency of the library. Organization is strengthened and efficiency is promoted by a good physical plan.[1]

The Wheeler and Githens monograph[2] is exceedingly helpful as a single source; aside from this, the librarian must piece together from many accounts a pattern for planning his technical departments and administrative areas. The very considerable detail involved in planning is nowhere conveniently summarized. This paper attempts to synthesize and describe the pattern and detail of this planning.

First consideration will be given to the development of a statement of functions which must initially shape and continually influence the physical plan. Then the experience of libraries and management will be quickly reviewed for suggestions and standards that may be useful. Finally, these suggestions and standards will be applied to the determination and utilization of floor space for activities normally carried on by the technical departments and administration.

The topic of this paper includes acquisition activities, cataloging activities, administration, and staff welfare. The paper does not attempt to discuss all local factors which may have a bearing upon any generalizations reached, for it will be necessary always for any librarian engaged in the planning of his own building to take cognizance of local situations and practices which require space provision. Neither does the paper seek to distinguish between large and small or between college and public libraries with respect to what must be essentially common problems and solutions. For example, the small library and staff will not need separate quarters for the technical departments, but this need is assumed in the paper.

FUNCTION AND PROCEDURE

The only valid basis upon which to rest a plan for an interior is that of function. This is an obvious statement to make when the whole of the building is being planned to serve one or more functions, but function is sometimes ignored in planning offices and work areas. It has happened that the technical departments have been given space left over, that staffrooms have been mired in the part of the basement not considered suitable

---

SOURCE: Reprinted from Robert A. Miller, "The Technical and Administrative Functions of the Library," in *Library Buildings for Library Service,* Chicago, American Library Association, 1947, pp. 37–55, by permission of the publisher.

for public use, and that the librarian's office has been thrust in the heart of the first floor where the public would be better served with the card catalog, a bibliography room, or a reading area.

In considering the functions of the technical departments I mean simply to consider the tasks which these departments are required to perform. With reference to both what these departments do now and what they will do in the predictable future, it is essential to prepare a complete checklist of the specific tasks to be undertaken. In the preparation of such a checklist our literature will provide much aid, for the standard books on acquisition, order work, serials work, and cataloging are full of practical experience and contain much that may be new in the way of suggestion. The checklist should be supplemented and verified by the local staff. It will be invaluable when the time comes to give a final approval to the plans developed by an architect. It should prevent a careless omission, and it may give one night of untroubled sleep!

Having prepared a checklist of tasks which is as inclusive as practical experience and foresight will permit, the librarian should seek assurance that, in the execution of these tasks, present procedures are satisfactory. Unless the librarian is ready to assume that all is going very well indeed and could probably go no better, the time is now appropriate to examine and study all procedures carefully, for it would be an indefensible error in planning and a serious professional error to permit a continuation of inefficient organization and practice in a new building.

The techniques of job description and analysis are well standardized. They can be and have been applied successfully by librarians to the study of technical departments. It may be necessary for strategical or tactical reasons to employ someone from the outside to conduct the analysis, but the administrator's responsibility is not lessened thereby. At this particular time, as he plans his new building, he must face the problem of organization realistically. He will need the facts revealed by the job analysis to make improvements in procedure as they may be indicated and to decide wisely in the confirmation or reassignment of jobs and personnel.

Following the job description and analysis and the determination of such changes in personnel and procedure as seem warranted, the librarian will be greatly helped in discussing building plans with the staff of his technical departments and with his architect if he will have prepared a chart of the organization, showing personnel and job relationships. Charts showing the activities involved in the major routines (such as the activities involved in cataloging a book new to the library) will be useful in discussing location of physical equipment with respect to the personnel involved and should be highly informative to the architect, who will, typically, have no experience with the complexities of cataloging.

The physical facts concerning the technical departments and procedures will not be completely stated without an accompanying list of each piece of equipment and its space requirements. If the equipment is listed separately, there must be a clear understanding of the needs of the personnel for ready access to those items of equipment which are required in the daily routines.

As a result of his study of function and procedure, the librarian should now have possession of the following: a checklist of tasks, an organization chart, job descriptions, routine charts, and lists of equipment. In the preparation of these guides and lists, he should have used such literature as he could find and the advice and counsel of his staff and colleagues.

LAYOUT SUGGESTIONS AND STANDARDS

Knowing in detail what the technical departments must produce in the new building and how, the librarian is next faced with the practical necessity of laying out personnel and equipment on a floor plan or sketch. Layout, as a problem, has had much attention from management, where, unfortunately all too often, the problem has been made difficult by the arbitrary assignment of space. Management defines layout as making the best possible use of available space and providing the most satisfactory working conditions for the staff. The literature of management provides guidance and suggestion to the librarian on many points of layout and arrangement.

Layout, obviously, should be based upon departmental divisions in order that supervisory control may be established, and these divisions should be as closely related on the floor as they are related by process or job. The flow of work in the technical departments should guide the location of personnel and equipment on the floor plan, in order that the book being processed may move in a continuous line through the various processes without any retracing or redoubling of the track.

Management has learned to look carefully at the future, for, while an estimate of space for expansion is not difficult to make, the availability of extra space creates problems. Since the librarian is constantly exhorted to look ahead, he is not likely to fail to estimate future growth. He need not fear an overestimate, for that is a mistake that no one has yet made in planning a library building. He may, however, not be aware of the lessons learned by management. Expansion should be planned for major departments and not for minor departments or divisions. In planning to accommodate the future needs of a catalog department, the plan should be made on a departmental basis and not for the various subdivisions, such as serials. If new plans provide more space than will actually be needed when possession is taken of new quarters, the layout should not attempt to utilize all available space. Extra space should be left vacant, for its premature use may prevent a proper later use, and there is every likelihood that efficiency will be impeded by dispersion. A good deal of space does not mean a good layout.

If the librarian has fortified his planning of the technical departments by an examination of his procedures through a job analysis, and, as a result, has some reorganization in view, he will be well advised not to assume that old space relationships should necessarily be continued in the new building. Neither should the pressures of personality, whim, or precedent prevail against a proper layout.

In estimating space needs for office layouts, management constantly refers to a survey made in 1930 in which it was determined that fifty to sixty square feet was a reasonable average amount of floor space for each clerical worker. These workers normally do not have need for shelving, book trucks, and reference materials. To provide a worker with space for this equipment, librarians have used the reasonable standard of one hundred square feet of floor space. This standard should not be revised upward in an attempt to provide expansion possibilities. It is better to estimate probable staff increases and provide sufficient extra space at the recommended standards. The librarian will need to differentiate clearly between the floor-space requirements of professional and clerical workers and to plan accordingly.

A typical arrangement of desks in large offices reveals a standardization of desk size so that aisles will be uniform. The main aisles measure from forty-eight to seventy-two inches, and subaisles are not less than thirty-six inches wide. Desks are normally placed side by side. A grouping of four desks side by side does not make access to an aisle difficult for any of the workers at these desks. Experience has shown that an arrangement which requires a desk to face another desk is not satisfactory, for when one worker faces another he may occasionally find it difficult to apply himself to his work. The side-by-side arrangement is not so likely to bring distraction. Between desks, from the back of one to the front of the desk immediately behind, forty-eight inches will suffice for desk chair and clear passage. In applying these suggestions and measurements to library layouts, it is obviously proper to place desks in horizontal rows and to leave sufficient space (not less than twenty-four inches) between desks on the sides for small book trucks. The necessity for all workers to have uninterrupted access to aisles must not be overlooked. It is essential also to have an aisle between an exterior wall and the first row of desks. This aisle may serve to prevent complaints about drafts from the windows and excessive heat from the radiators.

Shelving or files should not be placed back of a desk if that area is also to serve as more than an occasional passageway or aisle. At the same time, one of the important elements of good layout requires that the worker should have near at hand those tools and files which he uses constantly. The proper placement of files and equipment near the workers poses a real problem in the layout of a catalog department. Not less than forty-eight inches should be provided as working space in front of a single file. Where the files are faced, the working space should not be less than seventy-two inches.

Unless they are engaged in the same series of operations, there is no reason why professional and clerical workers cannot be physically separated. As a matter of fact, there are good reasons for this separation. The desks of the clerks will probably be smaller, and this will lead to different arrangements of desks and aisles. The personnel floor-space requirements are different. The activities of the clerical group can, with some exceptions, be centered in an area removed from the official records and working space of the professionals. The nature of the supervisory control for the two groups is different.

In attempting to control noise and to eliminate other distractions, it is customary to find that catalogers, particularly, have been secluded by partitions made either by an arrangement of card cases or by shelving. The experience of management would not favor this measure of separation, for such partitions lead to the establishment of assumed rights of possession, to the creation of separate group interest if two or more share the oasis, and to the abandonment of control.

Management, moreover, has in recent years moved consistently away from private offices. Supervisory control of personnel is best achieved by an officer who shares the working area with those responsible to him. Where private office space is needed for interviews, confidential conferences, and the like, it must, of course, be provided. But, if we may judge from the experience at Enoch Pratt, the private office is not satisfactory. There the office of the head cataloger was found to be too far removed physically and spiritually from the staff, and supervision was remedied by placing another desk for the head in the center of the professional working area.

The proper illumination of the working area should be carefully studied by a lighting expert. It is commonly observed that workers prefer daylight to any sort of artificial illumination. There are many instances where people work effectively in offices without natural light; nevertheless, management joins with the worker in preferring natural light. In more than one building where the interior is illuminated entirely by artificial light, it has proved necessary to issue weather reports regularly to the staff. Wherever natural light must be supplemented, the artificial light will be best designed as general, not individual, lighting. Overhead fixtures should not produce bright spots or lines of light, not only because of possible eye strain but also because many workers wear glasses and reflections on the rims of glasses can be disturbing. Other practical considerations include the placement of desks and personnel so that they shall not face light sources and the elimination of reflecting surfaces on walls, equipment, and desks. A horizontal arrangement of desks may not always provide sufficient natural light to the third or fourth desk away from the windows.

The worker in the technical departments should be provided with a quiet place to work. The noise of typewriters, adding machines, mimeographs, stamping machines, and the unpacking of boxes should be controlled. It has proved satisfactory to isolate the typing and card reproduction activities by providing separate quarters for the staff engaged in these activities. Supervision of this personnel can be secured either by designating a head typist who exercises supervision from her desk within the typing area or by building a parti-

tion, a portion of which is glass, so that casual supervision can be exercised from some removed point within the professional area. A completely soundproof room requires a method of construction that makes for permanence and may interfere with future flexibility within the general area. Proper soundproofing requires a double partition with no common or touching members, and insulating material between the partitions. Sound prevention to a high degree can be secured by the laying of rubber or cork flooring and by the use of acoustical plaster or other sound-absorbent materials on walls and ceilings.

The technical departments require storage facilities for both books and supplies. There is a common tendency to underestimate storage requirements for supplies, and care should be taken to assure adequacy. Book storage within the technical departments should be figured on the basis of normal, current loads. In the event of a large and unexpected acquisition, temporary shelving can take place within the stack area. There should be no thought of providing storage stacks within the technical departments. Neither should provision be made within the departments for those records and files which can go into dead storage, as, for instance, the old correspondence and card files of the order department, or for relatively inactive files, as, for instance, an abandoned accessions record.

As to provision for the staff in the technical departments, management has found that decentralization of lockers and restrooms is probably best, certainly within large organizations. Wardrobe space with forced circulation of air, such as might be secured by alcoves along an interior wall, is to be preferred to locker-rooms. This will be particularly true during wet weather, when a locker does not permit garments to dry and space is not available for the staff umbrellas.

Obscured, perhaps, in much of the foregoing is a principle learned of necessity. Flexibility must not be jeopardized by permanent installations. Layout should always be subject to the necessity of change. But management, by the way, insists that any layout should be worth a sixty-day trial.

The relation of the interior plan to the exterior design of the building should not be overlooked by the librarian and architect. An interior arrangement which seeks to accommodate itself to long, narrow spaces or to a series of odd-shaped spaces is not likely to be efficient. A large rectangular area is preferred, since it offers the best possibility for proper layout. Rectangular areas are available readily in buildings shaped H, T, or E, or within buildings of this type as they are modified to include or adjoin a stack area.

THE ORDER DEPARTMENT

With organization and routines established, and with knowledge of the experience of libraries and management, the librarian should now be in a position to attempt his first layout of the technical departments. At this time, preliminary to his conference with the architect on interior design, the librarian should simplify management's definition of layout somewhat as follows: to make the most efficient use of properly designed space. In other words, in sketching the new technical quarters, a conscientious attempt should be made to design the working area in terms of functions, in terms of the jobs to be done, and in accordance with accepted standards and principles of layout. At a later stage, architectural considerations and the limitations of location will require a modification of the sketch. But there is nothing to prevent, at this stage of planning, an attempt to visualize an ideal layout for the technical departments.

The librarian may find it relatively easy to sketch equipment and location directly on paper, but a convenient device to avoid too much sketching and erasing is to have cut to scale pieces of heavy paper or cardboard, each representing a single piece of equipment. These profile outlines can be moved into any number of locations and arrangements as the planner experiments with arrangements and seeks to establish his layout.

In considering first an ideal floor plan for the order department, the separate working areas should be defined and visualized. The following areas may be suggestive: ordering and receipt of books; preparation of materials for binding; receiving and checking in periodical issues and other serials; delivery of incoming boxes and packages; exchanges; and typing. According to the principle of locating these areas so that the flow of work shall be continuous, it will be necessary to arrange direct physical relationships, but only with respect to receiving activities. As directly as possible, and within the least possible distance, the receiving area should lead into the book, periodical checking, and binding areas. The book section should lead immediately into the first area of the catalog department. The binding area should have a similar relationship, perhaps to the serials cataloger. The area for exchanges and typing need not be within the other work areas, although the typing work area should not be too far removed.[3]

Figure 1 illustrates the flow of work in an order department as it might be indicated on a simple floor plan.

In laying out the detail of each working area, the librarian should consult his list of equipment and attempt to place each piece of equipment in its logical flow of work position. He should be

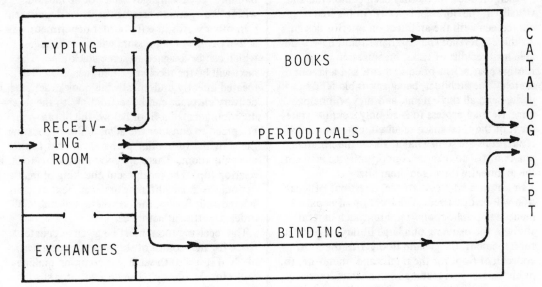

Figure 1 Flow of work in an order department.

guided by the recommended space standards for personnel, access to files, and aisles. He should not neglect to provide for wardrobe space, lavatories, drinking fountains, and storage of supplies.

While it is difficult to say what the shelving requirements of any order department are likely to be, it is advisable to plan the floor space in such a way as not to permit the holding of any large quantity of materials on order department shelves. Reliance should be placed squarely upon the book truck as a means of getting books into the department from the receiving room and on out of the department as quickly as they can be checked in and approved for forwarding. As suggested before, an unexpectedly large acquisition can be temporarily shelved in the stack area. A minimum number of shelves must be provided, of course, for current receipts and for those materials which are delayed for further correspondence or special treatment. These shelves should not interfere with the arrangements for workers and files but should be placed to one side of the working area.

The need of the book-ordering personnel for trade and other bibliographies will probably require the establishment of a trade bibliography and reference section within the book area. In some buildings it may be possible to provide adjacent space for a bibliography room which can be shared also by the cataloging staff, the reference librarians, and the public. The desirability of such a room is apparent, yet it has been achieved in relatively few library buildings.

When the ideal layout has been completed and visualized, the librarian is ready for his first conference with the architect on interior design. At this conference the librarian should have available his checklist of tasks, organization chart, routine charts, lists of equipment, and a layout sketch. The architect, being a sensible fellow, will understand all these items, and they will help him. He may profess to need only a simple statement of the total space required, but, since both reputations are somewhat at stake, the librarian must not fail to take this opportunity to acquaint the architect with all requirements.

In this or a later conference, questions of location will be discussed. The location of departments and public rooms requires much careful study in the planning of a large library. Consider, for a moment, the ground floor. It is the most convenient floor for the public and, therefore, for public service and reading-rooms. Public service requires the public catalog. The technical depart-

ments use the public catalog constantly. So does the reference department. All need a bibliography room. An ideal building situation would permit the location of all these departments and services on the ground floor. But this ideal can seldom be secured, for the horizontal space requirements are so great that they bear both on operational economy and on cost of construction.

As over-all plans for the interior are developed by the architect, the librarian must be prepared to accept the physical impossibility of securing an ideal location, and his first layout will probably be modified by considerations of final location. As building dimensions are determined and the possibilities of each floor are explored, the librarian may wish to develop a list of priorities, as follows: (1) Reading-room, public catalog, reference (including information services), and circulation must be kept together on one floor. (2) If space remains on this floor, the catalog department should have next priority. (3) The order department should have third priority, and, if not all order department activities can be accommodated on this floor, (4) the book-order and receipt activities should have fourth priority (with space for typists). (5) Periodical receipt and checking should have fifth priority (unless a separate serials department is created). (6) Binding preparation should have sixth priority. (7) The receiving room need not be located within the common area of the order department, but must be so located on ground or basement floor with respect to the exterior as to permit delivery directly into the building. (8) Exchanges need not be located within the common area of the order department.

In other words, the first order department activity to feel the pressure will be exchanges, which can be assigned to some stack area. The next will be the receiving room, which can be located directly underneath the book-order area if delivery entrance can be secured. With the receiving room located a floor below, the librarian may be forced to consider the advisability of locating the activities of binding preparation next to the receiving room. There are good arguments for this relationship. The receipt and checking of mail and periodicals in an adjoining area can next be considered and, finally, the complete removal of all order department activities.

The receiving room must be given adequate space for the storage of shipping supplies, particularly if it is also to serve as a common mailing room for the library. The necessity for storing boxes and chests used in binding shipments should not be overlooked. They do not look well in the corridor.

Location having been determined with respect to each area of activity in the order department, the librarian has now the difficult task of revising his ideal layout to suit location. At this stage he should base his revised layout on tracings taken from the architect's drawings, and he should not hesitate to inform the architect immediately of major difficulties, for the architect may be able to provide relief by small alterations or compromises in interior design. It is the responsibility of the architect to provide a physical solution for an imperative need; it is not required of the librarian that he must revise procedure or scramble a layout to serve an architectural appetite.

THE CATALOG DEPARTMENT

In discussing the catalog department and administrative areas, the suggestions already given on the devices of sketching, the timing of the various steps involved, and the conference with the architect will not need to be repeated. Planning for both catalog and order departments will usually proceed together, and the preliminary conference with the architect on interior design should not be held until layouts for all technical and administrative functions have been visualized and space requirements stated.

In considering the layout of the catalog department, the librarian may define working areas, as follows: accessioning, Library of Congress card orders, cataloging (including shelf listing), serials cataloging, card reproduction, marking, and filing.

In addition, the following files or aids may be listed, for they will require space provision and proper placement: union catalog (or depository or official), authority (if not in the above), serials (traveling cards), shelf list, and catalogers' reference collection.

As with the order department, the librarian should first chart the continuous flow on a simple floor plan. Figure 2 may be suggestive. This chart will obviously be more complex in a large department where personnel is differentiated as to job, i.e., subject heading, L.C. cataloging, original cataloging, shelf listing, serials, additions, etc. The complexity should be reduced to a chart, however, to assure continuity of operation and to avoid the losses of time and energy that will characterize a layout with unrelated or indirectly connected areas. Reference to the Wheeler and Githens monograph will provide further illustration.

A principle of management not always observed in present layouts of catalog departments requires the placement of files near the workers using them. In his first floor plan the librarian should attempt to accomplish this saving of steps, particularly for the professional catalogers. The catalogers will need convenient access to the union catalog (or its equivalent) and to the self list. They will next need access to the reference materials of cataloging, and the librarian now engaged in planning must not neglect to take cognizance of the probable issuance of a cumulative reprint of current L.C. cards. The proper use of this cumulative reprint, together with the *Catalog of Books Represented by Library of Congress Printed Cards,* will require both shelving and a table or ledge for

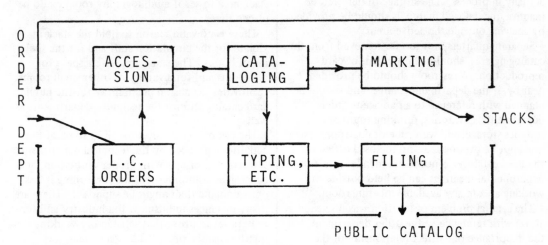

Figure 2 Flow of work in a catalog department.

reference. The serials cataloger will need direct access, of course, to any special catalog of serials or traveling cards that may be maintained.

It is difficult to suggest in a general way how best to secure the placement of official files near the catalogers. The solution of this problem will require much manipulation of the profile outlines upon the floor plan. Certain observations may be helpful. In a small department where the distances involved will not be great, the files should be grouped conveniently to the cataloger or catalogers. Except as a last resort, active files should not be located on a balcony or in the corridor. In a large department where professionals and clericals can be separated, the use of the files in the physical separation should be considered if supervision is not disturbed thereby. Certain clerical personnel will have little or no use of the files. Professionals who use the files only occasionally should be given preference over those clerks who work at the files only upon assignment, on the theory that clerical steps cost less than professional steps. Clerks who use certain files constantly—as, for example, the L.C. order clerk—have equal rights with professionals who use the files less constantly.

When the placement of files has been tentatively decided, the librarian should place each desk and piece of equipment on the plan, observing the standards recommended as to individual space, access to files, and aisles. He should refer to his list of equipment to be sure that no particular has been omitted.

As with the order department, it is desirable that no shelving be provided within the working areas of the catalog department for materials not actually in process. The storage of deferred or inactive uncataloged materials should be provided by shelving outside the active areas.[4]

Separate quarters, not too far removed from the cataloging area, should be provided for card reproduction. A restroom should be provided near by, if the department is large, and should be planned with reference to an adjacent order department. Lavatories, drinking fountains, supplies storage, and wardrobe or coatroom space must not be overlooked. An inclosed office for the head cataloger is not recommended; staff or departmental meetings can be held outside the working area in any available meeting room.

The general problem of location was discussed above with reference to the order department, but the importance of a direct relationship of the catalog department to the public card catalog should be stressed.

If the over-all plan will not permit the location of the catalog department on the same floor as the public card catalog (as in a plan in which reading-rooms surround the public catalog and circulation area), the librarian must answer to his own staff for the inconvenience of separation and must accept an unavoidable margin of increased cataloging cost. The maintenance of an official catalog, duplicating the main entries of the public record, cannot appreciably reduce this margin of increased cost, for it will have its own elements of cost. Also, since the official catalog normally does not provide answers to all questions, reference must still be made by catalogers to the public record.

If the catalog department must, by final necessity, be removed a floor from the card catalog, it should be so placed underneath or overhead as to hold to a minimum the separating distance. In such case, the librarian should provide a direct and normal rising staircase, unless convenient staircases are available in the general plan. It is hard to conceive of a situation requiring a floor separation which will not permit the order department to be planned adjacent to the catalog department.

The desirability of securing a direct relationship between the catalog department and the reference reading-room should not outweigh the necessity of securing a direct flow of work through the technical departments. Reference and cataloging come together principally in the use of bibliography. The large library needs a jointly shared bibliography room. Because limited space and priority of location may make it next to impossible to secure the area needed within the general building, a look might be taken at the stack area to see if a bibliography room could be placed there.

There is no valid reason to hold the stack inviolate for the circulation staff and for the shelving of books. The stack area offers space for restrooms and for a variety of other small rooms. It provides expansion possibilities for the public card catalog and for the technical departments as well.

The use of a stack level for all or some of the activities embraced by the technical departments is worth exploring. With proper ventilation, heat control, and illumination, the low ceiling is less objectionable than might be supposed. There are many instances in business and industry and some in libraries to prove that satisfactory working quarters can be provided in stack areas.

No one who will think seriously of the possibilities of using the stack for technical processes can ignore the next, inevitable question. Why have more than a minimum stack on the main floor? Why not utilize all of this floor, except for a minimum stack and circulation work area, for the ideal location of technical departments and public service? Rice Institute proposes to do so in its new building. A few university and many public libraries provide another answer by locating stacks under the main floor, which is then completely free for public and other departments.

One should reflect seriously on local needs and the use of a traditional stack level on a proposed main floor. The librarian who wishes to use this space for purposes other than the shelving of books can be reasonably assured of an architectural solution and should not postpone discussion with his architect.

ADMINISTRATION

Typical floor-space requirements for library administration are difficult to state because local factors and needs are the important determinants. A general list of administrative space needs would include the following: the reception area; the librarian's private office; the other executive offices; secretarial space; conference or board room; accounting, bookkeeping, or financial office; and supplies storage. Although local experience will indicate the proper space needs and relationships of these areas, certain general observations may have a bearing upon the local solution.

The location of the administrative office, particularly that of the librarian, should be convenient to the public in those communities where this office serves as the public relations nerve-center for the library. The public librarian should strive to find a location on the main or first floor. Except where the college librarian must share in supervision or must take his turn in serving at some public point, the college or university librarian need not be located on the main floor. The main floor location is, obviously, desirable; but administrative need has less priority on the main floor than the general needs of the public and the specific need of the technical departments for direct access to the public card catalog.

The planning of the reception area and the librarian's office should be in the nature of a reward to the librarian for his hard work on the plans of the rest of the building. Judging from the majority of present offices, there seems to have been a trend a number of years ago to make the librarian's office a miniature reading-room, with standard library furniture and a reading-room floor surface. The reasons that led us to these ascetic settings are difficult to appreciate. The librarian's office and his reception area should afford variety in furniture, floor covering, and fixture. They should be dignified, of course, but not threadbare. The library is an institution in which all who serve and are served can be proud. The librarian must transcend his traditional modesty and recognize the importance of appearance in the "front office." The reception area should not look like the interviewing office at a welfare agency. It should be professional and dignified, and it might even have a few new books on a table. A beautiful administrative suite will be a good investment in prestige and morale. The library staff and the public will share the librarian's pride in it. If possible, both office and reception area should have the attention of an interior decorator.

All administrative areas should be planned on the space needs of normal business. The reception or waiting-room area should be estimated in terms of normal maximum traffic. The receptionist should be so located as to permit direct and easy approach. Not more than two clerks, a receptionist and one other, should be located in the reception area, for office noise is not desirable there. A larger clerical force will require an adjacent office. The reception area should be informally arranged to avoid the institutional look. A barrier of desks, counters, or files must be avoided.

If there is need for additional offices for executives and assistant librarians, these should be arranged on the floor plan in such a way that the reception area serves all offices.

In some public and university libraries, there may be need for an accounting or business office area. This space need not be related directly to the librarian if he occupies a main floor area, but if he is located on a secondary floor a direct relationship should be secured. The standards of management will suggest desk arrangement and individual working spaces in the business office.

Most librarians will need a conference or board room adjacent to or near the administrative office. Such a room can serve not only for meetings of the official governing board or committee but for committee or departmental meetings of the librarian and staff. It will be an economy in planning to insist upon this wider use of the room. The librarian's office is not the place to hold committee meetings, official or staff.

General supplies will normally be handled by the librarian, his secretary, or his business office. The needs of storage can hardly be overestimated. Generous provision should be made for all administrative needs, for expansion will affect administration as surely as it will the stack, the reading-rooms and the technical departments.

STAFF WELFARE

In discussing the technical departments, some attention was given the staff with respect to restrooms, wardrobe space and drinking fountains. The experience of management favors decentralization of these necessities.

Additional staff facilities are often provided in large libraries and should be attempted in all new buildings, large and small. The conference room which may be available near the librarian's office is a professional necessity and should not be considered a staffroom.

The staff should have a club or lounge room which can be used in meeting friends and visitors and for group affairs. Adjacent to the lounge should be a rest area and a kitchen. The furnishing and layout of the staff rooms can be delegated to a staff committee, and this committee should be instructed to make every effort to secure comfort, color, and variety from the other library rooms.

Too often the staffrooms are located in the less desirable space of the basement. This leftover treatment is not recommended. Staff rooms placed on an upper floor can be designed as light, airy places with vistas. A visit to staffrooms should bring relaxation and refreshment. The staff will plan it that way, if the librarian permits.

SUMMARY

A summary of the detail of this paper would require an extended and repetitive paragraph. It might be useful, however, to try to set again the time schedule for the planning.

Before the architect is ready to consider interior design and the technical departments, the librarian should have prepared a list of functions, organization and routine charts, a list of personnel and equipment, and flow-of-work sketches. The latter he should attempt to visualize on an ideal floor plan, laying out each working area in detail so that the particular and total departmental floor-space requirements are defined. In the first conference with the architect on interior design, the librarian is then in a position to explain needs, routines, and organization. As the interior plan is developed, questions of location and priorities will arise; when these have been finally determined, the librarian must revise his layout for the final plan. In all this work, from the first statement of function to the last detail of final layout, the librarian must utilize the experience, common sense, and ability of his staff.

Planning a new building need not be a prelude to a nervous breakdown. To all questions comes an eventual architectural solution. The librarian who has confidence in himself will find competence in his staff and architect. To build is to have faith.

NOTES

[1] The author is indebted to Miss Lucile M. Morsch, Dr. Maurice F. Tauber, and Mr. Arnold H. Trotier for advice on certain matters discussed in this paper. These persons should not be held to account for any debatable or controversial position taken by the writer.

[2] Joseph L. Wheeler and Alfred Morton Githens, *The American Public Library Building* (New York: Charles Scribner's Sons, 1941).

[3] If a separate typing area is to be provided within or near the catalog department, consideration should be given to locating order department typists in the same area.

[4] The librarian should "provide only the book trucks and shelving required for a smooth flow of books through the department" (from a letter of Arnold H. Trotier dated June 11, 1946).

ABOUT THE AUTHOR—Robert Alexander Miller, Director of Libraries at Indiana University until his retirement in 1972, received his B.S. degree from Columbia's School of Library Service in 1930 and the PhD from the University of Chicago in 1936. From 1936 to 1942, he served as Director of Libraries at the University of Nebraska, having previously been supervisor of departmental libraries at the University of Iowa.

Technical Services and the Library Building

by Maurice F. Tauber

A second article on space for processing services provides further detail for planning efforts. In quoting Metcalf, Tauber cautions that "the first point to remember in connection with space for staff is the fact that in the past it has been this type of space that has been outgrown first in most library buildings."

In an address by Edwin Wolf, II, Librarian of the Library Company of Philadelphia, presented on April 13, 1959, on the occasion of the Cornerstone Ceremonies for Drexel's new Library Center, which marked the beginning of the celebration of National Library Week in Philadelphia, the following comment was made:

I am not a librarian with what is now called "professional training," but I am a librarian by profession in the old, theological sense of the word. I believe in books. By American Library Association standards I am nonetheless a heretic, for my concern has never been with circulation figures, Dewey decimal numbers, man-reading hours, or mechanical substitutes for reading. I would rather have had one Thomas Jefferson pore over books on politics and government in the room of the Library Company on the second floor of Carpenter's Hall in the spring of 1776, getting ideas for a certain Declaration of Independence, than show ten times the library attendance if those ten are teenagers copying from an encyclopedia in hopes that they can pass their solely manual efforts on their teachers as themes. I would rather get twenty books from the shelves for a voracious Walt Whitman than one for a genealogist paid to produce a pedigree. . . .

Let us assume that the first requisite for a librarian is a love of reading and a natural affection for other people who love reading; that the second is a contagious feeling of joyful wonderment at the explosive excitement in books; and the third is the technical knowledge necessary to perform a particular library job. Any intelligent person can, after all, learn how to type a catalogue card given a guide-book and a few easy lessons. It is amazing in literature how often we read of an author's happy recollections of hours spent in a library, rarely speaking of efficiency, often speaking of atmosphere. Occasionally, we read of the warmth with which a writer regarded a librarian, not because of his automation card-catalogue mind, but because of the ideas and unthought-of-leads he suggested. I sometimes think the most pleasant reading in a work of serious scholarship is the list in the prefatory acknowledgement of librarians to whom the author is indebted.[1]

This is an extremely long quotation, and can only be justified on the basis of its relevance to the topic under discussion, "Technical Services and the Library Building." Actually, Mr. Wolf has said little directly about technical services—acquisitions, cataloging, classification, binding, photographic reproductions. He mentions that he has not worried over classification, circulation figures, number of readers, or "mechanical substitutes for reading," which may be understood to be what we know as audio-visual equipment and materials. He talks about ideas being in minds, rather than in machines. He talks about librarians as readers, and how they should infect users to be readers. He talks about how easy it is to type a catalog card. He talks about how seldom we read in literature that writers of books comment about the library's efficiency or the "automation card-catalogue mind," whatever that may be.

In another part of the talk, he discusses briefly library buildings, about which one would have expected him to say somewhat more at a cornerstone laying. But perhaps this would have been out of focus, even though a new library in an educational institution is always a moment of great interest and pleasure.

It is about time that the exponents of the school of thought represented by Mr. Wolf say what they mean. I have just been surveying the library of a seminary in New York. This is an important in-

SOURCE: Reprinted from Maurice F. Tauber, "Technical Services and the Library Building," *Southeastern Librarian,* vol. 10, no. 2, Summer 1960, pp. 82–91, by permission of the publisher.

stitution, and its collections are among the richest in the world, if not the richest. The librarians are scholars in their field, but the library is in a bad state of inadequacy, which is probably as strong an understatement as one might make. The more than 200,000 volumes are improperly cataloged and inadequately classified, the bindings of rare volumes are deteriorating, and the physical relationships between the various technical units are such that money is being wasted in poor communication and difficult transportation, and general service to readers is handicapped. Scholars do come there and frequently find what they want—with great expenditure of time and with difficulty. Scholars as a rule do not complain much, and if they eventually get what they want they provide acknowledgements in prefaces that they had considerable help and cooperation from the librarians of specific institutions. But it is definitely clear that the library is deficient because of the poor physical conditions, the incorrect and incomplete records, the loss of control of the care of the collections, and the general slowdown of services. It is unfortunate perhaps that writers have not said more about the relation of technical services to their success in locating materials they need. Perhaps a book should be dedicated to a cataloging department.

Two years ago we completed a survey of the Columbia University Libraries. Columbia has rich collections, and its libraries attract endless groups of individuals who could be characterized as scholars and readers. Yet, even there we found that there is a constant need for a reconsideration of all of the problems related to the technical services, and quarters and facilities are among the most prominent of these. The contemplation of Wolf with its smoke-ring reflections of Franklin, Lincoln, Jefferson, John Dickinson and John Adams reading for specific purposes may be appealing, but all of these gentlemen would have welcomed some of the modern improvements in library buildings and facilities. It is quite likely that if Franklin and Jefferson, in particular, were alive today they would have their own contributions to make to both library architecture and technology.

There is no separate volume on the role of the physical quarters in the technical services in libraries. In our volume, *Technical Services in Libraries*,[2] some attention is given to the problems faced by librarians in the planning of quarters for acquisitions, cataloging and classification, binding, and photographic reproduction. Special

note was made of the records, equipment, personnel, and operations involved. Additional attention is given to these aspects as related to academic libraries in the volume, *The University Library*.[3] Various papers and the reports on the building conferences[4] sponsored by the old Cooperative Committee on Library Building Plans and more recently by the Association of College and Research Libraries contain material on both the relationships as well as the plans of technical services units.

The article by Miller in 1947 represented one of the few efforts to relate the technical functions of the library to building plans. One of Miller's general observations is worth noting at the outset:

A careful analysis of building and space requirements for technical and administrative functions is most important because the quality of public service depends directly upon the internal organization and efficiency of the library. Organization is strengthened and efficiency is promoted by a good physical plan.[5]

One of the ways in which the library program has been reviewed is through the library survey, which has been used, as have surveys of other aspects of American institutional life, as an instrument for the improvement of services and facilities. Joseph E. Wheeler, who retired as Librarian of the Enoch Pratt Free Library many years ago, has been one of the active surveyors in the development of building programs for various types of libraries.

Keyes Metcalf, Emeritus Director of the Harvard University Library, is another surveyor who most recently has concerned himself primarily with building problems. Donald Coney, Robert B. Downs, Ralph E. Ellsworth, William H. Jesse, Robert A. Miller, Robert H. Muller, Eugene H. Wilson, and others, as well as those librarians who have worked with the Library Building Consultants, of Evanston, Illinois, have assisted librarians in the development of library plans along with their programs. As a rule, librarians are not architects, but with the inclusion of them on building plans, either directly or as consultants, they have helped architects to avoid mistakes which have appeared in the past and can occur so easily.

There have been many library surveys which did not start essentially as building surveys, but as the activities and services of the library personnel were studied it was clear that a basic difficulty was derived from inadequate quarters or unsatisfactory building relationships. Poor quarters for staff, bad arrangements of rooms, insufficient reading rooms, exhausted space for books, no room for special services—these have been among the characteristics of the libraries which have been deficient in services.

FUNCTIONS AND PRINCIPLES

It is sometimes difficult to convince boards of trustees, either of public or academic institutions having libraries, that poor building quarters and equipment are deterrents to efficient library service, and over the years result in wastage of time and energy. Some people call these "hidden" costs—indeed they are not hidden; they are the most obvious defects that anyone, even without knowledge of library functions, could spot.

Miller, in his paper in the Chicago Institute in 1946, wrote:

The only valid basis upon which to rest a plan for an interior is that of function. This is an obvious statement to make when the whole of the building is being planned to serve one or more functions, but function is sometimes ignored in planning offices and work areas. It has happened that the technical departments have been given space left over, that staffrooms have been mired in the part of the basement not considered suitable for public use, and that the librarian's office has been thrust in the heart of the first floor where the public would be better served with the card catalog, a bibliography room, or a reading room.[6]

Miller suggests the development of a careful checklist of the tasks of the technical departments, now and in the future, so far as these can be foreseen. The development of such a list should be based upon a detailed analysis of the work so that inefficiencies in present organization are detected and can be eliminated in the new quarters. The perpetuation of inefficient organization or procedures from old to new buildings is not uncommon. The analysis of operations and practices also is important for convincing college or university administrators that waste occurs in the inadequate building quarters being used.

The principles for the technical units of public libraries were set down by Wheeler and Githens:

1. Provide the best possible lighting, preferably a north light, because most of the work will be exacting and very close; win-dow area should be generous, artificial lighting the best.
2. Eliminate noise.
3. Provide for sufficient space near desk and catalogs (Bishop estimates 100 square feet per cataloger) (Wheeler and Githens suggest this for all staff members of department).
4. Consider number of trucks, even though 100 square feet are supposed to include them.
5. Shelve every foot of wall space for books in process.
6. Provide separate soundproof room or enclosure for noisy machines.
7. Group interrelated work to limit movement.
8. Reduce further movement by having enough telephone stations.
9. Include booklift or elevator opening directly into cataloging department.
10. Provide washbowls with hot and cold water every 35 to 40 feet.
11. Provide sufficient space for reference books.
12. Provide space near catalogers and classifiers for shelflist and official catalog (if there is one) and for growth.
13. Out-of-date now for most libraries is the provision for an LC card depository.
14. Cupboards for supplies for each group.
15. Plan layout so that complete overseership of room is possible.
16. Future size of department must be visualized (determine size on basis of volume added and expenditures for books).[7]

Such needs are present in college or university library buildings. Similar functions require the same accommodations, regardless of the special type of library.

In the development of plans for technical services, various specific matters are worth attention. Among these are: 1) layouts and standards, 2) the question of partitions, and 3) physical conditions relating to personnel conveniences.

LAYOUTS AND STANDARDS

On the basis of the analysis of the work of the various technical departments, the problems of providing proper space for personnel and equipment are too difficult to solve. Miller has referred to the practice in some institutions in the past in giving the technical services the less desirable or the left-over space. Either of these actions results in grave problems of technical production later on. The two basic ideas of the layout for the technical services after sufficient space has been allotted, are 1) to have related activities physically located together, and 2) to reduce to a minimum (or better still, eliminate) any backtracking.

The technical services units of the library, especially acquisitions and cataloging, represent pretty much the same sort of office requirements that one finds in business houses. Keyes Metcalf, an astute observer of the inadequacies of library buildings, wrote in the 1955 proceedings of the Institute sponsored by the ALA Buildings Committee, as follows:

> The first point to remember in connection with space for staff is the fact that in the past it has been this type of space that has been outgrown first in most library buildings, and in general anything less than 100 square feet per person on duty at any one time is inadequate if it is to include space for a chair and a desk, and for the books and equipment that the staff member will be using. In addition, it is well to keep in mind that in the past library staffs have continued to grow, not as rapidly perhaps as the total size of the library's collections, but at least as rapidly as the student body. Space for staff must provide for administrative officers, for acquisition and cataloguing employees, and for those who are serving the public; that is, for the charging desk, the reference desk, etc.[8]

It is always easy to look backward and wish you had done something else about most things, and especially about library buildings. In connection with a general query which I asked Donald F. Cameron, librarian at Rutgers, about his new library building and the space relationships for the cataloging department and other technical units, he made some astute comments which should go down in the literature on space requirements, if they are not already there. However, in relation to a specific building they may be provocative. He wrote as follows:

> I don't know whether I can give you what you want, but let me state in general what I must have said in a more or less careless way to you about the cataloging space in our library.
> We had set aside an area of about 6,000 square feet. The 6,000 square feet was meant to accommodate our Periodical Department, our Order Department, and our Catalog Department. Mr. Van Horn and I assigned that amount and after cross-questioning we went ahead. In our innocence we didn't realize even in this sub-divided space, we would have to leave room for an elevator and fire-proof stairs, and we discovered

only after we had looked at the working drawings that those were substracted from the total available, and that came to 440 square feet. Then we discovered that our office suite so-called had to be subtracted from the total. Our office suite as it turns out sliced off another 1,000. Then we had an idea that each department head of the three departments mentioned ought to have a separate space inside the large area. By the time we had finished I found we had left something in the neighborhood of 1,800 square feet for cataloging.

> By all the known formulae this cannot take care of as many people as we are likely to have in the Cataloging Department before very long. Of course, there is some space on the floor below, and the separate offices which we have constructed will have to go by the board, and we will reclaim space there.

> The point that I was trying to make, however, was that in a more or less theoretical discussion of space allocations for processes, you can come to complete agreement with planners and architects about the square footage required, and then the poor innocent librarian finds out that decisions made subsequent to that time, such as the position of the librarian's office or the square footage used by elevators and stairs, have reduced the area far below the original intention. You will recognize that Keyes Metcalf has this problem well in hand, and has a formula to take care of it, but I think that was developed after our planning. . . .

> Purely on construction, there is one warning that I presume is superfluous for most people, and that is in a building which depends upon the air-conditioning for cooling and the enforced ventilation, it is very difficult to erect temporary walls for studies, offices, or seminar rooms without upsetting the entire ventilating system. The timing of the planning for these temporary quarters should come before the ventilating system has been decided upon. We did ours afterwards, and we have been suffering very much as the result of it.[9]

Of couse, it may be said that at any place when there is no provision for growth, there is going to be trouble in the future. Inadequate space for books or readers presents extreme difficulties for the library staff. It has been these inadequacies which have frequently been the reason for the erection of a new library. However, cramped quarters in circulation or in the several technical units create serious disturbances in the service of the library in ways similar to those arising from lack of seats or shelves. Take, for example, the statement of the librarian of Temple University in his annual report for 1957–58. He writes:

> Circulation cannot carry the load at peak periods, because in cramped quarters there is no room for handling both books going out in circulation and those being returned. The staff have no place to work. . . .
> The Acquisitions Division likewise is working under the handicap of insufficient space to handle the

volume of materials that comes on order or as gift. In fact, some of the work has to be done outside the room. The passage is often cluttered up with packages, waste baskets, and booktrucks. There is also the danger of passing readers helping themselves to books on the truck near the entrance, particularly since there is not constant direct observation of this area. . . . So many new tasks have been assigned to the present staff of the Catalog Division that there is scarcely enough space to handle the volume of work, but the quarters are already so crowded with desks that there is hardly room for a typist to work on catalog cards. . . . All this cramping and crowding adds up to a deterioration in service to readers, and poor working conditions for the staff. Our daily tasks are sufficiently trying without, indeed the added irritation of pressure for space. It seems wasteful to provide so generously in some ways to students, and then to serve them so badly through an inadequately housed library.[10]

This library is about twenty-five years old, and fits into the pattern of the developing university, with more students and more faculty members placing greater demands upon a library suitable for a smaller community of scholars. Actually, the building is of such a nature that adding more space to the various units concerned could not be done practically.

Although the new library building was completed in 1951 at the University of Houston, two years later the librarian reported that:

The fact that our Technical Services Division is already beginning to feel crowded points to the necessity for providing the members of this division with very generous space assignments. Fortunately, in our case, the modular type construction will permit the Technical Services Division to expand. . . .[11]

The presence of the modular type of construction at Houston is the saving factor. The permanent walls and beams, and heavy shelving built into the floors of some buildings would prevent easy expansion. It is pleasant to see that the new Louisiana State University Library has constructed its Technical Services area with the idea that easy changes may be made in the arrangements of work.

In addition to these issues of space relationships, mention may be made of two conditions which appear to arise constantly in libraries which have not been planned for efficient operation. These two factors involve 1) placing personnel who should be working together at opposite ends of the building, and 2) locating the card catalog on a different floor than the one on which the catalog department is located.

PARTITIONS

One of the interesting developments in library buildings was the inclusion of glass partitions between the technical services department and the adjoining corridor in the Massachusetts Institute of Technology Library. The idea, as expressed by staff members at the time, was to give a view to passersby,—faculty, students and others—of what goes on before books reached the library shelves, and to make the personnel of the Department feel less isolated from the public. From recent information,[12] it appears that the reaction to this innovation was favorable but not dramatic. There was a minimum of comment in the college newspaper, but on the whole it did not excite either the faculty members or the students. The staff members in the Department were said to like it. They soon ignored people who were observing their work, although my correspondent indicated that the open view may have some effect upon the orderliness and the clean desk top. It would appear to this observer that if such an effort really was achieved by this arrangement, it would be a formidable advantage!

My correspondent tells me that the most useful part of the glass partition was the opportunity of showing visiting groups the technical services area without bringing them directly into the department. While this outside view would not satisfy those who are interested in details of the work, many others were not particularly concerned about the individual operations in the Department.

My correspondent saved her last remarks for a mild shocker. She wrote:

This letter will tell you that the corridor is no longer used by the public. A year or two ago it was necessary to establish book-checker control, and that entrance to the library had to be closed off. In fact, we are now considering the possibility of incorporating the corridor into the technical services area.

Thus, the end of this bowlfish experiment at M.I.T., which at the outset appeared to have a good deal to commend it. But the idea itself is not a dead issue.

In her article on the new library at the University of New Hampshire, Thelma Brackett writes:

The visitor can see the length of the building and the technical processes staff preparing books for the reader

to use. The technical processes area extends through
seven modules (approximately 2930 square feet), and
has on one side, windows and desks, and, on the other,
book shelving. Down the center are catalog cases for
shelf lists and other tools. There are no dividing
walls. . . . The work is so planned that a truck of new
books, opened in the mail room two floors down,
goes up the elevator directly to the order department.
Checked in at that point, the books go to the
catalogers, the processors, the loan desk. If they are
not put on exhibit for a week, the electric booklift
at the loan desk carries them, still on trucks, to their
respective floors. The staff feels that the visibility of
this essential part of the life of a library is in itself
educational. And the production arrangement is
essentially sound.[13]

PHYSICAL CONDITIONS

A number of observations on the physical conditions for individual staff comfort should be
noted in this review. One of the most telling
descriptions of technical services quarters was
made by Wilhelm Munthe. He wrote:

At all events, there is one group of library workers
that always arouses my sympathy, namely, the women
in the order and catalog departments, who spend the
greater part of the day working at their desks in an
overcrowded and overheated room, the clatter of
typewriters constantly in their ears, books, catalog
cards, invoices and vouchers piled high about them, not
a hint of privacy, and no protection against draft and
disturbance. The room itself may be large in all its
dimensions, but nine cases out of ten will find it
utilized beyond its intended capacity, with the result
that the air is heavy and the light at most of the
desks bad—a harmful combination of daylight and
electricity. The temperature at which the room is
kept would alone be enough to drive the last man from
the catalog department, but it seems that women
librarians want a tropical temperature. Leaving this
out, there is still plenty to be done in the way of
humanizing the working quarters in American libraries.
It would certainly mean better health for the staff. Or
is it only my imagination that makes it seem that nowhere else have I ever found so many library assistants
with poor eyesight and poor hearing as I have in the
American metropolitan libraries.[14]

Other observations on difficulties arising from
poor flooring, noise, and inadequate light are
given in the following comments:

Some of our staff members have indicated that the
asphalt tile in the service areas offers too little
resiliency for comfort. Considerable strain would have
been avoided for these people, who must be on their

feet so much of the time, had cork, rubber tile, or
some other covering been used. Rubber tile is used
in the lobby, Bibliography Room, General Reference
Room, and on the patron's side of the loan desk, but
not on the staff side of the desk, nor in the Technical
Services Division. . . .[15]

Space for the Acquisitions Department area is
adequate, but higher than anticipated noise levels have
been such a deterrent to efficient work that some adjustments are necessary. . . . Because it serves as the
library's reception center, the two telephones at the
secretary's desk are in constant use. A noisy electric
typewriter is used nearly as much. Staff members
parade through the office area to draw supplies, to see
the librarian, to answer the telephone, and to perform
multitudinous other errands. The net result is distraction to those endeavoring to perform work requiring
concentration. For this reason a partition of some
type to enclose the work of the Acquisitions Department is considered a definite necessity. . . . (Also there
is a need to) provide a desirable barrier to separate a
"messy" activity (marking and mending) from the
catalog and circulation areas.[16]

The occupants of large open areas uniformly report
many distractions. Most professional librarians in
cataloging and acquisitions work have extensive
personnel responsibilities. However, few of these librarians are provided with the privacy essential to
proper interviewing, training guidance, discipline, and
other supervisory activities. These people must attempt
to work in an atmosphere in which there is almost
continual conversation, movement, mechanical
noise (e.g. from typewriter), etc. All visitors to the
room actually feel an obligation to speak for the entire group of personnel, if only to say good morning,
and the opportunities for passing the time of day are
irresistible to casual visitors, whether the seated person likes it or not. No business discussions of a confidential nature can be carried on without being over-
heard by the entire staff, whether it wishes to hear or
not. It is no wonder that the work output of many
catalog departments is no higher than it is.[17]

Levels of artificial illumination in the workrooms
appear to be inadequate. For most activities carried
on in libraries, values of from 30 to 50 foot-candles
are recommended. Ordinary seeing tasks, as in
intermittent reading, require a minimum of 30 footcandles. For prolonged close work, such as cataloging
and other activities generally carried on in the offices
and workrooms, a minimum of 50 foot-candles is
needed. Light readings taken in the Catalog Department at mid-afternoon on a clear day gave values of
33 and 44 foot-candles near the windows, and 25 footcandles at desks nearer the inner walls.[18]

In commenting on plans for the Adelphi College
Library, critics said that "west light" was "bad" for
cataloging.[19]

SUMMARY

Even though these remarks concerning the
technical services in libraries may be characterized
as random, they add up to several specific ob-

servations. These may be catagorized as follows:

1. Librarians, architects and academic officials generally do not give adequate attention to the needs of libraries in determining the layouts and space of technical units. The evidence suggests that over the years few libraries have been able to expand easily in these areas.
2. The formula developed by Wheeler and Githens for space for individual workers in the technical services appears to have had support in diminishing space of expanding technical services units. It is desirable when possible to relate the potential size of the library operation to the need for space in the future.
3. The straight-line arrangement of the units

of the technical services, so that no backtracking is necessary, has been demonstrated to be of significance from the standpoint of efficiency.
4. Much waste of manpower in time and waste in duplicating records can result from the separation of the several units of the technical services on different floors.
5. Since technical services personnel are required to spend a good portion of their time at desks and in examining records, proper lighting, ventilation, and temperature, as well as modern equipment, may be just as important in efficiency as sufficient space.
6. The effects of functional divisions upon the space needs of technical services of libraries has not been studied, and this problem needs examination for the guidance of librarians.

NOTES

[1] Drexel Institute of Technology, Philadelphia. Graduate School of Library Science. *Libraries and Librarians* (Drexel Library School Series, Number 2). Philadelphia, Drexel Institute of Technology, 1959, pp. 10–12.

[2] Tauber, Maurice F., ed. *Technical Services in Libraries* . . . New York, Columbia University Press, 1954.

[3] Wilson, Louis R., and Tauber, Maurice F. *The University Library,* 2d ed. New York, Columbia University Press, 1956.

[4] e.g. Cooperative Committee on Library Building Plans. Its various conferences held from 1945-1949. Later this work was done through ACRL and ALA building committees.

[5] Miller, Robert A. "The Technical and Administrative Functions of the Library." In Chicago. University. Graduate Library School. Library Institute. *Library Buildings for Library Service: Papers Presented Before the Library Institute at the University of Chicago, August 5-10, 1946.* Chicago, American Library Association, 1947, pp. 37-55.

[6] *Ibid.,* p. 38.

[7] Wheeler, Joseph L., and Githens, Alfred M. *The American Public Library Building.* New York, Scribner's, 1941, pp. 157–162. (paraphrased)

[8] Metcalf, Keyes, "The Librarian's Function in Programming." In American Library Association. Buildings Committee. *Planning a Library Building: Major Steps; Proceedings of the Institute Sponsored by the American Library Association Buildings Committee at St. Paul, Minnesota, June 19-20, 1954.* Hoyt Galvin, editor; Kathryn A. Devereaux, assistant editor. Chicago, American Library Association, 1955, p. 7.

[9] Letter from Donald F. Cameron, Librarian of the University, Rutgers, October 15, 1959.

[10] Philadelphia, Temple University Library. *Annual Report of the Librarian, 1957-58,* Philadelphia, Sullivan Memorial Library, Temple University, [n.d.], pp. 6-7.

[11] McGaw, Howard F. "The M. D. Anderson Memorial Library." In Muller, Robert H., "Critiques of Three Completed Library Buildings," *College and Research Libraries* 14:132-33, April, 1953.

[12] Letter from Natalie N. Nicholson, Associate Librarian, Massachusetts Institute of Technology, October 6, 1959.

[13] Brackett, Thelma, "Under One Roof: the University of New Hampshire's New Library." *College and Research Libraries* 20:199, May, 1959.

[14] Munthe, Wilhelm. *American Librarianship from a European Angle* . . . Chicago, American Library Association, 1939, p. 168.

[15] McGaw. *Op. cit.,* pp. 133-34.

[16] California. University. Santa Barbara College. Library. *Program for the Library Building, Unit No. 2.* [Santa Barbara], 1958, pp. 8-9.

[17] Dewey, Harry. *A Report to the Faculty, Staff and Students on the New Library Building for the Drexel Institute of Technology, April 22, 1957.* Philadelphia, [Drexel Institute of Technology], 1957, p. 39.

[18] Tauber, Maurice F., and Wilson, Eugene H. *Report of a Survey of Montana State University Library.* Chicago. American Library Association, 1951, pp. 134-5.

[19] Association of College and Reference Libraries. Building Committee. *The Fifth and Sixth Library Building Plans Institutes Conducted by the ACRL Buildings Committee. Proceedings of the Meetings at Wayne University . . . and at Rosemont College . . .* Edited by Walter W. Wright, (ACRL Monographs, Number 15). Chicago, Association of College and Reference Libraries, 1956, p. 59.

ABOUT THE AUTHOR—Maurice F. Tauber, currently Melvil Dewey Professor of Library Science at Columbia's School of Library Service, has served as surveyor and consultant to over one hundred libraries in the United States and abroad. He received a B.S. (1930), and an EdM (1939) degree from Temple University, a B.S. from Columbia University's School of Library Service (1934) and a PhD from the University of Chicago (1941). His professional career includes top departmental positions at Temple University, the University of Chicago and Columbia. A Fulbright Scholar to Australia in 1961, Mr. Tauber was also recipient of the Margaret Mann award and the Melvil Dewey medal. He is author of many books on library science, notably *The University Library* (with L. R. Wilson) 1945, 1956, *Technical Services in Libraries,* 1954, *Library Surveys* (with I. R. Stephens) 1967, was editor of *College and Research Libraries* from 1946-62, and has contributed numerous articles to professional journals.

Mind Over Mortar, or, Advanced Planning for Technical Services in a New Public Library Building

by Barbara M. Westby

Planning for processing services is carried forward in time with a glance toward future development. Of particular interest here are the remarks concerning provision for electronic data processing and the reader may wish to review this article when reading Unit VIII "Some Considerations for Newer Media and Automation Services in Library Buildings."

Is there a new library building in your future? As a technical services librarian you cannot afford to be a spectator. You must participate in the planning. Design a vehicle that will take your technical services department smoothly down the expressway to the new librarianship of the future. Someone has said that we tend to overestimate what can be done in a year but underestimate what can be done in five. Much advanced planning and thinking must be done before the architect comes. I hope your building has a sufficient gestation period so that you have time to consider all the factors that may affect your procedures and then have time to plan accordingly.

One of these factors is the Library Services and Construction Act. A new building, and a new technical services department, are perhaps more assuredly in your future because of its passage. More importantly, and more immediately, it means more money for more books, and I do not need to tell technical services directors what that means. But perhaps I should remind administrators that they must provide space and staff and that more abundantly. There is no such thing as providing the technical services department with too much space. The Wheeler-Githens formula of 100 square feet per person is still valid. One writer even recommended 150 square feet. Wheeler and Githens also recommended that there be an allowance for a fifty per cent expansion of the present staff. Is this unrealistic? I think not. By what percentage has

your library grown in the past 20–25 years. How much will it, or do you wish it, to expand in the future? The technical services department will grow by the same percentage. Miller and Metcalfe have both stated that one mistake that has not yet been made in planning a building is too much space.

Space costs money, and budgets for new buildings are never as big as they seem. Inflation shrinks them further. But please do not reduce the technical services department simply because it is a closed department. Too often in the past it has been allotted the space that is left over or that no one else wants. I am not minimizing the needs of the public service departments. I am only asking that technical services be given equal treatment. The quality of library service is dependent on internal organization and efficiency, which in turn are promoted by a good physical plan. The public library standards recommend planning for 20 years, but large public libraries will remain constant longer than that.

The Detroit Public Library opened its doors at its present location in 1921. Eight years later the Catalog Department, for example, had expanded into alcoves in the adjacent stacks. Seven more years found the official catalog and the shelf list moved into the corridor. Continuous consolidation throughout the years had jammed our desks together like sardines in a can by the time we moved into our new department. This time schedule of expansion is being repeated in other libraries even today. Denver Public Library has out-

SOURCE: Reprinted from Barbara M. Westby, "Mind Over Mortar, or, Advanced Planning for Technical Services in a New Public Library Building," *Library Resources and Technical Services*, vol. 11, no. 4, Fall 1967, pp. 479–487, by permission of the publisher.

grown its allotted space in six years. Although Kansas City (Missouri) Public Library has 4200 square feet, it will soon need more. The Technical Services Department at the University of Houston was too small after two years. Recently I visited a library which had a technical services department that was too small on the very first day of operations. And this is a library where the director traveled extensively for ideas and presumably did much advanced planning, but where was it when he laid out the floor plans for the technical services? He must never complain about the costs of cataloging. His administrative decisions in planning, which have resulted in inefficient and inadequate working conditions, will be a large factor in the costs.

Textual material in the future may not necessarily appear in book form. The Atomic Energy Commission Reports now appear only as $4 \times 5''$ microfiche. Do you catalog them? If so, will you need to provide for your catalogers various types of microform readers, if those in the public areas will be inaccessible either due to location or heavy use? Libraries now have microfilms, microcards, microfiche, films, phonograph records, tapes, etc. What will the future bring?

Another consideration in your advanced planning is the future organizational and service pattern of your library. The standards for public libraries recommend larger units of service. Will your library be a central unit in a metropolitan, regional, or multi-county system? Then your technical services operations will be affected. The number of titles to be purchased and cataloged will increase, and the number of copies to be ordered and processed will multiply, in proportion to the number of libraries added to your system.

Regionalization means cooperation. In the future we must do more than pay it lip service. The explosion in knowledge, the specialization of this knowledge, and the speed of communicating it means that we must cooperate in the housing and processing of it. Perhaps your library will purchase one or two subjects in depth while a neighboring library will stress another area of knowledge. This may require more catalogers with special skills. The cataloging or indexing information of these cooperatively acquired items must be interchangeable. What form will this take—accession lists, bibliographies, catalog cards, book catalogs, computer print-outs, or computerized information available on-line?

This input and output leads to the consideration of another aspect to your advanced planning, and that is mechanization. This is a major question and is the one which must be answered by any library planning to build in the future, for it affects all your operations, procedures, and organization. The critical part is to evaluate the influence of miniaturization and of electronic transmission systems on your future operations. Form follows function, but we are not compelled to give form to unknown functions. Automation is here and it is inevitable. I admit to fatigue in trying to keep up with the literature and trying to sift the wheat from the chaff. I am not interested in the plethora of words written on paper operations and how wonderful they are. They emphasize theoretical considerations rather than practical experience. I am not interested in a status symbol. I want to read honest appraisals of actual operations so that I can analyze their value in my own procedures. I am disturbed about references to compromises made to accommodate the machine. I do not favor the perpetuation of inefficient methods, but I believe that the machine should do our bidding, not we bending to the will of the machine. However, we cannot bury our heads in the sand ostrich fashion and expect only to feel the breeze of automation on our exposed posterior as it passes by. Like a good journalist we must answer the what, how, when, where and why in order to plot our new building.

Shall we automate everything or only order routines and serial records? We should plan for what we need fully and adequately but should not add fancy extras that we do not need. Will our automation produce catalog cards, book catalogs, or no visible catalog? Are you sure? One library planned its building with all systems go for automation. Later, when more practical considerations changed its orbit, it found that it had no space for a card catalog. If you have book catalogs, shall these be for the central library too or only for the branches and member libraries? Will copies be sold? Will you have full electronic data processing? Will it be based on a file of punched cards, or on disk storage of magnetic tapes? Then provision must be made for equipment and for space to store tapes or $3 \times 7''$ cards. Harry Bauer, in the *Wilson Library Bulletin*, once accused us of having a $3 \times 5''$ complex. Now perhaps we can add a $3 \times 7''$ complex. We must depart from the tradiional approach to our problems, but on the other hand all will not change. Various cataloging pro-

cesses at the routine level will be aided by mechanization. However, the intellectual processes: the
choice of entries according to ALA rules, verifica-
tion of authors, assignment of subject headings
and classification numbers will still be the function
of the librarian though he may be working with
an unwieldy 5 X 7" or 8 X 11" sheet instead of a
3 X 5" slip.

Ralph Parker, who practices as well as preaches
automation, has stated that librarians of the future will have little direct contact with the machines. Others would have us using video consoles
with key punch input, light pencils, teleprocessing
terminals with dial and dataphones, teletypes,
facsimile transmission, etc. Audio input of
numerical data will be available in the very near
future and audio output is here now.

Computers have been viewed by some as only
glorified slide rules, while others have endowed
them with man, or even god, like qualities. I suspect the truth lies somewhere in between. However, computers are stupid, until told what to do.
It is we in technical services who are going to tell
them what to do. Catalogers, already a scarce
commodity and in great demand, are going to be
in even greater demand. I have never been afraid
of unemployment. Henry Ford's assembly line
created more jobs, not less. Richard Shoemaker
of Rutgers, in the *Southeastern Librarian* for
Spring, 1964, stated that we once chained, or
locked in cages, books that were considered valuable or fearsome, and he suggested that catalogers,
being valuable or fearsome or both, should also be
chained or locked up before they are lured to
richer or more persuasive libraries. Now there's
an interesting sidelight on advanced planning!

Technical services are not only going to grow
but get noisier in the process. This suggests separate quarters for the machinery. Humans may be
smarter than machines, but they will put up with a
lot more in their physical surroundings and working conditions. The machine is more particular,
though the present third generation of computers
has become more tolerant. Transistors have replaced vacuum tubes and further microminiaturi-
zation by solid state technology has reduced the
weight and heat of computers. Fifty pounds per
square foot is the present requirement. A raised
floor is optional according to one IBM man since
the arrangement of the equipment allows the
cables to be laid out of the way, but another holds
that it is best to raise or depress the floor to house
the cables.

The amount of air conditioning and humidity
comfortable for humans is now acceptable to the
machines: 60°-80° Fahrenheit and 40-60% humidity. The present hardware is also equipped
with acoustical covers so no extra sound proofing is
needed. If you plan to mechanize, allow 600-800
square feet for the computer and peripheral equipment. This will permit expansion. The fourth
generation in 1970 will undoubtedly be smaller.
The key punch operations should be in a separate
room. So too should the supervisor and the pro-
grammer. The machine operator can have a desk
inside or just outside the data processing center.
There should be a conduit outside the building
leading to the room so that external storage machines in Washington or elsewhere can be tapped.
If you wish to make the center a show place, then
use glass walls and a raised floor.

Any automatic equipment installed today must
have several capabilities: It must be compatible
so that libraries can cooperate and exchange information via punched cards, tapes, teletype or whatever the future holds, or we will be back where we
are now, all repeating the same jobs in different
locations. It must be capable of sending and receiving catalog information to and from the Library of Congress. At the Detroit Public Library
we do 45-50% original cataloging, but if LC can increase this coverage I want to be able to get it.
And let us not kid ourselves that we can precata-
log all the materials we order. The original input
at ordering time must be correctable at cataloging
time.

Each university seems to be riding its own automation horse its separate way. Perhaps they can
afford this. They have computer complexes on
their campuses to which they have access, and
maybe even student programmers and research
funds. However, I think it is also true that too
many people have moved into this field with inadequate knowledge or study or ability to cover
the heavy expenses. But public libraries have no
such luxury and are bound by city budgets. We
need to pull together rather than compete. I
would like to see ALA or the public libraries or
both furnish leadership in this area. We must
analyze and devise the procedures best suited for
public library operations and then suggest the
hardware to carry out these tasks. EDP requires
standardization and uniformity, but let us devise
these for the sake of the efficiency of our operations, not for the sake of the machine.

Minder and Lazorick have suggested the following in their paper on the "Automation of the Pennsylvania State University Acquisitions Department":

> The traditional library organizational pattern may not be adequate in an automated system. Most technical service divisions are organized along lines of operation performance: acquisitions, cataloging, binding. A computer oriented system may work more efficiently if it is form oriented. Books separated from periodicals, serials, etc. A book is a one purchase transaction which is cataloged as a unit and sent to shelf as a unit. A periodical is a continuing type of transaction that theoretically has no ending and must be handled at predetermined periodic intervals. Serials too are continuing but somewhat irregular. These factors: unit transactions, continuity, and irregularity, are essential factors in computer utilization.
>
> Organization of work flow and programming by form allows for addition of other forms, such as Technical Reports, for example, later without disrupting the system. This is done by designing a separate system for each form. This does not necessarily mean that Technical Service Departments need be physically reorganized in an orientation. Records will be handled differently but output can be integrated: One listing of all forms or separate forms.

The data processing program suggested by IBM for the Detroit Public Library was a progressive one utilizing present equipment: an 026 key punch, 514 reproducer, 557 interpreter, 085 and 077 collators and an 082 sorter (650 cards a minute), and adding a 407 renting for $800 a month. This would be a card file system, printing upper case only, mechanizing orders and serials. This could progress to a card based system using a 360/20 model renting for $2500 a month. This would in addition produce book pockets and labels, and catalog cards alphabetized in filing order in both upper and lower case. A final stage could be a 360/30 at $5000 a month with both a card and disk storage. In the beginning we would add to our staff a supervisor and a programmer at $9000 and $7000 respectively. We have an operator, 2 key punch operators and a clerk-typist. The staff would increase as the operation increased. Automation creates jobs so your budgets will never be less, but more.

In the literature on the planning of library buildings, the Technical Services Departments have been sadly neglected. The chapter by Wheeler and Githens in their book the *American Public Library Building* and the paper by Robert A. Miller on "Technical and Administrative Functions in the Library" presented at the Building Institute in 1946 are still valid. There is an article by Maurice Tauber in the Summer 1960 issue of *Southeastern Librarian.* Little else exists.

However, the suggestions in the literature on library buildings are applicable to us. The first step in planning is to write a program, which is a statement of your philosophy and goals—your purpose, scope and function—and the requirements for carrying out your goals. The factors I have discussed so far must be considered in this planning. Make a detailed checklist of all the tasks now performed and to be performed, and the requirements of each as to staff, space, and equipment. Analyze your procedures and don't move an inefficient or outmoded practice into a new building. The new building may allow you to do an old job a new way. The organization chart resulting from this should reveal your work flow and the interrelationships of the various sections in your department. Your program should also show your need for proximity to the card catalog, bibliographical tools, and business office. Involve the staff. Visit libraries and learn their good and bad features. Be imaginative. Frank Lloyd Wright stated that a building grows out of conditions as a plant grows out of the soil. We must see that the soil is rich and fertile.

Following is a suggestive though incomplete checklist. I have already mentioned microform readers. Do you need a phonograph with earphones for the record cataloger? One music cataloger, whom I know, had permission to use the piano in the auditorium of the library. I do not recommend a piano, but it illustrates that you must consider many things. Electric typewriters? Copying and duplicating equipment? Pasting machines? Number and placement of electrical outlets? Of telephone outlets? Do you want telephone jacks on the catalog cases? Shelving? On all walls? Work tables? Trucks? Posture chairs. Types and sizes of desks? Storage space for supplies? Do you want a walk-in closet? They can look messy on open shelves.

The flow of work should follow an assembly line pattern. As a matter of fact for book processing I recommend an assembly line itself—be it roller, roller skate, or conveyor belt. It saves much tiring and wasteful lifting of books. In the Detroit Metropolitan Area both the Wayne County Library and the Detroit Public Library operate assembly lines. The latter is horseshoe in shape with the straight end that closes the shoe being located in the shipping room. Yes, the processing section is located next to the shipping room although it is two floors and a half a block away from the rest of the catalog department. There has been some inconvenience due to the fact that the processing section is located so far from the official catalog. In the shipping room boxes of books are opened and invoices checked on the line. Then the books are placed on masonite palette and pushed through a window into the processing room. After work on the books is completed they arrive back in shipping through another window at the other end of the line and are distributed into agency boxes for delivery. In processing new materials it is well to have on one level: loading dock, receiving area, space for unpacking, invoicing, cataloging and classification, preparation, mending. If steps of the work progress in logical order with no backtracking, on one level and on wheels, then more units or work will be performed per man hour. Horizontal access is cheaper than vertical access.

The second phase of a building program is the preliminary sketch—the architect's graphic translation of your program. You now see the location and shape given your quarters. You should check its location in relation to shipping, administrative office, business office, public catalog, other departments and the sections of your department to each other. Your work space must be planned for maximum economy and efficiency. As stated in the public library standards: "Efficient planning is obviously difficult if the work is physically hampered. Poor lighting results in a slow-down in work and increased error, too little equipment causes unnecessary handling of materials, crowding decreases concentration and increases irritation, poor machines produce poor work, distances between work-related areas mean wasted time and energy, and traffic through a workroom brings confusion and disruption." Keep these points in mind and be critical. Watch particularly for traffic from outside the department.

Blueprints look impossible, but like everything else if you proceed slowly and focus gradually, instead of trying to understand them at one glance, there is no difficulty. Make a layout of the space. Cut pieces of furniture and equipment to scale. Use a different color for each catagory: desks for clerks and catalogers, official catalog, shelf list, etc. This will facilitate an overall view. Experimenting with different arrangements will reveal the best utilization of space and the best supervisory control. If you are fortunate enough to obtain extra space, do not plan its use now. It will be easier then to expand in the future.

There should be a minimum of fixed walls to allow for maximum flexibility. The mechanical

and technological discoveries of the age will necessitate changes in procedure and room arrangement so one should plan for the most usable simplicity. One section of your department may increase while another decreases.

As a final check you should do some role playing. Wear several hats: that of the technical services director, the chief of the various sections of the technical services department, and order librarian, a cataloger, a clerk, etc. Then mentally walk through the tasks and spot unnecessary walking, backtracking, etc. Most important, pretend you are a book. This is, after all, our stock in trade. Does the book follow an orderly route from shipping carton to shelf? If so, you have it made. Advanced planning requires more than a superficial overview. It is drudgery to study your problem, develop new methods, and assemble necessary data to clarify your wishes to the planner and the architect. But then does not everything worthwhile require work?

From these working sketches come the detailed blueprints. This is your last chance before the mental image becomes mortar. You should check for the following: is there an acoustical ceiling; what kind of floor covering; a soundproof room for equipment; do the doors have thresholds—book trucks cannot pass over them easily; where are the elevators; are there book lifts; if so, will they hold a book truck or will you have to lift books off and onto a waist high lift; are there horizontal conveyors or vertical selective bookveyors; are they located so that you can make use of them; are there plenty of electrical outlets to accommodate all future electric and electronic devices; where are they located; where are the shelves; where are the light switches; are they at centralized positions or are they on several walls necessitating a complete walk around the room to turn lights off and on; what are the traffic patterns in your room and from outside your room; there should be none of the latter. Do not overlook the factor of human engineering. Francis McCarthy in his paper at the Buildings Institute for 1961, *Planning Library Buildings for Service,* has some charts on space for browsing, bending, pulling out trays, etc, which you will find interesting and useful.

About lighting I have no advice, except to avoid glare and contrast. The footcandle debate has found no agreement among illuminating engineers, architects, librarians, and opthamologists. I recommend windows with north light. I claim, but have no proof, that artificial light is better for the eyes if it is blended with natural light. I have some support from Robert O'Conner, New York architect, who states that there are both psychological and physiological advantages to such a mixture. Denver Public Library insisted on north light for its technical services department and has not regretted the decision. Kansas City (Mo.) Public Library has two glass walls and so loses that much shelving. Windows must be placed so as not to create glare.

The Catalog Department at the Detroit Public Library is an interior room and I might make a few comments on that. A nine foot ceiling creates no hardship. The walls are white but with four walls of shelving some of the starkness is relieved. I would recommend a slight tint of color, however. Clara Breed of the San Diego Public Library suggested pale yellow or pale peach. A bit of burnt umber added to white is also an idea. And pale blue is restful. Another touch of color could be used in the book trucks. One writer suggested fire engine red, mediterranean blue, etc. Each department could have its own color which would also identify ownership. The technical services department should not be neglected in the interior decoration plans. Color and decorative features will improve morale, and attractive and comfortable furniture should be considered. I am a firm believer in the Scandinavian formula of beautiful things for everyday use.

I have mentioned nothing about binding. You must provide for mending and repair, pamphlet binding, application of bookplates, pockets, plastic covers, etc. However, if you do not have a bindery, the best advice is do not start one. The costs are high both in equipment and union scale wages.

Approval of the blueprints is not a signal for relaxation. During construction, changes may be initiated due to structural requirements, higher costs, or second thoughts. Make certain that these do not seriously affect the operations of your department. Your final task will be the scale drawing which shows the arrangement of furniture and equipment and which will be used on moving day.

If you prepared your homework well, you and your staff will enjoy working in a cheerful and efficient department. Your mental image, skillfully developed, will produce a picture in mortar and brick that will be pleasant and practical.

ABOUT THE AUTHOR—Barbara M. Westby received her B.A. degree from Augustana College in South Dakota in 1941 and her B.S. in L.S. degree from the University of Denver in 1945. She worked in various library capacities before 1944, and after that became a cataloger, first in Detroit Public Library and then in the Army Medical Library in Washington, D.C. After several years with the U.S. Information Library in Stockholm, Sweden, she returned to Detroit Public Library where she advanced to Coordinator of Cataloging in 1963. She was Field Director for the Library of Congress Overseas Office, Oslo, Norway from 1966–69, and is currently Chief of the Catalog Management Division of the Library of Congress. Miss Westby has served on committees for various library organizations, has contributed to professional journals, and was Editor of the 9th Edition of *Sears List of Subject Headings* (1965).

Layout Planning for Plant Offices

by John Molnar

This short piece provides ideas and sketches for the layout of staff work spaces in industry and commerce which can be applied to the processing and administrative services of libraries.

Office space planning and layout would be simple, if it were possible to establish fundamental criteria for all needs—and if these needs would lend themselves to a modular plan. Experience has shown that this is impossible, but there is an optimum solution for all cases: Good ground rules, furniture, space and office standards, hard work and preseverance will provide that solution.

The following suggestions are based on experience and some measure of past success. While not a panacea for office space planning and layout, the guideline approach will provide the basic fundamentals for optimum space utilization.

First, the offices being considered are those associated with industrial plants, not commercial office buildings. The fundamentals can be used

SPACE LAYOUT PLANNING SHEET

Date Completed 10/1/68 By J. Molnar Current |X| Proposed | | Date___

Department Activity or Function	Managers	Supervisors	Group Leaders	Secretaries	Work Stations	Total Personnel	Total Space	Utilization Sq. Ft./Person	Total Female	Total Male	Special Areas
1. P. Brown	1D				1	2	210	105	1	1	
2. E. James		1H				1	100	100		1	
3. J. Lynn			1G			1	80	80		1	
4. -------					6	6	180	30	2		
8. A. Post				1	1	30	30		1		
9. -------					3	3	108	36		3	
10.							144				Central Aisle 4x36
Totals	2D	1H	1G	2	12	18	1140	63	4	14	

STANDARDS

Office:
A.____X____
B.____X____
C. 12 X 15
D. 10 X 12
E.____X____

Cubicles:
F.____X____
G. 8 X 10
H. 10 X 10
J.____X____

Work Stations:
K. 5 X 6
L. 5 X 8
M. 5 X 9
N.____X____

Comments:

FIGURE 1 A planning sheet similar to this one is a basic tool in office layout. Standards of office, cubicle and work station size may vary.

SOURCE: Reprinted from John Molnar, "Layout Planning for Plant Offices," *Plant Engineering,* March 6, 1969, pp. 88–89, by permission of the publisher.

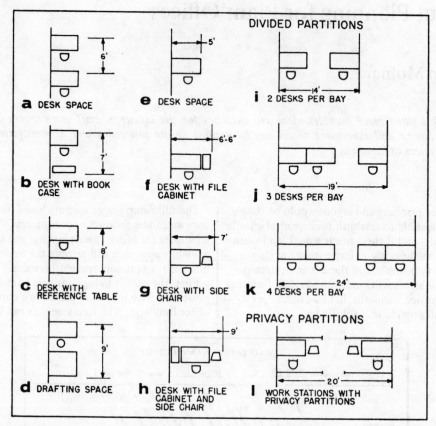

FIGURE 2 Basic dimensions of office work stations. At right, various combinations of work stations grouped to form work areas.

for planning and laying out: office functions in separate buildings; office functions combined with laboratories; and office functions combined with manufacturing operations.

First consideration in planning an office is the determination of the space needs that must be met. An excellent tool for finding these needs is the Space Layout Planning Sheet, Fig. 1. As shown, this sheet uses standard sizes of offices or work areas for varying levels of responsibility in the organization. Many companies have established these standards for office sizes; their use is essential to orderly planning. One such standard relates responsibility level to offices or work area size in this arrangement:

1. Division vice president   16 ft × 20 ft
2. Department manager   12 ft × 15 ft
3. Section manager   10 ft × 12 ft
4. Unit supervisor   10 ft × 10 ft
5. Group leader   8 ft × 8 ft
6. Individuals   5 ft × 6 ft

Space planning is begun with the basic building block—the *work station*. Several of these are combined to form *work areas*, and together they comprise the office layout.

A work station is, by definition, any area where someone performs work. It may be a plush, carpeted, paneled executive office or just desk space for an individual. In any case, work stations must be identified and areas assigned to them. These work stations may occupy space individually or may be grouped to form work areas. Work areas may then further be combined to form units, sections, departments, etc., depending upon the particular organization.

Work stations range in a wide variety of types and sizes. In an office, the smallest unit is the desk and swivel chair. Most companies use standard furniture, and a typical size for an office desk is 30 by 60 in.

In the preliminary planning stages, aisle space for every work station should be included, in order to develop a more realistic space requirement. While

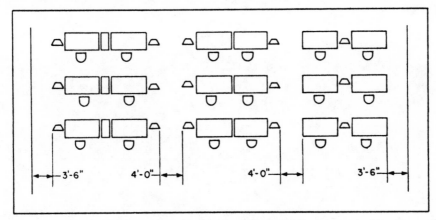

FIGURE 3 One version of no-partition 'bull pen' type of layout. In this type of layout, each work station is adjacent to an aisle.

aisles as narrow as 3 ft can be used on occasions, 4-ft aisle widths are preferred and should be used in the planning stages.

Desk space, front to front, can be as small as 5½ ft. but 6 ft is preferred. Therefore, using 6-ft (optimum) spacing between desks, and 2-ft aisle width (half of the 4-ft aisle) total area required for one desk work station is 6 ft by 7 ft, or 42 sq ft.

As the needs of work stations change, so does the space requirement. Figure 2 covers the basic needs of an individual working by himself, where there is no special need for privacy.

Various side-to-side and front-to-front dimensions for differing work station requirements in Fig. 2 will cover most needs, and can be tailored to space requirements. The partitions shown as work area dividers are 5-ft, 6-in.-high bank screen type, topped with 18-in. obscure glass panels. This partitioning provides privacy, yet does not interfere with air conditioning, ventilation and lighting.

Individually partitioned work spaces are usually preferred by those at the desks. However, groups of desks can be partitioned off for semi-privacy, particularly if the several individuals are performing similar or related tasks.

In a "bullpen" layout, no partitions are used in an area. Figure 3 shows typical possible combinations where every desk has direct access to an aisle. Three or four desks may be placed side by side, but this is usually undesirable. Whatever furniture layout plan is used, it must be arranged so that aisles are straight and relatively uniform in width.

A word of caution in planning bullpen space: limit the total open space; cross-talk and noise level could become intolerable. The maximum open space should not exceed 10,000 sq ft. with 5,000 to 6,000 sq ft considered good; judgment will dictate. One good practice is to limit the area to similar work functions—accounting (including budgets, payroll, etc.), purchasing, and others.

ABOUT THE AUTHOR—At the time this article was written (1969) Mr. Molnar was a planning consultant at Moorestown, New Jersey.

VII

MECHANICAL SPACES

Much of the comfort and flexibility of library buildings is dependent upon well planned mechanical spaces. The mechanical spaces include all the equipment required for plumbing, heating, ventilation, lighting, transportation and communication systems. Such equipment consumes much of the cost of the building and assumes major continuing expenses toward the building's proper functioning. Aesthetics are of concern here, too. For example, air must not only be circulated in a room but it must be introduced and removed through fixtures which are not offensive to the eye. Lighting fixtures must be easily cleaned or in time they will detract aesthetically and also diminish the intensity and quality of light.

Librarians cannot be expected to have the knowledge of the engineers and architects with whom they must deal. On the other hand, a basic understanding of some of the problems involved in the mechanical aspects of library buildings will enable the librarian to deal intelligently with consultant specialists in each of these areas of concern.

Lighting the Library—Standards for Illumination

by H. Richard Blackwell

Considering the primary task, reading, peformed in a library, lighting at once becomes an important aspect of the building planning process. It becomes a difficult aspect, and increases in importance, when we consider the variety of reading in the library environment: faded manuscripts and marginalia, rare or unique printings, deteriorated printings, contemporary print, microforms and computer printouts. It is obvious that a variety of lighting is required in the well illuminated library.

Few human environments are designed to make such concentrated use of the sense of sight as our modern libraries. Since lighting is intended to aid the sense of sight, we might well expect libraries to be among our best-lighted buildings. There is at least some evidence that this is not the case. Thus it is a happy challenge for me to be asked to present recommended standards of illumination for libraries to you. If libraries are not well lighted, no doubt it is because those of us who have devoted some years to the study of lighting needs for seeing have not made the results of our findings available in a sufficiently concise form. Let me attempt to summarize here the results of research studies conducted in my laboratories since 1950, first at the University of Michigan and more recently at Ohio State University.

Science devotes itself to phenomena which lend themselves to accurate study by known methods. This selective process does not necessarily ensure that the complex problems that often interest the user of scientific information the most will be studied first. Thus, in the field of the effect of light upon sight, we must admit that we have almost no knowledge about some of the most interesting aspects of the problem, simply because we do not know how to study them. We do have a considerable understanding of many effects of light upon sight, however, and I believe we know enough to specify reasonable standards for lighting a library.

BROAD ASPECTS OF THE EFFECT OF LIGHT UPON SIGHT

The physical characteristics of illumination, of interest to us, include the amount or intensity, the direction at which light rays strike an object to be seen, the color, and the plane of polarization. The pattern of luminescence or brightnesses of the entire environment is also of interest, and this depends upon the characteristics of the illumination and the reflectance characteristics of objects in the environment. Lighting is often described in terms of quantity (intensity) and quality, the latter term being used to refer to all aspects of illumination and brightness other than quantity. These words suggest that quality is an attribute that can be directly evaluated by a user of light, but that quantity is an intangible aspect of light, concerning the needs for which the designer of libraries must consult someone besides the user. Actually, of course, both quantity and quality of light must be evaluated in terms of their effect upon vision. Whereas a library user may be somewhat aware of some aspects of the effect of light upon sight, I hope to show that scientific evidence is our best guide in evaluating most aspects of light. In any case, light can be good or bad with respect to either quantity and quality or to both.

Seeing is a complex organic behavior involving a number of brain centers in addition to the eye.

SOURCE: Reprinted from H. Richard Blackwell, "Lighting the Library–Standards for Illumination," *The Library Environment: Aspects of Interior Planning*, Frazer G. Poole, editor, Chicago American Library Association, 1965, pp. 23–31, by permission of the publisher.

The eye receives light stimuli which are processed within the eye and in higher brain centers to provide information. Some of this information is used immediately to guide the behavior of the organism; in libraries, most of the information is stored as knowledge. An especially important class of information for our purposes is that which is used to program the adjustments of the eyes which aid in the collection of further information. What we see guides the adjustment of muscles in the eye; the adjustments then affect what we next see. I refer to the muscles which operate the iris (pupil) of the eye, those which alter the focus of the eyes, and those which direct the eyes toward one or another point in the space around them. The servo-loop involved in "simple" reading has almost incredible precision in programming the sequence of looking, seeing, and looking. The processing of information by the brain seems to follow a program which is itself largely dictated by the established sequence of eye movements and information assimilation.

So far as we know, the eyeball is not damaged by any kind of bad lighting, meaning either insufficient quantity or poor quality. It is easy to show that the effectiveness of information collection is reduced in bad light. There is some reason to believe that reading under bad light can lead to the development of ineffective programming of the information-collection process, which may become habitual. However, on this important

point we do not have clear scientific evidence. The effectiveness with which a human learns while reading is such a complex affair that we have not found a satisfactory method for studying the effect of variations in lighting upon it.

We also know that bad lighting, which reduces the effectiveness of information collection, can lead to localized or general discomfort. Some of this discomfort apparently can be traced to lighting conditions which overstimulate some of the eye-adjustment processes, as in the case of repeated constrictions and relaxations of the iris (pupil). More of the discomfort apparently can be traced to lighting conditions that lead to a reduction in information needed to guide the eye-adjustment processes. Thus, bad lighting interferes with the sensory stimuli needed to control both eye focus and eye pointing. Poorly programmed focus and pointing adjustments produce discomfort that develops slowly, and indeed may be delayed until after the offending use of the eyes has been terminated. These effects of lighting require further study but, again, the study of discomfort due to poor programming of eye-adjustment functions has proved comparatively difficult.

We have clear and comprehensive data in two areas. First, we can relate, with considerable precision, the degree of *visibility* of visual tasks to lighting variables. Visibility is obviously important because we cannot learn what we cannot see. As important as this is, at least equally as important

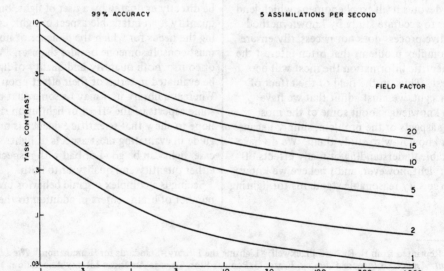

FIGURE 1   Lighting Variables and Task Visibility

FIGURE 2   Visual Task Evaluator

may be the fact that poor visibility leads to poor eye adjustments which lead to discomfort and perhaps to harmful habits of information collection. Secondly, we can describe the degree of discomfort produced immediately in a lighted environment by what is called "direct glare." Let me present recent findings in these two areas of our investigations before recommending lighting standards for libraries.

LIGHTING VARIABLES AND TASK VISIBILITY

Our investigations involved determining the degree to which more difficult visual tasks could be seen equally well when more illumination was used.[1] We required that our test subjects be correctly identified when we presented a small disc of light in a large field of uniform brightness. The disc subtended 4 minutes of arc, which made it about the overall size of a Snellen test letter legible with 20/20 vision. The subjects had to detect the presence of the disc in 1/5 second, since this is the length of time the eye normally pauses to fixate. We altered the physical contrast of the disc to vary its difficulty.

Data for 99 percent accuracy are presented in Figure 1. The curve labeled "1" represents the contrast needed by the test subjects just to detect the presence of the disc. This is "threshold" visibility. The other curves represent different degrees of ease of seeing or, as we have called them, different field factors. In our basic experiments, the subjects were able to adjust their eyes fully before the disc was presented so that they had no

need to search and scan. They were also especially well trained in detecting the discs. Other experiments suggested that a field factor of 15 would provide most users of light with sufficient ease of seeing under the dynamic conditions or ordinary seeing. The curve for the field factor of 15 is the "standard performance" curve which has been used to establish quantity requirements for different tasks.

The idea is simply this: Real visual tasks vary in their intrinsic difficulty due to their size, the distance at which they are viewed, their physical contrast, their color with respect to their background, and so on. We rate the difficulty of a task in terms of the physical contrast required to make the standard 4-minute disc equally difficult when viewed under the same conditions. The equation of difficulty of a real task to the standard task is made with an optical device known as the Visual Task Evaluator, shown in Figure 2. The task difficulty is designated by $\widetilde{C}$, the *equivalent contrast* of the disc of equal difficulty. The required quantity of illumination, E_r, for the task is read from the standard-performance curve at the value of $\widetilde{C}$ as shown in Figure 3. (The scales have been labeled in ordinary numbers, rather than in logarithms, to facilitate understanding of the process.) It is worth emphasizing that the level of ease of seeing represented by the standard-performance curve is only our best estimate of the illumination level needed. We can be much more positive, however, about the *relative amounts of light needed for different tasks.* These do not depend upon the field factor we select, but only upon the parallelism of the curves in Figure 1.

The required footcandles obtained in this manner for tasks likely to occur in libraries have been summarized in Table 1. Note that large, black print requires only about 1 footcandle, whereas the most difficult tasks require more than 100 footcandles. We must conclude that the light intensity we require depends drastically upon the task we are to perform. This conclusion supports the idea of localized lighting for areas where the *most* difficult tasks are performed. Seats near the windows in libraries have attracted those with difficult seeing tasks before this. The data certainly suggest that more light is needed for many tasks than is needed for well-printed books. Thus, if some of the more difficult tasks are performed at all generally in libraries, we have to stop thinking about general library lighting in terms of the problem of reading books alone. The Illuminating Engineering Society has recommended 70 foot-

TABLE 1

LIGHTING REQUIREMENTS FOR SAMPLE LIBRARY TASKS

Based on 1959 Standards for "Glare-free" Light

Task Description	Required Footcandles
10-point Textype print	0.9
8-point Textype print	1.1
Ink writing on white paper	1.4
12 easiest spirit-duplicated samples	2.1
Printed numerals*	8.3
No. 2 pencil on white paper	63.0
No. 3 pencil on white paper	76.5
5th carbon copy of typed material	133.0
12 most difficult spirit-duplicated samples	141.0

*Used by the German investigator, Bodmann.

candles for reading areas in libraries largely on the basis of the values for pencil writing. This recommendation makes the assumption that pencil writing is a task which must be performed throughout a library reading room—an assumption that does not seem unreasonable to me.

There has been some discussion of my selection of the level of ease of seeing represented by a field factor of 15. Use of a different field factor would influence the levels of recommended illumination considerably, as may be judged from the curves in Figure 1. It is interesting to evaluate my selection by comparing the footcandles recommended on this basis with the results of measurements of the increase of visual performance with illumination. Three published works were analyzed from this

point of view,[2] with the data presented in Figures 4–6. In each case, the solid curve shows the measured improvement in visual performance as illumination was increased; the vertical line represents the light intensity recommended on the basis of my field factor of 15. It is apparent that my selection of the degree of visibility represented by this field factor results in lighting intensities well below the levels producing the highest efficiency of seeing. This represents a safety factor which is undoubtedly prudent in view of the economics of installing and maintaining lighting.

The footcandle requirements contained in Table 1 represent what have been called "glare-free" light. We all know that a strong cone of light coming from the wrong direction can produce a specular reflection which will wash out task contrast and greatly reduce task visibility. Situations reducing task visibility in this way are said to produce "reflected glare." The measurements reported in Table 1 represented in effect the kind of perfectly diffuse lighting to be found with totally indirect light. We may well wonder to what extent different methods of modern lighting affect task difficulty due to the reflected glare effect. We have done considerable work on this point in recent years.[3]

Our basic technique involved making physical measurements of the contrast of a sample visual task, first under perfectly diffused lighting and then under real lighting installations. Recently, these measurements have been made with the Visual Task Photometer, shown in Figure 7. It was found that differences in physical contrast

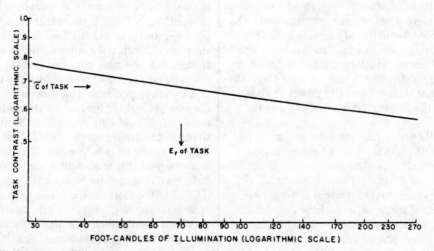

FIGURE 3 Quantity of Illumination Versus Task Contrast

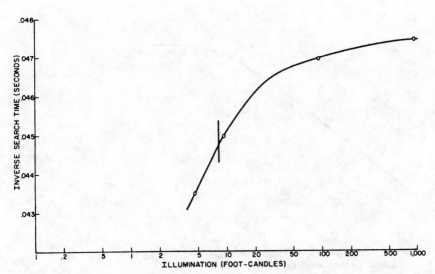

DATA FROM BODMANN (1962)

FIGURE 4   Improvement in Visual Performance with Increased Light Intensity

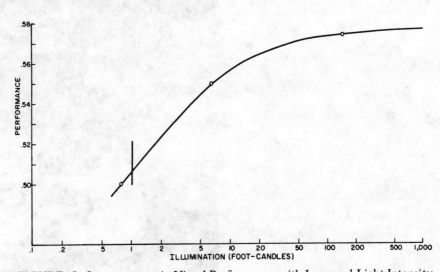

DATA FROM WESTON (1945)

FIGURE 5   Improvement in Visual Performance with Increased Light Intensity

produced corresponding differences in task difficulty as measured with the Visual Task Evaluator. Hence, measures of the task contrast under a real lighting installation relative to task contrasts under diffused lighting enable us to compute measures of equivalent contrast which apply to real lighting installations.

Figure 8 shows the establishment of the required illumination–E_r' for such a real lighting installation, when $\widetilde{C}'$ represents the equivalent task contrast obtained under real lighting installations. It will be noted that, in comparison with Figure 3, the value of $\widetilde{C}'$ is less than $\widetilde{C}$, and hence the value of E_r' is greater than E_r. This is the result generally found: Real lighting installations reduce task difficulty in comparison with perfectly diffused

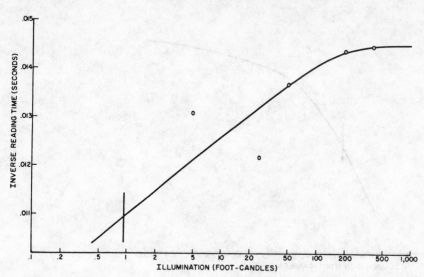

DATA FROM TINKER (1959)

FIGURE 6 Improvement in Reading Performance with Increased Light Intensity

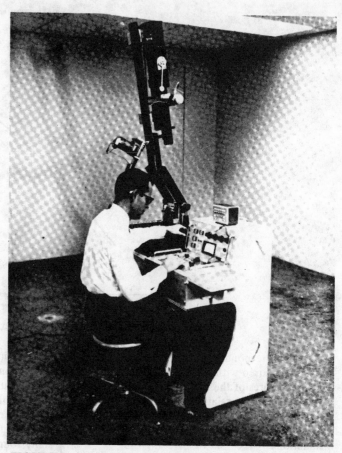

FIGURE 7 Visual Task Photometer

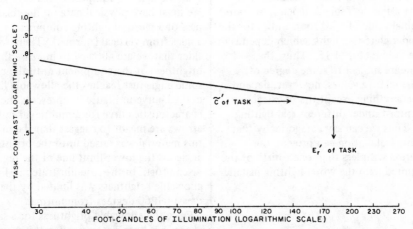

FIGURE 8 Required Illumination Versus Task Contrast in Real Lighting Situation

lighting. Paradoxical as it may sound, the only remedy is to use more of this comparatively poor light. The eye can be helped to see either by increasing task contrast or by increasing illumination. A little more contrast is as effective as much more illumination since the increase in illumination improves vision only in what must be agreed are a series of indirect ways. *This means that illumination quality, as measured by the task contrast a lighting system provides, is much more important than illumination quantity.*

The importance of illumination quality may be judged by the data summarized in Table 2. The required footcandles are for the No. 2-pencil task for which the glare-free illumination requirement was originally given as 63.0 footcandles. The values reveal that the requirement for illumination quantity depends upon both the layout of ceiling-mounted light sources and the lighting material used in each layout. For best task contrast, and hence best visibility, light should come to the task

from as large a percentage of the ceiling as possible. Increasing the area of the source of light reduces the deleterious effect of a light ray coming from just the wrong angle, which tends to conceal the task beneath a veil of reflected glare. The light-control materials are better than perfect diffusers in the same layouts because their control of the angle of emergence of light can be useful in reducing reflected glare. The multilayer polarizers have the light-control feature and, in addition, produce a preponderance of vertically plane-polarized light. It is a physical fact that vertically plane-polarized light reduces reflected glare, thus increasing the task contrast and visibility.

The data in Table 2 show that, with the best quality light, considerably lower footcandles can be used than with other methods of illumination. The greater *visual effectiveness* of lighting installations producing good visibility through higher task contrast certainly looms large in terms of the economics of installing and maintaining the light

TABLE 2

LIGHTING REQUIREMENTS (FOOTCANDLES) FOR NO. 2-PENCIL TASK

Based on 1964 Standards for Real Lighting Installations

18 by 24 foot room; 50% wall reflectance				
	Ceiling Coverage			
Lighting Material	100%	78%	56%	33%	16%
Perfectly diffusing panels	82.6	110.0	113.0	191.0	253.0
Light control panels A	67.2	85.6	92.3	129.0	148.0
Light control panels B	71.1	88.9	104.0	137.0	153.0
Multilayer polarizing panels	57.9	71.2	72.5	104.0	123.0

levels required with the various installations.

The absolute values in Table 2 depend, of course, upon the original value of 63.0 footcandles for the pencil task under glare-free light, which depends in turn upon the field factor of 15. Thus, these absolute values are subject to some degree of argument. The relative values, however, depend but little upon anything except the physical facts about task contrast under different real lighting installations. Thus we can say categorically that the best lighting installation can provide the visibility criterion with less than one fourth of the light level required with the worst lighting installation.

LIGHTING VARIABLES AND DIRECT COMFORT

In addition to preventing indirect discomfort, which results from trying to see in bad light, we must provide light in such a way as to prevent direct discomfort. The experience of direct discomfort has occurred to us all when we have entered a room with excessively bright light sources. These sources are said to produce discomfort due to direct glare (as distinguished from reflected glare).

It is possible to set a reasonable limit on the brightness a ceiling-mounted light source may reach before producing glare discomfort. The allowable brightness depends upon the point on the ceiling being considered with respect to the location of the user's eyes. Points on the ceiling across the room are much more glaring than points more nearly directly overhead, presumably because the former are nearer the line of sight used when a person looks casually about a room. Thus, points on the ceiling across the room cannot be so bright as points more nearly overhead. This characteristic of a lighting system may be described in terms of the brightness allowable from each element of ceiling at different angles from vertically beneath it. The stippled area in Figure 9 is bounded on the bottom by a line which represents the highest brightness allowable without glare discomfort. The brightness at large angles from vertical (normal) is the brightness which will be seen from points on the ceiling across the room. Accordingly, the allowable brightness is only about 165 foot-lamberts. The brightness at smaller angles can be much higher without discomfort.

This fact about discomfort glare enables us to evaluate lighting equipment in a very general way. We must have physical data on the relative brightness of a piece of lighting equipment at different angles from vertical (normal). Then, we can consider that we are allowed to increase the actual brightness of the equipment until the brightness at some angle just reaches the allowable limit. The dashed curve in Figure 9 represents the brightness characteristic curve for a multilayer polarizer. The arrows are meant to suggest that the brightness of this material was raised until the brightness at some angle hit the lower-limit line of the region of glare discomfort. In the case illustrated in Figure 9, the allowable brightness was limited by the brightness measured 60 degrees from normal.

Once the allowable brightness for a sample light source has been determined in this way, it is a simple manner to compute the illumination produced by a lighting installation limited in this way. This value of illumination may be considered the allowable illumination without glare discomfort. Values of this quantity are shown in Table 3. We see that the light-control materials allow us to have more footcandles without discomfort than perfect diffusers do. This is because the light-control materials reduce brightness at the large

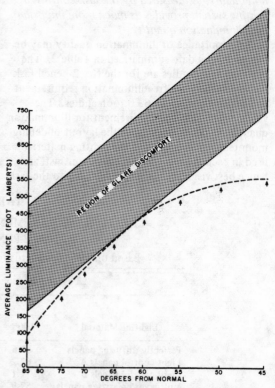

FIGURE 9 Glare Discomfort as Affected by Angle of Sight of User's Eyes

TABLE 3

ALLOWABLE FOOTCANDLES WITHOUT
DIRECT GLARE DISCOMFORT

18 by 24 foot room					
	Ceiling Coverage				
Lighting Material	100%	78%	56%	33%	16%
Perfectly diffusing panels	146.0	114.0	81.5	48.9	24.5
Light control panels A	421.0	328.0	235.0	141.0	70.5
Light control panels B	229.0	179.0	128.0	76.8	38.4
Multilayer polarizing panels	452.0	352.0	252.0	151.0	75.7

angles from normal at which the eye cannot tolerate high brightness. It is of interest to note that the multilayer polarizers have the same effect to an even greater extent.

Higher illumination levels are allowable when more of the ceiling is covered with light sources, simply because of the larger area of light source involved. Spreading out the light source obviously increases the allowable illumination by reducing the brightness at any point on the ceiling needed to produce a given number of footcandles.

It should be emphasized, as before, that the absolute values given in Table 3 are less dependable than the relative values. There is reason to believe that all the numbers in the table are too low for most modern installations. Disregarding the absolute values, however, we can say positively that the best material (the multilayer polarizing panels) permits use of more than three times as many footcandles without discomfort as the worst material (perfectly diffusing panels).

RECOMMENDED LIGHTING STANDARDS FOR LIBRARIES

Throughout the earlier sections of this paper, the theme has recurred that we can be much more positive about *relative* lighting requirements under different conditions than about *absolute* requirements. We are certain that different tasks require very different lighting levels, less certain exactly how many footcandles we must have. We are certain that lighting systems providing good task contrast can provide adequate visibility with much less light than is needed with systems providing poor contrast. We are certain that the allowable footcandles are much higher with the best than with the worst lighting materials. These statements emphasize the need for a more flexible view on

lighting requirements than is implied by a single footcandle standard. The data presented in the paper should provide the designer of a library with some idea of what is involved when a given lighting system is being considered. It is clear that some lighting systems are vastly superior to others producing the same number of footcandles. When designing lighting it would seem that illuminating engineering should be at least partially replaced by vision engineering.[4]

We can draw some very clear conclusions about the relative merits of different methods of providing lighting. The worst method of lighting involves use of a few rows of luminaries fitted with diffusing panels. If such a system covers only 16 percent of the ceiling with luminaires, the pencil task requires 253 footcandles. To make matters worse, the high brightness of these luminaires—particularly at large angles from the normal—limits the allowable illumination to 24.5 foot candles. Matters can be much improved by increasing the ceiling coverage of the light sources. Total ceiling coverage can represent the case of totally indirect lighting as well as of luminaires packed closely together. In this case, we require only 82.6 footcandles for the pencil task, and we can have 146 footcandles without discomfort. The light-control panels are helpful both in reducing required footcandles and in increasing allowable footcandles, but the multilayer polarizers are better still. The required footcandles can be reduced to as little as half, and the allowable footcandles increased by three times, when these panels are used in place of diffusers. The best system, from both points of view, is a full translucent ceiling of multilayer polarizers.

The overriding importance of lighting quality leads me to recommend strongly that this aspect of different systems be given first consideration in designing library lighting. The design must have quality, and then the quantity should be increased to the limit imposed by architectural and cost factors. Provided that we begin with quality, the "more light the better sight." As footcandles increase, more and more tasks will become adequately visible. With quality, increases in light intensity will prove helpful—at least up to 500 footcandles.

These statements imply that there is a gradation of desirability which parallels the level of illumination intensity used. At the risk of oversimplification, this gradation may be described in the following way with reference to quantity requirements in quality installations: Only the simplest visual tasks can be performed adequately with less than 30 footcandles. An increase to 50 footcandles represents a considerable improvement. A further increase to 70 footcandles is most helpful. A definite further improvement can be noted at 100 footcandles. Most visual tasks can be performed adequately at 150 footcandles.

In the entire range of visual tasks, the No. 2-pencil task is a common task of about median difficulty. Therefore, it does not seem at all unreasonable to use our extensive data on this task if a more quantitative approach to footcandle specifications is needed. The data in Table 2 show that the best lighting system studied, involving a complete ceiling of multilayer polarizers, requires 57.9 footcandles. Other systems with large ceiling coverage require from 67.2 to 110 footcandles.

Although color was noted as one of the physical characteristics of light, nothing further has been said about it. We know that the color of lighting has essentially no effect upon task visibility. It has a small effect upon direct discomfort, the warmer colors producing the least discomfort. Color, of course, has very important effects upon the pleasantness of a visual environment. Here, again, we know less about this aspect of light than we should because of difficulties encountered in measuring the pleasantness of lighting.

NOTES

[1] H. Richard Blackwell, "Development and Use of a Quantitative Method for Specification of Interior Illumination Levels on the Basis of Performance Data," *Illuminating Engineering*, 54:317–53 (June, 1959).

[2] H. W. Bodmann, "Illumination Levels and Visual Performance," *International Lighting Review*, 13:41–47 (1962); H. C. Weston, "The Relation between Illumination and Visual Efficiency—the Effect of Brightness Contrast," *Industrial Health Research Board Report No. 87* (London: H. M. Stationery Office, 1945); Miles A Tinker, "Brightness Contrast, Illumination Intensity and Visual Efficiency," *American Journal of Optometry and Archives of the American Academy of Optometry*, 36:221–36 (May, 1959).

[3] H. Richard Blackwell, "A General Quantitative Method for Evaluating the Visual Significance of Reflected Glare, Utilizing Visual Performance Data," *Illumintaing Engineering*, 58:161–216 (April, 1963).

[4] H. Richard Blackwell, "Vision Engineering," a continuing series of articles appearing in *Lighting*, beginning with the issue of July, 1963.

ABOUT THE AUTHOR—Dr. Blackwell has been associated with the Institute for Research in Vision at the Ohio State University since 1958 where he has also been Professor of Physiological Optics and Research Professor of Ophthalmology and is currently Professor of Biophysics. He holds degrees from Haverford College (B. S.), Brown University (M. A.), and the University of Michigan (PhD in Psychology). He has served as an international consultant to professional organizations, institutions and government agencies. His subject specialities are the psychophysics and psychophysiology of vision, psychophysical methodology and sensory theory, and atmospheric and physiological optics.

Library Lighting

by Keyes D. Metcalf

Lighting, particularly its intensity, is a controversial subject in library buildings today. This article by Metcalf created considerable stir when it was published. The following year Library Journal *published three brief articles, here reprinted, one of which presented opposing views. The others were to compromise or referee the dispute. One referee does perhaps offer the best possible advice: observe, analyze and evaluate. He concludes, "Precise design based on criteria established for the specific building will not only result in the best visual environment, but it is likely to be the most economical as well."*

Library lighting is a complicated and sometimes controversial matter whether approached as an engineering problem or a question of aesthetics; it is also, from the standpoint of the library's readers, a highly important matter. This short article can do little more than outline the questions involved and suggest factors to be weighed before decisions are made. Lighting problems are many, but they can be classified under three headings: quality, intensity, and costs.

I. QUALITY

Everyone agrees that quality of light is a basic consideration, but it is not easy to measure because it depends on several factors, particularly the light source, the fixtures used, and glare and contrast; moreover, it is closely related to intensity, which will be discussed in section II.

Light Sources

Until about the turn of the century the sun was the chief source of light in most libraries and the need for making full use of sunlight was a more important consideration in library architecture than any other single factor. The invention of the incandescent electric light bulb finally provided a reasonably satisfactory artificial method of lighting for libraries, though the quality and intensity of early incandescent lighting would seem completely inadequate today, and the cost of current was very high. Primitive though the fixtures were, by the end of the 19th century libraries could be lighted with electricity, readers could be admitted after the sun had set, and evening hours of opening were possible throughout the year. Today most libraries have windows—many of them have too many windows—but there is comparatively little dependence on natural light. Indeed, if costs alone were considered, it might be proved that natural light should be given up, but it is still important for psychological reasons, although in many libraries large areas used for reading as well as for book storage have no natural light today. Large window areas have the serious disadvantage of permitting cold to enter in the winter and heat in the summer. Moreover, natural light often brings unpleasant glare and shadows.

Electric lamps come in three main types: mercury, incandescent and fluorescent. Mercury lamps have been used comparatively little during recent years, although they provide greater intensity than incandescent bulbs using an equal amount of current. They are slow in reaching their full intensity after being switched on, but the delay has now been reduced and there is a prospect of their increased use in the years ahead, often in combination with one of the other types of lamp.

Incandescent bulbs, until some 20 years ago, were standard. Fluorescent tubes are a comparatively recent development. An incandescent bulb concentrates the source of light into a small space,

SOURCE: Reprinted from Keyes D. Metcalf, "Library Lighting," *Library Journal*, vol. 86, December 1, 1961, pp. 4081–4085, by permission of the publisher and the author.

making it easier to obviate dust and dirt but creating more glare unless protected. It should be realized, however, that any unshielded light source results in discomfort and should be avoided. There is still disagreement as to whether fluorescent or incandescent lamps are more satisfactory. In recent years the pendulum has been swinging in favor of fluorescent in spite of the flickering and noise that are still all too common faults. These problems cannot be ignored, but, with modern remote ballasts, the humming factor can be completely eliminated and the practice of using two parallel tubes in each fixture or two tubes end to end on the same ballast has largely overcome the stroboscobic effect. Some experts suggest that something about the quality of fluorescent light makes it desirable to use a higher intensity than with incandescent, but this apparently can be overcome by adding a small amount of incandescent light to the fluorescent installation. It should be added that at present there seems to be a tendency to go back to incandescent or a combination of the two.

Fluorescent lamps project light satisfactorily at right angles to the tubes, but their efficiency is greatly reduced beyond the ends, making it difficult to light shelves or individual tables along a wall at right angles to them, unless additional tubes are installed parallel to the wall and close to it. It is generally unwise to use fluorescent tubes if lights are turned on and off frequently, as this reduces the life of the tube considerably. On the other hand, fluorescent lamps can provide a good over-all illumination with great flexibility and make it possible to shift furniture and book stacks around without relocating lighting fixtures.

The advantages of fluorescent lamps can be summed up as follows: they use less than half the current required by incandescent lights for the same intensity and consequently produce less than one half the heat, a very important consideration if high intensity and air conditioning are to be used. They have a longer life, probably three or four times that of an incandescent bulb. They give greater flexibility. They have the disadvantage of higher installation and tube replacement costs, and fixture cleaning may take more time. If lights are required for a large percentage of the time during which the library is open, fluorescent light is cheaper, particularly if the cost of current is high. It should be remembered in this connection that most modern libraries rely completely on artificial light because of the depth of the rooms from the outside walls combined with compara-

tively low ceilings and in many cases with small window areas.

In any closed-access book stack incandescent lights may well be used. In a very large open-access stack the use of any one aisle is probably small enough so that incandescent lights are also indicated. But with a comparatively small collection and a large number of stack users, fluorescent lights are the economical arrangement.

Both incandescent and fluorescent light can by one means or another be given almost any color. At one time there was a vogue for blue bulbs in the belief that they were easier on the eyes. When fluorescent tubes first came into use their effect on the appearance of human skin, to which they gave a sickly pale green tint, was unpleasant, but experimentation and research has changed this and color is now a negligible factor because the client can select what he wants.

Fixtures

During the years that electric lamps have been used in libraries there has been a continuous improvement in fixtures as well as in the lamps themselves. In the old days lamps were placed so high that one seldom saw them and, when desk lamps were used close to the reading surface, shades directed the light to the table top and at the same time prevented the reader from looking at the bulb; then, as more general lighting seemed desirable, fixtures were designed that directed most of the light to the ceiling and indirect lighting resulted. Special shades for use over bulbs in stack aisles were developed. Frosting, which relieves the discomfort if one looks directly at the light, came into use for incandescent bulbs. Reflectors of various kinds were invented.

The first installations of new light sources and fixtures were often unsatisfactory. It seems to have been taken for granted that fluorescent lamps, since the source of light was distributed over the length of a long tube, would not require shielding. It is now obvious that this was absurd, and the need was soon met by protecting baffles, louvres, troffers, opaque glass or plastic. Any of these can be satisfactory, but the appearance of the installation is not always aesthetically acceptable. In reading rooms fluorescent lamps with troffers and reflectors are sometimes recessed into the ceiling, with acoustic tiles or plaster filling the space between the fixtures. The distance between the troffers depends upon the intensity desired, on whether the tubes are single or multiple, and on their wattage. The fixtures and tubes do not need to be in rows. Different patterns can be used. In selecting fixtures, methods of cleaning should be kept in mind. Air filtering helps because dust and dirt decrease the intensity of light. Any lamp gradually deteriorates to a point at which, even though it has not burned out, replacement is desirable. In rooms where scaffolding must be erected to change the light sources, it is economical to remove all the lamps at a set time before they begin to burn out and reinstall them in other parts of the building where changes can be made without ladders, thus permitting them to live out their natural lives.

Glare and Contrast

Discomfort is reduced if the surroundings provide comparatively little contrast with pages of the book that is being read, and it is recommended that table tops be fairly light in color, floors not too dark, and the walls, ceiling, and woodwork on the light side. Then when the eye wanders from book to table top or to the floor or walls there is no striking contrast in brightness to cause psychological discomfort. Glossy surfaces result in glare and should be avoided. Some architects and librarians feel that, even if dark surfaces in the reading room are less comfortable for the eyes, they make the whole room so much more attractive that they should be used.

Good over-all shielded lighting helps to prevent glare because the light comes from all directions and generally uniform illumination from multiple sources overlaps, producing a relatively shadowless room.

II. INTENSITY

The most desirable intensity of light on reading surfaces measured in foot candles is a controversial subject. Early in the century the intensity in some libraries was as little as one foot candle, and three or four were considered adequate. Since that time there has been a steady increase, averaging somewhere between five and ten percent a year in the number of foot candles recommended. Within the last three years the recommended level for libraries proposed by the Illuminating Engineering Society

has gone to 70 foot candles in reading areas. Representatives of the General Electric and Westinghouse companies say that this is a minimum figure and that as lighting methods improve it will be increased not only to 100, but to 200 foot candles. They report that in some administrative offices in their companies 500 foot candles are used already.

Most librarians, including the writer, are at a loss to know what to do about this increase and how to deal with it. We naturally tend to follow recommendations from the Illuminating Engineering Society and from the lighting experts, but we deplore any unnecessary increase in lighting cost. We are anxious to provide the most satisfactory lighting that is possible within our means, and we believe that the comfort of the reader and of the staff should receive very careful consideration. The effect of this increased intensity on library expenditures for electricity will be dealt with in section III.

A considerable number of architects, however, do not hesitate to say, in private at least, that they feel that the tendency toward very high light intensity is unfortunate. Ophthalmological research specialists generally have recommended levels well below those proposed by the trades involved. Dr. David G. Cogan, Director of the Howe Library of Ophthalmology, affiliated with the Harvard University Medical School and the Massachusetts Eye and Ear Infirmary, reports, "As far as health is concerned, it is a privilege and obligation of the medical profession, presumably the most qualified judge, to exercise its authority. The belief that relatively intense illumination is necessary for visual efficiency and that weak illumination induces organic disease of the eyes are probably the most widely held misconceptions pertaining to ophthalmology . . . These authors [in commercial laboratories] claim to have established a new science born of radically new concepts of the science of reading." Dr. Cogan goes on to say that the recommendations of this science have come as a considerable surprise to those familiar with man's ability to adapt himself to dark and to those who are acquainted with the previous reports that ten foot candles are adequate for ordinary purposes and that not more than 20 foot candles are required for exceptionally fine work. He also says that maximum visual acuity is reached at approximately ten foot candles, and that intensities greater than 20 have no practical significance. He made these statements 20 years ago and he repeats them today.

It should be remembered that light intensities may well be based on the conditions to be dealt with. Reading tasks vary. Good printing with a white background can be read comfortably with a lower intensity than a page having poor contrast which requires a higher intensity for the same reading comfort.

Under these circumstances what does a library planner do? One possibility is the course that was followed in the Lamont Library. Lighting there was installed to provide from 20 to 25 foot candles maintained, but so wired that with very little expense for alterations the intensity can be doubled. There seems to have been no need for an increase in 13 years. In this connection it should be borne in mind that fluorescent lamps have gradually increased in light efficiency in these years, and through good housekeeping and periodic replacement the intensities have increased considerably rather than decreased, as they tend to do in some installations.

III. COSTS

Lighting costs fall into three groups:

1. Installation includes wiring, switches, fixtures, lamps and effects on construction costs, to which should be added the problem of disposing of the heat generated by lighting. This last may be very considerable and should not be forgotten if high intensity light is to be used.
2. The cost of maintenance and upkeep includes the repair, cleaning and replacement of lamps.
3. The cost of electric current depends primarily, after the installation has been made, on the wattage of the lights used and cost of current per kilowatt. The latter varies a great deal from place to place, but with large users generally paying a lower rate. For many institutions, two cents per kilowatt will include the cost of current plus the maintenance and repair of the installation and lamp replacement, and the figures used in the next paragraph are based on that rate. A library is not satisfactory unless it is lighted well enough to enable the reader to work in comfort; cost should not be overemphasized, but disagreement on the desirable quality and intensity complicates the problem. It may be added that in many cases libraries have given little thought to lighting costs because these costs have not been included in the library budget but have been paid by the institution directly.

There are approximately 150 university (as distinguished from college) libraries in the country. The median of these libraries has a collection of 450,000 volumes and a student body of 7,500. Such a library, if we use generally accepted formulas, which will be discussed in detail in my book on library building planning, will require 100,000 square feet of floor space today. This figure can be expected to increase at the rate of five percent a year. Illuminating engineers report that $1\frac{1}{2}$ watts of light per square foot of floor space provides 20 foot candles in a typical installation today. A new installation ought to do 25 percent better, or 25 foot candles. The 100,000 square feet in the median university library would use 150,000 watts or 150 kilowatts an hour in order to obtain 20 foot candles throughout the building, and this, at two cents a kilowatt, would cost three dollars an hour. The average university library is open for 4,000 hours a year, which would mean $12,000 a year for lighting. This might be reduced to $10,000 because hallways may properly have a lower intensity and processing quarters are used shorter hours. If, however, the library uses 80 foot candles, the level that can be expected to be recommended within two or three years from now, lighting will cost $40,000 a year, or an extra $28,000 to $30,000.

The question that administrative officers must decide is whether it is more important to spend the money for increased intensity of light or for books and services. What is reasonable? As stated earlier, the writer does not know. Twenty to 25 foot candles were provided in 1948 for the Lamont Library and this can be doubled; but doubling would bring the intensity to a little more than half what is now proposed. If the recommended intensity doubles again in the next ten years, as there is every prospect that it will, the annual cost of lighting at that level would be eight times the sum that has sufficed up to now. It is only fair to repeat that this figure may well be reduced somewhat because lamps are becoming more efficient. On the other hand, it is certainly evident that, if we begin to use well over 100 foot candles, the heat generated, even with fluorescent tubes, will become so great as to place additional loads on our air conditioning equipment, if we have it, or to make our buildings almost impossibly hot if we do not have it.

Two final points might be made.

1. If the higher intensities are deemed best, ways and means should be worked out so that during the winter the buildings can be heated with the current used for lighting. This is now done to a considerable extent in some installations. It will not, however, help to relieve the problem of overheating during the summer.

2. If low intensities are used in most of a library's reading areas, it would seem desirable to provide higher intensities in one or more readily accessible areas for use for those who prefer more light, who have defective vision or who are working with small print or difficult to read manuscripts.

ABOUT THE AUTHOR—(See biographical note on page 79.)

More Light on Lighting

The following three articles were published in Library Journal *December 1, 1962. Lj introduced these brief articles as follows: "In our architectural issue last year, Keyes Metcalf, librarian emeritus of Harvard College Library, discussed some controversial aspects of adequate lighting for libraries. Here, another librarian takes issue with Mr. Metcalf, and Lj has brought in to referee the debate an illuminating engineer and a lighting and architectural consultant."*

Cost Is An Irrelevant Factor   by Robert T. Jordan

For some time now, I have been concerned about the potential mischief inherent in the article on "Library Lighting" by Keyes Metcalf in the December 1, 1961 issue of LIBRARY JOURNAL. It would be unfortunate if this article as it now stands should be incorporated without alteration in the major treatise he is compiling on college and university library buildings.

I was disturbed even before reading the article, at the introductory quotation above the title: "If the recommended intensity doubles again in the next ten years, as there is every prospect that it will, the annual cost . . . would be eight times the sum that has sufficed up to now." This is patently erroneous, by a factor of four.

However, the editor who selected this quotation (and inadvertently, I suppose, distorted its meaning by removal of certain words) was alert, at least, in indicating the most significant message in the article—a warning against unnecessarily high intensities of lighting because they would cost much more money.

More of the article is concerned with cost than with the optimum intensity of lighting. I think this is unfortunate in an article intended to be a general discussion of all aspects of library lighting. The importance of finding the optimum lighting intensity for maximum reader health, comfort, and efficiency is infinitely greater than the cost of this optimum intensity. The actual cost, per reader hour, of proper lighting, is so insignificant as to be irrelevant and hardly in good taste to even mention, at least in the wealthiest country in the world.

Suppose the median library of 450,000 volumes and 7,500 students (using Mr. Metcalf's example) has a staff of 65 and that the average student uses the library for 250 hours per year. This will be a total of approximately two million man-hours per year of use in the library, or a cost of approximately $1\frac{1}{4}$ cents per hour for each person in the library, for lighting at the intensities recommended by illuminating engineers of 80 foot candles in the reading areas, instead of the 10–20 foot candles suggested by Metcalf as sufficient. This cost is based on a total cost of $25,000 a year, which is in turn based on Metcalf's estimate of $40,000 a year for lighting at a maximum intensity of 80 foot candles in his postulated example. Metcalf assumes an *average* intensity of 66.7 foot candles, with his maximum of 80 foot candles. I submit that an *average* of 41.7 foot candles, for a total cost of $25,000 is more realistic, considering the high proportion of total library space that is used for exits, lobbies, corridors, staff rooms, stairways, stack and storage areas, and washrooms which require only 20 or 30 foot candles, and the large proportion of space used for auditoriums, utilities, janitors' closets, offices, work rooms, conference rooms, etc. that are in use for half or less of the 4,000 hours yearly that Metcalf has assumed the library will be open.

Metcalf proposes that 10 to 20 foot candles are sufficient in library reading rooms, and that any amount in excess of this is an unnecessary expense. Among illuminating engineers there is general agreement that a minimum of 50 to 70 foot candles is normally desirable in offices and library reading rooms. They have accepted the carefully documented, scientific research in this

SOURCE: Reprinted from Robert T. Jordan, "Cost Is An Irrelevant Factor" in "More Light on Lighting," *Library Journal*, vol. 87, December 1, 1962, pp. 4326–4329, by permission of the publisher and the author.

field, principally the studies of Dr. Richard Blackwell at the University of Michigan (not mentioned in the Metcalf article).

I have modified the generally accepted recommendation for 50 to 70 foot candles by use of the word "normally." Unfortunately, there does exist an inflexible and unreasoning pressure from lighting fixture manufacturers and power utility interests for truly excessive levels of illumination. Metcalf is aware of this, and he is correct in emphasizing that there should be no completely inflexible restrictions or requirements that do not take into consideration the entire visual environment (brightness, brightness differences, colors, textures, daylight controls, esthetic characteristics, and spatial and architectural considerations). It is true that Blackwell's findings can be interpreted to indicate that under *optimum* environmental conditions (i.e., size of print, contrast, lack of glare, etc.) that 10 to 20 foot candles are sufficient, but for *all around* utility at least 50 to 70 foot candles are indicated. Actually, a very good case can be made that library reading rooms should have higher lighting levels than classrooms, where the materials used are subject to more control (pencils versus pens, size of type, type of paper, etc.). Libraries typically include extreme varieties of material and visual tasks. For example, for efficient utilization of pencilled notes, at least 63 foot candles are required. Duplicated or dittoed material typically requires from 100 to 2000 foot candles, depending on the quality, for maximum visual efficiency and comfort. Thus, the recommendation for 50 to 70 foot candles is an attempt at a reasonable compromise for a situation where there cannot be any rigid control over the visual tasks.

In the text of the Metcalf article are references to the opinions of "illuminating engineers," "lighting experts," "architects," "ophthalmological research specialists" and the "medical profession." This sounds quite impressive, but may I respectfully submit that actually, only illuminating engineers can be considered as authoritative lighting experts, although the research of the illuminating engineers obviously requires the cooperation and teamwork of architects and biologists, the medical profession and psychologists, among others. For these other experts, concern for illumination standards represents only a small fraction of their total activities and interests. It is only the illumination engineer who has sponsored authoritative scientific research on this subject. This is tacitly acknowledged by Metcalf in the

sentence, "We naturally tend to follow recommendations from the Illuminating Engineering Society and from the lighting experts, but we deplore any unnecessary increase in lighting cost." But the scientific basis for the recommendations of the IES is not mentioned.

Metcalf refers to the *opinions* (my emphasis) of experts in *other* fields that the "lighting experts" are unreasonable in their recommendations. The only specific authority that he quotes is Dr. David G. Cogan, a respected ophthalmologist, who Metcalf states has repeated the same statements today as he made 20 years ago, that intensities of no more than 10–20 foot candles are required, even for exceptionally fine work. I submit that the opinion of one ophthalmologist who says that he hasn't changed his mind from the position that he held 20 years ago is not a sufficient scientific basis for recommendations that will affect hundreds of future buildings and millions of students.

Ophthalmologists, contrary to what one might expect, have not been responsible for any scientific research in the field of lighting standards.

The lighting level preferred by any one individual, or the subjectively expressed preferences of a group of individuals is not a scientific basis for determination of lighting levels. All too often one is influenced by the lighting levels experienced in one's environment as a child. Such psychological and associational factors can be very misleading.

The introduction to the November 1958 special issue on "Light & Vision" of *Industrial Medicine and Surgery* * states:

One of the virtues of science is the willingness to relegate to history and museums that which no longer is serviceable, or at least to mark all such as no longer the best. Prior to the Ann Arbor Conference too many sacred cows were being nurtured in the fields of vision and lighting. Recognizing the prior achievement of no ultimates, the Ann Arbor Conference was a mission of slaughter of vision and lighting fallacies.

H. C. Weston in an article titled "Lighting and Health" in the November-December 1960 issue of the *Royal Society of Health Journal* states:

Contemporary recommended levels for industry for different purposes are considerably higher than 20 years ago. This is in keeping with the general rise in standards of living which has occurred in this period. It has long been known that visual capacities, for example, acuity, contrast sensitivity, colour discrimination, and speed of perception, continue to improve as the level of illumination is increased up to outdoor lighting levels.

There is an unfortunate juxtaposition of sentences (on p. 4083 of the Metcalf article) that gives a strong impression that the recommendations of intensity by the Illuminating Engineering Society have in some manner been influenced by commercial considerations. This is reinforced by the general concern as to cost, and by the referral on the top of page 4084 to this "new science" as emanating from "commercial laboratories." It should be pointed out that the representatives of the large electric companies, who might conceivably be considered as representing "commercial" interests in selling more light bulbs, had a subordinate role in the studies of Dr. Richard Blackwell (now at Ohio State) at the University of Michigan, which were sponsored jointly by the departments of Psychology, Ophthalmology, Vision Research Laboratories, and School of Public Health, under a grant from the Illuminating Engineering Society.

The only factual justification in the Metcalf article for low levels of light intensity is Dr. Cogan's statement that maximum visual acuity is reached at ten foot candles. This might largely be true for material of extreme brightness contrast but what of eye fatigue, speed of perception, fine print material, or material with low brightness contrast? Mention should be made of the findings of scientists of the levels at which maximum speed of perception (assimilations per second) is reached, and at which eye fatigue is minimized.

The article is without reference to significant articles in the past on library lighting. At the very least, I would suggest that mention should be made of Blackwell's report, of Logan's article in Lj (see Dec. 1, '58, pp. 3392-93), of the pages on lighting in Ellsworth's report on library buildings in the "State of the Library Art" series and to the new "American Standard Guide for School Light-

ing" developed jointly by the Illuminating Engineering Society, the American Institute of Architects, and the National Council for Schoolhouse Construction. An extremely perceptive discussion of lighting requirements, critical of the tendency in America to completely eliminate daylight and to utilize uniformly high levels of illumination in a completely mechanically controlled environment can be found in Schools in the U.S.A., obtainable for $2.80 from British Information Services, New York 20, N.Y. Published in July 1961, this is probably the single best résumé of American school construction.

I am concerned that libraries have adequate lighting. If I am at all biased, it is toward moderation in lighting intensity, since a personal eye condition causes me to prefer a medium level of illumination, between the extremes of gross inadequacy that I have experienced in past years in many libraries (e.g., Berkeley Public, DC Public), and the extraordinary high levels of illumination of some modern banks, offices, etc. So I can truly appreciate Mr. Metcalf's apprehension that recommended levels of lighting might conceivably get out of hand. But I realize that this personal apprehension might be without validity for the average person, since the human eye was developed generally speaking for use under the open sky, with lighting intensities in the thousands or tens of thousands of foot candles. I am aware that very few individuals are without the capacity to contract their pupils sufficiently so as to read with comfort in light of hundreds of foot candles (as on an open porch).

There is much that is very useful in the remaining portions of the article, particularly in the discussion of lighting quality. Also, I like very much the realistic and useful suggestion in the article that as much as possible two different levels of lighting intensity be provided in a given area, to more nearly meet the differing requirements of various visual tasks.

NOTES

*The complete proceedings of the March 1958 conference on "Light and Vision," presenting the exhaustive studies made by Blackwell and associates, are available from the School of Public Health at the University of Michigan for $5.

ABOUT THE AUTHOR—Robert Thayer Jordan received his A.B. degree from Antioch College in 1947 and the M.L.S. degree in 1957 at the University of California. He has served as Librarian at Taft College, and from 1960-68, was Library Specialist in Higher Education for the Council on Library Resources, Inc. Mr. Jordan has written several books, his latest two being Tomorrow's Library: Direct Access and Delivery, and Media Power (both 1969). In 1968 he became Director of Media Services at Federal City College in Washington, D.C.

Observe Light, Evaluate Reports

by William M. C. Lam

Keyes D. Metcalf in "Library Lighting" has stated very well the dilemma of the thoughtful library consultant who must make a professional judgment regarding the value of increased expenditure for lighting. He is bothered by the inconsistency between his own experience, observations and common sense, and some of the recommendations of the Illuminating Engineering Society suggesting much higher lighting levels. He has witnessed the constant increases of the recommended levels and the suggestions of continued increases up to daylight levels as lighting methods improve.

He concludes with the very sensible suggestion: "If low intensities are used in most of the library's reading areas, it would seem desirable to provide higher intensities in one or more readily accessible areas for use for those who prefer more light, who have defective vision or who are working with small print or difficult to read manuscripts."

Robert T. Jordan, however, indicates the confusion that can be caused if the claims of lighting studies are not tested by observation and experience and if the readers are not careful to distinguish between recommendations "based on a research report" and the contents of "the report" itself. The actual Blackwell Report states that reasonable tasks require very little light: .6 footcandles for 12 pt. text type; 1 footcandle for typed original, good ribbon; 7 footcandles for no. 2 pencil on tracing paper over blueprint; while difficult tasks require very substantially more to be seen at the *same rate of speed and accuracy:* 77 footcandles for shorthand copy, no. 3 pencil; 3140 footcandles for typed original, poor ribbon; 5090 footcandles for white lines on blueprint, tracing paper overlay.

Mr. Jordan might have asked himself:

1. When am I limited by reading speed rather than thinking or writing speed?
2. On what basis was 70 footcandles selected, or 30 footcandles . . . years ago?
3. Do I know the time distribution of various "tasks" in my own library for a single day, week or year. If not, does the IES for all libraries?
4. Why not use no. 2 pencil, good typewriter ribbons, etc.?
5. If 3140 footcandles are "required," what is the difference between 20, 40, or 70?
6. Should I design around the most normal tasks, or the most difficult? Is safety involved (what evidence is there from medical sources)? Can I assume less than ideal conditions for the infrequent difficult task? Can there be a clear "right" or "wrong" answer to this question? Would I design a highway for "normal" speed on the 4th of July?

I would like to suggest some steps to be taken by those involved in building programs, libraries or otherwise:

1. Observe light. Learn how you see, and the many factors that influence your comfort.
2. Analyze "recommended light levels" with reference to your observations and experiences.
3. Recruit scientists (any field) on your staff to read and summarize various lighting research reports and to judge the recommendations reported to be "based on" the reports of Blackwell on reflected glare-polarization (quantity); Chorlton-Davidson on reflected glare; and Cogan (Massachusetts Eye & Ear Infirmary) giving the medical point of view.
4. Ask an ophthalmologist about lighting and eye health.

Lighting programs cannot be based on simple numerical recommendations, by me or anyone,

SOURCE: Reprinted from William M. C. Lam, "Observe Light, Evaluate Reports" in "More Light on Lighting," *Library Journal*, vol. 87, December 1, 1962, pp. 4329–4330.

but must take into consideration so many factors that nothing makes sense except individual judgments (by the best qualified professional available) for each specific design problem. Budget factors must also be considered along with physiological, psychological and aesthetic requirements in relation to the particular building design.

A librarian or library committee should be critical of the results with the simple criterion, "Is it a visual environment appropriate and comfortable for the purpose?" judging this only by eyes and brains. As to the details, such as fluorescent or incandescent, local or general illumination, select the best architect, give him the full responsibility and challenge him to do the best, not the minimum. Support him with a lighting consultant of his choice, if he desires the help, and if not fully confident of a proposed unconventional approach, reserve modest funds for evaluation of test installations (mocked-up in your own institution or demonstrated elsewhere).

Precise design, based on criteria established for the specific building will not only result in the best visual environment, but is likely to be the most economical as well.

ABOUT THE AUTHOR—At the time this article was written (1962) Mr. Lam was a consultant for Co-ordination of Lighting and Architecture, Cambridge, Massachusetts.

Too Much Light Is Poor Light

by C. L. Crouch

Unfortunately the standards of the Illuminating Engineering Society have been misquoted. The illumination levels recommended in the *IES Lighting Handbook*[1] are as follows:

	Footcandles on Task
Reading room	
Study and notes	70
Ordinary reading	30
Stacks	30
Book repair and binding	50
Cataloging	70
Card files	70
Check-in and check-out desks	70
Lobby*	20
Corridors,* elevators, escalators, stairways	20

*Not listed under "Library" but values for similar locations

In view of these values, I suggest that Mr. Metcalf might like to revise his economic analysis with the footcandle levels distributed as above according to the floor areas involved. It is certain that the average value for the 100,000 square feet will be considerably less than the figure of 80 footcandles that he attributes to the Society.

The Society has earnestly sought the right basis for its recommendations by sponsoring an eight-year program of basic research to determine a method of evaluating various visual tasks in terms of the amount of illumination necessary for efficient seeing. This was conducted by Dr. H.R. Blackwell of the University of Michigan.[2] Copies of the papers describing this work are available from the Society. In simple terms, each task requires a given amount of light depending upon its size and contrast. Dr. Blackwell's results point out that only low levels of illumination are needed for printed material, but that much more is needed for poorer contrast, e.g. No. 2 pencil writing on white paper (30 per cent contrast) as compared with black print on white paper (90 per cent contrast). Thus the recommendations for the Reading Room are in terms of the task: 30 footcandles for printed material; 70 footcandles for reading involving the taking of pencilled notes.

We appreciate the role of the ophthalmologist in guarding the health of the visual processes, but we do not find ophthalmologists themselves doing research in psychophysics to determine the response of the visual processes to light stimuli in their various complexities. The ophthalmologist does not study the light needed to see objects of various sizes and contrasts during the intervals of the eye pauses involved in visual scanning. He does not study the parameters of glare involved in overly bright sources. This sort of study is involved in such groups as the Armed Forces-National Research Council Vision Committee, the Optical Society of America and the Illuminating Engineering Society.

From this viewpoint, it is apparent that Dr. Cogan has not followed visual acuity studies in relation to illumination to the degree that he is acquainted with the work of R. J. Lythgoe, M.D., D.Sc. (1932),[3] in which he showed that visual acuity continued rising up to the limit of his illumination, 500 footcandles on white paper. Later in 1955, Stevens and Foxell[4] confirmed Lythgoe's work and went beyond it to show visual acuity increasing up to 1000 footcandles on white paper.

One could pursue Mr. Metcalf's economic argument in favor of further savings by cutting his 25 footcandles to 10 and save another $4000–$5000 for books and other services, if the illumination level has little significance. Why does he feel that 20–25 footcandles is a valid figure? Has he tried higher and lower levels of good quality lighting?

SOURCE: Reprinted from C. L. Crouch, "Too Much Light Is Poor Light" in "More Light on Lighting," *Library Journal*, vol. 87, December 1, 1962, pp. 4330–4331.

When all is said and done, we come back to the fact that a serious, sincere attempt has been made by Dr. Blackwell to determine the needs for quick, accurate seeing involved in scanning for reading and writing. The IES recommendations are based on this.

"Quality" is an equally important partner with "quantity." Light is thrown away if it is glaring and poorly distributed. Whenever there are complaints of "too much light," the quality is poor. Light is unobtrusive if properly controlled. There are 1000 footcandles in the shade of a tree on a sunny day. This is comfortable lighting. There is a simple test to use in interiors. If one sits or stands at the end of a room looking horizontally and shades the eyes with the hand and then suddenly removes the hand, there will be a shock of brightness if the lighting installation is glaring. If there is no shock, the lighting has passed its first test.[5]

Glossy reflections from books or notes are a further source of deleterious effects.[6] These reflections of overhead lighting equipment overlay the detail to be seen and greatly lower visibility. One can take a mirror and put it down on the desk. If the reflection of the overhead lighting is very bright, there is too much concentration of downward light which will cause the characters in the book or the pencil marks in the notes to be reduced in contrast. Much of the effectiveness of the light is lost if it is reflected in this way. Greater diffusion of the light will reduce this effect, such as large areas of low brightness luminaires.

NOTES

[1] *IES Lighting Handbook*, 3rd Edition, 1959. Illuminating Engineering Society, 345 E. 47th St., New York, N.Y.

[2] "Development and Use of a Quantitative Method for Specification of Interior Illumination Levels on the Basis of Performance Data," H.R. Blackwell, *Illuminating Engineering*, Vol. LIV, No. 6, July 1959; "New Methods of Determining Illumination Required for Tasks," C.L. Crouch, *Illuminating Engineering*, Vol. LIII, No. 8, August 1958.

[3] *The Measurement of Visual Acuity*, R.J. Lythgoe, M.D., D.Sc., Special Report No. 173 of the Medical Research Council, H.M. Stationery Office, London, 1932.

[4] "Visual Acuity," W.R. Stevens and C.A.P. Foxell, *Light and Lighting*, Vol. XLVIII, No. 12, December, 1955. Illuminating Engineering Society (London), 32 Victoria St., London S.W.1, England.

[5] *There is a technical solution which a photometric laboratory can give. If a lighting unit meets the "scissors curve" of the* American Standard Guide for School Lighting, *it will produce comfortable lighting.*

[6] *American Standard Guide for School Lighting*, ASA A23.1-1962, American Standards Assn., New York City.

ABOUT THE AUTHOR—Cazamer L. Crouch, a graduate of the University of Michigan, began his work in illumination in 1928 when he worked for electric companies, studying glare in lighting design. From 1944-67 he was Technical Director of the Illuminating Engineering Society, and won the IES Gold Medal. In late 1967 Mr. Crouch became Director of Research of the Illuminating Engineering Research Institute. He is an internationally known lecturer, the author of numerous papers, with world-wide renown for research on light and vision.

A Guide to the Librarian's Responsibility in Achieving Quality in Lighting and Ventilation

by Ellsworth Mason

Here Mason brings together for our consideration the two most important factors of comfort: lighting and ventilation. Quality in both is difficult to achieve and, particularly in the latter, to maintain. The following guidelines are exceptionally well conceived for our layman's level of understanding.

Quality, not intensity, is the keystone of good lighting. Low intensity of good quality is far superior to high intensity light of poor quality. Only in the last few months have I had any sympathy for Keyes Metcalf's contention long held, and still, I suspect, close to his heart, that 20 footcandles is high enough intensity for library lighting. I worked for eight years in about that intensity in the old Colorado College library, and it was miserable.

Last fall, after moving into a house about 15 years old, I discovered the best lighting for studying floor plans I have ever found in a dwelling, under a chandelier above the dining room table. It is a five-lamp incandescent fixture (a multiple light source), with the lamps pointed upward (semi-indirect light), each covered with a frosted globe (glare-free diffusion). The fixture is about three feet above table top and three feet below an eight-foot-high ceiling. The room is about 12' by 12'. The walls and ceiling are painted off-white, and, above table height, are comparatively unbroken, save for a few small paintings and one arched entryway. In a sense, this is the closest you can come in a cube to Dr. H. Richard Blackwell's experimental internal sphere, the best of all possible lighting environments. Noting the remarkable lighting, I tested it with my light meter. Placed on the table, the meter measured 26 footcandles. I therefore assure you that if you can split up your library into walled rooms 12' by 12' with an eight-foot ceiling, painted off-white, with a similar fixture, you have excellent reading light at 26 foot-candles intensity.

The condition is different in larger open spaces, but this example shows the two centrally important factors that make for good quality in lighting; the absence of glare, either direct or reflected glare; and the endless reflection of tiny points of light from multiple surfaces, creating an extremely complex interfiling of light rays within the room, with light bouncing off every surface in the room, instead of emanating, for example, in a cone from a single source. The interfiling and reverberation of the light rays are of the greatest importance.

The single most important problem in lighting is glare, caused by extremely intense centers of light. The glare problem became serious with the advent of fluorescent tubes, which are much more intensely bright over a longer span of space than incandescent lamps of the frosted globe type. Less glare is caused by incandescent lighting, but its heat load is so much greater than that of comparable fluorescent lighting that its use is impractical in an air-conditioned building, since the cost of the additional tonnage required of the refrigeration system is so great. Fluorescent lighting will be with us for a long time, and we must solve its problems.

Glare is of two kinds: *reflected glare,* from the reflection of overhead fixtures off a reading task; and *direct glare,* from an intense point of light at the most disturbing angle to the eye (which is generally the fixture at the most acute angle from the horizontal plane at eye level). In either case, glare has two effects: it causes the pupil of the eye to contract, restricting the amount of light that can enter; and it reduces the contrast on the read-

SOURCE: Reprinted from Ellsworth Mason, "A Guide to the Librarian's Responsibility in Achieving Quality in Lighting and Ventilation," *Library Journal,* vol. 92, January 15, 1967, pp. 201-206, by permission of the publisher and the author.

ing task between the print and its background. Both effects intensify the difficulty of reading. While no fixture can completely eliminate either direct or reflected glare (even the ceiling in indirect lighting can produce both types of glare), it is possible to reduce glare so that it is not an irritant. To do so is the central problem in selecting lighting fixtures.

Only by reducing direct glare can we hope to reduce reflected glare, and it is possible to control direct glare adequately by the use of properly designed eggcrate louvers. It can be nearly eliminated by the use of para-wedge louvers (which have the adverse psychological effect of leaving the entire ceiling dark, a condition that feels unnatural). Both of these fixture covers leave the bulb openly exposed, and reflected glare is intense directly below them.

If the fixture is covered with a diffusing lens, such as a prismatic or opalescent plastic lens, reflected glare can be controlled, unless the lamps in the fixture are so close to the lens that they show through badly. This kind of lens often has a very high surface brightness, which intensifies direct glare, and a lens with a low surface brightness must be chosen.

In recent years, Dr. H. Richard Blackwell of Ohio State University has proclaimed the use of multi-layer polarized lenses as the complete answer to the glare problem. These lenses are extremely expensive to install, and they reduce the intensity of the light source so drastically that to achieve a given lighting intensity, a much higher wattage is required, which greatly increases both operating costs and the heat load in the building. I have yet to see an installation of fixtures with polarized lenses in a library, probably because of the cost factor.

In my experience, the kind of fluorescent fixture that best diffuses light is a $2' \times 4'$ "can" fixture—one which holds the ballast and tubes in a metal box. This size fixture can hold from two to six tubes, and it diffuses best when only two are used, so positioned in the can that they distribute light evenly over the inner surface of the lens. The can should be no less than five inches deep, and the bulb should be positioned as far from the lens as possible. The lens should be a plastic diffusing lens.

Such a fixture will control reflected glare and go a long way toward providing the good quality lighting that comes only from totally good light diffusion. The problem of direct glare still re-

mains, but it can be nearly eliminated if the lighting fixture is placed within a ceiling coffer deep enough to place it out of sight. To accommodate a $2' \times 4'$ fixture, the poured ceiling will have to provide a coffer $4\frac{1}{2}'$ square, like that used in the Colorado College Library, which has, without exception, the best library lighting I have seen.

The second factor required in library lighting is the multiple interfiling of light rays (mentioned in connection with my home lighting). A fixture that diffuses light well is basic, because when light emerges from the fixture, it scatters widely, sending out multiple rays in many directions. To get the kind of interfiling that we need, this effect of a single fixture must be multiplied as many times as possible.

Blackwell has found that by one measurement, the quality of light is directly equivalent to the percentage of the ceiling covered by light. The larger the portion of the ceiling issuing light, the more multiple is the total scattering effect of the fixtures. In the case of a luminous ceiling, which is entirely covered by light, the scattering effect is so complete that it casts no shadow. Its diffusion is total. In the ordinary case, it will be impossible to provide this much light in a building because of cost, and the rule of thumb here is to separate the lighting fixtures from each other. Located singly, not touching each other, the fixtures will diffuse better and provide better quality lighting than if placed in strips.

Architects oppose this idea. In the first place, it is cheaper to hang and wire fixtures if they are in strips, rather than separated from each other. In the second place, architects consider lighting fixtures as decorative properties, and use them to paint the ceiling with light patterns for their esthetic value, which is generally quite minimal, with little regard for the quality of lighting that results from the arrangement. There is nothing totally esthetic (or unesthetic, for that matter) about a ceiling full of $2' \times 4'$ fixtures run on $6'$ centers, with a $4'$ space between them. Nevertheless, if good quality lighting is to result, assuming a good fixture, there must be as many separate sources of light as possible.

One final important factor in the diffusion of light within a room is the character of the "surround," as the technical term goes—the walls, floor, and any furniture or equipment within the lighted space. In my home lighting, the surround is off-white painted walls with little else to intervene, excellent reflecting surfaces. In a library, it will be the outer walls (which are sometimes glass, and glass at night is, for lighting purposes, black), inner walls, stacks, the floor covering, seats, tables, and equipment. The rule of thumb is that the darker they are, the lower the intensity and the poorer the quality of light that will result from any given ceiling light source. Interior decorators tend to use dark-colored woods, to the extent that they can afford it, which encourages the use of dark-tone harmonizing colors in the rest of the interior. Both to provide a cheerful interior and to achieve the best possible lighting, the librarian, working with an open mind, should encourage the use of light tones in the interior decor (but for heaven's sake *not* the pale, anemic, blonde wood that so besets libraries). The fact that spaces in modern libraries tend to be comparatively free of interior walls greatly reduces the area of vertical reflectance, and makes it all the more important that interior furniture and equipment, very especially the stacks, which are the highest vertical objects in the library, should be light-colored.

The question of how much intensity is desirable in library lighting is treated at length, and with important historical considerations, in Keyes Metcalf's book. I quite agree with his unstated opinion, inferred from the details he presents, that we are in the midst of a conditioning at the hands of the lighting industry that leads to our feeling the need for ever higher intensities. In a country where home lighting is nonexistent or, at the most, one footcandle, five footcandles is intense. In a country where supermarket lighting is a hundred footcandles, seventy-five is not intense. Where this ends, short of burning our eyeballs to cinders I, like Keyes, cannot predict. But at the present time, it means that low lighting intensities in libraries do not feel good to mid-20th Century Americans. In some libraries, this fact has led to the simple-minded insistence on very high lighting intensities, far above a hundred footcandles, with no concern at all for achieving good quality in the light. Not only is high intensity of no use if the quality of light is poor, it is worse than low intensity. If the quality of light is bad, *the higher the intensity, the worse the light is.*

The psychological effect of lighting on the feeling of a library interior is extremely important, and, to me, it does not feel good below about 55 f.c., even with good quality lighting. It feels totally good at about the 70 f.c. intensity recommended for reading areas by the Illuminating Engineering Society, no matter how they arrived at that figure. It does not feel any better in the very good quality lighting of Yale's Beinecke Library reading room at 120-140 f.c., and the very great difference in cost involved in such an increase of intensity is well described in Keyes' book.

What can a librarian do to help achieve good lighting in his new library? At least five things:

1. The librarian can alert the architect to the special importance of good quality lighting to a library building. Architects feel uncomfortable in dealing with lighting. They do not know much about it, and are impatient with its problems. They are much more interested in painting with light than in providing good reading light. Some of our most famous architects are incredibly ignorant about lighting. When appraising a potential architect, make sure that the buildings he has designed have good lighting.
2. Detail specific lighting fixtures, by catalog numbers, in the building specifications. With an "or equal" clause, it will get competitive bids. The engineers designing the building's lighting should obtain technical data about each lighting fixture from an independent testing laboratory (not from the manufacturer, or from a laboratory known to accept the manufacturer's data). Until these are subjected to independent appraisal, it is impossible to design either the quantity or the quality of the lighting in a building.
3. Hire a lighting consultant; you cannot depend on the engineers used by your architect to solve lighting problems. Someone on the library's side must appraise the lighting fixtures (or propose them, if needed), review the lighting layout plans, and advise whether the intensity and quality of the lighting is adequate. It will cost a few hundred dollars and save the waste of thousands. The minute a lighting consultant was hired in planning the new Hofstra University Library, the level of thinking about the lighting shot skyward from a very low level.
4. Have mock-ups made of the various lighting fixtures being considered. Install the fixtures at a characteristic ceiling height, spaced as you intend them to be in your building. The librarian can tell a great deal about the degree of surface brightness on a fixture lens, and this is an important factor in choosing them.
5. If any lighting fixtures proposed by the light-

ing subcontractor "as equal" are different from those specified, obtain the proper lighting data for the lighting consultant and have him review the lighting plans again. Nothing can be taken for granted in planning lighting.

VENTILATION

A good ventilation system is as important as good lighting in affecting the patron's reaction to a library. As in the case of lighting, good quality in the air *distribution* is more important than temperature settings. The basic requirements of a good quality ventilation system for a library are basically simple: it must distribute air throughout the building at the proper volume, at the proper temperature, from a proper distance (air blown from diffusers located too close to the reader greatly exaggerate the temperature), and at a suitable noise level. The last two requirements are comparatively easy to achieve with some intelligent planning. The first two are so difficult to achieve that I have never seen a building that is uniformly comfortable temperature-wise in all seasons of the year. Those that are uniformly comfortable at some seasons of the year are rare enough.

The greatest comfort difficulties are encountered in the interim seasons, or in climates where great differences in temperature occur within the same day. To achieve any pre-set temperature all the time, it is necessary to have both heat and refrigeration available constantly. Any time the outside temperature changes enough to make the internal temperature move above or below the temperature setting the air in the ventilation system must be either heated or cooled, depending on the direction of the outside change. Most buildings are run, for economic reasons, on the crude basis of banking the fires at the end of May, and turning off the refrigeration system at the end of September. As a result, it is impossible to heat the air on cold days during the summer, or to cool it on hot days during the winter, and in spring and fall, when the temperature flips randomly, the dislocations in comfort in a building can be extreme.

The control of air temperatures is crucial in ventilation, for a number of reasons, all due to space limitations in any building. In the first place, the ventilation system, in any cycle of air, i.e. any time it has circulated throughout the building and returned to the air intake fans again, will spill out of the building, through pre-designed exits, about 25 per cent of the air, picking up a new 25 per cent at the ventilation fans to freshen the recirculated air. The air added to the system comes into the building at outside temperature, which is a different temperature from the tempered air returning from the building to be recirculated. The two airs are mixed together before they reach the heating or cooling coils on their way to the air diffusers throughout the building, and they have a tendency to stratify, with the warmer air riding on top of the layer of cooler air. It is extremely important to homogenize the two temperatures before they reach the tempering coils, because if this is not done, the same amount of heat or cold is applied to the two strata of air, raising the temperature of one, for example, from 50° to 60° and of the other from 70° to 80°. In this case 60° air would come out of some diffusers in the building and 80° air out of others, neither temperature suitable.

By providing a properly designed mixing chamber it is possible to homogenize air of different temperatures, but this takes *space,* and engineers constantly complain that architects never provide adequate mixing chambers. If this is the case—and my experience convinces me that it is—the entire ventilation system is to a certain extent crippled from the start.

The second problem in temperature control involves the ducts, the great hollow metal shafts that conduct air from the fans vertically up through the floors, and horizontally out along the floor to the air diffusers that let the air out into the rooms. Ducts require an enormous amount of space, and there is never enough space to accommodate easily all that are needed. The horizontal duct runs are concealed in hollow ceilings, hung from the structural ceilings, and must compete for limited space with the plumbing and lighting of the building. Indeed, one of the marks of a skillful architect is how much duct work he can get into a ceiling.

The easiest way to distribute air is up through one continuous duct vertically, with one horizontal duct for each floor, from which are fed the individual ceiling air diffusers. This duct system is essentially one great, irregularly shaped box, with holes around the outer edge. With only a slight degree of sophistication, this kind of a system can feed any unit of space that needs only one single temperature control, such as a large unbroken bookstack and reading area, up to a certain size— say 10,000 square feet. However, if within that area one room is enclosed—a seminar room, for example—it must have its separate temperature control to provide satisfactory air conditioning. This means that it must be tempered by a separate re-heat coil within the duct system, which requires more space. Given six rooms on the same floor, the competition for space to locate the ducts can be extreme. Consequently, the architect always has a tendency to place too large or too complex an area on a single temperature control, and as a result somewhere in the zone, the control breaks down. This accounts for the hot and cold spots as you walk through most buildings.

One more complication in designing temperature control springs from the fact that in any area, the system must be designed to handle the peak occupancy of the area. If a room will hold 28 readers at peak load, then the system must be of such capacity that it can cool the room when 28 bodies are radiating heat in it. This it does by moving a volume of cooled air through the room. The volume of air can be varied, within limits, and the temperature can be dropped, within limits, to balance off the increased heat load that results from more people entering the room, but it is never flexible enough to accommodate just a few readers in the room. For the few it is always too cold. This is why supermarkets are generally freezing cold except when they are jammed with people on weekends.

I have said enough to indicate the magnitude of the problems involved in controlling temperature of internal spaces. There is one added problem on the outer walls, caused by the fact that a body sitting close to them will radiate heat to the outer wall if it is cooler than the air circulating in the room, especially if the walls are glass. This heat loss makes the reader feel cold, even though the air all around him may be of a comfortable temperature. To counterbalance this effect, the entire perimeter of a building must carry a supplementary heating system to produce a heat rise along the wall and a vigorous heat rise if the wall is glass. In drier climates where heat transfer is inhibited, this can be done by placing ducts from the central air-diffusing system around the entire perimeter. In a wet climate, it is most often produced by using fintube heaters or fan-coil units, or induction units along the wall. These systems take the already tempered air within the room and heat it further, sending it up along the wall by heat rise or by air movement.

Fin-tube units depend on the natural rise of the air passing over heated fins to produce upward air movement, which causes no noise problem. The air in fan-coil units is driven by a fan, which generally has two, and sometimes three, speed settings, and at high speed, most fan-coil units produce far too much noise for comfort in a library. This problem can be controlled by listening to sample units in the planning, discarding the noisy ones, and choosing for the building units that can produce the required cooling or heating capacity at *medium* speed. Induction units work by introducing air under high pressure into a chamber from which it escapes through nozzles, thereby inducing a movement of the room air upward over the tempering units. The passage of the compressed air through the nozzles at peak capacity can produce a very annoying whistle. Again the solution to the problem lies in choosing units of such capacity that they can temper the air at less than peak capacity.

I do not have space to explore the problem of distributing air through the building at the proper volume everywhere so that the total flow of air into the building is balanced, and not flowing too fast into one area at the expense of other areas. Engineers play with the balance of the ventilation system for a year after the building is in operation, adjusting dampers everywhere endlessly. All of this is done, they say, with the greatest scientific calculation. But there is nothing like moving into a new building to indicate clearly that the claims of the technologists are grossly exaggerated, and that, in the end, they produce a system that is made livable by trial and error, much as we adjust the "air-conditioning" in our living room by opening and closing the windows.

If the technologists are guessing to a certain extent, what then, can a librarian do to achieve a comfortably ventilated building? He can be prepared to think about a number of questions that arise in planning the building:

1. Should it be air-conditioned, by which is generally meant refrigerated as well as heated, or not? The answer is unequivocally yes. There is no question in the south or on the east coast. Even if the college does not have a summer session, there is enough hot weather in late spring and early fall to justify it, and sooner or later, everyone will have a summer session. In Colorado Springs, which has the mildest, driest climate summer and winter I have ever seen, I was at first convinced that it was not necessary, but, providentially, the summer before we completed planning, we had a scorcher that indicated

clearly the need for air conditioning. In that building of 50,000 square feet, the cost of adding refrigeration to a simple air-distribution system was $30,000, a mere drop in a total building cost of $1,250,000. Smaller ducts are needed for a fully air-conditioned system than for a ventilation only air-distribution system, and there is considerable saving in ductwork if the building is planned to provide refrigeration. If refrigeration is added to the building at a later date, as is sometimes the case, it must cope with a duct system not ideally suited to its needs.

2. What temperature setting should we choose in designing an air-conditioning system? So far as heating goes, the sky is the limit, up to heat absorption capacity of spiders, which sometimes is required in nonlibrary buildings. The difference between providing 65° and 75° is small, in terms of equipment and maintenance. For cooling, there is considerable difference in cost between achieving 75° and 72°. The former should be the aim. Much higher gets uncomfortable, especially in wet climates.

3. What kind of filtration should the ventilation system provide? Architects do not generally realize that library buildings require a much greater degree of filtration than most other buildings. They must be told that this is the case. A minimum filtration system should provide some kind of fixed or moving pad filter, to catch the large dust particles, backed by high-efficiency bag strainers that provide 85 per cent filtration. This combination is easy to maintain. In an industrial area where noxious chemicals are in the air, a library should investigate the cost of adding an activated charcoal filter to the above combination.

4. What about ventilation noise? It is desirable to maintain a comfortably low level background noise in the ventilation system to mask noises from the lighting fixtures and light conversation. It is extremely important to avoid humming and whistling noises, and noises of the movement of air in ductwork. This can be done in the design, and the program should specifically direct the architect's attention to this problem. Too many buildings have duct noises.

5. What about humidity control for the general library? The interesting thing about humidity control is that you never know what the humidity is in a building. Humidistats, though readily available, are seldom included in a building's atmospheric controls. Consequently, when a building has a humidity control system, no one, including the installers, the engineers, and the maintenance crew know if it is working accurately. There is no convenient basis to confirm your suspicion that the system is not working right, and to justify an indignant call to the plant department.

In extremely dry climates, there should be provision for adding humidity to the air, since for every 10 per cent rise in humidity, the folding strength of paper doubles. If humidity is added during winter, there is a problem of dripping on the coldest part of the outer wall, which is usually the metal window frames, and humidity will have to be adjusted below this drip point. At any time of year, it should not be above 50 per cent for human comfort.

In a wet climate, the problem is removing humidity for human comfort rather than adding it for the welfare of paper. On Long Island, relative humidity is sometimes 100 per cent. This sounds like the ideal element for fish, and it is; but we live through it, though not in comfort. Consequently, this humidity must be lowered, and buildings can now be held to 48 per cent relative humidity without great difficulty.

6. What about rare book areas? By this I refer to any special collections area that houses books of special value. These must be air-conditioned by a separate machine, not part of the central ventilation system, that feeds it alone. It must maintain a constant temperature of 70° (lower if you can stand it—Syracuse maintains 68°), and 50 per cent humidity, and must have a filtration system composed of 1) a pad filter or preferably a moving blanket filter such as Rollomatic; 2) a high-efficiency bag filter for 95 per cent filtration; and 3) an activated charcoal filter. To maintain constant humidity the system must contain a humidity removal feature in wet climates in addition to a humidity addition feature.

7. What about internal air pressure? The pressure inside the building should be adjusted to be slightly higher than outside air pressure

to produce a constant movement of air out through tiny cracks to inhibit the entrance of dust.

The librarian can also contribute to the planning a demand for a complete review of the ventilation system with the architects and engineers who designed it before the plans are sent out for bids. This is extremely difficult to achieve. The mechanical drawings (plumbing, electrical, ventilation) are the last drawings completed in the plans, and are always later than they should be. Everyone is eager to send them out to bid as soon as possible. Nevertheless, a ventilation review is extremely important, and the librarian can go over the entire building asking the following:

Question 1 – What are the temperature control zones, and where is the thermostat that controls them? A little common sense will indicate that some of them are in the wrong place—on a wall that gets sunned, for instance. Don't be surprised to find the control on a floor other than the zone you are considering, but ask whether the architect thinks this control sufficient, or whether there should be another added for this particular zone. You will find that the architect is not familiar with the mechanical drawings, and that the engineer also has to grope through the plans to find the temperature control location. Make them grope and ask the pertinent question. When we finished such a review of the Colorado College library building plans, the engineer in charge was asked in amusement by a member of his crew, "Are you released from the witness stand?" But we had improved the temperature control in one zone and three separate rooms in the process.

Question 2 – For every separate room, is there both an inlet *and an outlet* sufficient to carry the planned volume of air? Especially in very small rooms, such as group study rooms and faculty studies, the outlet is likely to be omitted. It can be provided easily by undercutting the door, but sometimes it is not provided, and the air quickly becomes foul.

Question 3 – For each separate room that has an odor problem such as the toilets and all areas in which smoking is permitted, is there a separate air vent for this room? Smoking rooms will quickly become stale and sour enough to make them unpleasant unless they are separately vented, but architects tend not to supply a separate vent, because doing so adds to the air conditioning load, which costs money. Nevertheless, if smoking is to be allowed in any area, separate vents must be provided.

I am convinced that the complexities of the ventilation system are such that they should be reviewed, both working drawings and specifications, by a ventilation engineer as a consultant. He will charge about as much per day as a library building consultant, but the end result in improvements in the system will greatly override the cost of a few hundred dollars, and the librarian should make sure that money to hire such a consultant is included in the consulting budget for the library planning. I am further convinced that it is never possible to balance the ventilation system with the scanty attempts bestowed on it by the engineers who install it, and by the do-it-yourself help available on most campuses. There are now companies who contract to balance out the ventilation system of new buildings, and one should be hired after the building is finished.

ABOUT THE AUTHOR–(See biographical note on page 116.)

Air Conditioning for Books and People

by Ian Grad and Alfred Greenberg

Practical experience is related here through the description of the air conditioning system for John M. Olin Library at the Washington University in St. Louis—one of the best planned library buildings constructed in recent years.

Libraries have a number of air conditioning problems not often encountered in other building types:

1. While the ratio of people to floor area in libraries with open stacks is quite low, still comparatively large quantities of air must be circulated to keep the books "conditioned" as well as the people.
2. Cooling load due to heat given off by people will vary widely. For example, conference and seminar rooms may have an occupancy load of 10 sq ft per person, while the stack area will average 80 to 100 sq ft per person. The areas with differing occupancies thus have to be carefully zoned.
3. Clean air is not only desirable, but necessary so that books will not become soiled.
4. The sound level of the air conditioning system must be low enough to prevent distraction, but cannot be so low that normal sounds will seem obtrusive. (It's well known that the air conditioning systems in some libraries have been so quiet that people complained the building was "noisy.")
5. A university library, such as described in this article, often operates 16 hours a day six days a week; somewhat less on Sunday. Thus ventilation equipment may have to run as much as 5000 hours per year. Such constant usage means that heavy-duty, long-life equipment must be used.

A search of both domestic and foreign literature disclosed that there is very little information available on the air conditioning criteria for modern libraries. However, the comfort criteria for people engaged in a variety of activities have been pretty

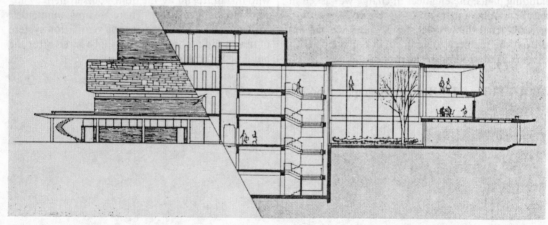

Figure 1 John M. Olin Library, Washington University, St. Louis. Murphy and Mackey, Architects; Neal J. Campbell, Structural Engineer; Fred S. Dubin Associates, Inc., Mechanical Engineers

SOURCE: Reprinted from Ian Grad and Alfred Greenberg, "Air Conditioning for Books and People," *Architectural Record,* vol. 121, June, 1957, pp. 231–234, by permission of the publisher and Fred S. Dubin Associates for the authors.

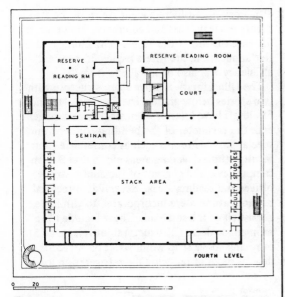

Figure 2

well established. To determine what would be the best atmospheric conditions for books we conferred with paper manufacturers, and, oddly enough were told that optimum conditions (76 degrees and 50 per cent relative humidity) for preserving paper were practically the same as those for people—certainly a fortunate coincidence. Since stack areas are normally in the interior of the library, the cooling load is mainly due to lights, and less air, at a lower temperature differential than is required for other areas, is needed. In this case, a minimum air movement of six air changes per hour was used to maintain uniform temperature conditions.

Temperature limits for the Olin library are 72 F (winter) and 78 F (summer). While 76 F is optimum for both people and books, to maintain this temperature under worst summer conditions would have required an increase of over 12 per cent in the refrigeration tonnage. In the winter it is planned to maintain exterior spaces at 72 F, so the stack areas will be 72 F also to have uniformity throughout. The humidity is controlled at 50 per cent with a permissible variation of plus or minus 5 per cent. Stack areas are conditioned 24 hours a day. The exterior areas are not normally conditioned at night. However, the humidity in areas fringing on the stacks is not allowed to go below 50 per cent. Due to the heat storage capacity of the masonry walls and the books in the library, it is anticipated that conditions late at night will not vary much from occupancy design conditions. Where there is lots of glass, such as the ground floor and the court, low limit controls will not let the temperature drop below 55 F at night.

The air conditioning system is designed to handle the most extreme conditions. Due to the uncertainties involved in thermal storage, undoubtedly field adjustments will be necessary to establish the best 24-hr control setup.

Research shows that from a practical and economic point of view an overall ambient sound level with the air handling systems running should be no greater than 40 db. A level of 35 db is considered by many the low limit since it is felt that below this, stray noises may be accentuated due to the low background noise level. In addition, the added cost of equipment and acoustical treatment would excessively increase the cost of the job.

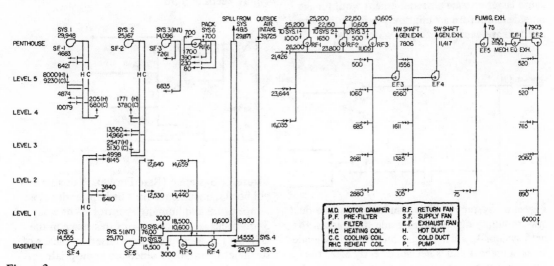

Figure 3

All equipment such as fans, pumps and refrigeration machines are set on proper vibration eliminating devices to minimize noise transmission from this source. The discharge ductwork of all double duct supply fans is lined with acoustic material to produce a maximum duct noise level of 52-55 db. Where necessary, the discharge end of all turbulators and mixing boxes is acoustically lined to produce a maximum sound level in the ducts of 37 db. This, when added to a 37 db room ambient with no air system being operated, will produce a 40 db level when the air systems are turned on.

One of the biggest maintenance problems in a library is keeping the books clean. All too often, even in air conditioned libraries, book stacks are covered with layers of dust due to the inadequacy of the air filtering system and/or the lack of proper maintenance. About 80 per cent filter

efficiency is considered adequate from the standpoints of cleanliness and economy. However, to increase the life of the 80 per cent filters used for this application, pre-filters having 35 per cent efficiency will also be installed.

The Olin Library is a five-story structure with two stories below grade. The 1st, 2nd, 4th and 5th levels have interior open stack areas. In general, the perimeter of the building contains the special purpose rooms such as conference rooms, faculty studies, reading areas etc. Level 3 is on campus level and consists of the administrative offices and reading areas. Several architectural design features were incorporated to eliminate almost all of the sun load. These include (1) a promenade deck, (2) structural louvers, and (3) overhang above strip windows. This served the dual purpose of reducing the refrigeration load

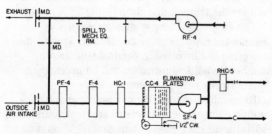

Figure 4 Systems 1, 2, 4. Dual duct supply feeds exterior spaces which have special rooms adjacent to one another with various occupancies, calling for separately controlled conditions. Hot and cold air is mixed to satisfy room or zone thermostats. System 4*, only, has a preheat coil after filters because larger outside air requirement would make outside and return air mixture too low otherwise, and perhaps cause freezing of water coils

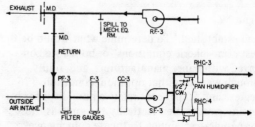

Figure 5 System 3. A single-duct system serves the stacks on levels 4 and 5. Pan humidifiers suit the purpose for a low-density area such as stacks. Reheat coils are employed on level 5 to compensate for roof heat loss, and on level 4 to temper supply air in summer which has to be quite cool for level 5 because of heat gain through the roof (spray keeps it at 90 F)

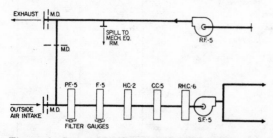

Figure 6 System 5. This is an interior single-duct system supplying the below-grade stack areas. As with system 4, which is dual-duct for below-grade areas, a preheat coil is needed directly after the filters because of the larger outside air requirement on the lower levels

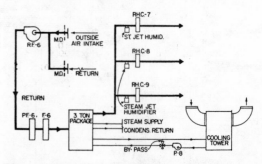

Figure 7 System 6 (Rare Books). Valuable and old books, documents must be kept under close temperature and humidity control 24 hr a day. A 3-ton package unit conditions this space in the Olin library. Moisture can be raised by means of steam jet humidifiers which are appropriate for this small, integrated system. A separate cooling tower is used

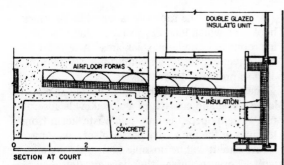

Figure 8 An unusual air distribution detail is the use of special metal forms to provide air channels while still allowing sufficient structural strength in the slab. Reason was that waffle slab had no space to run a conventional duct. Continuous air along glass at court counteracts drafts

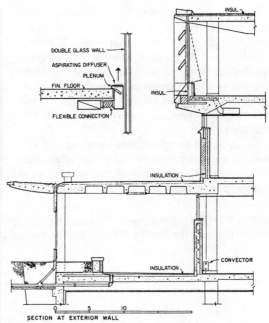

Figure 9 Sun control features—horizontal louvers, overhang and strip windows, and promenade deck—simplified air conditioning control. Areas did not have to be zoned for orientation as well as occupancy. The small detail shows how air is admitted where there is floor-to-ceiling glass. This occurs on some sides of court and on ground floor. Details may vary from place to place depending on construction

and eliminating the need for zoning of the air conditioning systems according to building orientation as well as function.

In addition evaporative spray piping will be installed on the roof to reduce air conditioning costs by about $8,000.

The two lower level and the two upper level stack areas each have their own conventional (single duct) air handling system including pan humidifier sections for humidity control. All other areas will be served by three modified dual duct air handling systems. Large areas which lend themselves to zone control will be handled by means of turbulator boxes which mix the hot and cold air proportionately for the right temperature.

An interesting application of zone control is being applied to the rows of faculty study rooms. Each row, consisting of from nine to 22 rooms will be handled by one turbulator box. The lights in each row will be ganged on a single switch so they are all on or off. For the floors above grade this will present a desirable uniform architectural appearance outside the building. Since these rooms will be occupied by only one person, most of the time, the major portion of the variable load will be due to outside air conditions. Therefore, an outside master thermostat can be tied into a submaster to re-set a discharge duet thermostat which will proportion the hot and cold air quantities as required. For rows of rooms below grade, only the preset discharge ductstat will be required. Here the human heat load is the only variable and can be compensated for by the setting of the discharge ductstat. The savings due to elimination of individual room control will offset increased lighting costs for at least 30 years.

All private offices, conference rooms, seminars, etc. will have individual room controls due to the nature of the periods, types and levels of occupancy.

All zone and individual mixing boxes will have thermostatic and static pressure controls. The latter, though adding slightly to the cost of the mixing boxes, will give the systems more stable operating characteristics.

The dual-duct systems are run at as low a velocity as is consistent with the space available for ductwork. These systems are in the medium velocity (4000 fpm is tops), high pressure range, and although initial ductwork cost is increased, the power economy effected by reducing the system static pressures due to the larger ducts justifies this procedure. In addition, it reduces the possibility of objectionable duct noise.

Ductwork is above hung ceilings where they occur. Since space conditions made it impossible to run a complete system of return ductwork, the hung ceiling is used as a return air plenum. Every effort was made to locate the return air registers for proper air circulation. This is complicated by the fact that registers nearer the shaft will tend to pull more air than those farther away. Therefore registers were placed equidistant from the return air shaft ducts which were run out 8–15 ft from the shaft wall and acoustically lined. Return air plenums at return air fan inlets were also acoustically lined to prevent noise transmission down the shaft.

Separate and complete systems of exhaust air were designed for areas or rooms that might have heavy smoking, toilets, photolabs., etc. All such rooms have 100 per cent exhaust.

A portion of the top floor is set aside for a rare book area which includes a vault, exhibit and reading room and rare book stack area. A separate 3-ton, direct expansion air conditioning system is used to provide 24 hour service.

The refrigeration equipment is located at the lowest level and consists of a closed cycle absorption system operating on 5 psig waste steam from turbines in the university power plant. At some future date it will be possible to provide the unit with 12 psig steam and thus have an additional 100 tons of air conditioning capacity for some other building in the area.

ABOUT THE AUTHORS—At the time this article was written (1957) Mssrs. Grad and Greenberg were associated with the firm of Fred. S. Dubin Associates, Inc., Consulting Engineers.

VIII

SOME CONSIDERATIONS FOR NEWER MEDIA AND AUTOMATION SERVICES IN LIBRARY BUILDINGS

In an article reprinted here, C. Walter Stone has written that "libraries of the future may not wisely be conceived as buildings at all but rather as parts of far-flung networks made up of units of varying sizes and types, each of which performs similar as well as some different functions, but all which may be linked together electro-mechanically." Preparing for that future day complicates further the building planning process. We cannot leap from today's book and print oriented library to that far-flung network of tomorrow. But better planned, more flexible buildings capable of adapting to future technologically oriented programs, systems and services will be one of the bridges to that future library.

This unit focuses attention on current building practices for automation services and the newer media technologies.

New Media Facilities

by John H. Moriarty

The shifting, changing needs of media services require new space utilization concepts. Libraries have successfully incorporated the ability to change space from books to readers and back again if necessary. Now we must consider group versus individual utilization of space, permanent versus flexible storage facilities, and adaptability to newer services through the newer media.

Physical quarters devoted to audio-visual service in libraries are often makeshift because of their location in old buildings and/or their secondary status. As a consequence, to write about them descriptively could be useless. However, when considering what A-V quarters to recommend, a library consultant is confronted with drafting an almost equally useless prescription: "Allocate every square foot that funds will allow, and provide conduit (of sewer pipe size, if possible) for electrical wiring with outlets placed in the floor, walls and ceiling every ten feet."

In his recent book on *Planning Academic and Research Library Buildings*,[1] Keyes Metcalf, a wise elder statesman in the field of library architecture, quite sensibly devoted some two pages out of four hundred to audio-visual service areas and, even here, his general advice was not to accept responsibility for planning such units. Nevertheless, this year hundreds of librarians will participate in planning new libraries in which they must work for a quarter of a century to come and, because of both the technological and educational changes anticipated, they should be helped to get ready to make the best of a complex, shifting situation.

Unlike the codex book—which was invented a millenium and a half ago and remained stable for about five hundred years—most audio-visual material is subject to change in form or format on an almost annual basis. Users of audio-visual materials are almost as unstable in their employment (in an architectural context, their deployment) of A-V materials. And so, with full knowledge of how ephemeral such remarks may prove, the writer offers personnel, practical, and very "down-to-earth" advice (most of which is not in books)

concerning what, in light of his experience, seems sensible "space and area" thinking about library service with "newer media." While change in communications technology and its increased educational use cause most of the uncertainties in planning A-V facilities, this article confines itself to demands placed by increasing use, and will not attempt either pedagogical or administrative justifications of A-V service as provided by librarians. Suffice it to say, that new media services and their staffing are assigned to libraries often enough to warrant interest and concern on the part of the library profession generally.

To restore some order in the chaos caused by A-V equipment and the space problems encountered in planning library service, the author has chosen to deal with these problems under headings relating to patron use rather than to emphasize differences in variant forms of equipment which the phrase "audio-visual" suggests. In this article, space problems will be discussed as they concern the allocation of space in libraries (1) for *individual* study or service, and (2) for *group* viewing or listening (as well as for exhibits and seminars).

Library use is predominantly on an individual basis, despite public library film showings, stories told in children's rooms or poetry readings held in a college library. While much audio-visual material originates in forms intended for mass consumption, a significant part of what is "published" in various audio-visual formats can be just as effective as information or as an emotional stimulus when addressed to the single student.

Prescriptions for individual study space intended for student viewing and listening have usually been understood in the past to mean requirements for

SOURCE: Reprinted from John H. Moriarty, "New Media Facilities," *Library Trends*, vol. 16, October, 1967, pp. 251–258, by permission of the publisher.

some type of booth having distinct physical isolation and/or resembling a darkened cubicle. This is still true; fortunately, however, it is becoming less so. Actually, current styles in library seating, often designed for one or two persons, allow as much space for listening as do the specialized tables or "booths" used frequently in A-V centers. While viewing films can present special problems, most projectors will accommodate individual use of earphones, and a plain white or neutral wall eight feet away will serve as a satisfactory screen. This is the same amount of space often allowed in designing carrels. The point to remember is that individual viewing and listening activities involving "mass" media can be scattered widely through a library, with little inconvenience or distortion of either book or audio-visual service utility.

To maximize individual use of A-V materials, the purchasing library must buy earphones for use with tape playback machines, record players, projectors, and other audio-visual equipment, and make sure from the outset that all such equipment is both portable and strong; it must also provide for the maintenance essential to ensure a continuing, as well as quiet, sanitary operation. Those planning a new or refurbished library which is to afford audio-visual service on an individual basis must be certain that special electrical outlets are installed as extensively as overhead lighting to ensure that all areas can be fully used as well as properly illuminated. It is a rule of thunb that the cost of putting in new power outlets after completing or remodeling a building may be ten times that of installation during original construction. All planned uses of library quarters shift and vary over the years, and a free, even lavish, provision of electrical outlets will ensure future flexibility for audio-visual and other needs.

In summary then, the allocation of space similar to that needed for a study carrel, probably $8' \times 8'$, and the installation of adequate electrical outlets in areas which otherwise would be used for stacks or reading rooms are the most that audio-visual service for individual study should require.

In some academic and public library buildings, individual listening booths have been grouped together in banks or clusters. Each booth is equipped separately with earphones so that a central desk or service attendant may play a record or tape desired by any user in any booth. An earlier arrangement was to have an attendant at a central service point who would play a disc by transmitting the sound to a full-volume speaker in a soundproof booth or room where the listener sat. Today, using modern "dial-access" equipment, a listener sitting in a booth can request a lecture or musical performance automatically simply by dialing the proper number or letter code which then activates a remote mechanism to retrieve the proper recording from a reservoir of tapes.

Grouping booths in libraries around a central service area can present both equipment and wiring problems. No architect or librarian should attempt to install such facilities without the benefit of expert consultation. Communications technology is changing so rapidly that generalizations cannot be made as to the most satisfactory arrangement. Of course, some space may be saved when A-V listening facilities are blocked together, but ordinarily this will mean staffing a special station and, thus, an increase in personnel costs.

Traditionally, librarians summon up thoughts of large and small group viewing and listening when thinking of audio-visual service areas. The relatively infrequent use of such space will fret a library administrator since, inevitably, other areas are often crowded with readers and books; it is true that planning such areas for libraries has too often been done poorly. Too many architects envision group space, especially if it is sizable, as a way to achieve theatrical rather than educational ends.

Therefore, shrewd librarians emphasize and re-emphasize to an architect the *educational* importance and use of large group space. Asking for tablet arms on movable chairs will at once alert an architect to the intended use of an area for instruction. Requesting room lighting that will permit reading, even studying, while the room is darkened for projection is another way in which librarians can make their A-V intentions clear. Slanted floors may be justified in some audio-visual presentation areas, but they normally bind the area to a single kind of use. Thus, in most public and college libraries, slanted floors are not recommended since the gains in convenience for A-V showings are small in comparison to gains to be made in flexibility when level floors are specified. For example, having a level floor area will permit a large library room to be used for exhibits or displays and, with only simple rearrangements, for lectures, the screening of motion pictures, and viewing of educational television.

Wherever feasible, large group spaces should be capable of division into smaller spaces by rolling doors or mobile partitions into place. While such areas can actually be made soundproof only in rare instances, they allow fuller deployment of what, without them, would be rarely-used facilities. Also, such room dividers will enable a library to hold several meetings at the same time, or to use part of one area as a short-term storage space without losing or harming the space remaining.

It would be nice if the auditorium in the average public or college library did not demand a special booth to quiet film projector noise. But, unfortunately, motion picture projection is noisy. So one answer here is simply to enclose a projector stand with a special wall so designed as to deaden sound. If the architect will provide a closet to do this, well and good. However, if a fixed enclosure handicaps the flexibility which might be needed to position a screen or projector properly for different locations or sizes of groups, a movable projection "barrier" lined with sound-deadening material should be provided, or else listeners must be asked to ignore the distraction. (The last is a counsel of despair which librarians as well as manufacturers of projectors should not ask of patrons.)

The problem of locating seats for film viewers and a screen or television set (or sets) for maximum visibility is actually not architectural. Only when a space will seat eighty to one hundred persons do the problems of screen size, audio-speaker positioning, and possible installation of a projection booth need to involve the architect. When proper lenses are used, most projectors in general use will throw an image of adequate size in a room which may seat up to one hundred people. However, building plans should specify a ceiling height of at least twelve feet so that a screen or television set may be positioned for good viewing, and so that a projector's throw will clear viewers' heads without obstruction. Speakers should be located at ceiling height or even in the ceiling itself.

The possibility of using a large open space in a library for an exhibit area or "art gallery" was noted above. If the amount of space required has been kept clear of permanent, fixed, specific-purpose A-V paraphernalia, such a service can be provided easily. Bare walls and a clear floor are the primary needs. One useful specification is that a picture rail or slot be provided along the walls of such an area. When not in use, the rail poses no problem. But, if it is available when the area is being used for exhibitions, much time and wall maintenance will be saved. In fact, it would be marked improvement in library halls and in all passages having a clear wall space ten feet or more in length, to specify installation of picture slots.

Sooner or later the inevitable makeshift posting of notices, show cards, or signs on such walls will yield eyesores. Providing a picture rail or slot at the start can at the least prevent some damage and at best facilitate optimum effective use of a potential display area.

The storage and security space required to house the various audio-visual media is analogous to "reading rooms." There cannot (and should not) be one universal standard reading room or mode of shelving; similarly, there cannot be a single design for optimum utilization, storage or security of audio-visual materials. Indeed, it cannot be over-emphasized that the search for flexibility, described above in relation to user-facilities, must apply equally to provisions made for storage and security. Too many locked equipment closets create both a nuisance and a delay in service as well as increased cost of use. Whatever neatness and security results from using such facilities almost certainly will not compensate for the loss in flexibility.

Since the average school, public or college library seldom possesses more than one piece of any kind of equipment, one can be rather casual about both storage and security. As with utilization, the main principle to follow when confronted with a problem of how much of any item should be ordered is to keep from over-specific assignments of space. The sizes of equipment, reels of film, discs, and tapes change so rapidly with technological improvement that precisely designed cupboards and slots can very soon become obsolete.

The large number of breakdowns which occur during A-V presentations contribute to much dissatisfaction with audio-visual library service. Frequently, these breakdowns are due to inadequate user preparation or mismatched equipment. But equipment failure is responsible for the hard core of poor staff performance. Few libraries are able to maintain large repair service units or staff. But some space at least should be provided for checking equipment, storing minor replacement parts, and inspecting films and tapes in order to prevent circulation of damaged material. These and similar maintenance activities are mandatory. An area of $10' \times 10'$ is minimal; an active audio-visual department would require probably twice the space. A repair bench area (or equivalent) having several power outlets and deep shelves (twelve or more) are necessities. As an alternative to transporting equipment to a local repair shop or sending it out of town to a factory, a repair shop will often pay for itself since it will enable a store or travelling service man to do needed repairs on library premises, thereby ensuring added days of equipment availability for A-V service.

From an architectural point of view, the space problems encountered in storing films, tapes, or other projected materials are not unique in the library. Regular library shelving is often adaptable for these materials since they are similar in size to books. Even TV tapes do not pose an unusual problem of storage for a librarian accustomed to shelving large, bound magazines.

However, slides, transparencies, and disc recordings do present special problems. Many sets of slides are sold in boxes to help their handling, and most discs come in attractive albums; both the boxes and album covers, however, are as fragile as a publisher's binding for a novel and usually are not suited to repeated use or long life on a library shelf. Librarians must be on the alert to find more suitable "packaging" for such materials. Furthermore, the basic role of space flexibility dictates that such collections, if they are large, be stored in movable shelving or cupboards which can be reached easily by persons of average height.

The facilities needed for most non-projected media present another and different story. Here the old problem of librarians—what to do with maps and globes—is compounded by the necessity of finding ways to store flat pictures, cartoons, clippings; models and mock-ups; specimens; posters, blueprints, charts, graphs, diagrams; felt, flannel, magnetic and other board materials; and exhibits. Problems of allocating space and facilities to these materials are numerous and almost always are rather specialized, depending on user practices, size of collection, and similar local considerations. Map cases have been adjusted to library use for a long time, and the floor space and strengths they require are calculated easily. Vertical files pose other problems; cupboards for specimens and objects (such as a doll collection) must usually be custom-made and adapted to the space allotted. Attics and cellars (if the ever-burgeoning book collection can be kept out, which is a large "if") can be a boon to the A-V specialist with ex-

hibits on his hands. In an architect's language, this problem calls for a large "circulation" or "turnaround" area that, periodically, will be empty. Since librarians use many book trucks on wheels, the problems of moving and shipping audio-visual equipment and materials are not unusual. Of course, mail and receiving rooms should be accessible from the outside by ramps, as in any well-planned library. Once the problem of handling materials in the general service area has been thought through (for example, provision for counters of the same height as carts used to move projectors and book trucks is vital), receiving exhibits and other bulky shipments is greatly facilitated, as are projector or equipment loans to library branches.

At one period or another in their professional lives most librarians all live in old or marcescent quarters where makeshift or downright awkward arrangements are unavoidable. The introduction of audio-visual (or newer media) services into such libraries sometimes, not always, will strain the long-tested adaptability of even the most experienced librarian. Since at the base of the newer media are technologies which change and usually "improve," the shape, size and special requirements of A-V equipment and materials will, inevitably, be fluid for an indefinite future. The wise librarian accepts this inevitability and, as with other elements of uncertainty in his milieu, meets the problems posed as standard elements in his over-all responsibility. At least, this is a "creative" approach. If, as is occasionally the case, a librarian feels newer media have been foisted on him, poor service will be virtually certain. But a diffident attitude toward the physical problems of accommodating new media is not warranted. The problems simply are not as large as all that.

In conclusion, whether new media are viewed negatively in comparison with a librarian's victories over past problems, or are regarded positively in the light of enrichments they may afford, they cannot be kept out of the libraries of today or tomorrow. Proper facilities must be provided, for which simple criteria have now been advanced.

NOTE

[1] Metcalf, Keyes D. *Planning Academic and Research Library Buildings.* New York, McGraw-Hill, 1965.

ADDITIONAL REFERENCES

"Audio Services and Facilities–A Panel Discussion." *In* Frazer G. Poole, ed., *The Library Environment: Aspects of Interior Planning.* (Proceedings of the Library Equipment Institute.) Chicago, ALA, 1965.

De Bernardis, Amo. "To Carrel or Not to Carrel? That is the Question," *Audio-visual Instruction*, 12:439-440, May 1967.

Green, Alan C., *et al. Educational Facilities with New Media.* (Interim report of a project being conducted by the Architectural Research Staff, School of Architecture, Rensselaer Polytechnic Institute, Troy, New York, under the terms of Contract Number OE-3-16-031 between Rensselaer and the United States Office of Education.) Jan. 1965. (Processed.)

Myller, Rolf. *The Design of the Small Public Library.* New York, R. R. Bowker Co., 1966.

Weber, David C. "Design for a Microtext Reading-Room," *Unesco Bulletin for Libraries,* 20:303-308, Nov.-Dec. 1966.

ABOUT THE AUTHOR–John H. Moriarty, a Phi Beta Kappa with B.A. (1926), B.S. (1934), and M.S. (1938) degrees in library science from Columbia University, held administrative positions at Cooper Union, Columbia University, the Library of Congress, and Purdue University. Mr. Moriarty was Director of Libraries and the Audiovisual Center at Purdue until his retirement in 1970. He taught library science at Columbia University and the University of Illinois, chaired numerous committees and was the author of *Directory Information for New York City Residents, 1626-1786* (1942). He died in 1971.

Planning for Media Within University Library Buildings

by C. Walter Stone

". . . No simple formulae or prescriptions exist which can be described honestly as 'definitive' guides useful to those interested in designing facilities for production, storage, or use of communications media on the university campus. . . In the author's opinion, the best place to begin planning for new media is by getting answers to some fundamental questions of purpose . . . and to questions concerning levels of teaching and research to be served as well as clear delineations of library responsibility. . ."

"Any teacher who can be replaced by a machine, should be." B. F. Skinner (Harvard University).

"Our aim is to have the computer instruct the researcher in how stored information is organized. He is led to browse in the general area of his inquiry and broaden or narrow it as he wishes. The [computer-based] system also helps him choose the best search strategy." Donald Hillman (Lehigh University).

"The dial-access retrieval system interconnects the library listening facilities with the thirty-two listening posts of the Office Practices Laboratory and forty positions of the Foreign Language Laboratory. Eighty-six students can listen at one time to any one of the selected programs over the earphones. . . . The library and all other instructional buildings are connected with the television studio by coaxial cables." Michael N. Slama (Ventura [California] County Junior College).

"Features of the library include an electronic operations system for automated circulation, teaching machines, computer and teletype consoles, and closed-circuit television. . . . The Mart Library also provides quarters for the Interdisciplinary Center for Information Science and will be central to the continuing growth of engineering and science education and research at Lehigh." Dedication brochure for the Mart Science and Engineering Library, Lehigh University.

"No surveys can be found that indicated how much the audiovisual materials are being used by our college students. Nor is there an easy way to arrive at even a guess as to the amount of use of visual materials on the college campus. There has been millions of dollars worth of research on the potential of audiovisual materials but there seems to be no research on their actual use." Richard Chapin (Michigan State University).

"The day when reading will be a primary form of information intake is . . . passing—my advice is to plan no more buildings for library use. Library space is a concession to the past." Sol Cornberg.

● ● ● ●

As yet, no simple formulae or prescriptions exist which can be described honestly as "definitive" guides useful to those interested in designing facilities for production, storage, or use of communications media on the university campus. In his 1965 book on *Planning Academic and Research Library Buildings*[1] Keyes Metcalf sensibly devoted just two pages out of some four hundred or more to audio-visual service areas. And, even here, the general advice given was not to accept responsibility for planning such units. Why?—To Metcalf the future must have appeared uncertain. And no wonder—witness the six statements quoted above. So then, given a desire to accept library planning responsibility, statements such as the half-dozen cited illustrate dramatically the numerous dilemmas which must be faced, and the fact is that one can no longer plan library buildings simply in terms of types of space to be allocated for traditional media acquisition, storage

SOURCE: Reprinted from C. Walter Stone, "Planning for Media Within University Library Buildings," *Library Trends*, vol. 18, no. 2, October, 1969, pp. 235-245, by permission of the publisher

and use. Rather the approach which is required calls for design of a total system of communication and information service, many ramifications of which suggest that library buildings as such are, indeed, passe'—not that many universities have as yet been willing to accept the advice offered by Cornberg. But perhaps this is because there has not yet (as Chapin suggests) been sufficient experience in using the newer media at such new learning center and laboratory facilities as are represented, for example, at Grand Valley in Michigan, in the Marywood College Library in Scranton, Pennsylvania, at Oklahoma Christian University, and in more recent years by the New York State University system (for example at Buffalo and Geneseo). Each of these institutions has facilities which feature electronic learning carrels and other hardware manifestations of modern learning techniques and technology. How then should the library planner proceed?

In the author's opinion, the best place to begin planning for new media is by getting answers to some fundamental questions of purpose (as enunciated by institutional size, age, avowed goals and methodologies of instruction) and to questions concerning levels of teaching and research to be served as well as clear delineations of library responsibility (such as will it provide independently or in cooperation with other agencies and departments prerequisite instructional and study spaces, equipment and special media service). Treatment of such factors tends either to be missing in much recent writing on the subject or to be notably ambiguous.

Next, library planners must acknowledge as a likelihood that it may be less necessary in the future to house all parts of any given media service program in one place so long as all units composing the program can be linked together in network-like systems and the resources of each can be deployed where and when needed to support overall functions. That is—libraries of the future may not wisely be conceived as buildings at all but rather as parts of far-flung networks made up of units of varying sizes and types, each of which performs similar as well as some different functions, but all of which may be linked together electromechanically. Within the total system at one time can be vestiges of past service programs of interest both to bibliophiles and antiquarians and avantgarde approaches to use of communications technology which could include telefacsimile and high-speed voice transmission aids capable of sending and receiving over 1,000 words per minute; electronic carrels distinguished by their typewriter-like keyboards and connections to on-line, time-sharing computers; audio jacks and sets of earphones; individual television display units capable of being augmented electronically through use of light pens, etc.

Apropos of these points, the student of contemporary library and information system design must acquire a new and, perhaps for some individuals, an alien vocabulary (but hopefully buttressed by personal experience with examples of the technology to which new labels refer) covering a broad variety of new electronic handwriting devices and ranging from Touch Tone dial systems to WATS (Wide Area Telephone Service) line service, TELPAK, and CCSA (Common Control Switching Arrangements); amplified telephone systems such as the so-called "Tele-lecture"; passive audio devices (such as "Code-a-phone"); visual transmission by audio phone lines; DAIRS (dial-access information retrieval systems); the various new forms of TWX service; and the latest generation of computers (known as "third generation") which features a time-sharing, multi-programming facility. Also to be considered as part of any long-range projection is Bell Telephone's new "Picturephone" system which offers two-way voice and picture communication transmitted over present telephone lines. It should become operational before the mid-1970's.[2]

The balance of this article concentrates on a few of the primary factors and functions which must be considered in planning facilities for all types of university library service and tries to state simply some of the more difficult problems in planning library space arrangements for the use of modern media. Noted in passing will be references to a number of sources of relevant information and to experimental programs conducted by several universities.

Listed below are some basic matters to be considered in planning an academic library. Concerning professional responsibility, it seems clear that university libraries of the future will be responsible for providing a very broad range of educational communication and information media and for *producing* new instructional aids as well as distributing materials. *Media evaluation* (as distinguished from simple cataloging and bibliographic description) will be needed. Active *partnership in instruction* (as the "library-college" idea suggests) has major implications for design of library facilities. Regular *participation in research* concerned with the effectiveness of using new teaching-study-learning resources implies new roles for librarians. *Switching center functions* to provide access to information wherever it may be located physically, as distinguished from access only to materials housed within given buildings, also opens up the world of computer applications to libraries and librarians.

At a minimum, augmenting the existing inventory of traditional library resources published in printed formats will be at least four types of new media for which library space must be reserved and equipment provided. These include *audio-visual materials* (e.g., slides, filmstrips, motion pictures, phonograph, disc and tape recordings); the *products of reprography* (the relatively rapidly produced, convenient and inexpensive media used for exact duplication of graphical representations); *miniaturized materials* and equipment needed to use such material (some late developments permit direct transfer of material in microform to computer printout); and the *products of automation* (perhaps the most dramatic and visible of which are the cathode ray tube display image).

Provision of these media and, indeed, of all library resources must be accomplished in an environment which reflects the current trends in education. Three important manifestations of these trends are evident in 1) the encouragement of independent study by students (utilizing aids to programmed learning); 2) academic integration (represented in a growing number of interdisciplinary instructional programs) and 3) use of special techniques of instruction representing in many cases what Dupuy has called the "audio-tutorial" methodologies[3] —in essence, simple extensions to other fields of the "language laboratory" idea. Use of these methodologies may be complemented by individual student and small group work with instructors or tutors who serve in adivsory roles and explain, interpret, or expand upon formal presentations given in audio or visual media. The effective teacher does not simply pass along facts and information—this can often be done more efficiently by a machine, audio type, film, slides, or a book. In recognition of this fact, the planner of modern library service will arrange the "library" programs conceived to accommodate a growing roster of library media service functions and take into account the stress now being given to methods of instruction which feature individualized approaches. The result may be a facility which through adequate design and the nature of resources provided can facilitate individualized study and teaching methods and deliver conveniently (vir-tually on demand, using electro-mechanical aids and systems) whatever types of new media service may be required to pursue given individual (or group) instructional objectives.

The management of such facilities requires close cooperation and joint planning by teams of specialists, all of whom are concerned, however, with the educational process and which may include as individual members some whose primary tasks will be represented in the work of advising students, others in testing, producing and/or distributing materials. Of note in this regard is the work being done in the new learning centers established at Stephens College in Missouri, at Oklahoma Christian College and Oral Roberts University. Other centers with similar goals have been established recently on the Santa Cruz campus of the University of California, by the University of Illinois on its Chicago campus, and in Florida at Florida Atlantic and at the University of South Florida. Orchard Ridge campus, one of three maintained by the Oakland Community College (located in the suburbs of Detroit), may represent the first complete campus designed specifically for individually-paced learning programs based on very heavy utilization of multi-media. Those responsible for planning libraries are urged to take cognizance of experience already gained at such institutions as those named.

Mandates given those responsible for constructing new college or university library buildings usually state that what must be provided is "maximum flexibility," "loft" space with a floor and/or ceiling "power grid" and, where feasible, "instantaneous access" to all specialized materials and equipment needed to assist the teaching-learning-study process.

Nor are such mandates, however vague, without merit. Contemporary thinking about university buildings and facilities suggests that any given instructional department, research laboratory, or library unit cannot be expected to remain in one physical form much longer than five years. Hence, the new Forbes Area complex of buildings being planned for the University of Pittsburgh (which is to house the humanities and social science departments as well as several professional schools) has been conceived and approved for construction as a modular, highly flexible unit capable of extension and virtually infinite rearrangement simply by changing wall, ceiling or floor locations much as one might restack boxes to permit larger, then smaller, and then again larger space utilization in three dimensions.

In the case of televised instruction, the experiences reported by Michigan State University[4] indicate that, given the present state of the art in design and use of closed-circuit television systems, the major expense to be associated with televised instruction involves staffing costs. Of course, size of enrollment is also a major factor. But in any event, until higher education is able to redeploy significantly its instructional staffs and related resources (e.g., space, equipment, and materials), very large courses enrolling as many as five hundred individuals will be needed frequently to reach a fiscal "break even" point.

One useful review of budget considerations is represented in the three-volume study entitled *Costs of Educational Media Systems*,[5] prepared by Michael C. Sovereign of the University of Illinois for the General Learning Corporation under a U.S. Office of Education grant. The study identifies cost components for a variety of educational tasks and affords a useful base for comparisons of alternate systems. However, when taken too literally, such studies can be misinterpreted so as to miss main points of technological innovation—which may involve improvements in quality as well as extension of educational opportunities, but the costs of which frequently can be evaluated only in terms of "have" or "have not" situations.

In the situation described, it really is not possible or practical to set forth basic costing principles covering such service since charges currently applied in schools and colleges (e.g., $1,000 to $4,000 per position for remote access video systems installed in a library) cannot be derived by simply summing figures, since once again the program of services was not conceived originally as a unified whole.

In addition to basic program conception, many technical factors must also be considered. And too much planning in the past has proceeded "by guess and by God" because it has been essentially "additive" rather than being conceived from the start as a total communication service planning task.

A first requirement to be noted immediately when "total" planning is undertaken is the need to provide more than normal power if television or computer equipment will be involved. The need for controllable incandescent lighting plus other requirements can easily lead to demands for an available current of 300 or more amperes. Additional air-conditioning tonnage required by new electronic resources and by heat generated from lights and equipment which must be carried off by some means suggests giving special attention to ventilation. Because audio recording may require "low pressure" air distribution systems and special ductwork to avoid noise factors, unusual ceiling heights may be specified.

Flexible use of a power grid system requires attention early in any design effort. Because walls and ceilings used in studio recording spaces must be capable of maintaining at least a forty decible noise reduction ratio, special attention is required at an early stage of planning. Simple loft plans can prove difficult to work with when one is considering space for development and use of graphic materials. And these, in general, must have special light control and ventilation as well as a reliable water supply free of normal sedimentation and capable of very accurate temperature and rates of flow control. Since these matters are highly technical they require consideration and knowledge on the part of library consultants as well as architects and engineers if a sound "total" plan is to be realized.

Often superimposed on traditional functional or subject division plans of library construction are individual study spaces, rooms for typing and group seminars, language laboratory facilities, photocopy rooms, temporary classrooms, reading laboratories, media distribution and equipment centers, television viewing and listening areas, electronic learning service stations (i.e., "wet carrels") and/or other special rooms. These are often added without proper attention being paid to such technical matters as ventilation. Aphorisms such as "less glass for readers and more for staff" which take into account distraction factors and/or needed relief from monotony—tend to be "pseudo" laws rather than valid guides for development of a total concept of a communication and information center.

Thus, respecting such centers, library planners, consultants and architects may have to consider possibilities for providing a much broader range of services and facilities than any previously noted. And indeed, such rather new and unusual facilities as child care units (cf. that developed for Federal City College in Washington, D.C.) may also have to be considered to meet the problems of part-time working mothers. And this point raises a host of others which concern the places in which individual learning and methods may best be accomplished by a commuting student population as well as the growing body of adults living in a given community who may be expected to use campus libraries—ranging from high school students and pre-college groups for purposes of orientation to post-retirement, vocational learning, and enrichment programs sponsored for senior citizens.

In short, in addition to lively educational imaginations, a variety of new and very technical knowledge is required of library planners, for example, knowledge of special effects of dryness upon ultra-microforms which have high reduction ratios and which are subject to damage by unfiltered air. A planner should know the special benefits which can accrue from the use of rear image rather than front image projection equipment for microforms. (The latter tends to be more sensitive to the image-destroying effects of higher levels of ambient light.)

Among a brief listing of references, of particular interest is unique work reported by Rensselaer, an institution which has featured problems of communications service in relation to design of university facilities.[6] A second volume on *New Media in Higher Education*,[7] edited by James W. Brown, represents an essential item for any reading list. The Licklider book[8] is obviously a "must" as are the reports of T. N. Dupuy on *Ferment in College Libraries*[9] and *Computers on Campus*[10] by John Caffrey and Charles J. Mosmann.

The single most comprehensive volume dealing with curriculum-related problems was issued some years ago at Stephens College.[11] This volume indicates clearly and almost uniquely the depth to which a local study should go if it is to be truly comprehensive in identifying needs of instruction and research for provision of newer media service. The best recent book is by Ellsworth.[12]

In concluding this statement on planning uses of media within the library it would seem important to offer a few cautioning words and then to suggest something positive in the way of suggestions for procedure. First, as a caution, the field suffers from a serious lack of common standards and definitions, not to mention a paucity of reliable statistical information on the basis of which sound cost effectiveness studies can be conducted. Despite ALA efforts and work being done by various bureaus of library research sponsored by universities and other non-profit organizations (such as the Systems Development Corporation in Santa Monica), planning in the area remains difficult. Obviously every effort should be made to ascertain costs responsibly and to relate these to local planning problems. But continuing study must be encouraged to derive as soon as possible the kinds of standards, definitions, and usage of terms which can be accepted generally.

A second caution has to do with the lack of sufficient experimentation on the basis of which one can truly study and project future needs, for instance, of the kinds of manpower needed to manage an optimum library program and plans for administrative organization which will operate effectively when the communications service is seen as a unified entity (as distinguished from random pieces of service which may or may not fit well together).

Finally to be offered as a positive aid, the following checklist of factors is recommended for consideration in planning future library development:

1. Educational goals of the institution and methods of instruction employed (including various levels of teaching and research to be served by undergraduate curricula laboratories, to meet graduate student or research staff needs, etc.)

2. A definition of the library function (what is to be included and what need not be considered)

3. The number and kinds of special facilities and equipment which must be provided (identified in terms of subjects, media forms and formats, clientele, and/or intended use)

4. Amounts and kinds of integrated versus decentralized media use facilities (e.g., multi-media carrels versus group listening or viewing rooms)

5. Degrees of administrative centralization versus decentralization to be afforded by the library system (through branches; in resource centers; by using satellite library arrangements)

6. Production and reproduction responsibilities (by whom? in what amounts? at what costs? to serve what purposes?)

7. The degree and nature of automated services (intended to help management, to provide information storage and retrieval services, to assist instruction and research. Who is to use the automation—individuals, classes, groups, *et al*?)

8. Such considerations as integrated versus separate cataloging of various forms of material; staffing patterns and budget arrangements; planned growth rates; special communications facilities; possibilities for cooperation with other agencies and institutions

9. Particular spaces, furnishings and equipment

(needed for materials and equipment storage; maintenance and repair; office activity; individual and group study and use of library resources; previewing; conference work; displays)

10. Lighting and ventilation (incandescent, fluorescent, ultraviolet; window drapes and blinds; plans for use of microtext; dimming controls; air-conditioning requirements; special humidity and temperature regulators; need for dark rooms)

11. Communication control systems (centralized and/or remote; one-way or multi-way; dial access audio and/or video; computer access and display mechanisms; individual browsing facilities for use of audio-visual media; loudspeakers versus use of headphones; special communication equipment needs)

12. Reproduction services (graphic, photographic, electronic reproduction)

To sum up, the day has arrived when it is no longer useful to talk much about planning or construction of university library buildings as if these were independent units. The future really does not encourage such efforts. Insofar as the words "library" and, indeed, "librarian" still have meaning, they represent a heritage from the past which recalls performance of functions without which civilizations could not have developed nor endured —that is the preservation and distribution of recorded knowledge. But today these are tasks which call for a broadening diversity of arts, skills, and intellectual talents not demanded previously and for maintenance of new and changing facilities which will permit rapid production, distribution and use of a very wide range of modern communications technology.

Once the terms "library" and "librarianship" are acknowledged to represent functional concepts rather than specific realities, it becomes easier for those made responsible to proceed with designing of facilities to provide optimum communication and information services. But let it be recognized at the outset that such facilities may not in the future look much like the traditional libraries of which universities have been so proud. Indeed, to recall an architectural adage, if form should properly follow function, then Cornberg's advice to campus planners quoted at the beginning of this article is worth recalling: "Plan no more buildings for library use. Library space is an anachronistic concession to the past which we can no longer afford."

• • • •

The author is indebted to David Crossman, assitant director of the University of Pittsburgh Libraries for Instructional and Research Services and nationally-known consultant on dial-access systems. Dr. Crossman provided an extensive review of current technical problems encountered in planning new media services for the college or university.

NOTES

[1] Metcalf, Keyes. *Planning Academic and Research Library Buildings.* New York, McGraw-Hill, 1965.

[2] Orlich, Donald C. and Hilen, Charles O., eds. *Telecommunications for Learning* (Seminar Report). General Telephone Company of the Northwest and Washington State University, February 1969.

[3] Dupuy, Trevor N. *Ferment in College Libraries.* Washington, D.C. Communication Service Corporation, 1968.

[4] Jones, Gardner, *et al.* "Educational Media," *College and University Business,* 47:124–130, April 1969.

[5] General Learning Corporation. *Costs of Educational Media Systems and their Equipment Components.* 3 vols. Washington, D.C., 1968.

[6] *Project Reward . . . and Campus Building.* Center for Architectural Research, Rensselaer Polytechnic Institute, 1969.

[7] Brown, James W. and Thornton, James W. *New Media in Higher Education.* Washington, D.C., Association for Higher Education, 1963. (See also revised edition, 1968.)

[8] Licklider, J. C. R. *Libraries of the Future.* Cambridge, Mass., M.I.T. Press, 1965.

[9] Dupuy, *op. cit.*

[10] Caffrey, John, and Mosmann, Charles J. *Computers on Campus.* Washington, D.C., American Council on Education, 1967.

[11] Leyden, Ralph C. and Balanoff, Neal. *The Planning of Educational Media for New Learning Centers* (A report by Stephens College, Columbia, Missouri). Washington, D.C., Office of Education, 1963.

[12] Ellsworth, Ralph E. *Planning the College and University Library Building.* Rev. ed. Boulder, Colo., Pruett Press, 1968.

ABOUT THE AUTHOR—C. Walter Stone is a graduate of Columbia University with the A. B. degree in 1946, the B. S. in L. S. in 1947, the M. A. in 1948 and the EdD in 1949. He has taught library science at the Universities of Illinois and Pittsburgh and has been Director of Educational Media for the U. S. Office of Education. Mr. Stone has been Director of the Center for Library and Educational Media Studies as well as Director of Libraries at the University of Pittsburgh, and a consultant in the field since 1952. In 1970 he established his own consulting firm. As author and editor, his interests lie in the fields of book activities and needs in Asian countries and in educational media.

Building-Planning Implications of Automation

by Robert H. Rohlf

Planning for automated services in libraries requires knowledge of new, different and changing procedures. The problem today is how frequently the changes occur that outdate a facility. "We should not be planning buildings now that in only ten years will be obsolete or will be as encumbering to our successors ten years from now as the Carnegie plans were to most of us." But, perhaps, until the library that is not a "place" is a reality, ten years is a reasonable period of function. Technology races ahead. Here Mr. Rohlf specifies some planning considerations that perhaps can be the optimum in planning today.

Mr. Becker has described in his usual clear and complete manner some of the automation devices for libraries now and in the future, and it has been left to me to attempt to discuss how library buildings should be planned for those automation possibilities. I would like to begin by pointing out an amusing feature of our present-day concern about automation. Mr. Becker explained to you in some detail the Bibliophone as it is used at the university in Delft and how this kind of mechanical or semiautomated device holds promise for certain applications.

The following is from the minutes of a former library association meeting:

The President then explained to the Conference a device for the automatic delivery of books which he had planned for use in the new [Harvard] building. At the delivery desk there would be a key board showing the digits to be combined into the various shelf numbers. As the number of the book wanted was struck by combination, it would appear by an automatic connection on the floor where the book was to be found. The attendant stationed there would take it from the shelf and place it in a box attached to an endless belt, whence it was tipped out at the other end into a cushioned receptacle close by the delivery desk, thus saving time, running, and expense.

This statement was made at the second annual conference of librarians in 1877. This evening, ninety years later, we are still discussing the same type of thing, but now we are calling it automation.

Discussing automated devices and their effects on planning in the future, I would like to divide my brief remarks into four areas, not all of which deal with building planning as such: the concept of some changes in library service, the problem of physical environment in library buildings, some specific physical requirements for fully automated systems as we can now see them, and some probable cost implications of automation insofar as buildings are concerned.

We must restrict our discussion to library planning now and in the next five to ten years. We are not talking about building planning thirty to forty years from now, although we must plan for thirty to forty years from now. First of all, I would like to discuss libraries in the sense of automated bibliographic files and limited facsimile reproduction. Because the directions were that our remarks were to be based on current library building planning, I am assuming that the book is still with us. It is proper to point out that the technology is here at the moment, of course, to reduce the Bible to the size of a pin and then to reproduce it page by page. However, considering that the cost would be $250 or more per page, and considering that the machines necessary to do this will take much more space than the Bible itself would, I am not going to discuss this technology because we must still concern ourselves with economics.

I mentioned that we would be concerned with limited facsimile reproduction. I qualify this by

SOURCE: Reprinted from Robert H. Rohlf, "Building-Planning Implications of Automation," in *Library Automation: A State of the Art Review,* (papers presented at the Pre-Conference Institute on Library Automation, San Francisco, 1967), Chicago, American Library Association, 1969, by permission of the publisher.

pointing out that we still have the problems of copyright and how they will be resolved. We also have the problem of cost. So, while it is tempting to discuss some of the very miraculous things which are taking place in the miniaturization of the actual material and in cross-country and even cross-continent facsimile transmission, my remarks are directed to the primary considerations which are here at this moment for libraries.

Now to the question of service. What type of library service must we plan buildings for in the next five to ten years that will still allow development for the future? First of all, libraries must be more "information outgoing"; by that I mean libraries will send information to people, whereas in the past, normally people came to the information. This change has obvious implications for building planning and for service. Another consideration is what will happen to the large main or central libraries, either university or public, in the future? I think that they will not only continue to be with us but that they will grow even larger and will increase in their services. We will have more storage buildings in the future, but the main libraries will still be with us and will be even more important than they are now.

However, I believe the branches—be they neighborhood, departmental, or divisional—may change. All library planners will have to consider whether or not their branch libraries might increase in number but decrease in physical size because of the possibilities of remote bibliographic access, print-outs, mail service, and perhaps a numerical reduction in the serial holdings necessary at multiple points.

Libraries should be able to send services out to businesses, to academic departments, and to area schools, but they will be sending out bibliographical information and requested follow-ups, for specific materials can then be fed back into the main library or into large area libraries or major divisional libraries to supply the material. In short, I think that libraries will be more outside oriented, not inside oriented. This conclusion assumes, of course, that library administrators and staffs will themselves become more outside oriented and think in terms of serving readers whom they may not see face to face but who may be only a voice over the telephone or a letterhead on the desk. This change is happening today in many libraries and it will accelerate in the future.

Given some of these service conditions, therefore, and given the ability to interrogate a library file by means of teletype-telephone or electronic data console, what are some of the environmental problems which library designers must not only consider but must successfully overcome in the future?

In the past ten to fifteen years, there has been a noticeable retreat from expansive, uninterrupted reading rooms to at least a visual breakup of the rooms into smaller areas by the use of smaller tables or groups of tables and more individual carrels or study tables. The rooms have been designed to maintain areas of expansiveness and yet to achieve some kind of personal, intimate feeling for the individual user.

One fact that is becoming more and more apparent to those people concerning themselves with the problem of planning space for automated service libraries of the future and of the present is that there is an increasing need for individual study space and individual bibliographic access. This will not necessarily mean more enclosed carrels as we see them or think of them today. It may mean simply more individual tables, although certainly an increase in enclosed electronic carrels is a necessity also. These individual reader spaces will come equipped with more wiring than existed in our grandfather's lifetime, simply because without this wiring the individual carrel and the individual table is useless for the special function which it will perform.

If you can envision rooms full of individual tables and rooms full of individual carrels, you can also envision a whole series of little boxes or blocks on the floor, a rather depressing scene, which the architect will have a real challenge to deal with aesthetically. The engineer will have a problem to allow for ventilation and the movement of air. The architect will have another problem to deal with in terms of light and the psychology of color. (Sometimes we are forced to wonder if all men are to be in boxes long before they are buried in them.)

Electronic carrels by their very nature are cocoons, but how many cocoons do we need or want in one room? This is a very real problem for the designer. I have seen some installations of individual carrels in larger rooms of which my first thought upon entering was of faceless men, and I wondered if some of the twentieth-century abstract impressionist painters were really prophets and if, while we may all have individual recesses, we will all become men without faces.

This is a future which I do not like to contemplate, and I give the challenge to the designers to overcome this problem and at the same time to the engineers to provide us with the electrical and mechanical facilities we need for library service—automation, video screens, facsimile reproductions, small computer consoles so that we can query the central bibliographic file from our study area—but to give us these things in such a way that we do not become faceless men. It has been pointed out that we need studies in depth on human engineering and behavioral studies to get persons and machines together in a way in which the machines are efficient and the people are happy. The challenge to architects will be to design these intimate electronic spaces and still provide us with space, color, visual beauty, and also a sense of the group or of humanity.

My third area of concern deals with some actual physical needs as I can foresee them at the moment. Formulas for reading space will of necessity have to allow for more space than those now used. It will take more square feet per reader on an individual basis—whether it be carrels or individual tables equipped with electronic devices—to achieve the same overall capacity as the 4-, 6-, and 8-place tables did in the past. Old reading space formulas will no longer be valid unless they take into account the need for increased individual study space. Another way to express the physical problems of the libraries of the future, insofar as their interior design is concerned, is that to a much greater degree than today, the libraries will become a series of spaces with connectors. This problem of the spaces and the design of the connectors is one of the prime interior design problems facing the library architects today.

The major share of my concern in the area of physical needs deals with flexibility and with electrical capacity. *Flexibility* is a word that has been used for some years now in library planning. It has often been pointed out that too much flexibility can be a bad thing, and that you cannot build full flexibility into a building because you simply cannot afford to or you do not really need to. On the other hand, libraries and librarians who have suffered for years with nineteenth-century totally inflexible buildings have emphasized flexibility in almost all postwar library buildings.

I am discussing flexibility in the sense that the prime need of today might be an inferior need in fifteen years and that a slight requirement today might be a very prime need in fifteen years. Our buildings must allow us to shrink or expand rooms and areas by moving or even removing walls. In this sense, we must have flexibility in our buildings, and I think that, by and large, libraries are achieving this.

Electrical capacity, a term used earlier, refers not simply to electrical power but more to electrical cables. One of the greatest considerations for library planning today is that of underfloor ducts, not conduits as we are used to thinking of them—$\frac{3}{4}$-inch pipe tubing or flexible tubing—but ductwork which is underneath the floor surface and which is nothing more than a tunnel framed in metal and laid in with the building floor when the building is constructed.

At one time, a single duct was used, then two underfloor ducts running side by side, and now some buildings are being planned and constructed with a 3-duct underfloor system. Let me describe these ducts briefly for those of you who are not certain what they are. They are a metal box, really. Each duct of a standard size will be approximately 3 inches across and approximately 2 inches deep. Today, there are super ducts on the market which measure approximately 2 inches deep and 7 inches across. One duct is used for telephone cabling, another duct is used for electrical cable, and a third duct is used for low-voltage requirements or for signaling controls. It is the third duct which is becoming so essential in modern library planning because this third duct, if properly sized and installed, is the duct which will carry the coaxial cables for the automation devices and, running side by side with the telephone ducts, will give the on-line accessibility that Mr. Becker talked about earlier.

These ducts have been spaced as close as 3 feet on centers. By that I mean that running in one direction every 3 feet on any floor you will have a series of these ducts. Sometimes the spacing is on 5, 6, 10, 15, or even 20 feet centers, depending upon the use of the building and, most importantly, upon the amount of money which is available to work with. I know one engineer who insists that ducts should be spaced 3 feet on centers and I know another one who says that 10 feet on centers is adequate because, after all, the ducts themselves take up anywhere from 1 to 2 feet in width depending upon the type of ducts used. This is an individual question which must be resolved for each building.

Many buildings have a cellular steel floor which may also be used for wiring raceways. It is my experience, however, that most libraries do not have cellular steel floors, primarily because of library load-bearing requirements and of our desire for large spans which normally make this type of construction uneconomical for libraries. While these cellular floors may be used as raceways, there are certain precautions which must be taken with them and an underfloor duct is often used in connection with the cellular floor.

There was a time when telephones operated on $\frac{1}{16}$-inch wires which were spliced together to form cables. Today the typical telephone instrument requires a 25-pair cable. For some telephones, such as those termed "call directors," the cabling has increased to 75-pair cable and the cable size has increased to $\frac{3}{4}$-inch diameter. In the past, telephone outlets and electrical outlets needed to be spaced along the walls, and in most cities, codes require certain spacing for these elements; but in large library workrooms and large library study rooms, we do not have a great wall expanse in relation to floor area and therefore the power must come from either above us or below us. Those of us who have seen some installations where telephone and power lines are hanging down from the ceiling or snaking along floors have been singularly unimpressed with the appearance and also with the safety of such installations.

Some libraries have had to go in and rip up flooring shortly after the library was occupied because the desks or listening booths were never in the right places on the floor where telephone or power sources could come up to their particular location. I know of one new large university library that is really a superbly designed and functioning building. Yet a short time after occupancy, some functions were automated and exposed coaxial cables had to be pushed through spaces between the floor slab above and the suspended ceilings below. Such alterations are possible, but they are far from desirable.

Underfloor duct is replacing conduit in many cases, even though we may still use the perimeter wall outlets, but underfloor duct is a prime consideration every library planner must discuss today before the library is built; and it must be discussed not in terms of today's use but tomorrow's use, a tomorrow of perhaps only five years from now.

Another physical problem that is surprisingly overlooked in some modern libraries is the problem of a computer center and the raised floor which generally is required for such an installation. This problem arises, of course, only in very large systems which will have their own computers. Computer machinery requires air conditioning, and while the amounts required have decreased because of the change from the old vacuum tubes to transistors, air conditioning of a greater capacity than that needed for other rooms in the library is required for those where computers are installed. The computers also require very extensive cabling and electrical power. This power is normally supplied under a raised floor to a particular machine. Another important consideration is that computer tapes, and to a lesser degree some microforms, are extremely sensitive to temperature and humidity changes, becoming in extreme cases unusable or even able to damage machines using them.

Another physical consideration is that of the illumination level. As you know, the lighting engineers and particularly the lighting companies have been raising the recommended light level each year to the point where one company now says that we need 1000 footcandles in order to have good reading and working light. But what happens to the use of viewing screens or video screens when we have such intense illumination? Now there are certain areas where the need for light will decrease, but the power level will, of necessity, increase because of the machines which will be used. This question of light level must be studied seriously, and we must make certain that we do not end up with machines whose screens are virtually unreadable because of the extremely bright light levels in the room.

Another physical change which we must plan for in buildings is that of shelving. The increasing amount of microform materials will require increasing amounts of special storage and shelving space. Normally, this material does not shelve efficiently or economically on standard library shelving and certainly not in standard library stack spacing. Careful consideration must be given to the question of center stack spacing when storing microform materials, for while a fixed stack may be an efficient and economical way to store books the fixed stack range based on the standard spacings of the past is not efficient for most microform storage. In effect, it would be very unfortunate to build any large library today where all storage shelving must be permanently fixed on a structural space. We must devote at least some portion, say one third as a minimum, to completely freestanding storage.

The problem of weight has been raised. Weight may be a problem with a computer facility which is going into an average office building, since offices are built on only a 50- to 60-pound live-load factor; however, the acceptable pound per square foot live-load weight for a library would be sufficient to handle computer machines now on the market, and the probabilities are that the machines will become lighter in the future, rather than heavier.

The last item to be discussed briefly is the unfortunate problem of cost. It should be fairly obvious to everyone that a fully electronic library will be a more costly one, physically, than the traditional library. We cannot build in sophisticated air conditioning and power requirements for machines and people, electrical flexibility, and telephone and audio flexibility, requiring extensive ductwork and conduit without increasing costs. These costs can be as much as $1 to $5 per square foot more than for a conventional library. It is possible, of course, that we will develop some cost savings in other ways in the future, but, for the present, we are forced to be virtually all things to all men and our costs reflect this.

It is safe to assume that storage costs will be less for microform materials than they are for standard materials. We are able to store more in the storage unit, but I must point out that the unit will cost more. In addition, microform storage areas should have very effective and sophisticated humidity and temperature control, and this is costly.

The cost of an electronic carrel and its equipment is obviously going to be much greater than the cost of an individual study table. The exact increase in its cost will depend upon how complete these carrels are in terms of equipment and access devices, but it will certainly exceed the cost of a 3 feet by 2 feet individual study table. One thing that disturbs me is that so far no designer has effectively tackled the challenge of designing an attractive electronic carrel from the ground up. All we see are electronic modifications of present study table designs.

I would like to add another disturbing problem here. In theory, an electronic carrel is quiet. But what happens in a large space with perhaps several hundred of these going at one time? How quiet will they be or how attractive? We may have an increase in acoustic cost because of this potential problem.

There are certain cost trade-offs, of course. How much does it cost us, for example, to store catalogs in card form in large catalog card rooms or areas, compared to what it would cost us to store them on magnetic tape or to have access to another's magnetic tape or drum?

There may also be totally different cost items tomorrow. For example, I understand that Bell Laboratories is now studying the possibility of developing a computer service similar to a public utility. There would be one computer center, or perhaps several regional centers, owned by the Bell Telephone Company. The consumer could rent a keyboard from Bell Telephone Company and then have access to the Bell Laboratories computers. Perhaps this will make our libraries empty in the future, but I rather doubt it.

In summary, we should not be planning buildings now that in only ten years will be obsolete or will be as encumbering to our successors ten years from now as the Carnegie plans were to most of us. The Carnegie plan buildings, however, served well for at least their first twenty to thirty years, and some of them were efficient much longer than that. Our challenge today is to see if we can do at least as well in view of onrushing technological change. We can do so only if we have the full cooperation, support, and imagination of everyone involved in the planning process. If we can intelligently and imaginatively present the service problems to our architects and engineers, they can solve the physical problems better than we.

ABOUT THE AUTHOR–Robert H. Rohlf received his B.A. degree (1949) from the College of St. Thomas, his B.S.L.S. (1950), L.S. (M.A.) (1952) and Certificate in Public Administration (1954) from the University of Minnesota. He has been an administrator in public and university libraries, the Library of Congress, and since 1969 has been Director of the Hennepin County Library System, Minneapolis.

Automation and Building Plans

by Robert H. Blackburn

The planning staff for the new University of Toronto library building assessed the present stage of computer technology and equipment, projected possible future developments in the field and then proceeded with their planning. Here the Chief Librarian shares their planning with us, not as a model, but as a hope "that we have provided amply for at least the near future." He concludes with sound advice that "to be safe, before a library commits itself, . . . it should get the latest prognostications from several sources."

The planning committee, the president, the architect and everybody else connected with a library building project will have read that computers are making possible great changes in the nature of libraries. They will react in various ways to the fact that one cannot tell precisely what the changes will be, or when, or exactly what the effect will be on their building requirements. They will probably be impatient at times, and suspect the librarian of dragging his feet, but at present there are some questions to which a librarian's only honest answer is a "definite maybe."

A part of the difficulty arises from the fact that those who write science fiction about "information retrieval" seldom make any distinction between *bibliographic* retrieval and *textual* retrieval. You may have to explain to your committee that the first operation, the identification and location of a book, is accomplished ordinarily through the use of bibliographies and catalogs and indexes, that the second operation consists of taking a book by hand from the shelf, and that computers may be applied to the first operation without altering the second.

It has been demonstrated that mechanized retrieval of bibliographic information is quite feasible technically, and adoption of the MARC II format now provides a basic standard for exchange of such information among libraries. Computer tapes are becoming available commercially for the current output of the British National Bibliography and part of the Shared Cataloging Program at the Library of Congress, and for dozens of "current-awareness" services which are unfortunately mutually incompatible. A great deal more experimentation is necessary before we have a clear picture of the most effective techniques and their economic limits, but a few of the large libraries which have been working on the problem for several years are now trying to develop "integrated" systems.

In such a system, a library will likely have its own resident computer in which the catalog records, shelflist, order file, subscription file, and loan records will all be inter-related and available "on-line," so that the record may be up-dated or consulted at any moment, and by many people at the same time. The cost-efficiency of an "on-line" system has not yet been demonstrated in practice, and it must be understood that the costs are high. Each installation will begin with something like a million dollars' worth of hardware, and perhaps as much again in development work over the first three or four years, plus ongoing adjustment and operation. However, it is in terms of "on-line" operation that automation could bring about really significant changes in bibliographic control, and for the moment we must assume that the potential improvements in library operation and in library use are great enough to offset a part of the cost and justify the rest.

It seems probable that many large universities within the next decade will have on-line computers in their central libraries, with multiple outlets in the various divisional or departmental libraries, and with some means of making prompt use of bibliographic records which have been generated elsewhere. It is not clear whether smaller universities and colleges will need to have computers and systems staff in their libraries; instead

SOURCE: Reprinted from Robert H. Blackburn, "Automation and Building Plans," *Library Trends*, vol. 18, no. 2, October, 1969, pp. 262–267, by permission of the publisher.

they may have local off-line operations, supplemented by access over telephone lines to information in larger centers. At any rate, every new academic library building should certainly make some provision for the use of mechanized bibliographic information. These provisions, of course, do not affect the normal need for reading rooms and shelf space. They may facilitate the co-operative building of collections and co-operative use, but they will not necessarily reduce the rate of growth. A helpful booklet discussing computers and some of their implications for library building is *The Impact of Technology on the Library Building.*[1]

The storage and retrieval of text, by computer, is a more difficult problem. It is true that a number of mechanized "data banks," mainly statistical, are now available commercially, and that the contents of some of them could be made accessible to users of university libraries. It is true also that some abstracting services and some collections of analyzed text are available commercially in coded microform which can be selected mechanically and projected on a screen or photocopy plate, and that these devices could be useful in handling limited bodies of data. It is true also that some knowledgeable people foresee the library of the future as a system of bibliographic retrieval linked automatically to a stackroom full of coded microtext—but here the crystal ball becomes very dark, and illumination awaits major changes in the arts and economics of publication, and miniaturization, transmission, and reproduction of text, as well as revision and clarification of copyright laws and acceptance by users of substitutes for the book. Whether these changes will come about, or when, or exactly what their effect would be is difficult to determine. For instance, if the whole body of the world's publications could be condensed into a desk-sized cabinet and called forth one page at a time at will, as has been seriously suggested is possible, then perhaps present library facilities such as reading rooms and stackrooms will have to be filled with hundreds or thousands of such desks. Meanwhile the annual production of print rises every year, in many languages and in many forms, and each library buys what it can to meet the most urgent local demands. Now that some factual data are being published only in machine-readable form, librarians will acquire it and find a way to make it available, but we are a very long way, I believe, from the use of computers for textual storage and retrieval of general library collections.

In planning a university library one cannot,

therefore, assume that computers will make any difference, at least in the next ten or fifteen years, to the growth of the book collection or to the need for study space. After that time one may hope that some technological and social miracle may begin to dampen acceleration in the growth rate of the book collection, and that it will not create too great a demand for new and specialized study space. Given the uncertainties, a librarian will want a building as flexible and adaptable as possible, within the ordinary economic limits of flexibility. Librarians should assume that within the next few years the library may have its own computer to serve a fairly comprehensive system of bibliographic control. It will be a new and better can-opener, not a new kind of diet.

The architect planning a new library building, having accepted the above generalities concerning the future of the library, will begin to ask for facts and figures, and for these you need to seek up-to-date advice. I suggest librarians not rely on the advice of computer consultants who have not worked on library systems: they will judge correctly that bibliographic control does not make heavy demands on computing power, but they are almost certain to underestimate the required storage capacity and the complexity of providing adequate access to that storage. They are likely to underestimate the high volume of input and output, the sophistication of the required system, and the time and money needed for adequate planning and development. Now that there are several libraries working in the field, librarians would do well to ask for their latest findings about scale and types of equipment to do the tasks required. Having developed a general idea of the scale, librarians will find local suppliers quite eager to give them specifications as to line-load, cabling, heat-load, floor-layout, and so on. Unless the library is already committed to a particular make of equipment, it should not become obligated to any one manufacturer at this point. The library market has not yet inspired anyone to design equipment that is really suited to library operations, and a library should be free to put together machines of various makes in order to arrive at a configuration which suits its particular needs.

During the design stage at Toronto, in the summer of 1966, we invited our architects and engineers to an all-day seminar with two imported consultants who had worked and published on information systems. The consultants had not met before and had different views of the future, but by the end of the day we had reached a consensus on the points that were important to the architects. In general, we agreed to gamble on computer cables becoming lighter rather than heavier as the equipment improves, so that eventually they might be carried in the regular three-duct underfloor system which is to be laid in most of our office floors for power, intercom, and telephone. For the initial stage, we had agreed that the data processing center would be connected to a vertical coaxial cable space running from an exit port in the basement up to a possible aerial connection on the roof. It was agreed that the vertical trunk line, which could be tapped at any floor, would feed a few horizontal trunk lines laid in the floor to serve these areas in which we could foresee the need for outlets, and that other horizontal lines would have to be installed later when and where they were needed. A complete grid of coaxial cable conduits in every slab would have been the neatest solution, but was thought to be more expensive than later modification to meet specific needs.

The horizontal cable trenches will run to nearly all public service points and control points, and the public catalog areas, as well as the technical service departments. They also serve a number of carrels in the audio-visual study area, so that we may be prepared for some preliminary experiments in the automated retrieval of text. New horizontal feeders which may have to be added in the future will be carried above false ceilings, where those exist, or else in trenches cut into the three-inch layer of light topping on the floor slabs. We may of course live to regret our gamble, and even now would sleep more soundly if we had been able to lace our floors with large cable conduits. The Library of Congress has a much safer provision in the plans for the Madison Memorial Building, which show a three-duct system laid at five foot centers in most of the floor slabs above the two basement levels. The ducts are to be three inches deep and six, six, and twelve inches wide to handle power, telephone, and coaxial cable respectively. The cost of this duct-work is estimated at about $1.50 per square foot over an area of about one million square feet.

In Toronto the computer will be near the center of the building and in a location which is convenient to staff, on the eighth floor, just above the technical service departments and just below the bookstacks. It could have been anywhere, really,

and there would have been some advantage in having it in the basement next to the supply of cooled water. We were tempted briefly by a suggestion that it be on a public service floor or at grade level, with a glass wall for the convenience of sightseers, but decided that we could not afford room for it on a public floor. The working drawings show approximately 4,000 square feet of raised floor to house the "customer engineering office" (twelve by twenty-five feet), the tape-disc-program library (twelve by thirteen feet) and the Sigma 7 computer which will be moved in from its present temporary quarters. The raised area has a ramped entrance and is completely enclosed to permit special air-conditioning. The raised floor is twelve inches above the finished floor level, and the walls enclosing it are largely glass, partly for the benefit of visitors. Alongside are offices for the systems manager and staff, amounting altogether to another 4,000 square feet of assignable work space. The space is assumed to be enough for the initial installation and a reasonable amount of development; any radical expansion in this part of the operation would presumably imply a reduction in technical service staff and office space or in stack space, and could be found by substitution in those contiguous areas. Beside the raised floor is another area which could eventually be raised and given extra supplies of power and cooled water.

I mention these details of planning at the University of Toronto not as a model to be followed, but simply as an example of what was accepted by one library in the summer of 1968. The detailed planning of our computer system is far from complete and will go on changing as we gain experience and as the machines improve. Since new generations of equipment tend to be smaller and faster and cooler, and to need lighter cables, we hope that we have provided amply for at least the near future. To be safe, before a library commits itself, however, it should get the latest prognostications from several sources.

To be absolutely safe, of course, in the face of present uncertainties, a library should tell its architect to go away and come back in twenty years, when more is known. However, if a university needs library service in the meantime, its librarian can only consult the omens, make a good guess and be prepared to find when the building is finished that his guess was not always completely accurate.

NOTE

[1] Educational Facilities Laboratory. *The Impact of Technology on the Library Building*, New York, 1967.

ABOUT THE AUTHOR–Robert H. Blackburn received his B.A. (1940) and M.A. (1941) degrees from the University of Alberta, his B.L.S. (1942) from the University of Toronto and his M.S. (1947) in library science from Columbia University. With varied public and academic library experience, Mr. Blackburn is now Chief Librarian at the University of Toronto as well as lecturer in library administration and author of articles, poems and short stories.

IX

FURNISHINGS AND EQUIPMENT

Although left until the end this last unit "Furnishings and Equipment" perhaps covers the subject about which the librarian can do most. The thought of "decorating" the library appeals naturally to most of us, and with a few simple guidelines we can do a fair job. If these comments sound a bit frivolous, they are meant to be so; but, in truth, the finishing of the interior is a professional job requiring the consultation and work of experts just as much as the planning, design, and construction of the building does.

The interior design should be planned at the earliest moment and must be considered during the building's design stages. Early, a decision for responsibility of interior design should be made. If the designing architectural firm does not employ a first rate interior design department charged with this responsibility, then an outside firm should be appointed to work with the planning agency and the designing architect. If there is close coordination of interior and exterior design, an integrated whole is assured. Unfortunately in too many cases, a decorator (as distinct from a designer) is called in at the last stages of building construction to hastily select upholstery fabrics, some drapery, and a color for the carpet. And yet, although we laymen cannot call out the fine detail, we can "sense" a well-designed interior, and will not be fooled by the decorator touch.

In much the same way as the architect needs the librarian to write the building program, the interior designer needs the librarian's help in deciding what pieces of furnishings and equipment are better or what layout or furniture arrangement will function best. It is in these areas that the practicing librarian can make a significant contribution to the building's interior. With matters of design (such as selection of materials, finishes, colors, proportion and scale) left to the designer, matters of function (such as spatial relations, work flow, maintenance) left to the librarian, and the two working together in close harmony, a warm, comfortable and functioning interior will be achieved.

This final unit of the *Reader* brings together a number of articles on library furnishings and equipment to serve as guidelines to the librarian in his endeavors toward realizing a functioning interior. First we concern ourselves with the bookstack, generally in both quantity and cost the largest item of equipment purchased for the building. Then follow articles on general considerations of furniture design, manufacture and arrangement. Finally we have included an article on the preparation of bidding documents.

Bracket Versus Case-Type Shelving

by Gladys T. Piez

A decision must first be made as to which of the two types of standard metal book-stack is desired. These two types are simply evaluated here and the author concludes that "bracket shelving appears to be the winner on points—far ahead in sales, usually less expensive, fully as stable and attractive, and much more flexible than case-type."

The relative advantages and disadvantages of bracket and case-type library shelving are a topic of continuing interest to many librarians, or so the Library Technology Project has concluded from the number of inquiries it receives on the subject. The following material has been gathered to provide some of the answers. (The designation "case" is used throughout the article for shelving which is also known as standard, panel, and lock-shelf.)

Important factors in the choice of shelving are cost, appearance, flexibility, and stability. The percentage of each type sold also has a bearing, since it reflects the choice or experience of others in the profession.

COST

To arrive at comparative cost figures, prices were obtained on bracket shelving with finished steel end panels but without tops and backs, and case shelving with tops and end panels (both are required for proper installation) but without backs. Costs are given on a percentage or dollar-value basis rather than on an individual cost basis, because the delivered and installed cost of a section of either single- or double-faced equipment can vary as much as 50 per cent, depending on quantity ordered and transportation charges.

One manufacturer says that it costs between $1400 and $1500 for the same quantity of case stacks that can be purchased by spending $1000 for bracket stacks. A like quantity of bracket shelving stripped (without tops, end panels, or backs) can be bought for $900. A second firm, on the same relative basis but not for the same quantity of shelving, quotes $450, $400, and $360.

Another manufacturer states that if bracket stacks stripped cost $1.00, bracket stacks with closed end panels will cost $1.10, and case stacks with either $\frac{1}{2}$- or 1-inch shelf adjustments will cost $1.50.

Two firms report that bracket shelving with finished end panels costs approximately the same as case-type, while without end panels the cost is almost 20 per cent less than case-type. A sixth manufacturer estimates that case-type costs from 10 to 12 per cent more than bracket-type. Still another firm reports that when bracket shelving is used with all such refinements as closed bases, end panels, and tops, the price differential in its favor is very small.

All of these estimates are based on shelving of comparable quality (gauge of metal, quality of finish, etc.).

APPEARANCE

A second element which affects choice of shelving is appearance. This is, of course, largely a subjective matter.

One manufacturer says that the librarians and architects he has dealt with have a very definite preference for case shelving but are under the impression that it costs more than bracket shelving, and that this is not necessarily true. He himself feels that case-type is more attractive, particularly when it is in color.

SOURCE: Reprinted from Gladys T. Piez, "Bracket Versus Case-Type Shelving, *ALA Bulletin*, vol. 55, November, 1961, 894–896, by permission of the publisher.

In the experience of another manufacturer, librarians and architects who prefer case shelving are definitely in the minority. Another has found that librarians and more particularly architects favor bracket shelving, and that a large number of architects choose it without end panels for the modern open look this gives. A fourth advises that a growing number of librarians prefer bracket shelving without end panels and consider it to be a more attractive modern design than the box-like appearance of case or bracket units with end panels. The same manufacturer believes, however, that the majority of librarians and architects judge case and bracket shelving equal in appearance when bracket shelving is fitted with end panels. This opinion is concurred in by another company. One manufacturer thinks that when closed ends are used with bracket shelving it compares very well in appearance with case type and that, in fact, when compared with certain kinds of case shelving, the bracket installation is the more attractive. In his experience, where appearance has been a factor, there has been no great inclination toward case-style units.

An alternative to the use of steel end panels as a way of dressing up bracket shelving is the addition of wood end panels to match a library's wood furniture—this makes a very attractive installation.

FLEXIBILITY

The biggest advantage attributable to bracket shelving is undoubtedly its greater flexibility. Experienced librarians and manufacturers (with one exception) with whom the subject has been discussed agree that it is much the more versatile of the two types.

In the average bracket installation, the fixed-base shelves are deep enough to allow complete inter-changeability of adjustable shelves of 8-, 10-, or 12-inch nominal depth within a given compartment. This is not possible with case equipment where all shelves are of the same depth except where special design of the base provides a deeper bottom shelf. Another advantage is that when bracket shelving is separated, one of the two existing columns can be used in the rearranged position, thus requiring only one additional column. When case shelving is separated, two additional end panels are necessary.

The absence of a top in the usual bracket installation permits placement of the shelves at greater intervals, and this in turn makes it possible to shelve books of greater height throughout a section, including the top shelf.

Because in bracket shelving (in contrast to case shelving) the ends of the shelf are actually part of the shelf itself, it is possible to move a fully loaded shelf without dropping any of the books. Such a shelf can be carried across a room or shifted up or down within the same section simply by unhooking the lugs, raising the shelf slightly, and bringing it forward. This may be an important consideration.

Such features as inverted-bracket, reference, sloping magazine-display, and bin shelves, hanging carrels, divided shelves, book lockers, and back stops are standard accessory items for the bracket stacks made by most companies. Some of these items can be furnished for case shelving on special order, but it is extremely difficult to furnish a hanging study carrel, for example, and still retain the adjustability which is possible with bracket equipment. For arrangement of periodicals, bracket shelving permits an unbroken line of sloping and flat shelves by the use of inverted or underside brackets; with case shelving there would be a full-depth upright every 3 feet. It is not practical to install 20-inch newspaper shelves and other large items in the smaller case units.

Case shelving is often used in rare book libraries because of the added protection against dust which backs and tops provide. Such shelving is also commonly found in law and other special libraries where books are uniform in height and frequent shelf adjustments are not necessary.

One manufacturer, who makes both types, specializes in bracket shelving for two reasons—first because the demand for it is so much greater, and second because specifications written around case shelving allow manufacturers to bid on welded cases of extremely light gauge material. Another firm continues to market case shelving simply to satisfy the small number of its customers who do not want to change to bracket-type.

STABILITY

Four companies report no appreciable difference in the stability of the two kinds of stacks. Another states that if all the refinements are added to bracket stacks there is no difference in the stability of the two types. He says, however, that since case shelving is supported on all four corners of the shelf and bracket shelving is cantilevered from a central column, theoretically, case-type stacks should be more stable.

Another manufacturer finds no great difference in stability, but states that if there is an advantage it is in favor of the bracket stack because the base parts may be readily adjusted for leveling purposes on irregular floors. By contrast, it is necessary to shim case shelving to compensate for floor irregularities. Still another manufacturer says that in modular buildings, where the trend is to install book stacks which are not tied to the building, the only way to guarantee the stability of free-standing case shelving is to anchor it to the floor. He points out that the base shelf on free-standing bracket stacks is 2 inches wider than the adjustable shelves, which increases stability.

Another feature which may provide a greater degree of stability in bracket shelving is the fact that, because of its design, books are always shelved closer to the center of gravity.

SALES

Seven manufacturers reported comparative percentages of sales as follows:

Number of Manufacturers	Percentage of Bracket Shelving Sold	Percentage of Case Shelving Sold
1	75 per cent	25 per cent
1	85 per cent	15 per cent
5	90–98 per cent	2–10 per cent

CONCLUSION

Bracket shelving appears to be the winner on points—far ahead in sales, usually less expensive, fully as stable and attractive, and much more flexible than case-type.

ABOUT THE AUTHOR–Gladys T. Piez attended Fargo College and the University of Minnesota. She was Information Specialist with the Federal Aviation Agency in Washington, D.C. from 1946–58, and then, until retirement in 1967, served with the Library Technology Project of ALA.

The Selection and Evaluation of Library Bookstacks

by Frazer G. Poole

"It is important ... that the individual responsible for drafting specifications for a library bookstack installation knows the criteria of good design, be able to evaluate the differences in the products of the several manufacturers, and knows something of the ways by which the performance of a bookstack may be tested." Thus in this article we look again at the two types of stack, and particularly installation methods, but with greater detail.

To the librarian, architect, or purchasing agent charged for the first time with the selection of bookstacks for a library, the task looks simple enough. In fact, at a glance, the products of the several manufacturers are so similar in appearance that it is difficult to tell them apart. Closer examination, however, reveals variations that may be the difference between a satisfactory installation and one that fails to perform as intended. It is important therefore that the individual responsible for drafting specifications for a library bookstack installation knows the criteria of good stack design, be able to evaluate the differences in the products of the several manufacturers, and knows something of the ways by which the performance of a bookstack may be tested.

Although some form of shelving has been used for the storage of books since Biblical days, shelving design continues to evolve slowly. In earlier times, most library book shelves were of wood, a material used with very handsome effect in many modern libraries. By the middle of the last century, many commercial bookstack installations used cast-iron uprights or side panels, with wood shelves. Steel shelving first appeared toward the end of the century, and is still the preferred material. Other materials, such as aluminum, have been tried, but have not proved suitable for this purpose. Steel, of course, offers the advantages of strength, durability, fire resistance, and lower cost, as compared with wood.

Although the terms are somewhat loosely and interchangeably used, most manufacturers refer to their product as "library bookstack" rather than "library shelving" and for this reason the word bookstack will be used throughout this paper to refer to installations using steel. Wood units are usually, but not always, called shelving.

Two types of steel bookstack are used in library installations, neither of which is to be confused with the steel shelving sold for use in stock rooms and similar industrial purposes. The latter product is totally unsuited for library use, although the low cost sometimes makes it attractive to those not familiar with its deficiencies. Such shelving usually consists of four upright angle irons, to which the metal shelves are bolted. These units have no flexibility of shelf arrangement and are very crude versions of the more refined units to be discussed below. Unfortunately, an occasional librarian finds that his purchasing agent has been led to believe that this product is suitable for library use. Rarely, the need for cheap shelving for the storage of little-used materials may justify this product, but the librarian should be very careful to determine that such shelving will indeed meet his needs before accepting it.

Of the two types of steel bookstacks to be considered here, the first is variously referred to as case-type, panel-type, lock-shelf, or standard. Case-type is perhaps the name most frequently used and refers to a design having full backs, tops, and end panels slotted, usually for the full depth of the case, to receive the shelves. The shelves, which slide in and out of the slots in the side panels, are designed to lock in position when

SOURCE: Reprinted from Frazer G. Poole, "The Selection and Evaluation of Library Bookstacks," *Library Trends*, vol. 13, no. 4, April, 1965, pp. 411–432, by permission of the publisher.

properly inserted. Most of the better known manufacturers of library bookstacks produce this style, as do other firms which do not normally supply libraries.

A few architects and librarians prefer case-type stacks because they believe the over-all design presents a neater and more finished appearance than the somewhat stripped-down effect of bracket-type bookstacks. Others prefer the more modern appearance of bracket-type stacks, as opposed to the rather box-like appearance of case-type stacks.[1] Case-type stacks are perhaps most frequently used in libraries where the collections run to long sets of uniform size, so that shifting of the collection can be kept to a minimum, e.g., law libraries. The same design is also used occasionally in rare book rooms, where the closed design offers some protection against dust. For the most part, however, the lack of flexibility and the higher cost, which for case-type may be from 10 to 30 per cent more than for bracket stack, usually leads to the selection of the latter. It is interesting to note that in the Library Technology Project (LTP) evaluation, five manufacturers reported that 90 per cent or more of their sales were of bracket stacks, one reported that 85 per cent of his sales were bracket stacks, and a seventh reported that bracket stacks accounted for 75 per cent of his sales as compared with case-type.[2]

In making a choice between case-type and bracket-type stack, adaptability for different needs is the most important consideration. Experienced librarians and manufacturers are in general agreement that the bracket stack is much the more flexible of the two styles. Case-type stacks are designed to accommodate shelves of only one depth in a given unit, i.e., an 8-inch section of case-type stack will accept only 8 inch shelves. In a bracket stack installation, on the other hand, there is, save for the fixed-base shelf, complete interchangeability of all widths of shelves in every section.

A major advantage of bracket stack is the ease with which a shelf, either partially or fully loaded with books, can be moved from one location to another. An entire shelf may be lifted from the uprights and carried to a new section of stack or it may be "walked" up or down the uprights by unhooking first one end and moving it to the new position, then unhooking and moving the other end. In a case-type installation, all books must first be removed from a given shelf, the shelf relocated, and the books shelved again.

Bracket stacks may also be rearranged more easily than case-type units, and require only one additional upright each time two sections are separated. Case-type stacks require two additional end panels when two sections are separated.

A further important advantage of bracket stacks lies in the availability of a variety of special shelves and other units. Magazine display shelves, pull-out reference shelves, inverted or flush-bracket shelves for shelving newspapers and large volumes, divided shelf units, carrels, book or typewriter lockers, coat rack units, and other features are available as standard items from most manufacturers of bracket stacks. A few such units, e.g., sloping display shelves, are available for case-type installations, usually on special order. Most of these features, however, do not lend themselves to use in this design.

There is some experience among librarians, unrecorded in the literature, to indicate that over a period of years, case-type stacks are more likely to suffer damage than a bracket installation. Careless placement of shelves may force the slotted portion of the end panels out of position, making shelves difficult to insert or remove thereafter. Designs in which the slots do not run the full depth of the shelf are less subject to such damage than those in which the slots extend the full depth. This is more likely to be a problem also, with the cheaper, case-type stacks in which relatively light gauges of metal are used.

Differences in stability of the two types appear to be negligible. In the LTP evaluation, four manufacturers reported no appreciable differences in the stability of bracket stacks versus case-type stacks.[2] One manufacturer stated that he believed bracket stacks should be more stable because the design is such that books are always shelved close to the center of gravity of the stack. Another manufacturer reported little difference in the stability of the two designs, if all refinements are added to the bracket stack. In the latter case, however, the only really important factor in stability is the end panels.

Aesthetics is, of course, a subjective matter. As indicated above, some architects and librarians like the appearance of the case-type design, although the majority seem to prefer the bracket stack. It should be remembered that metal or wood end panels can always be added to bracket stacks if a more finished appearance is desired.

Case-style stacks are manufactured by a large number of firms, only a few of which regularly supply the library trade. As a result, there is a wide range of quality and cost in the product. Since no performance standards for this design are available, the librarian who prefers the case-type stack is at a disadvantage. The best solution is to compare the products of the several manufacturers, noting such features as the design of the slots, the ease of inserting and removing shelves, the gauges of metal used, the presence of projecting screw heads or sharp edges that could damage books, the stability of the unit, and the ease of assembly. Evaluation from a catalog is difficult, if not impossible, and actual stack units should be examined either in the manufacturer's showroom or in a library installation.

Bookstacks of the bracket design were introduced by both Library Bureau and Art Metal just before the turn of the century. Today there are eight principal manufacturers of bracket-type stacks, and several others which produce this type but supply relatively small quantities to libraries.

The basic design of the bracket bookstack involves the use of vertical steel members (called uprights or columns) upon which the shelves are hung in cantilever fashion. If the uprights are supported at the base so that the unit will stand alone, the stack is called "freestanding." If the uprights support the loaded shelves but must be top-braced in order to remain standing, the stack is usually referred to as "non-freestanding." The latter is less expensive, but has the advantage of lacking a closed base and of being considerably less flexible. Freestanding units can be more easily re-arranged and moved from one location to another. Non-freestanding bracket stacks are usually considered less attractive than the closed-base, freestanding design. The latter, however, is a point the librarian will want to judge for himself, especially if cost is an important factor.

Bracket as well as case-type stacks are available in single-tier (one full-height unit, 7 feet-6 inches high), and in multi-tier. Multi-tier installations consist of two or more levels of stacks in which each level supports the weight of those above. In an earlier era, the spaces between vertical units were left open to allow the circulation of air around the books. These openings, however, promoted vertical drafts and considerably increased the hazards caused by fires. Today, air conditioning largely obviates the need for this circulation of air around the books and, as a result, the great majority of libraries are constructed with continuous, solid floors, each of which is capable of supporting, independently, the full load imposed by the stacks and the book collection. Thus, most present-day stack installations are single-tier. Where multi-tier installations are made, floors are continuous to reduce the fire hazard, but are not self-supporting. Because multi-tier stacks constitute such a small part of current installations and because they present special engineering problems, they will not be discussed further in this paper.

In a bracket stack, of either free or non-freestanding design, the uprights or columns are square or rectangular in cross section and measure from 2 by 2 inches to 2 by 3 inches. They may be formed in a variety of ways, each of which is calculated to produce a rigid column capable of withstanding the stresses placed upon the unit when it is loaded with books. Most commonly, the upright consists of two pieces of steel formed in a hat-shaped cross section and welded together with the flanges on the outside and at right angles to the longitudinal axis of the stacks. Other designs have a single flange on the inside, or have the two halves of a "C" shaped column turned back to back and bolted together. Although each manufacturer claims superiority for his column design, independent studies are desirable to determine both actual library requirements and the degree to which the several existing column designs meet these requirements.

Each tubular upright contains two vertical rows of slots. At intervals, depending upon the manufacturer, these slots, which are on 1-inch centers, differ slightly in shape, to permit easy alignment of shelves. Laterally, the slots may vary from ½ to $1\frac{1}{8}$ inches on centers. Adjustable shelves are hung from the uprights by means of hooks which engage the slots in the column.

The standard size of a single-faced section of bracket stack is 36 inches wide, by 7 feet-6 inches high, by 8, 10, or 12 inches deep. Two sections back to back, with the shelves on each side hung from the same pair of uprights, are referred to as a compartment, a double-faced section, or a bay. Most manufacturers will provide shorter or longer units on special order, and at least one manufacturer recently offered a standard 48-inch unit which will be discussed in more detail below. In addition to full-height (7 feet-6 inches) units, all manufacturers offer intermediate height (5 feet or 5 feet-6 inches) units, and standing height (3 feet-6 inches) units. The intermediate height is frequently used for installations in children's rooms or elementary school libraries, while the standing height units make convenient space dividers in open stack installations, or storage and work units in library work areas.

Rigidity in the longitudinal direction, i.e., in the long axis of the stack, is usually achieved by the use of steel cross braces. Under ordinary circumstances, sway braces are required only every fourth or fifth unit, although each manufacturer has his own recommendations. However, since the use of sway braces occasionally prevents large volumes from being pushed back on the shelves so that the spines line up with those of smaller books, some librarians object to them under any conditions. The alternative, for most manufacturers, is a very rigid design employing extra-heavy cross members in the base and some form of gusset or bracing at the top of each unit. Such designs are expensive, often adding as much as 10 per cent to the cost of a given job. Where gussets are employed, the shelving problem is alleviated only slightly, since the gussets themselves hamper the proper shelving of books. Whether the limited number of occasions when sway braces prevent an oversize volume from being shelved "through" is sufficient justification for the added cost of the specially reinforced design must be decided by the purchaser.

A second solution to the sway brace problem has appeared recently with the development of a stack unit in which the uprights are welded to the top and bottom spreaders, to form a rectangular frame. This is an economical design that provides great rigidity in the longitudinal direction.

Lateral rigidity, as well as lateral stability, depends primarily upon the strength of the uprights and upon that of the base support system. Strength of the uprights is achieved by the design of the cross section in relation to the gauge of metal used. For the least deflection in the lateral direction, the flanges in a two piece, welded upright are always at right angles to the longitudinal axis of the stacks. Where higher strength is required, an additional reinforcing strip of steel may be welded inside the column or bolted between the two halves of a non-welded column, or a heavier gauge of steel may be used.

Base support systems are of two general types. A few manufacturers offer both in order to meet a greater variety of specifications. In the more common design, the brackets at the ends of the bottom shelves are bolted to the uprights to form wings projecting at right angles to the longitudinal axis of the stack. In the second, and more rigid design, continuous support, from one side of the stack to the other, is provided either by a heavy duty member which wraps around and is bolted to the base of the column, or by a piece of heavy sheet steel which passes through the two halves of a non-welded upright. In some designs this may be the same as the reinforcing strip referred to

above. In either case, these members provide a far more rigid support for the upright than the design in which the end brackets of the base shelves are simply bolted to the columns.

No independent engineering studies of column strength or of base support systems have been conducted. However, recent testing by the University of Illinois for its stack installation in the library of the new Chicago Circle campus suggests that the usual design, in which the base brackets are simply bolted to the uprights, may not have sufficient strength to support heavy eccentric loads, whereas designs utilizing heavy gauge members that wrap around the upright, or reinforcing members that pass through the upright, can sustain such loads.

In view of the lack of accepted performance standards for bracket stacks, the author would like to suggest that the Library Technology Project of the American Library Association consider this a matter for investigation. Such a study should include a determination of reasonable performance standards for bracket stacks, as well as mathematical and engineering evaluations of existing designs, to determine their performance in accordance with such standards.

Although library floors are designed to be level, in practice it is impossible to make them so. Variations of one quarter inch or more in a distance of 9 to 12 feet are not uncommon, and in distances of 18 to 21 feet, variations of three-eighths to one-half inch or more may occasionally be encountered. It is important therefore that library bookstacks be equipped with proper leveling devices. Shims, although frequently used, are unsuitable for several reasons and should not be permitted. In the better designs, adjustable leveling clips or shoes are provided. These are usually covered with non-slip neoprene pads or sleeves. Such pads prevent damage to resilient tile flooring and decrease the tendency of stacks to "creep" when subjected to vibration.

The matter of stability in an installation of freestanding bookstacks is somewhat complicated. Every librarian has heard of occasional instances in which rows of bookstacks have been toppled, overturning others in succession, like dominoes. Under ordinary circumstances, a so-called freestanding stack is indeed freestanding. However, installations in those parts of the country subject to earthquake tremors may require special safety precautions. In California, the State Department of Public Works requires that freestanding stacks in the public schools be sufficiently stable to withstand a force equal to 20 per cent of the dead load of the books and the stacks.[3] Although not mandatory in other jurisdictions, many California libraries have included this requirement in their bookstack specifications. To provide an extra measure of safety, California law also requires that bookstacks in school libraries be able to withstand a force one and one-half times the overturning force.[3] Few freestanding stacks are able to meet the latter requirement without either anchoring or top bracing.

In cases where some fastening is required, floor anchoring is preferred because, in an earthquake, the bases of a stack installation can be displaced slightly, even if the tops are held in position by the top bracing.[4] Anchoring, however, is more expensive than top bracing and where earthquake tremors are not a problem the latter may be preferred.

Difficulties also arise when one tries to guard against vandalism. Many librarians consider this such a remote possibility that they take no further cognizance of the problem. Instances of deliberate over-turning of stacks have occurred, however, and to be on the safe side some librarians, as well as some library consultants, prefer to fasten the stacks in one manner or the other. A few of the manufacturers take a less conservative view and state that their freestanding stack installations do not require any fastening. In California, some type of fastening is mandatory in elementary and high school libraries. Elsewhere, the librarian makes his own decision.

Where top-bracing is preferred to floor anchors, "U" shaped channels of at least 18-gauge steel and with at least a one-inch flange should be used. One such channel is usually installed for every three bays or compartments. Thus a group of ranges, each eight bays long, would require three transverse channels. For the sake of appearance, channels are usually centered on the second upright from each end of the range, with other channels spaced at equal intervals along the remainder of the range, where possible. Transverse channels are located over the uprights, rather than in midsection, to provide maximum rigidity.

Metal end panels are widely used with bracket stack installations to give a neater appearance and, through the use of color, to enhance the decor. Although normally fabricated of smooth-surfaced sheet metal, at least one manufacturer now offers a textured surface. Others offer end panels with chromium plated trim strips or wood inserts, or panels faced with fabric-backed plastics, leather, or textiles. Full, wood end panels, available in a variety of different grains, are unusually handsome, but may add from 50 to 100 per cent to the cost of each panel.

Standard book shelves come in 8-inch, 10-inch, and 12-inch widths. Some manufacturers also offer a 9-inch shelf. It should be understood that the above figures are nominal widths and represent the distance from the front edge of the shelf to the center line of the stack. The actual widths of 8-, 10-, and 12-inch shelves are 7, 9, and 11 inches respectively. In almost all bracket stacks, the upright, between the inner edges of the shelves, is 2 inches thick, so that one inch is added to the actual widths of the shelves in calculating the usable depth of the section.

Since the wider the shelf, the higher the cost, no shelves should be wider than actually required. It is usually estimated that at least 80 per cent of the books in a comprehensive collection will fit on 8-inch shelves. Some bound periodicals of course require wider shelves, as do many medical, scientific, and art books. As a rule of thumb, it may be assumed that a normal installation will require 80 per cent 8-inch shelves, 15 per cent 10-inch shelves, and 5 per cent 12-inch shelves. Some special purpose shelves, e.g., sloping display shelves, have a nominal depth of 12 inches and should be used only in units with 12-inch bases.

Shelves of the several manufacturers vary from 35 to 35½ inches in usable length. It is easy to calculate that in a stack designed for 300,000 volumes at full capacity, one-half inch is the equivalent of 583 feet, in which could be stored an additional 4,500 volumes. On the other hand, since few libraries ever reach their absolute storage capacity, the additional space of the longer shelf design should not be given undue weight in writing specifications.

Within the last few years, one manufacturer has marketed a four-foot shelf for bracket stack installations. In theory, the longer shelf requires fewer uprights and in an installation of any size would result in substantial savings. It was assumed by the manufacturer that this shelf, as originally designed, would require no further reinforcement for all normal use. However, tests of the non-reinforced shelf, conducted by the University of California at Los Angeles, showed deflections of $\frac{1}{4}$ to $\frac{1}{2}$ inch under loads of 62 pounds per square foot. Although this loading was made heavy for test purposes, it was, in actuality, only 1.1 pounds per square foot greater than the average load in many areas of the UCLA stacks.[5] The four-foot shelf is available with a reinforcing steel channel welded to the lower surface but this reduces the cost advantage. Some librarians who have considered the matter carefully, also believe that the four-foot shelf has a functional disadvantage in that it is difficult, in a stack aisle of standard width, for the eye to encompass a span of four feet. Thus, locating a given item may be more difficult on the longer shelf than on a standard three-foot shelf. For some purposes, the longer shelf, without reinforcing, may be quite satisfactory and could result in definite economies. However, the several factors involved should be considered carefully before adopting the four-foot length.

All standard book shelves are presently designed to withstand loads of 40 pounds per square foot with no permanent deflection, and with no temporary deflection in excess of $\frac{3}{16}$ inch. While this standard is adequate for most library materials, bound copies of *Life*, for example, standing upright on a shelf, exert a load factor of 57 pounds to the square foot on a 12 inch shelf. Twleve-inch phonograph records produce a load factor of 49.5 pounds per square foot on a 12 inch shelf. Fortunately, most shelves are designed to withstand loads somewhat in excess of the 40-pound standard. This is not always the case, however, and there are recent installations in which the shelves sag to a degree noticeable to even the most casual observer. Strictly adhered to, the 40-pound standard is probably satisfactory in many situations, but the writer believes that a 60-pound per square foot standard, with an appropriate safety factor, is both desirable for the librarian and economically feasible for the manufacturer.

Although the U-bar shelf enjoyed considerable popularity some years back, such shelves are infrequent in present-day installations. They are still available, however, from at least one manufacturer. The split shelf, a fairly recent innovation, was designed to provide a more efficient type of book support which slides in a track down the center of the shelf. In use, these supports always remain upright and attached to the shelf. There is an additional cost for this design and as yet it has not been widely used; only two manufacturers are known to have it in their lines.

Hinged-bracket shelves were more popular some years ago than currently. This design is still available, however, from several manufacturers, and some librarians perfer it to the slightly cheaper detachable-bracket shelf. In the hinged design, the brackets are permanently attached to the shelf and fold flat for easy storage. The detachable bracket,

on the other hand, requires that the brackets be detached before the shelves are stored and reaffixed when the shelves are used. With the exception of one manufacturer who produces a bracket to fit either end of the shelf, brackets fit right or left ends of shelves only. There is little to choose between the two, except the greater convenience in storage of the hinged bracket type. Occasionally, one hears the objection that the hinged shelf is awkward to move, but this presents no problem if the proper technique is used.

A recent and very interesting innovation in shelving is known as Fold-a-shelf. Here the shelf and the end brackets are formed in one piece and the unit is slotted along the line at which the brackets would normally be attached to the shelf. In use, the brackets are simply folded upwards until they are in the vertical position. This design eliminates both hinges and loose end brackets and effects a saving over conventional shelves. If it is necessary to store the shelf, the ends are folded down to about 45 degrees, so that the units stack nicely. Although the metal eventually breaks from fatigue, it is good for at least 35 folds, if the end brackets are not bent downward more than 45 degrees.[6] In normal use, therefore, such shelves would last almost indefinitely. This design has gained acceptance on the West Coast where it was introduced.

The number of hooks used on shelf brackets may occasionally be a matter of importance. Such hooks, formed at the top of the brackets, engage the slots in the upright and support most of the weight of the books on the shelves. Lugs at the bottom of the bracket also fit into the slots of the upright, but serve only to keep the shelf from being moved sideways; they support no weight. Two hooks, if properly designed, are entirely adequate to support all possible loads. Three hooks, as furnished by some manufacturers, may tend to bind in the slots and make it difficult to shift shelves quickly and easily if hooks and slote are not properly sized and aligned. Sample shelves of three hook design should be carefully checked for proper clearances.

The normal capacity of a standard 90-inch stack is seven shelves—the fixed base shelf plus six adjustable shelves. for convenience and flexibility, uprights should have slots all the way to the top. With a 4-inch base, this permits separation of the shelves approximately $12\frac{1}{2}$ inches on centers, thus providing a clear filing space between shelves of $11\frac{3}{4}$ inches.

A variety of other types of shelves are available from the manufacturers, although these may not always be shown in their hand-out literature. Among the more common special-purpose designs are sloping display shelves for periodicals, flush bracket shelves for the storage of oversize volumes and newspapers, pull-out reference shelves, divided shelves for pamphlets, phonograph records, and similar items, book storage lockers, coat racks and umbrella stands, and desk units. Such units add greatly to the flexibility and convenience of the bracket stack installation. One new unit, which has not yet found its way into the catalogs, is a sloping newspaper display and storage shelf designed for the University of Notre Dame Library and used again in the Chicago Circle library of the University of Illinois. This special shelf, which eliminates the need for the traditional newspaper stick, holds the newspaper in a nearly vertical position under a plexiglas cover which lifts to permit access. Although users can leave newspapers in a state of disarray that is impossible with the traditional stick, experience at Notre Dame indicates that it requires little more staff time to straighten an issue and replace it behind its cover than to place the paper on the traditional stick.[7] The advantages of the new shelf are the ease with which a given title may be located, the convenience of access, and the ease of reading.

Although canopy tops are available for bracket stack installations, they are infrequently used in air-conditioned buildings. Such tops add appreciably to the cost and serve no useful purpose except to protect books from dust in areas that are not air-conditioned. They may occasionally be selected for aesthetic reasons, but against this must be balanced the fact that they prevent utilizing the full height of the stacks.

Bookstack accessories include such small but important items as book supports, range indicators, end-label holders, and shelf-label holders. Designs vary with the manufacturer. Choice of style, where available, rests with the purchaser, but there are some useful guidelines.

For general use, the wire-type book support is probably least satisfactory, although it is the most economical. The principal objection to this support is that it damages books carelessly shelved, by "knifing" into the pages. Plate-type supports are of two kinds. The first, and most common type, consists of a piece of sheet metal with a portion cut out and turned under to form a base. Although more expensive, this design is no better than the wire support and is to be avoided for the same reasons. A second design is frequently called the "findable" or "non-losable" support. In this type, the two sides are formed at right angles to

the main body of the support to produce a surface $\frac{1}{2}$ to $\frac{3}{4}$ inch in width. This eliminates the danger of "knifing" and makes it easy to locate the support when books are shelved on either side of the support. However, unless this type of support is provided with the proper non-skid surface on the base it will slide out of position when books are moved, and may scratch the surface of the shelf. For best results, the synthetic corks are superior to rubber-type materials as a non-skid surface. Application of these materials by pressure sensitive adhesives is unsatisfactory, and one of the solvent activated adhesives should be specified instead.

A third type of book support clips to the box edge at the front of the shelf, along which it slides as on a track. Usually known as a hook-type support, it also has a flange at right angles to the edge of the shelf to eliminate knifing the pages of books. This type of support should also be ordered with non-skid bottom.

Range index finders are "V"-shaped holders for 3 by 5 inch cards. Normally placed at the center of the end panel and close to the top, they identify a range at some distance and simplify the task of giving directions to users of open stack collections. Architects and designers occasionally object to these devices because they consider them unsightly, but the convenience they afford the library user compensates for any lack of aesthetic quality. Sometimes made in aluminum, range finders are better specified in steel. "V"-shaped range finders may be used with or without end panels. Where both ends of the range are open and accessible, it is necessary to use one range finder at each end. When both ends of a range are not accessible, as in those cases where one end is against a wall, only one range finder is required. Only one range finder is used at each end regardless of whether the range is single-faced or double-faced.

Three by five card holders, not to be confused with range index finders described above, are surface mounted on the end panels to identify the materials shelved within the range. One card holder is usually furnished for each end panel of a single-faced range, and two for a double-faced range. Although some manufacturers offer double holders for a double end panel, this design is less satisfactory than two single holders.

Even such small items as snap-on label holders can be unsatisfactory if not properly designed. Ordinarily these holders are used on periodical shelves to indicate the location of unbound issues. They should be designed of light weight metal with a high degree of spring, and it should be possible to remove them and relocate them quickly and easily, and without damage to the finish. Despite such obvious requirements, some manufacturers make these holders of fairly heavy-gauge steel with little or no spring. Better type holders are made of special aluminum alloys with sufficient spring to keep them in position but still permit easy adjustment.

A thorough knowledge of the several elements of good stack design is requisite for the development of proper specifications, but such knowledge alone does not guarantee a satisfactory installation. As with so many other products used in libraries, the development of specifications has been left largely to the manufacturers. Performance standards and specifications prepared by librarians to meet library needs do not exist. In consequence, nearly every specification for steel stacks is copied, in whole or in part, from specifications prepared by the several manufacturers for their own products. The result is often called a "nuts and bolts" specification. That is to say, the materials and methods of manufacture are specified, rather than the performance of the product. To date, the manufacturers concerned have shown little interest in developing performance standards for bookstacks.

Thus, if such specifications are to be developed, it appears that the work must be undertaken by an organization such as the Library Technology Project of the American Library Association. In fact, determination of the basic performance requirements of steel bookstacks, sponsorship of the required engineering tests, and the technical evaluation of existing designs are better conducted by an independent body. It is to be hoped that LTP will consider this a project that it might profitably undertake.

Despite the fact that carefully evaluated performance specifications are not yet available, there are tests that can be applied by the librarian, architect, or purchasing agent as a means of determining the performance of steel stacks. These tests are set forth in Appendix I.

We have not mentioned, thus far, the finishing of steel stacks. As with other elements of stack performance, finishes vary widely in quality and, unless specified in terms of performance, may not provide the durability, resistance to scratching, and other qualities desirable in a stack installation. Fortunately, performance specifications for steel finishes were developed by the LTP a few years ago and have been successfully used in some recent installations. These specifications, which deserve to be more widely known and used, are reproduced in Appendix II.

Wood has been used for library shelving since time immemorial. With the advent of sheet metal stacks, however, wood began to be used less frequently. Today, although still a popular material, wood is rarely used in large installations. There are exceptions, of course, and custom wood shelving is not infrequently found in rare book rooms, in browsing rooms, and in other areas of the library where shelving made of fine cabinet woods is used to enhance the decor.

Aside from these rather specialized uses, wood shelving today appears to be restricted mainly to installations in school and small public libraries. Despite its higher cost (wood shelving may run from twenty to thirty per cent more than steel) and its lack of flexibility, librarians justify their use of wood on the basis of its added "warmth," and on the fact that it is "less noisy."

As with steel, wood shelving may be obtained in both single- and double-faced units. Standard height shelving is 82 inches in wood instead of 90 inches, as in steel. Intermediate height shelving is 60 inches high, and counter height shelving is 42 inches high. These measurements will vary slightly from manufacturer to manufacturer. Shelf depths also parallel those used for steel shelving with 8-, 10-, and 12-inch shelves the accepted standards. In this instance, however, the depths given are actual rather than nominal. Again, as with steel units, the standard width module is 36 inches on centers.

As in case-type steel shelving, wood shelving may be purchased with backs, although this adds appreciably to the cost. If backs are not specified, full-height, double-faced shelving requires sway braces to provide longitudinal stability. Because of its lower height, wood shelving is not ordinarily anchored to the floor, nor is it top-braced as in the case of steel shelving.

Fixed bottom shelves may be flat (standard) or tilted at a ten degree angle. Some librarians prefer the latter design because it is easier to read titles on the bottom shelves. Against this advantage, however, must be weighed the tendency of books to slide to the back of the shelf, where they are often more difficult to see than if stored on a flat shelf. The cork or composition strips employed to overcome this difficulty usually are ineffective, especially under conditions where passing traffic sets up vibrations that affect the furniture in the building.

Both particle board and plywood shelves are used in the cheaper grades of wood shelving, but are subject to warping under sustained loads. The best shelving specifies solid hardwood (northern yellow birch or hard rock white maple) $\frac{13}{16}$ inch thick. Such shelves are "built-up" by edge-gluing a number of strips together.

Wood shelving is usually adjustable on one inch centers. A common method of providing for such adjustment uses vertical rows of holes drilled near the front and back edges of the end panels. Threaded brass pins inserted in the holes support the shelves, which are grooved at the ends so that the shelves drop over and cover the pins. This method is entirely satisfactory under ordinary circumstances, although school students have been known to replace the metal pins with wood pins or matches, which break when the shelf is loaded beyond a certain limit. Other methods of shelf support include the use of small metal hooks which fit into holes in the end brackets and at the same time project under the shelf to provide support. More expensive, but probably the most satisfactory if properly installed, are long metal standards which are set into grooves extending the full height of the end panels near the front and back edges. The shelves are supported on small metal angles which fit into slots in the standards. This system, which permits adjustments on one-half inch centers, is virtually fool-proof. It is available from most manufacturers at the option of the purchaser.

Although less varied than the line of accessory shelves available with bracket-type steel stacks, several special shelf types may be obtained. Among these are sloping display shelves for periodicals, newspaper holder racks, and divided shelves. Wood shelving is intermediate between case-type and bracket stacks in the ease of moving shelves loaded with books. In many cases, the position of a shelf may be adjusted without removing the books. In other instances, such adjustment is difficult if not impossible.

Wood shelving is similar to case-type, steel shelving in flexibility. In most cases a first unit consists of two end panels with appropriate shelves, base unit, and top. If additional sections are added, they are inserted between the original end panels. If a range is separated into two parts, two additional end panels are required to complete the modification.

Finishes used on wood bookstacks are the same as those used on other wood furniture. In general, the conversion varnishes (catalytic varnishes) are superior to the lacquer finishes. Tests of the conversion varnishes show that there are differences among different brands. Thus the only method by which quality can be assured is to subject representative samples to performance tests. Appendix I following the article, "The Materials and Construction of Library Furniture," lists tests by means of which the performance of both the finishes and the glues used in fabricating the shelving may be evaluated. These tests have been successfully used in many library furniture installations, but should be more widely known and used in specifications for wood furniture.

REFERENCES

1. Piez, Gladys T. "Bracket vs. Case-Type Shelving, the Pros and Cons," *ALA Bulletin,* 55:894–896, Nov. 1961.
2. *Ibid.,* p. 896.
3. Gallichotte, V. H. (W. R. Ames Co.) Letters dated Nov. 12 and Dec. 7, 1964.
4. *Ibid.,* Letter dated Nov. 12, 1964.
5. Cox, James. Letter dated Nov. 25, 1964.
6. Gallichotte, V. H. (W. R. Ames Co.) Letter dated Dec. 15, 1964.
7. Schaefer, Victor A. Letter dated Jan. 7, 1965.

APPENDIX I

Performance Tests for Bracket-Type Steel Bookstacks

Although in theory it should be considerably easier to develop complete performance specifications for steel bookstacks than for wood furniture, such specifications are not now available. Before they can be made available, engineering studies of bookstack requirements and complete evaluations of existing designs are required. In the absence of such specifications, the following tests may prove helpful.

These tests are designed to evaluate the actual strength of the uprights; the lateral stability of the bookstack as measured by the strength of the base support system; longitudinal stability as measured by the strength of the sway braces, welding, or other reinforcing designed to provide rigidity in the longitudinal direction; and the strength of the shelves. In a weak or unstable unit, the eccentric loading of so much weight could cause the unit to topple sideways. Care should be exercised, therefore, in conducting these tests. A properly designed and erected bookstack, on the other hand, can withstand all such loading and still be so stable that it can be lightly rocked from side to side without danger.

These tests may be included in bookstack specifications under the heading: On Site Testing. They can be conducted in many cases by the owner, or they can be performed for the owner by an independent engineering laboratory. In addition to ordinary mechanic's tools, a platform scale for weighing the materials used to load the shelves, a spring scale reading 100 pounds or more for measuring longitudinal stability, and sufficient weight, in the form of steel or iron scraps or small ingots of pig iron or lead, to load all shelves as indicated, are required. Most cities have foundries or iron works where such weights may be obtained for temporary use. It is recommended that each bidder be permitted to observe the testing of his product. All samples for testing purposes should, of course, be delivered before bids are opened, but the tests should be conducted after such opening.

Although the following tests have been used successfully by a few institutions, most recently by the University of Illinois at Chicago Circle, it is to be hoped that they will be replaced by more comprehensive specifications resulting from sound engineering studies.

Samples for testing and evaluation should consist of one range of two, double-faced sections with 20-inch bases, complete with fixed base shelves and 24, 10-inch adjustable shelves. Sway braces, if included in the specifications, should be required with the sample. End panels are desirable for purposes of general evaluation, but should not be installed while the tests are being conducted.

If possible, samples should be erected on a concrete floor rather than a resilient tile floor. In any case, all neoprene pads should be removed so that direct contact between the base of the stack and the floor is achieved.

On Site Testing

1. When the sample bookstack has been properly installed and leveled by the bidder, it shall be tested by loading first the shelves in one complete section from the top down. One hundred seventy-five pounds shall be added to the topmost shelf, adjusted to the highest position in the section, after which one hundred seventy-five pounds (uniformly distributed over the shelf) shall be added progressively to each lower shelf until the section is completely loaded with one hundred seventy-five pounds on each of six adjustable shelves and on the base shelf. The first measurements of deflection shall be made at this time. The same procedure shall then be followed on the section opposite that first tested, and the deflection measured again. Any deflection of the upright from a straight line[1] in excess of $\frac{3}{8}$ inch, shall be considered a failure and shall result in disqualification of the bidder. Further, any deflection of the upright from the vertical[2] in excess of $\frac{3}{8}$ inch shall also be considered a failure and shall likewise result in the disqualification of the bidder.

2. The sample bookstack shall be further tested by applying a 100 pound force, horizontal and parallel to the long axis of the range, against the uprights at a point 48 inches above the floor. This test may be conducted with or without adjustable shelves, but one hundred seventy-five pounds shall be added to each of the four base shelves before testing. Any temporary deflection from the vertical in excess of $\frac{3}{8}$ inch and any permanent deflection exceeding $\frac{1}{16}$ inch[3] shall be considered failure and shall result in disqualification of the bidder.

3. At least five adjustable shelves shall be tested, after placing them in position in the sample range and loading them with the equivalent of 50 pounds per square foot. Any temporary deflection of the shelf in excess of $\frac{3}{16}$ inch, and any permanent deflection of any of the five shelves,[4] shall be considered failure and cause for disqualification of the bidder.

NOTES

[1] Such deflection is best measured by stretching a chalk line along the loaded side of the upright from extreme top to extreme bottom edges and measuring the maximum deviation from a straight line. Ordinarily, such deviations will occur somewhere between 12 and 30 inches above the floor line.

[2] Prior to loading the stack, a plumb line should be suspended from the top of the column so that the bob, which must swing freely, is at rest not more than two inches above floor level and in the exact center of the column. (The center line should be marked on the column as a reference point.) Deflection of the column from the vertical is measured by the distance the bob swings from the mark on the center of the column.

[3] As in note 2 above, a plumb line should be suspended from the top of the column so that the bob swings freely and rests over an established mark on the floor. The necessary force may be exerted by a spring scale hooked to the upright at the proper height and pulled to the 100 pound mark by two men, or by a lever with one end fixed to the floor.

[4] A nominal 10-inch shelf (actual depth 9 inches), 35.5 inches long, contains 2.2 square feet. Thus a loading factor of 50 pounds per square foot requires a shelf load of 110 pounds for testing purposes. Shelves should be loaded with the narrow edges of all weights at right angles to the length of the shelf, to avoid the "bridging" effect. Measurement may be made with a stretched chalk line or, preferably, with a metal straight edge. If desired, the sample may also include five nominal 8-inch shelves (actual depth 7 inches) which contain 1.7 square feet and require a shelf load of 85 pounds to develop a load factor of 50 pounds per square foot.

APPENDIX II

Performance Tests for Finishes on Steel Bookstacks

In steel bookstacks, as in the case of wood furniture, it is easier to test the finish than to test other elements of performance. The following tests for finishes on steel bookstacks were developed for the Library Technology Project a few years ago. They have been used successfully in a few instances, but deserve wider dissemination. In slightly modified form, they are included here by permission of the LTP.

In practice, these tests should be included in the specifications as a means of determining the qualifications of the several bidders. The tests should be conducted by an independent laboratory qualified to conduct tests on paints and related products.

As in the case of samples for testing the finish on wood, the samples required here should be submitted not later than the opening of bids and the award, other elements of the bids being equal, should be made on the basis of the satisfactory performance of the samples under testing.

Performance Tests for Finishes on Steel Bookstacks

1. Manufacturer's Obligations—Failure of the finish on the test samples in any portion of the following tests shall be cause for disqualification of the bid. Further, the owner reserves the right to conduct such tests, on a random basis, on stack components delivered to the job. Failure of such components to meet these specifications may result in an order to stop fabrication until the condition is corrected. The cost of such random testing will be borne by the owner, except in the event of failure of the finish to meet the specifications, in which case the charges will be assessed to the manufacturer.

2. Samples Required—Prior to the opening of bids on this contract, bidders shall furnish to the owner twelve, 4-inch by 6-inch and two, 4-inch by 4-inch panels of 20-gauge cold rolled steel for testing purposes. These panels shall have been prepared by running them through a production line similar in all respects to the procedures to be used in finishing the bookstacks to be supplied on the contract, including cleaning and rustproofing, followed by a finish coat as close as practicable to the color to be furnished on this contract. The test panels shall be fully representative of the quality of paint finish for the entire installation.

3. Testing Agency—All tests will be made by a testing engineer, laboratory, or agency selected by the owner, and in accordance with applicable standard methods of the American Society for Testing Materials (ASTM), or by the procedures described herein.

4. Tests—The following tests shall be conducted on the test panels.

(a) *Film thickness.* Thickness of enamel shall be measured by a General Electric film thickness gauge or equivalent (See ASTM Method D1005-21 and ASTM 1400-58). Measurements of less than 1.5 mil. thickness shall be considered a failure and cause for disqualification of the bidder.

(b) *Gloss.* Gloss shall be not less than 50 nor more than 70 as determined on a 60 degree gloss meter (See ASTM Method D523-53T).

(c) *Bend test (adhesion).* Two specimens prepared as outlined above shall be bent 180 degrees over a $\frac{1}{4}$ inch diameter mandrel, one parallel to and one transverse to the grain of the steel, as follows: place the coated side uppermost on a mandrel at a point equidistant from the edges of the panel and bend the panel double in approximately one second. Cracks occurring at either end and extending no more than $\frac{1}{4}$ inch shall be disregarded.

(d) *Print Resistance.* Panels prepared as previously described shall be subjected to the following tests:

Cold print–A piece of 2 inch × 2 inch cheesecloth shall be placed on the finished panel. A five pound metal weight shall be placed on the cloth. The contact surface of the weight shall be a smooth surface and one square inch in area. The weight shall remain unmoved in the position for 24 hours at 75 degrees F.

Hot print–The same procedure shall be used for the hot print test as used for the cold print, except that the weight shall be two pounds instead of five pounds, and the temperature during the pressure shall be 110 degrees F. instead of 75 degrees F. Immediately after removal of the weights the exposed area shall be rubbed with a soft cloth and examined. Any printing discernible after rubbing shall be considered a failure.

(e) *Impact test (adhesion and flaking).* Two specimens shall be prepared as described above. One specimen shall be placed over a $1\frac{1}{4}$ inch diameter opening. A ball of 530 gram weight shall be dropped 10.5 inches on the section of the panel over the opening. The test shall be repeated on the other specimen on the reverse side. Cracks, hairline cracks, or chipping of the impact area shall be considered a failure of the test and cause for disqualification.

(f) *Abrasion resistance (Taber).* Two, 4-inch by 4-inch panels shall be prepared as described above. The film thickness, which shall be measured at four places equidistant from the center of each panel, shall not vary more than 0.2 mils. After weighing each panel, place one panel on the platform of the Taber Abrader using a CS10 wheel and two, 1,000-gram weights. Subject the panel to 1,000 cycles, cleaning the panel by brushing every 100 cycles. Repeat with the second panel. Loss in excess of .650 grams per 1,000 cycles (average of two results) shall be considered a failure and cause for rejection and disqualification.

(g) *Salt spray.* This test shall be run in accordance with ASTM Method B287-57T, using panels prepared as previously specified. After fifty hours of salt spray, specimens showing any evidence of discoloration or scratched areas showing lifting or rusting more than $\frac{1}{8}$ inch outside of the scribe lines shall be considered failure and cause for disqualification.

(h) *Acid and chemical resistance to cleaning chemicals, etc.* Five wells $\frac{1}{2}$ inch in diameter and $\frac{1}{2}$ inch deep shall be formed on the face of test specimens with modeling clay. Into each of four individual wells, one of the following shall be poured: alcohol (95 per cent), mineral or vegetable oil, acetic acid (10 per cent), and undiluted household ammonia. At the end of fifteen minutes, a 10 per cent lye solution shall be poured into the fifth well. At the end of thirty minutes from the time the first four solutions were poured into the wells, the five wells shall be removed and the test panel rinsed thoroughly and wiped dry. Evidence of discoloration, softening, or blemish of the finished surface shall be considered failure and cause for disqualification.

(i) *Cigarette burns.* A well-lighted cigarette shall be laid on the finished panel and allowed to remain in one position for $1\frac{1}{2}$ minutes. After removing the cigarette, the test panel shall be rinsed with water only and wiped dry. Any evidence of stain or blemish on the finish shall be considered failure and cause for disqualification.

ABOUT THE AUTHOR–Frazer G. Poole received the B.A. degree from Catawba College in 1937, and the B.L.S. degree from the University of California at Berkeley in 1949. He has held various professional library positions at the University of California in Berkeley and in Santa Barbara, was Director of the Library Technology Project for ALA, and Director of Libraries at the University of Illinois, Chicago Circle. Presently Mr. Poole is Assistant Director for Preservation in the Administrative Department of the Library of Congress, a consultant on library buildings and contributor to professional journals.

What to Look for When Buying Shelving

by Martin Van Buren

Before finally deciding which bookstack to purchase it is well to study the finished product. In bookstacks, the finished product is a completed installation. A visit to several installations to evaluate them is advised. Here Mr. Van Buren gives us guidelines for the evaluation process.

On January 25, 1964, seven major manufacturers of steel shelving were indicted in the Federal Courts for price-fixing and collusion. The remarkable thing about the indictment is the fact that the perpetrators were caught at all, for very few librarians, architects, or members of building committees are familiar with the details of price structures in the furniture market. Even the terminology can be misleading. How can they be expected to know if a competitive bid is fair?

The intricacies of pricing, profits, commissions, and rebates are carefully guarded secrets of the trade. Yet there exists no law that forbids an outsider from learning them. The objectives are obvious: in one corner is the manufacturer who hopes to sell his product for a profit ranging from "fair" to "all the market can bear." In the other corner is the library which hopes to buy a quality product as cheaply as possible. In the center is the equalizing factor—competition. But when is competition truly effective? The library committee is often the last to know.

The practice of taking competitive bids can be an efficient method of creating a fair trade between buyer and seller. But the process of bidding can also become a farce. For example, it is not considered unethical for a bidder to seek "courtesy bids" from competitors who are not interested in a particular contract because they are currently under a full production load. This means that a sincere bidder approaches a disinterested firm asking it to enter a bid in order to assure the usual three-bid requirement. The disinterested bidder deliberately quotes an excessive figure. Collusion? The practice is not considered so.

The terms cost, net, wholesale, retail, and list, can be confusing to the layman. Cost means exactly what the word implies—the cost to a manufacturer to produce his goods, or the cost to a dealer when he buys goods from a manufacturer and applies shipping costs and basic overhead for handling. Net and wholesale are so closely similar that they can be regarded as synonymous; it is the base price that a manufacturer offers to a distributor or dealer after his profit has been applied. Retail and list are also synonymous, meaning the price asked by a retail store when it is selling to the general public.

Furniture is sold by any of three methods:

1. Through distributors who stock and distribute from their own warehouses. In this case the distributor commissions his own salesmen. The distributor operates within a franchised area and solicits only within his defined territory. He may sell through dealers or directly to the consumer, the latter involving competitive bidding to institutions or public buildings such as libraries. If a distributor offers a direct bid he may offer a "courtesy" commission to his dealer in the immediate sales vicinity.

2. Through retail dealer outlets. These are usually established retail stores that maintain their own showrooms, handling certain lines on a selective basis. In selecting retail outlets a manufacturer looks for the type of store that caters to his grade of product; i.e., a furniture maker who specializes in low-price produce will seek that type of outlet, whereas a manufacturer of very high grade furniture will search out more exclusive stores.

3. Directly from manufacturer to consumer. This method is more common among manu-

SOURCE: Reprinted from Martin Van Buren, "What to Look for When Buying Shelving," *Library Journal*, April 1, 1965, pp. 1614–1617.

facturers who make only specialized contract furniture—such as steel library shelving. No middle man is involved other than the regional representative, who receives a commission against sales in his area.

These three methods of selling cause differing attitudes in pricing processes. Where distributors and retail dealers are involved, the manufacturer normally issues printed price lists indicating "suggested" retail prices from which certain discounts are allowed. Sometimes a manufacturer will insist that his retail prices be maintained exactly as prescribed, regardless of the area, distributor, or dealer. This is known as "fair trading."

When a manufacturer is constantly faced with the bidding processes common to institutional and public buildings (again, such as library shelving) he will often refrain from publishing any price lists; each bid is judged and prepared on the basis of existing business conditions and a calculated estimate of competitors' current production demands, plus the manufacturer's own present need for new business. The policy is merely a day-by-day adaptation of the law of supply and demand.

The practice of refusing to offer printed price lists contains all the dangers and temptations of collusion. What librarian knows the current status of material and labor costs, plus local business conditions, when he takes bids for shelving? How can he know whether competition is fierce because business is slow, or whether the entire manufacturing market is operating to capacity?

For example, in the indictment of 1964 it was not determined exactly *how long* the proven collusion among the seven manufacturers had been going on. On the other hand it would also be extremely difficult to prove whether the practice had been resumed, or whether it might be resumed at some future date. The question is not to imply further collusion on the part of any manufacturer, but it raises an academic question: is a resumption of the practice a possibility?

There are some protective devices that will help librarians and others concerned to determine if a steel stack manufacturer is competent, and if his bid is a reasonable one.

The first is a knowledge of pricing and distributing methods, as described above.

The second is the writing of fair but exacting shelving specifications. But who is to do this? Will the burden fall on the librarian, who perhaps does not understand either the terminology of legal requirements or the technical jargon of construction standards? Or will it fall to the architect, who

understands specification writing but perhaps does not know the functional requirements of library equipment? Or to a competent library shelving manufacturer who understands both, but who will naturally slant his specifications toward his own product specialties? Or to an interior decorator, who understands neither?

We are faced, then, with two questions:

1. Are the low bidders under consideration competent manufacturers?
2. Are the low bids in line with truly competitive situations?

To answer the first question, the following procedures are suggested:

The manufacturer being considered is asked to submit his own literature and specifications. This data is studied carefully and compared with the specifications written into the bid documents. Any discrepancies are weighed further to determine if they will affect the quality of the equipment.

If there is the slightest doubt or question—and to further protect the library's interests—the bidder is asked to submit a letter stating in detail if his equipment varies in any way whatsoever from the written specifications; if so, he is asked to explain in detail the deviations. Many shelving specifications require such a letter, to be included in the initial bid submittal.

The bidder should be asked to submit a list of installations: some requests ask for installations over five years old, some ask for installations within the past five years. I prefer to ask for both, since production quality can either deteriorate or improve.

The list of installations should be thoroughly checked, first by letter of inquiry to the library where it was installed, then, if necessary, by visiting and inspecting some of the listed installations.

The exchange of information among librarians is a vital and revealing means of protection within the library field. If records of bid tabulations and procurement procedures were kept and freely exchanged, the library field would benefit greatly by such knowledge.

Inspection of existing installations can be helpful only if the librarian or others know what to look for. Perhaps the best way to offer pointers is to describe my own procedure:

The librarian, the architect, or a member of the Board is asked to accompany the inspection party. An appointment is made with the librarian of the installation in question. During the visit, other members of the visiting group are asked to engage the local staff in conversation; this is a diversionary measure done for two reasons: first, to allow the inspection to proceed as fast as possible; second, if critical notes are taken in an objective manner, there is no point in hurting a prideful librarian's feelings, should she happen to look over your shoulder.

The inspection proceeds as follows:

1. Check alignment of ranges. Sight along the end panels to see if they are in a perfect row, and that each end panel is in vertical alignment with the others. Then sight down each range to determine if each section is in line or whether some sections "stagger." This is a matter of installation, but since most manufacturers make their own installations, careful alignment, both horizontally and vertically, is a sign of efficiency.

2. Check for rough edges. Even turned back edges should be felt for burrs or ragged spots that might snag books or fingers. The underside of shelves, both flat and sloping, as well as the back edges of end panels, should be checked.

3. Check welded joints. Do they meet; are they true; do they have ragged joints?

4. Check the "true" condition of flat sheet-metal members such as shelf surfaces. Are they warped? Is there any sign of twist?

5. Check end panels for warp or twist or wrinkle. By reflected light, a waver in an end panel surface can be easily detected. In the case of the three-member end panel such as some manufacturers install (in double-faced shelving), each of the three vertical members should align true, without waver or wrinkle, and joints between the three units should be perfectly tight and true.

6. Check to see if adjacent shelf brackets join neatly without a break between. Most shelf brackets have a curved turn outward from the shelf, intended to meet the outward turn of the adjacent shelf bracket. If the design of the slots in the uprights and the outward curve of the shelf brackets is such that they do not meet, the resulting gap can cause "knifing" of books as well as a sloppy appearance.

7. Check to see that right-angle bends in sheet steel members are truly at right angles. For example, canopy tops require a right angle bend, then an additional return. At corners a proper right angle bend will fit snugly with its counter member. "Breaking" sheet material at true right angles is a simple manufacturing procedure. If right angles are not true, this indicates negligence in production control.

8. Check the quality of paint finishes, and do not overlook inside and underside surfaces. Also inspect for sags and areas where the coating is too thin to withstand hard usage. In one (new) installation it was noted that some areas exposed surface coatings that were in places, so thin that the bare metal could be seen.

9. Check for stability of ranges, especially full height ranges. Can they be swayed, even when loaded with books?

The above pointers do not comprise all the finer elements to look for when inspecting a stack installation, but they cover the more important ones.

In determining whether bid figures are fair and in line with current market values, probably the best recourse open to the librarian is comparison with other bid figures of recently completed jobs. The various library periodicals carry news of recently completed libraries. Contact can be established with these sources.

However, to make a fair analysis for comparative purposes, certain factors must be known, such as:

- The size of the installation. A small installation will receive considerably higher bids per section than a very large one.

- The location of the installation. Shipping and labor costs vary extensively, from manufacturing location to site, and with regard to costs of local labor hired to assist in installation.

- The time of bidding. For example, if shelving is bid under the general contract covering the erection of the building, at least a year will take place before delivery is wanted. Any shelving manufacturer bidding against such a lengthy installation date will naturally add a contingency allowance to his bid in case of increases in material costs during the interim period. If shelving is bid at a later date, with perhaps a six-month delivery period, the manufacturer can more accurately determine his bid.

- Any known fluctuations in material prices, such as steel; national labor strikes or disputes; etc. A librarian may not be able to determine the extent to which such events will affect cost, but events of this kind on a national scale can sound a warning on price changes.

Possibly the ideal exchange of information and accurate analysis of bids for protective purposes would be a computer system, perhaps maintained by the American Library Association or the Library Technology Project, that would maintain a running tabulation of bids from all libraries; but that is a far-fetched thought in terms of the economics involved.

In the past the method was to rely on the past reputation of the manufacturer, but this method also is clearly not infallible, for even the most reputable names are not always above reproach. Possibly there will always be dubious practices in merchandising furniture as with other products. But the best defense against such practices is knowledge.

ABOUT THE AUTHOR–Martin L. Van Buren attended Ohio State University and Georgia Institute of Technology. He worked as an industrial designer before becoming proprietor of Martin Van Buren, Inc., Planning Consultants, Charlotte, N.C. Mr. Van Buren has been a UNESCO and Ford Foundation grantee and contributor to professional journals.

Economics of Compact Book Shelving

by Robert H. Muller

The planning team must attempt an efficient use of the space being planned. Compact shelving is often considered as a space saver. Mr. Muller looks at the economics of compact shelving and raises some doubts concerning their true economy.

Librarians are concerned primarily with the content of publications, their selection from the world's publishing output, their bibliographic organization, their efficient retrieval, their interpretation, and the stimulation of reading. Despite the primacy of these intellectual functions, library operation requires attention to many mundane tasks, one of which is the housing or shelving of the materials acquired. In libraries where space is ample and many empty shelves are still waiting to be filled, librarians tend to pay little attention to shelving methods; but when library shelves become overcrowded, as most of them eventually do, the librarian is temporarily diverted from educational and intellectual concerns and forced to focus attention on the economics of book storage. Interest in book storage systems should not be taken as a sign of predilection for gadgetry or mechanics but as a task imposed upon librarians by the requirement that they make the best possible use of the resources placed at their disposal.

Much has been written about the predicament of libraries that have run out of space for books. Various alternatives have been carefully compared by many authorities. To cite just a few of the more recent discussions, in 1954, Metcalf considered six possibilities, including innovations in shelving;[1] in 1960, Orne reviewed all aspects of book storage warehouses,[2] and Ellsworth briefly summarized much of what is known about book storage capacities, storage alternatives, and the economics of the situation.[3] In 1961, Hopp succinctly recapitulated some of the most crucial policy questions relating to the handling of infrequently used books.[4]

Also, in 1961, the preliminary edition of a study conducted at the University of Chicago, entitled *Patterns in the Use of Books in Large Research Libraries,* by Fussler and Simon,[5] assumed that research collections can be divided into a more frequently and a less frequently used portion, and the substantial savings could be achieved by housing the less frequently used portion in a more compact manner than with conventional stack shelving. As the authors put it, "the costs of housing a large stack book collection will be substantially less if some reasonable fraction of the total collection is placed in compact storage."[6] Weber, who reviewed the study, agreed that "the economic factors involved in housing a research collection may make it desirable to segregate books into two or more levels of accessibility."[7] Reviewer Logsdon, in enumerating the principal findings and conclusions of the study, included among them the following: "Compact storage of books can save significant operating and capital sums, possibly ranging from 60 to 77 per cent of the costs of conventional housing."[8] Logsdon also stated that "the carefully marshalled evidence in this study . . . offer(s) much, not only in support of lower cost of housing by compact storage of little-used material, but also in support of going further toward cooperative storage and the reduction of the number of copies of little-used books held by research libraries as a group."[8] A third reviewer, Mackenzie, wrote similarly that "the conventional book-storage methods are no longer adequate to meet with reasonable financial economy the demands which are being made upon them in ever-greater measure."[9]

Fussler and Simon wrote hopefully of possible savings through compact storage, but did not in-

SOURCE: Reprinted from Robert H. Muller, "Economics of Compact Book Shelving," *Library Trends,* vol. 13, no. 4, April, 1965, pp. 433–447, by permission of the publisher.

dicate the kind of equipment, if any, they would recommend; their sophisticated-looking, but exasperatingly inconclusive chapter on "The Economics of Book Storage" failed to come to grips with the problem in any concrete sort of way, except to say that ". . . some combination of book sizing, shelving books on edge, narrower range aisles, fewer main aisles, shelving somewhat higher than the usual 7′6″, and the elimination of empty shelving, will yield a capacity of at least 30 volumes per square foot."[10] These compactions are the familiar methods advocated in 1949 by the late Fremont Rider in preference to special compact equipment.[11] They have been used at Yale University, where a capacity of sixty-four volumes per square foot (as compared to twenty-one for shelving without gaps) was actually achieved.[12] Yale's book retirement study, as reported by Ash, also referred primarily to Rider's methods rather than to the use of compact storage hardware, although cost computations were included for Art Metal and Ames shelving, and unsuccessful experiments with mobile stacks were referred to in passing.[13]

Both the Chicago and the Yale studies reflected a nagging suspicion among librarians and the Council on Library Resources, Inc., which financed the studies, that conventional book shelving for infrequently used books may be wasteful. When expectancy of book use is low, it does not seem justified to array books in a manner that utilizes only about 10 per cent of the cubage (which as Rider pointed out was true of most conventional shelving arrangements).[14] Such lavishness is presumed to be extravagant and, therefore, indefensible. Since compaction à la Rider involves no significant added equipment, it is tantamount to cost reduction; but such is not necessarily the case to a sufficient extent if equipment especially designed for compact storage has to be purchased and installed. Rider's methods involve some serious drawbacks; books are no longer displayed continuously by subject classification in the storage area (although the "ribbon" arrangement[15] suggested by Rider may offset this disadvantage somewhat); books shelved on the long edges may cause damage to bindings; marking the call numbers on the narrow edge may also be objectionable or involve expense in the boxing of books; working in 22-inch aisles may prove exceedingly uncomfortable and annoying; and very high shelves and very long book ranges may prove operationally inefficient.

At institutions where Rider's methods have not been considered acceptable (and relatively few have resorted to it), other methods of improved cubage utilization have been explored; these methods all involve equipment especially engineered for compact book storage and, therefore, entail substantial added costs.

There are basically three types of compact book storage equipment currently available in the United States.

1. One type involves swinging or revolving *hinged book cases* (single or double rows), usually placed in front of, or attached to, regular stationary book cases. An example is the COM-PAC-CASE unit made by Art Metal, Inc., of Jamestown, New York, which consists of two halves of a book case that swing open like a French door. It comes in two versions: (a) one swinging book case or, (b) two swinging book cases in front of each stationary case. (The Snead compact stacks, installed in the 3,150,000-volume Midwest Interlibrary Center (MILC) in 1951, but no longer marketed, represent a variant of this type, in which the entire 3-foot book case swings out into the aisle.) A COM-PAC-CASE installation can be seen in the Illinois State Archives, Springfield. An intriguing-looking variant of the swinging type consists of convex cases on casters that are connected with struts to a center point and can be manually pulled out of their fixed storage frame. These cases are manufactured by Pivoted Wings, Blackburn, England; the applicability of the latter equipment to libraries has been advertised but not tested.

2. A second type consists of a stationary frame with *sliding drawers* available in varying dimensions. Current manufacturers of single-headed drawer equipment include the Hamilton Manufacturing Company, Two Rivers, Wisconsin (COMPO) and C. S. Brown & Company, Wauwatosa, Wisconsin, the latter offering what is claimed to be an improved version of the COMPO, but similar in basic design. This equipment has been installed in many libraries, e.g., in the St. Louis Public Library's Compton Regional Annex and the Oklahoma City Public Library. The manufacturing of a double-headed type of sliding drawer, known as STOR-MOR, which was installed in the 400,000-volume storage building of the University of Michigan in 1954, has been entirely discontinued, except for occasional reorders to expand existing installations.[16]

3. The third type consists of *blocks of ranges of movable cases,* with only one inter-range aisle

per block; the cases rest on tracks sunk in the floor and are activated either manually or pulled by a small motor connected to a continuous link chain drive or a cable, which is located at the center of the range. This type is marketed under the trade name COMPACTUS; it was invented and patented by the engineer Hans Ingold, of Zürich, Switzerland, in 1947. It has been installed in many libraries in Europe, Great Britain, Australia, etc. and has recently become available in the United States through Jackson Compactus, Los Angeles, California, which acquired the sole rights to manufacture and sell this system in the United States, Canada, and Mexico. COMPACTUS equipment has so far not been installed in any research library in the United States although early commercial installations can be found in Toronto, Canada (in the Orenda Engine Co., Canada Life Insurance Co., Trader Finance Co., and Canada General Insurance Co.), and in Halifax, Nova Scotia (in the T.B. Wing of the Victoria General Hospital). There is a semi-automatic textbook storage installation in the Anaheim Union High School, California, and a semi-automatic storage area for biological specimens at Arizona State University at Tempe; and installations are under consideration for the West San Gabriel Valley (California) Regional Library and for rare books and manuscripts at Yale University. The company does not consider itself to be in the shelving manufacturing business as such but primarily supplies the patented basic tracks, undercarriage, motor, etc., which can be joined to any case-type shelf unit to form a compact stack installation. It should be noted that whereas ordinary shelving requires a live floor load capacity of 100 to 150 lbs./sq. ft. (depending on shelf depth, width of aisles, height, and safety factor) and the Art Metal, Hamilton, and Brown compact designs require a minimum of 160 lbs./sq. ft., a *Compactus* installation has been said to require up to 287 lbs./sq. ft. (Stromeyer specifies a maximum of 1,400 Kg./sq. meter, which equals about 287 lbs./sq. ft.[17] Jackson Compactus, however, claims a requirement of only 180 to 240 lbs.[18]

The COMPACTUS type of installation comes in three versions: manually operated, semi-automatic, and automatic. A semi-automatic installation contains one stationary range, usually between two blocks of several ranges each; the stationary range may or may not contain the motor and the switch panel. In an installation designated as completely automatic, all book ranges are movable. Most installations are semi-automatic. Safety devices to prevent attendants from becoming sandwiched and injured between ranges have been judged as perfectly adequate.[19] Electric power consumption is considered negligible in the total operating picture, considering that the motor needs to be only a small one and an optional device for having the motor automatically switched off after designated intervals is part of the installation. H. Strahm, the director of the Municipal and University Library of Bern, Switzerland, called inventor Ingold the Galileo in the library field for having solved the motorization of book stacks in a most elegant manner; he expressed surprise that such stacks had not been invented by a librarian, who as a result undoubtedly would have won professional fame. The library basement at Bern has a semi-automatic COMPACTUS installation that increased storage capacity from 53,700 volumes to 130,440 volumes (octavos only).[20]

A system similar to COMPACTUS, installed in the National Diet Library of Japan, is marketed under the trade name ELECOMPACK (Tokyo, Japan). Whether or not this equipment can be economically imported into the United States and installed here is not known. The Company president Hanichiro Naito has stated: "My staff and I should be very happy if our ELECOMPACK filing system were widely adopted in your country."[21] Negotiations are underway. The equipment is so designed that, at the press of a button, an aisle can be created between any two book ranges within a block of nine ranges placed on each side of a single stationary book range that contains the control panel. The ranges portrayed in the company's catalog consist of five 3-ft.-wide double-faced book cases movable on rails by means of two feeders.[22]

Another system of movable rolling stacks, not yet developed in the United States to the point of marketability, are laterally moving single book cases activated manually or by an electric motor. The cases are placed in the aisles of a regular stationary installation; they are suspended from a rail (like a monorail car) and move in a track on the floor. A mock-up was displayed at the 1964 American Library Association Conference, St. Louis, by the Aetna Steel Product Corporation, New York, which reports that it is still compiling engineering data.

There may well be other manufacturers than those mentioned which are offering compact storage equipment. No attempt has been made at complete coverage since the chief concern in this review is the identification of types. There are also additional book storage conceptions which have not yet been developed into marketable products in the United States and are, therefore, of only theoretical interest.

Any type of equipment not offered commercially in the United States, such as, a scheme of motor-driven bookcases that can be propelled laterally into a main access aisle, is not worth serious consideration by librarians until a manufacturer is ready to risk marketing it. It is partly for this reason (in addition to patent restrictions) that COMPACTUS was not installed in any United States institution until a franchised manufacturer was available, even though it had been successfully used in Switzerland, England, Sweden, Germany, etc. as long as ten years ago.

Several evaluative reviews of compact storage equipment have been published in the past decade. The most comprehensive and penetrating of such studies was made by the Czechoslovakian librarian Drahoslav Gawrecki in 1960.[23] He surveyed all possible compact storage ideas for the purpose of developing recommendations as to the most serviceable types of equipment for compact book storage which the state-controlled steel fabricators of socialist Czechoslovakia might provide. He developed ingenious layouts to achieve maximum compaction with a combination of different types of equipment on the assumption that such equipment might be manufactured when needed. He concluded that the COMPACTUS type is best, that laterally moving cases and the drawer-type are also useful, and that the swinging type is least applicable. He particularly stressed the advantage of combination arrangements involving more than one type in a given area, and questioned the value of capacity calculations made for a single type of equipment in isolation. A great deal of interest in compact storage is in evidence in other countries in the Soviet orbit. This interest may stem from the overcrowdedness of the book stacks of research libraries in these countries during a period when the chances for constructing additions or new buildings are rather slim; hence, there may be a strong desire to utilize existing space to the best advantage. Capacity increase rather than cost savings has been the predominant if not the only interest in this connection. For Poland, Przybylo has offered a competent review of the literature, including developments in other Slavic countries.[24] For the USSR, Pashchenko evaluated different types of equipment; his conclusion favored revolving book cases in preference to the drawer-type.[25] Pashchenko claimed to have been the first to plan a compact storage installation in the USSR (Academy of Sciences, Moscow, which involved blocks of movable cases in groups of twenty-four). He regarded movable pull-out bookcases as particularly promising.

In the Federal Republic of Germany, Stromeyer's authoritative and thorough treatise on book stack problems in 1958 contained a chapter on space saving through new types of shelving systems.[26] This chapter offered a detailed and critical account of COMPACTUS, which the author compared, point by point, with the Snead (MILC) system; COMPACTUS was judged to be preferable despite some reservations. Stromeyer considered other systems (notably sliding drawers) less suitable and only rarely applicable, but failed to give reasons for such negative evaluation. He paid some attention to the economics of book shelving, concluding that local circumstances will determine whether COMPACTUS involved a higher or lower over-all cost (including building construction) and implying perhaps that cost considerations were not of paramount importance.

In England, ten years ago Hill presented a descriptive review of all types of compact equipment, including rolling book cases, COMPACTUS, the Snead system, the Art Metal system, Hamilton drawers, and Ames drawers.[27] His conclusions as to the economics of book storage were exceedingly cautious and hedged with qualifications. He expressed doubt as to the applicability of compact storage in public access situations.

In the United States, Kaplan in 1960 traced compact storage developments and expressed criticism of unsubstantiated claims made in the literature; he reported that evidence of savings in cost effected by compact shelving was almost non-existent.[28] In 1962 Metcalf presented a lucid review of compact shelving methods as well as equipment. He recommended that ". . . movable shelving be regarded as a last resort, and that the library first consider whether portions of its collections might be placed in a stack with narrower shelves and aisles, shelved by size, or perhaps transferred to a cooperative storage building. . . ."[29]

Despite an abundance of information on, and

attention to, compact storage equipment as well as a considerable amount of competitive advocacy, no conclusively valid and reliable data are presently available on the basis of which one can determine which type of storage equipment, if any, is most suitable for a given situation. What are lacking are rigorously controlled comparative cost-accounting evaluations of existing installations, with full data on original capital outlay, including building construction and cost of operation and maintenance. The need for this sort of information, grounded in actual operating situations rather than imagined constructs and theoretical computations, is evident; in Kaplan's words:

Savings developed by systems of compact shelving must be regarded with suspicion when presented theoretically. In any actual installation the shape of the room and other factors will seriously affect savings. The library profession would benefit from a demonstration of how these factors influence the capacity of each type of compact shelving.[30]

It is possible to compute theoretically achievable savings for the *combined cost* of compact shelving equipment and a given building construction cost in a specific situation, as was done by Muller,[31] who showed that storage equipment becomes more applicable as building cost goes up. Studies at Yale University,[32] following a similar methodology for a specific assumed construction cost of $20 per square foot, concluded that per-volume cost for 22-inch aisles spacing would be about one-fourth of that for conventional spacing, and that compact equipment would not substantially reduce the cost per volume as compared to conventional shelves with 36-inch aisles. The Yale method was later applied by Elecompack, Ltd., Tokyo, in one of its advertising brochures, in which an illustrative

TABLE 1

NUMBER OF VOLUMES THAT CAN BE SHELVED IN A $500,000[1] BUILDING WITH DIFFERENT TYPES OF SHELVING EQUIPMENT

(1) Type of Equipment	(2) Shelving Cost Per Sq. Ft. of Area Occupied by Shelving[2]	(3) Shelving Plus Building Cost of $25 Per Sq. Ft.[3]	(4) No. of Sq. Ft. of Floor Area Obtainable for $500,000[4]	(5) Maximum Volume Capacity Per Sq. Ft. of Floor Areas (Compactness)[5]	(6) Total Volumes in Bldg. Costing $500,000[6]
COMPO (Brown)	$13.98	$38.98	12,827	40	513,080
COMPO (Hamilton)	19.33	44.33	11,278	44[7]	496,276
COM-PAC-CASE (Art Metal)	19.04	44.04	11,353	41	465,473
COMPACTUS semi-automatic	46.44	71.44	6,999	52[8]	363,948
Conventional (Art Metal)	3.02	28.02	17,844	19	339,036
Conventional (Brown)	3.86	28.86	17,325	20	346,500

1. Gross area cost, including stairways, main corridors, toilets, elevators, heating and ventilating equipment, et cetera.
2. Quoted price for a layout of equipment divided by the number of square feet occupied.
3. The building cost unit price is assumed to be constant, i.e., equal for different types of equipment. Actually, a somewhat higher cost may be associated with compact equipment since greater floor load capacity must be provided for. A cost of $25 per sq. ft. without equipment is based on experience at the University of Michigan where recent air-conditioned buildings cost $23 to $26 per square foot, exclusive of the cost of land.
4. Obtained by dividing $500,000 by the building cost per square foot as shown in column 3.
5. Number of lineal feet of shelving in an installation layout divided by number of square feet multiplied by eight, since shelving is assumed to accommodate eight volumes per lineal foot. (Figures are rounded off to the nearest digit.)
6. Column 4 multiplied by column 5.
7. This capacity figure is higher than the figures computed for the Brown equipment since the theoretical layout and drawings do not show structural columns, which would reduce capacity to some extent. The drawers are 36 inches deep, 18 inches wide, each drawer having a shelving capacity of 72 lineal inches.

block diagram implied that the combined cost of conventional stacks plus building construction cost would be about 44 per cent higher than the combined cost of ELECOMPACK plus building construction, at least for Japan: "The difference of overall cost between ELECOMPACK and conventional shelves widens as the value of the combined total of construction cost of conventional book shelves per unit floor space increases, which means that the overall cost can be reduced greatly."[33]

Lester Mattison showed that, for 23 by 23 ft. bays in a modular building, "savings effected by substituting COMPO-type compact shelving for standard bracket shelving in a $20 per sq. ft. building amount to only 4% ... Compact shelving in a low cost storehouse building is 59% costlier than wood utility shelving and 35.4% costlier than bracket shelving." He concluded that "cheap shelving in an expensive building and expensive shelving in a cheap building appear to be equally incongruous."[34]

For shelving equipment currently on the United States market, Tables 1 and 2 present comparative data on the crucial question of the economics of compact storage. The question is posed in terms of the number of volumes that can be shelved in the storage portion of a storage building for a fixed amount of money, viz., $500,000. (A constant construction cost of $25 per square foot, exclusive of equipment, is assumed although the required greater floor load capacity for compact equipment will probably involve a higher cost of about $1 per square foot to provide increased concrete slab thickness, wider column-footings, and stronger bottom structure.) Caution is in order since the figures are based on informal quotations supplied by manufacturers, and no attempt was made to determine the reliability of such quotations.

This hypothetical tabulation shows that a building with conventional shelving will house maximally about 348,000 volumes (assuming eight volumes per lineal foot). Semi-automatic

TABLE 2

BASIC REFERENCE DATA FOR COMPUTING SHELVING COSTS USED IN TABLE 1

(1) Source of Quotation	(2) Type of Equipment	(3) No. of Lineal Ft. of Shelving for the Project Quoted	(4) No. of Sq. Ft. of Floor Area Occupied by Shelving	(5) Total Cost Quoted	(6) Shelving Cost Per Sq. Ft. of Area Occupied by Shelving
Brown & Co.[9] 7/17/64	COMPO	10,444	2,075	$ 29,000	$13.98
Hamilton Mfg. Co. Estimate 11/3/64	COMPO	111,720	20,000	386,635	19.33
Art Metal, Inc. Estimate 5/25/64	COM-PAC-CASE	32,182	6,255	119,100	19.04
Jackson Compactus 12/18/63	COMPACTUS semi-automatic	30,576	646	30,000	46.44
Art Metal, Inc. 3/25/64	Conventional ranges 39' long	14,942	6,255	18,800	3.02
Brown & Co. 7/17/64	Conventional	5,187	2,075	8,000	3.86

8. This figure was initially computed as being 36 volumes per square foot, based on an installation involving 24 "cars," each 9.1 foot long, equipped with 12.5-inch wide shelves, each car containing seven shelves, i.e., 9.1 times 7 times 2 times 24 equals 30.576 lineal feet. Assuming eight volumes per lineal foot, the capacity of the installation is 244,608 volumes. Dividing this figure by the number of square feet (646) results in a figure of 36 volumes per square foot. The capacity, however, would be much higher with narrower shelves (eight inches) and a narrower main aisle that provides access to two stack blocks instead of only one as in this installation. Reducing shelf width from 12.5 to 8 inches allows for an increase of over 50 per cent in the number of cars. Hence to assume a capacity figure of 52 volumes per square foot for eight-inch shelves does not seem unreasonable (as against twenty-six volumes per square foot with 12.5 inch shelves). At Bern University, volume capacity was computed to be 559 square meters, or 52 volumes per square foot. (See Stromeyer, op. cit., Tabelle).

9. Brown reported in a letter dated 10/14/64 that on two recent small jobs where both Brown and Hamilton submitted bids, the bids compared as follows: (1) Brown $6,043, Hamilton $8,310, and (2) Brown $8,275, Hamilton $9,914. The situation may be different in the case of larger jobs. The Brown cost figures relate to drawer units that are 48 inches deep.

COMPACTUS, although unquestionably providing the densest type of compact shelving, surprisingly yields space only for about 16,000 volumes more (4.6 per cent). It does increase capacity per square foot by about 150 per cent but provides a negligible cost advantage in original construction and equipment outlay at the prices currently quoted. It should be mentioned, however, that the quotations relate to relatively small installations and may be assumed to be lower for larger installations. Rider's familiar adage evidently applies to COMPACTUS: "The only place where saving would be effected would be in the amount . . . of the stack building 'shell'. . . . What we have here . . . is greater compactness of storage, but no over-all economy."[35] It is possible that the cost of such mobile stacks is lower abroad. A librarian who recently returned to the United States from a study tour, during which he visited compact stack installations, stated in a letter to the writer in July 1964 that "What it all comes down to is simply this: if in Europe a proposed eleven-story building with conventional book stacks can be reduced in size to a four-story building, with mechanized bookstacks, then the savings in building costs alone more than compensate for the higher expenditure for mechanized bookstacks." To which one might reply: To be sure, a 64 per cent shrinkage in building size is impressive and a source of fascination and amazement; but conclusions as to savings do not necessarily follow. If COMPACTUS type shelving were to come down in price in the United States, it would probably become the preferred type of compact equipment.

For the time being, the two other types of compact shelving seem to offer the most appreciable cost advantages. *Hinged cases* with two swinging cases and narrow aisles (2 ft.) result in savings that are reflected in an increase of book capacity by about 34 per cent. Savings obtainable through *sliding shelves* can be assumed to result in a book capacity increase of about 47 per cent, minus a correction for the higher floor load requirement. Both of these types of equipment show similar compactability, i.e., nearly 100 per cent as compared with the tightest kind of conventional shelving model illustrated by Stromeyer.[36] Assuming that the cost quotations are trustworthy, both hinged and sliding shelves but particularly the sliding shelves, appear to be worth serious consideration in the planning of storage stacks for research collections which are to be housed in a building costing $25 or more per square foot, exclusive of equipment. (It is noteworthy, however, that even the most advantageous type of compact equipment, economically speaking, achieves only a somewhat better result, than the increase of about 40 per cent in capacity that can be achieved by reduction of range-aisles from 36 to 22 inches, which Yale University has found to be "practical."[37]) In cases where building costs per square foot are much lower, the appropriateness of compact shelving equipment becomes increasingly questionable.

Advantages other than cost have also been claimed for compact storage; among them are lower custodial service, repair, maintenance, utilities, security, ground maintenance, overhead cost, and lower cost in book delivery and reshelving (since distances have been shortened). Although some of these advantages may appear self-evident, no studies have been found that satisfactorily quantify all these alleged operational economics. Since library budgets of universities rarely include utility costs, library administrators are not likely to be overly concerned about such cost factors; and the alleged economy in book delivery and reshelving is likely to be cancelled out to a considerable extent by the increased labor involved in shelf manipulation (sliding, rotating, etc.). In any case, all such factors combined probably account for savings of less than 2 per cent per year of original construction plus equipment cost. If a $500,000 building of, say, 17,500 square feet could be reduced in size to 7,000 square feet by the use of COMPACTUS-type stacks, the savings in plant maintenance would amount to about $10,500 a year ($1.00 a square foot per year). On a 5 per cent compound-interest basis, it would take twenty-five years to build up enough capital to construct another building of the same dimension. Obviously, from the long-range institutional (rather than the more narrow librarian's annual budgetary) point of view, such savings should not be disregarded. However, since all types of compact shelving installation do involve some reduction in direct and easy access to books, over-all cost savings will have to be very substantial before librarians will resort to such measures for this reason.

NOTES

[1] Metcalf, Keyes D. "When Bookstacks Overflow," *Harvard Library Bulletin*, 8:204, Spring 1954.

[2] Orne, Jerrold. "Storage Warehouses." *In* Ralph R. Shaw, ed., *State of the Library Art.* New Brunswick, N.J., Graduate School of Library Service, Rutgers, The State University, 1960, Vol. 3, Part 3, p. 16.

[3] Ellsworth, Ralph E. "Library Buildings." *In* Ralph R. Shaw, *op. cit.,* Vol. 3, Part 1, pp. 59–66.

[4] Hopp, Ralph H. "Problems of Storing University Library Materials," *College and Research Libraries,* 22:435–437, Nov. 1961.

[5] Fussler, Herman H., and Simon, Julian L. *Patterns in the Use of Books in Large Research Libraries.* Chicago, University of Chicago Library, 1961. (Published originally in a limited edition for review and criticism by University of Chicago Library.)

[6] *Ibid.,* p. 245.

[7] David C. Weber, review of Herman H. Fussler and Julian L. Simon's *Patterns in the Use of Books in Large Research Libraries,* in *The Library Quarterly,* 32:79, Jan. 1962.

[8] Richard H. Logsdon, review of Herman H. Fussler and Julian L. Simon's *Patterns in the Use of Books in Large Research Libraries,* in *College and Research Libraries,* 23:79, Jan. 1962.

[9] A. G. Mackenzie, review of Herman H. Fussler and Julian L. Simon's *Patterns in the Use of Books in Large Research Libraries,* in *Journal of Documentation,* 18:35, March 1962.

[10] Fussler and Simon, *op. cit.,* p. 248.

[11] Rider, Fremont, *Compact Book Storage.* New York, The Hadham Press, 1949.

[12] Ash, Lee, ed. *Yale's Selective Book Retirement Program.* Hamden, Conn., The Shoe String Press, Inc., 1963, pp. 58–59.

[13] *Ibid.,* p. 53.

[14] Rider, *op cit.,* p. 8.

[15] *Ibid.,* p. 54.

[16] A representative of this company, in analyzing the recent decline of demand for STOR-MOR equipment, expressed the view that most librarians with a storage problem would rather build a new building or addition than purchase a compact storage system, for they fear that the consideration of compact storage would cause governing authorities to lower the priority of their request for a new facility. Also, librarians are reluctant to conceive of any of their materials being placed in what may appear to be inaccessible or "dead" storage since all books are presumably being used constantly. Moreover, double-headed drawers are admittedly less applicable to small rooms and corners of large rooms than the single-headed type of drawer design of Brown's or Hamilton's. (This information was obtained by the author in April 1964 from the W. R. Ames Company, Milpitas, Calif.)

[17] Stromeyer, Rainald. "Platzersparnis durch neuartige Regalanlagen," *In* Chapter 5, *Moderne Probleme des Magazinbaues in Deutschland und seinen Nachbarländern* (Arbeiten aus dem Bibliothekar-Lehrinstitut des Landes Nordrhein-Westfalen, Heft 15). Köln, 1958, p. 63.

[18] Jackson Compactus Company of Los Angeles, Calif. Letter dated Oct. 14, 1964.

[19] Stromeyer, *op. cit.,* p. 60.

[20] Strahm, H. "Eine umwälzende Neuerung im Magazinsystem," (Vereinigung Schweizerischer Bibliothekare), *Nachrichten,* 31:161–165, 1955.

[21] Naito, Hanichiro. Letter dated June 6, 1964.

[22] Miura, Michio. *Library and Elecompack.* (A translation of the textual portion of this brochure was supplied to the author and has been sent, along with the brochure, to the American Library Association Library Technology Project, 50 E. Huron Street, Chicago, Illinois.) For a brief description, see "Goods and Gadgets," *ALA Bulletin,* 58:651, July-Aug. 1964. The company president states that ELECOMPACK differs in structure from COMPACTUS, and he expects to obtain a patent of his own. ELECOMPACK has two feeders as compared to only one per bay for COMPACTUS. Each range of bookcases is fastened to the feeders independently, thus keeping the ranges from shoving against each other when moved. It is equipped with safety devices, and it is possible to centralize control for several blocks of stacks.

[23] Gawrecki, Drahoslav. *New Shelving Equipment in Libraries Abroad.* (Title translated from Czech). Martin, Matica Slovenska, 1960. Five volumes are issued in three booklets. Volumes 1 and 2 contain 67 pages; volume 3 contains 40 pages; and volumes 4 and 5 contain 98 pages. (A typewritten translation, uncorrected, has been deposited with the American Library Association Library Technology Project, 50 E. Huron Street, Chicago, Illinois, and is also available on microfilm or copyflow enlargement, OPB 22289, $8.20, from University Microfilms, Inc., Ann Arbor, Michigan.)

[24] Przybylo, Zofia. "Compact Storage of Collections in Libraries," (Title of article translated from Polish). *Przeglad Biblioteczny,* 27:29–44, 1959.

[25] Pashchenko, F. N. "New Methods for Organizing and Equipping Library Stacks," (Title of article translated from Russian). *Biblioteki SSSR,* 12:199–234, 1959.

[26] Stromeyer, *op. cit.,* pp. 56–77.

[27] Hill, F. J. "The Compact Storage of Books: A Study of Methods and Equipment," *Journal of Documentation,* 11:202–216, 1955.

[28] Kaplan, Louis. "Shelving." *In* Ralph R. Shaw, *op. cit.,* Vol. 3, Part 2, pp. 9–14.

[29] Metcalf, Keyes D. "Compact Shelving," *College and Research Libraries,* 23:103–111, 1962.

[30] Kaplan, *op. cit.,* p. 27.

[31] Muller, Robert H. "Evaluation of Compact Book Storage Systems," *ACRL Monograph No. 11,* Spring 1954, p. 86.
[32] Ash, *op. cit.,* p. 55.
[33] Information in an advertising brochure of Elecompack, Ltd., Tokyo. (Translated from the Japanese.)
[34] Mattison, Lester. "A Comparison of Shelving Costs for a Library Storehouse." Unpublished M.S. thesis prepared for the Library School, University of Minnesota, 1961, p. 46.
[35] Rider, *op. cit.,* p. 34.
[36] Stromeyer, *op. cit.,* p. 139; Model C3: 21 volumes per lineal foot.
[37] Muller, *op. cit.,* p. 81. See also Ash, *op. cit.,* p. 52.

ABOUT THE AUTHOR—Robert H. Muller was born in Germany, attended Victoria University in England, received a B. A. degree from Stanford in 1936, an L.S. certificate from the University of California in 1937, and M.A. (in L.S.) and PhD degrees from Chicago in 1942. He was Head Librarian at Bradley University and at Southern Illinois until he went to the University of Michigan in 1954, becoming Associate Director there in 1959. Since 1971 he has been Librarian of the Queens College Library in New York, N.Y. Besides being a library administrator, he has taught, acted as building consultant for many libraries, and served on numerous and varied committees.

Design of Library Furniture

by Martin Van Buren

Furniture for the library must be selected for its appearance, to be sure. But we must also consider how it will appear after use, when it is five or twenty-five years old. We must also be concerned with how a particular piece of furniture appears in its place in the building, how well it relates to other furniture and to the building itself. And, of course, we must consider how the furniture carries out its intended function. These and other factors of design are related by the author.

The physical environment of a library depends on two factors: the architectural quality of the building and the design of its furniture. These closely related elements must be harmonious if a successful aesthetic result is to be achieved. Architecture and furnishings must be compatible in color, texture, material, and form. This relationship is particularly important in the library building, with its large open spaces which the eye can distinguish as a single entity; such areas appear either unified or disjointed according to the correlation of elements.

This relationship creates two problems in library furniture design. First, the design of the library building must be developed before other elements —including the furniture—are considered. Second, the design of library furniture must fulfill certain functional requirements. Aesthetic and utilitarian needs, as they relate to the design of the building and to library operations, must be determined simultaneously.

A third problem in furniture design, not related to library architecture, arises from the fact that library furniture undergoes excessive abuse and wear. Not only is it subjected to long hours of use day after day, but some users mistreat the furniture. Further, certain areas of the library may be multi-purpose, involving frequent handling of folding or stacking furniture. Janitorial services such as waxing, mopping, and vacuum cleaning are also hard on furniture. Finally, library furniture is costly and cannot be replaced frequently; normally a life span of at least ten years must be expected.

Many samples can be seen of library furniture that succeed or fail in fulfilling these design requirements. Lewis Mumford, after praising the architecture of the American Embassy in London, has this to say about its library:

I cannot say as much in praise of the furniture. The clumsy, armless, almost immovable chairs were obviously chosen by someone with little experience in sitting or reading, much less in note-taking; they achieve a maximum of cushioned discomfort with a minimum of efficiency.... Here was a place for a dexterous innovation in modern library furniture, to match the high standard we have achieved in the conduct, if not always the design, of lending libraries.[1]

Fortunately, such criticisms of library furniture are becoming less valid. Manufacturers are beginning to explore new materials and technologies. Furniture makers from other fields are showing increased interest in the expanding market of library technical furniture, thus creating keener competition and introducing new concepts in design. The stigma of sameness is disappearing from the American library scene as each year sees more examples of imaginative library furniture. Creativity and functional design in library furniture are not only overdue, these qualities are now vital to future library planning.

At the Institute for Library Consultants held at the University of Colorado in the summer of 1964, the effects of mechanization upon library planning were discussed. Of particular interest to the participants was the manner in which computer development and improvements in the miniaturization of graphic information might enable libraries to provide a type of service hitherto im-

SOURCE: Reprinted from Martin Van Buren, "Design of Library Furniture," *Library Trends*, vol. 13, no. 4, April, 1965, pp. 388–395, by permission of the publisher.

possible. It seemed possible that such developments might lead to complex carrel designs for individual study that would require more space than traditional types of study space. Designs incorporating some of these ideas have already been developed by Ralph Ellsworth and others.[2] The use of these and similar designs may mean that the accepted formula of 25–30 square feet per reader may no longer be adequate for such situations.

Despite the extended discussion of these subjects, there seemed to be no general agreement of what the future would bring in this area of concern. Some of the best known authorities in library planning could not predict the future requirements of certain types of library furniture and equipment. This suggests the need for additional study and research on the part of the library profession, both by individual librarians and by such agencies as the Library Technology Project of the American Library Association, as well as on the part of the manufacturers of library equipment and furnishings.

The principles of library furniture design include six factors.

1. *Function.*—This relates to comfort, convenience, efficiency of operation, and serviceability. How well a unit of furniture performs its function determines its degree of usefulness. Comfort, for example, implies a state of ease free from distress or pain. Furniture of proper dimensions, proportions, and materials is pleasant to use for reading, working, and lounging. Comfort in library furniture requires proper pitch and height of seating units, adequate area allowances of work surfaces, comfortable colors and light-reflecting qualities of top surfaces, and easy-moving working parts such as doors and drawers.

2. *Construction.*—Durability and resistance to wear are important. Surfaces must withstand abrasion and impact. Joints should not loosen. Moving parts should be sturdy and simply designed to minimize complex mechanical failure, as, for example, in folding furniture that is handled frequently and sometimes roughly.

3. *Materials.*—Increasingly rapid development of new materials such as synthetics (plastics and other man-made derivatives), as well as new methods of handling and fabricating traditional materials, have opened endless opportunities in the selection of furniture materials. Materials in furniture are selected for the following characteristics: beauty, versatility in forming and fabricating, strength, resistance to wear, resistance to dirt, adaptability to various finishing techniques, and cost.

4. *Finish.*—The main purpose of the finish is to protect the surface of the material and to enhance its natural beauty. Finishes may be surface-coated, penetrating, or integral. Surface-coated finishes include paint, lacquer, varnish, epoxy, and metal plating. A typical penetrating finish on wood surfaces is linseed oil. Integral finishes are those in which pigment is introduced into the material before it is formed and hardened, e.g., molded fiberglas chairs.

5. *Scale.*—This defines a certain value in size or degree within a group or system of related items. Furniture should be scaled to pleasing proportions with relation to the size and bulk of surrounding furniture, the dimensions of the room in which it is placed, and the mass of related architectural elements.

6. *Proportion.*—Whereas scale relates to other elements, proportion is an inherent quality in the design of a unit of furniture, implying the relationship of the parts to the whole. Proper proportions among the various parts result in aesthetic overall balance and symmetry.

The quality of beauty has been deliberately avoided in the above list because aesthetic values cover all aspects of furniture design. To a competent designer this quality underlies all other considerations. There is library furniture on the market which satisfies all the requirements listed above, including aesthetic compatibility with certain styles of architecture, but still lacks beauty. Beauty is the abstract feature that adds the final touch and brings pleasure to the senses. It is the mark of true design excellence when all of the practical requisites are met, yet overall beauty still emerges. This is particularly true of library technical furniture, where functional needs carry such a demanding—and sometimes difficult—burden.

Of all the objectives to which the library aspires, comfort of the user is perhaps the foremost. It is the objective most closely associated with the design of library furniture. The trend is comparatively recent; early libraries, such as those in Europe, ignored comfort as an aspect of library service. During the last half-century, however, the idea of emphasizing reader comfort along with efficient service has become accepted. In 1934, Angus Snead Macdonald stated: "If only a small part of the money saved on the building structure is put into comfortable furniture, the best available equipment, and attractive interior decoration, it will be possible to secure an atmosphere of comfort . . . wherein a love for reading can be readily cultivated."[3] Macdonald was stating a premise that is widely accepted today—that of encouraging patrons to use the library by making it an inviting place in which to work.

Once the aim was established, modern research techniques offered some logical solutions to the problem. It has long been known that comfort in furniture design is directly related to human measurements. But the accurate determination of these measurements, particularly in a mass society, was not scientifically attempted until recent years.

An example can be made of table-reader seating. Some studies of military personnel were conducted during World War II, mostly to determine human measurements for use in the design of military clothing, equipment, and aircraft seating. In 1945, the Heywood-Wakefield Company instituted a study by Earnest A. Hooton of Harvard on railway coach seating.[4] The main purpose of this survey was to determine the dimensions and proportions of seating required to fit the majority of passengers. A more general survey of seating was conducted by Bengt Akerblom at the Karolinska Institutet in Stockholm in 1948.[5]

Perhaps the most revealing and comprehensive study of seating and seat-to-table relationships was made at the University of Arkansas in 1959.[6] Whereas the Hooton studies relied on sand molds to determine restful spinal curvatures in the sitting position, and the Akerblom survey employed the bone structure to arrive at human measurements, the University of Arkansas tests utilized a unique seating contraption.

The experimental "chair" consisted of metal plungers inserted into holes in a wood frame (seat and back). The plungers, or pins, were in rows placed 1½ inches apart, supported on springs and capped by rubber discs. The angle between the seat and back frames was adjustable. For purposes of the study, basic sitting positions were established for the following activities: dining, writing, card playing, talking, and relaxing. For library use the most important of these are reading, writing, and relaxing (lounge seating).

Exhaustive tests were first made to determine average or mean dimensions of the human body. Both age and sex were considered and tabulated separately. Activities that involved table use, such as reading and writing, included studies on seat-and-table relationships. A summary of the conclusions covering the proper dimensions of chairs to be used for reading or writing follows:

Height of seat: 17 inches at front at highest point.
Slope of seat: 0.5 inches from front to back.

Depression of seat: 2.5 inches from highest to lowest point.
Depth of seat: 16.5 inches from front to back.
Width of seat: 17 inches at widest point.
Height of chair back: 17.5 inches from seat to top of back.
Width of chair back: 13.5 inches across top; 10 inches across bottom.
Slope of chair back: 2.4 inches backward, or 15 degrees from vertical.
Included angle (seat-back) 103.3 degrees (Derived from data furnished, not given in this form in the report.).

Depth of chair back: determined at 1½ inch intervals up the center of the back starting 4.5 inches above the seat:

16.3 inches at 4.5 inches above seat.
16.6 inches at 6 inches above seat.
17 inches at 7.5 inches above seat.
17.3 inches at 9 inches above seat.
17.8 inches at 10.5 inches above seat.
18.3 inches at 12 inches above seat.
18.7 inches at 13.5 inches above seat.

In addition, data on the height, free depth, angle, and distance apart of arm rests were determined.

Another interesting test, made during the University of Arkansas survey, compared preferences of the most comfortable table height for reading or writing among the subjects cooperating in the tests. Table I summarizes the results.

From these data the investigators concluded that table heights for the tested seat heights should be 27 inches, or 10 inches above the highest point of the seat. For readers above average in dimension, a one-inch increase in this dimension was allowed. This table height allows a two-inch top thickness, to permit adequate knee space or clearance.

TABLE I

PERCENTAGE OF SUBJECTS SELECTING VARYING HEIGHTS OF TABLES

Height (inches)	Percent of subjects
23.0 to 23.9	1.9%
24.0 to 24.9	9.9
25.0 to 25.9	22.8
26.0 to 26.9	31.5
27.0 to 27.9	22.8
28.0 to 28.9	7.4
29.0 or more	3.7
Mean height (in inches): 26.5	

Another factor in table reader requirements is the amount of work surface required per user. Again human measurements serve as a guide. For activities such as seminar discussion (talking), a minimum width based on the width of the human torso plus a clearance allowance between seats can be established. Thus one recent investigation specifies a minimum table width of 15 inches for knee space, plus 6 inches on each side, or a total clearance of 27 inches per user.[7] *Anatomy for Interior Designers* suggests a minimum width of 24 inches for such activities as typing.[8]

Obviously, the usual library activities such as note-taking and the spread of reference materials require more table surface than typing. The most logical measure for library use is the span from elbow to elbow with arms akimbo—that is, spread horizontally. The Damon studies of military personnel give a median span of 36.5 inches, while an earlier study by Brackett offers a median span of 39.25 inches.[9] However, these studies were conducted solely on military males; it can be assumed that female measurements will be less.

Analysis of data from the above studies indicates the following table widths are desirable for library use: (1) discussion and seminar activities: 24–27 inches per person, (2) general library-reader use: 36 inches per person, and (3) for graduate students in academic libraries: 42 inches per person.

Statistics generally support the accepted table depth dimension of 24 inches per user. For example, the Damon studies of military males show a mean anterior arm reach of 34.8 inches;[9] this means the distance from wall to tip of middle finger when the subject assumes forward reach with his back to the wall. Subtracting the average chest depth or thickness of 8.2 inches, a clear arm reach of 26.6 inches results. The reaching distance of women will be somewhat less. Thus we can scientifically accept a work surface depth of 24 to 26 inches per person.

The above examples are intended to illustrate the trend toward the use of the scientific method in determining standards of comfort and efficiency in library furniture design. An analytical approach to such problems is important, both to improve library furniture in its present functional role, and to prepare for unforeseeable future requirements in this field of design. These future requirements include not only the question of electronic miniaturization potentials, but the expanding scope of library services as well. Increasingly, the library is becoming a center in community or academic life, with facilities for such things as exhibits, graphic art collections, music listening, language laboratories, special meeting rooms, and the like. Library furniture manufacturers must remain abreast of these trends and be prepared to meet new functional requirements on sound principles. In library furniture, the day of hit-or-miss design is past.

NOTES

[1] Mumford, Lewis. "The Sky Line: False Front or Cold-War Concept," *The New Yorker*, 38:174–185, Oct. 20, 1962.

[2] Ellsworth, Ralph E., and Wagener, Hobart D. *The School Library: Facilities for Independent Study in the Secondary School.* New York, Educational Facilities Laboratories, 1963.

[3] Macdonald, Angus Snead. "Some Engineering Developments Affecting Large Libraries," *Bulletin of the American Library Association*, 28:631, Sept. 1934.

[4] Hooton, Earnest A. *A Survey in Seating.* (Instituted by the Heywood-Wakefield Company.) Cambridge, Harvard University, Department of Anthropology, Statistical Laboratory, 1945.

[5] Akerblom, Bengt. *Standing and Sitting Posture.* Stockholm, A. B. Nordiska Bokhandeln, 1948.

[6] Ridder, Clara A. *Basic Design Measurements for Sitting* (Agricultural Experiment Station, Bulletin 616). Fayetteville, University of Arkansas, 1959, pp. 1–91.

[7] Woodson, Wesley E. *Human Engineering Guide for Equipment Designers.* Berkeley, University of California Press, 1954, pp. 1–51.

[8] Panero, Julius. *Anatomy for Interior Designers.* 3rd ed. New York, Whitney Library of Design, 1962, p. 81.

[9] Woodson, *op. cit.*, pp. 4–16, 4–17.

ABOUT THE AUTHOR—(See biographical note on page 291.)

The Materials and Construction of Library Furniture

by Stephen D. Pryce

Because furniture design does change, the author has written this paper so that the librarian "may be better able to evaluate current trends and developments." Here we look closer at some wood furniture criteria. Appended are some performance tests and suggestions for evaluating library wood furniture.

Lightness of line, strength and durability without bulk, and utility without severity have been the theme for architecture and its furnishings over the last few years. In its wake have come revised concepts in materials, in material applications, and in construction. The trend to designer-conceived interiors, and demands for imaginative, colorful, yet practical furnishings, both technical and casual, have opened a wide field of interest. This, coupled with the expanding growth and opportunity in the library furnishings field, has resulted in a refreshing competition for the library furnishings market and has stimulated expansion of research and facility improvement programs among the manufacturers.

The result of this trend may be seen in the furniture of new libraries: in the design, shape, thickness, and materials that make up table tops; in leg design and the mechanics of leg attachment; in the design, weight, material, and construction of reading chairs; in the improvement and acceptability of plastic laminates, extruded and formed plastic parts; and in the mating of fiberglas and polyester resin to give durable, colorful seating.

The objective of this paper is to provide the librarian with basic information on the materials and methods used in the manufacture of library furniture, so that he may be better able to evaluate current trends and developments.

A library table is a functional piece of furniture which must provide a working surface at a height convenient to the seated patron. This surface must be rigid, smooth, and decorative to meet today's standards. The whole is the sum of its parts. Therefore, as we consider a table and its purpose,

we study the top, its manufacture, and the nature of its support. The manner of fabrication is critical to the serviceability of the piece.

Table top construction usually employs one of two methods: (1) solid wood (lumber) or (2) ply-construction. Solid wood construction uses solid, unmodified wood components. Ply-construction employs several layers of materials, which may be all wood, or may be a combination of wood and modified wood products, i.e., fiberboard, particle board, laminated plastics, etc.

Solid wood tops are made of lumber strips or boards edge-glued under pressure, to form a panel. When the glue is set, the panel is surfaced in a planer, cut to size, and sanded to a uniform, smooth surface. If the component strips are narrower than they are deep, i.e., narrower than the thickness of the table top, the panel is often referred to as of "butcher block" construction. If the dimensions are reversed, it is simply a solid wood panel or top. This method of construction is sometimes used for the tops of charging desks and for catalog reference table tops which are subject to abrasive wear of books or the bottoms of catalog card trays.

Wood, by nature, picks up and gives off moisture proportionate to the relative humidity of its environment. In doing this, wood shrinks or swells. In the case of a solid wood panel, the whole panel expands or contracts as an expression of the movement of each of the component strips. Although each strip has its own individual grain pattern and reacts differently to moisture, these differences are minimized by proper kiln drying, machining, and gluing methods. The inevitable small differences

SOURCE: Reprinted from Stephen D. Pryce, "The Materials and Construction of Library Furniture," *Library Trends,* vol. 13, no. 4, April, 1965, pp. 396–410, by permission of the publisher.

are, for the most part, submerged in the panel as a unit. Because movement is inevitable, a solid top must be flexibly mounted, allowing it to ride with dimensional changes in the wood. Any effort to tie it down rigidly can result in splitting of the top, or in the distortion of the top and any framework to which it is attached. A solid top, particularly one of large components, must be well made to hold up over the years. Today's use of solid tops in libraries is primarily a matter of design, since, with the possible exception of tops for charging desks and catalog tray consultation tables, there is no use to which library furniture is subjected that requires this construction—that is, in the same sense that dictates solid wood tops for work benches.

Ply-construction, as indicated earlier, is used in multiple combinations. By definition, the term implies the use of three or more plies or layers of materials face-glued together to make up the full thickness of the panel or top. In all cases, the panel should be balanced, i.e., it should have an equal number of plies on each side of the center ply or core. With such construction there will always be an odd number of plies or layers. A given ply-construction has specific merits, and its components, depending upon the type, have definite purposes. These will be pointed out as we discuss the basic types.

Lumber core, ply-construction employs a core, or center ply, of solid lumber strips made up in the same manner as a conventional solid panel or top. The core materials, however, should be low density, straight grained wood species, such as basswood, or yellow poplar. On each face of the core, normally with the grain direction at right angles to that of the core, are the "cross-band" veneers. Firmly glued and with the grain so oriented, the cross bands restrain and thereby minimize the movement of the core, as it naturally seeks to respond to atmospheric moisture changes. The "face" and "back" veneers are, in turn, face glued to the cross-band veneers. The grain directions are normally at right angles to that of the cross bands and in the same direction as that of the core.

Here then, we have an all wood top that has its several elements oriented to restrain the major movements of the core, and balanced to restrain it equally on each side and thus avoid distortion. Over an extended period, even when subjected to extreme moisture changes, a well made ply-construction table top will not fail because of fatigue. In addition to the physical advantages of balanced, lumber core construction, this method has the advantage of permitting the use of decorative face veneers with wider grain patterns and, consequently, more pleasing wood figures.

It is worth mentioning that there is a form of lumber core construction employing wood blocks, rather than full-length strips, for the core components. This is common practice in the fabrication of commercial exterior door panels. However, since it is very difficult to produce a permanently attractive and satisfactory top surface using block construction, the method is not suitable for use in library tables. The difficulty arises from the fact that each piece of wood has its own movement pattern, and only if block components are uniformly kiln dried and securely bonded end-to-end and edge-to-edge will the core move as a unit. Movements of the individual blocks show up through the face veneers as outlines of the separate pieces, a condition usually referred to as "telegraphing."

Lumber core construction is traditionally and properly considered the best all-around manner of making library table tops. Properly made, such construction is stable, has good screw holding capacity, permits machining and edging or banding, has good tensile strength and stiffness, and is not subject to splitting through fatigue or abuse.

Veneer core construction, as implied, is that in which the full thickness is made up of wood veneers glued face to face. The grain directions of adjacent plies are at right angles. A familiar example of this type of construction is a decorative wood veneer laid up on a sheet of douglas fir plywood. The same method, using hardwood veneers throughout, is used in producing panels and tops for household furniture. When all hardwood veneers are used, this is a quality construction, employed successfully with decorative wood veneer faces, and as an underlayment for decorative high pressure laminates.

Particle board (a term employed here to cover all types of wood flake, fines, and splinter boards) is made by mixing wood particles with glue and subjecting the mixture to high heat and pressure. This material is gaining increased acceptance as the industry improves the quality control of its products. The subject of particle board is an important one. For this writing, suffice it to say that there are many types of particle board, determined by the form and combination of wood elements employed and by the method of manufacture.

A good quality board, properly used, makes an excellent panel or top for many purposes. It has not, however, found any widespread use in the manufacture of quality library furniture and cannot be generally recommended for large tops or for structural or load bearing members until it has been improved by further research. As of the present time, particle board has been used largely for certain types of library work room furniture and for shelves in wood installations. In the latter use, it has been found to warp under loading and should not be used for this purpose.

Table tops for library use run the gamut, from small study tables for single occupancy, to large tables for general reading and conference purposes. Requirements for each type differ, based on the use and abuse to which the table may be subjected.

The strength and durability of a table top depends upon its construction. We have discussed the major types. The appearance of a top and its use as a working surface is, for the most part, a matter of the surface material and the finish. There are two major top materials: wood, either solid or veneer, and high-pressure, plastic laminates.

Wood, which is unchallenged as the material most easily and gracefully lived with, both in the home and in the library, has been the traditional material for library table tops. However, the advent of high-pressure, plastic laminates brought a competitor, particularly in those instances where there is a need for a hard, stain-free surface.

Vast improvements in these materials, in quality, uniformity, and selection of patterns, have come in recent years and have paved the way for the laminates to take an increasing share of the market for top surface treatment. To counter the recognized advantages of plastics, yet keep the traditional values of wood, the wood finishing industry has developed both new film overlays for low pressure application on wood veneered panels, and durable catalyzed synthetic finishing materials, including the polyesters, epoxies, and polyurethanes, for spray application. These materials rival the plastics in stain and abrasion resistance. For the most part, however, these finishes are in their infancy, and because of their present high cost and difficulty of application have not found wide use in the production of library furniture.

For general finishing, most manufacturers continue to rely upon the traditional nitrocellulose lacquers applied either hot or cold. These are extremely versatile, relatively inexpensive, clear, easily maintained and repaired finishes. However, library furniture manufacturers are making increased use of the conversion varnishes (catalyzed alkydurea resin solutions) sometimes referred to as catalytic varnishes. Properly formulated, these synthetics are definitely superior in solvent and abrasion resistance to the conventional lacquer finishes.

It should be noted that not all finishes of the same type are equally good. Thus, one manufacturer's conversion varnish may give better (or poorer) performance than another's, depending upon the formulation and upon the way in which the material is applied. Since the most satisfactory method of evaluating finish performance is by laboratory testing, the methods outlined in Appendix I, which have been successfully used in many instances, may be useful.

Of interest because of their present vogue are the oil finishes. These are penetrating rather than film finishes, as are the lacquers, varnishes, etc. They are most pleasing when used with hardwoods such as walnut and teak, and are most practical for furniture in casual and low traffic areas. Softness, low sheen, and easy maintenance are special characteristics favoring the oil finishes.

Both wood veneer faces and plastic laminates can be made burn-resistant by inserting an aluminum foil laminate directly beneath the face element. The foil serves as a heat dissipator, and saves loss from the careless cigarette. Fabrication with inserted foil laminates is very exacting and expensive. It is justifiable only for table tops in areas where smoking is permitted or hot elements are used.

A support-free panel would be the ideal, and almost every contemporary designer works toward this end, making every effort to give firm, unyielding support to the table top, yet trying for the effect of a top with minimum support. Answers have come in the form of slim line center pedestals and in the slim line metal leg bases, but primarily in the use of plate mounted legs, individually attached to the underside of the top. The latter obviates the need for complete base construction, and has made it possible to eliminate the apron which, in earlier designs, was required for the solid attachment of the legs.

To make a table with four separately attached legs as stable as the traditional solid design of top on a full base calls for good materials and good engineering. Three elements are involved: the top, the legs, and the tie-in between the two, the mounting plate. All three must be rigid if the whole construction is to be so. Since the legs are mounted to the top, the top must be strong and rigid. The legs themselves must not flex. Whether the legs are laminated or solid is not material to this, assuming proper lamination. The steel plate used for mounting the leg to the top is normally at least $\frac{1}{4}$ inch in thickness and seldom less than 4 or 5 inches square. Usually the leg is bolted to the plate. A hanger bolt screwed into the leg and then threaded into the plate, although occasionally used, is the least effective method. The best type of library furniture construction uses a bolt through the mounting plate inserted into a boring in the top of the leg and then threaded into a cross-inserted steel pin or bushing. In this system, the wood is bypassed in developing strength, by tightening the leg to the plate. This system is very effective.

The plate, in turn, may be screwed to the underside of the top with wood screws, or, in better construction, with bolts that are received by steel bushings or pins inserted into the panel from the edge and parallel to the surface of the top. Using bolts and pins, the wood is again bypassed in tightening the joint. The advantage in the latter system is that in the metal to metal joint there is less concern for fatigue caused by the many cycles of racking and twisting to which library tables are inevitably subjected.

A discussion of table construction, no matter how brief, is incomplete without mention of bridging. A table top spans the distance between leg supports. When individual legs are used without benefit of stretchers or aprons, there comes a point when the natureal stiffness of the top must be supplemented by using a bridge or keel. As a general rule, the wider the span, the heavier and deeper the bridge member or keel. When table lengths exceed a certain point, it is usually more practical to use a center supporting leg than to go overboard in bridge construction.

A sharp edge is easily damaged, and in turn, can inflict damage if struck by the user. For these practical reasons, and for purposes of design, table tops are usually edged. A solid lumber top can be given an edge of any shape without supplementary edging material, but ply-construction using lumber or veneer core, normally needs an edge banding to protect the elements of the construction. Exceptions, of course, are found where the edges are tapered back and under or, in the case of wood core, are given a shape that allows the core to project beyond the face element so that any impact is absorbed by it, rather than by the more fragile veneers or plastics. Edge bandings may be wood, veneer, wood strips, densified wood, plastic, or metal. For most applications, wood edging is more elegant and imparts more warmth.

In discussing table tops, we have briefly covered general construction methods, core materials, finishes, and edgings. The points made here hold true for all types of panels, although most panels are not judged as harshly or are so demandingly used as table tops. Where the term "panel" is used, it applies to the full range of furniture components, including the backs, sides, tops, and bottoms of card catalog cases, book truck panels and shelves, magazine rack sides, wood book shelving, and similar items.

The library chair used at a table for reading or writing presents the greatest challenge to the furniture manufacturer in that it must be strong, rigid, resistant to abuse, and—most important of all—comfortable. At the same time, it must be reasonably light in weight for ease of handling.

The conventional, easily tipped, straight-back chair with its scooped seat, slats, straight posts, and straight top back rail has been largely replaced by so-called "wall-saver" designs. Here the back posts are curved, allowing the lower or leg portion of the posts to strike the floor molding, thus preventing the back posts from hitting the wall.

Equally important in the above construction is its "no-tip" feature. Tipping is so difficult in such designs that the user is discouraged from doing so. This adds immeasurably to the life of the chair. The back posts can be curved by band-sawing a solid or laminated block, or by steam-bending a straight post, and cutting to pattern after bending. Both methods are practical and normally perform well. However, the steam-bent post can boast continuous grain throughout its length and for this reason it is less liable to breakage or splitting than is sometimes the case with band-sawn posts.

Wall-saver designs, although less susceptible to tipping by the occupant, must nevertheless be strong enough to resist the tremendous strains put on them if so abused. When tipped backward, the major stresses on the chair occur at the points where the side stretchers join the back posts; when tipped forward, at the stretcher to leg joints. For these reasons, machining of these joints must be accurately done to assure a tight fit. Assembly calls for a strong adhesive, adequate doweling (at least two dowels per joint), and the support of well-fitted, glued and screwed corner blocks bridging each joint.

Bottom stretchers and rungs make table chairs stronger, but their use is often in conflict with contemporary design and its need for uncluttered simplicity.

Some recent designs in wood table chairs use straight back posts positioned at an angle to the floor. Although the wll-saver feature is still present in this design, as is the resistance to tipping, the seat does not extend to the back posts, thereby giving the floating seat appearance so desirable in some contemporary designs.

Molded plywood and molded reinforced fiberglas seating have also gained acceptance for library use. Properly made, such seating is useful, attractive, and normally light in weight. Each type has been extensively used for stacking chairs. The compound curve construction of these designs explains why both great strength and low weight are possible. The weakness of this design is usually in the attachment of the legs, although this has been largely resolved by the use of a rubber grommet coupling.

Molded plastic chair shells are made either by intrusion molding or by forming with fiberglas and polyester resin; the same basic procedure and materials used in making boat hulls. Of the two systems, the latter is that referred to as reinforced fiberglas. Those chairs longest in use and of highest reputation are of this construction. Color is an important factor when using plastics. In such application, however, coloring must be integral and not merely a surface treatment.

As in other products of complex manufacture, furniture is best judged by the expert. Experts, however, are not always at hand, and librarians, although otherwise trained and experienced, are often called upon to specify, evaluate, and purchase furniture.

The criteria in Appendix II will be helpful to the librarian called upon to judge the general quality of library furniture. Such criteria, however, cannot substitute for proper specifications, the development of which is a job for an expert in wood furniture design and construction. The performance of wood finishes is more readily evaluated and for this purpose, the tests found in Appendix I will prove helpful.

APPENDIX I

Performance Tests for the Gluing and Finishing of Wood Furniture

Tests which determine actual performance are highly desirable as a means of evaluating the durability and general quality of library wood furniture. Such tests are exceedingly difficult to develop, however, and as a consequence, relatively little work has been done in this area.

A few years ago, the Library Technology Project of the American Library Association instituted a study to develop a satisfactory performance test for library reading chairs made of wood. The result of this work, which was conducted by the Department of Engineering Research, North Carolina State College at Raleigh, was a procedure by which the strength of various types of chair construction could be evaluated. The method, unfortunately, is difficult to apply because of the size of the equipment required, but it does form the basis for further work that might well be carried on by the LTP to provide chair endurance standards acceptable to the industry and to librarians alike.

Despite the lack of suitable methods for testing durability and general quality of construction, there are methods for testing the finishes used on wood furniture and one accepted test for evaluating the quality of glue and the methods used in the fabrication of wood panels and table tops. These tests, which are not new, have been widely used for the purchase of institutional furniture. They have also been used in the purchase of library furniture but are not as well known as they should be. Incorporated into wood furniture specifications, these tests can help library purchasers obtain finishes with the beauty, durability, and resistance to abuse required for library furniture.

It should be realized, of course, that it is not enough to write these tests into the specifications. Nor is it enough to ask prospective bidders to certify that their finishes meet these specifications. Samples of the finish to be furnished by the bidder should be submitted to the purchaser who should, in turn, see that they are tested and the results certified to him by a qualified independent testing laboratory. Assuming compliance by bidders with all other aspects of the bid documents, the award can be based on the results of the laboratory evaluation. While these tests are incomplete, as regards all the performance characteristics of wood furniture, they are sufficiently rigorous to ensure the elimination of cheaper grades of furniture.

Most large cities have one or more qualified testing laboratories which may be located through the yellow pages of the telephone directory. In some cases, the city purchasing agent will have knowledge of such laboratories. Lacking other sources of information, the librarian may write to the Library Technology Project of the American Library Association for a list of testing laboratories in his area.

The cost of these tests, which must be borne by the purchaser, will be approximately one hundred twenty-five dollars per set, although charges vary somewhat from one laboratory to another. Testing costs, however, are negligible when compared with their effectiveness in eliminating poorly finished furniture.

Although these tests are in general use, variations are used by different laboratories. Usually, however, it will be better to insist that the methods cited here be used. In any case, the laboratory requested to conduct such tests should be identified and the tests discussed with the personnel who are to run them, before the specifications are completed.

In the event of non-award of a bid because of failure to pass these tests, the unsuccessful bidder should receive a copy of the certified report on his product submitted by the testing laboratory.

Samples required for these tests will vary somewhat with the number of panels to be tested for delamination. The sizes given here are those usually preferred for such tests, although this point should be checked with the laboratory conducting the tests.

Samples for testing delamination (where applicable to the specifications concerned) include:

1. Two unfinished test panels, each 6 inches by 6 inches, fully representative of the five-ply, lumber-core construction (or solid, edge-glued construction) to be used in the table tops furnished in response to the specifications.
2. Two unfinished test panels, each 6 inches by 6 inches, fully representative of the five-ply, lumber-core construction (and/or solid, edge-glued construction) to be used in the shelving or other panels to be furnished in response to the specifications.
3. Two unfinished test panels, each 6 inches by 6 inches, fully representative of the plywood veneers to be furnished in response to these specifications.

Samples for testing finish include twelve test panels, finished in complete accordance with the specifications, each 6 inches by 12 inches, plywood veneer construction. Samples should be of the same wood veneer specified, and should be similar in color to that required in the specifications.

Performance Tests for Wood Furniture (Delamination and Finish)

Test No. 1. Cold Soak Test (Delamination)—This test should be conducted in accordance with pro-

cedures established and approved by the Commodity Standard Division of the General Services Administration, Test CS-35-49. Samples, (In writing specifications, a description of the exact sample or samples to be tested should be included here.) fully representative of the materials to be used in the tables furnished on this contract, shall be submerged in water at room temperature for four hours, then dried at temperatures of 70 to 100 degrees F. for twenty hours. After fifteen such cycles, no delamination shall be apparent. Failure to meet this requirement shall be cause of disqualification.

Test No. 2. Hot and Cold Check Test (Finish)—A sample of finished wood shall undergo ten cycles without evidence of checking or finish failure. Each cycle shall consist of exposure for one hour to a temperature of 120 degrees F., one hour at room temperature, one hour at −10 degrees F., and one hour at room temperature. Specimens for this test shall have aged not less than five days after completion of finishing.

Test No. 3. Resistance to Stains (Finish)—The test panel shall be exposed to the following materials:

A. Lipstick—as manufactured by Revlon under the name "Lanolite."
B. Permanent writing ink—as manufactured by the Parker Pen Company, under the name "Permanent Black."
C. Carbon paper—as manufactured by Carter under the trade-mark "Midnight."
D. Coca-Cola.
E. Reclaimed rubber such as used in rubber heels.
F. Rubber stamp pad ink—as manufactured by Sanford under the name "Sanford Opaque."
G. De-natured alcohol.
H. Acetone.

Liquid agents are to be applied one-half teaspoon directly to the surface, while solid agents, such as carbon paper and lipstick, are to be rubbed on the surface. All should be allowed to stand four hours, after which the surfaces are to be washed with distilled water, followed with lacquer thinner. Any change in the appearance of the finish following this final treatment shall be deemed a failure.

Test No. 4. Resistance to Fading (Finish)—Specimen of finished wood shall have one-half of the surface suitably masked and then exposed to two General Electric 275 watt R.S. sunlamps for sixteen hours. Specimen is to be placed 24 inches from the lamp, and temperature of sample is not to exceed 100 degrees F. At the end of the test, any appreciable difference between the masked and unmasked portions of the specimen shall be considered failure and cause for disqualification. Color of the sample must match as closely as possible that submitted by the owner.

Test No. 5. Resistance to Heat (Finish)—A specimen of finished wood shall tolerate a well-lighted cigarette laid flat on the surface with the burning end in actual contact with the finish for a period of 30 seconds, without permanent damage. Inability of the finish to meet this minimum requirement shall be considered a failure.

Test No. 6. Resistance to Scratching (Finish)— Using method 6303 of Federal Test Method Standard No. 141, with an applied maximum load on the Hoffman Scratch Tester, but with only *one* stroke of the scratch tool across the surface, the finish must not be completely removed at the completion of this stroke.

Test No. 7. Resistance to printing (Finish)— Using method 6211 of Federal Test Method Standard No. 141, a specimen of finished wood shall be subjected to a weight of not less than two pounds per square inch at 110 degrees F., applied over a surface 8 inches square covered with 00440B, Type III, cheesecloth, for 24 hours. Any evidence of printing shall be considered a failure.

Test No. 8. Resistance to Humidity (Finish)— The finish shall withstand 100 per cent relative humidity and 110 degrees F. for a period of 72 hours, without any permanent discoloration or softening of the varnish film.

Test No. 9. Resistance to Hot Water (Finish)— Twenty-five cc. of boiling water shall be poured on the finished surface and allowed to cool to room temperature. The water shall then be wiped from the surface and the finish examined for spotting, blushing, or softening. Any evidence of these conditions shall be considered a failure.

Test No. 10. Resistance to Cleaning Compounds (Finish)—A 5 per cent solution of trisodium phosphate shall remain in contact with the finished surface for a period of twelve hours and shall cause no permanent discoloration or softening of the film.

Test No. 11. Resistance to Normal Wear and Abrasion—This test is to be conducted in accordance with the following procedure: A wood block with rounded edges, approximately 4 inches by 6 inches, faced with 1.05-54 sateen and loaded with a total weight of 10 lbs., plus or minus $\frac{1}{2}$ pound, shall be moved reciprocally across the surface of the sample. The pad shall be saturated with Dutch Cleanser paste (20 grams of Dutch Cleanser in one ounce, liquid measure, tap water). Rewet with paste every fifty reciprocations. The finish shall withstand at least 100 motions in each direction without being worn through to the wood.

APPENDIX II

General Criteria for Evaluating Library Wood Furniture

In the space available here, it is possible to provide only a partial list of the criteria used by an expert in judging the quality of library furniture. Further, these criteria, depending as they do largely upon visible characteristics, cannot be fully indicative of the durability of the construction or the quality of the finish. Nevertheless, close attention to such details will help the untrained person to be a better judge of library furniture, whether it be in the showroom, in an exhibit, or in a library installation. Librarians with some experience in the purchase of library furniture are already familiar with many of these principles.

General Criteria

Stability—Subject the piece to normal use or occupancy. Shifting the weight several times will enable the user to determine if the joints are strong and if the elements of the piece are individually and collectively rigid.

Finish—The quality of the finish depends upon the preparation of the wood by sanding, as well as upon the finishing materials and their method of application. An experienced furniture man can judge quality with his hands, by the smoothness of the exposed edges and, more important, by the unexposed edges which are, nevertheless, subject to contact by hand or leg, i.e., by the smoothness of the undersides of the top, the aprons, stretchers, rungs, and similar parts. Smoothness of the unexposed parts normally indicates the quality climate surrounding the manufacture of the piece.

In judging furniture for library use, the finish need not be of the same quality as a piece of fine living room furniture which has been hand-rubbed many times. In all cases, however, the film thickness must be substantial and continuous. The unexposed surfaces should have a good finish, even if not of the same quality as used in the exposed areas. The back and the undersides of all panels and tops should have at least a coat of sealer.

The above follows the rule of furniture economics. Sanding and finishing are the most expensive operations in the plant. Unless required by the quality standards of the manufacturer or by the trade he solicits, these operations are not extended beyond the minimum. Keep in mind, therefore, that a reasonably well-constructed piece of furniture may not have a high quality sanding and finishing job, but rare indeed is the piece of well-sanded and finished furniture that is not of real quality in both material and manufacture.

Specific Criteria

Check chairs for:

1. *Comfort*—the chair should support the user's legs and back when the chair is in position of normal use; *height of chair arms*—arms should not be too low or too high to be comfortable; *contour of seat*—some depression in the center makes chairs more comfortable; *slope of seat from front to back*—an excessive slope tilts body away from the surface of the table and is uncomfortable for writing or for reading with the book on the top of the table.
2. *Strength*—there should be no flex or wobble of any joints. The best construction uses a minimum of two dowels where seat rails join back posts.
3. *Finish*—feel arm rests, seat edges, and stretchers.
4. *Joints*—should be tight and well fitted.

Check tables for:

1. *Stability*—stand at one end and lean, exerting forward and downward pressure; table should neither tip nor rock. (Adjustable glides should be furnished.)
2. *Top construction*—judge for proper support

and top thickness by having someone sit on the table near the center. Deflection should not exceed $\frac{1}{8}$ inch in 6 feet. No permanent deflection should be observed. Larger tables, depending upon design, may require a keel for rigidity. Poor construction can frequently be detected by the interior elements telegraphing through face veneers. Throw a beam of light across the table surface at a low angle. Poorly dried interior elements and joints will stand out in relief.

3. *Leg attachment*—turn table on side and attempt to move leg. No motion of leg at point of attachment and no flexing normally indicates good construction.

Check card catalog cabinets for:

1. *Proper fit of drawers*—they should slide readily but not be loose. Interchange several drawers—the degree of fit should be the same. Drawer runners are of solid hardwood in good construction; beware of plywood runners.
2. *Joint construction*—wide, close fitting dovetails should be used in attaching drawer sides to tray fronts. Attachment of tray backs to sides may be by dovetails or box joints, although the locking characteristic of the dovetail favors its use. Small glue blocks in the back corners add strength and help to protect the tray against damage when dropped.
3. *Hardware*—check tray pulls for rough surfaces or sharp edges. Try card compression mechanism for ease of motion.
4. *Sliding reference shelves*—shelves should slide easily, but not be a loose fit. Examine stops for sturdiness; light wood screws soon pull out or break.

Check case goods generally for:

1. *Joints*—should be tight, well fitted.
2. *Moving parts*—drawers, doors, pull-out slides, all should be smooth running and well-fitted.

ABOUT THE AUTHOR—At the time this article was written (1965) Mr. Pryce was a furniture consultant in Grand Rapids, Michigan.

Furniture and Equipment: Sizes, Spacing, and Arrangement

by Keyes D. Metcalf

As the planning process progresses, the librarian must try actual arrangements in detail to realize the best function and utilization of space. Achieving an effective layout is usually done by the trial and error process—a tracing paper—working and re-working the layout until the optimum arrangement is reached. Mr. Metcalf gives us expert advice for the layout of seating accommodations, shelving and card catalog cases.

Equipment layout is not an exact science. "Circumstances alter cases." Compromises are inevitable due to financial and space limitations. The architect's training and experience enable him to visualize and determine equipment as well as space relationships; in library planning, in which the equipment fulfills such an important function and is so closely related to the lighting, ventilation, and structural concepts, the architect should generally be responsible for the first proposals. However, a library building consultant or a librarian with knowledge and experience in the functioning of libraries can almost always make valuable contributions.

The following requirements should be kept in mind in preparing library layouts:

A. They should not give an appearance of congestion. This is important, since a library's use is inevitably affected by the first impression received by a newcomer.

B. The reader who is occupying his chosen seating accommodation or who is consulting the catalog, the reference and bibliography collections, or working at the shelves, should not feel that he is in an unpleasantly crowded situation; he should not be interfered with unnecessarily by his neighbors, and he should not interfere with them.

C. The reader should have satisfactory seating accommodations with suitable privacy, an adequate working surface, and a comfortable chair. At the same time it should be remembered that square footage is the greatest single factor in building costs, that it should be utilized to the full, and that unused space rarely adds as much to the general effect as does quality equipment.

D. The areas required for furniture and equipment include both the space occupied by the equipment and that used for access to it. The latter takes more than the former. Six square feet may be generous for a working surface for one person, and a good-sized chair occupies less than four square feet, but to provide one suitable accommodation in a reading area may take twenty-five square feet, over sixty per cent of it for access purposes. Book shelves rarely take more than thirty per cent of the total stack area. The same is true for catalog cases in the catalog room.

This article will confine itself to three types of library equipment: seating accommodations, shelving, and card catalog cases. Between them they present an opportunity to discuss basic layout principles:

1. The size of the equipment to be used must be determined.

2. Aisles, as already stated, are the greatest users of square footage. They should be considered with the same care as the equipment. Most access aisles should be used on both sides in order to obtain full value from them. An aisle along a wall used from one side only is generally wasteful. The width of an aisle should depend on appearance and on the

SOURCE: Reprinted from Keyes D. Metcalf, "Furniture and Equipment: Sizes, Spacing, and Arrangements," *Library Trends*, vol. 13, no. 4, April, 1965, pp. 488–502, by permission of the publisher.

amount of use it will receive. Aisles and corridors with solid walls on both sides, feel and look narrower than those of the same width which are completely or partially open on one or both sides at table top level, or even anywhere below eye level. A cross stack aisle with book stack ranges at right angles, seems wider than one of the same width between two parallel stack ranges.

3. In planning layouts watch for visual and auditory distractions. Acoustic protection is as important as visual protection. Seating accommodations adjacent to heavily travelled traffic arteries are generally unsatisfactory in both of these connections.

4. Long and much used corridors should generally be kept straight, although many architects very properly like to introduce visual barriers in them. Often this can be done with light as well as by equipment, walls, or doors.

Long rows of regimented tables and chairs in a large reading area tend to make the room look like a railroad station. One possible exception may be the use of carrels along a wall. This arrangement will seem like part of the structure, rather than equipment, but even here it may be desirable to break up the rows by the occasional use of a small lounge chair in place of a carrel.

6. Wall shelving around a reading area is not economical in space use because of the wide adjacent aisle that is required. Moreover, if the books are heavily used, consulting them will disturb unnecessarily the readers within the area.

7. Curved walls and acute or obtuse angles waste between ten and twenty-five per cent of the floor area, even with the most careful layout.

SEATING ACCOMMODATIONS

These basic principles for equipment layout apply to seating accommodations in a library. The problem has become more complicated than it was a generation ago, because seating is no longer confined almost entirely to standard library chairs at long tables placed in parallel rows. Academic libraries are being planned today with up to eighty-five per cent individual seating at tables for one, in carrels in a wide variety of positions so arranged that the user has no one sitting immediately beside him, or in lounge chairs—sometimes with tablet arms—separated from each other by an aisle or

a small low table. This change has stemmed primarily from two facts.

1. Most readers today come to academic libraries primarily to read and study, and prefer a reasonable amount of visual and acoustic privacy.
2. Methods have been developed in the past ten years that make it possible to provide adequate individual quarters which use little if any more square footage than was formerly involved in multiple seating at long tables, and thus individual seating has become economically feasible.

This article cannot go into detail in regard to all possible types of seating, but will outline some of the requirements that make them satisfactory for academic readers. These involve adequate working surfaces, space for comfortable access without interfering with or disturbing others, a comfortable chair, of course, and a desirable amount of visual and acoustic privacy.

At a table for two or more persons without partitions between the different accommodations, at least six square feet for each reader is desirable, preferably a surface three feet wide by two feet deep. These dimensions can be reduced in a reserve book room or in an undergraduate library for women to 33 inches by 21 inches if necessary, but the smaller size is not recommended. The shorter dimensions, that is, 33 inches by 21 inches, are as adequate, however, for individual quarters which are cut off from others as the larger ones are at multiple seating tables, because no other reader can overlap onto the space. For advanced and graduate students a table 3 feet, 6 inches wide is preferred, and for one writing a doctoral dissertation, four feet in width is not excessive but is not necessary. If there is even a narrow shelf over the

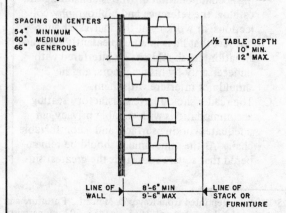

FIGURE 1 Double Staggered Carrels

back of the working surface, a depth of 27 inches is recommended, because the shelf tends to interfere with overhead lighting. (Fluorescent tubes placed under a shelf tend to result in unpleasant reflection and glare because of the angle at which the light reaches the book page. It is sometimes preferable to place shelves over one end of the table instead of at the rear, or to assign a shelf in an adjacent stack section for books wanted for use later.

Access to seating accommodations involves two problems: space for cross aisles and that for direct access to the chairs. Twenty-six inches would seem to be the minimum width for the latter if no other chair is in a position to back into the same space and no other reader needs to pass. This gives 18 inches beyond the front of the table for the chair itself, and 8 additional inches to push the chair back in getting into it. With only 26 inches available, the chair itself should not be overly large, should not have arms, and the corner leg of the table should be set back some 6 inches.

Twenty-six inches of access space is inadequate, however, if one has to pass another's chair to reach his own; here, thirty-two inches should be the minimum, and even then the tables or carrels can well be staggered as shown in Figure 1. Thirty-six inches of access space is generous for carrels staggered in this way.

If carrels or tables for multiple seating have chairs backing into an aisle from both sides, five feet in the clear should be available between the tables; and if the tables are long and passing is frequent, an aisle of six feet is preferable.

Cross aisles, which are not used for seating and are at right angles to tables should preferably be not less than three feet wide, and a wider one is desirable if long tables are on one or both sides. Main cross aisles in a large reading room can well be up to as much as five or six feet in width.

A third requirement for seating is suitable privacy, both visual and acoustic. Partial visual privacy can be obtained by not placing readers so that they face each other over a table; tables with readers on one side only and all facing the same direction will help. A table with chairs on both sides should be four feet across, if possible.

If a table for one can have a partition at its back, it becomes a carrel, but the back should be high enough so that when a reader sits up straight he cannot see the top of the head of the person in front of him bob up from time to time, as that is more distracting than seeing the full torso continuously. An intermittent appearance is as distracting

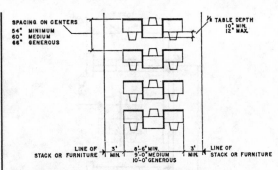

FIGURE 2 Triple Staggered Carrels

as an intermittent sound. A partition to be adequate should be at least fifty inches high for women and at least fifty-two to fifty-four inches for men.

Partitions can also be placed on either side of a reader, as well as in front, but preferably not at both sides. Many readers shut off on both sides feel like a horse with blinders. If partitions are used on both sides, it is suggested that they be omitted in front or held down to ten inches above the table top, as in the triple staggered carrels shown in Figure 2.

Acoustic distraction is increased by hard surfaces, floors, table tops, ceilings, and walls which reflect undesirable noise. Breaking up hard surfaces by projections or indentations helps. Resilient floor coverings, such as cork or rubber tile, will be beneficial also. Carpeted floors and acoustic tile on ceilings are the most useful in this regard. Watch out for noise from wood, vinyl asbestos, and asphalt tile on floors, or from formica on table tops. Occasionally, acoustically treated

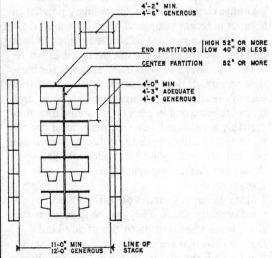

FIGURE 3 Double Carrels in Stack Area

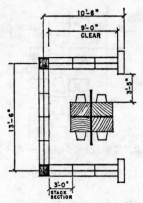

FIGURE 4   Reading Alcove, with Table for Four

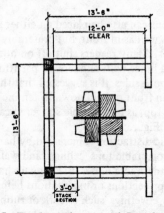

FIGURE 5   Reading Alcove, with Pinwheel Carrels

walls are indicated and one should remember that books themselves have acoustical properties. Heavy traffic in a reading area increases the chances of both visual and acoustic distraction.

Lounge chairs have been increasingly popular in libraries in recent years, and some have used them for twenty-five per cent of all the seating. Others find that lounge chairs are not occupied as much as those in carrels or even those at tables for multiple seating. It depends somewhat on the seriousness of the students. Lounge chairs are most useful in browsing and in periodical rooms; they may desirably constitute five to ten per cent of the total seating in a library, and very rarely over fifteen per cent. Properly placed and selected, they should not increase equipment costs or square footage used.

Many different varieties of carrels have been devised in recent years. They can be in single rows along walls, screens or partitions of any kind. Double rows that are staggered can be very satisfactory with the readers sitting in opposite direc-tions, as shown in Figure 1. Triple rows of staggered carrels can be used in a large reading area with fairly good-sized aisles on each side as shown in Figure 2. Double rows of carrels all facing the same way, with the partitions at the back of each table and on one side, can be placed in a reading area or substituted for two stack ranges (see Figure 3). Tables for four with partitions running in both directions can be used in a reading room or a reading alcove, as shown in Figure 4. In an alcove the clear space for this arrangement should be at least 10 feet, 6 inches wide and 9 feet deep. If it is 12 feet deep, a pinwheel or swastika arrangement can be used, as in Figure 5. Double carrels 5 feet wide are sometimes used in coeducational institutions for couples, and this may help to make the areas quieter, rather than otherwise.

Small areas in a book stack called oases have been used in Princeton University and elsewhere, but unless individual seating with partitions is arranged, they may become trouble spots. Large stack oases, occupying the space of the full module or perhaps more, can be used to advantage in a very large stack to break the monotony. Individual seating, special lighting, and perhaps a carpeted floor may be indicated.

SHELVING

The volume capacity for a book stack can be estimated only roughly because of irregular volume sizes. Leaving that factor out of consideration, it depends on the square footage required for the average single-faced standard size section three feet wide overall and 7 feet, 6 inches high. (This height will give space for a protective base four inches high and seven shelves twelve inches on centers, plus an extra two inches at the top to make it easier to withdraw and replace books there.) The square footage required depends on these several factors.

1. The non-assignable space for stairs, lifts, and entrances should not exceed more than ten per cent of the total area, except in a very small stack, and in a large one less than that. It is not considered further in this statement.

2. Section or shelf depths with the commonly used bracket shelves are generally seven or nine inches "actual" or eight or ten inches "nominal." With the two inches left vacant in the center of a double-faced range, this means sixteen inches or twenty inches over-

all depth. The writer prefers in most cases to use eight-inch "actual" shelves with eighteen inches overall depth, and with the bottom shelves no wider than the upper ones. The bottom shelf is the critical point for light, for book trucks, and for squatting or kneeling users. Each additional inch depth of shelves, including that for the base, reduces the capacity by two per cent. A twenty-four inch base in a double-faced section reduces capacity by approximately twelve per cent below that for an eighteen-inch base, if aisle widths are uniform. The narrow base requires safety precautions to insure stability, but these are relatively inexpensive.

3. The stack aisle width should depend on the amount of traffic and the length of the ranges. The longer the range, the more often two persons will have to pass each other. A twenty-six inch aisle width is possible for closed access storage, and one of thirty inches is generous even with very long ranges with closed access. Thirty-three inches with thirty foot long ranges will be adequate in a university library with large collections and access restricted to advanced students and faculty. Thirty-six inches can be called standard for a heavily used stack.

    Range length is also of importance, and like aisle widths should vary according to use. Nine to fifteen feet may be long enough for ranges in a heavily used reference collection, and fifteen for an undergraduate collection. Thirty feet in length has generally been considered the maximum for university libraries but, with limited access and collections of one million volumes or more, can be extended to as much as forty-two feet. Great national libraries with closed access stacks have used ranges up to sixty feet in length satisfactorily when proper labeling is provided. Remember that range spacing with long ranges in a modular stack must be based on column spacing.

4. The final factor to be considered is the frequency and the width of the cross aisles at right angles to the ranges. Three feet (minus two inches for the uprights on each side) should ordinarily be considered a minimum; if the stack is large, a main cross aisle should be not less than four or four and a half feet. An aisle of five or six feet is generous, and the latter may be extravagant in space use. Remember that three feet is ten per cent of

thirty feet, and an extra three-foot aisle cutting a thirty-foot range in two reduces capacity by ten per cent, and a six-foot wide aisle where a four-foot one will do is a factor worth keeping in mind.

In a modular stack the distance between column centers should be an exact multiple of the distance between the range centers. Of less but still of considerable importance, the clear distance between columns in the direction of the ranges should be a multiple of three feet, plus four inches to allow for any irregularity in the building columns and for the adjacent stack uprights.

In laying out a stack, remember to provide a simple arrangement for the books and the traffic. Avoid what might be called blind areas that interfere with the regular order of book shelving, and if small areas behind stairs or in corners are necessary, use them for special collections rather than for parts of the main collection.

Avoid odd-length sections as far as possible, as they will always be a nuisance. If, because of columns, odd length sections seem to be required from time to time, it may be preferable to use lecterns or consultation tables in their place.

Narrow aisles reduce the available light on the backs of the books on the lower shelves. If fluorescent tubes are used and the ceiling height permits it, the intensity on the lower shelves can be increased by placing the light tubes at right angles to the ranges.

Watch out for places used to house oversize books; they may require deeper shelves and the aisles will be unduly narrowed. Suitable locations can often be found along walls, stairs, or elevators.

Remember that carrels, placed along a wall adjacent to a three-foot cross aisle, or used in place of the last stack section, are space savers.

With the above in mind, it should be repeated that the square footage required per single-faced stack section depends, if non-assignable space is omitted, on the depth of the shelves, the width of stack aisles and of the cross aisles, and the length of ranges. Figures 6 and 7 show examples and indicate also the effect of carrel seating along walls. Changes in square footage requirements result from a change in any of the dimensions. But it is fair to state that if non-assignable space is left out of consideration, $8\frac{1}{3}$ square feet per single-faced section is adequate with what can be called standard university library spacing, but it is better to use between that figure and ten square feet for smaller libraries with heavy stack use. In figuring

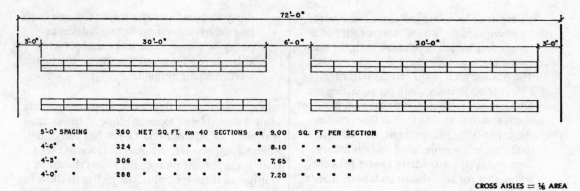

5'-0" SPACING   360 NET SQ. FT. FOR 40 SECTIONS OR 9.00 SQ. FT PER SECTION
4'-6"   "   324 "   "   "   "   "   "   "   " " 8.10 "   "   "
4'-3"   "   306 "   "   "   "   "   "   "   " " 7.65 "   "   "
4'-0"   "   288 "   "   "   "   "   "   "   " " 7.20 "   "   "

CROSS AISLES = ⅙ AREA

FIGURE 6   Stack Layout

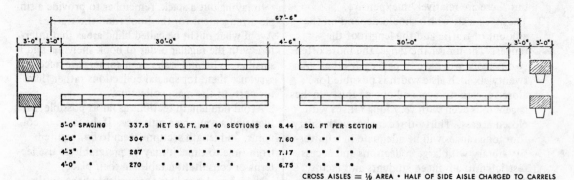

5'-0" SPACING   337.5 NET SQ. FT. FOR 40 SECTIONS OR 8.44 SQ. FT PER SECTION
4'-6"   "   304   "   "   "   "   "   "   "   " " 7.60 "   "   "
4'-3"   "   287   "   "   "   "   "   "   "   " " 7.17 "   "   "
4'-0"   "   270   "   "   "   "   "   "   "   " " 6.75 "   "   "

CROSS AISLES = ⅙ AREA • HALF OF SIDE AISLE CHARGED TO CARRELS

FIGURE 7   Stack Layout

volume capacity per single-faced standard section, 125 books should be considered as working capacity, but that is another story which cannot be dealt with here.

CARD CATALOG CASES

In most libraries, the primary problem in arranging catalog cabinets or cases is the provision of adequate space for the readers at the time of peak load, rather than space for the cards, although this is too seldom realized. It is possible, in a very large library with millions of cards, to provide for 4,000 of them for each square foot of floor space in the catalog room. On the other hand, in a large university with a small collection 1,000 cards to a square foot is often all that should be installed. There are three space users to be kept in mind in connection with catalog case layout: the cases themselves, the consultation tables, and the aisles for access required by those who consult the cards. These will be considered in that order.

The cases vary widely in overall dimensions. The Widener Library Building at Harvard Univer-

sity has catalog cases holding over 500 trays, but these can be called "white elephants." In order to obtain flexibility, cases today are generally constructed in units 5 or 6 trays wide and measuring from just over 33 inches to approximately 40 inches in width. The depths may vary from 12 inches up to just over 19 inches, although 24 inches is used occasionally, but the generally considered standard length is 17 inches. Whatever the overall depth of a tray, approximately 3 inches should be subtracted from it, because of the unusable space at the front and back, and then between 70 and 75 per cent of the remaining space will represent that available for storing cards before the drawers become so full as to be more or less unmanageable. One hundred cards to an inch of usable filing space is a safe figure to use. This will mean that a tray 17 inches long will house comfortably 1,000 cards (17" - 3" = 14" and 14" × 72% = 1008), and one 19 inches long will house 1,150 cards (19" - 3" = 16" and 16" × 72% = 1152).

The height of the case does not affect the floor space it occupies, but is an important factor in the amount of floor space required to house a given number of cards. Standard cases in the United States have generally been 10 to 12 trays high, but many colleges and universities have used and are using successfully cases 14 or 15 trays high. One with 15 trays will give 50 per cent greater capacity in the same area than one with ten. It is possible to buy cases in units, and those 10 trays high can be installed to start with and a 5-tray high case placed on top of it later. This may not look as well and will cost more per tray, but with careful design should not be too unsatisfactory.

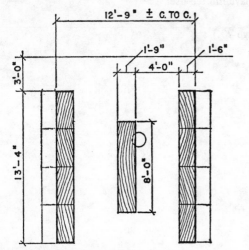

FIGURE 8 Catalog Case Layout

One decision that must be made in connection with catalog case arrangements is whether or not there should be a sliding reference shelf in them at a suitable height for consultation. This is rarely to be recommended because its use will block the access to a good many trays above and below and at each side, and it will tend to be a space user, rather than a space saver.

Consultation tables on which the user of the catalog places the tray that he wishes to consult are almost always desirable. Again, there is the problem of their height, width, and length. Tables should rarely be more than 6 to 8 feet long, because it will make it too difficult to go around them to reach the trays on the other side. The width can be anywhere from 20 inches (or even less) up to 3 feet. Tables 3 feet wide can be used to better advantage from both sides at the same time than narrower ones, and sometimes should be selected if the use anticipated is very heavy. Thirty-nine inches used to be the standard height for consultation tables, but many libraries have found that 41 inches or 42 inches is preferable, as it prevents a tall person from leaning over the ta-

ble or having his feet stick out behind him so far as to cause trouble. Experience indicates that persons no less than 5 feet tall can use a table 42 inches high with little inconvenience.

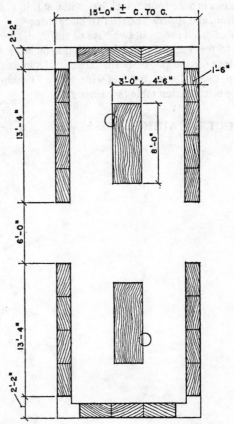

FIGURE 9 Catalog Case Layout for a Large Library

The third and greatest user of space in a catalog room is that for the aisles, those between the cases and the consultation tables, and also the cross aisles at right angles to the case ranges. The former can be as narrow as 2 feet, 6 inches where the cases are available only to the staff. Aisles up to 5 feet, 6 inches wide are not uncommon, but are unfortunate as they result in unused space and, of equal importance, the reader and the filer often object to carrying the tray to the consultation table and will often try to use it at the catalog where they will get in the way of others. For such aisles, 4 feet, 6 inches is generous, 4 feet, 3 inches is adequate, and 4 feet will not cause congestion if the consultation tables are not over 6 feet or 8 feet long.

In trying to arrange spacing for a large catalog in

a modular building, note that two full ranges of catalog cases will fit in a 25 feet, 6 inch column spacing, giving 12 feet, 9 inches on centers for the cases. Thirteen feet, six inches, or two to a 27-foot column spacing, is generous; but two ranges of cases in a 22 foot, 6 inch bay will result in congestion, and it may be better to place three double-faced ranges in two bays of this size, giving 15 feet each. Twelve feet and nine inches will provide for the two cases that are each 18 inches deep, two aisles, each 4 feet wide, and a 21 inch-wide consultation table (see Figure 8).

There is still the problem of cross aisles to be considered. There must, of course, be an adequate cross aisle at at least one end of the case ranges and preferably at both, if space is available. To two parallel ranges, it is possible to add a third range at right angles, making a three-sided alcove which will give larger capacity. Double rows of alcoves with cases on three sides and with one cross aisle are possible and provide the greatest space utilization (see Figure 9). However, this is recommended only with very large collections which have limited use.

ABOUT THE AUTHOR—(See biographical note on page 79.)

Selecting Informal Seating for University and College Libraries

by Donald D. Powell

One way to attract library usage is by providing "the comforts of home." But providing such comforts can bring problems of informality leading to unwanted noise and abuse of the library and its furnishings. "Informal furnishings must stand up not only to the eye, but to the hardest usage, to dust-laden air, to moisture, smoke, grit, chemicals, stains, spills, friction and other attacks on their integrity, attacks both frontal and insidious." To aid us in selection of furniture that does "stand up" Mr. Powell has written these guidelines.

The selection of informal library seating is directly related to its intended function and location within the library. It must fit the environment and achieve a character suitable for the purpose its serves. It must, above all, be comfortable, no matter what use it is required to satisfy. Within each of these characteristics, recognition must be given to varying reader demands and to the manner in which, for example, bibliographic materials, periodicals, and browsing collections are handled. Special elements, such as audio-visual facilities, lounges, typing rooms, and similar areas, are aspects of informal use in which the character of the space relates to its special function. Group study rooms and separate smoking rooms are relatively new and important definitions of specialized, informal readers' space. The use and disposition of informal furnishings develops out of the recognition of new demands created by changes in the sociological habits of readers.

Basic planning for informal furnishings should begin with a coordinated design program which will result in a selection of items which will complement each other, which will produce an environmental expression suitable for an informal readers' area in the library, and which will achieve proper harmony with the library as a whole.

Careful study must be made of the location and individual placement of informal seating. The classic lounge chair grouping around a coffee table, frequently used in libraries but so closely related to the home living room environment, encourages oral communication between students occupying such seats. In many instances this is not an appropriate use of library facilities. The desirability of using sofa units in these informal areas should also be carefully evaluated because of the risk that such furniture will not be properly used. Reclining or sleeping on sofas in lounge areas is not only inappropriate for the library environment, but results in one person using space designed for two or three.

Today, library planning emphasizes the individual reader and his environment. Informal seating should limit rather than encourage oral communication and the consequent distraction of others in areas where quiet is required. At the same time, there is a need for the design of better informal seating. Such seating should emphasize comfort and provide for a variety of postures and uses suited to individual needs within that portion of the library in which it is to be placed. In instances where informal seating for group use is desired, this may well be assigned to a separate space such as a smoking room, where talking and lounging will not disturb or distract others.

Coordinated planning, identification of proper functional designs, and a carefully evaluated layout of informal furnishings are important preliminaries to final selection. Here, durability and suitability of construction are of prime importance.

Since adults and teen-agers can do a great deal of

SOURCE: Reprinted from Donald D. Powell, "Selecting Informal Seating for University and College Libraries." *Library Trends*, vol. 13, no. 4, April, 1965, pp. 455–460, by permission of the publisher.

damage to library furniture merely by using it, construction must be durable enough to withstand the attacks of these users. It should be remembered, however, that it is up to the designer to provide a library environment that will arouse both respect and affection for these items. The use of steel legs, laminated plywood bonded to foam rubber, zippered upholstery, and other new methods of construction should be investigated when choosing and selecting informal furniture for a library.

The following construction features, characteristic of well-made, good quality furniture, should be kept in mind when selecting upholstered furnishings. Frame construction may be of any American hardwood, kiln-dried to approximately 5 per cent moisture content. All joints should be double dowelled with birch spiral dowels and glued.

Springing should contain approximately sixteen heavy-duty coil springs per seating space. Spring construction should be of the type usually referred to as "wire edge or spring edge," or that referred to as "tied to frame on hard edge" construction. In either case, springs should be tied 8-ways with jute spring twine, with eight knots per spring, using the French method (criss-cross), or the German method (straight double tie). Covering of springs should be 10 ounce burlap tied through to the springs, with a one-half inch rubberized hair pad on top and a sixteen ounce cotton batting top layer.

Webbing should be used on all inside arms and backs of units, and be covered with a layer of cotton if required by style. Muslin is applied on all first class upholstering jobs before the final upholstery fabric is applied. Upholstery should be of the best standard of workmanship, neatly tailored with all joints straight, welt seams double-stitched, and sufficient returns on the fabric to prevent ripping or tearing. Exposed fabric seams should not be allowed on visible areas of the units. When foam rubber cushions are used, all corners should be mitered and hand-stitched to the covering fabric to prevent movement of the cushion within the cover.

Casters or glides should be carefully chosen for the floor finish in the area where they are to be used. Carpet protectors should be used on all bases where installation is on carpeting or on area rugs, to prevent damage to carpet and to stabilize furniture and prevent movement. Rolling casters (either wheel or ball type) may be

chosen where floor conditions make them desirable. Rubber treads on casters can be used to cut down noise and prevent damage to floor surfaces. Ball-type casters are preferable for use on soft surfaces such as carpeting. Rust proof glides should be furnished where floor mopping and washing is required. Glides should be of proper size to support the weight of the furniture units to prevent imprinting and marking of floors.

Where fire-resistant upholstery is mandatory, the choice of fabric is between vinyl or vinyl-coated fabrics, and tightly woven mohair. Other fibers may be acceptable if they have been given suitable fireproofing treatment. The choice is predicated not only on the initial cost of each unit but on other factors. For example, in temperate climates under high soil conditions, the vinyls may be acceptable. In warm climates and non-air-conditioned buildings, the vinyls can be uncomfortable and are usually not to be recommended. Under low soil conditions, where the interval between cleanings may be long, woven fabrics may be suitable. Here the choice is between fiberglas fabrics and treated fabrics of natural fibers. Fiberglas fabrics, however, although easy to clean, are highly vulnerable to abrasion and wear. Fabrics woven from one of the better synthetic fibers, such as nylon, possess excellent wearing qualities and are available in a good color range. Where soil conditions are sufficiently bad to warrant the choice, removable cushions or zipped-on covers may be used. Special fabric treatments such as "Scotchguard" are recommended where furniture may be exposed to food and liquid stains, or where general soil should be kept to a minimum.

Fabrics should be selected to complement the design of the building and to harmonize with the character and design of the furniture. Fabric texture, print, color, weight, and weave should be carefully selected for each item or type of item in the library. Some fabrics show good wear characteristics when used on a flat surface, but when used on a curved surface, such as the edges of an upholstered seat pad, they split and tear, exposing the inner fibers of the material to abrasion and thereby reducing durability. Other fabrics, when stretched on a tight fitting, upholstered unit reflect light in such a manner that they give the appearance of a stained or soiled fabric. Furnishings which will normally be occupied for relatively long periods at a time should not be covered in vinyl, leather, or other hard-coated surfaces since they become too warm and too moist for comfortable seating. Under such conditions, textured and plush fabrics of woven construction should be specified.

The color scheme should be carefully thought out in planning fabric use. Natural, undyed yarns mixed with dyed yarns in textured fabrics take washing, wear, and soil with little loss of vitality. Synthetic fabrics, such as nylon, should be used where frequent maintenance, such as repeated cleaning, is likely. The type of weave and the color of the fabric are important factors in the durability of the fabric under conditions where constant maintenance is required. A natural colored yarn, for example, is much less subject to discoloration by repeated cleaning than is a dyed yarn. Similarly, the dye characteristics of a loosely woven fabric are superior to those of a tightly woven fabric.

The cost of the labor required to maintain any item of furniture is a valid factor in evaluating its worth. Informal furnishings must stand up not only to the eye, but to the hardest usage, to dust-laden air, to moisture, smoke, grit, chemicals, stains, spills, friction, and other attacks on their integrity, attacks both frontal and insidious. The specifications, implied by the popular word "functional," include both ease of maintenance and the ability to survive the damages inflicted by soil and wear on the one hand and those inflicted by cleaning agents on the other. The most important motivation of the reformation in furniture design which we call "contemporary" was the need to improve maintenance characteristics. Today, institutions should demand interiors that are easy to keep clean and in good repair. The high cost of labor places an enormous financial benefit in the hands of any institution whose premises have been so planned and designed that cleaning and repair are kept to a minimum, both in labor and in time.

The interior designer must provide for the soundness of the interiors he designs, in the fabrication and detailing of the materials he selects as well as in the cleanability and ease of repair thereof. The librarian's responsibility is to provide information about those areas in which wear and tear and soil will occur, and about the equipment, personnel, and work schedules available to maintain them. Proper upkeep in libraries requires both daily care and periodic repair to keep an interior looking its best within the usual amortization period, or until it is more profitable to replace it than to continue maintaining it. Initial investment versus running expense is a major concern in selecting all furnishings for libraries.

In budgeting funds for the interior of a library, the librarian and designer usually have a choice between a high investment in quality materials and workmanship balanced against low maintenance costs in the future, or a low initial investment balanced against higher maintenance costs. The known immediate costs of the furnishings are weighed against unknown future costs consisting largely of labor expenses.

In the present article, it is not possible to treat all the details of this subject. However, the check-list that follows poses a series of questions for which the librarian must have answers before making a final selection of the informal furnishings for the library. For additional information, he should seek the assistance of the architect or interior designer responsible for the building.

1. The cleanliness standard—what is the desired level of cleanliness?
2. Invasion of dirt—what is the location of entry of dirt and traffic?
3. Heating and air-conditioning—will high soil and coating residues affect furniture maintenance?
4. Maintenance versus obsolescence—can the wearability and life of furniture be estimated?
5. Redesign of furniture—must furniture be redesigned to meet changing library needs and requirements?
6. Contingencies of climate—what effects will climate have on maintenance schedules?
7. Fire code requirements—will this affect treatment of upholstery fabrics?
8. Interior structure—what are the limitations on placement of furniture?
9. Lighting fixtures—what will be the relumping and cleaning cycle?
10. Floor cleaning hazards—how and by what type of cleaning equipment will floors be cleaned, what type of baseboards should be specified, what type of legs on furniture should be detailed to resist marks from vacuum cleaners, waxers, and mops? (Fabrics should be out of the way of solvents used on floors. Heavy furniture should be on casters.)
11. Furniture materials and finishes—to what

conditions of wear and soil will furniture be exposed?

12. Types of windows and doors—are dust-catching installations and light control devices required to prevent fading of fabrics?

13. Furniture materials—what are the relative advantages of oiled, lacquered, varnished, and painted finishes on wood furniture and where is metal furniture preferable for low maintenance requirements?

ABOUT THE AUTHOR—At the time this article was written (1965) Mr. Powell was a member of the architectural firm of Skidmore, Owings and Merrill, Chicago, Illinois.

Furniture for Library Offices and Staff Work Areas

by James V. Jones

"There exists a dearth of material about equipping library offices and staff work areas." To remedy the situation Mr. Jones has written the following article to specifically aid planners in selecting furniture for these areas.

When one reflects upon the concentration of interest concerning library buildings and equipment since 1950, and the countless words written and spoken about this subject, it is most surprising that the needs of the library staff itself have been largely ignored. There exists a dearth of material about equipping library offices and staff work areas. However the library profession need not feel too badly about this. Neither has the subject received adequate attention in office management literature.

How would a library continue to give service without an acquisitions department, a cataloging section, periodical records, physical preparation? And yet all of the building and equipment institutes, their resultant publications, and other professional literature expiate at length only about such things as modules, ceiling heights, stack spacing, and lounge furniture. In truth our attention has been given over to the public areas of libraries and the impression and impact that these will make on our public and our peers. As a result we have relegated to hit and miss methods those areas which are truly the nerve centers of our libraries.

Quite obviously, then, the author cannot draw upon a survey of existing literature in order to lay down the doctrines of good furniture selection for library offices and work areas. At the 1962 Library Furniture and Equipment Institute, at Coral Gables, Florida, Martin Van Buren adequately described the lack of references; the librarian, he said, ". . . is left with very little to go on other than manufacturers' catalogs and a few elemental principles."[1]

With today's emphasis on data processing, the term "system analysis" is becoming rather common. No less than a particular routine should the entire "office" operation of a library be subjected to systems analysis. It is here that proper selection of furniture and equipment must start. Only when one is sure that he has achieved the most efficient and effective work distribution, that the work flows smoothly and without interruption, and that proper forms have been designed and useless items eliminated can he sit down to lay out the physical arrangement of furniture and equipment.

A well-done analysis will reveal the optimum number of people or positions needed to accomplish the current work load and the additional positions likely to be needed in the foreseeable future. After preparing a list of equipment used, the planner is ready for a preliminary layout plan.

The listing of equipment used is a critical point. Too often librarians have thought of their work processes as something unique with no counterpart in the business world. As a result, they have been blind to equipment innovations and improvements in business and industry. Not only the administrator definitely planning a new installation, but all library administrators should constantly be aware of new ways of doing things in banks and other business offices which they visit, even in supermarkets and drugstores. Many excellent designs of loan desks have started from the design of new equipment in other fields.

Not only have managers been relatively uninterested in their office layout and equipment in the recent past, but even the manufacturers of such equipment have made no attempt to stimulate their market. One does not have to review manufacturers' catalogs for too many years back

SOURCE: Reprinted from James V. Jones, "Furniture for Library Offices and Staff Work Areas," *Library Trends*, vol. 13, no. 4, April, 1965, pp. 448–454, by permission of the publisher.

to find the era of "Model T" desks. Happily this has now changed radically. One can now find desks designed for any ordinary use in standardized, interchangeable units. Such desks are available in wood or metal, in traditional or modern design, with linoleum or plastic tops, with any variety of drawers and drawer accessories, in colors that are standard or custom. Like comments can also be made in regard to chairs, files, tabulating equipment accessories—even typewriters now vie in design and color.

A relatively recent concept in the design of office furniture and office layout has been that of the work station. This has come about with the use of the L-return unit that is a type of credenza joined to the desk unit to form an L. The depth and height as well as the type of cabinets or drawers of the L-return is determined by the work to be done at that work station. The variety of units available to customize work stations had led to the labeling of such units as modular units.

In planning work areas just as in the public areas, a keynote today is space economy. The modular units make possible the ultimate in space conservation while providing, at the same time, a more efficient work station than was possible with traditional office furniture. Thoroughly planned use of modular office furniture has not yet been fully exploited in libraries. It should be in the future.

In the past, perhaps as a "fringe benefit" to compensate for low pay, we have tended to be too lavish with space allocated for work stations. Every clerk was assigned to a secretarial desk no matter what his duties. The keynote of space conservation noted above no longer allows us this luxury. Even though one does not use the new modular furniture, desks should be selected to fit the job. For the typist whose regular assignment is the preparation of catalog cards, a 42-inch fixed bed typewriter desk is adequate and satisfactory.

On the other hand it is equally important to provide a large and versatile desk for the position that demands it. When space saving cuts into the efficiency and morale of a staff member, it is no longer a saving.

In any desk the selection of the proper drawers and drawer inserts is important and very often overlooked. The girl typing catalog cards finds a drawer with a stationery rack completely useless. The administrator will gladly give up two standard storage drawers to have a file drawer in which he may keep frequently used files at ready call.

Metal or wood, plastic or linoleum top, tra-

ditional or contemporary design, bright colors or office grey—most of these decisions must be left to the librarian or his consultant. One can find convincing arguments on either side and quite often the selection will depend upon one's personal taste or the location of the installation. Two hints of caution need to be mentioned. One will not find a concise explanation of the fine points of office furniture construction, and therefore one cannot base his selection of furniture on established standards. It is recommended that the planner examine carefully several grades of furniture to determine the quality that best suits him and the funds available. In general, the reputable manufacturers will be his best guide.[2]

Secondly, once he has determined this grade or quality, he should purchase all of his furniture from one manufacturer. This will not only prevent many headaches at installation time, but will provide for interchangeability as needs and functions change—which they will, all too soon. It is also the only insurance against a crazy quilt pattern when new furniture is added in the future.

For those in the library who must operate by the seat of their pants, it is very important that they be seated with maximum comfort. This demands a true posture chair; one that can be adjusted in height and depth, and which has a vertically adjustable backrest. Two other adjustments can also be provided: a backrest pitch adjustment and a spring tension adjustment. For the ultimate in comfort and thus in staff efficiency, the office equipment dealer should be contracted to check chair adjustments regularly.

So long as the chair selected is of the true "posture" type, it matters little for worker efficiency what its design, its fabric, or its base may be. As with desks, these are matters of taste, total decor, and available funds. Certainly there will be gradations of quality and certainly reputable manufacturers should set the standard.

Library offices *per se* will range from the private enclosed space assigned to the higher administrators, to the smaller, semi-enclosed type formed by movable partitions and occupied by various supervisors. Selection of type of furniture, its finish, supporting units, and accessories will depend upon the position of the administrator and the nature and variety of his duties.

The top administrator will ordinarily have the finest desk in the library although not necessarily or even desirably the highest quality. The modular U station is becoming the standard in executive offices. There is no end to the accessories that can be provided in a custom-built desk for the administrator. Most librarians, even if they could, would not expect their desk to be fitted with television, refrigerator, bar, etc. But executive desks of today have as standard such things as built-in dictation stations, personal files, and other convenient work organizers.

As one moves from one administrative office to another, the differing duties will dictate the furniture needs. This man uses dictating equipment, Miss S needs a typewriter, Mr. T is a regular user of a calculator, etc.

Quite often it will be necessary to custom design equipment for special needs. This will most often happen when one is planning a new library and has the opportunity to employ designers from the architect's or interior decorator's staff. Rather universally, comments are made that these people really do not understand the work of librarians and so prepare a faulty design. More likely, the librarian is not sufficiently aware of what he needs himself and so does not adequately describe his needs to the designer. If a table is needed to carry a special piece of equipment such as a cutter, the dimensions of the equipment must be made known to the designer. Likewise if the cutter is to be used with the operator standing up, one does not want the table to be at desk height of 29 inches. The librarian should carefully check the final drawings and specifications of all specially designed equipment for just such mistakes. He should above all not be reluctant to ask for an explanation of anything not clear to him in such specifications. Far better to admit ignorance at this point than to be stuck with a $500 piece of white elephant.

Quite easy to overlook, but of great importance are many items of everyday humdrum use. What will be done with wraps, boots, and umbrellas? Will there be staff lockers? Wardrobes? Costumers? What provision is there for trash? Wastebaskets at each desk? Type? Style? Color? What of waste from incoming shipments? How to store packaging materials for interlibrary loans? Binding shipments? Where and how will everyday supplies be housed? Is there duplicating equipment in ordinary working areas, such as a mimeograph and office photocopiers? What provision is made for housing these and their supplies? What provision is made for clocks and water fountains? Obviously all of the above items are minor. But enough minor irritants piled one on another soon lead to bad staff morale, bickering, and reduced efficiency and production.

The increasing rapidity with which larger libraries are using data processing equipment raises new problems of equipment selection. In this case, it is necessary that librarians seek the advice and guidance of those who have had such installations for some time. University libraries will likely find departments on their own campus which can advise them. Others must seek the advice of local businesses. There are companies specializing in the manufacture and sale of supporting equipment for data processing departments. As with library and office furniture, many will furnish guidance in actual layout of an efficient department based upon the data processing equipment to be installed.

At this point, one has presumably designated his personnel needs and the equipment which will be used to complete the necessary tasks in an efficient and economical fashion. Now these must be reduced to a scale model drawing fitting them into the space available. Not to be overlooked at this time is the location of electric outlets, telephone stations, plumbing such as sinks and running water, doors and their direction of swing (which are interior and which exterior?), conditioned air outlets—hot or cold, windows, columns, and other building details. Desks for typists using electrical typewriters should not be placed fifty feet from the nearest electrical outlet. A desk is not wanted in the natural corridor of traffic that a door will provide. All of which is quite obvious, but surprisingly quite often overlooked.

When the scale diagram is drawn, the librarian should sit down and trace the work flow through the various areas. Where are orders prepared? Where mailed? At what point is incoming mail received, unpacked, and sorted? This flow of work needs to be charted throughout the area from the time an operation starts until it is finished. When such tracing is completed, the librarian can readily see whether the proposed layout is actually the most efficient possible. Most likely it will not be. Then comes shifting, redrawing, and retracing of work flow. Eventually the optimum will be reached.

This is still not the end, however. There are certain space factors to be considered over and above the worker, his furniture, and equipment. The most obvious is the traffic flow. The need for secondary and intermediate aisles could not possibly be determined until the optimum layout for work flow was determined. Traffic flow must now be studied and adequate aisle space provided: three to four feet for secondary and intermediate aisles, five feet for main aisles, and six to eight feet for corridors to the exits.[3]

At this point one may ask why the worry and trouble over a few extra feet of walking. After all we do need exercise, and the entire length of the cataloging area can be walked in just one-half minute! But let us take those thirty seconds and suppose that they are lost at each of ten steps a book takes from ordering to shelving. We now have five minutes of lost time per book. Should the library be growing at 10,000 books per year, these extra five minutes total 833 hours in a year.

Those 833 hours represent over $1,000, or quite a few more books that could have been added for the public's use.

Eventually one looks at paper diagrams until no further progress can be made in bettering work flow or traffic movement. At this point there is nothing more to be done. Most likely the schematic drawing will suffice to provide an efficiently functioning department for at least the first year—that is unless Miss P happens to have her chair right below that noisy air diffuser!

NOTES

[1] American Library Association, Library Administration Division in cooperation with the University of Miami. *Proceedings of a Three-Day Institute on Library Furniture and Equipment Conducted at Coral Gables, Florida, June 14–16, 1962.* Chicago, American Library Association, 1963, p. 7.

[2] Ellsworth, Ralph E. *Planning the College and University Library Building: A Book for Campus Planners and Architects.* Boulder, Pruett Press, Inc., 1960, pp. 89–93.

[3] National Stationery and Office Equipment Association. *How to Plan Your Office Space.* Washington, National Stationery and Office Equipment Association, 1964, p. 29.

ABOUT THE AUTHOR—James V. Jones was graduated from John Carroll University (B.S.) in 1949 and from Western Reserve University (M.S.) in 1950. After holding the position of Director of Libraries at St. Louis University and Cleveland State University he became Director of the Case Western Reserve University library system. Mr. Jones writes for professional journals and since 1963 has been a library examiner and consultant.

Preparation of Bidding Documents for Library Furnishings and Equipment

by Frazer G. Poole

The planning agency (the city or county, the college or university) will have experts on its staff who are qualified to write specifications, prepare bidding documents and evaluate bids. The librarian will be called upon to contribute his special knowledge of library furniture and equipment. The success of all other planning efforts can be endangered by sloppily or hastily prepared bidding documents and the librarian must carry ultimate responsibility for review of the documents. Very little has been written to aid him in understanding bidding routines and procedures. The following article by Mr. Poole has filled this gap in the literature. This paper should be studied by all who are contemplating placing major purchase orders for library furnishings and equipment.

Any librarian who has searched for information on the preparation of contract documents for library furnishings and equipment has been surprised to find that this subject is scarcely mentioned in the library literature and treated only in the most cursory fashion in the literature of purchasing or business management. Indeed, one suspects that this aspect of purchasing procedures is passed from one practitioner to another as were medieval crafts.

In consequence, this discussion is based upon personal experience and upon the experience of librarians and purchasing agents who, of necessity, have prepared or reviewed bidding documents for library furnishings. I am grateful to the several librarians who have shared their experiences with me, as well as to those who have sent me copies of the bidding documents used in furnishing their libraries. I am likewise indebted to those manufacturers of library furnishings who offered suggestions based upon their experiences with the bidding problems of library furnishings.

Some aspects of bidding procedures are subject to varying opinions and to different legal requirements. For some problems there is no one accepted solution. Where possible, both points of view are discussed.

One can hardly suggest that the furnishings of a library are more important than the building. Yet, there is general agreement that the best of new buildings can be enhanced by properly selected furnishings, or that much of the effect created by the architect can be lost if library furnishings are not appropriate in design and in quality. Furniture that does not withstand the rigorous treatment it receives by library users, bookstacks with finishes that abrade too rapidly or with shelves that will not support the loads to which they are subjected, table legs that soon come loose, upholstery that pulls away from the frame, desks with drawers that do not slide properly—these and others are defects that reduce efficiency and add to the cost of library management. Thus, problems affecting the efficient procurement of library furnishings are of special concern to the librarian responsible for modernizing an old building or equipping a new building.

Disappointing—often critical—delays, rebidding, wasted funds, inappropriately designed or badly constructed furniture, even lawsuits may result from poorly written purchase or contract documents. Ordinarily, these problems do not receive wide publicity, but they are perhaps more common than is realized. They happen to large institutions as well as to small.

This discussion of the documents required for the purchase of library furnishings and equipment is based primarily upon procedures used in taking

SOURCE: Reprinted from Frazer G. Poole, "The Preparation of Bidding Documents for Library Furnishings and Equipment," in *The Procurement of Library Furnishings,* edited by Frazer G. Poole and Alphonse F. Trezza, Chicago, American Library Association, 1969, pp. 25-33, by permission of the publisher.

competitive bids. Competitive bidding is nearly always used where tax funds are involved, and the procedure is of interest therefore both to public libraries and to academic libraries which operate under state, county, or municipal control. Competitive bidding is less frequently employed by private institutions, although here, too, it is frequently used if the purchase is of appreciable cost. Even where competitive bidding is not used, detailed specifications are often desirable in order to ensure that the products furnished on the contract are of the requisite quality and design.

In situations in which competitive bids are required by statute, they are also used for routine purchases if the cost exceeds some minimum figure, as well as for those special situations in which substantial quantities of new items are required on a one-time basis; for example, in furnishing a new library. Even when not required by law, the cost of furnishings for a new building will almost always be such as to suggest the desirability of taking competitive bids.

It should be emphasized that competitive bids are taken to ensure (1) the purchase of required items in the appropriate quality at the lowest possible price, and (2) the distribution of public money on a wide basis rather than to the favored few. Competitive bidding does not imply, however, that a contract will be awarded to the lowest bidder, although there is always a presumption that this will be the case. For the purchaser, competitive bidding provides a means of analyzing and judging generally comparable merchandise on the basis of quality as well as of cost.

The above statement is probably more true in theory than in practice, and I am sure many librarians have been involved in situations in which only the lowest bid has been considered, regardless of the quality of the product offered. There is no good solution to such situations, although it is often a matter of educating the purchasing agent or other responsible official on the need for a given level of performance. It also helps if the librarian is prepared to offer assistance in writing specifications that will assure the needed quality.

In actual practice some bid documents are precise and detailed; others are abbreviated and loosely written. Nor is there a wholly accepted terminology for contract documents. In some instances the word *specifications* is used, either alone or as part of a longer phrase, to designate the entire package of bidding or contract documents related to a single job. Properly, however, the term *specifications* is restricted to those portions of the documents that describe in detail the specific characteristics of the furnishings or equipment to be supplied.

Rarely, a library may be successful in obtaining the furnishings it needs without going to the trouble of preparing detailed bidding documents; but when this happens, it is a matter of luck. In most cases problems with vendors, misunderstanding of the library's requirements, the purchase of unsatisfactory furniture and equipment, and the legal difficulties that not infrequently follow are directly attributable to the lack of proper bidding documents and, in particular, to improperly written General Conditions and poorly prepared specifications.

Colleges, universities, and schools with purchasing agents normally place responsibility for the preparation of contract documents on these officers. In a municipality it is usually the city purchasing agent who prepares bid documents. In some instances the architect or designer prepares the documents, or he may be called upon to assist the purchasing agent. In other instances the task will be divided, with the purchasing agent assuming responsibility for those aspects of the documents that must follow a prescribed legal pattern and the architect preparing the technical portions or specifications.

In either case the librarian or library consultant, or both, may be asked for comments, or he may, if qualified to do so, actually write portions of the specifications. Even if the librarian is not qualified to assist in writing the specifications for library furnishings, he ought to be sufficiently knowledgeable to review these documents intelligently and to make suggestions for their improvement.

Both the number and the form of contract documents vary widely, depending upon the experience of the persons responsible for their preparation, the general nature of the furnishings involved, the applicable legal requirements, and whether the furnishings are part of a larger contract.

PRINCIPAL PARTS OF THE CONTRACT DOCUMENT

Generally, a complete set of the contract document will include the following materials, which are here organized into seven principal sections. This is not the only way in which this material can be arranged, but it does follow a generally established and logical pattern. The arrangement used here provides for most variations necessitated by local laws and practices.

Invitation to Bid. This section of the document, also called Notice to Bidders or Bidding Instructions, usually takes the form of a letter in which notice is given to potential suppliers that bids will be taken for specified items or a class of items. The title Invitation to Bid is more appropriate, however, and, since it avoids confusion with the section Instruction to Bidders, is to be preferred. The invitation should provide at least the following information:

Place and time of bid opening
Name of item or class of items involved
Name and address of individual from whom bid documents may be obtained
Amount of deposit required for a set of bid documents
Cost of additional sets of documents
Conditions governing refund of the bidder's deposit.

Also, included, where applicable, may be such information as the following:

Data pertaining to submission of samples—if these are to be required prior to opening of bids
Notice of publication of bidding information in newspapers or other media.

Usually, this notice is mailed separately to those suppliers from whom bids are particularly desired. Later, it may be bound with the other bid documents even though distributed previously.

Index. If the bid documents are voluminous, an index is convenient for the user. Shorter documents may not require an index.

Instructions to Bidders. This section of the contract document provides information covering the legal and practical matters relating to the bids. Not infrequently the section designated Instructions to Bidders is confused with that known as the General Conditions. Sometimes the Instructions are included and the General Conditions omitted, or vice versa. Normally, however, both are used. Occasionally, in two sets of documents containing both sections, some of the information in the Instructions in one document will be included in the Conditions in the other. Despite the variation in practice, there is a fairly clear distinction in the purposes of the two sections and it is better if the titles are not used interchangeably.

To repeat, Instructions to Bidders is used to inform potential suppliers about the legal aspects of the bid, bidding procedures, the general qualifications of bidders, the list of documents which make up the contract, and similar matters.

General Conditions. This section of the contract document relates more specifically to the job in hand and provides information about such items as the use of materials other than those required in the specifications, the owner's right to terminate the contract if the supplier fails to conduct the work properly, the conditions under which the contractor may stop work, the general requirements for shop drawings, the owner's right to do work on the premises, indemnity agreements, liability insurance, guarantees to be furnished by the contractor, payment of royalties and fees, the need for compliance with applicable statutes—such as wage and hour laws, state and local purchasing acts—and similar matters.

Not infrequently the General Conditions will be those used by the institution for its building contracts, modified for the furnishings contract. This, however, is a dubious practice at best and sometimes results in contract documents in which the requirements set forth in the Instructions to Bidders are in contradiction to the General Conditions because the latter section was not properly adapted to a new situation.

It is hardly the task of the librarian to reconcile such differences or to suggest the makeup of these sections of the contract documents. Nevertheless, insofar as he is qualified and can afford the time to review these materials, he may be able to prevent serious problems from arising at a later date. Clearly, he can assist here only to the extent that he and his purchasing agent are able to work together cooperatively and effectively.

We do not have space in this paper to discuss all of the elements which make up the General Conditions, but the importance of requiring shop drawings for those items which vary in any degree from standard design or construction should be emphasized. Although this requirement is customary practice, it is not always followed, and more than one instance of the delivery of the wrong item or of an item that does not function properly is traceable to the fact that the manufacturer or supplier was not required to submit shop drawings. Again, the librarian has the ultimate responsibility for his building. The more active and knowledgeable his interest, the better the building will be. Occasionally, a section designated Special Conditions is used. This is applicable where the General Conditions have been originally developed for a different job—for example, for a building contract—and it is desirable to indicate certain special requirements of the furniture installation, such as delivery schedules, installation dates, storage facilities at the site, or refinishing of items damaged during installation. Usually, however, it is preferable to include this information in the General Conditions.

Standard Forms and Agreements. No two sets of contract documents ever contain the standard forms in the same place. The makeup of such forms, of course, as well as the number, will vary, depending upon applicable legal requirements. Typically, these forms and agreements (which preferably should constitute a separate section of the documents) include: an owner's protective bond (also called a performance bond) to be submitted by the contractor and his surety; a materials performance bond, an Agreement form to be signed by the contractor and the purchaser or owner; and various releases and waivers of lien for both the contractor and his subcontractors, together with any other forms required by law. These several forms, when properly completed and endorsed, constitute the legal basis for the agreement between supplier and purchaser.

Miscellaneous Items. Following the above, there are usually a number of other sections, including a list of approved wage scales, lists of approved surety and fire insurance companies, as well as addenda, if any, to the General Conditions. These several sections form both the legal and the general basis for the contract, and the librarian should be aware of their nature and their importance.

Furnishings Requirements by Bid Group. Finally we come to those aspects of the contract document that relate directly to the furnishings of the library and are, therefore, of the most significance to the librarian.

When all furnishings for a new library are to be purchased at the same time, it is desirable to divide them into several reasonably homogeneous groups. This division greatly simplifies the taking of bids, as compared with issuing specifications for a single mixed group of furnishings. In most instances bids are taken on all groups at the same time. The advantage to the owner, in bidding all groups simultaneously, as opposed to bidding each group separately, is that some bidders will bid two or more groups at a reduction in cost over the total cost of separate bids.

The categories used for bidding vary according to the size and complexity of the building, but the following segregates the usual items of library furnishings into groups that may be bid satisfactorily under most circumstances:

Group A. Library steel bookstacks and accessories.

Group B. Library technical furniture—wood (circulation desks—if not part of the building contract, card catalog cabinets, book trucks, reading tables, study carrels and tables, chairs, etc.)

Group C. Standard office furniture and equipment

Group D. Lounge and upholstered furniture (occasional furniture, tables, and chairs)

Group E. Carpets and draperies.

Occasionally, it may be desirable to subdivide the above groups. Thus, under some conditions bids may be taken on carpets and draperies separately, or upholstered items may be bid separately from other items of occasional furniture. Again, certain items of office furniture, if desired in wood, may be bid with the technical library furniture, or office furniture may be divided into two sections if composed of both wood and steel items.

The important point is that furnishings should be divided into groups which bidders can bid in their entirety. Many bid complications arise because some bidders cannot supply all of the items called for in a particular group. Carpeting, as an extreme example, should never be included in the same bid group with steel office furniture.

When all bid groups are to be put "on the street," they are usually made up as a single package, with the general sections of the documents bound with those sections that pertain directly to the several groups of furnishings. An alternate procedure is to issue the general sections bound as a unit and to issue separately, upon request of the potential suppliers, those sections relating specifically to the furnishings. In either case each section pertaining to a separate group of furnishings should normally consist of the following: Part I. Detailed Specifications and Part 2. Schedule of Equipment.

Part 1, Detailed Specifications, is required for items to be especially designed or with features that make them different from stock items. In specifying furnishings for which only a catalog number is to be shown—as is often the case, for example, with steel office furniture—detailed specifications are sometimes omitted. Even here, however, it is much better practice to include essential specifications. For office furniture such details include those features necessary to define the level of quality desired, e.g., the locking arrangement on desk drawers, the type of suspension to be used on file and desk drawers, fabric types and colors, material for tops, etc.

Specification in this section of those features considered essential in the furnishings is a means of defining the desired level of quality and provides added assurance of obtaining that quality in those instances in which performance specifications cannot be used. In addition, it is better to include here such items as color of finish and upholstery and the color and type of material for desk tops than to show them only on the drawings, as is sometimes done.

The lack of a standard arrangement for contract documents, the manner in which they are sometimes put together, and the number of addenda required to correct mistakes in the original documents are among the common causes of problems in competitive bidding. Documents which are poorly written and difficult to interpret occasionally discourage suppliers from submitting bids. Listing page after page of items of office furniture in the schedule of equipment while the color, upholstery, and top material are detailed only on the blueprints—thus requiring the estimator in the manufacturer's office to work back and forth from floor plans to specifications in order to establish a list of the number of items in each color—is one way to lose a potential bidder. Coordinating such details is more easily and quickly done when the documents are being prepared by the purchasing agent or architect. Even less defensible is the situation in which the documents contain no schedule of equipment and the supplier is forced to make his own list before he can prepare his bid.

It should be emphasized that many of the problems encountered in the award of bids are traceable to improperly prepared documents. A detailed, accurate, complete set of contract documents is well worth the effort required.

The Detailed Specifications section normally consists of:

A general paragraph(s) explaining the coding system, defining the type of items required, stating the scope of the work required for the group, and providing any other general or background information pertaining to the bid group involved

A paragraph listing the items of furniture required as samples. For samples representing stock items, the requirements should include delivery twenty-four hours before bid opening and retention of the successful bidder's samples to be used as controls until completion of the job

Paragraphs setting forth requirements for materials, hardware, workmanship, and installation; requirements for shop drawings; performance requirements (both structural and finish); testing to be conducted; samples of finished wood or steel to be tested for compliance with performance requirements; cleanup; and a guarantee statement.

Not all of these subjects must be covered for each bid group, although those mentioned will ordinarily be needed for bookstacks and technical library furniture.

Part 2. Schedule of Equipment, is required for all groups including carpets and draperies. The schedule should include:

Code numbers of all items as used on the floor plans
Catalog numbers of the items (if the "or equal" procedure is used)
Quantity of each item (the determination of quantities is the responsibility of the owner) and
Description of the item, including all dimensions and other essential features.

COROLLARY DOCUMENTS

The seven sections, beginning with the Invitation to Bid and concluding with the Furnishings Requirements by Bid Groups, constitute the principal contract documents. With these, several corollary or supporting documents are usually required. The latter include one or more sets of floor plans with all items of furniture shown in their proper positions and coded to the Schedule of Equipment and sketches of all special equipment or of equipment that differs in any way from standard items selected from a catalog.

The "Or Equal" Procedure. In preparing specifications for furnishings and equipment, two general methods are used: (1) "or equal" and (2) performance and testing. The first is used in situations in which it may be desirable to accept standard items listed and described in a supplier's catalog and identified by a specific catalog number. In other instances the architect and owner may elect to provide custom-designed furnishings. Then, performance specifications, including drawings, will be required.

Where standard items are to be used, the librarian—or other person responsible for preparing the order—is faced with the task of knowing all the principal characteristics of the items he wishes to order. In competitive bidding it is usually necessary to use the term "or equal" as an indication of the buyer's willingness to accept comparable products of other firms.

Despite the fact that the "or equal" clause is often required by law, it is often an unsatisfactory method of procurement. The very term "or equal" is abstract and has little significance when used without qualification. Since the evaluation of quality and performance in such situations is often made on the basis of personal opinion, potential bidders, when attempting to relate "or equal" to cost, are forced to guess who it is that will make the final decision. In some instances the General Conditions state that wherever the term "or equal" (or "or approved equal") is used, the decision is to be made by the architect, the interior decorator, the consultant, the owner, or some combination of these individuals. Although not a universally acceptable solution, identification of the person responsible for the decision does make it possible to use the "or equal" procedure with less fear of later complications. Where such an escape clause is used, it should be carefully worded. The following is an example of suitable phrasing for this situation:

"Where any article or thing in these documents is specified by a proprietary name, a trade name, or the name of a manufacturer, with the addition of the expression 'or equal,' it is understood: (1) that the architect, (or interior designer, or consultant) acting as the owner's representative, will use his own judgment in determining whether or not any article proposed as an alternate is the equal of any article specified herein; (2) that the decision of the architect on all such questions of equality shall be final; and (3) that in the event of any adverse decision by the architect, acting as the owner's representative, no claim of any sort shall be made or allowed against the architect or the owner by the manufacturer, jobber, or other supplier of the articles involved."

Where the phrase "or equal" is used, a further modification is often helpful. This procedure, which requires the catalog number of at least three different suppliers (the minimum number normally required in competitive bidding) followed by the phrase "as manufactured by the XYZ Corporation," establishes the general level of quality desired more precisely than citation of a single product and makes it more difficult for a supplier to bid on articles of substandard quality. However, the individual responsible for preparing the specifications must know the product lines of more than one firm. This procedure also requires that the term "as manufactured by" be defined in the General Conditions. A suitable statement for such use is as follows:

"Wherever, in these contract documents, any material, or any item of equipment is defined by describing a proprietary product or by using the statement 'as manufactured by,' it is the intent of the owner that this shall describe the quality of material to be used, the quality of craftsmanship desired, the method of manufacture, and the dimensions. This procedure is not intended to limit bidding to such items, but rather to establish, by reference to acceptable existing products, a standard of quality to which the items furnished on this contract must conform."

Performance Specifications and Testing. The alternative to specifying a proprietary article, and nearly always the only really satisfactory procedure when possible, is to prepare performance specifications for each product involved. Performance specifications differ from the typical nuts-and-bolts specifications so frequently used in specifying library furnishings in that they are based upon the actual performance expected of the article. In other words, the important consideration is how well the product performs, not how it is made. The librarian who requires an installation of bookstacks should be concerned with how this equipment supports books, not with the method of assembly, the gauge of steel, or the dimensions of the supporting columns.

One of the original charges to the Library Technology Program of the American Library Association was to develop standards and specifications for library furnishings and equipment. Studies in this project showed clearly (what industry generally had known for years) that the only way to obtain a given level of quality in the purchase of library furnishings was to develop specifications based upon actual performance rather than upon the materials and methods of manufacture. Yet, desirable though they may be, such specifications have proved extraordinarily difficult to produce.

For many years, and this is largely true today, the majority of specifications for library furnishings have specified only the methods and materials to be used in their production. Since such specifications are usually the standard of a particular manufacturer, they point directly to one product, with the result that other manufacturers are often unable to bid or must submit a qualified bid which is then subject to rejection by the owner.

In too many instances the manufacturer's specifications emphasize special features which may be standard with one firm but require special tooling and dies or costly changes in production methods of others. Requesting such specifications results in increased costs or may simply reduce bidders to an unacceptably low number. Sometimes special features are actually required, but they should not be included in the specifications unless they are.

It was the need for specifications based upon performance, rather than upon methods and materials, that led the Library Technology Program to spend nearly six years in an effort to develop performance specifications for bracket-type bookstacks. Hopefully the Program will be able to develop performance specifications for other items of library furnishings as well.

Wood furniture poses a much more difficult problem in the development of performance specifications than do steel bookstacks. The only approach to such specifications at this time is a series of tests for the durability of the finish. However, such tests provide at least an indirect measure of the general quality of furniture. It is characteristic of the wood furniture business that finishing operations are the most costly element of the entire manufacturing process. No manufacturer of poor-quality merchandise can afford an expensive finish, and no manufacturer of first-line quality dares risk a poor finish. It is logical to assume, therefore, that if the finish is good, the design and construction will be generally satisfactory. For this reason no buyer of library furniture interested in a quality product should fail to include in his specifications a detailed set of tests for finish.

Normally, the stated requirements for such tests as well as the tests themselves should be incorporated in the Detailed Specifications for the group of furniture under consideration. Occasionally, specifications will call only for certification by the manufacturer that his product will pass the tests, but this is not always an adequate safeguard. To ensure compliance, the owner should require finish samples in advance of the bid opening and should have these samples tested by a competent laboratory. Award of the contract should then be contingent, other factors being equal, upon the degree to which the bidder's samples have passed the specified tests.

Nothing said above, however, should be construed to mean that it is unnecessary to spell out in detail the requirements for such aspects of furniture as gluing, drying of wood used in construction, methods of fastening, etc. On wood furniture, tests for finish are useful in separating generally good-quality furniture from poor-quality furniture. In the absence of tested performance specifications covering basic design and construction, however, the nuts-and-bolts type of specification is still necessary.

Coding Furnishings on Blueprints. When furnishings for a new building are involved, it is desirable practice, again not always followed, to prepare floor plans showing each item of furniture in its proper position. All items shown should be identified with code numbers keyed to the various equipment schedules in the bid documents. Some architects and planners prefer to show the complete schedule of equipment on the blueprint. This method has some advantages, but it should not be a substitute for the listing in the Schedule of Equipment. In any case, the coding system should be consistent and as simple as possible. It is good practice to make the first unit of the code number correspond to the letter or number which designates the bid group.

Responsibility for Quantities. The problem of whether the manufacturer or the owner should be responsible for identifying and counting the number of items in each category is a matter of disagreement among specification writers. Some insist that the specifications be so written as to make the manufacturer or supplier responsible for the count; others believe that the owner should specify quantities. The rationale behind the first procedure is that the supplier can be held responsible for any mistakes he makes. Thus, if at final delivery the manufacturer is short two tables, or ten stacks, or three map cases, it is his obligation to supply these items. The other argument states that the owner is in the best position to know the quantities involved and that it too frequently leads to complications in bidding, as well as in final delivery, to leave the matter of quantities to the manufacturer. In practice, even with an expert preparing the specifications, code numbers become transposed, one number is made to look like another, units immediately next to each other in the drawings are misconstrued, and, in the end, the bidder quotes on the wrong quantity. Thus, although the argument that the owner can always hold the supplier responsible sounds logical, experience shows that better and more uniform bids are likely to result if the owner specifies the quantities.

Requirement of Unit Prices by Bidder. Competitive bidding requires, as a matter of course, that the bidder state a total sum for furnishing the articles included in any one bid group. It is also good practice to require that the bidder provide unit prices for all items of furniture "delivered, uncrated, and set in place."

Provision for Adjustment of Quantities. In some situations it may also be desirable to be able to purchase additional quantities of a given item during the period of the contract or for some stated period thereafter. When this is the case, a requirement that the bidder furnish unit prices on the basis of an increase or decrease in the quantity not to exceed some given percentage may be included. Often this is 10 percent of the total bid for the group, but it may be more or less.

Guarantee Period. Contracts should provide a stated guarantee period, although this will differ with the type of product. For this reason, if the bid documents are issued as a package, each group requires a different guarantee period and this normally is a part of the detailed specifications. On the other hand, if each group is bid separately, the guarantee statement may be included in the General Conditions. Guarantee periods in general effect at this time are as follows:

Group A. Library steel bookstacks—5 years
Group B. Library technical furniture (wood)—3 years; except upholstery—2 years
Group C. Standard office furniture—5 years
Group D. Lounge and upholstered furniture construction—5 years; upholstery—2 years
Group E. Carpeting—3 years; draperies—3 years.

Shop Drawings. Wherever items of furnishings are of special design, the owner should call for shop drawings. Ordinarily, the general requirement that shop drawings must be provided will be stated in the General Conditions. Specific requirements for shop drawings should be repeated in the Detailed Specifications covering each group.

Many errors in the interpretation of blueprints and design sketches will be revealed in shop drawings. These should, of course, be examined by the architect or designer *and* by the librarian. Only experience will indicate the several kinds of mistakes that can occur, but a major problem area is in dimensions. Whether the shop drawings are for stacks or furniture, the librarian should check all dimensions on them with the greatest care.

Bidder Qualifications. The problem here, of course, is how to restrict bidding to manufacturers who are fully qualified, without being illegal and without eliminating those who may be qualified but not well known. There is no easy answer to this difficulty. The proper use of performance specifications serves in instances where engineering or laboratory tests can be conducted on the products involved. In some instances such tests may not be feasible. Where this is the case, other criteria may be used to determine the qualifications of the bidders.

Those most frequently used for library furniture and technical equipment are the following:

The manufacturer must have produced items of the type required by the specifications for at least five years.

The manufacturer must have published a catalog of his products for at least five years.

The manufacturer must be able to furnish the names of at least three installations, of equal or greater magnitude than that required in the installation for which he is bidding, made within the past five years.

The ostensible manufacturer of the furniture must be in fact the manufacturer of some major portion of the items required. (In any case the bidder is usually required to list the name and location of the factory where the furniture will be manufactured.)

Obviously, the purpose of such restrictions is to eliminate those bidders who are unqualified by virtue of their lack of experience, inadequately equipped plants, or production of cheap and poorly made products. In some cases these criteria may be too restrictive. A given manufacturer, for example, may have been in the field for several years but only lately issued a catalog of his products. He will not be able to meet the requirements of a "catalog for five years." Yet his products may be generally acceptable otherwise. In general, however, these criteria are reasonable and serve their purpose. If they are used, they must be followed or legal complications may result. In one recent instance a large contract was to be awarded to a firm which, although the low bidder, failed to meet one of the established criteria. One bidder, who had met the criteria but was high bid, objected and threatened to take the matter to higher authority. The result was nearly disastrous.

This matter warrants emphasis. To avoid problems, sometimes serious problems, the owner must be scrupulously honest and fair in awarding contracts. Bidders who cannot meet established qualifications or who do not meet specifications should be disqualified. When all bidders submit qualified bids, the situation will be complicated, but it is far less likely to cause trouble than if a firm which does not meet the requirements is selected for award of a contract. If the owner cannot properly evaluate qualified bids, then an outside expert should be called in.

Omissions in Specifications and Drawings. There are frequent instances in which items are omitted in either the drawings or the specifications. Unless the owner is protected by special phrasing, he may "lose" such items. It is, therefore, desirable to include in the "general" paragraph of the Detailed Specifications a sentence similar to the following:

"Items shown in the drawings and coded to the specifications, or referred to and required in the specifications but not shown on the drawings, shall be furnished just as though fully covered by both drawings and specifications."

Samples. Samples of several kinds may be required depending upon whether stock or special design items are specified. It is usually unnecessary, for example, to require samples of steel office furniture. These products are nearly always uniform in quality within the same line and may be inspected in any office furniture store.

Library technical furniture of wood, on the other hand, is less well known. Further, it is often difficult to find showrooms where representative items can be examined except in major cities, and there is less uniformity of quality in general. Thus, when specifying from the catalog, it may be advantageous to inspect representative pieces prior to awarding the contract. In such instances samples of tables, chairs, card catalog cabinets, and book trucks may be called for. To avoid complications, it is important that such samples be delivered before the date of bid opening. Practice varies, but it is usually wise to specify that such samples be delivered at least twenty-four hours prior to the opening of bids.

At the same time, it should be noted that the preparation and shipping of samples may be a serious inconvenience to the manufacturer and can result in increased costs to the consumer. If the bidders can be prequalified (and this is not possible in all situations) so that bidding can be restricted to those bidders whose products are known to be satisfactory, then samples are seldom necessary and only tend to add one more complexity to the bidding situation. When bidders cannot be prequalified, there is more justification for requiring samples.

Samples of non-stock items, that is to say items to be custom designed, may also be required, but these should be preproduction samples, required only of the successful bidder. There are instances in which custom-designed samples have been required prior to the opening of bids. This is nearly always an unreasonable requirement and may be—in fact, has been—cause for a serious reduction in the number of bidders. Where preproduction samples are required, the specifications should make clear that the cost of such samples is to be added to the total cost and that they will become the sole property of the owner.

The requirement of preproduction samples ap-plies primarily to furniture on which it is impossible to conduct satisfactory tests for performance. It does not apply to steel bookstacks if on-site or laboratory testing is planned. For testing, samples should be required for delivery prior to the opening of bids. Tests may be conducted before or after bid opening. Samples of the successful bidder should be retained as controls against which to measure stacks delivered to the job. Test panels of finished metal and wood will also be required if laboratory testing is to be conducted. The requirements of such test panels should be carefully spelled out in the specifications covering the items in question.

Sketches. Sketches are clearly necessary where new designs are contemplated. Too often, however, sketches are omitted when minor changes from regular designs are called for. Rather than depend upon verbal descriptions, even for minor changes, the owner should include sketches as a part of the contract documents.

General Problems in the Award of Contracts. Even the tightest, most competently written specifications will not produce the desired results unless the owner is willing to be fair and consistent in his treatment of bidders. In too many instances care is taken to write good specifications, but the offer of the lowest bidder is accepted even though the bid does not meet specifications. Occasionally, legal action is threatened against an owner who has accepted a bid that fails to meet specifications, but in most cases manufacturers who actually met specifications shrug their shoulders and accept the situation.

On the owner's side, manufacturers are too often unwilling to meet librarians' specifications. In many instances the manufacturer simply bids his standard model XYZ. Librarians and purchasing agents must constantly be on the alert for such practices. To accept a qualified or limiting bid negates every aspect of the most carefully drawn specification and leaves the owner vulnerable to anything the bidder wants to supply.

Acceptance of qualified bids, except for very compelling reasons, is a slap at every conscientious bidder who sincerely tries to meet the specifications. Legally, a qualified bid is cause for automatic rejection, and the owner should not hesitate to take such action when it is indicated. Sometimes every bid may be qualified, in which case it may then be necessary to evaluate all of the products offered. For this reason the General Conditions should contain a clause requiring that any and all deviations from the written specifications be explained in detail in an accompanying letter. Bids qualified in any way without such explanation should be rejected.

Another practice of the alternate or qualified bidder is to propose a different design. To the nontechnical person or committee—and this is a not infrequent occurrence in small and medium-sized public or academic libraries—the alternate proposal looks satisfactory and is accepted. The result, of course, is that the owner has approved the bidder's specifications, which may represent a cheaper quality.

In summary, the following six points should be emphasized:

1. Make certain that the contract documents for library furnishings are as clear, detailed, and complete as possible.

2. Use performance specifications, including laboratory tests wherever possible.

3. If the term "or equal" is used, cite three comparable items instead of one and identify the person or persons who will determine what is "equal."

4. Do not establish criteria for bidders unless such criteria will be followed.

5. Do not establish specifications which are not required.

6. Do not accept qualified bids; legally they may be thrown out without further consideration.

ABOUT THE AUTHOR—(See biographical note on page 287.)

Appendix

Formulas and Tables

The appendices to the major work by Keyes D. Metcalf, Planning Academic and Research Library Buildings, are as important and easily consulted as the text itself. Perhaps of greatest utility to the library planner is Metcalf's Appendix B, Formulas and Tables. We reprint it here for the reader's use as a quick reference source. The many references to chapter headings, pages, and figures are, of course, to the original full text of Metcalf's work as published by McGraw-Hill in 1965.

The figures given here are at best only approximations and may be altered by local conditions; they are not arrived at by exact scientific calculation.

Six groups are dealt with; those relating to:

I. Column spacing. See also Chapter 4.

II. Ceiling heights and floor size areas. See also Chapter 5.

III. Reader accommodations. See also Chapter 7.

IV. Book storage (excluding problems that are affected by column spacing). See also Chapter 8.

V. Card catalogues. See also Sections 11.2 and 16.3.

VI. Government standards.

I. *Column Spacing*

A. *Stack Areas.* No one size is perfect for column sizes or column spacing.

Other things being equal, the larger the bay size, the better, so long as it does not unduly increase construction costs, floor to floor heights, or column sizes.

Column spacing—that is, the distance between column centers—is generally more important in concentrated stack areas than in combined stack and reading areas because in the latter suitable adjustments are easier to make.

Clear space between columns—this is not the space between column centers—in a column range should preferably be a multiple of 3 ft (plus an additional 4 in. to provide for irregularities in the column sizes and for the end uprights in the range).

Range spacing and range lengths have a greater effect on book capacity than the distance between columns in a column range. The reduction of space between range centers by 1 in. increases book capacity by approximately 2 per cent. The reduction of space used for cross aisles at right angles to the ranges is also of importance. (See Figures 16.19 to 16.23).

If practicable, columns should be no greater than 14 in. in the direction of a range, and the dimension in the other direction should be kept down to 18 in. If over 14 in. in the direction of the range is necessary, the column might almost as well be 32 in. in that direction. It could then occupy the space of a full stack section and perhaps enclose a heating duct. If a column is wider than the range, it will jut into the stack aisle. Irregular length stack sections are inconvenient, unduly expensive, and can often be replaced to advantage by a lectern or consultation table.

Tables B.1*A* and B.1*B* deal with standard layouts in commonly used module sizes.

The following comments may be useful in connection with Tables B.1*A* and B.1*B*.

1. Spacing 3 ft 9 in. or less should be used for closed-access storage only, with ranges not more than 30 ft long and not more than 18 in. deep.

2. Spacing 3 ft 9 in. to 4 ft 1 in. can be used to advantage for large little-used, limited-access stacks, with ranges up to 30 ft long. Closed-access ranges up to 60 ft long have been used successfully with ranges 18 in. or less deep, 4 ft or 4 ft 1 in. on centers.

3. Spacing 4 ft 2 in. to 4 ft 6 in. can be used for open-access stack, preferably held to 18 in. in

SOURCE: Reprinted from Metcalf, Keyes D., *Planning Academic and Research Library Buildings;* sponsored by The Association of Research Libraries, under a grant by the Council on Library Resources; copyright 1965 by The American Library Association and published by McGraw-Hill Company, New York.

TABLE B. 1*A*

SQUARE MODULES WITH THE COLUMN SPACING A MULTIPLE OF 3 FT (PLUS $1\frac{1}{2}$ FT FOR THE COLUMN ITSELF)*

Bay size	Sections between columns, standard 3′	Ranges to a bay	Range spacing on centers
19′6″ × 19′6″	6	5	$3'10\frac{4}{5}''$
	6	4	$4'10\frac{1}{2}''$
	6	3	6′6″
22′6″ × 22′6″	7	6	3′9″
	7	5	4′6″
	7	4	$5'7\frac{1}{2}''$
25′6″ × 25′6″	8	7	$3'7\frac{5}{7}''$
	8	6	4′3″
	8	5	$5'1\frac{1}{5}''$
	8	4	$6'4\frac{1}{2}''$
28′6″ × 28′6″	9	8	$3'6\frac{3}{4}''$
	9	7	$4'0\frac{6}{7}''$
	9	6	4′9″
	9	5	$5'8\frac{2}{5}''$

*Columns should not be wider than the depth of range. 14 × 14 in. up to 14 × 18 in. is suggested.

TABLE B. 1*B*

SQUARE MODULES WITH COLUMN SPACING A MULTIPLE OF 3 FT*

Bay size	Sections between columns standard 3′	Ranges to a bay	Range spacing on centers
18′ × 18′	5	5	$3'7\frac{1}{5}''$
	5	4	4′6″
	5	3	6′
21′ × 21′	6	6	3′6″
	6	5	$4'2\frac{2}{5}''$
	6	4	5′3″
24′ × 24′	7	7	$3'5\frac{1}{7}''$
	7	6	4′
	7	5	$4'9\frac{3}{5}''$
	7	4	6′
27′ × 27′	8	8	$3'4\frac{1}{2}''$
	8	7	$3'10\frac{2}{7}''$
	8	6	4′6″
	8	5	$5'4\frac{4}{5}''$
	8	4	6′9″

*Columns should not be wider than the depth of the range. 18 × 32 in. is suggested.

depth with the range length based on the amount of use.

4. Spacing 4 ft 6 in. to 5 ft is generous even for heavily used open-access undergraduate stack if ranges are 15 ft long and 4 ft 6 in. on centers, and in some circumstances up to 30 ft if 5 ft on centers.

5. Spacing 5 ft to 5 ft 10 in. is unnecessarily generous for any regular stack shelving and is often adequate for periodical display cases and for heavily used reference collections.

6. Spacing 6 ft or greater is adequate for newspaper shelving and generous for periodical display cases.

Square bays are more flexible than those that form a long rectangle and are generally somewhat cheaper if the ceiling height is limited. But if the latter are used, the number of suitable sizes can be greatly increased. Table B.2 shows possibilities with 22 ft 6 in. in one direction and different spacing in the other one.

Similar tables can be prepared for long rectangular bays 18 ft, $19\frac{1}{2}$ ft, 21 ft, 24 ft, $25\frac{1}{2}$ ft, 27 ft, and $28\frac{1}{2}$ ft in one direction.

If section lengths are changed from 3 ft to some other size, such as 3 ft 1 in., 3 ft 2 in., 3 ft 3 in., 3 ft 4 in., 3 ft 5 in., or 3 ft 6 in., or in countries using the metric system to 90, 95, 100, or 105 cm, tables comparable to Tables B.1*A*, B.1*B*, and B.2 above should be prepared with those lengths as a base.

Always keep in mind the probable cost advantages available if standard sizes are used. Remember that columns so large that they interfere with aisles are seldom necessary.

B. *Seating Accommodations*. Column spacing is

TABLE B. 2

LONG RECTANGULAR MODULES, 22 FT 6 IN. IN ONE DIRECTION*

Bay size	Ranges to a bay	Range spacing on centers
22′6″ × 18′	4	4′6″
22′6″ × 20′	5	4′
22′6″ × 20′10″	5	4′2″
22′6″ × 21′8″	5	4′4″
22′6″ × 24′	6	4′
22′6″ × 25′	6	4′2″
22′6″ × 26′	6	4′4″
22′6″ × 27′	6	4′6″

*A bay of this size will give seven sections 3 ft long between 14-in. columns in the direction of the column range. The column sizes suggested in Table B.1*A* are suitable here.

TABLE B. 3

CARRELS*

Bay size	Open†	Double- or triple-staggered‡	Small closed §	Large closed ¶
18′	4	4	4	3
19½′	4	4	4	3
21′	5	4	4	4
22½′	5	5	5	4
24′	6	5	5	4
25½′	6	5	5	5
27′	6	6	6	5

*A carrel, as used here, is an area in which a reader is cut off from any neighbor who is closer than 3 ft on either side or front and back and one side. The minimum desirable width of an adequate carrel working surface is 2 ft 9 in., which is as useful as 3 ft for each person at a table with two or more persons sitting side by side. Minimum depth suggested is 20 in.

†Distance apart on centers should be not less than 4 ft 3 in., unless the front table leg is set back 4 to 6 in., and armless chairs are used, in which case the distance on centers can be reduced to 4 ft. Any distance over 4 ft 6 in. is unnecessarily generous. A clear space of 27 in. or more between working surface and partition at the rear is recommended. A shelf above the table interferes with overhead lighting and makes a deeper table desirable.

‡Distance between centers should seldom be less than 4 ft 6 in.; 5 ft is preferred; anything greater is unnecessarily generous. With triple-staggered carrels, the back of the center one should be held down to no more than 10 in. above the table top.

§The distance between centers should be not less than 4 ft 6 in.; and 5 ft is preferred. Watch out for ventilation. A window is psychologically desirable. Closed carrels are not recommended for undergraduates or any student not actually engaged in writing a dissertation. Glass in the door or grills should be provided for supervision.

¶A room less than 6 ft long at right angles to the desk will permit shelves above the desk or a bookcase behind the occupant but preferably not both. One less than 6 ft parallel to the desk will not permit a 4-ft long desk, and a second chair, and may make it necessary to open the door outward. See Figs. 7.1, 10.2, and 16.7*B*.

TABLE B. 4

FACULTY STUDIES AND SMALL MULTIPURPOSE ROOMS

Bay size	Small faculty study*	Small conference room or generous faculty study†
18′	3	2
19½′	3	2
21′	3	2
22½′	3	2
24′	4	3
25½′	4	3
27′	4	3

*A room of this size can house a large desk, shelving, a filing case, and permit a door to open in. (See Fig. 7.1.)

†This will provide for conference rooms for four, an adequate small staff office, or a generous faculty study. It should be at least 8 ft in the clear in one direction and have a total area of over 70 sq ft. (See Figs. 7.1 and 7.4.)

Any small room will seem less confining if it has a window, and since window wall space is generally at a premium, a room can well have one of its short sides on the window wall.

of less importance in connection with seating accommodations than with shelving. Tables B.3 and B.4 show the maximum number of carrels available on one side of standard-size bays and the number of studies available in such bays.

II. *Ceiling Heights and Floor Areas*. Minimum and maximum ceiling heights and floor areas involve basic functional and aesthetic problems. Suggestions from the functional point of view are proposed as an aid in reaching decisions.

A. *Ceiling Heights*. Ceiling heights greater than functionally necessary may be desirable aesthetically but involve increased cost, unused cubic footage, and larger areas to allow the stairs to reach a higher level. Ceiling heights have desirable functional minimums also, and if reduced beyond them may be unpleasant to the users, may seriously affect book capacity and flexibility, and may needlessly complicate lighting and ventilation. Table B.5 suggests functional minimums and maximums.

B. *Floor Areas*. Both the number of floors in a library and the area of each floor may be important functionally and aesthetically. Decisions in regard to them may properly be influenced by the site surroundings, the slope of the ground, and the value of the property. It is obvious, however, that a skyscraper with only 5,000 sq ft on each floor would be undesirable and that a 250,000 sq-ft area on one floor would involve unnecessary and undesirable horizontal traffic.

Table B.6 makes suggestions, which at best are only approximations, as to the percentage of the gross square footage of a library building which functionally should be on the entrance or central-services level in a typical academic library.

III. *Accommodations for Readers*. Seating accommodations for readers and the service to readers are the largest space consumers in most libraries. The required areas depend on:

A. The number of accommodations provided

TABLE B. 5

CLEAR CEILING HEIGHTS

Area	Suggested minimum[a]	Suggested functional maximum[b]
Book stacks[c]	7'6"	8'6"
Stacks with lights at right angle to ranges[d]	8'4"	8'9"
Stacks with lights on range tops functioning by ceiling reflection	9'0"	9'6"
Reading areas under 100 sq ft . .	7'6"	8'6"
Individual seating in large areas .	8'4"	9'6"
Large reading rooms over 100 ft long broken by screens or bookcases[e].	9'6"	10'6"
Auditoriums up to 1,500 sq ft .	9'6"	10'6"
Entrance or main level with over 20,000 sq ft	9'6"	10'6"
Floor with mezzanine[f].	15'6"	18'6"

[a]Heights lower than specified have been used successfully on occasion, but ceiling lights should be recessed and good ventilation assured. Financial savings will be comparatively small.

[b]Greater heights may be useful aesthetically and provide added flexibility by making areas available for a wider range of purposes.

[c]7 ft 6 in. is the lowest height which permits an adequate protective base and seven shelves 12 in. on centers (standard for academic libraries) with suitable clearance at the top. The top shelf will be 6 ft 4 in. above the floor, the greatest height that can be reached without difficulty by a person 5 ft tall. (See Fig. 8.7.) Space above 7 ft 6 in. is not useful for storage of open-access collections and will be confusing if used for other shelving.

[d]This height used with fluorescent tubes, at right angles to the ranges, permits stack ranges to be shifted closer together or farther apart without rewiring, and is high enough so that heat from the tubes will not damage the books on the top shelf. If the fixtures are flush or nearly flush with the ceiling, the clear height can be reduced a few inches.

[e]Fig. 16.4 shows the arrangements for the reading room 131 ft long in the Lamont Library, with a clear ceiling height of 9 ft 6 in.

[f]Mezzanines provide inexpensive square footage if they occupy at least 60 per cent of the floor area (building codes may prohibit them unless mezzanine is partitioned off and made a separate unit), and if the over-all height of the two resulting levels is not much more than 6 ft greater than would be provided if there were no mezzanine.

B. The types of accommodations and the percentage of each

C. Dimensions of the working surfaces for each type of accommodation

D. Average square footage required for each type of accommodation

E. Additional space required for service to readers

TABLE B. 6

SUGGESTED FORMULAS FOR PERCENTAGE OF GROSS SQUARE FOOTAGE FUNCTIONALLY DESIRABLE ON THE CENTRAL-SERVICES LEVEL*

Gross building area in sq ft	Size of collections in volumes	Minimum percentages of gross area on central-services level
Under 20,000	Under 100,000	40–50
20,000–45,000	100,000–250,000	$33\frac{1}{3}$–40
40,000–80,000	250,000–500,000	25–$33\frac{1}{3}$
75,000–150,000	500,000–1,000,000	20–30
135,000+	1,000,000+	$16\frac{2}{3}$–25

*Central services as used here include the main control point, circulation and reference services, reference and bibliographical collections, the public catalogue, and acquisition and catalogue departments.

These computations are approximations only, but smaller figures than those in the last column will often necessitate shifting part of the central services to other levels and incidentally may add considerably to staff payrolls.

A. *Formulas for Percentage of Students for Whom Seating Accommodations Are Required.* The formula used should depend on:

1. The quality of the student body and faculty. The higher the quality, the greater the library use.

2. The library facilities provided. The more satisfactory the seating accommodations and the services provided, the greater the use.

3. The quality of the collections. Superior collections increase use.

4. The curriculum. In general, students in the humanities and social sciences use the library more than do those in the pure and applied sciences.

5. The emphasis placed on textbook instruction, which tends to reduce library use.

6. Whether the student body is resident or commuting and, if the former, whether the dormitories provide suitable study facilities. Heaviest library use in most residential institutions is in the evening; in commuting ones, during the daytime hours.

7. Whether the location is rural, suburban, or urban. Large population centers tend to decrease evening use because of other available activities and attractions.

8. Whether the institution is coeducational or for one sex only. Coeducation tends to increase library use, particularly in the evening.

9. The emphasis placed by the faculty on the library and on nontextbook reading.

10. The percentage of graduate students and the fields in which they work.

11. The institution's policy in regard to use by persons other than those connected with it.

12. The departmental library arrangements which may make available other reading facilities and reduce the use of the central library. Table B.7 suggests formulas for percentage of students for whom seating is suggested.

B. *Suggestions for Types of Seating Accommodations and the Percentage of Each Type*

1. For Undergraduates:

a. Tables for four or more. Not more than 20 per cent. Should be largely restricted to those in reserve-book and reference rooms.

b. Lounge chairs. Not more than 15 per cent. Should in general be restricted to lounge areas, smoking rooms, current-periodical rooms, or used to break up unpleasantly long rows of other types of accommodations. In many libraries 8 to 10 per cent of seating of this kind is adequate.

c. Individual accommodations. Up to 85 per cent. These should provide in most cases for working surfaces cut off from immediately adjacent neighbors, by aisles or partitions on one, two, or three sides. The partitions should be high enough—52 in. for men—so that heads do not bob up or down above them and cause visual distraction. These accommodations may include:

1. Tables for one. These can be quite satisfactory along a wall or screen if the readers all face in the same direction. When placed in a reading area, as shown in Fig. 7.10, they are not recommended.

2. Tables for two with partitions down the

TABLE B.7

FORMULAS FOR PERCENTAGES OF STUDENTS FOR WHOM SEATING ACCOMMODATIONS ARE SUGGESTED

Type of institution	Percentage
Superior residential coeducational liberal arts college in rural area or small town . . .	50–60
Superior residential liberal arts college for men or women in rural area or small town	45–50
Superior residential liberal arts college in a small city	40–45
Superior residential university	35–40
Typical residential university	25–30
Typical commuting university	20–25

center. See Fig. 7.11*B*. For limited use only.

3. Tables for four or more with partitions in both directions. See Fig. 16.12. A great improvement over a table for four without partitions.

4. Pinwheel arrangement for four. See Fig. 16.12. Satisfactory, but requires more space than (3) above.

5. Double carrels with readers facing in different directions. See Fig. 16.8. Not as satisfactory as (6) below.

6. Double-staggered carrels. See Fig. 16.10*A*.

7. Pairs of double-staggered carrels on both sides of a screen. See Fig. 16.10*B*.

8. Triple-staggered carrels in place of three stack ranges or in a large reading area. See Fig. 16.11.

9. Rows of single carrels at right angles to a wall in book-stack or reading area. See Fig. 16.5*A*.

10. Single carrels in place of last stack section at the end of a blind stack aisle. See Fig. 16.5*B*.

11. Typing carrels similar to (10) above, but with special acoustic protection. See Fig. 7.6.

12. Rows of double carrels in a reading area or in place of two stack ranges. See Fig. 7.12*A*, *B*, and *C*.

Closed carrels are rarely recommended for undergraduates. Shelves in carrels tend to encourage undesirable monopolization. A shelf outside the carrel with an open or locked cupboard provides for books and papers to be reserved and makes possible longer hours of carrel use.

2. Graduate Student Accommodations:

a. At tables for multiple seating. Not recommended.

b. Open carrels of any of the types proposed in 1 above. Graduate carrels may have shelves over the working surface, but this will require deeper table tops because of lighting problems, unless the shelves are installed at one side. See Figs. 16.6, *A*, *B*, and *C*.

c. Closed carrels. See C and D below for working surface dimensions and square-footage requirements. Closed carrels require special care for satisfactory lighting and ventilation. Unless larger than necessary to provide adequate working surfaces, claustrophobia tends to result. A window for each carrel or an attractive grill on at least one side will help.

3. Faculty Accommodations: If possible,

closed studies should be provided for faculty members engaged in research projects which require the use of library materials. Limited assignment periods are suggested. They should not be used as offices. See C and D below for working surface dimensions and square-footage requirements.

C. *Dimensions of Working Surface for Each Type of Seating Accommodation.* Table B.8 gives suggested minimum and adequate dimensions. No attempt is made to propose maximum or generous sizes.

D. *Average Square Footage Required for Different Types of Accommodation.* The square-footage requirements suggested in Table B.9 are at best approximations, but may be helpful in preliminary stages of planning.

E. *Additional Space Required for Service to Readers.* Space for direct access to seating accommodations is dealt with in Table B.9 and elsewhere.

Additional space required includes:
Assignable Areas:
The public catalogue.

TABLE B.8

SUGGESTED WORKING SURFACE AREA FOR EACH PERSON

Type of accommodation	Minimum size	Adequate size
Table for multiple seating . .	33" × 21"*	36" × 24"
Individual table or open carrel for undergraduate . .	33" × 20"†	36" × 22"
Open carrel for graduate student without book shelf over it	36" × 24"‡	42" × 24"
Carrel, open or closed, for graduate student writing dissertation, with a book shelf	36" × 27"§	48" × 30"
Faculty study	48" × 30"	60" × 30" if there is shelving over it

*Recommended only for reserve-book use or for a college for women.

†A space of 33 × 20 in. goes farther in an individual accommodation than at a large table because others do not intrude on the space.

‡Shelves are not recommended over open carrels because they make it easier for an unauthorized student to monopolize one.

§A shelf over a carrel table requires additional depth because it interferes with lighting. A closed carrel should preferably have a window, glass in the door, and more space around the table than an open one, or claustrophobia may result.

TABLE B.9

APPROXIMATE SQUARE-FOOTAGE REQUIREMENTS FOR DIFFERENT TYPES OF SEATING ACCOMMODATIONS[a]

Type of accommodations	Requirements in sq ft		
	Minimum	Adequate	Generous
Small lounge chair[b]. . .	20	25	30
Large lounge chair[c] . . .	25	30	35
Individual table[d]	25	30	35
Tables for four[e]	$22\frac{1}{2}$	25	$27\frac{1}{2}$
Tables for more than four[f]	20	$22\frac{1}{2}$	25
Individual carrels[g]	20	$22\frac{1}{2}$	25
Double carrels[h]	$22\frac{1}{2}$	25	$27\frac{1}{2}$
Double-staggered carrels[i]	$22\frac{1}{2}$	25	$27\frac{1}{2}$
Triple-staggered carrels[j].	$22\frac{1}{2}$	25	$27\frac{1}{2}$
Double row of carrels with partitions between, placed in a reading room or in place of two stack ranges[k]	$22\frac{1}{2}$	25	$27\frac{1}{2}$

[a]The figures used here include: (1) area of working surface if any; (2) area occupied by chair; (3) area used for direct access to the accommodations; and (4) reasonable share of all the assignable space used for main aisles in the room under consideration.

[b]These chairs if in pairs should be separated by a small table to prevent congestion and to hold books not in use. See Fig. 7.14B, C, and D.

[c]Large lounge chairs are expensive, space-consuming, and an aid to slumber. See Fig. 7.14A. Rarely recommended.

[d]Individual tables are space-consuming, are generally disorderly in appearance because they are easily moved, and result in a restless atmosphere from traffic on all sides. See Fig. 7.10. Not recommended except along a wall or screen.

[e]Tables for four are the largest ones recommended, unless pressure for additional capacity is great.

[f]Tables for more than four are space savers, but few readers like to sit with someone on each side. They will avoid using them as far as possible.

[g]Individual carrels are economical in use of space if placed at right angles to a wall, adjacent to an aisle that must be provided under any circumstances. They reduce visual distraction if partitions 52 in. or more in height are provided on at least two of the four sides. See Fig. 7.11A and D.

[h]Double carrels are useful, but the staggered ones described below are preferred. See Fig. 16.8.

[i]Double-staggered carrels are as economical of space as tables for four and reduce visual distraction. See Fig. 16.10A.

[j]Triple-staggered carrels are as economical of space as tables for six or more and reduce visual distraction. See Fig. 16.11.

[k]Double rows of carrels are economical in space use and reduce visual distraction. See Fig. 7.12.

Space around the bibliographical and reference and current-periodical collections which is required because of heavy use.

Public areas outside service desks.

Special accommodations for microfilm reproductions, maps, manuscripts, archives, and other collections not shelved in the main stack area. These may include audiovisual areas of various types.

Staff working quarters, which were dealt with in section 7.4.

Non-Assignable Areas, discussed in section 16.2:
Entrances, vestibules, and lobbies
Corridors
Areas used primarily as traffic arteries
Stairwells and elevator shafts
Toilets
Walls and columns

It is suggested that not less than 25 sq ft per reader in assignable or non-assignable areas will be required for the services in these groups, and that unless the special accommodations mentioned above are held to a reasonable minimum and careful planning is provided throughout, the 25 may have to be increased to 35 sq ft.

IV. *Book-stack Capacity.* Book-stack capacity is based on:

A. The number of volumes shelved in a standard stack section.

B. The square-footage requirements for a standard stack section

A. *The Number of Volumes Shelved in a Standard Stack Section.* The number of volumes that can be shelved in a standard stack section depends on: (1) Book heights and the number of shelves per section; (2) book thickness; (3) the decision in regard to what is considered a full section.

1. Book Heights and Shelves Per Section: Stack sections in academic libraries are considered standard if they are 7 ft 6 in. high and 3 ft wide. Sections of this height make possible seven shelves 12 in. on centers over a 4-in. base. This spacing is adequate for books which are 11 in. tall or less, which, as shown in Table B.10, include 90 per cent of the books in a typical collection.

It is suggested that most of the remaining 10 per cent will be concentrated in a comparatively few subjects, that 70 per cent of this 10 per cent will be between 11 and 13 in. tall, and that six shelves 14 in. on centers will provide for them.

2. Book Thickness and the Number of Volumes That Can Be Shelved Satisfactorily on Each Linear Foot of Shelving: No two libraries are alike in this

TABLE B.10

BOOK HEIGHTS*

8" or less	25%	12" or less	94%
9" or less	54	13" or less	97
10" or less	79	Over 13"	3
11" or less	90		

*Adapted from Rider's *Compact Storage*, p. 45, which was based to a considerable extent on research done by Van Hoesen and Kilpatrick on the height of books in academic libraries.

connection. The average thickness will depend on (*a*) The definition of a volume; (*b*) binding policy, particularly for pamphlets and serials and periodicals; (*c*) the collection under consideration.

A commonly used formula for thickness of books is shown in Table B.11.

3. The Decision on When a Section is Full: In Table B.11 a suggested number of volumes per single-faced section is proposed. It is evident that if books are shelved by subject, it is unwise to fill the shelves completely, and any estimate must be an approximation. For many libraries 125 volumes per stack section is considered safe, although Robert Henderson's cubook formula, which was noted in section 8.2, proposed only 100 volumes per section.

Shelving 125 volumes to a single-faced section, as suggested by Wheeler and Githens, is a practice often used, but it is safer and preferable to estimate the number of standard sections the collec-

TABLE B.11

VOLUMES PER LINEAR FOOT OF SHELF FOR BOOKS IN DIFFERENT SUBJECTS*

Subject	Volumes per foot of shelf	Volumes per single-faced section
Circulating (nonfiction)	8	168
Fiction	8	168
Economics	8	168
General literature	7	147
History	7	147
Art (not including large folios)	7	147
Technical and scientific	6	126
Medical	5	105
Public documents	5	105
Bound periodicals	5	105
Law	4	84

*This table is in common use by stack manufacturers. It was used by Wheeler and Githens, who suggest that 125 volumes per single-faced section be considered practical average working capacity.

TABLE B.12

YEARS REQUIRED FOR A COLLECTION TO INCREASE FROM TWO-THIRDS TO SIX-SEVENTHS OF FULL CAPACITY

Rate of growth	Years					
	$3\frac{1}{3}$%	4%	5%	6%	8%	10%
Geometric increase*	7+	6+	5+	4+	3+	2+
Arithmetic increase†	8+	7+	6−	5−	4−	3−

*A geometric increase represents an increase of a given percentage each year of the total number of volumes at the end of the previous year.

†An arithmetic increase represents an increase each year of a given percentage of the total number of volumes at the time used as a base and so does not become larger year by year.

tion now fills completely and then add 50 per cent to that number to determine the present requirements for comfortable shelving arrangements. This would make the shelves two-thirds full on the average and would leave 1 ft of unused space available on each shelf. If collections are growing eacy year by 5 per cent of the collection at the end of the previous year, it will take between five and six years for the shelves to become six-sevenths full, and to leave an average of 5 in. vacant on each shelf. By the time this occurs, the annual cost of labor for the constant moving of books that will be necessary, plus the damage done to bindings by the moving, leaving out of consideration the resulting inconvenience, may well be greater than the interest on the capital sum required to provide for additional shelving.

Table B.12 shows the period required for a collection that now occupies two-thirds of available space to reach six-sevenths or between 85 and 86 per cent of absolute capacity at different rates of growth.

Table B.13 shows the period required for a

TABLE B.13

YEARS REQUIRED FOR A COLLECTION TO INCREASE FROM 50 TO 85 PER CENT OF FULL CAPACITY

Rate of growth	Years					
	$3\frac{1}{3}$%	4%	5%	6%	8%	10%
Geometric increase	16+	13+	11+	9+	7+	5−
Arithmetic increase	27+	18−	14+	12−	9−	7+

collection that now occupies one-half of the available shelving to grow to the point where it occupies six-sevenths of the shelving, with the growth at various percentage rates. In both tables the rates are figured with the annual increase estimated at a given percentage of (1) the previous year's total, and (2) by a percentage of the total at the time the estimate is made, that is, arithmetically instead of geometrically.

B. *Square-footage Requirements for a Standard Stack Section.* The square-footage requirements for a standard stack section depend primarily on: (1) range spacing; (2) range lengths; (3) the number of cross aisles and their widths; (4) cross aisle area charged against adjacent reader accommodations; (5) non-assignable space.

1. Range Spacing: Range spacing should be based on column spacing, which was discussed at the beginning of this appendix; on shelf depths, which are discussed in *a* below; and on stack-aisle widths, dealt with in 2 below.

a. Shelf depths. Depths as used here are based on double-faced bracket shelving with 2 in. between the back of the shelf on one side of the range and the back of the shelf on the other side. Shelf depths specified by stack manufacturers are 1 in. greater than the actual depth, that is, a 7-in. "actual" shelf is called an 8-in. "nominal" shelf, because 8 in. is available if half the 2 in. noted above is assigned to the shelves on each side of a double-faced shelf section.

Table B.14 shows depths of books. If these figures are correct (the author believes they represent the average in research and academic libraries), a shelf with 8 in. actual depth, together

TABLE B.14

PERCENTAGE OF BOOKS IN AN ACADEMIC COLLECTION BELOW DIFFERENT DEPTHS MEASURED FROM THE BACK OF THE SPINE TO THE FORE EDGE OF THE COVERS*

5" or less	25%	9" or less	94%
6" or less	54	10" or less	97†
7" or less	79	Over 10"	3
8" or less	90		

*Adapted from Rider's *Compact Book Storage*, p. 45.

†An 8-in. actual, i.e., a 9-in. nominal depth shelf, will house a 10-in.-deep book without difficulty, unless there is another deep book immediately behind it. Most books over 10 in. deep will be more than 11 in. tall and should be segregated on special shelving which is more than 9 in. in nominal depth.

with the space available between shelves on the two sides of a double-faced section, will provide for practically any book that does not have to be segregated because of its height, and 8-in. actual depth shelves (they are designated by the manufacturers as 9-in. shelves) are recommended in place of the 7- or 9-in. actual-depth shelves which are commonly used. In many libraries a 7-in. actual-depth shelf is suitable for a large part of the collections.

2. Stack-Aisle Widths and Stack-Range Lengths. Stack-aisle widths should be based on the amount of use by individuals and by trucks and the length of the ranges before a cross aisle is reached. Other things being equal, the longer the range, the wider the aisle should be. Table B.15 suggests desirable stack-aisle widths in conjunction with stack-range lengths under different types and amounts of use.

Do not forget that stack-aisle widths must be based, indirectly at least, on the column spacing,

TABLE B.15

SUGGESTED STACK-AISLE WIDTHS AND STACK-RANGE LENGTHS*

Typical use of stack	Aisle width† Min.	Aisle width† Max.	Range lengths‡ Min.	Range lengths‡ Max.
Closed-access storage stack. .	24"	30"	30'	60'
Limited-access, little-used stack for over 1,000,000 volumes	26"	31"	30'	42'
Heavily used open-access stack for over 1,000,000 volumes	31"	36"	24'	36'
Very heavily used open-access stack with less than 1,000,000 volumes	33"	40"	15'	30'
Newspaper stack with 18" deep shelves	36"	45"	15'	30'
Reference and current-periodical room stacks . . .	36"	60"	12'	21'
Current-periodical display stacks	42"	60"	12'	21'

*These are suggestions only and not to be considered definite recommendations. Circumstances alter cases.

†Stack-aisle widths of 24 in. should be considered an absolute minimum and are rarely justifiable. Anything under 26 in. is difficult with a book truck, even when the use is light. The minimum width proposed should generally be used only with the minimum range lengths suggested.

‡Stack-range lengths are often determined by available space, rather than by their suitability. The maximum lengths shown in the table should generally be used only with the maximum aisle widths suggested.

TABLE B.16

SUGGESTED CROSS-AISLE WIDTHS*†

Typical use of stock	Main aisle Min.	Main aisle Max.	Subsidiary cross aisle‡ Min.	Subsidiary cross aisle‡ Max.
Closed-access storage . . .	3'	4'6"	2'6"	3'6"
Limited-access stack. . . .	3'	4'6"	3'	3'6"
Heavily used open-access stack	4'	5'	3'	4'
Heavily used open-access stack for large collection and ranges 30' or more long	4'6"	6'	3'3"	4'6"

*These are suggestions only and not to be considered definite recommendations. Circumstances alter cases.

†In determining minimum or maximum widths, keep in mind the length and width of the book trucks used, as well as the amount of use. Minimum width stack aisles should not be accompanied by minimum cross aisles. From the widths shown in the table, up to 4 in. may have to be subtracted to provide for adjacent stack uprights and irregularities in column sizes.

‡If open carrels adjoin a subsidiary aisle, they will make it seem wider, but traffic will tend to be disturbing to the carrel occupants. Fig. 16.17 shows a method of reducing undesirable and unnecessary traffic. If closed carrels open from a subsidiary aisle, they will make it seem narrower.

dealt with at the beginning of this appendix, and are affected as well by the shelf depths discussed in 1a above, if columns are not to obstruct the aisles. The distance between column centers should be an exact multiple of the distance between the center of parallel stack ranges within the stack bay, which in turn is determined by the sum of the depth of a double-faced range and the width of a stack aisle.

3. Widths for Main and Subsidiary Cross-Stack Aisles: Cross-aisle widths should be based on amount of use and are inevitably affected by the column spacing. Column spacing often makes it difficult to provide any cross-aisle widths except 3 ft or a multiple of 3 ft. If standard column spacing is altered or if columns 14 in. long in the direction of the ranges are used and the column range is filled out with a lectern, 4 ft 6 in. aisles can be made available. (See Figs. 4.9 and 4.10.)

Table B.16 suggests desirable cross-aisle widths under different types and amounts of use.

4. Cross-Aisle Area Charged Against Adjacent Reader Accommodations: The effect on square-footage requirements per stack section and volume capacity per net square foot of stack area, resulting from the provision of reader accommodations in

TABLE B.17

SQUARE FOOTAGE REQUIRED FOR ONE SINGLE-FACED STANDARD SECTION

Range spacing	Square feet with minimum cross aisles*	Square feet with generous cross aisles†	Square feet with adequate cross aisles combined with carrels‡
5'0"	8.25	9.00	8.4375
4'6"	7.425	8.10	7.60
4'3"	7.0125	7.65	7.225
4'0"	6.60	7.20	6.75

*Based on Fig. 16.19, with a 15-ft blind-aisle range on each side of a 3-ft center aisle.

†Based on Fig. 16.20, with two 3-ft side aisles and a 6-ft center aisle separated by 30-ft stack ranges.

‡Based on Fig. 16.21, with 3-ft side aisles between carrels and 30-ft stack ranges, the latter separated by a 4 ft 6 in. center aisle. One-half of the side aisles are charged against the carrels, but even on 5-ft centers the carrels occupy only 22½ sq ft, and square footage for a section is low.

the form of stack carrels, is shown in Figs. 16.18 to 16.23. These indicate that the assignment of one-half of the adjacent cross-aisle areas to reader space when carrels are on one side of the cross aisles and book-stack ranges are on the other, may increase rather than decrease book capacity per square foot of net stack area, and in addition provide desirable and economical seating accommodations adjacent to the books. See Table B.17.

It is evident that a large number of variables are involved in book-stack capacity. Table B.17 is based on the square footage required for a single-faced standard section in stack layouts, with different range spacing, range lengths, and cross-aisle widths, as well as stack carrels, as shown in Figs. 16.19 to 16.21.

Table B.18 shows stack capacity per square foot of area if 100, 125, 150, or 160 volumes per standard stack section is used in connection with 7, $8\frac{1}{3}$, 9, or 10 sq ft occupied by each section.

5. Non-Assignable Space: Non-assignable space was discussed in some detail in section 16.2. It includes, as far as its effect on book capacity is concerned, the floor space occupied by columns, mechanical services, and vertical transportation of all kinds. We mention it here simply to call attention to it. In a carefully designed stack for 25,000 volumes or more on one level, non-assignable space should not amount to more than 10 per cent of the gross stack area, and with a larger installation considerably less than that.

TABLE B.18

VOLUME CAPACITY PER 1,000 SQUARE FEET OF STACK AREA WITH DIFFERENT NUMBER OF SQUARE FEET AND DIFFERENT NUMBER OF VOLUMES PER SECTION

Sq ft per section[a]	No. of sections in 1,000 sq ft	Volumes per 1,000 sq ft with different no. of vols. per section[b,c]			
		100[h]	125[i]	150[j]	160[k]
10[d]	100	10,000	12,500	15,000	16,000
9[e]	111	11,100	13,875	16,650	17,760
$8\frac{1}{3}$[f]	120	12,000	15,000	18,000	19,200
7[g]	143	14,300	17,875	21,450	22,880

[a]Examination of Table B.17 and Figs. 16.18–16.23 should help in determining area to allow for a single-faced section. This matter has been covered in IVB of this appendix.

[b]Volumes per section has been covered in detail in IVA of this appendix.

[c]If a period is used instead of a comma in the volume count in the last four columns shown above, it will give the number of volumes per square foot available under different conditions.

[d]10 sq ft per section is the cubook formula proposed by R. W. Henderson.

[e]See Table B.17 for an example.

[f]The Author suggests that this is a satisfactory and safe figure to use for a large collection accessible to graduate students and a limited number of undergraduates.

[g]Adequate for a very large collection with limited access.

[h]100 volumes per section is the cubook formula.

[i]The author suggests that this is a safe figure for comfortable working capacity in an average library. See IVA of this appendix and section 8.2 for a full discussion.

[j]The number of 150 volumes per section is too often proposed by architects and librarians. While it is a possible figure, it should be realized that it approaches full capacity and should be used only in cases where additional space is immediately available when capacity is reached. The time to consider what comes next will have passed.

[k]The number of 160 volumes per section should not be considered for most academic libraries, unless the collection has an unusually high percentage of abnormally thin volumes and individually bound pamphlets.

V. *Card Catalogue Capacity.* In planning a card-catalogue room, estimates quite similar to those used for book-stack capacity must be made. They should include:

A. The capacity for each card catalogue unit used

B. The square footage of floor space required to file 1,000 cards comfortably

A. *The Capacity of Each Card Catalogue Unit.*

The capacity of each card catalogue unit depends on:

1. The number of trays it contains.
2. The depth of each tray and the number of inches of cards that can be filed in it without undesirable and uneconomical congestion.
3. The thickness of the card stock, that is, the number of cards that will occupy 1 in. of filing space.

1. The Number of Trays in a Card Cabinet: This depends on the number of trays in each direction, that is, vertically and horizontally. Cabinets are made in a great many different sizes, but for large installations six trays wide and 10 to 12 high are considered standard, giving 60 or 72 to a unit.

A cabinet with trays 14 or even 16 high is possible, with fairly low bases so that the top one will be within reach. This will give 84 or 96 trays to a unit.

Cabinets five trays wide of different heights are also available, but may be more expensive per tray unless purchased in large quantities. They have the advantage of fitting into standard 3-ft-wide stack units.

2. The Depth of the Trays: Trays can be purchased in almost any depth, but just over 15, 17, and 19 in. might be considered standard. A tray under 15 in. is uneconomical in floor space used if the catalogue is large. Those over 19 in. are so heavy when full as to make their use a doubtful blessing.

3. The Thickness of Cards and the Number That Will Occupy 1 Inch of Filing Space: Experience indicates that 100 average cards to 1 in. of filing space is a safe figure to use today. Cards tend to thicken somewhat as they get older. Cards used earlier in the century averaged considerably thicker than those used today.

Table B.19 shows the capacity for cabinets six trays wide with different heights and different tray depths, based on 100 cards to 1 in., with the net available filing space filled to a comfortable working capacity. The term "tray depth" refers to the over-all depth of the cabinet in which the trays are housed. From it 3 in. should be subtracted to obtain the gross filing space available, and comfortable working capacity can be estimated at between 70 and 75 per cent of the gross filing space, with a somewhat larger percentage usable with the longer trays.

The capacities noted above can be increased by at least 10 per cent before they become completely unmanageable, but it is strongly recom-

TABLE B.19

CARD CAPACITY FOR STANDARD CARD CABINETS SIX TRAYS WIDE*

Trays high	Tray length		
	15"†	17"‡	19"§
10	51,000	60,000	69,000
12	61,200	72,000	82,800
14	71,400	84,000	96,600
16	81,600	96,000	110,400

*Cabinets six trays wide occupy approximately 40 in. in width. Five-tray-wide cabinets occupy approximately $33\frac{1}{3}$ in. in width and can be placed in a standard 3-ft-wide stack section. They will probably cost more per tray, but they may fit into the available space to advantage, sometimes combined with the wider units.

†A 15-in. tray is estimated to provide 12 in. of net filing space, which, if filled to 71 per cent capacity, will house comfortably approximately 850 cards which average 1/100 in. in thickness.

‡A 17-in. tray is estimated to provide 14 in. of net filing space, which, if filled to 72 per cent of capacity, will house comfortably approximately 1,000 cards which average 1/100 in. in thickness.

§A 19-in. tray is estimated to provide 16 in. of net filing space, which, if filled to 73 per cent of capacity, will house comfortably approximately 1,150 cards which average 1/100 in. in thickness. These trays may be uncomfortably heavy when filled to capacity.

mended that the lower figure be used in estimating comfortable working capacity.

B. *Square Footage of Floor Space Required to File 1,000 Cards Comfortably.* The space requirements depend on:

1. The depth of the trays is a somewhat variable factor, as already noted.
2. The height of the cabinets.
3. The space between cabinets set aside for consultation tables and for those who use the catalogue. This should depend on the intensity of use at the time of peak loads. A small catalogue with heavy use requires much more square footage for 1,000 cards than does a large one with light use.
4. The space assigned to main and secondary aisles used to approach the cards.

Figs. 16.29 to 16.32 show different arrangements based primarily on the intensity of use and secondarily on the size of the catalogue which result in all the way from 1,000 to 4,000 cards per sq ft of floor space for the whole area.

Every library building program should indicate the number of cards that should be housed and any available information about the amount of use at the time of peak loads.

VI. *Government Standards*. It is possible and in some cases necessary to base space-assignment figures on standards promulgated by governmental authorities supervising the institutions concerned. These standards can be helpful but, like all formulas and tables, they should be used with caution because, as has been emphasized throughout this volume, situations differ and circumstances alter cases. Do not put yourself into a strait jacket. With this word of warning, standards for three different groups are noted:

A. *California State Colleges Library Standards.* Based upon library volumes to be housed, the following space standards are to serve as guidelines for the design of new buildings or additions to existing buildings:

1. Book-stack areas at the rate of 0.10 sq ft per volume.
2. Readers' stations at the rate of 25 sq ft per station, with stations to be provided for 25 per cent of predicted FTE (full-time equivalent students).
3. Special materials. An additional area equal to 25 per cent of the bound-volume area should be the budget standard for special materials: unbound periodicals, maps, courses of study, and sample textbooks.
4. Special functions:

(These data relate to each person employed in any of these categories)

Square feet

Administration	150
Administrative conference room	150
Secretary-reception	160
Technical services	
Division head	150
Department head	110
Asst. catalogue librarian	110
Asst. order librarian	110
Serials librarian	110
Documents librarian	110
Clerical—per position	80

Public services	
Division head	150
Department head	150
Reference librarian	110
Special services	110
Circulation librarian	110
Clerical—per position	80
Public services points	
Per librarian's station	125
Per clerical station	80

B. The California State Department of Education in 1955 included this statement in *A Restudy of the Needs of California in Higher Education.*

Libraries.—Total library space requirements, including study halls and all library-staff work areas, were computed on the basis of the following estimates:

1. Reading rooms and study halls, including circulation desks and staff offices: 30 net square feet per station and one station for every four full-time students, or 7.5 net square feet per full-time student.

2. Collections housing the volumes listed below, including work areas, assuming progressively greater use of closed stacks as collections increase in size, and the use of central storage facilities for the larger collections:

First 150,000 volumes	0.10 net sq ft per volume
Second 150,000 volumes	0.09
Next 300,000 volumes	0.08
Next 400,000 volumes	0.07
Second 1,000,000 volumes	0.05

(Note: The total floor area allowed by 1 and 2 above will, it is estimated, provide for the necessary carrels, microfilm and audio-visual facilities, etc.)

3. Size of collection:

State college: 30 volumes per full-time student for the first 5,000 students, plus 20 volumes per full-time student beyond 5,000 students.

University: 100 volumes per full-time student for the first 10,000 students, plus 75 volumes per student for the second 10,000 students, plus 50 volumes per student beyond 20,000 students.

C. The United States Veterans Administration has prepared tables to indicate library space assignments which are based on the number of beds in different types of hospitals. They are hoping by the use of these tables to determine through a computer the square footage to be assigned in a library for each group of space users, library staff, hospital staff, patients, shelving equipment, and so forth.

Index

This index comprises personal names, institutional names, subjects, journal titles, and the appendix. Not included are conference participants and the information in footnotes.